HIPPOCRENE PRACTICAL DICTIONARY

ALBANIAN-ENGLISH
ENGLISH-ALBANIAN

HIPPOCRENE PRACTICAL DICTIONARY

ALBANIAN-ENGLISH
ENGLISH-ALBANIAN

Prof. Dr. Ilo Stefanllari

HIPPOCRENE BOOKS
New York

For information, address:
HIPPOCRENE BOOKS, INC.
171 Madison Avenue
New York, NY 10016

Cataloging-in-Publication Data.
Stefanllari, Ilo.
    Albanian-English, English-Albanian/Ilo Stefanllari.
        p.   cm. — (Hippocrene practical dictionary)
    ISBN 0-7818-0419-1
    1. Albanian language—Dictionaries—English.
    2. English language—Dictionaries—Albanian. I. Title.
    II. Series.
PG9591.S73   1996   95-50678
491'.991321—dc20   CIP

Printed in the United States of America.

CONTENTS

THE ALBANIAN ALPHABET
(Alfabeti I Gjuhes Shqipe)

Aa Bb Cc Dd Dh/dh Ee Ëë Ff Gg
Gj/gj Hh Ii Jj Kk Ll LL/ll Mm Nn
Nj/nj Oo Pp Qq Rr Rr/rr Ss Sh/sh Tt
Th/th Uu Vv Xx Xh/xh Yy
Zz Zh/zh

THE ENGLISH ALPHABET
(Alfabeti I Gjuhes Angleze)

Aa Bb Cc Dd Ee Ff Gg Hh Ii Jj Kk
Ll Mm Nn Oo Pp Qq Rr Ss Tt Uu Vv
Ww Xx Yy Zz

ALBANIAN-ENGLISH
DICTIONARY
(Fjalor Shqip-anglisht)

PREFACE

The bilingual English-Albanian/Albanian-English Practical Dictionary is useful to several kind of people, to those who study foreign languages, to those who speak fluent Albanian and those who have just acquainted themselves with the Albanian alphabet, to travellers, visitors, tourists and businessmen.

This dictionary contains over 20,000 entries, alphabetically arranged and supplied with the basic grammatical information and simple pronounciation. The headword is in bold type. The headwords in this dictionary include all the important words needed in everyday life. In this dictionary the compound words appear as headwords with their own entries. If several headwords have the same spelling they are in alphabetical order. Derivatives are in bold type like the headwords.

After every word we give the phonetic transliteration and stress mark to show how to say the word.

We give the part of speech in a short form after every headword and derivative. We show whether a verb is transitive or intransitive.

Idioms are given in bold type. If an idiom has more than one meaning, we divide the meaning by means of a semicolumn. If the idiom contains a noun but has a verb it will be in that entry for that verb.

The dictionary provides an adequate translation in the target language of every word and expression in the source language.

PARATHENIE

Fjalori dygjuhësh Shqip-Anglisht/Anglisht-Shqip destinohet për një rreth të madh njerëzish, përfshirë nxënësit, studentët, udhëtarët, vizitorët, turistët dhe biznesmenët. Fjalori përmban mbi 20.000 fjalë e shprehje që kanë përdorim të lartë në jetën e përditshme. Fjalori është realizuar duke u mbështetur në një literaturë të pasur gjuhësore e leksikografike. Ai është realizimi i parë i autorit me mjete kompjuterike.

Fjalët shqipe janë shtypur me shkronja të zeza. Fjala jepet me theksin tonik dhe karakteristikat e saj gramatikore.

Pas karakteristikave gramatikore jepen përkthimet e ndryshme që ndahen me shifra arabe. Kuptimet e përafërta sinonimike ndahen me presje, ndërsa ato paksa më të largëta me pikëpresje.

Përveç kuptimit të parë të fjalës jepen edhe kuptime dytësore e të prejardhura të cilat ilustrohen në një masë të mirë me mikrokontekste. Në fjalor jepen me shkronja të theksuara edhe shprehjet idiomatike me denduri të lartë përdorimi.

LIST OF ABBREVIATIONS
(Shkurtimet)

as.	asnjanës	neuter
f.	femërore	feminine
f.jk.	folje jokalimtare	intransitive verb
f.jv.	folje joveprore verb	passive, reflexive
f.k.	folje kalimtare	transitive verb
gj.dis.	gjuhë bisedore	spoken language
lidh.	lidhëz	conjuction
m.	mashkullore	masculine
mb.	mbiemër	adjective
ndajf.	ndajfolje	adverb
num.rresht.	numër rreshtor	ordinal numeral
num. them.	numër themelor	cardinal numeral
paraf.	parafjalë	preposition
pasth.	pasthirmë	interjection
p.d.	përemër dëftor	demonstrative pronoun
p.l.	përemër lidhor	relative pronoun
p.pk.	përemër i pakufishëm	indefinite pronoun
p.p.	përemër pyetës	interrogative pronoun
p.pr.	përemër pronor	possessive pronoun
p.v.	përemër vetor	personal pronoun
sh.	shumës	plural
amer.	amerikane (gjuhë)	American
anat.	anatomi	anatomy
astron.	astronomi	astronomy
biol.	biologji	biology
bujq.	bujqësi	agriculture
dr.	drejtësi	law
ek.	ekonomi	economy
el.	elektricitet	electricity
fet.	fetare	religious
fig.	figurativ	figurative
filoz.	filozofi	philosophy
fin.	financë	finance
fiz.	fizikë	physics
gram.	gramatikë	grammar
gjeog.	gjeografi	geography
gjeol.	gjeologji	geology
gjeom.	gjeometri	geometry
kim.	kimi	chemistry
let.	letërsi	literature
mat.	matematikë	mathematics
mek.	mekanikë	mechanics
mjek.	mjekësi	medicine
muz.	muzikë	music
sport.	sport	sport
teat.	teatër	theater
tek.	teknikë	technique
treg.	tregti	commerce
usht.	ushtri	military
zool.	zoologji	zoology

TRANSLITERATION GUIDE
(Tejshkronjëzimi)

Aa - a   in arm
Bb - b   in boy
Cc - ts   in Tsar
Çç - tʃ   in charm
DH/dh - ð in they
Ee - e(ɛ) in estuary, elm
Ëë - ə   in around
Ff - f in fleet
Gg - g in game
Gj/gj -
Hh - h   in hunter
Ii - i   in interest
Jj - j   in yesterday
Kk - k   in cream, come
Ll - l   in little, list
Mm - m   in mine, monster
Nn - n   in nine, name
Nj/nj - ŋ in new, knew
Oo - o   in all, or
Pp - p   in post, pepper
Qq -
Rr - r   in roar, remember
Rr rr -
Ss - s   in sister
SH/sh - ʃ in shame, shall
Tt - t   in tell, talk
Th/th - θ in thick, thank
Uu - u   in foot, cook
Vv - v   in volley, very
Xx - dz   in ads(e)
Xh/xh -dʒ in joke
Yy - y
Zz - z   in zero
ZH zh - ʒ in vision

ENGLISH-ALBANIAN DICTIONARY
(Fjalor Anglisht-shqip)

A

a, A (letter of the Albanian alphabet) a, A; **conj.** or
abací,~a f. sh. ~ , ~të. abbey
abát, ~i m. sh. ~ ë, ~ët. abbot
abazhúr, ~i m. sh. ~ë, ~ët. lampshade
abetár/e, ~ja f. sh. ~e, ~et. primer
absolút, ~e mb. absolute; besim absolut absolute trust
abstením, ~i m. sh ~e, ~et. abstention
absten/ój kal. ~ova, ~uar. abstain; **abstenoj në votime**
abstain from voting
abstrákt, ~e mb. abstract; **ide abstrakte** abstract notion;
emër abstrakt abstract noun
absúrd, ~e mb. absurd, nonsensical; ridiculous
abuzím, ~i m. sh. ~e, ~et. abuse, mistreatment
abuz/ój kal. abuse, maltreat, ill-use
acarím, ~i m. sh. ~e, ~et. aggravation, irritation
acar/ój kal. irritate, aggravate
acártë (i,e) mb. freezing
acarúar (i,e) mb. irritated, aggravated; **marrëdhënie të**
acaruara aggravated relations
acíd, ~i m. sh. ~e, ~et. acid
açík ndajf. bised. plainly, openly
adekuát, ~e. mb. adequate
ader/ój jokal., óva, úar. adhere
administrát/ë, ~a f. sh ~a, ~at. administration
administrím, ~i m. administration
administr/ój kal., ~óva, ~úar. administer, manage, run
admirím, ~i m. admiration
admir/ój kal., óva, ~ úar. admire
admirúes, ~i m. sh. ~, ~it. admirer
admirúesh/ëm (i), ~me (e) mb. admirable
adoptím, ~i m. sh. ~e, ~et. adoption
adopt/ój kal., ~óva, ~úar. adopt; **adoptoj një jetim** adopt an
orphan; **adoptoj një rezolutë** adopt a resolution
adrés/ë, ~a f. sh. ~a, ~at. address; **adresa e shtëpisë** home
address
adhurím, ~i. m. adoration; worship
adhur/ój kal., ~óva, ~úar. adore; worship
adhurúesh/ëm (i), ~me (e) mb. adorable; **fëmijë i adhurueshëm**
an adorable child
aeroplán, ~i m. sh. ~ë, ~ët. aeroplane, airplane
aeroport, ~i m. sh. ~e, ~et. airport
afaríst, ~i m. sh. ~ë, ~ët. businessman
afát, ~i m. sh. ~e, ~et. term; timetable; schedule; **para**
afatit before the schedule; **në afat** on schedule
áfer ndajf. near, nearby, close
afersí,~a f. nearness, proximity, vicinity
afersísht ndajf. approximately
áfert (i,e) mb. 1. next, near; 2. close; **njerëzit e afërt**
close relatives; 3. related
afrím,~i m. sh. ~, ~et. approach, approaching, nearing
áfro pj. about, approximately
afróhem vetv. near, come closer; approach

áftë (i,e) mb. able, capable; **punëtor i aftë** an able worker; **nxënësi më i aftë i klasës** the ablest student in the class

aftësí, ~a f. sh. ~, ~të. 1. aptness, ability, capability; 2. capacity; **aftësi prodhuese** productive capacity

agím, ~i m. sh. ~e, ~et. 1. dawn, daybreak; **në agim** at dawn; 2. **fig.** dawn, beginning

agoní, ~a f. agony; **jam në agoni** be in agony

agrar, ~ e mb. agrarian **agresión, ~i m. sh. ~e, ~et.** aggression; **agresion i hapur** open aggression

agresív, ~e mb. aggressive

agresór, ~i m. sh. ~ë, ~ët. aggressor

agronóm, ~i m. sh. ~ë, ~ët. agronomist

agronomí, ~a f. agronomy

agrúme, ~t f. vet. sh. bot. citrus

agjencí, ~a f. sh. ~, ~të. agency

agjént, ~i m. sh. ~ë, ~ët. agent

ah, ~u m. sh. ~e, ~et bot. beech, beech tree

ai përem. vet. he

áj/ër, ~ri m. air; **në ajër të pastër** in the open air; **kështjella në ajër** castles in the air

ajo përem. vet. she

ajr/ój kal., ~óva, ~úar. air, ventilate

ajrór, ~e mb. air, aerial

akademí, ~a f. sh. ~, ~të. academy; **akademi ushtarake** military academy

akademík, ~e mb. academic

akóma ndajf. yet, still; more

akredit/ój kal., ~óva, ~úar dipl. accredit

aksidént, ~i m. sh. ~e, ~et. accident; **aksident automobilistik** a car accident

aksidentalísht ndajf. accidentally, by chance

aksión,~i m sh. ~e, ~et. 1. action; 2. **fin.** share

ákt, ~i m. sh. ~e, ~et. 1. act, deed, exploit, feat; 2. **zyrt.** act; 3. **teatr.** act

aktív, ~i m. sh. ~e, ~et fin. assets; **aktivi dhe pasivi** assets and liabilities

aktív, ~e mb. active; **bëj një jetë aktive** lead an active life; 2. active, functioning, in operation

aktivitét, ~i m. sh. ~e, ~et. activity

aktivizój kal., óva, ~úar. activate

aktór, ~i m. sh. ~ë, ~ët. actor

aktúal, ~e mb. 1. actual, current, present-day; **gjendja aktuale** the actual situation; 2. urgent, pressing

aktualitét, ~i m. sh. ~e, ~et. actuality

aktualizój kal., ~óva, ~ úar. actualize

akuariúm, ~i m. sh. ~e, ~et aquarium

áku/ll, ~lli m. sh. ~j, ~jt. ice

akullóre, ~ja, f. sh. ~e, ~et. ice-cream

ákullt (i,e) mb. icy; **fig.** icy, chilly, frigid

akumul/ój kal., ~óva,~úar. accumulate

akustík, ~e mb. acoustic

akúzë, ~a m. sh. ~a, ~at drejt. accusation, charge, indictment; **ngre një akuzë kundër dikujt** bring in an indictment against smb

akuz/ój kal., ~óva, ~úar. accuse, charge, indict

akuzues,~e mb. accusing, accusatory

alarm, ~i m. sh ~e, ~et. alarm; **jap alarmin** give (raise, sound) the alarm

alarmój kal., ~óva, ~úar. alarm

albúm, ~i m. sh. ~e, ~et. album

aleáncë, ~a f. sh. ~a, ~at. alliance

aleát, ~i m. sh. ~ë, ~ët. ally

alergjí, ~a f. sh. ~i, ~të. allergy

alfabét, ~i m. sh. ~e, ~et. alphabet

alfabetík,~e mb. alphabetical

algjéb/ër, ~ra f. algebra

alibí, ~a f. sh. ~, ~të drejt. alibi

alkoól, ~i m. sh. ~e, ~et. alcohol, spirit

alkoolik,~e mb. alcoholic; **pije alkoolike** alcoholic drinks

alternatív/ë, ~a f. sh. ~a, ~at. alternative

aluzión, ~i m. sh. ~e, ~et. allusion

amator, ~i m. sh. ~ë, ~ët. amateur

ambalazhim, ~i m. packing

ambalazhoj kal., ~ova, ~uar. pack, wrap

ambasád/ë, ~a f. sh. ~a, ~at. embassy

ambasadór, ~i m. sh. ~ë, ~ët. ambassador; **ambasador i jashtëzakonshëm** ambassador extraordinary

ambíci/e, ~a, f. sh. ~e, ~et. ambition; envy

ambicióz, ~e mb. ambitious, aspiring

ambiént, ~i m. sh. ~e, ~et. environment

ambientóhem vetv. 1. accustom oneself to; 2. acclimatize

ambulánc/ë, ~a f. sh. ~a, ~at. polyclinic

amerikan,~e mb. American

amfiteát/ër, ~ri m. sh. ~ra, ~rat. amphitheater

amnistí, ~a f. sh. ~, ~të drejt. amnesty; **amnisti e përgjithshme** a general amnesty

amtar,~e mb. maternal, motherly, mother; **gjuhë amtare** mother tongue

amvis/ë,~a f. sh. ~a, ~at. housewife

anakronik,~e mb. anachronistic

analfabet,~e mb. illiterate

analitik,~e mb. analytic, analytical

analíz/ë, ~a f. sh. ~a, ~at. analysis; **në analizë të fundit** in the final analysis

analiz/ój kal., ~óva, ~úar. analyze

analogjí,~a f. sh. ~, ~të. analogy

ananás,i m. sh. ~e, ~et bot. pineapple

anekdót/ë,~a f. sh. ~a, ~at. anecdote

aneksím,~i m. sh. ~e, ~et. annexation

aneks/ój kal., ~óva, ~úar. annex

án/ë, ~a f. sh. ~ë, ~ët. side

anëtár, ~i m. sh. ~ë, ~ët. member

angazhím, ~i m. sh. ~e, ~et. 1. engagement, involvement; 2. pledge

angazhóhem vetv. 1. engage in, involve in, commit oneself to 2. pledge one's word

aníj/e, ~a f. sh. ~e, ~et. ship, boat; **anije me vela** sailing boat; **anije peshkimi** fishing boat; **anije lufte** warship

ankánd, ~i m. auction; **nxjerr (vë) në ankand** auction off

ankésë, ~a f. sh. ~a, ~at. complaint, grievance; **bëj (paraqit) një ankesë** lodge (submit) a complaint

ankétë, ~a f. sh. ~a, ~at. questionnaire

ankóhem vetv. complain

ankth, ~i m. sh. ~e, ~et. anxiety, anguish

an/ój jokal., ~óva, ~úar. incline, lean

anoním, ~e mb. anonymous

ansámb/ël,~li m. sh. ~le, ~let. ensemble

antagoníst, ~e mb. antagonistic

antén/ë, ~a f. sh. ~a, ~at. aerial; antenna

antík, ~e mb. antique

antík/ë,~a f. sh ~a, ~at. antique; **dyqan antikash** an antique shop

antikuár,~i m. sh. ~ë, ~ët. antiquarian

antipati, ~a f. sh. ~, ~të. antipathy; **tregoj antipati** show antipathy

antipatik, ~e mb. antipathetic

antitéz/ë, ~a f. sh. ~a, ~at. antithesis

antologji, ~a f. sh. ~, ~të. anthology

antoním,~i m. sh. ~e, ~et gjuh. antonym

anul/ój kal., ~óva, ~úar. 1. repeal, revoke, abrogate; 2. annul, invalidate

aparát, ~i m. sh. ~e, ~et. 1. apparatus; **aparat fotografik** camera; 2. **mjek.** apparatus; **aparati i frymarrjes** the respiratory aparatus

apartamént,~i m. sh. ~e, ~et. flat, apartment

apatí,~a f. apathy

apatík,~e mb. apathetic

apél,~i m. sh. ~e, ~et. 1. roll call; 2. **drej.** appeal

apendicít,~i m. mjek. appendicitis

apó lidh. or; **sot apo nesër** today or tomorrow

ar,**i** m. gold

árdhm/e, ~ja (e) f. future

árdhsh/ëm (i), ~me (e) mb. future, coming; **koha e ardhshme** gram. future tense

árdhur, ~a (e). f. sh. ~a, ~at (të) income, revenue; **të ardhurat vjetore** yearly income; **tatim mbi të ardhurat** tax income

arén/ë,~a f. sh. ~a, ~at. arena; scene

argëtím,~i m. sh. ~e, ~et. amusement, entertainment

argëtóhem vetv. amuse oneself

argët/ój kal., ~óva, ~úar. entertain, amuse

argumént, ~i m. sh. ~e, ~et. argument, reasoning

argument/ój kal. ~óva, ~úar. argue, give reasons for

argjénd,~i m. kim. silver

argjéndte (i, e) mb. silver; silvery

arí,~u m. sh. ~nj, ~njtë zool. bear

aristokratík, ~e mb. aristocratic

aritmetík, ~e mb. arithmetic/al

aritmetík/ë, ~a f. arithmetic

arkaík,~e mb. archaic

arkeológ,~u m. sh. ~ë, ~ët. archaelogist

arkeologjí, ~a f. archaeology

árkë, ~a f. sh. ~a, ~at. chest, box; cash-desk, cashier's window

arkitékt, ~i m. sh. ~ë, ~ët. architect

arkitektúr/ë, ~a f. architecture

arkív,~i m. sh. ~a, ~at. archives

armatím, ~i m. sh. ~e, ~et. armament; **gara e armatimeve** arms race

armatós kal., ~a, ~ur. arm

árm/ë ~a f. sh. ~ë, ~ët. 1. arms, weapons; **armë zjarri** firearms; 2. **fig.** weapon

armëpushím,~i m. sh. ~e, ~et. armistice, cease-fire, truce

armí/k, ~ku m. sh. ~q, ~të. enemy, foe; **armik i betuar** sworn enemy

armiqësí, ~a f. sh. ~, ~të. enmity, hostility

armiqësísht ndajf. hostilely

armiqësór, ~e mb. hostile; **qëndrim (aktivitet) armiqësor** hostile attitude (activity)

árn/ë, ~a f. sh. ~a, ~at. patch

arním,~i m. sh. ~e, ~et. patchwork

arn/ój kal., ~óva, ~úar. patch

arsím, ~i m. education

arsimór, ~e mb. educational

arsimtár, ~i m. sh. ~ë, ~ët. teacher

arsimtáre, ~ja f. sh. ~e, ~et. woman teacher

arsye, ~ja f. sh. ~, ~t. 1. reason, sense; **për arsye se** by reason of; 2. reasons, cause

arsyesh/ëm (i), ~me (e) mb. 1. reasonable, rational; 2. fair

arsyet/ój jokal., ~óva, ~úar. 1. reason; 2. justify

art, ~i m. sh. ~e, ~et. art; **vepër arti** work of art; **artet e bukura** the fine arts

artéri/e,~a f. sh. ~e, ~et. 1. **anat.** artery; 2. **fig.** artery

ártë (i,e) mb. golden; **unazë e artë** a golden ring; 2. **fig.** golden, precious; fortunate

artificiál, ~e mb. 1. artificial; **lule artificiale** artificial flowers; 2. artificial, affected; insincere

artificialísht ndajf. artificially

artiku/ll, ~lli m. sh. ~j, ~jt. 1. article; **artikuj veshmbathje** articles of clothing; 2. article

artilerí,~a f. përmb. usht. artillery

artíst, ~i m. sh. ~ë, ~ët. artist

artistík,~e mb. artistic

artizán,i m. sh. ~ë,~ët. artisan, craftsman

artrít,i m. sh. ~e, ~et mjek. arthritis

arrést, ~i m. sh. ~e, ~et. arrest; **në arrest** under arrest

arrestím, ~i m. sh. ~e, ~et. arrest, custody

arrest/ój kal., ~óva, ~úar. arrest, put under arrest, take into custody

árr/ë,~a f. sh. ~a, ~at bot. walnut; walnut tree

arrí/j jokal. ~ta, ~tur. 1. arrive at (in), get to, reach; **arrij herët (vonë)** arrive early (late); **arrij në kohë** arrive on time; 2. attain; **arrij qëllimin** attain one's goal; 3. reach; 4. catch somebody up; 5. suffice

arrírë (i,e) mb. 1. ripe, mellow; **pemë e arrirë** ripe fruit; 2. mature, grown

arrítj/e,~a f. sh. ~e, ~et. 1. achievement, attainment; accomplishment; **arritjet shkencore** the scientific achievements; 2. arrival; **data e arritjes** date of arrival
arrítsh/ëm (i), ~me (e) mb. 1. accesible; 2. attainable
arrogánc/ë,~a f. arrogance
arrogánt,~e mb. arrogant
as,~i m. sh. ~e, ~et. 1. ace; 2. **fig.** ace; **futbollist as** an ace footballer
as lidh. neither, nor, either; **as ftohtë as ngrohtë** neither cold nor warm
asamblé, ~ja f. sh. ~të. assembly; **asambleja kushtetuese** the constituent assembly; **asambleja ligjvënëse** the legislative assembly
asfált,~i m. min. asphalt
asfalt/ój kal., ~óva, ~úar. asphalt
asgjë pakuf. nothing; **nuk di asgjë** I know nothing; **e bleu për asgjë** he bought it for nothing
asgjëkúnd(i) ndajf. nowhere
asgjësím, ~i m. annihilation, extermination
asgjës/ój kal., ~óva, ~úar. annihilate, exterminate, destroy
asimil/ój kal., ~óva, ~úar. 1. assimilate; **asimiloj ushqimin** assimilate the food; 2. **fig.** assimilate
asnjánës,~e mb. neutral; **shtet asnjanës** a neutral country; **jam (qëndroj) asnjanës** be (remain) neutral
asnjanësí,~a f. neutrality
asortimént, ~i m. sh. ~e, ~et. assortment
aspák ndajf. not at all
aspékt, ~i m. sh. ~e, ~et. aspect **aspirátë, ~a f. sh. ~a, ~at.** aspiration
aspirínë, ~a f. sh. ~a, ~at. aspirin
aspir/ój kal dhe jokal. ~óva, ~úar. aspire
ástmë, ~a f. mjek. asthma
astronáut,~i m. sh. ~ë, ~ët. astronaut
astronomí, ~a f. astronomy
ashensór,~i m. sh. ~ë, ~ët. lift, elevator
ashk/ël,~la f. sh. ~la, ~lat. splinter
áshpër (i,e) mb. harsh, rough, severe; **gjykim (dënim) i ashpër** a harsh judgment (punishment)
ashpërsí, ~a f. harshness, roughness
ashpërsím,~i m. aggravation, exacerbation
ashpërs/ój kal., ~óva, ~uar. aggravate, exacerbate
ashtú ndajf. so; **nuk është ashtu** it is not so; **ashtu qoftë!** so be it!
atashé,~u m. sh. ~të dipl. attaché; **atashe ushtarak** military attaché
atash/ój kal., ~óva, ~úar. attach; affiliate
atdhé, ~u m. country, fatherland, motherland
atdhetár, ~i m. sh. ~ë, ~ët. patriot
atdhetár, ~e mb. patriotic
atdhetarí, ~a f. patriotism
ateíst, ~i m. sh. ~ë, ~ët. atheist
ateíz/ëm,~mi m. atheism

atentát, ~i m. **sh. ~e, ~et.** attempt on someone's life; **i bëj atentat dikujt** make an attempt on someone's life
át/ë, ~i m. **sh. étër, étërit.** father
atëhérë ndajf. then
atërór, ~e mb. paternal
atësí,~a f. paternity, fatherhood
atjé ndajf. there
atlás, ~i m. **sh. ~e, ~et.** atlas
atlét, ~i m. **sh. ~ë, ~ët.** athlete
atletík,~e mb. athletic
atmosférë, ~a f. atmosphere; **atmosferë e ngrohtë e miqësore** a warm and friendly atmosphere
atmosferík, ~e mb. atmospheric; **trysni atmosferike** atmospheric pressure
atóm, ~i m.**sh. ~e, ~et.** atom
atomík, ~e mb. atomic; **bombë atomike** atomic bomb; **energji atomike** atomic energy; **peshë atomike** atomic weight
atribút, ~i m. **sh. ~e, ~et.** attribute
áthët (i,e) mb. sour, tart
audiénc/ë, ~a f. **sh. ~a, ~at.** audience
auditór, ~i m. **sh. ~ë, ~ët.** lecture room
autentík,~e mb. authentic
autoambulánc/ë, ~a f. **sh. ~a, ~at.** ambulance
autobiografí,~a f. **sh. ~, ~të.** autobiography **autobús,~i** m. **sh. ~ë, ~ët.** bus; **stacion autobusi** a bus station; **shkoj me autobus** go by bus
autográf,~i m. **sh. ~e, ~et.** autograph
automát,~i m. **sh. ~ë, ~ët.** automat
automatík, ~u m. **sh. ~ë, ~ët.** automatic
automatík, ~e mb. automatic
automjét,i m. **sh. ~e, ~et.** vehicle **automobíl, ~i** m. **sh. ~a, ~at.** automobile, car
autonóm, ~e mb. autonomous, self-governing; **republikë autonome** an autonomous republic
autonomí, ~a f. autonomy
autór, ~i m. **sh. ~ë, ~ët.** author; **e drejta e autorit** copyright
autoritár, ~e mb. authoritative
autoritét, ~i m. **sh. ~e, ~et.** authority
autorizím,~i m. **sh. ~e, ~et.** authorization
autoriz/ój kal., ~óva, ~úar. authorize
aváncë,~a f. **sh. ~a, ~at.** 1. advance, headway, progress; 2. fin. advance
avanc/ój kal., ~óva, ~úar. advance, progress
avantázh, ~i m. **sh. ~e, ~et.** advantage
avarí,~a f. **sh. ~, ~ të.** break-down
aventúr/ë,~a f. **sh ~a, ~at.** adventure
aviación, ~i m. aviation
avokát,~i m. **sh. ~ë, ~ët.** advocate
ávull, ~i m. steam, vapour
avullím,~i m. evaporation
azíl, ~i m. **sh. ~e, ~et.** asylum

B

babá, ~i m. sh. ~llárë, ~llárët. father; papa, dad, daddy
babagjysh, ~i m. sh. ~ër, ~ërit dhe ~a, ~at. grandfather
babë, ~a m. sh. baba
babëzitur (i, e) mb. greedy, insatiable
bagázh, ~i m. sh. ~e, ~et. baggage, luggage; **biletë bagazhi** luggage ticket
bagëtí, ~a f. sh. ~, ~të. përmbl. cattle; **ahur bagëtish** cattle shed; **kope bagëtish** herd (pack) of cattle
báhç/e, ~ja f. sh. ~e, ~et. garden; kitchen garden, flower garden
bahçeván, ~i m. sh. ~ë, ~ët. gardener
bajám/e, ~ja f. sh. ~e, ~et. 1. bot. almond, almond-tree; 2. anat. tonsils
baját, ~e mb. 1. stale; **bukë bajate** stale bread; 2. fig. stale, banal, trite, overdone; **shaka bajate** stale joke
bajonét/ë, ~a f. sh. ~, ~at. bayonet
bák/ër, ~ri m. kim. copper; **ngjyrë bakri** copper-colored; **tel bakri** copper wire
bákërt (i,e) mb. copper, coppery, copper-colored
bakshísh, ~i m. sh. ~e, ~et. tip, gratuity; **i jap dikujt bakshish** tip someone
baktér, ~i m. sh. ~e, ~et. kim. bacterium
bakteriológ, ~u m. sh. ~ë, ~ët. bacteriologist
bakteriologji, ~a f. bacteriology
baláo/ë, ~a f. sh. ~a, ~at. ballad
balánc/e, ~a f. sh. ~a, ~at. 1. balance, scales; 2. fig. balance
balancim, ~i m. balance, equilibrium, equipose
balanc/ój kal., ~óva, ~úar. balance
balén/ë, ~a f. sh. ~a, ~at. zool. whale
balerín/ë, ~a f. sh. ~a, ~at. ballerina, ballet dancer
balét, ~i m. sh. ~e, ~et. ballet
balonë, ~a f. sh. ~a, ~ at. balloon; kite
balsam/ój kal., ~óva, ~úar. embalm
bált/ë, ~a f. sh. ~a, ~at ose ~ëra, ~ërat. mud, mire, slush; **kasolle balte** mud hut; **spërkatem me baltë** be spattered with mud
ballafaqím, ~i m. sh. ~e, ~et. confrontation
ballafaq/ój kal., ~óva, ~úar. confront, bring face to face, set opposite
báll/ë, ~i m. 1. forehead; 2. face, front, frontage, façade; **ballë për ballë** face to face; face-on; **i bëj ballë** face up to, meet head on, cope with; **në ballë të** in the van; in the vanguard of
ballkón, ~i m. sh. ~e, ~et. 1. balcony; 2. teatr. balcony
ballor, ~e mb. frontal, facial
ballúk/e, ~ja f. sh. ~e, ~et. forelock
bamírës, ~e mb. beneficent, charitable
bamirësí, ~a f. sh. ~, ~të. beneficence, charity
bámj/e, ~a f. sh. ~e, ~et. bot. okra
banák, ~u m. sh. ~ë, ~ët. counter; **nën banak** under the counter
banakiér, ~i m. sh. ~ë, ~ët. barman
banál, ~e mb. banal; commonplace
banalitet, ~i m. sh. ~e, ~et. banality
banán/e, ~ia f. sh. ~e, ~et. bot. banana

banderól/ë, ~a f. sh. ~a, ~at. streamer
bánd/ë, ~a f. sh. ~a, ~at. 1. **muz.** band; 2. band; **bandë hajdutësh** a band of robbers
bandít, ~i m. sh. ~ë, ~ët. bandit
banditiz/ëm, ~mi m. sh. ~ma, ~mat. banditry, brigandage
banés/ë, ~a f. sh. ~a, ~at. dwelling house, lodging house, residence
baním, ~i m. sh. ~e, ~et. dwelling, inhabitation; **banim i përkohshëm** sojourn
bankét, ~i m. sh. ~e, ~et. banquet; **jap (shtroj) një banket** give a banquet
bánk/ë, ~a f. sh. ~a, ~at. bank; **banka tregëtare** commercial bank; **banka kombëtare** national bank; **banka botërore** World Bank; **hap një llogari në bankë** open an account with (in) a bank
bánk/ë, ~a f. sh. ~a, ~at. 1. bench; 2. work-bench
bankënót/ë, ~a f. sh. ~a, ~at. bank note
bankiér, ~i m. sh. ~e, ~et. banker
ban/ój kal., ~óva, ~úar. dwell, reside, live, lodge
banór, ~i m. sh. ~ë, ~ët. dweller, resider, habitant, inhabitant
banúeshëm (i) mb. inhabitable
bánj/ë, ~a f. sh. ~a, ~at. 1. bath; **bëj banjë** take a bath; **banjë me avull** steam bath; **banjë dielli** sunbathe; 2. public baths; bath- house; 3. **spec.** bath
bar, ~i m. sh. ~ëra, ~ërat. **bot.** grass; herb; **bar i thatë** hay; **barërat e këqija** weeds; **korr bar** mow the grass
bar, ~i m. sh. ~na, ~nat. 1. medicine, medicament; 2. **fig.** remedy
bar, ~i m. sh. ~ë, ~ët. bar
barabár ndajf. equally
barabártë (i,e) mb. equal
barák/ë, ~a f. sh. ~a, ~at. barrack, hut
báras (bárazi) ndajf. equally
barasvlérës, ~i m. sh. ~, ~it. equivalent, counterpart
barasvlérsh/ëm (i), ~me (e) mb. equivalent
barazí, ~a f. sh. ~, ~të. equality
baraz/ój kal., ~óva, ~úar. 1. equalize, equate, even up, square; 2. level, level off; 3. **sport.** tie
barbár, ~i m. sh. ~ë, ~ët. barbarian
barbár, ~e mb. barbarian, barbarios, barbaric
barbarísht ndajf. barbarously, barbarically
barbaríz/ëm, ~mi m. sh. ~ma, ~mat. barbarism
barbúnj/ë, ~a f. sh. ~a, ~at. **bot.** runner beans, French beans
bárdh/ë, ~a (e) f. sh. ~a, ~at (të). white; **veshur në të bardha** dressed in white; **e bardha e vezës** the white of the egg
bárdhë (i,e) mb. white; **e bardhë si bora** as white as snow; **me flokë të bardha** greyhaired
bardhësí, ~a f. whiteness
barél/ë, ~a f. sh. ~a, ~at. stretcher
barésh/ë, ~a f. sh. ~a, ~at. shepherdess
barí, u m. sh. ~nj, ~njtë. shepherd, herdsman, herder
barísht/e, ~ja f. sh. ~e, ~et. greens, greenery, herbage
baritón, ~i , m. sh. ~ë, ~ët. **muz.** baritone
baritór, ~e mb. pastorial; **jetë baritore** pastorial life

bar/k, ~ku m. sh. ~qe, ~qet. 1. **anat.** belly, abdomen; **me barkun bosh** with an empty belly; 2. **mjek.** diarrhea
barkaléc. ~e mb. big-bellied, pot-bellied
bárk/ë, ~a f. sh. ~a, ~at. boat
barkúsh/e, ~ja f. sh. ~e, ~et **anat.** ventricle
baromét/ër, ~ri m. sh. ~ra, ~rat. barometer
barút, ~i m. sh. ~e, ~et. powder; **mbaj barutin të thatë** keep the powder dry
bárr/ë, ~a f. sh. ~ë, ~ët. 1. burden, load; 2. **fig.** burden, duty, obligation, responsibility; 3. pregnancy; **jam me barrë** be pregnant, be in a family way
barrikád/ë, ~a f. sh. ~a, ~at. barricade
bas, ~i m. sh. ~ë, ~ët. **muz.** bass
basketbóll, ~i m. **sport.** basketball
basketbollíst, ~i m. sh. ~ë, ~ët. basketball player
básm/ë, ~a f. sh. ~a, ~at. chintz, calico, printed cotton fabric
bast, ~i m. sh. ~e, ~et. bet; **vë bast** make a bet; **humb (fitoj) bastin** win (lose) the bet
bastárd, ~e mb. 1. bastard, fatherless, illegitimate, misbegotten; 2. adulterated, corrupted, debased, impure; 3. cross-bred
bastárd, ~i m. sh. ~ë, ~ët. bastard, scoundrel, knave, villain
bastís kal., ~a, ~ur. raid; **bastis shtëpinë** raid the house
bastísje, ~a f. sh. ~e, ~et. raid
bastún, ~i m. sh. ~ë, ~ët. cane, walking stick
bash, ~i m. sh. ~e, ~et. **det.** stem (of a ship)
bashkatdhétar, ~i m. sh. ~ë, ~ët. compatriot, fellow-countryman
bashkautór, ~i m. sh. ~ë, ~ët. co-author
báshkë ndajf. jointly, together, in common
bashkëbaním, ~i m. cohabitation
bashkëban/ój kal., ~óva, ~úar. cohabit
bashkëbisedím, ~i, m. sh. ~e, ~et. interlocution, colloquy
bashkëbised/ój kal., ~óva, ~úar. talk with, converse with, discourse with
bashkëbisedúes, ~i m. sh. ~, ~it. interlocutor
bashkëfshatár, ~i m. sh. ~ë, ~ët. fellow-countryman
bashkëjetés/ë, ~a f. coexistence; **bashkëjetesë paqësore** peaceful coexistence
bashkëjet/ój jokal., ~óva, ~úar. coexist
bashkëkohór, ~e mb. contemporary, modern, up-date
bashkëkryetár, ~i m. sh. ~ë, ~ët. co-chairman
bashkëluftëtár, ~i m. sh. ~ë, ~ët. comrade-in-arm
bashkëngjít kal., ~a, ~ur. 1. conjoin; 2. enclose
bashkëngjítur ndajf. enclosed
bashkënxënës, ~i m. sh. ~, ~it. school-mate; class-mate
bashkëpronár, ~i m. sh. ~ë, ~ët. co-owner
bashkëpunëtór, ~i m. sh. ~ë, ~ët. collaborator, cooperator
bashkëpuním, ~i m. sh. ~e, ~et. collaboration, co-operatio; **në bashkëpunim me** in co-operation with
bashkëpun/ój kal., ~óva, ~úar. collaborate, cooperate
bashkërendít kal., ~a, ~ur. co-ordinate
bashkërenditj/e, ~a f. co-ordination
bashkësí, ~a f. sh. ~, ~të. community

bashkëshórt, ~i m. sh. ~ë, ~ët. husband, spouse
bashkëshórt/e, ~ja f. sh. ~e, ~et. wife, spouse
bashkëtingëllór, ~e m. f. sh. ~e, ~et. consonant
bashkëtrashëgimtár, ~i m. sh. ~ë, ~ët. co-heir
bashkëveprím. ~i m. sh. ~e, ~et. interaction, interworking
bashkëvepr/oj jokal., ~ova, ~uar. interact
bashkí, ~a f. sh. ~, ~të. municipality; town-hall
bashkiák, ~e mb. muncipal; **zgjedhjet bashkiake** municipal
elections
bashkím, ~i m. sh. ~e, ~et. 1. union; 2. unity; 3.
confederation; 4. affiliation ; 5. unification **bashk/ój kal.**,
~óva, ~úar. 1. unite, unify; 2. combine, mix; 3. connect,
link; 4. join, bond, fuse, cohere, stick together; 5.
cooperate, work together, concert; 6. associate, affiliate; 7
mate, couple
báshku (së) ndajf. together
bashkuar (i,e) mb. united, unified; joined, linked; merged,
combined
bashkudhëtár, ~i m. sh. ~ë, ~ët. co-traveller
bashkúes, ~e mb. joining, connecting, connective,
connectional
baták, ~u m. sh. ~ë, ~ët. slough, mire
batakçí, ~u m. sh. ~nj, ~njtë. swindler, defrauder, sharper
batalión, ~i m. sh. ~e, ~et. usht. battalion
bataníj/e, ~a f. sh. ~e, ~et. blanket
baterí, ~a f. sh. ~, ~të. 1. battery; 2. **sport.** heat; 3.
usht. battery
batíc/ë, ~a f. sh. ~a, ~at. high tide
báth/ë, ~a f. sh ~ë, ~ët. bot. broad bean
báz/ë, ~a f. sh. ~a, ~at 1. base; basis; foundation; 2.
gjeom. base; **baza e trekëndshit** the base of the triangle; 3.
kim. base; 4. usht. base; **bazë ajrore** air base; 5. **mat.** base
bazóhem vetv. base oneself upon; depend on; rely on
baz/ój kal., ~óva, ~úar. base, found, ground
be, ~ja f.sh. ~, ~të. oath, vow; **zë be** take an oath
béb/e, ~ja f. sh. ~e, ~et. baby
béb/e, ~ja f. sh. ~e, ~et. pupil, apple of the eye
béfas ndajf. suddenly, unexpectedly, all of a sudden,
abruptly
befasí, ~a f. suddenness, unexpectedness, abruptness; **zë**
(kap, gjej) në befasi take smb by surprise
befasísh/ëm (i) ~me (e) mb. sudden, abrupt
befasísht ndajf. of a sudden, instantly
befasóhem vetv. be surprised, be taken by surprise
befas/ój kal. ~óva, ~úar. surprise, take by surprise; storm,
take by storm
béftë (i, e) mb. sudden, abrupt
begatí, ~a f. sh. ~, ~të. affluence, opulence
begat/ój kal., ~óva, ~úar. enrich, richen
begátsh/ëm (i) ~me (e) mb. opulent, affluent, wealthy, well-
to-do
begenís kal., ~a, ~ur. deign, condescend
behár, ~i m. sh. ~e, ~et. summer
beháre, ~t f. sh. spices, condiments
bekím, ~i m. sh. ~e, ~et. blessing; **jap bekimin** give the
blessing
bek/ój kal., ~óva, ~úar. bless
bekúar (i, e) mb. blessed

bel, ~i m. sh. ~e, ~et. spade
bel, ~i m. sh. ~a, ~at. waist; **bel i hollë** a slender waist
belá, ~ja f. sh. ~, ~të (~ra, ~rat.) trouble; **futem në bela**
get into trouble
belbëzím, ~i m. sh. ~e, ~ et. stammering, stuttering
belbëz/ój jokal. dhe kal., ~óva, ~úar. stammer, stutter
benzín/ë, ~a f. benzine; gasoline
benzól, ~i m. benzol
beqár, e mb. unmarried, single, celibate
beqarí, ~a f. bachelorhood, celibacy, singleness
berbér, ~i m. sh. ~ë, ~ët. barber, hairdresser
bereqét, ~i m. sh. ~e, ~et. harvest; **mbledh bereqetin** gather
in the harvest
bés/ë, ~a f. troth; **jap besën** plight one's troth
besím, ~i m. sh. ~e, ~et. 1. confidence, faith, trust; **kam**
besim have confidence in smb; 2. **fet.** belief **besimtár**, ~e mb.
devout, pious, religious
besník, ~e mb. faithful, loyal
besnikërí, ~a f. faithfulness, loyalty, fidelity
besnikërísht ndajf. faithfully, loyally
bes/ój kal., ~óva, ~úar. 1. trust in (to), have faith in,
believe in; 2. entrust; 3. think, believe
besúar (i, e) mb. trusted, trusty
besúesh/ëm (i), ~me (e) mb. credible, trustworthy, believable
betéj/ë, ~a f. sh. ~a, ~at. battle; **bie në fushën e betejës**
die in battle
betím, ~i m. sh. ~e, ~et. swear, oath, vow; **bëj betimin**
swear(take) an oath
betóhem vetv. swear, take an oath
betón, ~i m. concrete
beton/ój kal., ~óva, ~úar. concrete
betúar (i,e) mb. sworn; **armik i betuar** sworn enemy
bezdí, ~a f. sh. ~, ~të. annoyance, nuisance, bother
bezdís kal., ~a, ~ur bised. annoy, bother
bezdíssh/ëm (i), ~me (e) mb. bised. annoying, bothersome
bëhem vetv. become; grow
bë/j kal., ~ra, ~rë. 1. do, make; **bëj një gabim** make a
mistake; 2. effect, cause, bring about, accomplish; 3. set
up, put up; 4. compose, write; 5. make do; 6. make for; **bëj**
një vizitë pay a visit to; **bëj ç'është e mundur** do one's best
bërt/ás jokal., ~íta, ~ítur. shout, cry out, call out
bërtham/ë ~a, f. sh. ~a, ~at. 1. kernel, stone; 2. **fig.**
nucleus, core
bërzóll/ë ~a, f. sh. ~a, ~at. chop; **bërzollë derri** pork chop
bërryl, ~i m. sh. ~a, ~at. 1. elbow; **mbështetem në bërryl**
lean on one's elbow; 2. bend
bíb/ël, ~la f. sh. ~la, ~lat. Bible
bibliografí, ~a f. sh. ~, ~të. bibliography
bibliotekár, , ~i m. sh. ~ë, ~ët. librarian
bibliotek/ë ~a, f. sh. ~a, ~at. library; book-case
biçák, ~u m. sh. ~ë, ~ët. pocket knife
biçiklét/ë ~a, f. sh. ~a, ~at. bicycle, bike; **ngas biçikletën**
ride a bicycle

bidon, ~i m. sh. ~ë, ~ët. can; churn; **bidon qumështi** milk can
bíe jokal., **ráshë**, **rënë**. fall, fall down, come down, drop
down; **bie shi (borë)** it rains (snows); **bie në dashuri** fall in
love; **bie në gjumë** fall asleep
bíe kal., **prúra**, **prúrë**. 1. bring; 2. cause, bring about
bifték, ~u , m. sh. ~ë, ~ët. beefsteak
bíj/ë ~a, f. sh. ~a, ~at. daughter
bilánc, ~i m. sh. ~e, ~et. balance sheet
bilárdo, ~ja f. sh. ~, ~t. billiards
bilbíl, ~i m. sh. ~a, ~at. zool. nightingale
biletarí, ~a f. sh. ~, ~të. booking-office
bilét/ë, ~a f. sh. ~, ~at. ticket; **biletë treni** railway
ticket; **biletë parkimi** parking ticket
bilión, ~i m. sh. ~ë, ~ët. billion
bim/ë, ~a f. sh. ~ë, ~ët. plant; crops
bind kal., ~a, ~ur. convince, persuade
bíndës, ~e mb. convincing, persuasive; **arsye bindëse**
persuasive reasons
bíndje, ~a f. sh. ~e, ~et. conviction, persuasion; **kam
bindjen se** I am convinced that
bíndshëm ndajf. convincingly
bíndur (i,e) mb. 1. convinced, persuaded; 2. obedient; **fëmijë
i bindur** an obedient child
binják, ~e mb. twin; **vëllezër binjakë** twin brothers
biografí, ~a f. sh. ~, ~të. biography
biologjí, ~a f. biology
bi/r, ~ri m. sh. ~j, ~jtë. son
birúc/ë ~a, f. sh. ~a, ~at. cell
birrarí, ~a f. sh. ~, ~të. alehouse
bírr/ë ~a, f. sh. ~a, ~at. beer, ale
biséd/ë ~a, f. sh. ~a, ~at. chat, talk, conversation; **bisedë
e përzemërt** cordial talk
bisedím, ~i m. sh. ~e, ~et. talk, conversation; negotiation;
zhvilloj bisedime hold talks, conduct negotiations; **hyj në
bisedime** enter into negotiations
bised/ój jokal., ~óva, ~úar. chat, talk, converse
bisedór, ~e mb. gjuh. conversational
bis/k, ~ku m. sh. ~qe, ~qet. shoot
biskót/ë ~a, f. sh. ~a, ~at. biscuit, bun, cookie
bísh/ë ~a, f. sh. ~a, ~at. wild beast
bisht, m. sh. ~a, ~at dhe ~ra, ~rat. 1. tail (of a dog etc.);
2. tail (of a comet, aircraft etc.); 3. handle
bishtáj/ë ~a, f. sh. ~a, ~at. bot. pod
bitúm, ~i m. sh. ~e, ~et. bitumen
bizéle, ~ja f. sh. ~e, ~et. bot. pea
bjéshk/ë, ~a f. sh. ~ë, ~ët. alpine land
blegërí/j jokal., ~ta, ~tur. bleat
blegtorí, ~a f stock-breeding
ble/j kal., ~va, ~rë. buy, purchase
blérës, ~i m. sh. ~, ~it. buyer, purchaser
blérës mb. purchasing; **fuqi blerëse** purchasing power
blerím, ~i m. greenery, verdure, greens

blérj/e, ~a f. sh. ~e, ~et. purchase
blértë (i,e) mb. green
blét/ë. ~a f. m. ~ë, ~ët. zool. bee
blu mb. blue
blúaj kal. **blóva, blúar**. 1. grind; **bluaj kafenë** grind coffe
beans; 2. crush; 3. **fig**. chew over, meditate on, ruminate
blúz/ë, ~a f. sh. ~a, ~at. blouse
bllo/k, ~ku m. sh. ~qe, ~qet. 1. block; **bllok mermeri** a block
of marble; 2. block (of flats); 3. pad
bllokád/ë, ~a f. sh. ~a, ~at. blockade; **çaj bllokadën** break a
blocade; **heq bllokadën** raise the blockade
bllok/ój kal., ~óva, ~úar. blocade; obstruct; **bllokoj rrugën**,
kalimin block (a road, passage); **bllokoj pagat** freeze the
wages
bobín/ë, ~a f.sh. ~a, ~at. 1. coil; 2. bobbin, spool
bodéc, ~i m. sh. ~ë, ~ët. goad, prod; **shpoj me bodec** prick
with a goad
bodrúm, ~i m. sh. ~e, ~et. cellar
bojatís kal., ~a, ~ur. 1. paint; 2. color, tinge
bój/ë, ~a f.sh. ~ëra, ~ërat. 1. paint; 2. polish; 3. colour,
tint
bojkotím,~i m. boycott
bojkot/ój kal., ~óva, ~úar. boycott
boks, ~i m. **sport**. boxing
boksiér, ~i m. sh. ~ë, ~ët. boxer
boksít, ~i m. sh. ~e, ~et. bauxite
boll ndajf. enough
bollëk, ~u m. abundance, plenty; **me bollëk** abundantly,
abounding in
bóllsh/ëm (i), ~me (e) mb. abundant, plentiful, bountiful,
copious
bombardím, ~i m. sh. ~e, ~et. bombardment
bombard/ój kal., ~óva, úar. bomb, bombard
bombardúes, ~i m. sh. ~, ~it. bomber
bómb/ë, ~a f. sh. ~a, ~at. bomb; **bombë me gaz lotsjellës**
tear-gas bomb
bonifikím, ~i m. sh. ~e, ~et. reclamation
bonifik/ój kal., ~óva, ~úar. reclaim
bord, ~i. m. sh. ~e, ~et. board; **në bord** on board
borderó, ~ja f. sh. ~, ~të. pay-roll
bór/ë, ~a f. sh. ~ëra, ~ërat. snow
borí, ~a f. sh. ~, ~të. trumpet; **bori makine** a car horn; **bori
gjahu** a hunting horn
borizán, ~i m. sh. ~ë, ~ët. trumpeter
borxh, ~i m. sh. ~e, ~et. 1. debt; **jam borxh** be in debt;
futem (hyj) borxh get (run) into debt; **shlyej (laj) borxhin**
settle (pay) off the debt; 2. obligation
borxhlí, ~u m. sh. ~nj, ~njtë. debtor; **i jam borxhli** I am
indebted (obliged) to somebody
borzilok, ~u m. sh. ~ë, ~ët. **bot**. basil
bostán, ~i m. sh. ~e, ~et. **bot**. watermelon
bosh, ~e mb. 1. empty, void, vacant; 2. hollow; 3. **fig**.
empty, futile; **fjalë boshe** words empty of meaning; **me barkun
bosh** on an empty stomach
boshatís kal., ~a, ~ur. 1. empty; **boshatis sirtarin** empty out
the drawer; 2. vacate; 3. evacuate

boshllë/k, ~ku m. sh. **~qe, ~qet.** 1. void; 2. vacuum; 3. **fig.**
gap
bosht, ~i m. sh. **~e, ~et.** 1. axle; 2. axis; **boshti i tokës**
the earth's axis
botaník, ~e mb. botanical; **kopshti botanik** botanical garden
botaník/ë. ~a f. botany
botaníst. ~i m. sh. **~ë, ~ët.** botanist
bót/ë, ~a f. sh. **~ë, ~ët.** 1. world; universe; 2. the world;
human affairs; active life; 3. "the world"; everybody;
everything; 4. **the world** (of art, politics, sports); 5.
people; society; mankind; 6. sphere, realm, domain, kingdom
botëkuptím, ~i m. sh. **~e, ~et.** world-outlook
botërísht ndajf. openly, publicly
botërór, ~e mb. world, global, world-wide, universal; **luftë
botërore** a world war
botím, ~i m. sh. **~e, ~et.** edition; publication
bot/ój kal., ~óva, ~úar. publish, issue; **botoj libra
(artikuj)** publish books (articles)
botúes, ~e mb. publishing; **shtëpi botuese** publishing house
botúes, ~i m. sh **~, ~it.** publisher
braktís kal., ~a, ~ur. abandon, forsake, desert; **braktis
anijen** abandon the ship
braktísje, ~a f. abandonment, desertion, forsaking
bráv/ë, ~a f. sh. **~a, ~at.** lock
brázd/ë, ~a f. sh. furrow
bredh, ~i m. sh. **~a, ~at.** bot. fir, fir-tree
bredh jokal., bródha, brédhur. wander, roam, ramble
bredharák, ~e mb. wandering, rambling, roving
breg, ~u m. sh. **brígje, brígjet.** 1. shore, coast; 2. knoll,
mound, small hill
bregdét, ~i m. sh. **~e, ~et.** coast, seashore, seaside
bregdetár, ~e mb. coastal, seaside
bregór/e, ~ja f. sh. **~e, ~et.** hillock, mound
brej kal., ~ta, ~tur. 1. nibble, gnaw; 2. **fig.** gnaw; **faji i
brente ndërgjegjen** guilt gnawing away at his conscience; 3.
corrode, eat into (away)
brékë. ~t f. **vet.** sh. drawers, underpants, shorts
brénda ndajf. in, inside; within; parfjal. in, inside, within
brendësí, ~a f. interior, inside, inner part
brendí, ~a f. content
bréndsh/ëm (i), ~me (e) mb. interior, internal, inner
bréng/ë, ~a f. sh. **~a, ~at.** grief, sadness, sorrow
brengós kal., ~a, ~ur. grieve, sorrow, aggrieve
brengósur (i,e) mb. aggrieved, grief-stricken, sad, sorrowful
brésh/ër, ~ri m. 1. hail; **iku nga shiu e ra në breshër** jump
out of the frying pan into the fire; 2. **fig.** volley
breshërí, ~a f. sh. **~, ~të.** volley, salvo
bréshk/ë, ~a f. sh. **~a, ~at.** zool. tortoise
bretkós/ë, ~a f. sh **~a, ~at.** zool. frog
brez, ~i m. sh. **~a, ~at.** 1. belt; **brez shpëtimi** lifebelt; 2.
gjeog. strip, belt; 3. generation
bri, ~ri m. sh. **~rë, ~rët.** horn; **me brirë** horned; **prej briri**
horny
bri paraf. aside, alongside, beside

brigád/ë. ~a f. sh. ~a, ~at. 1. brigade; **brigadë zjarrfiksash** the fire brigade; 2. **usht.** brigade
brím/ë, ~a f. sh. ~a, ~at. hole
brim/ój kal., ~óva, ~úar. bore, drill, pierce
brínj/ë, ~a f. sh. ~ë, ~ët. **anat.** rib
bris/k, ~ku m. sh. ~qe, ~qet. 1. razor, safety-razor; 2. pocket- knife, penknife
bríshtë (i,e) mb. 1. brittle, breakable, fragile, frail; 2. **fig.** brittle
brítm/ë, ~a f. sh. ~a, ~at. cry, shout, outcry, scream, yell; **britmë gëzimi** a cry of joy
brohorít (brohorís) jokal., ~a, ~ur. cheer, acclaim, applaud
brohorítj/e, ~a f. sh. ~e, ~et. cheer, acclamation, applause
brók/ë, ~a f. sh. ~a, ~at. jug, pitcher
bronkít, ~i m. sh. ~e, ~et. **mjek.** bronchitis
bronz, ~i m. sh. ~e, ~et. bronze, brass
brónztë (i,e) mb. brazen
broshúr/ë, ~a f. sh. ~a, ~at. booklet, brochure
brúmbu/ll, ~lli m. sh. ~j, ~jt **zool.** beetle
brúm/ë, ~i m. dough; paste
brumós kal., ~a, ~ur. **fig.** mold, shape
brutál, ~e mb. brutal, cruel, savage, ruthless, merciless
brúto mb. 1. raw, crude; **material bruto** raw material; 2. **fin.** gross; **pesha bruto** gross weight
brym/ë, ~a f. sh. ~a, ~at. rime, frost
búa/ll, ~lli m. sh. ~j, ~jt. buffalo
bubullím/ë, ~a f. sh. ~a, ~at. thunder
bubullí/n jokal., ~u, ~rë. thunder
bucél/ë, ~a f. sh. ~a, ~at. 1. cask, keg; 2. **tek.** hub
buç/ét jokal., ~íti, ~ítur. rumble, peal, boom, resound
buçím/ë, ~ f. sh. ~a, ~at. roar, rumble, boom
budall/á, ~áqe mb. **bised.** foolish
budall/á, ~ai m. sh. ~énj, ~énjtë. **fig.** fool, dolt
budallallë/k, ~ku m. sh. ~qe, ~qet **bised.** foolery, stupidity
budíng, ~u m. sh. ~ë, ~ët. pudding
budíst, ~i mb. Buddhist
budíz/ëm, ~mi m. Buddhism
buf, ~i m. sh. ~ë, ~ët. dhe ~ër, ~ërit. 1. **zool.** screech-owl; 2. **fig.** numskull, dolt
bufé, ~ja f. sh. ~, ~të. 1. cupboard, sideboard; 2. buffet
bujár, ~e mb. 1. gentle; generous, bountiful, munificent, open- handed; large-hearted
bujár, i m. sh. ~ë, ~ët. **hist.** gentleman
bujarí, ~a f. generosity, munificence, bounty
búj/ë, ~a f. sensation; commmotion, ado; **bën bujë** cause sensation
buj/k, ~ku m. sh. ~q, ~qit. farmer, tiller; agriculturist
bujqësí, ~a f. agriculture, farming
bujqësór, ~e mb. agricultural, farm; **prodhime bujqësore** agricultural produce; **makineri bujqësore** agricultural machinery
bújsh/ëm (i), ~me (e) mb. sensational; **lajm i bujshëm** sensational news
bujtín/ë, ~a f. sh. ~a, ~at. inn, boarding house

búk/ë, ~a f. sh. ~ë, ~ët. bread; **bukë e zezë** brown bread;
fetë buke slice of bread; **bukë e ndenjur** stale bread;
thërrime buke breadcrumbs; **i heq bukën e gojës** take the bread
out of one's mouth
bukëpjékës, ~i m. sh. ~, ~it. baker
bukëshítës, ~i m. sh. ~, ~it. baker
búkur, ~a (e) f. sh. ~a, ~at (të). beauty
búkur (i,e) mb. beautiful, pretty, handsome, good-looking
búkur ndajf. nicely, finely, handsomely
bukurí, ~a f. sh. ~, ~të. beauty, prettiness; **për bukuri**
excellently, superbly
bukurshkrím, ~i m. handwriting; calligraphy
bulb, ~i m. sh. ~e, ~et. bot. bulb; **bulbi i qepës** onion bulb
buletín, ~i m. sh. ~e, ~et. bulletin
bulevárd, ~i m. sh. ~e, ~et. boulevard, avenue
bulmét, ~i m. sh. ~ra, ~rat. dairy produce
bulmetór/e, ~ja f. sh. ~e, ~et. dairy
bulón, ~i m. sh. ~a, ~at. tek. bolt
bum, ~i m. sh. ~e, ~et. ek. boom
bumeráng, ~u m. sh. ~ë, ~ët. boomerang
bunkér, ~i m. sh. ~ë, ~ët. 1. **usht.** bunker; 2. **tek.** bunker
buqét/ë, ~a f. sh. ~a, ~at. bunch, nosegay (of flowers)
burbúqe, ~ja f. sh. ~e, ~et. bot. bud
bur/g, ~gu m. sh. ~gje, ~gjet. jail, prison, gaol
burgím, ~i m. sh. ~e, ~et. imprisonment, confinement; **burgim
i përjetshëm** life imprisonment
burgós kal., ~a, ~ur. imprison, jail
burgósur, ~i (i) m. sh. ~, ~it (të). prisoner
burím, ~i m. sh. ~e, ~et. 1. spring, fountain; 2. source,
origin
burimór, ~e mb. source; **material burimor** source material
búrm/ë, ~a f. sh. ~a, ~at. screw
burokrát, ~i m. sh. ~ë, ~ët. bureaucrat
burokratík, ~e mb. bureaucratic
bur/ón jokal., ~ói, ~úar. 1. spring; gush; 2. **fig.** derive,
stem from
búrs/ë, ~a f. sh. ~a, ~at. scholarship
búrs/ë, ~a f. sh. ~a, ~at. stock exchange; stock-market
búrr/ë ~i m. sh. ~a, ~at. 1. man; male; 2. husband
burrërí, ~a f. 1. manhood; virility; 2. bravery, valour
burrërór, ~e mb. 1. manly, manful; 2. brave, valiant,
courageous
bust, ~i m. sh. ~e, ~et. art. bust
búsull, ~a f. sh. ~a, ~ at. compass
bush, ~i m. sh. ~e, ~et. bot. box, box-wood
but, ~i m. sh. ~e, ~et. tun
bútë (i,e) mb. 1. soft, smooth; **zë i butë** soft voice; 2.
mellow; **qëndrim i butë** a mellow attitude; 3. meek, lenient;
4. tender, gentle, sweet; 5. mild; **mot i butë** mild weather;
6. tame **butësí**, ~a f. softness, smoothness
butësísht ndajf. softly, gently
buxhét, ~i m. sh. ~e, ~et. fin. budget
búz/ë, ~a f. sh. ~ë, ~ët. 1. **anat.** lip; **buza e sipërme (e
poshtme)** the upper (lower) lip; **mbledh (rrudh) buzët** curl
one's lips; **var buzët** hang one's lips; 2. lip, edge, brim,
brink; **në buzë të varrit** on the brink of the grave

buzëqésh jokal., ~a, ~ur. smile
buzëqéshj/e, ~a f. sh. ~e, ~et. smile
buzëqéshur ndajf smilingly
buzëvárur mb. sulky, sullen
byrék, ~u m. sh. ~ë, ~ët gjell. pie
byró, ~ja f. sh. ~, ~të. bureau
byzylyk, ~u m. sh. ~ë, ~ët. bracelet

ca pakuf. bised. some; **ca njerëz** some people
ca ndajf. some; a few; **ca nga ca** little by little
ca/k, ~ku m. sh. ~qe, ~qet. 1. limit, boundary, border line;
2. **fig.** limit
caktím, ~i m. 1. fixation, fixing; 2. delimitation; 3.
appointment; 4. allocation
cakt/ój kal., ~óva, ~úar. 1. fix, set, settle, determine;
caktoj çmimin fix the price; **caktoj datën** set the date; 2.
define, limit, delimit; 3. appoint, designate, nominate
caktúar (i,e) mb. 1. fixed, settled; 2. appointed, fixed; 3.
definite, specific, particular
car, ~i m. sh. ~ë, ~ët. tsar, tzar, czar
cékët (i,e) mb. 1. shallow, shoal; **ujë i cekët** shallow water;
2. **fig.** shallow, superficial
cektësí, ~a f. sh. ~, ~të. 1. shallowness; shallows, shoal;
2. **fig.** superficiality
cen, ~i m. sh. ~e, ~et. blemish, defect, fault (edhe **fig.**)
cením, ~i m. sh. ~e, ~et. 1. **mjek.** lesion; 2. violation;
infringement; 3. intrusion, encroachment
cen/ój kal., ~óva, ~úar. 1. infringe; violate; 2. encroach,
intrude
censúr/ë, ~a f. censorship
censurím, ~i m. sh. ~e, ~et. censorship
censur/ój kal., ~óva, ~úar. censor
centigrád/ë, ~a f. sh. ~ë, ~ët. centigrade
centigrám, ~i m. sh. ~ë, ~ët. centigram
centilít/ër, ~ri m. sh. ~ra, ~rat. centiliter
centimét/ër, ~ri m. sh. ~ra, ~rat. centimeter
centrál, ~i m. sh. ~e, ~et. power-station, power plant;
central atomik a nuclear power-station
centralíst, ~i m. sh. ~ë, ~ët. telephone operator,
telephonist
centralíz/ëm, ~mi m. centralism
centraliz/ój kal., ~óva, ~úar. centralize
centríst, ~i m. sh. ~ë, ~ët. centrist
centríz/ëm, ~mi m. centrism **centr/ój kal., ~óva, ~úar.** 1.
center; 2. **sport.** center
cep, ~i m. sh. ~a, ~at. edge, brink; **në cep të tavolinës** on
the edge of the table
ceremoní, ~a f. sh. ~, ~të. ceremony; **ceremoni martese** a
wedding (marriage) ceremony
ceremoniál, ~i m. ceremonial
ceremoniál mb. ~, ~le. ceremonious
ceremoníal, ~i m. ceremonial
cérm/ë, ~a f. mjek. gout
certifikát/ë, ~a f. sh. ~a, ~at. certificate; **certifikatë
lindjeje (martese, vdekjeje)** a birth (marriage, death)
certificate
cicërím/ë, ~a f. sh. ~a, ~at. chirp, tweet
cicër/ój kal., ~óva, ~úar. chirp, tweet, warble
cíf/ël, ~la f. sh. ~la, ~lat. splinter; **cifël druri (metali,
xhami)** a splinter of wood (metal, glass) **ciflóhet vetv.** scale
off
cigán, ~i m. sh. ~ë, ~ët. Bohemian, gypsy

cigáre, ~ja f. sh. ~e, ~et. cigarette; **letër cigareje**
cigarette- paper; **një paketë cigare** a packet of cigarettes;
cigare me filtër filter-tip (filter-tipped cigarette)
cigarísht/e, ~ja f. sh. ~e, ~et. cigarette-holder
cík/ël, ~li m. sh. ~le, ~lat. cycle; series
ciklik ~e mb. cyclic
ciklón, ~i m. sh. ~e, ~et. meteor. cyclone
cilësí, ~a f. sh. ~, ~të. 1. quality; **mallra të cilësisë më
të lartë** goods of the highest quality; 2. attribute,
characteristic; 3. special (distinguishing) feature
cilësisht ndajf. qualitatively
cilës/ój kal., ~óva, ~úar. qualify
cilësór, ~e mb. 1. qualitative; **përmirësim cilësor**
qualitative improvement; 2. **gram.** qualificative
cilësúar (i,e) mb. qualified
cíl/i, ~a sh. ~ët, ~at. pyet. who; which; whom
cíli (i), ~a (e) lidhor. sh. ~ët (të), ~at (të) who; that
cilidó, ciladó pakuf. sh. **cilëdó, cilatdó.** whoever
cilínd/ër, ~ri m. sh. ~ra, ~rat. 1. **gjeom.** cylinder; 2. **tek.**
cylinder **cilindrík.** ~e mb. cylindrical
cimbídh kal., ~a, ~ur. pinch, nip
cingërím/ë, a f. sh. ~a, ~at. freeze, frost
cingún, ~i m. sh. ~ë, ~ët. miser
ciník, ~u m. sh. ~ë, ~ët. cynic
ciník mb. ~, ~e. cynical
ciníz/ëm, ~mi m. cynicism
cíp/ë, ~a f. sh. ~a, ~at. 1. film, coating, layer; 2.
membrane, skin
cipëplásur mb. shameless, impudent
cir/k, ~ku m. sh. ~qe, ~qet. circus
cirónk/ë, ~a f. sh. ~a, ~at. **zool.** bleak
cist, ~i m. sh. ~e, ~et. **mjek.** cyst
cistérn/ë, ~a f. sh. ~a, ~at. **tek.** cistern, tank
citát, ~i m. sh. ~e, ~et. quotation
civíl, ~i m. sh. ~ë, ~ët. civilian
civíl, ~e mb. civil; **të drejtat civile** civil rights; **gjendja
civile** civil status; **luftë civile** civil war
cjap, ~i m. sh. cjep, cjéptë he-goat, billy-goat
cóp/ë, ~a f. sh. ~a, ~at. bit, piece, particle, scrap, crumb,
morsel
copët/ój kal., ~óva, úar. break, smash, tear to pieces
cun/g, ~gu m. sh. ~gje, ~gjet. 1. stump; 2. **anat.** stump
curríl, ~i m. sh. ~a, ~at. trickle

Ç

çád/ër, ~ra f. sh. **~ra, ~rat.** 1. umbrella; 2. parasol, sun-
shade, beach umbrella; 3. tent; 4. **fig.** umbrella
çáfk/ë, ~a f. sh. **~a, ~at.** zool. mew
çaj ~i m. bot. tea; **një gotë çaj** a cup of tea; **lugë çaji**
teaspoon; **takëm çaji** tea-service
ça/j kal., ~va, ~rë. 1. cleave, split, devide; **çaj dru** cleave
wood; 2. **fig.** hack, hew; 3. cleave a path through, make one's
way; 4. penetrate, pass through, plough through
çajník, ~u m. sh. **~ë, ~ët.** tea-kettle, teapot
çak/áll, ~álli m. sh. **~áj, ~ájt.** zool. jackal
çák/ëll, ~lli m. gravel
çakërr, ~e mb. squint-eyed
çakmák, ~u m. sh. **~ë, ~ët.** cigarette lighter
çakord/ój kal., ~óva, ~úar. muz. put out of tune
çalamán, ~e mb. lame
çálë (i, e) mb. lame, limping
çálë-çálë ndajf. limpingly
çalím, ~i m. sh. **~e, ~et.** hobble
çal/ój kal., ~óva, ~úar. hobble, limp
çálthi ndajf. limpingly
çamarrók, ~e mb. naughty, mischievous; **fëmijë çamarrok** a
naughty child
çamçakëz, ~i m. chewing-gum
çanák, ~u m. sh. **~ë, ~ët.** bowl
çáng/ë, ~a f. sh. **~a, ~at.** gong; **i bie çangës** beat (sound)
the gong
çánt/ë, ~a f. sh. **~a, ~at.** bag; handbag; **çantë shkolle**
satchel; **çantë veglash** toolbag
çap, ~i m. sh. **~a, ~at.** step; **çap i shpejtë** quick step
çapkën, ~i m. sh. **~ë, ~ët.** imp, urchin
çap/úa, ~oi m. sh. **~ónj, ~ónjtë.** spur; claw; **çaponjtë e
këndesit** cock's spur; **çaponjtë e maces** cat's claws
çarçáf, ~i m. sh. **~ë, ~ët.** sheet
çar/ë, ~a (e) f. sh. **~a, ~at.** crevice, crack, fissure, rift,
split
çar/k, ku m. sh. **~qe, ~qet.** trap; **ngre çarkun** lay (set) a
trap; **çark minjsh** mouse-trap
çarmatím, ~i m. disarmament
çarmatós kal., ~a, ~ur. 1. disarm; 2. **fig.** disarm
çast, ~i m. sh. **~e, ~et.** instant, moment; **këtë çast** at this
moment; **në çast** in a moment; **për një çast** for a moment
çatí, ~a f. sh. **~, ~të.** roof
çdo pakuf. every, any; each
çdokúsh pakuf. everyone, everybody
çdonjër/í, ~a pakuf. everyone
çéhr/e, ~ja f. sh. **~e, ~et.** mien, complexion, countenance
çe/k, ~ku m. sh. **~qe, ~qet.** cheque, check; **çek i bardhë** a
blank cheque
çekán, ~i m. sh. **~ë, ~ët.** hammer
çekíç, ~i m. sh. **~ë, ~ët.** small hammer
çel kal., ~a, ~ur. 1. open, unlock; 2. open out, bloom,
blossom (the flowers); 3. open (an account, etc.); 4. open (a
meeting, debate, etc.); 5. hatch

çélem vetv. 1. brighten up, cheer up; 2. clear up; **koha u çel** it cleared up; 3. bloom, blossom

çélës, ~i m. sh. ~a, ~at. 1. key; **çelësat e makinës** the car keys; 2. spanner, wrench; 3. **tek.** key; 4. **fig.** key; 5. **muz.** key, clef

çelësbërës, ~i m. sh. ~, ~it. locksmith

çelët (i, e) mb. light (color)

çelí/k, ~ku m. sh. ~qe, ~qet. steel

çelikós kal., ~a, ~ur. steel, strengthen

çelikósem vetv. steel oneself, harden

çelíktë (i, e) m. 1. steely; 2. **fig.** steely, solid as a rock

çélur (i, e) mb. 1. open; 2. light (color)

çengél, ~i m. sh. ~a, ~at. hook; grapnel

çérdh/e, ~ja f. sh. ~e, ~et. 1. nest; 2. créche; 3. **fig.** nest; **çerdhe hajdutësh** a nest of thieves; 4. **usht.** nest; **çerdhe mitralozi** a machine-gun nest

çerék, ~u m. sh. ~ë, ~ët. quarter; **një çerek ore** a quarter of an hour

çét/ë, ~a f. sh. ~a, ~at. unit

çézm/ë. ~a f. sh. ~a, ~at. drinking-fountain

çështj/e, ~a f. sh. ~e, ~et. question, matter, issue, problem, matter; cause; **çështje për jetë a vdekje** a matter of life and death; **Si qëndron çështja?** What is the matter?

çfárë përem. pyetës **(lidhor)**. what; whatever

çfarëdó pakuf. whatever, any

çfarëdósh/ëm (i) ~me (e) mb. whatever, of any kind

çibúk, ~u m. sh. ~ë, ~ët. smoking-pipe

çiflí/g, ~gu m. sh. ~gje, ~gjet. estate

çift, ~i m. sh. ~e, ~et. pair, couple

çift, ~e mb. even; **numër çift** even number

çíft/e, ~ja f. sh. ~e, ~et. double-barrelled gun

çifút, ~i m. sh. ~ë, ~ët. Jew, Israelite, Hebrew

çik/ë, ~a f. sh. ~a, ~at. bit; **çikë e nga një çikë** bit by bit

çiklíst, ~i m. sh. ~ë, ~ët. cyclist

çiklíz/ëm, ~mi m. **sport.** cycling

çikrík, ~u m. sh. ~ë, ~ët. pulley; capstan

çilimí, ~u m. sh. ~nj, ~njtë. kid, child

çíltas (çíltazi) ndajf. frankly, openly; **flas çiltas** speak openly (frankly)

çíltër (i, e) mb. frank, candid, straightforward

çíltëri, ~a f. candidness, sincerity, open-heartedness, frankness

çiltrísht ndajf. frankly, candidly

çiménto, ~ja f. cement

çiment/ój kal., ~óva, ~úar. 1. cement; 2. **fig.** cement

çímk/ë, ~a f. sh. ~a, ~at. **zool.** bed-bug

çinteresúar (i, e) mb. disinterested, unconcerned

çirák, ~u m. sh ~ë, ~ët. apprentice

çírrem vetv. 1. be, get torn; 2. get scratched, scratch oneself; 3. shout oneself hoarse

çízm/e, ~ja kreys. sh. ~e, ~et. boot; **çizme lëkure** leather boots; çizme gome rubber boots

çjerr kal., ~óra, çjérrë. 1. tear, rip; 2. split (one's ears); 3. tear off, pull off

çjérrë (i, e) **mb.** 1. torn; 2. hoarse
çjérrës, ~e **mb.** piercing, jarring
çka përem. pyet. (lidhor). what
çka ndajf. so-so
çlírët (i, e) **mb.** loose, slack, flaccid
çlírët ndajf. 1. easily; 2. loosely
çlirím, ~i m. 1. liberation; **çlirimi kombëtar** national
liberation; 2. emancipation
çlirimtár, ~i m. **sh.** ~ë, ~ët. liberator
çlirimtár, ~e **mb.** liberation; **luftë çlirimtare** liberation war
çlir/ój kal., ~óva, ~úar. 1. liberate, emancipate; 2. loose;
3. exempt; 4. emit, release
çlódh kal., ~a, ~ur. rest
çlódhem vetv. rest, repose, have (take) a rest
çlódhës, ~e **mb.** restful; **ngjyra çlodhëse për sytë** colors
restful to the eye
çlódhje, ~a f. rest, repose
çmbësht/jéll kal., ~ólla, ~jéllë. unfold, unwrap, unroll;
uncoil, unfurl
çmend kal., ~a, ~ur. madden, make (send, drive) crazy
(insane)
çméndem vetv. 1. go mad (crazy, insane); 2. **fig.** be crazy
about
çmendínë, ~a f. **sh.** ~a, ~at. mental home, mental hospital
çméndur (i, e) **mb.** crazy, mad, insane, deranged
çmendurí, ~a f. **sh.** ~, ~të. insanity, lunacy, madness,
derangement
çmësóhem vetv. unaccustom, break the habit of
çmës/ój kal. ~óva, ~úar. break off, give up, wean oneself
from, rid oneself from
çmilitariz/ój kal., ~óva, ~úar. demilitarize
çmim, ~i m. **sh.** ~e, ~et. 1. price, charge, cost; **çmimi me
pakicë (me shumicë)** retail (wholesale) price; **ulja e çmimit**
the reduction in (of) the price; 2. prize, reward, bounty
çmobiliz/ój kal., ~óva, ~úar. usht. demobilize
çmobilizúar (i, e) **mb.** demobilized
çmoj kal., çmóva, çmúar 1. estimate, evaluate, value, assess;
2. appreciate, estimate
çmont/ój kal., ~óva, ~úar. dismantle, disassemble, take to
pieces
çmos pakuf. bised. everything; **bëj çmos** do one's best, do
one's utmost, try one's best, do all one can, do the best one
can
çmúar (i, e) **mb.** 1. precious, valuable, priceless; 2. **gur i
çmuar** precious gem, stone; 2. **fig.** estimable, highly esteemed
çmúesh/ëm (i), ~me (e) **mb.** precious; appreciable, estimable
çnder/ój kal., ~óva, úar. 1. dishonor, disgrace, shame; 2.
rape, violate
çnjerëzór, ~e **mb.** inhuman, heartless, pitiless; **trajtim
çnjerëzor** inhuman treatment
çobán, ~i m. **sh.** ~ë, ~ët. herdsman, shepherd
çóhem vetv. 1. get up, stand up; **çohem më këmbë** stand up; 2.
wake up; 3. rise
çoj kal., çóva, çúar 1. send, dispatch, forward; **çoj një
letër** send a letter; 2. send (word, greetings,
congratulations); 3. transmit, convey, carry, conduct; 4.
lead, guide, direct; 5. fare, get on, get along

çoj kal., çóva, çúar. 1. raise, lift, elevate; **çoj dorën** raise one's hand; 2. put up, pull up; 3. wake somebody up; 4. raise (the voice etc.)

çokollát/ë f. sh. ~a, ~at. chocolate

çoráp, ~i m. kryes. sh. ~ë, ~ët edhe **~e, ~et.çorape burrash** socks; **çorape grash** stocking; **një palë çorape** a pair of socks (stockings)

çórb/ë, ~a f. 1. porridge; 2. **fig.** hotch-potch, hodge-podge

çorganizím, ~i m. sh. ~e, ~et. disorganization

çorganiz/ój kal., ~óva, ~úar. disorganize

çorganizúes, ~e mb. disorganizing

çorientím, ~i m. sh. ~e, ~et. disorientation

çorient/ój kal., ~óva, ~úar. 1. disorientate; 2. **fig.** confuse

çorodít (çorodís) kal., ~a, ~ur. deprave, debauch, lead astray

çorodítj/e, ~a f. sh. ~e, ~et. depravity, corruption

çorodítur (i, e) mb. depraved, debauched, degenerate

çrregullím.~i m. sh. ~e, ~et. 1. disorder, clutter, confusion, disarray, mess; 2. **mjek.** disorder; **çregullim mendor** mental disorder

çrregull/ój kal., ~óva, ~úar. mess up, disorder

çrrégullt (i, e) mb. 1. disordered, irregular; 2. messy, untidy

çrrënjós kal., ~a, ~ur. 1. uproot; 2. **fig.** root out, eradicate, tear up by the roots

çudí. ~a f. sh. ~, ~të. 1. wonder, amazement; **si për çudi** for a wonder; 2. marvel, miracle; **çuditë e natyrës** the marvels of the nature

çudibërës, ~e mb. miraculous, marvellous

çudít (çudís) kal., ~a, ~ur. marvel, wonder, look aghast

çudítem vetv. be astonished, surprised, amazed

çuditërísht ndajf. surprisingly

çudítshëm (i), ~me (e) mb. strange, odd, unusual, uncommon, peculiar

çudítur (i, e) mb. surprised, astonished, amazed, flabbergasted

çukít (çukís) kal., ~a, ~ur. peck

çukítje, ~a f. sh. ~e, ~et. peck

çun, ~i m. sh. ~a, ~at. boy, lad, youngster

çúp/ë, ~a f. sh. ~a, ~at. girl, lass

çur/g, ~gu m. sh. ~gje, ~gjet. gush

çurg/ón jokal., ~ói, ~úar. gush out

dac, ~i m. sh. ~a, ~at. tom-cat, male cat
dáck/ë. ~ f. sh. ~a, ~at. slap, smack; **i jap dikujt një dackë turinjve** slap somebody on the face
dádo, ~ja f. sh. ~, ~t. baby-sitter
dádo, ~ja f. sh. ~, ~t **tek**. nut (of a screw)
dafin/ë, ~a f. sh. ~, ~at. **bot**. laurel; **fle mbi dafina** rest on one's laurels
daják, ~u m. sh. ~ë, ~ët. cudgel; **i dha dajak** gave him a good beating
dáj/ë, ~a m. sh. ~a, ~at **dhe** ~llárë, ~llárët. uncle (mother's brother)
dájr/e, ~ja f. sh ~e, ~et. tambourine
daktilografí, ~a f. typing
daktilografím, ~i m. typing, type-writing
daktilografíst, ~i m. sh. ë, ët. typist
daktilograf/ój ~óva, ~uár. type
dal jokal., dóla, dálë. 1. exit, go out; **dal jashtë** go out; 2. break away, withdraw from; 3. come out, appear; **dal faqebardhë** come out successfu; 4. get out of; **të dalë ku të dalë** happen what may
dalëngadálë ndajf. slowly; gradually; little by little, bit by bit
dálj/e, ~ f. sh. ~e, ~et. 1. exit, way out; 2. appearance; 3. emergence
dált/ë, ~a f. sh ~a, ~at. chisel
dalt/ój kal., ~óva, ~úar. chisel
dallaveraxhí, ~u m. sh ~nj, ~njtë. swindler, defrauder
dallavér/e, ~ja f. kryes. sh. ~e, ~et. swindle, fraud
dallëndysh/e, ~ja f. sh. ~, ~et. swallow; **me një dallëndyshe s'vjen pranvera** one swallow does not make a summer
dállg/ë, ~a f. sh. ~ë, ~ët. 1. wave, ripple; **dallgë të mëdha** huge waves; 2. **fig**. wave
dallgëz/ón jokal., ~ói, ~úar. wave
dallím, ~i m. sh ~e, ~et. distinction, differentiation, discrimination
dallóhem vetv. be distinguished, be notable
dall/ój ~óva, ~úar. 1. distinguish, discern, descry; 2. differentiate, discriminate
dallúar (i,e) mb. distinguished, celebrated, noted, eminent
dallúes, ~e **mb**. distinctive
dallúesh/ëm (i), ~me (e) **mb**. distinguishable, evident
damár, ~i m. sh. ~ë, ët. **biol**. 1. vein; 2. grain; 3. **gjeol**. lode; 4. **fig**. vein, mood
dámk/ë ~a f. sh. ~a, ~at. brand
damkos kal., ~a, ~ur. brand
dárdh/ë, ~a f. sh. ~a, ~at **edhe** ~ë, ~ët. pear; pear tree
dár/ë, ~a f. sh. ~ë, ët. pinchers
dárk/ë, ~a f. sh. ~a, ~at. dinner, supper; **jap një darkë** give a dinner; **ha darkë** have dinner, sup, have supper
dark/ój jokal., ~óva, ~úar. dine, sup, have dinner
dásm/ë, ~a f. sh. ~a, ~at. wedding
dasmór, ~i m. sh. ~ë, ~ët. wedding guest
dash, ~ m. sh. desh, déshtë. **zool**. ram
dasha/ ~kéq, ~kéqe **mb**. malevolent

dashamír, ~i m. sh. ~ë, ~ët. benevolent; **njeri dashamir** a benevolent person

dashamirësí, ~a f. benevolence, kindness

dáshj/e, ~a. f. willingness; **me dashje** willingly; **pa dashje** reluctantly, unwillingly

dashnór, ~i m. sh. ~ë, ~ët. lover, boyfriend, beau

dashnór/e, ~ja f. sh. ~e, ~et. lover, girlfriend

dáshur, ~a (e) f. sh. ~a, (të) darling, sweetheart

dáshur, ~i (i) m. sh. ~, ~it (të) lover, boyfriend

dáshur (i,e) mb. 1. dear, beloved; 2. lovable

dashurí, ~a f. love; **bie në dashuri** fall in love; **bëj dashuri** make love to somebody; **me dashuri** lovingly

dashuróhem vetv. 1. fall in love; 2. be in love

dashur/oj kal., ~óva, ~úar. 1. love; 2. be fond of, be keen on

dát/ë, ~a f. sh. ~a, ~at. date; **Sa është data sot?** What's the date today?

datëlindj/e, ~a f. sh. ~e, ~et. birthday, date of birth; **Gëzuar ditëlindjen!** Happy birthday!

dat/ój kal., ~óva, ~úar. date

daúll/e, ~ja f. sh. ~e, ~et. drum; **i bie daulles** beat the drum

debát, ~ m. sh. ~e, ~et. debate, argument, controversy; **hap debatin** open the debate; **debat i gjallë** a heated debate

debí, ~a f. sh. ~, ~të. fin. debit

debitór, ~i m. sh. ~ë, ~ët. debtor

debut/ój jokal., ~óva, ~úar. make one's debut

decilít/ër, ~ri m. sh. ~ra, ~rat. deciliter

decimét/ër, ~ri m. sh. ~ra, rat. decimeter

deduksión, ~i m. sh. ~e, ~et. deduction

dedukt/ój kal., dhe jokal., ~óva, ~úar. deduce **deficít**, ~i m. sh. ~e, ~et. fin. deficit

deformím, ~i m. sh. ~e, ~et. deformation

deform/ój kal., ~óva, ~úar. deform

dég/ë, ~a f. sh. ~ë, ~ët. 1. branch, limb, stem, bough; 2. section, division, affiliate; 3. branch, tributary

degjenerím, ~i m. sh. ~e, ~et. degeneration

degjener/ój jokal. dhe kal., ~óva, ~úar. degenerate

deh kal., ~a, ~ur. 1. intoxicate; 2. **fig.** intoxicate

déhem vetv. 1. get drunk, intoxicated; 2. **fig.** get intoxicated

déhur (i,e) mb. drunk, drunken, intoxicated

dekadént, ~e mb. decadent

dekád/ë, ~a f. sh. ~a, ~at. decade

dekán, ~i m. sh. ~ë, ~ët. dean; **dekani i fakultetit** dean of the faculty

deklarát/ë ~a f. sh. ~a ~at. declaration, statement; **bëj një deklaratë** make a statement

deklar/ój kal, óva, ~úar. declare

dekompozím, ~i m. decay, decomposition

dekorát/ë, ~a f. ah. ~a, ~at. decoration, medal

dekor/ój kal., ~ó, ~úar. decorate, give a medal to somebody

dekrét, ~i m. sh. ~e, ~et. decree

dekret/ój kal., ~óva, ~úar. decree

dél/e, ~ja f. sh. ~e, ~et dhe dhen, ~të. zool. ewe, sheep

delegación, ~i m. sh. ~e, ~et. delegation
delegát, ~i m. sh. ~ë, ~ët. delegate
deleg/ój kal, ~óva, ~úar. delegate
delfín, ~i m. sh. ~ë, ~ët. zool. delphin
delikát, ~e mb. 1. delicate, smooth, soft; 2. fragile, frail; 3. delicate, difficult, ticklish
dem, ~i m. sh. ~a, ~at. zool. bull; **e zë (e kap) demin për brirësh** take the bull by the horns
demagóg, ~u m. sh. ~ë, ~ët. demagogue
demagogjí, ~a f. sh. ~, ~të. demagogy
demagogjík, ~e mb. demagogic
demask/ój kal, ~óva, ~úar. expose, unmask
dembél, ~e mb. lazy, idle, indolent, slothful
demografí, ~a f. demography
demokrací, ~a f. sh. ~, ~të. democracy; **demokraci parlamentare** parliamentary democracy
demokrát, ~i m. sh. ~ë, ~ët. democrat
demokratík, ~e mb. democratic; **qeveri demokratike** democratic government; **shoqëri demokratike** a democratic society
demokratizím, ~i. democratization
demokratiz/ój kal., ~óva, ~úar. democratize
demonstrát/ë, ~ë, ~a, ~at. demonstration; **demonstratë masive** mass demonstration; demonstratë proteste protest demonstration
demonstratív, ~e mb. demonstrative
demonstrím, ~i m. sh. ~e, ~et. demonstration
demonstr/ój kal, ~óva, ~úar. 1. demonstrate, show; 2. demonstrate, take part in a public rally
demoraliz/oj kal, ~óva, ~úar. demorilize, dispirit, dishearten
dendësi, ~a f. density; **dendësia e popullsisë** population density
déndur (i,e) mb. dense; thick
déndur ndajf. often, frequently; **ndodh dendur** it happens often
deng, ~u m. sh. déngje, déngjet. bundle, bale
denigrím, i m. sh. ~e, ~et. denigration
denigr/ój kal, ~óva, ~úar. denigrate
denonc/ój kal., ~óva, ~úar. denounce
dentár, ~e mb. dental
dentíst, ~i m. sh. ~ë, ~ët. dentist
dénjë (i,e) mb. worthy, deserving
denj/ój kal., ~óva, ~úar. deign, condescend
departamént, ~i m. sh. ~e, ~et. departament
depërtím, ~i m. sh. ~e, ~et. penetration
depërt/ój kal., ~óva, ~úar. penetrate
depërtúes, ~e mb. penetrating
dépo, ~ja f. sh. ~, ~t. depot, storehouse, warehouse
depozit/ój kal., ~óva, ~úar. 1. deposit, store; 2. fin. deposit, bank, save
depresión, ~i m. sh. ~e, ~et. 1. gjeogr., gjeol. depression; 2. ek. depression; 3. mjek. depression
deputét, ~i m. sh. ~ë, ~ët. deputy
derdh kal., ~a, ~ur. 1. pour (out); 2. spill; 3. shed; **derdh lot** shed tears; 3. tek. cast, mould
dérdhem vetv. 1. spill over; 2. overflow; 3. fig. overflow

dér/ë, ~a f. sh. dyer, dyert. door; derë **më derë** from door to door; **hap (mbyll) derën** open (close) the door; **trokas në derë** knock at the door

déri parafj. till, until, up to; **deri tani** up to now

derisá lidh. till; as long as

derr, ~i m. sh. ~a, ~at. 1. pig, hog, swine; **mish derri** pork; 2. **fig.** pig

deshifr/ój kal., ~óva, ~úar. decipher, decode

det, ~i m. sh. ~e, ~et. sea; **Deti Adriatik** Adriatic Sea; **Deti Mesdhe** Mediterranian Sea

detál, ~i m. sh. ~e, ~et. tek. component

detár, ~i m. sh. ~ë, ~ët. seaman, sailor, mariner

detár, ~e mb. 1. sea, maritime; 2. nautical, naval

detashmént, ~i m. sh. ~e, ~et. usht. detachment

detektív, ~i m. sh. ~ë, ~ët. detective

detyr/ë, ~a f. sh. ~a, ~at. 1. duty, task, assignment; **kryej detyrën** do one's duty; 2. post, position, office, job

detyrím, ~i m. sh. ~e, ~et. 1. obligation; **përmbush një detyrim** fulfil an obligation; 2. compulsion

detyr/ój kal., ~óva, ~úar. compel, oblige, force

detyrúes, ~e mb. compelling, constraining

detyrúesh/ëm (i), ~me (e) mb. necessary, obligatory, compulsory; **shërbim i detyrueshëm ushtarak** compulsory military service

devé, ~ja f. sh. ~, ~të. zool. camel

devij/ój kal., ~óva, ~úar. deviate, veer, digress

devoción, ~i m. libr. devotion

devótsh/ëm (i), ~me (e) mb. devoted, dedicated; **mësues i devotshëm** a devoted teacher

devotshmërí, ~a f. libr. devotion

dezertím, ~i m. sh. ~e, ~et. 1. usht. desertion; 2. desertion, defection

dezert/ój jokal., ~óva, ~úar. 1. usht. desert; 2. desert, defect

dezinfekt/ój kal., ~óva, ~úar. disinfect, decontaminate

dezinfektúes, ~i m. sh. ~, ~it. disinfectant

dëbím, ~i m. sh. ~e, ~et. 1. banishment; 2. expulsion; 3. discharge, dismissal

dëb/ój kal., ~óva, ~úar. 1. banish; 2. expel; 3. dismiss, discharge; 4. drive out, force out, put out

dëfrím, ~i m. sh. ~e, ~et. entertainment, amusement

dëfr/éj jokal., ~éva, ~yer. entertain, divert, amuse

dëft/éj kal., ~éva, ~yer. 1. tell, narrate; 2. show, indicate; 3. disclose, reveal, tell

dëftés/ë, ~a f. sh. ~a, ~at. receipt, sales slip, voucher

dëftór, ~e mb. gjuh. indicative; **mënyra dëftore** indicative mood

dëgjimór, ~e mb. libr. hearing, auditory, aural

dëgj/ój kal., ~óva, ~úar. 1. hear, listen; 2. listen to

dëgjúar (i,e) mb. noted, renowned, celebrated, famous; **piktor i dëgjuar** a noted painter

dëgjúes, ~i m. sh. ~, ~it. listener, auditor

dëlírë (i,e) mb. chaste, pure

dëm, ~i m. sh. ~e, ~et. 1. damage, harm; 2. loss; destruction, devastation; 3. detriment

dëmsh/ëm (i), ~me (e) *mb.* harmful, noxious; **duhani është i dëmshëm** smoking is harmful
dëmtím, ~i *m. sh.* **~e, ~et.** damage; injury
dëmt/ój kal., ~óva, ~úar. damage, injure, impair, hurt
dëním, ~i *m. sh.* **~e, ~et.** 1. sentence, condemnation; 2. punishment **dënim me vdekje** capital punishment; 3. penalty
dën/ój kal., ~óva, ~úar. 1. sentence, condemn; 2. punish; penalize
dënúesh/ëm (i), ~me (e) *mb.* punishable, blamable; condemnable
dërg/ój kal., ~óva, ~úar. 1. send; **dërgoj një pako** send a parcel; 2. dispatch, forward
dërgúes, ~i *m. sh.* **~, ~it.** sender, dispatcher, conveyer
dërrás/ë, ~a *f. sh.* **~a, ~at.** plank
dërrm/ój kal., ~óva, ~úar. 1. crush, break into pieces; 2. *fig.* crush, defeat, overwhelm
dëshir/ë, ~a *f. sh.* **~a, ~at.** wish, desire, longing; **plotësoj dëshirat e dikujt** satisfy one's desires
dëshir/ój kal., ~óva, ~úar. wish, desire, yearn
dëshirúesh/ëm (i), ~me (e) *mb.* desirable
dëshmí, ~a *f. sh.* **~, ~të.** 1. testimony, witness, evidence; 2. testimonial
dëshmitár, ~i *m. sh.* **~ë, ~ët.** witness, testifier, attestant
dëshm/ój kal., ~óva, ~úar. witness, testify, give testimony; attest, certify
dëshmór, ~i *m. sh.* **~ë, ~ët.** martyr
dëshpërím, ~i *m. sh.* **~e, ~et.** despair, desperation
dëshpërúar (i,e) *mb.* desperate, despairing, despondent, downcast
dështím, ~i *m. sh.* **~e, ~et.** 1. *mjek.* miscarriage, abortion; 2. failure, miscarriage
dësht/ój jokal., ~óva, ~úar. 1. *mjek.* miscarry; 2. fail, miscarry
di kal., ~ta, ~tur. 1. know; **me sa di unë** as far as I know; 2. know how to
diabét, ~i *m. mjek.* diabetes
diafrágm/ë, ~a *f. sh.* **~a, ~at. anat.** diaphragm
diagnóz/ë, ~a *f. sh.* **~a, ~at. mjek.** diagnosis
diagrám, ~i *m. sh.* **~e, ~et.** diagram
dialékt, ~i *m. sh.* **~e, ~et. gjuh.** dialect
dialektík, ~e *mb. filoz.* dialectical
dialektór, ~e *mb.* dialectal
dialóg, ~u *m. sh.* **~ë, ~ët.** dialogue
diamánt, ~i *m. sh.* **~e, ~et.** diamond
diamét/ër, ~ri *m. sh.* **~ra, ~rat. gjeom.** diameter
diametrál, ~e *mb.* diametrical
diatéz/ë, ~a *f. sh.* **~a, ~at. gram.** voice; **diateza veprore (pësore)** the active (passive) voice
diçká pakuf. something
diçká ndajf. somewhat; so-so
didaktík, ~e *mb.* didactic
díel, ~a (e) *f. sh.* **~a, ~at (të).** Sunday
díe/ll, ~lli *m. astr.* sun; **dritë dielli** sunlight, sunshine; **lindja e diellit** sunrise; **perëndimi i diellit** sunset
diellór, ~e. sunny; solar
diét/ë, ~a *f. sh.* **~a, ~at. mjek.** diet; **mbaj dietë** be (go) on a diet

diferénc/ë, ~a f. sh. ~a, ~at. difference
diferenc/ój kal., ~óva, ~úar. differentiate
díg/ë, ~a f. sh. ~a, ~at. dike, dam
dígjem vetv. dógja (u), djégur. burn; be burning; be (get)
burnt (scorched)
dijení, ~a sh. ~, ~të. knowledge; **s'kam dijeni** have no
knowledge of
díjsh/ëm (i), ~me (e) mb. learned
diktatór, ~i m. sh. ~ë, ~ët. dictator
diktatoriál, ~e mb. dictatorial
diktatúr/ë, ~a f. sh. ~a, ~at. dictatorship
diktím, ~i m. dictation
dikt/ój kal., ~óva, ~úar. detect, track down; ferret out
dikt/ój kal., ~óva, ~úar. 1. dictate; **i diktoj një letër
sekretarit** dictate a letter to the secretary; 2. dictate,
impose
dikú ndajf. somewhere
dikúr ndajf. formerly, at one time, in times past, once upon
a time
dikúrsh/ëm (i), ~me (e) mb. former, past, long past, bygone,
long- ago, ancient
dikúsh (gjin., dhan. dikújt, kallëz. dikë) pakuf. somebody,
someone
dilém/ë, ~a f. sh. ~a, ~at. dilemma; **jam në dilemë** be in a
dilemma; **vë në dilemë** put (place) somebody in a dilemma
diletánt, ~i m. sh. ~ë, ~ët. dilettante
dím/ër, ~ri m. sh. ~ra, ~rat. winter
dimërór, ~e mb. wintry
dinák, ~e mb. foxy,cunning, crafty, artful, sly
dinakërí, ~a f. sh. ~, ~të. craftiness, foxiness, artfulness
dinamík, ~e mb. mek. dynamic
dinamík/ë, ~a f. dynamics
dinamít, ~i m. dynamite
dinámo, ja f. sh. ~, ~t. tek. dynamo; generator
dinastí, ~a f. sh. ~, ~të. dynasty
dinjitét, ~i m. dignity
diplomací, ~a f. diplomacy
diplomát, ~i m. sh. ~ë, ~ët. diplomat
diplomatík, ~e mb. diplomatic; **trupi diplomatik** diplomatic
corps; **imunitet diplomatik** diplomatic immunity
diplóm/ë, ~a f. sh. ~a, ~at. diploma; degree
dirék, ~u m. sh. ~ë, ~ët. det. mast
direktív/ë, ~a f. sh. ~a, ~at. directive, instruction
dirigjént, ~i m. sh. ~ë, ~ët. muz. conductor
dirigj/ój kal., ~óva, ~úar. 1. **muz.** conduct; 2. direct, lead,
guide
disá pakuf. some, several
disfát/ë, ~a f. sh.~a,~at.defeat; **pësoj disfatë** suffer defeat
disí ndajf. somehow, somewhat
disiplín/ë, ~a f. sh. ~a, ~at. discipline; **disiplinë e rreptë**
strict discipline
disiplin/ój kal., ~óva, ~úar. discipline
disiplinór, ~e mb. disciplinary; **masa disiplinore**
disciplinary measures
dis/k, ~ku m. sh. ~qe, ~qet. 1.**sport.** discus; 2.disc, disk,
record
diskredit/ój kal., ~óva, ~úar. discredit
diskreditúes, ~e mb. discreditable

diskriminím, ~i m. sh. **~e, ~et.** discrimination
diskrimin/ój kal., **~óva, ~úar.** discriminate
diskriminúes, ~e mb. discriminating
diskutím, ~i m. sh. **~e, ~et.** discussion, debate
diskut/ój kal., **~óva, ~úar.** discuss, debate, dispute
diskutúesh/ë (i), ~me (e) mb. debatable, disputable, arguable, controversial
dispozicíon, ~i m. sh. **~e, ~et.** disposal; **në dispozicion të** at one's disposal
distánc/ë f. sh. **~a. ~at.** distance
distil/ój kal., **~óva, ~úar.** distill
distinktív, ~i .sh. ~ë, ~ët. badge
dita-ditës ndajf. day after day; day by day
ditár, ~i m. sh. **~ë, ~ët.** diary; **mbaj ditar** keep a diary
dít/ë, ~a f. sh. **~ë, ~ët.** 1. day; daytime, daylight; 2. period, time, age; 3. date, time, particular day; **çdo ditë** every day, day after day; **një ditë** one day, some day; **ditë për ditë** day in, day out; **tërë ditën** all day long
ditëlíndj/e, ~a f. sh. **~e, ~et.** birthday; **festoj ditëlindjen** celebrate one's birthday; **mbrëmje (dhuratë) për ditëlindjen** birthday party (present)
dítën ndajf. during daytime
ditë-púnë, ~a f. sh. **~ë, ~ët.** workday, working day
ditór (i, e) mb. daily; **pagë ditore** daily pay
dítur (i, e) mb. learned, erudite, knowledgeable, well-read; **ia bëj të ditur dikujt** inform somebody of (about) something
diturí, ~a f. sh. **~, ~të.** learning, erudition, knowledge
diván, ~i m. sh. **~e, ~et.** couch, divan, settee, sofa
dividénd, ~i m. sh. **~ë, ~ët. ek.** dividend
divizión, ~i m. **~e, ~et.** usht. division
divórc, ~i m. sh. **~e, ~et.** divorce
djál/ë, ~i m. sh. **djem. djemtë.** 1. boy, guy, lad, chap; 2. son
djalërí, ~a f. boyhood
djall, ~i m. sh. **djaj, djajtë.** devil, demon
djallëzór, ~e mb. devilish, fiendish, hellish
djallëzúar (i, e) mb. mischievious, elfish
djáth/ë, ~i m. sh. **~ëra, ~ërat.** cheese
djáthtas (djathtazi) ndajf. right, rightwards, to the right side; **kthehem djathtas** turn right
djáthtë (i, e) mb. right; **ana e djathtë** the right side
djathtíst, ~e mb. rightist
dje ndajf. yesterday
djeg kal., **dógja, djégur.** 1. burn; 2. scorch, char; 3. nettle, sting; 4. scald; 5. cremate
djégur (i, e) mb. burned, burnt; scorched, parched, singed, charred
djep, ~i. m. sh. **~a, ~at dhe ~e, ~et.** 1. cradle; **tund djepin** rock the cradle; 2. **fig.** cradle; **djepi i kulturës** the cradle of culture
djérs/ë, ~a f. sh. **~ë, ~ët.** sweat, perspiration; **me djersën e ballit** with the sweat of one's brow
djersít jokal., ~a, ~ur. sweat, perspire
djerr, ~e mb. waste, barren

djésh/ëm (i), ~me (e) mb. yesterday's; **gazeta e djeshme** yesterday's paper

d.m.th. lidh. shkurt. **i domethënë.** i. e.

dobësi, ~a f. sh. ~, ~të. weakness, feebleness, fraility

dobës/ój kal., ~óva, ~úar. weaken, enfeeble

dóbët (i, e) mb. 1. weak, frail, feeble; 2. meager; lean, thin; 3. feeble, faint, low; 4. fragile, breakable; 5. poor, deficient; **dritë e dobët** weak light; **rrymë e dobët** weak current

dóbët ndajf. weakly

dobí, ~a f. sh. ~, ~të. good, benefit, utility

dobiprúrës, ~e mb. beneficial

dobísh/ëm (i), ~me (e) mb. useful, profitable

doemós ndajf. necessarily

dogán/ë, ~a f. sh. ~a, ~at. customs house; customs duty; **kaloj doganën** get through customs

dogmatík, ~e mb. dogmatic

dógm/ë, ~a f. sh. ~a, ~at. dogma

dok, ~u m. tekst. duck

doktór, ~i m. sh. ~ë, ~ët. 1. doctor, physician; 2. doctor (degree)

doktrin/ë f. sh. ~a, ~at. doctrine

dokumént, ~i m. sh. ~e, ~et. document; **dokument juridik** legal document

dokumentár, ~e mb. documentary

dokument/ój kal., ~óva, ~úar. document

dolláp, ~i m. sh. ~ë, ~ët. cupboard, sideboard

dollár, ~i f. sh. ~ë, ~ët. dollar

dollí, ~a f. sh. ~, ~të. toast; **ngre një dolli** raise a toast

domát/e, ~ja f. sh. ~e, ~et. tomato; **salcë domatesh** tomato sauce; **sallatë me domate** tomato salad

domethënës, ~e mb. meaningful, significant; telling

dominó, ~ja f. sh. ~, ~të. domino

domosdósh/ëm (i), ~me (e) mb. necessary, indispensable, essential; **ajri, ushqimi dhe uji janë të domosdoshëm për jetën** air, food and water are indispensable to life

domosdoshmërí, ~a f. sh. necessity

doracák, ~u m. sh. ~ë, ~ët. handbook, manual

doréz/ë, ~a f. sh. ~a, ~at. 1. glove; **doreza boksi** boxing gloves; 2. handle; **dorezë dere** the handle of a door

dór/ë, ~a f. sh. dúar, dúart. 1. hand; 2. hand, labourer, workman; 3. handful; 4. quality; **heq dorë** give up, renounce; **ndërron dorë** change hands; **me dorë** by hand; **nga dora në dorë** from hand to hand; **dorë për dore** hand in hand; **larg duart** hands off (sth/smb)

dorëheqj/e, ~ja f. sh. ~e, ~et. resignation

dorëshkrím, ~i m. sh. ~e, ~et. 1. manuscript; 2. handwriting

dorështrëngúar mb. stingy, miserly, parsimonious, tight-fisted, close-fisted

dorëzán/ë, ~i m. sh. ~ë, ~ët. guarantor, voucher, warrantor

dorëzóhem vetv. give up, surrender

dorëz/oj kal., ~óva, úar. 1. hand in; 2. consign, hand over to smb; 3. hand smb over to smb

dósj/e, ~a f. sh. ~e, ~et. file

dramatík, ~e mb. dramatic

dramatiz/oj kal., ~óva, ~úar. dramatize
dramatúrg, ~u m. sh. ~ë, ~ët. dramatist
drám/ë ~a f. sh. ~a, ~at. drama, play
dráp/ër, ~ri m. sh. ~ínj. ~ínjtë. sickle
dre, ~ri m. sh. ~rë, ~rët. zool. deer, stag, buck
dredh kal., **dródha**, **drédhur**. 1. twist, twine, weave, knit; 2. roll; 3. revolve, spin; 4. curl, coil
drédh/ë ~a f. sh. ~a, ~at. curve, bend, turn
drédhur (i, e) mb. 1. curly; 2. bendy, winding; 3. vibrating
drejt ndajf. 1. straight; **rri drejt** sit up straight; 2. directly; 3. fig. honestly, frankly
dréjtë (i, e) mb. just, righteous, upright; right
dréjt/ë, ~a (e) f. sh. ~a, ~at (të). right; truth, verity
drejtësi, ~a f. justice
drejtím, ~i m. sh. ~e, ~et. 1. direction, course, way; 2. information, instructions; 3. direction, orientation; 4. management; guidance; 5. directions
drejt/ój kal., ~óva, ~úar. 1. direct, manage; 2. guide, lead; 3. address; 4. point, orient, position towards; 5. steer; 6. straighten
drejtór, ~i m. sh. director
drejtorí, ~a f. sh. ~, ~të. directorate
drejtpërdrejt ndajf. 1. directly; 2. face-to-face; 3. live
drejtpërdréjtë (i, e) mb. 1. direct; live; 2. straight; 3. immediate; 4. first hand
drejtshkrím, ~i m. gjuh. orthography
drejtúes, ~i m. sh. ~, ~it. head, director, leader, manager
drejtúes, ~e mb. leading, directing, guiding
drék/ë, ~a f. sh. ~a, ~at. lunch; **ha drekë** eat lunch; **koha e drekës** lunch-time
drek/oj jokal., ~óva, ~úar. lunch
drídhem vetv. shudder, shiver, shake, tremble; **dridhej i tëri nga të ftohtit** shivering all over with cold
drídhje, ~ja f. sh. ~e, ~et. 1. vibration; 2. shudder, quiver, shiver, tremor
dritár/e, ~ja f. sh. ~e, ~et. 1. window; **hap dritaren** open the window; 2. fig. window
drít/ë, ~a f. sh. ~a, ~at. 1. light; **drita e diellit** the light of the sun; 2. source of light; 3. electric lamp; **ndez (shuaj) dritat** turn (switch) the lights on (off); 4. enlightenment; 5. art. light; **dritë dhe hije** light and shade; **nxjerr në dritë** bring to light; **hedh dritë mbi** shed (throw) light on; **në dritën e** in the light of **dritëshkúrtër mb.** 1. mjek. short-sighted; 2. fig. short-sighted; **politikan dritëshkurtër** a short-sighted politician
dríth/ë, ~i m. sh. ~ëra, ~ërat. cereals; grains
dróg/ë. ~a f. sh. ~a, ~at. drug; **marr drogë** take drugs **dru**, ~ri m. sh. ~rë, ~rët. 1. wood; **dru zjarri** fire-wood; kindling; 2. timber, lumber; 3. fig. cudgeling
drúaj kal., dhe jokal., ~ta, ~tur. shy of smb (doing) smth; fight shy of, shy away from
drúajtur (i, e) mb. shy, timid, bashful
drúnjtë (i, e) mb. wooden; woody
dry, ~ni m. sh. ~na, ~nat. pad-lock

dúa kal., **désha**, **dáshur**. 1. love; 2. like, be fond of; 3. want, need; 4. wish; **si të duash** as you like it

duarbósh ndajf. empty-handed

duartrok/ás kal., dhe jokal., ~íta, ~ítur. applaud, clap

duartrokítj/e, ~a f. sh. ~e, ~et. applause

duét, ~i m. sh. ~e, ~et. muz. duet, duo

duhán, ~i m. sh. ~e, ~et bot. tobacco; **pi duhan** smoke; **Ndalohet duhani!** No smoking!

dúhem vetv. 1. be in love with; 2. **veta III.** be wanted, be necessary; 3. **pavet.** ought, should

dúhur (i,e) mb. due, proper, necessary; **marr masat e duhura** take the necessary measures; **në kohën e duhur** in due time

dúkem vetv. 1. appear, emerge, show up, come into view; 2. seem, look; **më duket se** it seems that

dúkje, ~ja f. appearance, mien, look; **vë në dukje** point out; call attention to

dúksh/ëm (i), ~me (e) mb. visible, apparent, evident

durím, ~i m. 1. endurance, perseverance; 2. forebearance; 3. patience; **bëj durim** be patient

dur/ój kal., ~óva, ~úar. 1. bear, endure, stand; 2. tolerate

durúesh/ëm (i), ~me (e) mb. 1. bearable, endurable; **temperaturë e durueshme** bearable temperature; 2. tolerable

dush, ~i m. sh. ~e, ~et. shower; **bëj dush** take a shower

duzin/ë, ~a f. sh. ~a, ~at. dozen

dy num. them. two

dyánsh/ëm (i), ~me (e) mb. two-sided; bilateral

dyfíshtë (i, e) mb. double, two-fold

dylbí, ~a f. sh. ~, ~të. field-glasses, binoculars

dyll/ë, ~i m. wax

dymbëdhjétë num. them. twelve

dyqán, ~i m. sh. ~e, ~et. shop, store

dyshék, ~u m. sh. ~ë, ~ët. mattress

dyshemé, ~ja f. sh. ~, ~të. floor

dyshím, ~i m. sh. ~e, ~et. doubt, suspicion; **në dyshim** in doubt; **pa asnjë dyshim** beyond (past) doubt

dyshímtë (i, e) mb. doubtful, suspicious

dysh/ój jokal., ~óva, ~úar. doubt, suspect

dytë (i, e) num. rresht. second

dytësór, ~e mb. secondary

dyzét num. them. fouty

dhe, ~**u** m. sh. ~**ra,** ~**rat.** 1. soil, ground; 2. earth; 3. land, country

dhe. lidh. and

dhelparák, ~**e** mb. foxy, cunning

dhélp/ër,~**ra** f. sh. ~**ra.** ~**rat.** 1. **zool.** fox; 2. **fig.** fox; **dhelpër e vjetër** a crafty old fox

dhemb jokal., ~**i,** ~**ur.** ache, pain; **më dhemb koka** my head aches (is aching)

dhémbj/e, ~**a** f. sh. ~**e,** ~**et.** ache, pain; **dhembje dhëmbi** toothache; **dhembje veshi** earache

dhémbsh/ëm (i), ~**me (e)** mb. 1. painful; 2. distressing; **përjetim i dhembshëm** a painful experience

dhémbshur (i,e) mb. affectionate

dhembshurí, ~**a** f. affection

dhen, të f. vet. **sh.** sheep

dhëmb, ~**i** m. sh. ~**ë,** ~**ët.** 1. tooth; **pastë dhëmbësh** toothpaste; **furçë dhëmbësh** tooth-brush; **heq një dhëmb** have a tooth pulled out; **mbush një dhëmmb** have a tooth filled; **dhëmb për dhëmb** tooth for tooth; 2. **tek.** cog, notch

dhëmbáll/ë, ~**a** f. sh. ~**ë,** ~**ët.** molar

dhënd/ër, ~**ri** m. sh. ~**úrë,** ~**úrët.** bridegroom

dhën/ë, ~**a (e)** f. sh. ~**a,** ~**at (të).** data, fact; information; **të dhëna statistikore** statistical data

dhënë (i,e) mb. 1. given, donated, bestowed, granted; 2. given, specified, stated; **i dhënë pas** be given to smth (doing smth)

dhi, ~**a** f. sh. ~, ~**të.** zool. goat, nanny-goat; **dhi e egër** wild goat

dhiát/ë, ~**a** f. sh. ~**a,** ~**at.** testament; **Dhiata e Vjetër** The Old Testament; **Dhiata e Re** The New Testament

dhímbs/em vetv., ~**a (u),** ~**ur.** compassionate, be (feel) sorry for

dhjám/ë, ~**i** m. sh. ~**ëra,** ~**ërat** dhe **dhjamë,** ~**t** fat, grease, lard

dhjámur (i,e) mb. fatty, greasy, lardy; **proshutë me dhjamë** fatty bacon

dhjétë num. them. ten

dhjetor, ~**i** m. December

dhóm/ë, ~**a** f. sh. ~**a,** ~**at.** room; chamber; **dhomë gjumi** bedroom

dhún/ë, ~**a** f. violence

dhun/ój kal., ~**óva,** ~**úar.** 1. violate; 2. rape

dhúnsh/ëm (i), ~**me (e)** mb. violent

dhuntí, ~**a** f. sh. ~, ~**të.** gift, flair, genius, talent

dhurát/ë, ~**a** f. sh. ~**a,** ~**at.** gift, keepsake, souvenir

dhurím, ~**i** m. sh. ~**e,** ~**et.** donation, endowment, gift, gratuity, offering

dhur/ój kal., ~**óva,** ~**úar.** donate, present, bestow

dhurúes, ~**i** m. sh. ~, ~**it.** donor, giver, donator, grantor

E

éc/i jokal., ~**a**, ~**ur.** 1. walk, saunter, stroll, amble; 2. move, go; 3. proceed, advance; 4. go, fare

écj/e, ~**a f. sh.** ~**e**, ~**et.** 1. walk, stroll, saunter; 2. gait, pace, step

ecurí, ~**a f.** 1. procedure; 2. development, progress

edukát/ë, ~**a f.** education; **edukatë morale (fizike)** moral (physical) education

edukatór, ~**i m. sh.** ~**ë**, ~**ët.** educator

edukím, ~**i m.** education

eduk/ój kal., ~**óva**, ~**úar.** educate

edukúes, ~**e mb.** educational; **film (libër) edukues** educational film (book)

edhé ndajf. yet, more, still

edhé lidh. and; also, too

efékt, ~**i m. sh.** ~**e**, ~**et.** effect, consequence, result, outcome

efektív, ~**i m. sh.** ~**e**, ~**et. dhe** ~**a**, ~**at. librr.** staff, personnel, force

efektív, ~**e mb. librr.** effective, efficacious; **masa efektive** effective measures

eféktsh/ëm (i), ~**me (e) mb.** effectual; **kurë e efektshme** an effectual cure

égër (i,e) mb. 1. wild; **mace e egër** a wild cat; 2. savage; 3. uncultivated, desolate; 4. fierce, ferocious; 5. severe

egërsí, ~**a f.** cruelty, ferocity

egërsir/ë, ~**a f. sh.** ~**a**, ~**at.** wild beast

egërsóhem vetv. vet. 1. grow wild; 2. be infuriated

egoíst, ~**e mb.** selfish, egotistic(al)

egoíz/ëm, mi m. egoism, selfishness

ekíp, ~**i m. sh.** ~**e**, ~**et.** 1. crew; 2. **sport.** team; **skuadër futbolli** football team

eklíps, ~**i m. sh.** ~**e**, ~**et. astr.** eclipse; **eklips i plotë (i pjesshëm) i diellit** a total (partial) eclipse of the sun; 2. **fig.** eclipse

ekologjí, ~**a f.** ecology

ekonomí, ~**a f. sh.** ~, ~**të.** 1. economy; 2. thrifty management, economizing, saving

ekonomík, ~**e mb.** 1. economic; **zhvillimi ekonomik** economic development; **sanksione ekonomike** economic sanctions; 2. economical

ekonomíkísht ndajf. economically

ekonomíst, ~**i m. sh.** ~**ë**, ~**ët.** economist

ekonomiz/ój kal., ~**óva**, ~**úar.** economize, use sparingly, save, go easy on

ekrán, ~**i m. sh.** ~**e**, ~**et.** screen; **ekran i gjerë** wide screen

ekraniz/ój kal., ~**óva**, ~**úar.** screen

ekskavatór, ~**i m. sh .** ~**ë**, ~**ët.** excavator

ekskursión, ~**i m. sh.** ~**e**, ~**et.** excursion; **bëj një ekskursion** go on an excursion

ekspansión, ~**i m. sh.** ~**e**, ~**et.** expansion

ekspedít/ë, ~**a f. sh.** ~, ~**at.** expedition; **ekspeditë gjeologjike** a geological expedition

eksperíenc/ë, ~ **f. sh.** ~**a**, ~**at.** experience

eksperimént, ~i m. sh. ~e, ~et. experiment; **bëj një eksperiment** perform (carry out, conduct) an experiment
eksperimentál, ~e mb. experimental
eksperiment/ój kal., ~óva, ~úar. experiment
ekspért, ~i m. sh. ~ë, ~ët. expert
eksplorím, ~i m. exploration
eksplor/ój kal., ~óva, ~úar. explore
eksplozív, ~i m. sh. ~a, ~at. explosive
ekspórt, ~i m. export
eksport/ój kal., ~óva, ~úar. export
eksportúes, ~i m. sh. ~, ~it. exporter
ekspozít/ë, ~a f. sh. ~a, ~at. exhibition, display
ekspoz/ój kal., ~óva, ~úar. display, exhibit, show
eksprés mb. 1. express; **tren ekspres** an express train; 2. instant; **kafe ekspres** instant coffee
ekstensív, ~e mb. extensive; **bujqësi ekstensive** an extensive agriculture
ekstrém, ~e mb. extreme
ekstremíst, ~i m. sh. ~ë, ~ët. extremist; **ekstremistët e majtë (e djathtë)** the left (right) extremists
ekuatór, ~i m. gjeogr. equator
ekuipázh, ~i m. sh. ~e, ~et. crew
ekzamin/ój kal., ~óva, ~úar. libr. examine; inspect
ekzekutív, ~e mb. executive
ekzekut/ój kal., ~óva, ~úar. 1. execute; 2. drejt. execute; 3. perform
ekzemplár, ~i m. sh. ~ë, ~ët. copy; sample; specimen
ekzisténc/ë, ~a f. existence, being
ekzist/ój jokal., ~óva, ~úar. be, exist
ekzistúes, ~e mb. libr. existing
elastík, ~e mb. elastic, flexible, pliant; resilient
elb, ~i m. bot. barley
elefánt, ~i m. sh. ~ë, ~ët. elephant
elegánt, ~e mb. elegant
elektorál, ~e mb. libr. electoral; **fushatë elektorale** the electoral campaign
elektricíst, ~i m. sh. ~ë, ~ët. electrician
elektricitét, ~i m. electricity
elektrík, ~e mb. electric, electrical; **rrymë (dritë) elektrike** electric current (light)
elektroník, ~e mb. spec. electronic; **makinë elektronike** electronic calculator
elektroník/a, ~a f. spec. electronics
elemént, ~i m. sh. ~e, ~et. element
elementár, ~e mb. elementary; **grimcë elementare** elementary particle
elimin/ój kal., ~óva, ~úar. 1. eliminate; **eliminoj gabimet** eliminate mistakes; 2. eliminate, wipe out; 3. sport. eliminate
elít/ë, ~a f. elite
emancipím, ~i m. emancipation
emancip/ój kal., ~óva, úar. emancipate **embárgo**, ~ja f. drejt. embargo
embrión, ~i m. sh. ~e, ~et. 1. biol. embryo; 2. fig. embryo; **në embrion** in embryo

ém/ër, ~ri m. sh. **~ra, ~rat.** 1. name; **Si e kini emrin?** What is your name?; 2. name, reputation, fame; **me emër të mirë** with a good name (reputation); **fitoj emër** win a name for oneself; 3. **gram.** noun; **emër i përveçëm (i përgjithshëm)** proper (common) noun; **në emër të** in the name of

emërím, ~i m. sh. **~e, ~et.** appointment, nomination, assignment

emër/oj kal., **~óva, ~úar.** nominate, appoint, designate

emërór, ~e mb. nominal

emërtím, ~i m. sh. **~e, ~et.** name, denomination

emërt/ój kal., **~óva, úar.** name

emigránt, ~i m. sh. **~ë, ~ët.** emigrant

emigrím, ~i m. sh. **~e, ~et.** emigration

emigr/ój jokal., **~óva, ~úar.** emigrate

emisár, ~i m. sh. **~ë, ët.** emissary

emisión, ~i m. sh. **~e, ~et.** 1. program, show, telecast, series; 2. emission (of bank notes)

emoción, ~i m. sh. **~ e, ~et.** emotion

emocionúes, ~e mb. emotional, stirring, thrilling, touching

enciklopedí, ~a f. sh. **~, ~të.** encyclopedia

end kal., **~a, ~ur.** weave

éndem vetv. roam, wander, rove

energjí, ~a f. sh. **~, ~të.** 1. energy; 2. **fiz.** energy; **energji bërthamore (elektrike)** nuclear (electrical) energy; 3. energies

energjík, ~e mb. energetic; **fëmijë energjik** an energetic child

én/ë, ~a f. sh. **~ë, ~ët.** utensil, container, receptacle, holder

éngjë/ll, ~lli m. sh. **~j, ~jt.** angel

enígm/ë, ~a f. sh. **~a, ~at.** enigma

entuzíast, ~e mb. enthusiastic

entuziáz/ëm, ~mi m. enthusiasm

epidemí, ~a f. sh. **~, ~të.** mjek. epidemic

epidemík, ~e mb. epidemic

epík, ~e mb. epic

epík/ë, ~a f. epic

episód, ~i m. sh. **~, ~et.** episode

epók/ë, ~a f. sh. **~a, ~at.** epoch

ér/ë, ~a f. sh. **~ëra, ~ërat.** wind; **erë e ngrohtë (e ftohtë)** a cold (warm) wind; **era e veriut (e jugut, e lindjes, e perëndimit)** the north (south, east, west) wind; **fryn erë** it blows

ér/ë, ~a f. sh. **~ëra, ~ërat.** smell, fragrance, scent, odour

ér/ë, ~a f. era

errësír/ë, ~a f. sh. **~a, ~at.** darkness

errës/ój kal., **~óva, ~úar.** darken, blacken

érrët (i,e) mb. 1. dark, black; 2. **fig.** obscure, vague

esénc/ë, ~a f. sh. **~a, ~at.** 1. essence; 2. **kim.** essence

estetík, ~ mb. esthetic

etáp/ë, ~a f. sh. **~a, ~at.** phase

etikét/ë, ~a f. sh. **~a, ~at.** label

étj/e, ~a f. 1. thirst; **shuaj etjen** quench one's thirst; 2. **fig.** thirst, craving

etník, ~e mb. ethnic

evolución, ~i m. evolution

evol/uón jokal., **~uói, ~úar libr.** evolve

ëmbël (i,e) mb. 1. sweet; **verë e ëmbël** sweet wine; 2.
melodious, mellow, pleasing; 3. sweet, amiable, loveable
ëmbëlsí, ~a f. sweetness
ëmbëlsir/ë, ~a f. sh. ~a, ~at. dessert, sweet; sweetmeat
ëmbëls/oj kal., ~ óva, ~úar. sweeten
ënd/ërr, ~rra f. sh. ~rra, ~rrat. dream
ëndërrím, ~i m. sh. ~e, ~et. dreaming
ëndërrimtár, ~e mb. dreamy
ëndërr/oj jokal., ~óva, ~úar. dream
ëndj/e ~a f. sh. ~e, ~et. gratification, satisfaction,
contentment

F

fabrík/ë, ~a f. sh. ~a, ~at factory, plant, mill; **fabrikë e letrës** a paper mill; **fabrikë e këpucëve** a shoe factory
fábul/ë, ~a f. sh. ~a, ~at folk., let. fable; **fabulat e Ezopit** Aesop's fables
faj, ~i m. sh. ~e, ~et. 1. blame; **ia hedh fajin dikujt** lay (put) the blame for smth on smb; 2. guilt
fajësí, ~a f. drejt. guiltiness
fajës/ój kal., ~óva, ~úar. 1. blame; 2. incriminate, declare guilty
fajk/úa, ~ói m. sh. ~ónj, ~ónjtë. zool. hawk, falcon
fajtór, ~e mb. guilty
fakt, ~i m. sh. ~e, ~et. 1. fact, truth, reality; **në fakt** in fact; 2. facts; evidence, data, proof
fakt/ój kal., ~óva, ~úar. proof, evidence, document
faktór, ~i m. sh. ~ë, ~ët. 1. factor; 2. **mat.** factor
fakultét, ~i m. sh. ~e, ~et. faculty
fal kal., ~a, ~ur. 1. drej. acquit, absolve; 2. pardon, forgive; 3. make smb a present of something
fála, ~t (të) f. vet. sh. greetings, regards; **U bëj të fala!** Give my regards to them!
fálas ndajf. gratis, free of charge
fálem vetv. pray
falemindérit pasth. thank you
falënder/ój kal., ~óva, ~úar. thank
falimentím, ~i m. sh. ~e, ~et. bankruptcy
faliment/ój jokal., ~óva, ~úar. go bankrupt
fálj/e, ~a f. sh. ~e, ~et. 1. pardon, forgiveness; 2. donation
falsifikím, ~i m. sh. ~e, ~et. forgery, falsification
falsifik/ój kal., ~óva, ~úar. falsify, forge, counterfeit
fálsh/ëm (i), ~me (e) mb. pardonable, excusable, forgivable; **gabim i falshëm** a pardonable error
faltór/e, ~ja f. sh. ~e, ~et fet. shrine, sanctuary, tabernacle, temple
fám/ë, ~a f. fame, reputation, celebrity; **fitoj famë** achieve fame **famëmádh**, ~e mb. famous, famed, renowned
familjár, ~e mb. family; **planifikimi familjar** family planning; **jeta familjare** family life
familjarizóhem vetv. familiarize
famílj/e, ~a f. sh. ~e, ~et. 1. family; 2. **biol.** family
fámsh/ëm (i), ~me (e) mb. famous, renowned, illustrious; **artist i famshëm** a famous artist
famullí, ~a f. sh. ~, ~të fet. perish
fanatík, ~u m. sh. ~ë, ~ët. fanatic
fantastík, ~e mb. 1. fantastic; 2. marvellous, excellent; 3. ficticious, imaginary
fantazí, ~a f. fantasy, imagination; fancy
fáq/e, ~ja f. sh. ~e, ~et. 1. cheek; 2. page; 3. face
farmací, ~a f. sh. ~, ~të. drugstore, pharmacy
farmacíst, ~i m. sh. ~ë, ~ët. pharmacist
fasád/ë, ~a f. sh. ~a, ~at. facade, front, frontage
fasúl/e, ~ja f. sh. ~e, ~et. bot. beans
fásh/ë, ~a f. sh. ~a, ~at. bandage, gauze
fashíst, ~i m. sh. ~ë, ~ët. fascist

fat, ~i m. sh. ~e, ~et. luck, fate, fortune; **fat i mirë** good luck; **fat i keq** bad luck; **për fat të mirë** fortunately, as good luck would have it; **jam me (pa) fat** be in (out) of luck; **për fat të keq** unfortunately
fatál, ~e mb. libr. fatal; **gabim (aksident) fatal** a fatal mistake (accident)
fatalíst, ~e mb. libr. fatalistic; **qendrim fatalist** a fatalistic attitude
fatbárdhë mb. fortunate, lucky
fatbardhësísht ndajf. fortunately, luckily
fatkéq, ~e mb. unlucky, unfortunate, ill-starred
fatkeqësí, ~a f. sh. ~, ~të. misfortune, calamity
fatkeqësisht ndajf. unfortunately
fatlúm, ~e mb. lucky
fatmirësísht ndajf. fortunately
fatúr/ë, ~a f. sh. ~a, ~at. bill, invoice; receipt
fáun/ë, ~a f. fauna
favór, ~i m. sh. ~e, ~et. favor; **në favor të** in favor of; **i bëj dikujt një favor** do smb a favor
favoriz/ój kal., ~óva, ~úar. favor
favórsh/ëm (i), ~me (e) mb. libr. favorable; **kushte të favorshme** favorable conditions
fáz/ë, ~a f. sh. ~a, ~at. phase, stage
fe, ~ja f. sh. ~, ~të. religion
federál, ~e mb. federal
federát/ë, ~a f. sh. ~a, ~at. federation **fejés/ë**, ~a f. sh. ~a, ~at. engagement, betrothal
fej/ój kal., ~óva, ~úar. engage, betroth
fejúar (i,e) mb. engaged, betrothed
fém/ër, ~ra f. sh. ~ra, ~rat. female
femëror, ~e mb. 1. female; 2. feminine; 3. **gram.** feminine
fenér, ~i m. sh. ~ë, ~ët. 1. lantern; 2. beacon
fenomén, ~i m. sh. ~e, ~et. phenomenon
férm/ë, ~a f. sh. ~a, ~at. farm, ranch
ferr, ~i m. hell
férr/ë, ~a f. sh. ~a, ~at. bot. brier
fést/ë, ~a f. sh. ~a, ~at. holiday, festival, fiesta
festím, ~i m. sh. ~e, ~et. celebration
festivál, ~i m. sh. ~e, ~et. festival
fest/ój kal., ~óva, ~úar. celebrate
fetár, ~e mb. religious, pious, holy, godly
fét/ë, ~a f. sh. ~a, ~at. slice; **një fetë bukë** a slice of bread
feudál, ~e mb. feudal
fëllíq kal., ~a, ~ur. 1. soil, sully; 2. **fig.** disgrace, defile
fëllíqur (i,e) mb. 1. soiled, sullied, dirtied; 2. **fig.** dirty, mean, disgraceful
fëmíj/ë, ~a m. sh. ~ë, ~ët. child
fëmijërí, ~a f. childhood
fëmijërór, ~e mb. childish; childlike
fërg/ój kal., ~óva, ~úar. fry
fërgúar (i,e) mb. fried; **patate të fërguara** fried potatoes
fërkím, ~i m. sh. ~e, ~et. friction; rubbing

fërk/ój kal., ~óva, ~úar. rub
figuratív, ~e mb. figurative
figúr/ë, ~a f. sh. ~a, ~at. figure; **bën figurë të mirë (të keqe)** cut a fine (poor) figure
fíj/e ~a f. sh. ~e, ~et. 1. yarn, thread, fiber; 2. sheet (of paper); 3. hair; 4. matchstick
fi/k, ~ku m. sh. ~q, ~qtë bot. fig; fig-tree
fildísh, ~i m. ivory
filíz, ~i m. sh. ~a, ~at. shoot, sprout
film, ~i m. sh. ~a, ~at. 1. film; 2. motion picture; **xhiroj një** film shoot a film
filológ, ~u m. sh. ~ë, ~ët. philologist
filologjí, ~a f. philology
filozóf, ~i m. sh. ~ë, ~ët. philosopher
filozofí, ~a f. philosophy
filozofík, ~e mb. philosophical
fílt/ër, ~ri m. sh. ~ra, ~rat. filter
filtr/ój kal., ~óva, ~úar. filter
filxhán, ~i m. sh. ~ë, ~ët. cup; **filxhan çaji** tea-cup
fi/ll, ~lli m. sh. ~je, ~jet. thread, yarn (**edhe fig.**)
fill ndajf. right (straight) away (off)
fillestár, ~e mb. 1. elementary, rudimentary; 2. initial
fillím, ~i m. sh. ~e, ~et. beginning, start, outset; **në fillim** at first, in the beginning; **nga fillimi në mbarim** from start to finish; **që në fillim** from the very beginning, from the start
fillimísht ndajf. initially, primarily, firstly
fill/ój kal., ~óva, ~úar. begin, start, commence
fillór, ~e mb. primary, elementary; **shkollë fillore** primary school, grade school
finál/e, ~ja f. sh. ~e, ~et. sport. final; **finalet e tenisit** the tennis finals
finánc/ë, ~a f. sh. ~a, ~at. finance
financiár, ~e mb. financial; **gjendja financiare** financial standing; **vështirësi financiare** financial difficulties
financiér, ~i m. sh. ~ë, ~ët. financer
financ/ój kal., ~óva, ~úar. finance; fund
fírm/ë, ~a f. sh. ~a, ~at. 1. firm; 2. signature; **hedh firmën** put one's signature to
fisník, ~e mb. 1. noble; **qëndrim fisnik** noble aim; 2. **hist.** noble; **familje fisnike** a noble family
fisnikërí, ~a f. nobility
fisnór, ~e mb. tribal
fishék, ~u m. sh. ~ë, ~ët. cartridge
fishekzjárr, ~i m. sh. ~ë. ~ët. fireworks **fishkëll/éj jokal., ~éva, ~yer.** whistle
fishkëllím/ë, ~a f. sh. ~a, ~at. whistle
fitíl, ~i m. sh. ~a, ~at. wick
fitím, ~i m. sh. ~e, ~et. profit, gain
fitimprúrës, ~e mb. profitable, gainful; **investim fitimprurës** profitable investment
fitimtár, ~e mb. victorious, triumphant; **dal fitimtar** come out victorious

fit/ój kal., ~óva, ~úar. 1. earn, gain; **fitoj para** earn
money; 2. get, acquire; 3. win
fitór/e, -ja f. sh. ~e, ~et. victory, triumph; **korr fitore**
gain (win, score) a victory over
fitúes, ~i m. sh. ~, ~it. winner, victor
fitúes, ~e mb. victorious, triumphant, winning
fizarmoník/ë, ~a f. sh. ~a, ~at. accordion
fizík, ~e mb. physical; **forcë fizike** physical strength;
gjeografi (kimi) fizike physical geography (chemistry)
fizikán, ~i m. sh. ~ë, ~ët. physicist
fizík/ë, ~a f. physics
fizikísht ndajf. physically
fjalamán, ~e mb. talkative, verbose, wordy
fjál/ë, ~a f. sh. ~ë, ~ët. 1. word; **fjalë për fjalë** word for
word; **me fjalë të tjera** in other words; 2. news, information,
message;
 dërgoj fjalë send word; 3. promise, pledge; **jap fjalën** give
one's word; **mbaj fjalën** as good as one's word, keep one's
word; 4. speech; 5. quarrel, argument, angry discussion; **bëj
fjalë** have words with somebody; 6. hearsay, gossip
fjalkryq, ~i m. sh. ~e, ~et. crossword
fjalëshúmë mb. talkative
fjalí, ~a f. sh. ~, ~të. gram. sentence
fjalím, ~i m. sh. ~e, ~et. speech, discourse
fjalór, ~i m. sh. ~ë, ~ët. dictionary; **fjalor shpjegues**
explanatory dictionary; **fjalor dygjuhësh** bilingual dictionary
fjalórth, ~i m. sh. ~ë, ~ët. glossary
fjalósem vetv. speak, talk, chat
fjétur (i,e) mb. 1. sleepy, drowsy; 2. **fig.** sleepy
fjóngo, ~ja f. sh. ~, ~të. ribbon
flagránt, ~e mb. flagrant; **shkelje flagrante** flagrant
violation
flak kal., ~a, ~ur. 1. throw, hurl, fling, cast; 2. discard,
throw away, cast off
flák/ë, ~a f. sh. ~ë, ~ët. 1. flame, blaze; 2. **fig.** fervor,
passion
flakër/ój jokal., ~óva, ~úar. hurl, fling
flakër/ój jokal., ~óva, ~úar. flame, blaze, flare
flamúr, ~i m. sh. ~ë, ~ët. banner, flag, standard
flas jokal., fóla, fólur. 1. speak; 2. talk, converse; 3.
discourse, make a speech, deliver a talk; 4. make known; **flas
të vërtetën** speak the truth
fláut, ~i m. sh. ~e, ~et. muz. flute
fle jokal., fjéta, fjétur. sleep; **fle mirë (keq)** sleep well
(badly)
flét/ë, ~a f. sh. ~ë, ~ët. 1. wing (of a bird); 2. leaf (of a
tree, book); 3. foil, sheet (of metal); 4. fin (of a fish)
fletór/e, ~ja f. sh. ~e, ~et. copy book, exercise book
flij/ój kal., ~óva, ~úar. sacrifice, immolate
flok, ~u m. sh. ~ë, ~ët. hair; **kreh flokët** comb one's hair;
qeth flokët have one's hair cut
florí, ~ri m. gold
florínjtë (i,e) mb. golden; **unazë e florinjtë** a golden ring
flót/ë, ~a f. sh. ~a, ~at. fleet, navy
flútur, ~a f. sh. ~a, ~at. zool. butterfly
flutur/ój jokal., ~óva, ~úar. fly, glide

fluturúes, ~e mb. flying
fllad, ~i m. sh. ~e, ~et. breeze **fók/ë**, ~a f. sh. ~a, ~at.
zool. seal
folé, ~ja f. sh. ~e, ~të. nest
fólës, ~i m. sh. ~, ~it. speaker
fólj/e, ~a f. sh. ~e ~et. gram. verb; **folje e regullt** regular
verb; **folje e paregullt** irregular verb; **folje kalimtare**
(jokalimtare) transitive (intransitive) verb
foljór, ~e mb. gjuh. verbal
folklór, ~i m. folklore
fóluri, ~it (të) as. speech, discourse
fólur (i,e) mb. spoken; **gjuhë e folur** spoken language
fond, ~i m. sh. ~e, ~et. 1. ek., fin. fund; 2. stock
fonetík, e mb. phonetic
fonetík/ë, ~a f. gjuh. phonetics
fórc/ë, ~a f. sh. ~a, ~at. 1. force, strength, power; 2.
usht. force; **forcat paqeruajtëse** peace-keeping forces; 3.
force, violence; 4. legal authority; 5. **fiz.** force
forcím, ~i m. consolidation; strengthening; hardening
forc/ój kal., ~óva, ~úar. strengthen, brace, reinforce,
consolidate, fortify
formál, ~e mb. formal; **kërkesë (vizitë) formale** formal
request (visit)
formalísht ndajf. formally
formalitét, ~i m. sh. ~e, ~et. formality
fórm/ë, ~a f. sh. ~a, ~at. 1. form, appearance, shape; 2.
let., art. form; 4. **gram.** form; 3. strength, fitness, form;
jam në formë të shkëlqyer I am in a superb form; 5. **tek.**
mould, cast; 6. kind, variety
formím, ~i m. sh ~e, ~et. 1. formation
form/ój kal., ~óva, ~úar. 1. form, shape, give shape; 2.
form, found, set up; 3. **fig.** mould
formulár, ~i m. sh. ~ë, ~ët. form
formúl/ë, ~a f. sh. ~a, ~at. formula
formul/ój kal., ~óva, ~úar. formulate
fort. ndajf. hard, tight, tightly
fórtë (i,e) mb. 1. strong, mighty; 2. hard; heavy; 3. firm,
resolute, unyielding; 4. intense, bright, powerful
fóshnj/ë, ~a f. sh. ~a, ~at. baby, babe, infant, neonate,
newborn
foshnjór, ~e mb. infantile; **sëmundje foshnjore** infantile
diseases
fotografí, ~a f. sh. ~, ~të. picture, photograph
fotograf/ój kal., ~óva, ~úar. photograph, take a picture
fotokopj/ój kal., ~óva, ~úar. photocopy
fqinj, ~i m. sh. ~ë, ~ët. neighbor
fqinjësí, ~a f. neighborhood
fragmént, ~i m. sh. ~e, ~et. fragment
fráz/ë, ~a f. sh. ~a, ~at. phrase
fre, ~ri m. sh. ~rë, ~rët. rein
frekuent/ój kal., ~óva, ~úar. frequent, visit often
fren, ~i m. sh. ~a, ~at. brake; **mbaj frena** put on the brakes
fren/ój kal., ~óva, ~úar. 1. brake; 2. **fig.** curb, bridle,
restrain; 3. harness

fréskët (i,e) mb. 1. fresh, cool, breezy; 2. fresh, new, latest; 3. garden-fresh; 4. bracing, cool, refreshing; 5. energetic, full of vim and vigour

freskí, ~a f. freshness

fresk/ój kal., ~óva, ~úar. freshen up, refresh

freskór/e, ~ja f. sh. ~e, ~et. fan

freskúes, ~e mb. refreshing

frigorifér, ~i m. sh. ~ë, ~ët. refrigerator, icebox, cooler

frikacák, ~e mb. cowardly, fainthearted

frík/ë, ~a f. fear, fright; **kam frikë** I am afraid of

frikës/ój kal., ~óva, ~úar. frighten, scare, intimidate

fríksh/ëm (i), ~ me (e) mb. frightening, fearful **fron, ~i m. sh. ~e, ~et.** throne, the throne; **hipi në fron** mount the throne

front, ~i m. sh. ~e, ~et. front

frút/ë, ~a f. sh. ~a, ~at. fruit

fry/j kal., ~va, ~rë. 1. inflate, pump up; 2. blow; **fryj hundët** blow one's nose; 3. swell; 4. **fig.** blow up; 5. wind

frym/ë, ~a f. 1. breath; **marr frymë** breathe; **me një frymë** in the same breath; **mbaj frymën** hold one's breath; 2. capita; **për frymë** per capita

frymëzím, ~i m. sh. ~e, ~et. inspiration

frymëz/ój kal., ~óva, ~úar. inspire

frymëzúes, ~e mb. inspiring; **shembull frymëzues** an inspiring example

frytsh/ëm (i), ~me (e) mb. fruitful; **diskutim i frytshëm** a fruitful discussion

fshat, ~i m. sh. ~ra, ~rat. 1. village; 2. country

fshatár, ~i m. sh. ~ë, ~ët. peasant, villager, countryman

fshatarësí, ~a f. përmb. peasantry

fsheh kal., ~a, ~ur. hide, conceal

fshéhtë (i,e) mb. 1. hidden, concealed; 2. secret

fshés/ë, ~a f. sh. ~a, ~at. broom

fshij kal., ~va, ~rë. 1. sweep; brush; dust; 2. wipe, dry; 3. rub, erase; 4. **fig.** wipe out, exterminate

ftés/ë, ~a f. sh. ~a, ~at. invitation; invitation card

ftoh kal., ~a, ~ur. 1. cool, chill; 2. **fig.** cool

ftóhem vetv. 1. catch cold; 2. **fig.** grow cool

ftóhtë, ~t (të) as. cold, coldness; **dridhem nga të ftohtët** shiver with cold; 2. cold; **marr të ftohtë** catch cold

ftóhtë (i,e) mb. 1. cold, chilly, cool; 2. **fig.** cool, frigid, unemotional, unfeeling

ft/ój kal., ~óva, ~úar. invite

ftúa, ftói m. sh. ftonj, ftónjtë. quince; quince-tree

fuçi, ~a f. sh. ~, ~të. barrel, butt, hogshead; drum

fund, ~i m. sh. ~e, ~et. 1. bottom; **fundi i shishes** the bottom of the bottle; 2. end; **në fund** in the end; **më në fund** at last; 3. skirt

fundit (i,e) mb. 1. last; 2. latest; 3. conclusive, final, ending

funksión, ~i m. sh. ~e, ~et. 1. function, role, operation; 2. function, charge, duty; 3. **mat.** function

funksionál, ~e mb. functional

funksionár, ~i m. sh. ~ë, ~ët. functionary

fuqí, ~a f. sh. ~, ~të. 1. might, strength; 2. power; **fuqi mendore (fizike)** mental (physical) power; **hipi në fuqi** came in(to) power; 3 **fiz.** power, energy; 4. powerful state; 4. **drejt.** force

fuqísh/ëm (i), ~me (e) mb. powerful, mighty, strong

fuqiz/ój kal., ~óva, ~úar. strengthen

fúrç/ë, ~a f. sh. ~a, ~at. brush; **furçë rroje** shaving brush

furnél/ë, ~a f. sh. ~a, ~at. cooker; **furnelë elektrike** an electric cooker

furnizím, ~i m. sh. ~e, ~et. supply, provision

furniz/ój kal., ~óva, ~úar. supply, provide

furtúnë, ~a f. sh. ~a, ~at. storm, tempest

fustán, ~i m. sh. ~e, ~et. dress

fúsh/ë, ~a f. sh. ~a, ~at. 1. field, plain; 2. field, domain, realm, sphere; 3. battleground; 4. playing field

fut (fus) kal., ~a, ~ur. 1. put in(to); 2. usher, let in; 3. introduce; instil; 4. get into

futbóll, ~i m. football

futbollíst, ~i m. sh. ~ë, ~ët. footballer

fútem vetv. 1. get in; 2. get into something

fytyr/ë, ~a f. sh. ~a, ~at. face

G

gabím, ~i m. sh. ~e, ~et. mistake, error, fault; **bëj një gabim** make (commit) a mistake
gabimísht ndajf. mistakenly
gab/ój jokal., ~óva, úar. 1. mistake, blunder, err; 2. deceive, delude
gabúar (i,e) mb. 1. wrong, mistaken; **pikëpamje të gabuara** mistaken views; 2. deceived, deluded
gadíshu/ll, ~lli m. sh. ~j, ~jt gjeogr. peninsula
gafórr/e, ~ja f. sh. ~e, ~et zool. crab
gájd/e, ~ja f. sh. ~e, ~et muz. bag-pipe
galerí, ~a f. sh. ~, ~të. 1. gallery; **galeria e arteve** gallery of arts; 2. **teatr.** gallery, 3. **min.** gallery
gangrén/ë, ~a f. mjek. gangrene
gangstér, ~i m .sh. ~ë, ~ët. gangster
garancí, ~a f. sh. ~, ~të. warranty, guarantee
garánt, ~i m. sh. ~ë, ~ët. guarantor, voucher
garánt/ój kal., ~óva, ~úar. guarantee
garantúar (i,e) mb. guaranteed, ensured
garázh, ~i m. sh. ~e, ~et. garage
gardh, ~im .sh. ~e, ~et dhe gjérdhe, ~t. fence, railing, rail
gardh/ój kal., ~óva, ~úar. fence
gár/ë, ~a f. sh. ~a, ~at. race; competition, contest; **në garë me** in competition with
garúzhd/ë, ~a f. sh. ~a, ~at. laddle
gáti. ndajf. 1. ready; **jam gati** be ready; **bëhem gati** get ready; 2. almost, nearly, about
gatím, ~i m. sh. ~e, ~et. cooking
gatishmërí, ~a f. readiness
gatít (gatís) kal., ~a, ~ur. 1. prepare, make ready; 2. fix, make, do (all of a meal)
gátsh/ëm (i), ~me (e) mb. 1. ready; 2. prompt; 3. willing, eager, game; 4. ready-made; **rroba të gatshme** ready-made clothes
gatúaj kal., ~óva, ~úar. 1. knead; 2. cook; 3. **fig.** cook, scheme
gaz, ~i m. sh. ~e, ~et dhe ra, ~rat. gas; **balonë me gas** a gas balloon; **sobë me gas** gas-cooker, gas stove
gaz, ~i m. merriment, gaity, mirth
gazetár, ~i m. sh. ~ë, ~ët. newspaperman, journalist, newsman, pressman, reporter
gazetarí, ~a f. journalism
gazét/ë, ~a f. sh. ~a, ~at. newspaper; **gazetë e përditshme (e përjavshme)** daily (weekly) paper
gazmór, ~e mb. joyful, joyous, merry, mirthful, cheerful, gleeful
gazolín/ë, ~a f. gasoline, gasolene
gáztë (i,e) mb. gaseous
gaztór, ~i m. sh. ~ë, ~ët. jester; clown
gdhend kal., ~a, ~ur. 1. carve; 2. chisel, engrave, etch, sculpt; 3. **fig.** engrave, imprint
géte, ~t f. vet. sh. tights, pantyhose
gëlqér/e, ~ja f. lime
gëlltít (gëlltís) kal., ~a, ~ur. 1. swallow, gulp; 2. **fig.** swallow
gënj/ej kal.,~éva, ~yer. 1. lie, tell a lie; 2. dupe, deceive, mislead, trick
gënjeshtár, ~i m. sh. ~ë, ~ët. liar, fibber

gënjeshtár, ~e mb. lying
gënjésht/ër, ~ra f. sh. ~ra, ~rat. lie, fib
gënjéshtërt (i,e) mb. 1. false, sham; 2. feigned
gërh/ás jokal., ~íta, ~ítur. snore
gërmádh/ë, ~a f. sh. ~a, ~at. ruin, ruins, remains
gërm/oj kal., ~óva, ~úar. 1. dig, excavate; 2. fig. probe; 3.
rummage
gërshét, ~i m. sh. ~a, ~at. plait
gërshet/oj kal., ~óva, ~úar. 1. plait, braid; 2. fig. entwine
gërshër/ë, ~a f. sh. ~ë, ~ët. 1. scissors; 2. shears; 3.
clippers
gërvisht kal., ~a, ~ur. 1. scratch, claw, scrape, skin; 2.
fig. grate, grind, rasp
gërvíshtj/e, ~a f. sh. ~e, ~et. scratch
gërr/yej kal., ~éva, ~yer. erode, abrade, wash away; eat out,
corrode
gërryes, ~e mb. erosive, eroding, corrosive; caustic
gështenj/ë, ~a f. sh. ~a, ~at. bot. chestnut; chestnut tree
gëzím, ~i m. sh. ~e, ~et. joy, bliss, gaity, merriment,
mirth, glee; kërcej (hidhem përpjetë) nga gëzimi jump for joy
gëzóhem vetv. be glad, rejoice
gëz/oj kal., ~óva, ~úar 1. enjoy; gëzoj shëndet të plotë
enjoy good health; 2. gladden, delight, cheer
gëzuar (i,e) mb. joyful, glad, delighted
gëzuar pasth. cheers; Gëzuar Vitin e Ri! A Happy New Year!
gëzuesh/ëm (i), ~me (e) mb. merry, jolly, mirthful, jovial,
cheering, cheerful
gisht, ~i m. sh. ~a, ~at dhe ~ërinj, ~ërinjtë. finger; gishti
i madh (i vogël, i mesëm) thumb (little, middle) finger;
gishti tregues forefinger (index finger); gishti i unazës
ring finger; kam gisht në have a finger in the pie
glob, ~i m. sh. ~e, ~et. globe
globál, ~e mb. global
gllabërój jokal., ~óva, ~úar. 1. devour; 2. swallow up,
engulf
góc/ë, ~a f. sh. ~a, ~at. girl, lass
godín/ë, ~a f. sh. ~a, ~at. building
godít kal., ~a, ~ur. strike, hit
godítj/e, ~a f. sh. ~e, ~et. 1. hit, blow, stroke, knock; 2.
throb, beat, pulsation
gojarísht ndajf. orally, verbally
gój/ë, ~a f. sh. ~ë, ~ët. mouth; hap (mbyll) gojën open
(close) the mouth
gójëz, ~a f. sh. ~a, ~at. muzzle
gojór, ~e mb. oral, verbal; shpjegim gojor a verbal
explanation
gol, ~i m. sh. ~a, ~at. sport. goal; shënoj një gol score
(kick) a goal
golf, ~i. sport. golf
gomár, ~i m. sh. ~ë, ~ët. 1. donkey, ass; 2. fig. donkey, ass
góm/ë, ~a f. sh. ~a, ~at. 1. rubber; 2. eraser, rubber; 3.
tire
gónxh/e, ~ja f. sh. ~e, ~et. bud
gostí, ~a f. sh. ~, ~të. feast
gót/ë, ~a f. sh. ~a, ~at. glass, tumbler
gózhd/ë, ~a f. sh ~ë, ~ët. nail
grabít (grabís) kal., ~a, ~ur. plunder, pillage

grabitqár, ~e mb. rapacious; predatory; **sulm grabitqar** a predatory attack

grád/ë, ~a f. sh. ~ë, ~ët dhe ~a, ~at. 1. degree; 2. rank; 3. **gjeom.** degree

grad/ój kal., ~óva, ~úar. 1. promote; 2. grade, graduate, calibrate

graduál, ~e mb. gradual; **rritje (rënie) graduale** a gradual rise (fall)

grafík, ~u m. sh. ~ë, ~ët. graph

grafík, ~e mb. graphic

gram, ~i m. sh. ~ë, ~ët. gram, gramme

gramatík/ë, ~a f. gjuh. grammar

gramafón, ~i m. sh. ~a, ~at. record player, gramaphone; **pllaka gramafoni** gramaphone records

gramatík/ë, ~a f. grammar

gramatikór, ~e mb. grammatical

granát/ë f. sh. ~a, ~at. usht. grenade

gremín/ë, ~a f. sh. ~a, ~at. abyss, chasm

grep, ~i m. sh. ~a, ~at. 1. a fish hook; 2. a crochet hook

grérëz, ~a f. sh. ~a, ~at. zool. wasp, hornet

grév/ë, ~a f. sh. ~a, ~at. strike; **bëj grevë** go on strike; **grevë e përgjithshme** a general strike

grevíst, ~i m. sh. ~ë, ~ët. striker

gri mb. grey

gri/j kal., ~va, ~rë. mince; grate

gríl/ë, ~a f. sh ~a, ~at. grill, grating

grímc/ë, ~a f. sh. ~a, ~at. particle

grndavéc, ~e mb. fretful, peevish; **fëmijë grindavec** a fretful child

grindém vetv. quarrel, bicker, squabble

gríndj/e, ~a f. sh. ~e, ~et. quarrel, brawl, wrangle

grip/ ~i m. mjek. flu, influenza

grírë (i,e) mb. minced; **mish i grirë** minced meat

gris kal., ~a, ~ur 1. tear, rip; 2. wear out

grísur, ~a (e) f. sh. ~a, ~at (të). tear, rip

gróp/ë, ~a f. sh ~a, ~at. hole

grósh/ë, ~a f. sh. ~ë, ~ët. bot. bean

grúa, ~ja f. sh. gra, grátë. 1. woman; 2. wife, spouse

grúmbu/ll, ~lli m. sh. ~j, ~jt. heap, pile, mound, stack, mass

grumbullím, ~i m. sh. ~e, ~et. 1. accumulation, accretion; 2. gathering

grumbull/ój kal., ~óva, ~úar. 1.gather, collect, accumulate, heap up, pile up; 2. glean, take in; 3. mass, crowd, congregate

grup, ~i m. sh ~e, ~et. group

grup/ój kal., ~óva, ~úar. group

grúr/ë, ~i. wheat

grusht, ~i m. sh. ~e, ~et. 1. fist; 2. blow; 3. handful

gryk/ë, ~a, f. sh ~ë, ~ët dhe ~a, ~at. 1. **anat.** throat; 2. neck; **gryka e shishes** the neck of a bottle; 3. **gjeog.** mouth

guásk/ë, ~a f. sh. ~a, ~at. 1. shell; 2. **fig.** shell; **mbyllem në guaskën e vet** go (retire, withdraw) into one's shell; **dal nga guaska e vet** come out of one's shell

gudulís kal., ~a, ~ur. tickle

gúng/ë, ~a f. sh. ~a, ~at. hump, bulge, bump, lump, swelling

gur, ~**i m. sh.** ~**ë,** ~**ët.** 1. stone; 2. jewel, gem, precious stone; 3. **mjek.** stone; **gur në veshka** kidney stone
gusht, ~**i m.** August
guvernatór, ~**i m. sh.** ~**ë,** ~**ët.** governor
guxím, ~**i m.** daring, boldness, courage, guts
guximsh/ëm (i), ~**me (e) mb.** daring, bold
gúx/ój jokal., ~**óva,** ~**úar.** dare, brave

GJ

gjah, ~u m. 1. hunt; hunting; 2. game
gjahtár, ~i m. sh. ~ë, ~ët. hunter, huntsman
gjak, ~u m. sh. ~ra, ~rat. 1. blood; **enët e gjakut** blood vessels; **analizë gjaku** blood test; **tension gjaku** blood pressure; **lidhje gjaku** blood relationship; 2. kinship
gjakatár, ~e mb. bloody, bloodthirsty; **vepër gjakatare** a bloody deed
gjakdérdhj/e, ~a f. sh. ~e, ~et. bloodshed; **evitoj gjakderdhjen** avoid the bloodshed
gjakftohtë mb. cold-blooded
gjaknxéhtë mb. hot-blooded
gjálp/ë, ~i m. butter
gjállë (i,e) mb. 1. alive, living, live; **peshk i gjallë** live fish; 2. active, lively, sprightly; 3. raw
gjallëróhem vet. cheer up, brighten, enliven
gjallër/ój kal., ~óva, ~úar. animate, vivify
gjallërúes, ~e mb. enlivening, invigorating; bracing
gjárp/ër, ~ri m. sh. ~ërinj, ~ërinjtë. zool. snake, serpent
gjás/ë, ~a f. sh. ~a, ~at. likelihood, probability; **sipas gjasës** in all likelihood
gjáshtë num. them. six
gjáshtë (i,e) num. rresht. sixth
gjashtëdhjetë num. them. sixty
gjashtëmbëdhjétë num them. sixteen
gjashtëqínd num. them. six hundred
gjátë (i,e) mb. long; tall
gjátë ndajf. long, for a long time, at length
gjátë parafj. 1. along; 2. during, in the course of
gjatësí, ~i f. sh. ~, ~të. 1. length; 2. **gjeog.** longitude
gje/j kal., ~ta, ~tur. 1. find, come upon (across), chance upon; 2. find, discover; 3. recover, retrieve
gjel, ~i m. sh. ~a, ~at. zool. cock
gjélbër (,) mb. green; **fushë e gjelbër** green field
gjelbërúar (i,e) mb. verdant
gjéll/ë, ~a f. sh. ~ë, ~ët. dish
gjemb, ~i m. sh. ~a, ~at. prickle, thorn; **rri mbi gjemba** be (sit) on thorns
gjéndem vetv. ~a (u), ~ur. 1. happen to be; 2. find oneself
gjéndj/e, ~a f. sh. ~e, ~et. 1. condition, state; 2. circumstances, situation; 3. status
gjenerál, ~i m. sh. ~ë, ~ët. usht. general
gjeneratór, ~i m. sh. ~ë, ~ët. generator
gjenetík, ~e mb. genetic
gjenetík/ë f. genetics
gjení, ~u m. sh. ~, ~të. genius
gjeografí, ~a f. geography; **gjeografia fizike** physical geography
gjeografík, ~e mb. geographical
gjeológ, ~u m. sh. ~ë, ~ët. geologist
gjeologjí, ~a f. geology
gjeologjík, ~e mb. geological
gjeometrí, ~a f. geometry
gjeometrík, ~e mb. geometric(al)

gjer parafj. till, up to, to; **gjer nesër** till tomorrow
gjérë (i,e) mb. 1. wide, broad; 2. large; large-scale, far-ranging; 3. vast; 4. loose; 5. roomy, spacious
gjérë ndajf. widely, broadly, on all sides, at length
gjerësí, ~a f. sh. ~,~të. width, breadth
gjerësísht ndajf. broadly, widely, extensively
gjersá lidh. until
gjest, ~i m. sh. ~e, ~et. 1. gesture; **komunikoj me gjeste** communicate by gesture; 2. **fig.** gesture; **një gjest simpatie** a gesture of sympathy
gjetíu ndajf. elsewhere
gjéth/e, ~ja f. sh. ~e, ~et. leaf
gjë, ~ja f. sh. ~ra, ~rat. thing; **ç'do gjë** everything; **në ç'do gjë** in everything
gjë pakuf. something, anything; nothing
gjëegjëz/ë, ~a f. sh. ~a, ~at. puzzle
gjëkáfshë pakuf. something
gjëkúndi ndajf. somewhere, anywhere
gjëmím, ~i m. sh. ~e, ~et. 1. roar; 2. thunder
gjëm/ój jokal., ~óva, ~úar. 1. roar; 2. thunder
gjënd/ër, ~ra f. sh. ~ra, ~rat. anat. gland
gji, ~ri m. sh. ~nj, ~njtë. bosom, breast
gjigánt, ~i m. sh. ~ë, ~ët. giant
gjigánt, ~e mb. gigantic, enormous, immense
gjilpër/ë, ~a f. sh. ~a, ~at. 1. needle; 2. hypodermic needle; 3. stylus
gjimnastík/ë, ~a f. gymnastics
gjimnáz, ~i m. sh. ~e, ~et. junior high school; high school
gjiní, ~a f. sh. ~, ~të. 1. kinship; 2. **biol.** genus; 3. **gjuh.** gender; 4. **let. art.** genre
gjinkáll/ë f. sh. ~a, ~at. zool. cicada
gjiráf/ë, ~a f. sh. ~a, ~at. zool. giraffe
gjithandéj ndajf. everywhere, in every place; far and wide; here, there and everywhere
gjithánsh/ëm (i), ~me (e) mb. all-round; **edukim i gjithanshëm** an all-round education
gjithashtú ndajf. also, too; **kjo tregon gjithashtu se ...** it also shows that ...
gjithçká pakuf. everything, all; **ai di gjithçka** he knows everything
gjíthë pakuf. all; **gjithë bota** all the world; **gjithë kohën** all the time; **me gjithë zemër** with all one's heart; **gjithë e gjithë** all in all
gjithësí, ~a f. universe
gjithfárë pakuf. various; all kinds of, all sorts of
gjithkúnd ndajf. everywhere
gjithkúsh pakuf. everyone, everybody
gjithmónë ndajf. always
gjithnjë ndajf. always; **si gjithnjë** as always
gjithséj ndajf. in all, altogether, as a total
gjithsesí ndajf. anyhow, in any way, in any case
gjób/ë, ~a f. sh. ~a, ~at. fine, penalty
gjobít (gjobís) kal., ~a, ~ur. fine

gjoks, ~i m. sh. ~e, ~et. chest, breast
gjórë (i,e) mb. poor, unfortunate
gju, ~ri m. sh. ~një, ~njët. knee; **bie në gjunjë** go down to one's knees
gjúaj kal., ~ta, ~tur. 1. hunt; 2. shoot
gjuetí, ~a f. hunting
gjúh/ë, ~ f. sh. ~ë, ~ët. 1. **anat.** tongue; 2. language, tongue; **gjuhë amtare** mother tongue
gjuhësí, ~a f. linguistics; **gjuhësia e krahasuar** comparative linguistics
gjuhësór mb. linguistic
gjum/ë, ~i m. sleep, nap, slumber; **marr një sy gjumë** take a nap; **vë në gjumë** put smb to sleep
gjúrm/ë, ~a f. sh. ~ë, ~ët. 1. track, trace, footprint, footstep; 2. vestige; 3. imprint
gjykát/ë, ~a f. sh. ~a, ~at drejt. court, tribunal
gjykátës, ~i m. sh. ~, ~it. drejt. judge, magistrate
gjykím, ~i m. sh. ~e, ~et. 1. judgment; 2. trial
gjyk/ój kal., ~óva, ~úar. 1. judge, consider; 2. try; 3. referee, umpire
gjymtyr/ë, ~a f. kryes. sh. ~ë, ~ët. **anat.** limb
gjyq, ~i m. trial, hearing
gjyqësór, ~e mb. drejt. judicial
gjyqtár, ~i m. sh. ~ë, ~ët. 1. judge, magistrate; 2. referee, umpire
gjysm/ë, ~a f. sh. ~a, ~at. half
gjysh, ~i m. sh. ~ër, ~ërit dhe ~a, ~at. grandfather, granddad
gjysh/e, ~ja f. sh. ~e, ~et. grandmother

H

há kal., hëngra, ngrënë. 1. eat, take a meal; 2. bite; 3. corrode, eat away, wear away; 4. eat somebody up; 5. itch

habí, ~a f. surprise, amazement, astonishment, wonder; **me habi** with astonishment

habít (habís) kal., ~a, ~ur. astonish, astound, overwhelm, surprise

habítsh/ëm (i), ~me (e) mb. 1. surprising, amazing, astounding, astonishing; **vendim i habitshëm** a surprising decision; 2. wonderful, fabulous, marvellous, stupendous

hájde,~ni pasth. come!

hajdút, ~i m. sh. ~ë, ~ët. thief, robber

hakmárrës, ~e mb. revengeful

hakmárrj/e, ~a f. sh. ~e, ~et. revenge, vengeance

hak/mérrem vetv., ~móra (u), ~márrë. revenge, avenge **hál/ë, ~a f. sh. ~a, ~at.** 1. fish-bone; 2. pine-needle

hall, ~i m. sh. ~e, ~et. trouble, scrape, fix, plight

háll/ë, ~a f. sh. ~a, ~at. aunt

hállk/ë, ~f. sh.~, ~at. 1. link; 2. a cuff link; 3. **fig.** link

ham/áll, ~álli m. sh. ~áj, ~ájtë dhe ~éj, ~éjtë. porter

haméndj/e, ~a f. sh. ~e, ~et. guesswork, supposition, conjecture, surmise; **me hamëndje** by guesswork

hap, ~i m. sh. ~a, ~at. 1. step; **me hapa të shpejtë** with quick steps; 2. footstep; 3. gait; stride

hap kal., ~a, ~ur. 1. open; **hap derën** open the door; 2. unfasten; 3. spread out, unfold; 4. unlock; 5. start

hápur (i,e) mb. 1. open, overt; 2. unclosed; 3. wide, wide-open; 4. candid, frank

hápur ndajf. openly

hardhí, ~a f. sh. ~, ~të. bot. vine; **gjethe hardhie** vine leaves

hardhúc/ë, ~a f. sh. ~a, ~at zool. lizard

har/k, ~ku m.sh. , ~qe, ~qet. 1. bow; 2. arc; **harku i ylberit** the arc of a rainbow; 3. **el.** arc; **hark elektrik** electric arc; 4. **muz.** bow

harmoní, ~a f. 1. harmony; **jetoj në harmoni me** live in harmony with; 2. **muz.** harmony

harmonísh/ëm (i), ~me (e) mb. harmonious

harmoniz/ój kal., ~óva, ~úar. harmonize

hárt/ë, ~a f. sh. ~a, ~at. map; **harta e Shqipërisë** the map of Albania

hartím, ~i m. sh. ~e, ~et. 1. composition; 2. compilation

hart/ój kal., ~óva, ~úar. 1. compile; 2. compose; 3. work out

harxhím, ~i m. sh. ~e, ~et. expenditure

harxh/ój kal., ~óva, ~úar. spend, expend; use up, exhaust; **harxhoj kohën** expend the time

harrés/ë, a f. oblivion, forgetfulness

harr/ój kal., ~óva, ~úar. forget; **Mos më harro!** Don't forget me!

has kal., ~a, ~ur. meet, encounter, come across; run into; **has vështirësi** meet with difficulties

hatër, ~i m. sh. ~e, ~et. favor

hedh kal hódha, hédhur. throw, hurl, toss, cast, fling, toss

hédhur (i,e) mb. 1. discarded, cast-off; 2. frisky

hedhurín/ë, ~a f. kryes. sh. ~a, ~at. trash, garbage, refuse, rubbish, litter

hektár, ~i m. sh. ~ë, ~ët. hectare

hékur, ~i m. sh. ~a, ~at. 1. iron; 2. flat-iron
hekurós kal., ~a, ~ur. iron
hékurt (i,e) mb. iron; ferrous; **vullnet i hekurt** a will of iron
hekurúdh/ë, ~a f. sh. ~a, ~at. railway, railroad
hekurudhór, ~e mb. railway; **stacion hekurudhor** railway station
helikoptér, ~i m. sh. ~ë, ~ët. helicopter
helm, ~i m. sh. ~e, ~et. poison, toxin, venom; bane
helmét/ë, ~a f. sh. ~a, ~at. helmet
hélmët (i,e) mb. poisonous
helmím, ~i m. sh. ~e, ~et. poisoning; intoxication
helm/ój kal., ~óva, ~úar. poison; intoxicate
helmués, ~e mb. poisonous, toxic, venomous
hemisférë, ~a f. sh. ~a, ~at. hemisphere
hendbóll, ~i m. sport. handball
hendé/k, ~ku m. sh. ~kë, ~kët dhe ~qe. 1. ditch; 2. **fig.** gap
heq kal., hóqa, héqur. 1. remove, take off, pull out; 2. drag, pull; 3. inhale; puff at
hér/ë, ~a f. sh. ~ë, ~ët. time; **çdo herë** every time; **herë pas here** now and then; **një herë e mirë** once and for all
hérë-hérë ndajf. at times, sometimes,
hérët ndajf. 1. early; 2. prematurely; 3. long ago, in the old days; remotely
heró, ~i m. sh. ~nj, ~njtë. 1. hero; **hero kombëtar** national hero; 2. **let.** hero
heroík, ~e mb. heroic
heroikísht ndajf. heroically
heroíz/ëm, ~mi m. sh. ~ma, ~mat. heroism
hérsh/ëm (i), ~me mb. 1. ancient; 2. early
hesáp, ~i m. sh. ~e, ~et. count, calculation, computation, reckoning
hesht jokal., ~a, ~ur. be silent, be quiet
héshtj/e, ~a f. sh. ~e, ~et. silence; **në heshtje** in silence; **thyej heshtjen** break silence
héshtur (i,e) mb. 1. silent; 2. tacit
hetím, ~i m. sh. ~e, ~et. inquiry, inquest
het/ój kal., ~óva, ~úar. inquire, inquest
hën/ë, ~a f. astr. moon; **hënë e re (e plotë)** new (full) moon; **një herë në hënë** once in a blue moon
hënór, ~e mb. lunar
hëpërhë ndajf. for the time being
hi, ~ri m. ash, cinders
hiç, ~i m. nothing; nothingness; **filloj nga hiçi** start from scratch
hidraulík, ~u m. sh. ~ë, ~ët. plumber
hidrocentrál, ~i m. sh. ~e, ~et. hydropower-station
hidrogjén, ~i m. kim. hydrogen
hidroplán, ~i m. sh. ~ë, ~ët. hydroplane
hídhem vetv. spring, jump, hop
hidhër/ój kal., ~óva, ~úar. 1. embitter; 2. afflict, grieve
hídhur (i,e) mb. 1. bitter, acrid; 2. **fig.** bitter
hién/ë, ~a f. sh. ~a, ~at. zool. hyena, hyaena
higjién/ë, ~a. f. hygiene
higjeník, ~e mb. hygienic

híj/e, ~a f. sh. ~e, ~et. 1. shadow, shade; 2. silhouette, outline; 3. grace

hijeshí, ~a f. sh. ~, ~të. grace

híjsh/ëm (i), ~me (e) mb. graceful, charming; **kërcimtar i hijshëm** a graceful dancer

hilé ~ja f. sh. ~, ~të dhe híl/e,~ja f. sh. ~e, ~et. trick, trickery

himn, ~i m. sh. ~e, ~et. hymn, anthem; himni kombëtar national anthem

hínk/ë, ~a f. sh. ~a, ~at. funnel

híp/i jokal.,~a, ~ur. 1. get on; 2. mount, climb, ascend; 3. increase, rise

hipodróm, ~i m. sh. ~e, ~et. hippodrome

hipokrít, ~e mb. hypocritical; **njeri hipokrit** hypocritical man

hipokrizí, ~a f. sh. ~, ~të. hypocrisy

hir, ~i m. sh. ~e, ~et. 1. sake; **për hir të** for the sake of; 2. grace

hírsh/ëm (i), ~me (e) mb. graceful

histerí, ~a f. sh. ~, ~të. hysteria

histerík, ~e mb. hysterical

historí, ~a f. sh. ~, ~të. 1. history; 2. story

historían, ~i m. sh. ~ë, ~ët. historian

historík, ~e mb. historic; historical

hóllë (i,e) mb. 1. thin; 2. delicate; 3. watery

hollësir/ë, ~a f.kryes. sh. ~a, ~at. detail, minutia, particulars

hollësish/ëm (i), ~me (e) mb. detailed; **analizë e hollësishme** a detailed analysis

holl/oj kal., ~óva, ~úar. 1. thin out; thin down; 2. dilute

homoseksuál, ~e mb. homosexual

horizónt, ~i m. sh. ~e, ~et. horizon

horizontál, ~e mb. horizontal

hotél,~i m. sh. ~e, ~et. hotel; **qendroj në hotel** stay at a hotel

húa, ~ja f. sh. ~, ~t. loan

huadhënës, ~i m. sh. ~, ~it. lender

húaj kal., ~ta, ~tur. lend, loan

húaj (i,e) mb. foreign, alien

húajtur (i, e) mb. loaned, lent

huazím, ~i m. sh. ~e, ~et. borrowing

huaz/ój kal., ~óva, ~úar. borrow

húdh/ër, ~ra f. sh. ~ra, ~rat. bot. garlic

humaníst, ~i m. sh. ~ë, ~ët. humanist

humanitár, ~e mb. humanitarian; **punë humanitare** humanitarian work

humaníz/ëm, ~mi m. humanism

humb kal., ~a, ~ur. 1. lose; **humb rrugën** lose one's way; 2. be defeated; 3. waste

húmbj/e, ~a f. sh. ~e, ~et. 1. loss; **pësoj humbje** suffer losses; 2. waste; **humbje e kohës** waste of time

húmbur (i,e) mb. lost

humnér/ë, ~a f. sh. ~a, ~at. abyss, precipice

humór, ~i m. 1. humor; 2. temper, spirit; **në humor të mirë** in good spirits

humoríst, ~i m. sh. ~ë, ~ët. humorist

humoristík, ~e mb. humorous

hund/ë, ~a f. sh. ~ë, ~ë. nose; **fut hundët në punët e** poke
one's nose in smb's affairs; **shfryj hundët** blow one's nose
hungërím/ë, ~a f. sh. ~a, ~at. grunt, growl
hungër/ój jokal., ~óva, ~úar. grunt, growl, snarl
huq, ~i m. sh. ~e, ~et. vice
húrm/ë, ~a f. sh. ~a, ~at bot. date
hy/j jokal., ~ra, ~rë. 1. enter, come in; 2. join, inscribe
hyrj/e, ~a f. sh. ~e, ~et. entry, entrance

I

ibrík, ~u m. sh. ë, ~ët. kettle
idé, ~ja f. sh. ~, ~ë. idea; **nuk e kam idenë** I have no idea;
më lindi ideja it occurred to me
ideál,~i m. sh. ~e, ~et. ideal
ideál, ~e mb. ideal; **kohë ideale për pushim** ideal weather for
a holiday
idealíst, ~e mb. idealistic
idealíz/ëm, ~mi m. idealism
idealiz/ój kal., ~óva, ~úar. idealize
identifikím, ~i m. sh. ~e, ~et. identification; **identifikimi**
i viktimës the identification of the victim
identifik/ój kal., ~óva, ~úar. identify
identík, ~e mb. identical; **pikëpamje identike** identical views
identitét, ~m. sh. ~e, ~et. identity; **kartë identiteti**
identity card
ideologjí, ~a f. sh. ~, ~të. ideology
ideologjík, ~e mb. ideological
idíom/ë, ~a f. sh. ~a, ~at. gjuh. idiom
idiót, ~i m. sh. ~ë, ~ët. idiot, fool, dolt
idiotësí, ~a f. idiocy, stupidity; imbecility
ídhu/ll, ~lli m. sh. ~j, ~jt. idol
íj/ë, ~a f. sh. ~ë, ~ët. side, flank
ík/i jokal., ~a, ~ur. 1. go; leave; 2. pass, lapse; 3.
vanish, disappear
ikón/ë, ~a f. sh. ~a, ~at. icon
íkur (i,e) mb. gone; departed
iláç, ~i m. sh. ~e, ~et. 1. medicine; 2. **fig.** remedy
ilegál, ~e mb. illegal; unlawful
ilustrím, ~i m. sh. ~e, ~et. illustration
ilustr/ój kal., ~óva, ~úar. illustrate
iluzíon, ~i m. sh. ~e, ~et. illusion; **s'kam iluzione** I have
no illusions
im, ~e pron. my; **im atë** my father
imagjinár, ~e mb. imaginary, ficticious, unreal; **qenie**
imagjinare imaginary being
imagjinát/ë, ~a. imagination, fancy
imagjin/ój kal., ~óva, ~úar. imagine, envision
imázh, ~i m. sh. ~e, ~et. image
imedíat, ~e mb. immediate, urgent, pressing; **nevoja imediate**
urgent needs
imët (i,e) mb. minute, fine; **përshkrim i imët** a minute
description; **grimca të imëta** minute particles
imigránt, ~i m. sh. ~ë, ~ët. immigrant
imigrím, ~i m. sh. ~e, ~et. immigration
imigr/ój jokal., ~óva, ~úar. immigrate
imitím, ~i m. sh. ~e, ~et. imitation
imit/ój kal., ~óva, ~úar. imitate
imorál, ~e mb. immoral
impórt, ~i m. import
import/ój kal., ~óva, ~úar. import
impúls, ~i m. sh. ~e, ~et. impulse; **i jap impuls** give an
impulse to

impulsív, ~e mb. impulsive; **njeri impulsiv** an impulsive man;
natyrë impulsive an impulsive nature
imtësí, ~a f. sh. ~, ~të. minutia, detail; **përshkruaj me
imtësi** explain in detail
imunitét, ~i m. 1. **biol.**, **mjek.** immunity; 2. **drej.** immunity;
imunitet diplomatik diplomatic immunity
imuniz/ój kal., ~óva, ~úar. immunize
inát, ~i m. sh. ~e, ~et. ill will, spite; **nga inati** out of
(from) spite; **e kam inat dikë** have a spite against smb
inatçí, ~e (dhe **inatçëshë**) mb. rancorous, spiteful
inatós kal., ~a, ~ur. anger, enrage
inatósem vetv. get angry
incidént, ~i m. sh. ~e, ~et. incident; **incident kufitar**
frontier incident
inciz/ój kal., ~óva, ~úar. record
ind, ~i m. sh. ~e, ~et. **anat.** tissue
indéks, ~i m. sh. ~e, ~et. index
indiferénc/ë, ~a f. indifference
indiférent, ~e mb. indifferent
indivíd, ~i m. sh. ~ë, ~ët. individual; **të drejtat e
individit** the rights of an individual
individuál, ~e mb. individual
individualiz/ój kal., ~óva, ~úar. individualize
induksión, ~i m. sh. ~e, ~et. induction
induktív mb. inductive
industrí, ~a f. sh. ~, ~të. industry; **industri e rëndë (e
lehtë)** heavy (light) industry
industriál, ~e mb. industrial; **zhvillimi industrial**
industrial development
industrialíst, ~i m. sh. ~ë, ~ët. industrialist
infeksión, ~i m. sh. ~e, ~et. infection
infekt/ój kal., ~óva, ~úar. 1. infect; 2. **fig.** infect
infermíer, ~i m. sh. ~ë, ~ët. male nurse
inflacíon, ~i m. ek. inflation
influénc/ë, ~a f. influence
influenc/ój jokal., ~óva, ~úar. influence
informacíon, ~i m. sh. ~e, ~et. information; **jap informacion**
give (pass on) information
informatív, ~e mb. informative
inform/ój kal., ~óva, ~úar. inform
ingranázh, ~i m. sh. ~e, ~et. gear
iniciatív/ë, ~a f. sh. ~a, ~at. initiative; **marr iniciativën**
take the initiative
iniciatór, ~i m. sh. ~ë, ~ët. initiator
inkuraj/ój kal., ~óva, ~úar. encourage
inorganík, ~e mb. inorganic; **kimia inorganike** inorganic
chemistry
insékt, ~i m. sh. ~e, ~et. insect
inspektím, ~i m. sh. ~e, ~et. inspection
inspekt/ój jokal., ~óva, ~úar. inspect
inspektór, ~i m. sh. ~ë, ~ët. inspector
instalím, ~i m. sh. ~e, ~et. installation
instal/ój kal., ~óva, ~úar. install

instínkt, ~i m. sh. ~e, ~et. instinct; **veproj me instinkt** act on instinct

institucíon, ~i m. sh. ~e, ~et. institution

institút, ~i m. sh. ~e, ~et. institute

instruksión, ~i m. sh. ~e, ~et. instruction

instrukt/ój kal., ~óva, ~úar. instruct

instruktór, ~i m. sh. ~ë, ~ët. instructor

instrumént, ~i m. sh. ~e, ~et. 1. instrument; **instrument muzikor** musical instrument; 2. **fig.** tool

integrím, ~i m. sh. ~e, ~et. integration

integritét, ~i m. integrity

integr/ój kal., ~óva, úar. integrate

intelékt, ~i m. intellect

intelektuál, ~i m. sh. ~ë, ~ët. intellectual

intelektuál, ~e mb. intellectual; **zhvillimi intelektual** intellectual development

intensifik/ój kal., ~óva, ~úar. intensify

intesitét, ~i m. intensity; **punoj me intesitet më të madh** work with greater intensity

intensív, ~e mb. intensive; **bujqësi intensive** intensive farming

interés, ~i m. sh. ~a, ~at. 1. interest; **zgjon interes** arouses interest; 2. interest, advantage, beneifit; **mbroj interesat e** protect the interests of; 3. **fin.** interest; **përqindja e interesit** the rate of interest

interesánt, ~e mb. interesting; **bisedë interesante** interesting conversation

interes/óhem vetv., ~óva, ~úar. interest oneself in, be interested in, have an interest in

interes/ón jokal., ~ói, ~úar. interest

interesúar (i,e) mb. interested

internacionalíst, ~e mb. internationalist

intern/ój kal., ~óva, ~úar. intern

interpretím, ~i m. sh. ~e, ~et. interpretation

interpret/ój kal., óva, ~úar. interpret

interpretúes, ~i m. sh. ~, ~it. interpreter

intervál, ~i m. sh. ~e, ~et. interval; **gjatë intervaleve (me intervale)** at intervals

intervíst/ë, ~a f. sh. ~a, ~at. interview; **jap një intervistë** give an interview

intervist/ój kal., ~óva, ~úar. interview

intím, ~e mb. intimate

intonación, ~i m. sh. ~e, ~et. intonation

intrígë, ~a f. sh. ~a, ~at. intrigue

intuít/ë, ~a f. intuition

invalíd, ~i m. sh. ~ë, ~ët. invalid

inventár, ~i m. sh. ~ë, ~ët. inventory

inventariz/ój kal., ~óva, ~úar. inventory, take stock of

investím, ~i m. sh. ~e, ~et ek. investment; **investimi i kapitalit** investment of capital; **investimet e huaja** foreign investments

invest/ój kal., ~óva, ~úar. ek. invest

inxhiníer, ~i m. sh. ~ë, ~ët. engineer

injoránt, ~i m. sh. ~ë, ~ët. ignorant

iríq, ~i m. sh. ~ë, ~ët. **zool.** hedgehog
ironí, ~a f. 1. irony; 2. **let.** irony; **ironi e fatit** the irony
of fate
ironík, ~e mb. ironic(al); **buzëqeshje ironike** ironic smile
ishu/ll, ~lli m. sh. ~j, ~jt. island
izolánt, ~i m. sh. ~e, ~et **fiz., elektr.** insulator
izolím, ~i m. **libr.** 1. isolation; 2. insulation
izol/ój, ~kal., ~óva, ~úar. 1. isolate; 2. **tek., elektr.**
insulate
izolúes, ~e mb. insulating

ja pj. here, there, here is, there is; here are, there are
ják/ë, ~a f. sh. ~a, ~at. collar; **masa e jakës** collar size; **ngre jakën** turn up the collar
jam jokal., qéshë, qénë. be; **jam jashtë** be out; **jam gjithë veshë** be all ears; **jam si në shtëpinë** time be at home; **jam për** be for
janár, ~i m. January
jap kal., dháshë, dhënë. 1. give; 2. confer, grant, award, accord; 3. deal, deliver; 4. render
jargaván, ~i m. sh. ~ë, ~ët. bot. lilac
járg/ë, ~a f. sh. ~ë, ~ët. saliva; spittle
jastëk, ~u m. sh. ~ë, ~ët. pillow; cushion
jáshtë. ndajf. out, outside
jáshtë parafj. out of, beyond, off; **jashtë qytetit** out of town; **jashtë përdorimit** out of use; **jashte teme** off the point
jásht/ëm (i), ~me (e) mb. 1. exterior, external, outer, outward; 2. foreign; **politikë e jashtme** foreign policy; **faktor i jashtëm** external factor
jashtázakonsh/ëm (i), ~me (e) mb. extraordinary; exceptional; **mbledhje e jashtëzakonshme** extraordinary meeting; **i dërguar (ambasador) i jashtëzakonshëm** envoy (ambassador) extraordinary
jáv/ë, ~a f. sh. ~ë, ~ët. week; **ditët e javës** the days of the week; **javë për javë** every week; **një javë si sot** a week today; **brenda një jave** in a week
javór, ~e mb. weekly
jehón/ë, ~a f. sh. ~a, ~at. resound, echo
jelék, ~u m. sh. ~ë, ~ët. waistcoat
jépem vetv. 1. given to, inclined towards, disposed towards, addicted to; 2. give up, surrender
jeshíl, ~e mb. bised. green; **sallatë jeshile** lettuce
jetés/ë, ~a f. living, subsistence, livelihood; **mënyra e jetesës** way of living, lifestyle; **standard i jetesës** standard of living
jét/ë, ~a f. 1. life, existence; **gjithë jetën** all my life; **vë në jetë** carry into execution; **erdhi në jetë** came into being; **ndërroi jetë** died; 2. activity; 3. liveliness; 4. way of living
jetësór, ~e mb. 1. living; 2. vital
jetëshkrím, ~i m. sh. ~e, ~et. biography
jetëshkúrtër mb. short-lived
jetík, ~e mb. vital
jetím, ~i m. sh. ~ë, ~ët. orphan
jetimór/e, ~ja f. sh. ~e, ~et. orphanage
jet/ój jokal., ~óva, ~úar. 1. live, be alive; remain alive; 2. live, subsist, exist; 3. reside, dwell; 4. remain in existence; survive; 5. enjoy life
jo pj. no, not
jod, ~i m. kim. iodine
jónë pron. our
jorgán, ~i m. sh ~ë, ~ët. quilt
josh kal., ~a, ~ur. allure, seduce, tempt
jóshës, ~e mb. alluring, enticing
jóte pron. your
ju përem. vetor. you

júaj *pron.* your
jug, ~u *m.* south
jugór, ~e *mb.* southern
juridík, ~e *mb.* juridical
juríst, ~i *m. sh.* ~ë, ~ët. jurist
justifik/ój *kal.,* ~óva, ~úar. justify

ka, ~u m. sh. qe, qétë. ox
kabinét, ~i m. sh. ~e, ~et. the Cabinet
kabín/ë, ~a f. sh. ~a, ~at. cabin
kábllo, ~ja f. sh. ~, ~t. cable
kaçavíd/ë, ~a f. sh. ~a, ~at. screw-driver
kaçúb/ë, ~a f. sh. ~a, ~at. bush
kaçurrél, ~e mb. curly; **flokë kaçurrela** curly hair
kád/e, ~ja f. sh. ~e, ~et. barrel, keg
kadifé, ~ja f. sh. ~, ~të. velvet
kafáz, ~i m. sh. ~e, ~et. cage
káfe, ~ja f. sh. ~e, et **dhe káfe**, ~ja f. sh. ~, ~të. 1. bot.
coffee tree; 2. coffee; **kafe ekspres** instant coffee; **mulli
kafeje** coffee grinder; 3. coffee-house; coffee bar
kafené, ~ja f. sh. ~, ~të. café
kafshát/ë, ~a f. sh. ~a, ~at. mouthful
káfsh/ë, ~a f. sh. ~ë, ~ët. animal; **kafshë ngarkese** beast of
burden; **kafshë e egër** wild beast; **kafshë shtëpijake** domestic
animal
kafshím, ~i m. sh. ~e, ~et. bite; **kafshim gjarpëri** snake bite
kafsh/ój kal., ~óva, ~úar. bite
kajsí, ~a f. sh. ~, ~të. bot. apricot; **reçel kajsie** apricot
jam
kakáo. ~ja f. sh. ~, ~t. bot. cocoa
kakarís jokal., ~i, ~ur. cackle
kakarísj/e, ~a f. sh. ~e, ~et. cackle
káktus, ~i m. sh. ~e, ~et. bot. cactus
kalá, ~ja f. sh. ~, ~të. 1. fort; castle; 2. **shah.** castle,
rook
kalamá, ~ni m. sh. ~j, ~jt. kid
kalb kal., ~a, ~ur. rot, decay
kálbur (i,e) mb. rotten, decayed
kalendár, ~i m. sh. ~ë, ~ët. calendar
kál/ë, ~i m. sh. kúaj, kúajt zool. 1. horse; **hip në kalë** get
on a horse; **ngas kalin** ride a horse; **punoj si kalë** work like
a horse; **bie nga kali** fall off the horse; 2. vault, vaulting
horse
kálë-fuqí m. sh. kúaj-fuqí fiz. horsepower
kalimtár, ~e mb. 1. transitory; **periudhë kalimtare** transitory
period; 2. **gjuh.** transitive; **folje kalimtare** transitive verb
kalímthi ndajf. in passing
kalít (kalís) kal., ~a, ~ur. 1. temper, forge; 2. harden
kalítj/e, ~a f. 1. temper; 2. **fig.** hardening
kal/ój jokal., ~óva, ~úar. 1. pass; 2. go past; 3. go by,
elapse, expire; 4. pass (the exam); 5. approve by voting
kalórës, ~i m. sh. ~, ~it. rider, horseman
kalorí, ~a f. sh. ~, ~të. calorie
kalorífer, ~i m. sh. ~ë, ~ët. radiator
káltër (i,e) mb. sky-blue, azure
kalúar, ~a (e) f. sh. ~a, ~at (të) past; **në të kaluarën** in
the past
kalúar ndajf. mounted
kalúes, ~e mb. passable
kalúesh/ëm (i), ~me (e) mb. passable, traversable, crossable
kalláj, ~i m. kim. tin
kallám, ~i m. sh ~a, ~at. bot. reed, cane; **kallam sheqeri**
sugar- cane

kallëp, ~i m. sh. ~e, ~et. 1. last; shoe-tree; 2. mould; 3. piece; ear

kallëz/ój kal., ~óva, ~úar. tell, narrate; 2. inform against, denounce

kallëzúes, ~i m. sh. ~, ~it. gjuh. predicate

kallí, ~ri m. sh. ~nj, ~njtë. spike, ear

kam kal., **páta**, **pásur** 1. have, own, possess; 2. be, feel; **kam ftohtë** I feel cold

kambán/ë, ~a f. sh. ~a, ~at. bell

kameleón, ~i m. sh. ~ë, ~ët. zool. chameleon

kamerdár/e, ~ja f. sh. ~e, ~et. tire

kameriér m. sh. ~ë, ~ët. waiter **kameriér/e**, ~ja f. sh. ~e, ~et. waitress

kamión, ~i m. sh. ~ë, ~ët. truck, lorry; **kamion vetëshkarkues** tipper lorry, tipper truck

kamp, ~i m. sh. ~e, ~et. camp; **kamp pushimi** rest home, holiday camp; **kamp përqëndrimi** concentration camp

kampión, ~i m. sh. ~ë, ~ët. sport. champion; **kampion boksi** boxing champion

kampionát, ~i m. sh. ~e, ~et. championship; **kampionati botëror** world championship

kamxhík, ~u m. sh. ~ë, ~ët. whip

kanál, ~i m. sh. ~e, ~et. 1. canal, channel; **Kanali i Suezit** the Suez Canal; 2. radio. telev. channel; 3. fig. channel

kancér, ~i m. mjek. cancer

kandidát, ~i m. sh. ~ë, ~ët. candidate, applicant, runner

kandís kal., ~a, ~ur. convince, persuade

kangúr, ~i m. sh. ~ë, ~ët. zool. kangaroo

kaós, ~i m. chaos

kap kal., ~a, ~ur. 1. catch, seize; 2. capture; take captive; 3. fasten; 4. overtake; 5. take by surprise; 6. understand, get it

kapacitét, ~i m. capacity; **me kapacitet të plotë** at full capacity

kapák, ~u m. sh. ~ë, ~ët. 1. lid; cap; cover; 2. anat. eyelid

kapél/ë, ~a f. sh. ~a, ~at. hat, cap; **kapelë republikë** bowler

kápem vetv. cling to, hold on tightly to

kapërc/éj kal., ~éva, ~yer. 1. cross, pass over, get over; 2. tide over, surmount, overcome; 3. swallow

kápës/e, ~ja f. sh. ~e, ~et. peg, pin; **kapëse rrobash** clothes-peg; **kapëse flokësh** a hairpin

kapitál, ~i m. sh. ~e, ~et. ek. capital; **kapital qarkullues** floating (circulating) capital

kapitál, ~e mb. capital; **dënim kapital** capital punishment

kapitalíst, ~i m. sh. capitalist

kapitalíst, ~e mb. capitalist

kapitalíz/ëm, ~mi m. capitalism

kapitén, ~i m. sh. ~ë, ~ët. captain; **kapiten i anijes** captain of a ship

kapítu/ll, ~lli m. sh. ~j, ~jt. chapter

kaq ndajf. so, so much, such

karafíl, ~i m. sh. ~a, ~at. bot. carnation

karaktér, ~i m. sh. ~e, ~et. 1. character; **njeri me karakter të fortë** a man of stong character; 2. moral strength; 3. art.,let. character

karakterístik, ~e mb. characteristic; **tipar karakteristik** characteristic feature
karakteristík/ë, ~a f. sh. ~a, ~at. characteristic
karakteriz/ój kal., ~óva, ~úar. characterize
karamél/e, ~ja f. sh. ~e, ~et. candy, sweet
karantín/ë, ~a f. sh. ~a, ~at. quarantine; **mbaj në karantinë** keep in quarantine
karát, ~i m. sh. ~ë, ~ët. karat, carat; **unazë 20 karatësh** a ring of 20 carats
karbón, ~i m. kim. carbon
karburánt, ~i m. sh. ~e, ~et. fuel
kardiák, ~e mb. mjek. cardiac; **sëmundje kardiake** cardiac disease
karfíc/ë, ~a f. sh. ~a, ~at. pin, breastpin, brooch, hair-clip
karkaléc, ~i m. sh. ~a, ~at. zool. grasshopper
karót/ë, ~a f. sh. ~a, ~at. bot. carrot
karshí ndajf. opposite, face to face, facing, vis-a-vis
kartél, ~i m. sh. ~e, ~et ek. cartel
kárt/ë, ~a f. sh. ~a, ~at. 1. paper; 2. charter; **Karta e OKB-së** Charter of the United Nations
kartolín/ë, ~a f. sh. ~, ~at. post-card
kartón, ~i m. sh. ~ë, ~ët. cardboard; **kuti kartoni** a cardboard box
karriér/ë, ~a f. sh. ~a, ~at. career
karríg/e, ~ia f. sh. ~e, ~et. chair
karróc/ë, ~a f. sh. ~a, ~at. 1. cart; 2. wheel-barrow, push cart; 3. perambulator
kasafórt/ë, ~a sh. ~a, ~at. safe
kasáp, ~i m. sh. ~ë, ~ët. butcher
kasóll/e, ~ja f. sh. ~e, ~et. hut, shack
kastíle ndajf. purposely, intentionally
kásht/ë, ~a f. sh. ~ëra, ~ërat. straw
kat, ~i m. sh. ~e, ~et. floor, storey; **kati i parë (përdhes)** first (ground) floor; **në katin e dytë** on the second floor
katalóg, ~u m. sh. ~ë, ~ët. catalogue
katarákt, ~i m. sh. ~e, ~et. cataract
katastróf/ë, ~a f. sh. ~a, ~at. catastrophe
katéd/ër, ~ra f. sh. ~ra, ~rat. chair
katedrál/e, ~ja f. sh. ~e, ~et. cathedral
kategorí, ~a f. sh. ~, ~të. category, class
kategorík, ~e mb. categorical, flat; **mohim kategorik** a categorical denial
kategoríkisht ndajf. categorically, flatly
kategoriz/ój kal., ~óva, ~úar. categorize
kát/ër, ~ra f. sh. ~ra, ~rat. 4
kátër num. them. four
katërmbëdhjétë num. them. fourteen
katërqínd num. them. four hundred
kátërt (i,e) num. rresht. fourth
katolík, ~e mb. catholic; **kisha katolike** catholic church
katrór, ~i m. sh. ~ë, ~ët. gjeom. square
katúnd, ~i m. sh. ~e, ~et. village
káuz/ë, ~a f. sh. ~a, ~at. cause
kavanóz, ~i m. sh. ~a, ~at. jar; **kavanoz me reçel** a jar of jam

kázm/ë, ~a f. sh. ~a, ~at. pick, pickax
kec, ~i m. sh. ~a, ~at edhe ~ër, ~ërit. kid
kek, ~u m. cake
keq (i) ~e (e) mb. sh. këqíj, këqíja (të). bad, evil, wicked;
kohë e keqe bad weather; **lajm i keq** bad news
keq ndajf. badly; **luaj keq** play badly
keqárdhj/e, ~a f. regret; **shpreh keqardhje** express regret
kéqas ndajf. badly
keqdáshës, ~e mb. malevolent; **njeri keqdashës** a malevolent
person
keqdáshj/e, ~a f. malevolence
keqës/ój kal., ~óva, ~úar. worsen, make worse
keqësúes, ~e mb. aggravating
keqkuptím, ~i m. sh. ~e, ~et. misunderstanding
keqkupt/ój kal., ~óva, ~úar. misunderstand
keqpërdor/ój kal.,~óva, ~úar. 1. misuse, ill-use; 2. mistreat
keqtrajtím, ~i m. sh. ~e, ~et. ill-treatment
keqtrajt/ój kal., ~óva, ~úar. ill-treat
két/ër, ~ri m. sh. ~ra, ~rat. zool. squirrel
këlysh, ~i m. sh. ~ë, ~ët. cub; whelp; puppy
këmb/éj kal., ~éva, ~yer. change, exchange
këmb/ë, ~a f. sh. ~ë, ~ët. 1. foot; **më këmbë** on foot; 2. leg;
këmba e karriges the leg of a chair
këmbëngúl jokal., ~a, ~ur. insist, persist
këmbëngúlës, ~e mb. insistent, persistent
këmbëngúlj/e, ~a f. sh. ~e, ~et. insistence, persistence
këmbím, ~i m. sh. ~e, ~et. change, exchange; **këmbim i
mendimeve** exchange of views
këmísh/ë, ~a f. sh. ~ë, ~ët. shirt; **këmishë me mëngë të
shkurtra** a short-sleeved shirt
kënáq kal., ~a, ~ur. please, satisfy, content, gratify
kënáqem vetv. enjoy, delight in, take pleasure in
kënaqësí, ~a f. sh. ~, ~të satisfaction, pleasure,
gratification; **me kënaqësi** with pleasure
kënáqsh/ëm (i), ~me(e) mb. satisfactory; **përgjigje e
kënaqshme** a satisfactory answer
kënáqur (i,e) mb. satisfied, pleased, content
kënd, ~i m. sh. ~e, ~et. 1. gjeom. angle; 2. corner
kënd/ój kal., ~óva, ~úar. 1. sing; chant; 2. tweet, chirp
këndsh/ëm (i), ~me(e) mb. pleasing, nice, agreeable,
pleasant; **zë i këndshëm** a pleasing voice
kënét/ë, ~a f. sh. ~a, ~at. marsh, swamp
këng/ë, ~a f. sh. ~ë, ~ët. song; **këngë popullore** folk song;
kënga e zogjve birdsong
këngëtar, ~i m. sh. ~ë, ~ët. singer
këpucár, ~i f. sh. ~ë, ~ët. shoemaker
këpúc/ë, ~a f. sh. ~ë, ~ët. shoe; **vesh këpucët** put on the
shoes
këpút (këpús) kal., ~a, ~ur. 1. pick, pluck; 2. break; 3.
exhaust, tire out
këpútem vetv. get tired, get exhausted
këpútur (i,e) mb. 1. broken; 2. interrupted; 3. exhausted,
tired out
kërc/ás jokal., ~íta, ~ítur. 1. crackle;. 2. snap; **kërcas
gishtërinjtë** snap one's fingers

kërc/éj jokal ~**éva,** ~**yer.** 1. jump; 2. dance
kërcëním, ~**i m. sh.** ~**e,** ~**et.** menace, threat
kërcën/ój kal., ~**óva,** ~**úar.** threaten, menace
kërcënúes, ~**e mb.** threatening, menacing
kërcím, ~**i m. sh.** ~**e,** ~**et.** jump, bounce, leap, spring
kërkés/ë, ~**a f. sh.** ~**a,** ~**at.** request, demand, requirement;
bëj një kërkesë make a request
kërkím, ~**i m. sh.** ~**e,** ~**et.** 1. search; **në kërkim të** in search
of; 2. research
kërk/ój kal., ~**óva,** ~**úar.** 1. look for, seek, search; **kërkoj
punë** look for a job; 2. ask, require
kërkúes, ~**e mb.** demanding, exigent; **mësues kërkues** a
demanding teacher
kërmí/ll, ~**lli m. sh.** ~**j,** ~**jtë. zool.** snail
kërpúdh/ë, ~**a f. sh.** ~**a,** ~**at. bot.** mushroom
këshíll, ~**i m. sh.** ~**a,** ~**at.** council; **Këshilli i Ministrave**
Council of Ministers
këshíll/ë, ~**a f. sh.** ~**a,** ~**at.** advice, counsel; **zbatoj
këshillën e** follow one's advice
këshill/ój kal., ~**óva,** ~**úar.** advise
këshillúesh/ëm (i), ~**me (e) mb.** advisable
kështjéll/ë, ~**a f. sh.** ~**a,** ~**at.** citadel, castle
kështu ndajf. so; thus
këta dëft. these
këtíllë (i,e) dëft. such
këtú ndajf. here; **deri këtu** up to here
kikirík, ~**u m. sh.** ~**ë,** ~**ët. bot.** peanut
kilográm, ~**i m. sh.** ~**ë,** ~**ët.** kilogram
kilomét/ër m. sh. ~**ra,** ~**rat.** kilometer
kilovát, ~**i m. sh.** ~**ë,** ~**ët.** kilowatt
kimí, ~**a f.** chemistry
kimík, ~**e mb.** chemical; **reaksion kimik** chemical reaction
kimíst, ~**i m. sh.** ~**ë,** ~**ët.** chemist
kinemá, ~**ja f. sh.** ~**,** ~**të.** 1. cinema, movie house, movie
theater; 2. the cinema, the movies
kinostúdio, ~**ja f. sh.** ~**,** ~**t.** film-studio
kirúrg, ~**u m. sh.** ~**ë,** ~**ët.** surgeon
kirurgjí, ~**a f. mjek.** surgery
kirurgjík, ~**e mb.** surgical
kísh/ë, ~**a f. sh.** ~**a,** ~**at.** church; the Church
kishtár, ~**e mb.** churchly, ecclesiastical
kitár/ë, ~**a f. sh.** ~**a,** ~**at.** guitar
kjo dëft. this
klarinét/ë, ~**a f. sh.** ~**a,** ~**at. muz.** clarinet
klás/ë, ~**a f. sh.** ~**a,** ~**at dhe** ~**ë,** ~**ët.** 1. class; **lufta e
klasave** class struggle; 2. class; 3. course, subject, lesson;
4. class, category
klasifikím, ~**i m. sh.** ~**e,** ~**et.** classification
klasifik/ój kal., ~**óva,** ~**úar.** classify
klasík, ~**e mb.** classic, classical
kliént, ~**i m. sh.** ~**ë,** ~**ët.** client; customer
klím/ë, ~**a f. sh.** ~**a,** ~**at.** climate

kliník, ~e mb. clinical
kliník/ë, ~a f. sh. ~a, ~at. clinic
klub, ~i m. sh. ~e, ~et. club
kllóçk/ë, ~a f. sh. ~a, ~at. brooding-hen
koalicíon, ~i m. sh. ~e, ~et. coalition
kóck/ë, ~a f. sh. ~a, ~at. bone
kod, ~i m. sh. ~e, ~et. code; **kodi penal** the penal code
kód/ër, ~ra f. sh. ~ra, ~rat. hill
kóh/ë, ~a f. sh. ~ë, ~ët. 1. time; **s'kam kohë** I have no time;
gjithë kohën all the time; **në atë kohë** at that time; **për ca
kohë** for some time; **në të njëjtën kohë** at the same time; **në
çdo kohë** at any time; 2. length of time; period; 3. times;
age, epoch, era; 4. weather; 5. occasion; instance; 6. **muz.**
time; 7 **gjuh.** tense; 8 while, moment
kók/ë. ~a f. sh. ~ë, ~ët dhe ~a, ~at. 1. head; **ngre (kthej,
tund) kokën** raise (turn, nod) one's head; 2. ability to
reason; intellect; imagination; mind; 3. head (of cattle); 4.
head, leader; 5. head (of a nail, pin)
kokëfórtë mb. stubborn, obstinate
kokëfortësí, ~a f. stubborness
koktéj, ~im. sh. ~e, ~et. cocktail
kolég, ~u m. sh. ~ë, ~ët. colleague
kolegj, ~i m. sh. ~e, ~et. college
koleksión, ~i m. sh. ~e, ~et. collection; **koleksion pullash**
stamp collection
koleksioníst, ~i m. ~ë, ~ët. collector
kolektív, ~e mb. collective; **përpjekje kolektive** collective
efforts
kolér/ë, ~a mjek. cholera
kolón/ë, ~a f. sh. ~a, ~at. column; pillar
koloní, ~a f. sh. ~, ~të. colony
koloniál, ~e mb. colonial; **sundim kolonial** colonial rule
koloniz/ój kal., ~óva, ~úar. colonize
kolovájz/ë, ~a f. sh. ~a, ~at. swing; seesaw
kollásj ndajf. easily
kóll/ë, ~a f. cough; **kollë e mirë** whooping cough
kollítem vetv. cough
kolltúk, ~u m. sh. ~ë, ~ët. armchair
komandánt, ~i m. sh. ~ë, ~ët. commander
komand/ój kal., ~óva, ~úar. command
komandúes, ~e mb. commanding
komb, ~i m. sh. ~e, ~et. nation; **kombi shqiptar** the Albanian
nation; **Organizata e Kombeve të Bashkuara** the United Nations
kombësí, ~a f. sh. ~, ~të. nationality
kombëtár, ~e mb. national; **flamuri kombëtar** national flag;
himni kombëtar national anthem
kombinát, ~i m. sh. ~e, ~et. combine
kombiním, ~i m. sh. ~e, ~et. combination
kombin/ój kal., ~óva, ~úar. combine
komedí, ~a f. sh. ~, ~të. 1. **let.**, art. comedy; 2. comedy
komént, ~i m. sh. ~e, ~et. comment
koment/ój kal., ~óva, ~úar. comment
komét/ë, ~a f. sh. ~a, ~at. **astr.** comet

komík, ~e mb. comic; **opera komike** comic opera
kominóshe, ~t f. vet. sh. overalls
komisión, ~i m. sh. ~e, ~et. commission
komitét, ~i m. sh. ~e, ~et. committee
komodínë, ~a f. sh. ~a, ~at. bed-side table
kompaní, ~a f. sh. ~, ~të. usht. company
kompás, ~i m. sh. ~e, ~et. compasses
kompeténc/ë, ~a f. sh. ~a, ~at. competence
kompetént, ~e mb. competent; **mjek kompetent** a competent doctor
kompil/ój kal., ~óva, ~úar. compile
kompléks, ~i m. sh. ~e, ~et. complex; **kompleks industrial** industrial complex
kompléks, ~e mb. complex; **sistem kompleks** a complex system
komplimént, ~i m. sh. ~e, ~et. compliment
komplót, ~i m. sh. ~e, ~et. plot, conspiracy
komplót/ ój jokal., ~óva, ~úar. plot
komponént, ~i m. sh. ~ë, ~ët. component
kompozitór, ~i m. sh. ~ë, ~ët. composer
kompoz/ój kal., ~óva, ~úar. muz., art. compose
komunál, ~e mb. communal
komún/ë, ~a f. sh. ~a, ~at. commune
komunikím, ~i m. sh. ~e, ~et. communication
komunik/ój kal., ~óva, ~úar. communicate
komunitét, ~i m. sh. ~e, ~et. community
koncépt, ~i m. sh. ~e ~et. concept
koncérn, ~i m. sh. ~e, ~et. concern; company
koncért, ~i m. sh. ~e, ~et. concert; **jap koncert** give a concert
konfederát/ë, ~a f. sh. ~a, ~at. confederation
konferénc/ë f. sh. ~a, ~at. conference
konflíkt, ~i m. sh. ~e, ~et. conflict
kongrés, ~i m. sh. ~e, ~et. congress
konkrét, ~e mb. concrete; **propozim konkret** concrete proposal; **masa konkrete** concrete measures
konkúrs, ~i m. sh. ~e, ~et. competition
konkurénc/ë. ~a f. competition, rivalry
konkurrúes, ~e mb. competitive
konkurr/ój jokal., ~óva, ~úar. compete
konsekuént, ~e mb. consistent
konservatór, ~e mb. conservative; **qëndrim konservator** conservative stand
konsérv/ë, ~a f. sh. ~a, ~at. canned food
konserv/ój kal., ~óva, ~úar. can, preserve
konsiderát/ë, ~a f. sh. ~a, ~at. consideration
konsider/ój kal., ~óva, ~úar. consider
konstruktív, ~e mb. constructive; **propozim konstruktiv** constructive proposal
kónsu/ll, ~lli m. sh. ~j, ~jt. consul
konsullát/ë, ~a f. sh. ~a, ~at. consulate
konsullór, ~e mb. dipl. consular
konsúm, ~i m. consumption
konsumatór, ~i m. sh. ~ë, ~ët. consumer
konsum/ój kal., ~óva, ~úar. consume

kontákt, ~i m. sh. ~e, ~et. 1. contact; **në kontakt me** in contact with; 2. **elektr.** contact
kontinént, ~i m. sh. ~e, ~et. continent
kontinentál, ~e mb. continental; **klimë kontinentale** a continental climate
kontrabandánd/ë, ~a f. sh. ~a, ~at. smuggling
kontrabandíst, ~i m. sh. ~ë, ~ët. smuggler
kontradíkt/ë, ~a f. sh. ~a, ~at. contradiction
kontradiktór, ~e mb. contradictory; **raporte kontradiktore** contradictory reports
kontrást, ~i m. sh. ~e, ~et. contrast
kontrát/ë, ~a f. sh. ~a, ~at. contract; **bëj (lidh) kontratën** make (enter into) a contract
kontrib/uój jokal., ~uóva, ~úar. contribute
kontribút, ~i m. sh. ~e, ~et. contribution
kontróll, ~i m. sh. ~e, ~et. control, check; **jam jashtë** kontrollit be out of control; **dal jashtë kontrollit** get out of control; **humb kontrollin e** lose the control of
kontroll/ój kal., ~óva, ~úar. control, check
konvént/ë, ~a f. sh. ~a, ~at. convention **konvíkt**, ~i m. sh. ~e, ~et. hostel
kooperatív/ë, ~a f. sh. ~a, ~at. cooperative
kooperím, ~i m. cooperation; **në kooperim me** in cooperation with
kooper/ój jokal., ~óva, ~úar. cooperate
kópj/e, ~a f. sh. ~e, ~et. copy
kopj/ój kal., ~óva, ~úar. copy
koprác, ~i m. sh. ~ë, ~ët. miser
kops/ë, ~a f. sh. ~a, ~at. button
kopsít kal., ~a, ~ur. button up; **kopsit këmishën** button up one's shirt
kopsht, ~i m. sh. ~e, ~et. 1. garden; 2. kindergarten
kopshtár, ~i m. sh. ~ë, ~ët. gardener
kor, ~i m. sh. ~e, ~et. chorus
korál, ~i m. sh. ~e, ~et. coral
kór/e, ~ja f. sh. ~e, ~et. crust
korníz/ë, ~a f. sh. ~a, ~at. frame
korporát/ë, ~a f. sh. ~a, ~at. corporation
korsé, ~ja f. sh. ~, ~të. corset, stays
korr kal., ~a, ~ur. 1. reap; 2. **fig.** achieve, gain, attain; **korr fitore** gain victory
korrékt, ~e mb. correct
korrespondenc/ë, ~a f. sh. ~a, ~at. correspondence; **mbaj korrespondencë me** keep correspondence with
korrigj/ój kal., ~óva, ~úar. correct, rectify
korrík, ~u July
korruptím, ~i m. sh. ~óva, ~úar. corruption
korrupt/ój kal., ~óva, ~úar. corrupt
kos, ~i m. yoghurt (yogurt, yoghourt)
kósto, ~ja f. sh. ~, ~t. cost; **kostoja e jetesës** the cost of living
kostúm, ~i m. sh. ~e, ~et. suit
kot ndajf. in vain, vainly, to no avail
kótë (i,e) mb. vain, futile, useless, pointless

kóv/ë, ~a f.sh. ~a, ~at. 1. pail, bucket; 2. bucketful; **dy kova me ujë** two buckets (bucketfuls) of water; 3. scoop
kozmetík, ~e mb. cosmetic
kozmík, ~e mb. cosmic
kozmonáut, ~i m. sh ~ë, ~ët. cosmonaut
kózmos, ~i m. cosmos
krah,~u m. sh. ~ë, ~ët. 1. arm; **krah për krah** arm in arm; 2. armful; 3. hand; 4. power, might, force, strength
kráhas paraf. along with something
krahasím, ~i m. sh. ~e, ~et. comparison, compare; **në krahasim me** in comparison with
krahas/ój kal., ~óva, ~úar. compare
krahasór, ~e mb. gjuh. comparative
krahín/ë ~a f. sh. ~a, ~at. region
krahinór, ~e mb. regional
kravát/ë, ~a f. sh. tie, neck-tie
kredí, ~a f. sh. ~, ~të. credit; **kredi bankare** bank credit; **ble (shes) me kredi** buy (sell) on credit
kreditór, ~i m. sh. ~ë, ~ët. creditor
kreh kal., ~a, ~ur. comb
kréh/ër, ~ri m. sh. ~ra, ~rat. comb
krejt. ndajf. wholly, completely, entirely, fully, thoroughly
krejtësísht ndajf. totally
krem, ~i m. sh. ~ra, ~rat. cream
kremt/ój kal., ~óva, ~úar. celebrate
krenár, ~e mb. proud
krenarí, ~a f. pride
krenarísht ndajf. proudly
kren/óhem vetv., ~óva, ~úar. boast, pride oneself, take pride
krésht/ë, ~a f. sh. ~a, ~at. 1. mane; 2. comb; 3. **gjeog.** ridge
krevát, ~i m. sh. ~e, ~et. bed
krijím, ~i m. sh. ~e, ~et. creation
krij/ój kal., ~óva, ~úar. 1. create; 2. cause, produce
krijúes, ~i m. sh ~, ~it. creator
krijúes, ~e mb. creative; **procesi krijues** the creative process
krim, ~i m. sh. ~e, ~et. crime; **kryej një krim të rëndë** commit a serious crime
krimb, ~i m. sh. ~a, ~at. zool. worm; **krimb i tokës** earthworm; **krimb mëndafshi** silkworm
kriminál, ~e mb. criminal
kriminél, ~i m. sh. ~ë, ~ët. criminal, convict
kríp/ë, a f. sh. ~ëra, ~ërat. 1. salt; 2. **fig.** salt
krípur (i,e) mb. salty, briny
kris jokal., ~a, ~ur. 1. crack; 2. break out
kristál, ~i m. sh. ~e, ~et. crystal
krishtérë (i,e) mb. christian
krishtlíndj/e, ~a f. kryes. sh. ~e, ~et. Christmas
kritér, ~i m. sh. ~e, ~et. criterion
kritík, ~e mb. 1. critical; **vërejtje kritike** a critical remark; 2. decisive; crucial
kritík/ë, ~a f. sh. ~a, ~at. 1. criticism; **i hapur ndaj kritikës** open to criticism; 2. critic

kritik/ój kal., ~óva, ~úar. criticize
kríz/ë, ~a f. sh. ~a, ~at. crisis; **krizë politike (ekonomike)** political (economic) crisis
krokodíl, ~i m. sh. ~ë, ~ët. crocodile; **lotë krokodili** crocodile tears
krom, ~i m. kim. chromium
krúa, krói m. sh. króje, krójet. spring
krúaj kal., króva, krúar. scratch
krye, ~t as. head; **në krye të faqes** at the head of the page; **ngre krye** revolt, rebel
kryefjál/ë, ~a f. sh. ~ë, ~ët. gjuh. subject
kryej kal., kréva, kryer. 1. perform, accomplish; 2. make, commit; **kryej një krim** commit a crime
kryengrítj/e, ~a f. sh. ~e, ~et. uprising, insurrection; **kryengritje e armatosur** an armed uprising
kryeqytét, ~i m. sh. ~e, ~et. capital
kryesí, ~a f. sh. ~, ~të. chairmanship
kryesór, ~e mb. main, chief, principal
kryetár, ~i m. sh. ~ë, ~ët. chairman, head
kryq, ~i m. sh. ~e, ~et. cross; **Kryqi i Kuq** Red Cross
kthéhem vetv. return, come back
kthej kal., kthéva, kthyer. 1. turn; 2. move something round; 3. change, convert
kthés/ë, ~a f. sh. ~a, ~at. turn, bend, curve
kthét/ër, ~ra f. sh. ~ra, rat. claw
kthim, ~i m. sh. ~e, ~et. return
kthjéllët (i,e) mb. 1. clear, serene; 2. sober
ku ndajf. where; **Ku shkon?** Where are you going?
kualifikím, ~i m. sh. ~e, ~et. qualification
kualifik/ój kal., ~óva, ~úar. qualify
kualifikúar (i,e) mb. qualified
kub, ~i m. sh. ~e, ~et. gjeom. cube
kudó ndajf. everywhere
kufí, ~ri m. sh. ~j, ~jtë. border, boundary
kufiz/ój kal., ~óva, ~úar. 1. bound, border; 2. restrict, restrain
kufizúar (i,e) mb. limited, confined, restricted
kujdés, ~i m. sh. ~e, ~et. care, caution; **bëj (tregoj) kujdes për** take care of
kujdés/em vetv., ~a (u), ~ur. care for, look after, take care of
kujdéssh/ëm (i) ~me (e) mb. careful, cautious
kujtés/ë, ~a f. memory; **kujtesë e mirë (e dobët)** good (poor) memory
kujtím, ~i m. sh. ~e, ~et. 1. memory, recollection, remembrance, reminiscence; 2. token, keepsake, memento
kujt/ój kal., ~óva, ~úar. recollect, recall, bring back to mind
kúkull, ~a f. sh. ~a, ~at. doll, puppet
kulét/ë, ~a f. sh. ~a, ~at. purse
kulm, ~i m. sh. ~e, ~et. 1. summit, top; 2. **fig.** height, peak, apogee, acme
kultiv/ój kal., ~óva, ~úar. 1. cultivate, till; 2. **fig.** cultivate, develop, educate
kultúr/ë, ~a f. sh. ~a, ~at. 1. culture; 2. **bujq.** crop
kulturór, ~e mb. cultural

kull/ój kal., ~óva, ~úar. 1. filter, percolate, strain; 2. drain; 3. drip

kullót (kullós) kal., ~a, ~ur. graze, pasture; **kullot dhentë** pasture one's sheep

kullót/ë, ~a f. sh. ~a, ~at. pasture

kúmbull, ~a f. sh. ~a, ~at. plum

kun/át, ~áti m. sh. ~étër, ~étërit. brother-in-law

kunát/ë, ~a f. sh. ~a, ~at. sister-in-law

kúndër parajf. against, counter

kundësúlm, ~i m. sh. ~e, ~et. counter-attack

kundërshtár, ~i m. sh. ~ë, ~ët. opponent, adversary, rival

kundërshtím, ~i m. sh. ~e, ~et. 1. opposition; 2. objection; **nuk kam kundërshtim** I have no objection; **A ka kundërshtime?** Any objections?

kundërsht/ój kal., ~óva, ~úar. oppose, object

kúndërt (i,e) mb. opposite, contrary

kundër/vë kal., ~vúra, ~vënë. counterpose

kundréjt paraf. against, opposite to

kundrín/ë, ~a f. sh. ~a, ~at. gjuh. object; **kundrinë e drejtë (e zhdrejtë)** direct (indirect) object

kúngu/ll, ~lli m. sh. ~j, ~jt. 1. **bot.** pumpkin; 2. **fig.** greenhorn

kúp/ë, ~a f. sh. ~a, ~at. 1. glass; 2. cup

kuptím, ~i m. sh. ~e, ~et. 1. meaning, sense 2. understanding, comprehension

kuptimplótë mb. meaningful

kuptúesh/ëm, ~(i), ~me (e) mb. understandable, comprehensible, intelligible

kuq (i), ~e (e) mb. red

kur ndajf. when

kur lidh. when

kurdís kal., ~a, ~ur. 1. wind up; **kurdis orën** wind up the watch; 2. **fig.** tune up; 3. **fig.** cook up, concoct

kurdohérë ndajf. always, at any time

kureshtár, ~e mb. curious; **jam kureshtar të di** I am curious to know

kuréshtj/e, ~a f. sh. ~e, ~et. curiosity

kúr/ë, ~a f. sh. ~a, ~at. cure, treatment

kurím, ~i m. sh. ~e, ~et. treatment

kurnác, ~e mb. miserly, stingy

kur/ój kal., ~óva, ~úar. cure

kurór/ë, ~a f. sh. ~a, ~at. 1. wreath; 2. crown; 3. wedlock

kurs, ~i m. sh. ~e, ~et. 1. course; 2. rate; **kursi i këmbimit** rate of exchange

kursé lidh. whereas

kurs/éj kal., ~eva, ~yer. 1. save; **kursej paratë** save money; 2. conserve; 3. spare

kurth, ~i m. sh. ~e, ~et. trap, snare

kúrrë ndajf. never

kurríz, ~i m. 1. back; spine; 2. back (of a chair)

kusí, ~a f. sh. ~, ~të. saucepan, casserole

kusúr, ~i m. sh. ~e, ~et. 1. change; 2. rest

kush (kujt; kë) përem. who, whose, whom

kushedí ndajf. perhaps

kushërí, ~ri m. sh. ~nj, ~njtë. cousin
kusht, ~i m. sh. ~e, ~et. 1. condition; 2. terms
kushtetúes, ~e mb. constitutional
kushtetút/ë, ~a f. sh. ~a, ~at. constitution
kusht/ój kal., ~óva, ~úar. 1. dedicate; 2. devote; 3. pay, show
kushtúesh/ëm (i), ~me (e) mb. expensive, costly, dear
kutí, ~a f. sh. ~, ~të. box, case
kuzhín/ë, ~a f. sh. ~a, ~at. kitchen, cookery
kyç, ~i m. sh. ~e, ~et. 1. key; 2. wrist

L

laboratór, ~i m. sh. **~ë, ~ët.** laboratory
lag kal., **~a, ~ur.** 1. wet, dampen, moisten; 2. water
lágem vetv. get wet, get a wetting
lágësht (i,e) mb. damp, humid
lagështí, ~a f. dampness, humidity
lágët (i,e) mb. wet, drenched, soaked
lágur (i,e) mb. wet, drenched, soaked
lágj/e, ~ja f. sh. **~e, ~et.** quarter
láhem vetv. 1. wash oneself; 2. bathe; 3. settle up with, pay up, discharge
la/j kal., **~va, ~rë.** 1. wash; **laj duart (rrobat)** wash one's hands (clothes); 2. liquidate, pay up; **laj borxhin** pay up (settle) a debt
lajkat/ój kal., **~óva, ~úar.** flatter, adulate
lajm, ~i m. sh. **~e, ~et.** news; the news; **lajm i mirë (i keq)** good (bad) news; **lajmi i fundit** the latest news; **dëgjoj lajmet** listen to the news
lajmërím, ~i m. sh. **~e, ~et.** notice, announcement
lajmër/ój kal., **~óva, ~úar.** notify, announce
lajthí, ~a f. sh. **~, ~të.** bot. hazlenut; hazel
lak, ~u m. sh. **léqe, léqet.** 1. noose, lasso, slip-knot; 2. trap, snare
lákër, ~ra f. sh. **~ra, ~rat.** bot. cabbage
lakmí, ~a f. sh. **~, ~të.** envy, covetousness
lakmitár, ~e mb. covetous, envious
lakm/ój kal., dhe jokal., **~óva, úar.** covet, crave, envy
lak/ój kal., **~óva, ~úar.** 1. bend; 2. gjuh. decline
lakrór, ~i m. sh. **~ë, ~ët.** pie
lakuríq, ~i m. sh. **~ë, ~ët. zool.** bat
lakuríq, ~e mb. nude, naked
lamtumír/ë, ~a f. sh. **~a, ~at.** farewell; **i lë lamtumirën dikujt** bid farewell to somebody
lamtumírë! pasth. farewell!
laps, ~i m. sh. **~a, ~at.** pencil
lárë (i,e) mb. 1. washed; 2. **fig.** clean
lárës, ~e mb. washing; **makinë larëse** washing machine
larg ndajf. far, far off, far away
largësí, ~a f. sh. **~, ~të.** distance; **në një largësi prej** at a distance from
lárgët (i,e) mb. 1. distant, far-off, far-away; 2. distant (of people)
largóhem vetv. leave, depart, go away, go off
larg/ój kal., **~óva, ~úar.** 1. remove; 2. draw away; 3. **fig.** avert, banish
largpámës, e mb. far-sighted, foresighted, far-seeing
larmísh/ëm (i), ~me (e) mb. varied, assorted, diverse
lart ndajf. above, up, aloft
lártë (i,e) mb. 1. high; 2. tall; 3. lofty
lartësí, ~a f. sh. **~, ~të.** 1. height; 2. **gjeogr.** altitude
lartës/ój kal., **~óva, úar.** 1. raise, put up; 2. elevate, uplift
lárv/ë, ~a f. sh. **~a, ~at zool.** larva
láshtë (i,e) mb. ancient

lavdërím, ~i m. sh. ~e, ~et. commendation, praise
lavdër/ój kal., ~óva, ~úar. praise, commend
lavdërúes, ~e mb. commendatory, laudatory
lavdërúesh/ëm, (i), ~me (e) mb. praise-worthy, commendable, laudable
lavdí, ~a f. sh. ~, ~të. glory
lavdíshëm (i), ~me (e) mb. glorious; **vepër e lavdishme** a glorious deed
le pj. let
léckë, ~a f. sh. ~a, ~at. 1. rag, cloth, dishrag; 2. tatters
ledh, ~i m. sh. ~e, ~et. bank
ledhatím, ~i m. sh. ~e, ~et. caress
ledhat/ój kal., ~óva, ~úar. caress
ledhatúes, ~e mb. caressing
legál, ~e mb. legal
legátë, ~a f. sh. ~a, ~at. legation
legén, ~i m. sh. ~ë, ~ët. basin, wash-basin
legjendár, ~e mb. legendary; **hero legjendar** legendary hero
legjéndë, ~a f. sh. ~a, ~at. legend
legjislación, ~i m. sh. ~e, ~et. legislation
legjislatív, ~e mb. legislative
leh jokal., ~a, ~ur. bark, yap, yelp
léhje, ~a f. sh. ~e, ~et. bark, yelp
léhtë (i,e) mb. 1. easy; 2. light; **peshë e lehtë** light weight; **muzikë e lehtë** light music
léhtë ndajf. 1. easily; 2. lightly; 3. slightly
lehtësí, ~a f. sh. ~, ~të. ease, facility
lehtës/ój kal., ~óva, ~úar. 1. ease, alleviate; 2. facilitate; 3. lighten
lehtësúes, ~e mb. alleviating, easing, relieving, mitigating, lentive, soothing
léj/e, ~a f. sh. ~e, ~et. 1. permission; **pa leje** without permission; 2. permit; 3. leave; **jam me leje** be on leave
lejlék, ~u m. sh. ~ë, ~ët. zool. stork
lej/ój kal., ~óva, úar. let, allow, permit; **më lejoni t'ju njoh** me allow me to introduce to
leksík, ~u m. gjuh. vocabulary, lexicon
leksikór, ~e mb. gjuh. lexical
leksión, ~i m. sh. ~e, ~et. lecture; **mbaj leksione** give (deliver) lectures
leopárd, ~i m. sh. ~ë, ~ët. zool. leopard
lépur, ~ri m. sh. ~j, ~jt. zool. hare; rabbit
lesh, ~i m. sh. ~ra, ~rat. wool
léshtë (i,e) mb. woolly, woollen
leshtór, ~e mb. hairy; fleecy; furry
lét/ër, ~ra f. sh. ~ra, ~rat. 1. paper; **letër shkrimi** writing paper; 2. letter
letërnjoftím, ~i m. sh. ~e, ~et. passport
letërsí, ~a f. sh. ~, ~të. literature
letrár, ~e mb. literary; **vepër letrare** literary work
lév/ë, ~a f. sh. ~a, ~at. 1. lever; 2. **fig.** lever
lexím, ~i m. sh. ~e, ~et. reading

lex/ój kal., **~óva**, **~úar**. read
lexúes, **~i** m. sh. **~**, **~it**. reader
lexúesh/ëm (i), **~me (e) mb**. readable; legible; **shkrim i lexueshëm** a legible writing
lezétsh/ëm (i), **~me (e) mb. bised**. 1. nice; 2. pleasant; 3. good- looking
lë kal., **láshë**, **lënë**. 1. leave; 2. put, place; 3. let; 4. entrust smth to smb; 5. bid; 6. give up, abandon
lëkúnd kal., **~a**, **~ur**. shake, quake, rock; **lëkund djepin** rock the cradle
lëkúndem vetv. waver, vacillate
lëkúndës, **~i** m. sh. **~**, **~it**. swing
lëkúr/ë, **~a** f. sh. **~ë**, **~ët**. 1. skin; 2. rind; 3. hide
lëm/ë, **~i** m. sh. **~énj**, **~énjtë**. 1. threshing floor (ground); 2. **fig**. field, domain, realm
lënd/ë, **~a** f. sh. **~ë**, **~ët**. 1. substance, material, matter; 2. timber, lumber; 3. content; **pasqyra e lëndës** table of contents; 4. subject
lëndín/ë, **~a** f. sh. **~a**, **~at**. lawn, grass
lën/g, **~gu** m. sh. **~gje**, **~gjet**. 1. fluid, liquid; 2. juice; **lëng limoni** lemon juice
lëngsh/ëm (i), **~me (e) mb**. 1. fluid; 2. juicy
lëpí/j kal., **~va**, **~rë**. lick
lësh/ój kal., **~óva**, **~úar**. drop, let fall
lëvdát/ë, **~a** f. sh. **~a**, **~at**. praise
lëvd/ój kal., **~óva**, **~úar**. praise
lëvíz kal., **~a**, **~ur**. 1. move, budge, stir; 2. advance, go ahead; 3. remove, move out; 4. turn, revolve; 5. transfer
lëvízj/e, **~a** f. sh. **~e**, **~et**. movement, motion
lëvízsh/ëm (i), **~me (e) mb**. movable, mobile
lëvózhg/ë, **~a** f. sh. **~a**, **~at**. shell, hull, husk, pod, bark, rind, cortex
li, **~ja** f. **mjek**. small pox
liberál, **~e mb**. liberal
líbër, **~ri** m. sh. **~ra**, **~rat**. book; **libër leximi** reader (reading book)
librarí, **~a** f. sh. **~**, **~të**. bookshop
lidh kal., **~a**, **~ur**. 1. tie, bind, fasten; 2. connect, join; 3. lace
lídhëz, **~a** f. sh. **~a**, **~at**. **gjuh**. conjunction
lídhj/e, **~a** f. sh. **~e**, **~et**. 1. connection; 2. tie, link, bond; 3. affinity; 4. league; 5. binding
lig (i), **~ë (e) mb**. wicked, evil, bad
líg/ë, **~ a (e)** f. sh. **~a**, **~at (të)** evil
líg/ë, **~a** f. sh. **~a**, **~at**. league
ligj, **~i** m. sh. **~e**, **~et**. law
ligjërísht ndajf. legally, lawfully
ligjër/ój jokal., **~óva**, **~úar**. discourse
lígjsh/ëm (i), **~me (e) mb**. lawful; legitimate
limón, **~i** m. sh. **~ë**, **~ët**. **bot**. lemon; lemon-tree
lind jokal., **~a**, **~ur**. 1. be born; 2. give birth; 3. rise; 4. issue, arise, spring up, come forth
líndj/e, **~a** f. sh. **~e**, **~et**. 1. birth; 2. rise; 3. **gjeogr**. East
lindór, **~e mb**. 1. eastern; 2. natal

liqén, ~i m. sh. ~e, ~et. lake
lírë (i,e) mb. 1. free; 2. unoccupied, unengaged, at leisure;
3. unconfined, at large, freed, loose; 4. vacant; 5.
unreserved; 6. cheap
lirí, ~a f. sh. ~, ~të. freedom; liberty; **liri e fjalës**
freedom of speech; **liri e shtypit** press freedom
liridáshës, ~e mb. freedom-loving
lirísht ndajf. freely; fluently
lir/ój kal., ~óva, ~úar. 1. free, release, set free; 2.
liberate; 3. loose, let loose; 4. dismiss; 5. untie, unbind;
6. cheapen; 7 relieve; 8 empty
lírsh/ëm (i), ~me (e) mb. free; loose
lírshëm ndajf. 1. loosely; 2. freely, fluently
lis, ~i m. sh. ~a, ~at. bot. oak
líst/ë, ~a f. sh. ~a, ~at. list
litár, ~i m. sh. ~ë, ~ët. rope
lít/ër, ~ra f. sh. ~ra, ~rat. liter
lód/ër, ~ra f. sh. ~ra, ~rat. toy, plaything
lodh kal., ~a, ~ur. 1. tire, fatigue; 2. bore, weary
lódhem vetv. get tired
lódhsh/ëm (i), ~me (e) mb. 1. tiring; **udhëtim i lodhshëm** a
tiring journey; 2. boring
lódhur (i,e) mb. tired, weary
logjík, ~e mb. logical; **përfundim logjik** a logical conclusion
(outcome)
logjík/ë, ~a f. logic
logjiksh/ëm (i), ~me (e) mb. logical
lój/ë, ~a f. sh. ~ëra, ~ërat dhe ~na, ~nat. 1. play; game; 2.
art. interpretation; 3. fig. fun, joke
lojtár, ~i m. sh. ~ë, ~ët. player
lokál, ~i m. sh. ~e, ~et. local, public house
lokál, ~e mb. local
lokomotív/ë, ~a f. sh. ~a, ~at. engine
lopát/ë, ~a f. sh. ~a, ~at. spade; shovel
lóp/ë, ~a ~f. sh. ~ë, ~ët. zool. cow
lord, ~i m. sh. ~ë, ~ët. lord
lot, ~i m. kryes. sh. ~, ~ët. tear; **derdh lot** shed tears;
shpërtheu në lot burst into tears
lotarí, ~a f. sh. ~, ~të. lottery
luaj jokal., ~ta, ~tur. 1. play; **luaj me top** play with a
ball; **luaj futboll** play football; 2. act; execute, perform;
3. move
lúajtur (i,e) mb. crazy, demented, deranged
luán, ~i m. sh. ~ë, ~ët. zool. lion; **pjesa e luanit** lion's
share
luftarák, ~e mb. 1. military; 2. militant, fighting
lúft/ë, ~a f. sh. ~ëra, ~ërat. war; battle; struggle
luftënxítës, ~e mb. warlike
luftëtár, ~i m. sh. ~ë, ~ët. fighter, warrior
luftím, ~i m. sh. ~e, ~et. combat, action, fighting
luft/ój jokal., ~óva, ~úar. fight, battle, combat, struggle;
strive
luftúes, ~e mb. warring
lúg/ë, ~a f. sh. ~ë, ~ët. spoon
lugín/ë, ~a f. sh. ~a, ~at. valley

lúl/e, ~ja f. sh. ~e, ~et. bot. flower
lulëz/ój jokal., ~óva, ~úar. 1. bloom, blossom, flower; 2.
fig. thrive, flourish, prosper
lulëzúar (i,e) mb. 1. blooming, flowering; 2. thriving,
flourishing
lúm/ë, ~i m. sh. ~énj, ~énjtë. river
lúmtur (i,e) mb. happy
lumturí, ~a f. happiness
lumtur/ój kal., ~óva, ~úar. make happy
lundr/ój jokal., ~óva, ~úar. 1. sail, navigate; 2. float
lundrúes, ~i m. sh. ~mb. navigating
lútem vetv. 1. ask, implore, beg; 2. please; 3. pray
lútj/e, ~a f. sh. ~e, ~et. 1. prayer; 2. request
lyp kal., ~a, ~ur. 1. ask, beg; 2. beg, ask alms; 3. require

llaç, ~**i** m. mortar
llaf, ~**i** m. sh. ~**e,** ~**et.** word
llahtársh/ëm (i), ~**me (e)** mb. terrible, dreadful
llámb/ë, ~**a** f. sh. ~**a,** ~**at.** lamp; **llampë elektrike** electric lamp
llast/ój kal., ~**óva,** ~**úar.** pamper
llastúar (i,e) mb. pampered; **fëmijë i llastuar** pampered child
llogarí, ~**a** f. sh. ~, ~**të.** account, reckoning, computation, calculation; **llogari bankare** bank account; **llogari rrjedhëse** running account (account current)
llogarít (llogarís) kal., ~**a,** ~**ur.** count, calculate, compute
llogór/e, ~**ja** f. sh. ~**e,** ~**et.** trench, ditch
lloj, ~**i** m. sh. ~**e,** ~**et.** kind, sort, type
llojshmërí, ~**a** f. sh. ~, ~**të.** variety, assortment
llomotít (llomotís) jokal., ~**a,** ~**ur.** babble, gibber; mutter
llomotítj/e f. sh. ~**e,** ~**et.** gibberish, gab; muttering
lloz, ~**i** m. sh. ~**e,** ~**et.** bolt
llúll/ë, ~**a** f. sh. ~**a,** ~**at.** pipe

M

mác/e, ~ja f. sh. **~e, ~et.** zool. cat; **mace e egër** wild cat; **iku macja, lozin minjtë** when the cat is away, the mice will play

maçók, ~u m. sh. **~ë, ~ët.** tom-cat, he-cat

madje pj. even, yet

madh (i), ~e (e) mb. 1. big, large, huge, enormous; 2. grand; 3. great, vast, immense; 4. elder; senior

madhësí, ~a f. sh. **~, ~të.** 1. size; 2. quantity

madhështí, ~a f. magnificence, grandeur

madhështór, ~e mb. magnificent

madhór, ~e mb. 1. major; **moshë madhore** the age of majority; 2. usht. ranking; **oficer madhor** ranking officer; 3. major, important, principal

magazín/ë, ~a f. sh. **~a, ~at.** warehouse, storehouse, depot, storeroom

magazin/ój kal., **~óva, ~úar.** store

magnét, ~i m. sh. **~e, ~et.** magnet

magnetík, ~e mb. 1. magnetic; **forcë magnetike** magnetic force; **fushë magnetike** magnetic field; **shirit magnetik** magnetic tape; 2. **fig.** magnetic

magnetiz/ój kal., **~óva, ~úar.** 1. magnetize; 2. **fig.** magnetize

magnetofón, ~i m. sh. **~a, ~at.** tape-recorder

magjeps kal., **~a, ~ur.** 1. bewitch; 2. charm, enchant

magjepsës, ~e mb. bewitching; charming, fascinating, enchanting; **bukuri magjepsëse** enchanting beauty

magjí, ~a f. sh. **~, ~të dhe ~ra, ~rat.** 1. witch-craft; witchery; 2. magic, spell

magjík, ~e mb. magic(al); **fjalë magjike** a magic word

mahnít kal., **~a, ~ur.** marvel, amaze, astound, strike with wonder

mahnítem vetv. be amazed, be astonished

mahnitës, ~e mb. astonishing, amazing, marvellous

mahnítj/e, ~a f. sh. **~e, ~et.** amazement, astonishment, marvel

mahnítsh/ëm (i), ~me (e) mb. striking; miraculous, marvellous, wonderful

maj, ~i m. May

máj/ë, ~a f. sh. **~a, ~at.** 1. peak, summit; **maja e malit** the peak of the mountain; 2. tip; **maja e hundës** the tip of the nose; 3. brim; **është mbushur me majë** full to the brim

májm/ë (i), ~e (e) mb. 1. fat; **mish i majmë** fat meat; 2. **fig.** fat; **fitim i majmë** a fat profit

majmún, ~i m. sh. **~ë, ~ët.** zool. ape, monkey

majonéz/ë, ~a f. sh. **~a, ~at.** mayonnaise

májtas dhe májtazi ndajf. left; **Majtas kthehu!** About left turn!

májtë (i,e) mb. left; **syri (veshi, krahu) i majtë** the left eye (ear, arm); **dora (këmba, ana, këpuca) e majtë** the left hand (foot, side, shoe)

makaróna, ~t f. vet. sh. macaroni, pasta

makinerí, ~a f. sh. **~, ~të.** machinery

makín/ë, ~a f. sh. **~a, ~at.** 1. machine, engine; **makinë qepëse a** sewing machine; **makinë shkrimi** typewriter; **makinë larëse** washing- machine; 2. vehicle, automobile, car, motorcar; 3. machinery, apparatus

maksimál, ~e mb. libr. maximal, maximum, greatest, utmost, highest, top
maksimúm, ~i m. sh. ~e, ~et. maximum
mal, ~i m. sh. ~e, ~et. mountain
malësór, ~e mb. highland, upland
malór, ~e mb. mountainous
mall, ~i m. longing; **malli për shtëpi** a longing for home
mall, ~i m. sh. ~ra, ~rat. commodity, article, ware
mallëngjéhem vetv. get moved
mallëngj/éj kal., ~éva, ~yer. touch, move
mallëngjyes, ~e mb. touching, moving; **film mallëngjyes** a touching film
mallkím, ~i m. sh. ~e, ~et. curse, damnation
mallk/ój kal., ~óva, ~úar. curse, damn, maledict
mallkúar (i,e) mb. damned, cursed
mamá, ~ja f. sh. ~, ~të. mamma, ma
man, ~i m. sh. ~a, ~at. bot. mulberry; mulberry tree
manaférr/ë, ~a f. sh. ~a, ~at. bot. blackberry
manár, ~i m. sh. ~ë, ~ët. pet
manastír, ~i m. sh. ~e, ~et. monastery, abbey, convent, nunnery
mandarín/ë, ~a f. sh. ~a, ~at. bot. tangerine
mandát, ~i m. sh. ~e, ~et. drejt. mandate
mángët (i,e) mb. deficient, lacking, defective, incomplete
maní, ~a f. sh. ~, ~të. mania
manifest/ój jokal., ~óva, ~úar. manifest
manipul/ój kal., ~óva, ~úar. manipulate
manovr/ój kal., ~óva, ~úar. maneuver, manoeuvre
mantél, ~i m. sh. ~e, ~et. mantle
manuál, ~i m. sh. ~e, ~et. manual, handbook
manusháq/e, ~ja f. sh. ~e, ~et. bot. violet
marangóz, ~i m. sh. ~ë, ~ët. carpenter, joiner
marifét, ~i m. sh. ~e, ~et. trick
marinár, ~i m. sh. ~ë, ~ët. sailor, seaman, seafare, mariner
márk/ë, ~a f. sh. ~a, ~at. trade-mark; brand
markúç, ~i m. sh. ~ë, ~ët. hose
marmelát/ë, ~a f. sh. ~a, ~at. marmalade
mars, ~i m. March
marsh, ~i m. sh. ~e, ~et. tek. gear
marshím, ~i m. sh. ~e, ~et. march
marsh/ój jokal., ~óva, ~úar. march
martés/ë, ~a f. sh. ~a, ~at. marriage, matrimony, wedlock
martesór, ~e mb. matrimonial
márt/ë, ~a (e) f. sh. ~a, ~at. Tuesday
martír, ~i m. sh. ~ë, ~ët. martyr
martóhem vetv. get married
mart/ój kal., ~óva, ~úar. marry, wed
martúar (i,e) mb. married
marúl/e, ~ja f. sh. ~e, ~et. bot. lettuce
marr kl., móra, márrë. 1. take; 2. get; 3. remove something; 4. receive; 5. catch; 6. choose; buy; 7 need, require; 8 obtain; 9 go by; 10 consider
márrë (i,e) mb. crazy, insane, mad

marrdhëní/e, ~a f. sh. **~e, ~et.** relation, relationship;
marrëdhënie diplomatike diplomatic relations
márrës, ~i m. sh **~, ~it.** 1. receiver, recipient; 2. **tek.**
receiver
marrëvéshj/e, ~a f. sh. **~e, ~et.** agreement, accord; **arrij në**
marrëveshje come to (arrive, reach) an agreement; **nënshkruaj**
një marrëveshje sign an agreement
marrëzí, ~a f. sh. **~, ~të.** stupidity, craziness, foolishness
marrósem vetv. go mad, go crazy
marrósur (i,e) mb. mad, crazy
masázh, ~i m. sh. **~e, ~et.** massage
más/ë, ~a f. sh. **~a, ~at.** 1. measure; 2. size; 3. limit;
jashtë mase beyond measure; 4. **muz.** measure
más/ë, ~a f. sh. **~a, ~at.** measure; precaution; **masa kundër**
krimit measures against crime; **masat e sigurimit** safety
measures
másë, ~a f. sh. **~a, ~at.** mass; **masë dheu** a mass of earth; 2.
the masses
masív, ~e mb. massive
maskar/á, ~ái m. sh. **~énj, ~énjtë.** knave, scoundrel, villain,
rogue
másk/ë, ~a f. sh. **~a, ~at.** 1. mask; 2. **fig.** mask, guise
mask/ój kal., **~óva, ~úar.** 1. mask; 2. **fig.** mask, conceal; 3.
usht. camouflage
másh/ë, ~a f.sh. **~a, ~at.** 1. poker; 2. **fig.** tool
máshkull, ~i m. sh. **méshkuj, méshkujt.** male; man
mashkullór, ~e mb. 1. male; 2. masculine
mashtr/ój kal., **~óva, ~úar.** trick, delude, take in
mat (i) kal., **~a, ~ur.** 1. measure; 2. **fig.** assess; gauge;
3. consider, weigh
matánë ndajf. on the other side
matematík, ~e mb. mathematical
matematik/ë, ~a f. mathematics
materiál, ~i m. sh. **~e, ~et.** 1. material; **material ndërtimi**
building material; 2. fabric, cloth; 3. data, facts, figures,
information
materiál, ~e mb. material; **bota materiale** the material world;
dëshmi materiale material evidence
materialíst, ~e mb. materialistic
matéri/e, ~a f. filoz. matter
maternitét, ~i m. sh. **~e, ~et.** maternity home
mátës, ~i m. sh. **~, ~it.** gauge
mátur (i,e) mb. prudent, discreet
maturí, ~a f. prudence
mbáhem vetv. 1. support oneself; 2. keep up; 3. hang on, hold
on; 4. abide by
mbaj kal., **~ta, ~tur.** 1. hold; 2. keep; 3. rear; 4. preserve;
5. bear, carry; 6. retain, reserve
mbar/ój kal., **~óva, ~úar.** 1. finish, complete, conclude,
terminate; 2. finish off, dispose of, use up, consume
mbart kal., **~a, ~ur.** carry, convey, transport
mbarúar (i,e) mb. 1. finished, ended, completed; 2. highly
accomplished; perfect, masterful
mbáse pj. perhaps
mbasí lidh. as, for, because
mbath kal., **~a, ~ur.** 1. put on; 2. shoe (the horse)

mbe/s jokal., ~ta, ~tur. 1. stick; 2. remain
mbés/ë, ~a f. sh. ~a, ~at. niece
mbeturín/ë, ~a f. kryes. sh. ~a, ~at. remains, remnants, leftovers, leavings
mbërth/éj kal., ~éva, ~yer. 1. button (up); 2. nail smth up; 3. grab, grib; 4. fix
mbështét (mbështés) kal., ~a, ~ur. 1. lean, rest, repose; 2. back up, support; 3. base, ground
mbështétem vetv. 1. lean, rest, stand; 2. rely on
mbësht/jéll kal., ~ólla, ~jéllë. 1. wrap up; 2. roll up; coil
mbi parafj. on, upon; over; above; on; about
mbiçm/ój kal., ~óva, ~úar. overvalue, overrate, overestimate
mbiém/ër, ~ri m. sh. ~ra, ~rat. 1. gjuh. adjective; 2. surname
mbijetés/ë, ~a f. survival
mbijet/ój jokal., ~óva, ~úar. survive, outlive
mbikëqyr kal., ~a, ~ur. supervise, oversee, watch over
mbikëqyrës, ~i m. sh. ~, ~it. supervisor
mbi/n jokal., ~u, ~rë. sprout, germinate, shoot, strike roots
mbinatyrsh/ëm (i), ~me (e) mb. supernatural; **qënie e mbinatyrshme** supernatural being
mbingark/ój kal., ~óva, ~úar. overload, overburden, overcharge
mbinjer/í, ~íu m. sh. mbinjérëz, mbinjérëzit. superman
mbivlér/ë, ~a f. sh. ~a, ~at. surplus value
mbivlerës/ój kal., ~óva, ~úar. overvalue, overestimate
mbizotër/ój jokal., ~óva, ~úar. predominate, prevail, overwhelm
mbizotërúes, ~e mb. prevalent, dominant, predominant, prevailing; **mendim mbizotërues** prevalent opinion
mbjell kal., mbólla, mbjéllë. 1. sow; 2. fig. sow, spread, introduce
mbledh kal., mblódha, mblédhur. 1. collect; 2. gather, rally; 3. pick up; 4. mat. add, sum up; 5. accumulate
mblédhje, ~a f. sh. ~e, ~et. 1. meeting, gathering; 2. mat. addition; 3. collection, collecting
mbrés/ë, ~a f. sh. ~a, ~at. 1. scar, sore; 2. fig. impression; **mbresat e para të** one's first impressions
mbret, ~i m. sh. ~ër, ~ërit. 1. king; 2. fig. king; **mbreti i kafshëve** the king of beasts
mbretërí, ~a f. sh. ~, ~të. 1. kingdom; 2. fig. realm, kingdom
mbretër/ój kal., ~óva, ~úar. reign
mbretërór, ~e mb. royal, regal
mbrëmj/e, ~a f. sh. ~e, ~et. 1. evening, dusk, nightfall, sundown; 2. party
mbrój kal., ~ta, ~tur. protect, defend, guard
mbrójtës, ~i m. sh. ~, ~it. defender, protector
mbrójtes, ~e mb. defensive, protective
mbrójtj/e, ~a f. sh. ~e, ~et. 1. defence, guard; 2. protection
mbul/ój kal., ~óva, ~úar. 1. cover; 2. protect, shield; 3. enwrap, shroud; 4. conceal, cloak, cover up
mburój/ë f. sh ~a, ~at. shield, armour
mbúrrem vetv. boast, brag, pride oneself
mbush kal., ~a, ~ur. 1. fill; 2. fig. fill; 3. fill in (out); 4. stuff; 5. mjek. fill, stop (a tooth)
mbúshur (i,e) mb. filled; stuffed

mbyll kal., ~a, ~ur. 1. shut, close; 2. lock; 3. lock in; 4. switch off; turn off; 5. close up; seal; 6. shut up, confine; 7 shut down, close down
mbyllur (i,e) mb. 1. shut, closed; 2. locked; 3. reticent; 4. dark **mbyt (mbys) kal., ~a, ~ur.** 1. strangle, choke, throttle; 2. smother, suffocate, stifle; 3. drown
mbytem vetv. get drowned; get suffocated
me parafj. with; by
medálj/e, ~a f. sh. ~e, ~et. medal; **ana tjetër e medaljes** the reverse (the other side) of the medal
megjíthatë lidh. yet, notwithstanding, nevertheless
mekaník, ~u m. sh. ~ë, ~ët. mechanic
mekaník, ~e mb. mechanical (edhe **fig.**)
mekaníkisht ndajf. mechanically
mekaníz/ëm, ~mi m. sh. ~ma, ~mat. mechanism, gadget, device
mekaniz/ój kal., ~óva, ~úar. mechanize
melankolík, ~e mb. melancholic; **natyrë melankolike** a melancholic nature
melodí, ~a f. sh. ~, ~të. muz. melody
melodík, ~e mb. melodic, melodious
meméc, ~e mb. mute, dumb
ménçur (i,e) mb. wise, clever
mençurí, ~a f. wisdom
mend, ~të f. vet. sh. 1. mind, intellect, intelligence; 2. mind, intention; **ndërroj mend** change one's mind; 3. memory; **mbaj mend** keep (bear) in mind; **sjell ndër mend** bring (call) smth to mind; 4. imagination
mendím, ~i m. sh. ~e, ~et. 1. thought; 2. idea, notion; 3. opinion; 4. mind; **për mendimin tim** to my mind
méndj/e, ~a f. sh. ~e, ~et. 1. mind, intellect, wit, head; **jam i një mendjeje me** be of one mind; **ndryshoj mendje** change one's mind; 2. advice
mendóhem vetv. think over, turn over in one's mind
mend/ój jokal., ~óva, ~úar. think, meditate, ponder
mendúar (i,e) mb. thoughtful, meditative, pensive
menjëherë ndajf. at once, instantly, immediately, right away
menjëhersh/ëm (i) ~me (e) mb. immediate, instant, instantaneous sudden, prompt
meqénëse lidh. for, as, since
merimáng/ë, ~a f. sh. ~a, ~at. zool. spider
merit/ë, ~a f. sh. ~a, ~at. merit
merit/ój kal., ~óva, ~úar. merit, deserve
mermér, ~i m. sh. ~ë, ~ët. marble
mérrem vetv. occupy oneself, engage in smth, be occupied in smth, take up
mes, ~i m. sh. ~e, ~et. middle, mid, midst; **në mes të natës** in the middle of the night
mes parafj. between, amidst
mesatár, ~e mb. average; mean, medium, middle
més/ëm (i), ~me (e) mb. middle
metafór/ë, ~a f. sh. ~a, ~at. metaphor
metál, ~i m. sh. ~e, ~et. kim. metal

metalík, ~e mb. metallic
metalurgjí, ~a f. metallurgy
meteór, ~i m. sh. ~ë, ~ët astr. meteor
mét/ë, ~a (e) f. sh. ~a, ~at (të). defect, fault, flaw
métë (i,e) mb. 1. deficient, incomplete; 2. not quite right
mét/ër, ~ri m. sh. ~ra, ~rat. meter; **metër katror** square
meter
metód/ë, ~a f. sh. ~a, ~at. method
metodík, ~e mb. methodical
metrík, ~e mb. metric
metró, ~ja f. sh. ~, ~të. subway, underground, tube
mezí ndajf. hardly, barely, scarcely
më ndajf. more
mëkát, ~i m. sh. ~e, ~et. sin
mëkatár, ~i m. sh. ~ë, ~ët. sinner
mëkat/ój jokal., ~óva, ~úar. sin
mëlçí, ~a f. sh. ~, ~të. anat. liver
mëndáfsh, ~i m. silk
mëndáfshtë (i,e) silken; silky
mëng/ë, ~a f. sh. ~ë, ~ët. 1. sleeve; 2. gjeog. armlet
mëngjés, ~i m. sh. ~e, ~et. 1. morning; **mëngjes për mëngjes**
every morning; 2. breakfast; **ha mëngjes** have breakfast
mënyr/ë, ~a f. sh. ~a, ~at. 1. manner, way, mode, fashion; **në
këtë mënyrë** in this way; **me çdo mënyrë** by any means; **në asnjë
mënyrë** by no means, in no way; 2. gjuh. mood
mënjánë. ndajf. aside; **heq (vë) mënjanë** set aside
mëpársh/ëm (i), ~me (e) mb. preceding, foregoing, previous
mërgím, ~i m. sh. ~e, ~et. emigration
mërg/ój kal., ~óva, ~úar. emigrate
mërkúr/ë, ~a (e) f. sh. ~a, ~at (të). Wednesday
mërmërít (mërmërís) jokal., ~a, ~ur. murmur
mërzí, ~a f. sh. ~, ~të. boredom, ennui
mërzítem vetv. get bored
mërzítsh/ëm (i), ~me (e) mb. boring, annoying; **libër i
mërzitshëm** a boring book
mësím, ~i m. sh. ~e, ~et. 1. teaching; 2. lesson; 3. class,
school; 4. fig. lesson
mësimdhënës, ~i m. sh. ~, ~it. teacher
mësimór, ~e mb. teaching
mësóhem vetv. get accustomed, get used to
mës/ój kal., ~óva, ~úar. 1. teach; 2. learn; 3. hear of,
learn of(about)
mësúes, ~i m. sh. ~, ~it. teacher
mëshír/ë, ~a f. mercy; **në mëshirën e** at the mercy of; **tregoj
mëshirë për** show mercy to
mëshir/ój kal., ~óva, ~úar. pity
mëshírsh/ëm (i), ~me (e) mb. merciful
mëtéjsh/ëm (i), ~me (e) mb. further
mi, ~u m. sh. ~nj, ~njtë zool. mouse, rat
mía (e) pron. my
midís parafj. among, amid, between, amidst
míell, ~i m. sh. ~ra, ~rat. flour
míj/ë, ~a f. sh. ~a, ~at dhe ~ëra, ~ërat. thousand

mi/k, ~ku m. sh. **~q, ~qtë.** 1. friend; **miku im më i mirë** my best friend; **miku i mirë njihet në ditë të vështirë** a friend in need is a friend indeed; 2. guest

mikprítës, ~e mb. hospitable

mikprítj/e, ~a f. hospitality; **mikpritja shqiptare** the Albanian hospitality

mikrób, ~i m. sh. **~e, ~et.** biol., mjek. microbe

mikrofón, ~i m. sh. **~a, ~at.** microphone

mikroskóp, ~i m. sh. **~ë, ~ët** opt. microscope

miliárd, ~i m. sh. **~ë, ~ët dhe ~a, ~at.** milliard

milimét/ër, ~ri m. sh. **~ra, ~rat.** millimeter

milingón/ë, ~a f. sh. **~a, ~at.** zool. ant; **fole milingonash** ant-hill

milión, ~i m. sh. **~ë, ~ët dhe ~a, ~at.** million

milionér, ~i m. sh. **~ë, ~ët.** millionaire

mílj/e, ~a f. sh. **~e, ~et.** mile

mimóz/ë, ~a f. sh. **~a, ~at.** bot. mimosa

minatór, ~i m. sh. **~ë, ~ët.** miner

minerál, ~i m. sh. **~e, ~et.** mineral

minerál, ~e mb. mineral; **ujë mineral** mineral water

mín/ë, ~a f. sh. **~a, ~at.** mine; **vë mina** lay mines

miniér/ë, ~a f. sh. **~a, ~at.** mine

minimál, ~e mb. minimal; **shpenzime minimale** minimal expenses

minimiz/ój kal., **~óva, ~úar.** minimize

minimúm, ~i m. sh. **~e, ~et.** minimum; **ul në minimum** reduce to the minimum

miníst/ër, ~ri m. sh. **~ra, ~rat.** minister

ministrí, ~a f. sh. **~, ~të.** ministry

min/ój kal., **~óva, ~úar.** mine

minoritár, ~ mb. minority

minút/ë, ~a f. sh. **~a, ~at.** minute; **një minutë, të lutem!** just a minute, please!

miqësí, ~a f. sh. **~, ~të.** friendship

miqësór, ~e mb. friendly; **marrëdhënie miqësore** friendly relations; **ndeshje miqësore futbolli** a friendly game of football

miratím, ~i m. sh. **~e, ~et.** approval, approbation

mirat/ój kal., **~óva, ~úar.** approve

mír/ë, ~a (e) f. sh. **~a, ~at (të).** 1. good; **ndryshimi mes të mirës dhe të keqes** the difference between good and evil; 2. benefit, advantage

mírë (i,e) mb. 1. good, generous, kind, gentle, amiable; 2. fine; 3. able, competent; 4. well-behaved

mírë ndajf. good, well, all right, okay

mirëdáshës, ~e mb. kind, benevolent

mirëdíta pasth. good day!

mirëkuptím, ~i m. understanding

mirëmbáj kal., **~ta, ~tur.** maintain

mirënjóhës, ~e mb. grateful

mirënjóhj/e, ~a f. gratitude

mirënjóhur (i,e) mb. well-known, renowned, celebrated

mirëpó lidh. but

mirëpr/és kal., **~íta, ~ítur.** make somebody welcome, receive somebody hospitably

mirëqéni/e, ~a f. well-being, welfare
mirëseárdhj/e, ~a f. welcome
mirësí, ~a f. sh. ~, ~të. benevolence, goodness, amiability
mirupáfshim pasth. good-bye! by-by! so long!
mís/ër, ~ri m. sh. ~ra, ~rat bot. corn, maize
misión, ~i m. sh. ~e, ~et. mission
misionár, ~i m. sh. ~ë, ~ët missionary
mish, ~i m. sh. ~ra, ~rat. 1. meat; 2. flesh
mitín/g, ~gu m. sh. ~gje, ~gjet. meeting
mítur (i,e) mb. infant
míz/ë, ~a f. sh. ~a, ~at. zool. fly
mjaft. ndajf. enough
mjaftúesh/ëm (i), ~me (e) mb. sufficient, adequate
mjált/ë, ~i m. honey; muaji i mjaltit honeymoon
mjedís, ~i m. sh. ~e, ~et. environment, surrounding
mjégull/ë, ~a f. sh. ~a, ~at. fog, mist, haze
mjek, ~u m. sh. ~ë, ~ët. doctor
mjék/ër, ~ra f. sh. ~ra, ~rat. 1. chin; 2. beard
mjekësí, ~a f. medicine
mjekësór, ~e mb. medical; ndihmë mjekësore medical health
mjek/ój kal., ~óva, ~úar. cure, medicate, treat
mjérë (i,e) mb. poor
mjet, ~i m. sh. ~e, ~et. 1. implement, tool; 2. means; me të
gjitha mjetet by all means
mobíli/e, ~a f. sh. ~e, ~et. furniture
mobiliz/ój kal., ~óva, ~úar. mobilize
moçál, ~i m. sh. ~e, ~et. marsh, bog
móç/ëm (i), ~me (e) mb. 1. old, aged; 2. ancient
modél, ~i m. sh. ~e, ~et. 1. model; 2. pattern, example; 3.
mould, die modérn, ~e mb. modern, contemporary, up-to-date
moderniz/ój kal., ~óva, ~úar. modernize, update
modést, ~e mb. modest
modestí, ~a f. modesty
mód/ë, ~a f. sh. ~a, ~at. fashion; moda e fundit the latest
fashion; ndjek modën follow the fashion; në modë (jashë mode)
in (out of) fashion
moh/ój kal., ~óva, ~úar. 1. negate; 2. disown; 3. deny
mohúes, ~e mb. negative
móll/ë, ~a f. sh. ~ë, ~ët. bot. apple; apple tree
momént, ~i m. sh. ~e, ~et. moment, instant
monédh/ë, ~a f. sh. ~a, ~at. coin; currency
monetár, ~e mb. monetary; politika monetare monetary policy
monopól, ~i m. sh. ~e, ~et. monopoly
mont/ój kal., ~óva, ~úar. assemble, fit (put) together
monumént, ~i m. sh. ~e, ~et. monument
morál, ~i m. 1. moral; 2. morale; ngre moralin e raise
(boost) the morale of
morál, ~e mb. moral; çështje morali a moral question
mos pj. don't
mosbesím, ~i m. disbelief, distrust
mosmarrëvéshj/e, ~a f. sh. ~e, ~et. disagreement
mósh/ë, ~a f. sh. ~a, ~at. age

mot, ~i m. sh. ~e, ~et. 1. weather; 2. year; **një herë në mot** once in a blue moon
mót/ër, ~ra f. sh. ~ra, ~rat. sister
motív, ~i m. sh. ~e, ~et. 1. motive; 2. motif
motór, ~i m. sh. ~e, ~et. tek. 1. motor; 2. motorcycle
mposht kal., ~a, ~ur. 1. vanquish, defeat; 2. overpower, overcome, surmount; 3. restrain
mpreh kal., ~a, ~ur. sharpen, whet
mpréhtë (i,e) mb. 1. sharp; 2. shrill, piercing; 3. keen; acute; alert
mrekullí, ~a f. sh. ~, ~të. miracle
mrekullúesh/ëm (i), ~me (e) mb. wonderful, marvelous
múaj, ~i m. sh. ~, ~t. month
mujór, ~e mb. monthly; **rrogë mujore** monthly pay
mullí, ~ri m. sh. ~nj, ~njtë. mill; **mulli me erë** wind-mill
mund jokal., ~a, ~ur. can
mund kal., ~a, ~ur. 1. defeat; 2. suppress, overcome, subdue
mundësí, ~a f. sh. ~, ~të. possibility, probability
mundóhem vetv. 1. strive, attempt, endeavor, labor, try; 2. toil, sweat, work hard, strain oneself
múndsh/ëm (i), ~me (e) mb. possible, probable
mungés/ë, ~a f. sh. ~a, ~at. 1. lack, want, scarcity; 2. absence
mur, ~i m. sh. ~e, ~et. 1. wall; **mur ndarës** dividing wall; **edhe muret kanë veshë** walls have ears
músku/l, ~li m. sh. ~j, ~jt. muscle
mustáq/e, ~ja f. kryes. sh. ~e, ~et. mustache; moustaches
mushamá, ~ja f. sh. ~, ~të. raincoat, waterproof, mackintosh
múshk/ë, ~a f. sh. ~a, ~at. zool. mule
mushkërí, ~a f. sh. ~, ~të. lung
mushkónj/ë, ~a f. sh. ~a, ~at. zool. mosquito
muzé, ~u m. sh. ~, ~të. museum
muz/g, ~u m. sh. ~gje, ~gjet. twilight, dusk
muzikánt, ~i m. sh. ~ë, ~ët. musician
muzík/ë, ~a f. music
muzikór, ~e mb. musical
my/k, ~ku m. sh ~qe, ~qet. mold

N

nacionalíst, ~e mb. nationalist
náft/ë, ~a f. naphtha
naiv, ~e mb. naive
naivitét, ~i m. naivety
najlon, ~i m. nylon
nam, ~i m. bised. fame, reputation, repute, name; **nam i mirë (i keq)** good (bad) reputation
narkotík, ~u m. sh. ~ë, ~ët. narcotic
narkotík, ~e mb. narcotic
nát/ë, ~a f. sh. net, nétët. night; **gjatë natës** at night; **ditë e natë** day and night; **Natën e mirë!** Good night!
nátën ndajf. at night, by night, nightly
natyralíst, ~e mb. letr.,art. naturalistic
natyr/ë, ~a f. 1. nature; 2. nature, character; 3. sort, kind
natyrísht ndajf. of course
natyrór, ~e mb. natural
natyrsh/ëm (i), ~me (e) mb. natural; **vdekje e natyrshme** natural death
natyrshëm ndajf. naturally
ndáhem vetv. 1. part, part company; 2. separate, divorce
nda/j kal., ~va, ~rë. 1. divide; 2. separate; 3. divorce; 4. share
ndaj parafj. by; towards; to
ndajfólj/e, ~a f. sh. ~e, ~et. gjuh. adverb
ndal kal.,~a, ~ur. 1. stop, discontinue, quit, cease; 2. halt
ndálem vetv. 1. stop, come to a stop; 2. pause; 3. stop by (round); 4. refrain
ndalés/ë, ~a f. sh. ~a, ~at. 1. stop, pause; 2. stopover; 3. station
ndal/ój kal.,~óva, ~úar. 1. stop; 2. cease, discontinue; 3. prohibit, forbid, inhibit; 4. halt
ndalúar (i,e) mb. forbidden, prohibited
ndánë parafj. by, along
ndárj/e, ~a f. sh. ~e, ~et. 1. division; 2. separation; 3. partition
nde/j kal., ~va, ~rë. 1. hang (the clothes); 2. stretch
ndénjur (i,e) mb. 1. stagnant; 2. stale
nder, ~i m. 1. honor; 2. favor
ndérë (i,e) mb. 1. stretched, extended; 2. tense; 3. shallow
nderím, ~i m. sh. ~e, ~et. honor, respect, homage
nder/ój kal., ~óva, ~úar. honor
ndérsh/ëm (i), ~me (e) mb. 1. honest; **njeri i ndershëm** an honest man; 2. honorable; upright
ndershmërí, ~a f. honesty, probity, uprightness
ndershmërísht ndajf. honestly
nderúar (i,e) mb. honored; honorable
ndesh kal., ~a, ~ur. 1. meet, encounter, come across; 2. run into **ndéshem vetv.** 1. meet with; 2. face; 3. run (bump) into; 4. contend, confront, clash
ndéshj/e, ~a f. sh. ~e, ~et. 1. combat, battle, fight; 2. contest, match; 3. collision
ndez kal., ~a, ~ur. 1. light, ignite; **ndez zjarrin** light the fire; 2. turn on; switch on; 3. **fig.** kindle
ndézur (i,e) mb. 1. lighted, lit, alight; 2. **fig.** alight
ndër parafj. among, amongst

ndërgjégj/e, ~ja f. conscience; **ndërgjegje e pastër** a clear conscience

ndërgjegjsh/ëm (i), ~me (e) mb. conscientious; **nxënës i ndërgjegjshëm** a conscientious pupil

ndërhy/j jokal.,~ra, ~rë. 1. interfere; 2. intervene; 3. intercede; 4. mediate, go between

ndërhyrj/e, ~a f. sh. ~e, ~et. 1. interference; 2. intervention; 3. intercession; 4. mediation

ndërkáq ndajf. meanwhile, meantime

ndërkóhë ndajf. in the meanwhile

ndërkombëtár, ~e mb. international; **situata ndërkombëtare** international situation

ndërkombëtariz/ój kal., ~óva, ~úar. internationalize

ndërlikím , ~i m. sh. ~e, ~et. complication

ndërlik/ój kal., ~óva, ~úar. complicate

ndërlikúar (i,e) mb. complicated, intricate; **gjendje e ndërlikuar** a complicated situation

ndërmárrj/e, ~a f. sh. ~e, ~et. 1. enterprise; 2. undertaking, venture

ndërmjét. parajf. between

ndërmjét/ëm (i), ~me (e) mb. intermediary, intermediate, in-between

ndërmjétës, ~i m. sh. ~, ~it. go-between, mediator, intermediator

ndërmjétës, ~e mb. intermediary, intermediate

ndërmjetës/ój jokal., ~óva, ~úar. mediate, intercede

ndërpré/s kal., ~va, ~rë. 1. interrupt; 2. discontinue, leave off, suspend; 3. **gjeom.** intersect

ndërsá lidh. while, whereas, whilst

ndërsjéllë (i,e) mb. reciprocal; **ndihmë e ndërsjellë** reciprocal help

ndërtés/ë, ~a f. sh. ~a, ~at. building

ndërtím, ~i m. sh. ~e, ~et. building, construction

ndërtimór, ~e mb. structural

ndërt/ój kal., ~óva, ~úar. build, construct

ndërtúes, ~i m. sh. ~, ~it. builder

ndërtúes, ~e mb. constructive

ndërthúr kal., ~a, ~ur. interweave, interlace; combine

ndërvárur (i,e) mb. interdependent

ndërrím, ~i m. 1. substitution; 2. change, exchange; **pjesë ndërrimi** spare parts; 3. shift

ndërr/ój kal., ~óva, ~úar. 1. change; 2. exchange; 3. moult, cast (the feathers, hair, skin); 4. change, switch

ndërrúeshëm (i), ~me (e) mb. 1. interchangable; 2. convertible

ndëshkím, ~i m. sh. ~e, ~et. 1. punishment, chastisement, castigation

ndëshkimór, ~e mb. punitive, punishing; **masa ndëshkimore** punitive measures

ndëshk/ój kal., ~óva, ~úar. 1. punish; 2. penalize

ndíej kal., ndjéva, ndíer. feel, experience, sense

ndíhem vetv. 1. feel; 2. be felt, be heard

ndihmés/ë, ~a f. sh. ~a, ~at. contribution

ndíhm/ë, ~a f. sh. ~a, ~at. help, aid, assistance; **me ndihmën e** with the help of

ndíhmës, ~e mb. 1. auxiliary, back-up; 2. ancillary
ndihm/ój kal., ~óva, ~úar. help, aid, assist
ndijím, ~i m. sh. ~e, ~et. sensation
ndij/ój kal., ~óva, ~úar. sense
ndikím, ~i m. sh. ~e, ~et. influence; **ndikimi i mjedisit** the influence of the environment; **përdor ndikimin** use one's influence with smb; **nën ndikimin e** under the influence of
ndik/ój jokal., ~óva, ~úar. influence
ndikúes, ~e mb. influential
ndje/j kal., ~va, ~rë. forgive, excuse, pardon
ndjek kal., **ndóqa**, **ndjékur.** 1. follow, go after, go behind; 2. chase, pursue, run after; 3. trace, track, run down; 4. attend
ndjékës, ~i m. sh ~, ~it. follower, pursuer
ndjékj/e, ~a f. 1. pursuit; 2. attendance; 3. prosecution
ndjénjë ~a f. sh. ~a, ~at. feeling, sense; sensitivity
ndjésh/ëm (i), ~me (e) mb. 1. sensitive; 2. sensible; 3. compassionate, sentimental
ndjeshmërí, ~a f. sensibility, sensitivity
ndodh jokal., ~a, ~ur. happen, take place, occur, befall, come to pass
ndódhem vetv. 1. be, be present, happen to be; 2. be located, be situated
ndodhí, ~a f. sh. ~, ~të. happening, occurence, incident
ndokúnd ndajf. somewhere
ndokúsh pakuf. somebody; anybody, anyone
ndonjë pakuf. any, some
ndonjëhérë ndajf. 1. sometimes; 2. never; **s'e kam parë ndonjëherë** I have never seen him
ndóshta pj. perhaps, maybe
ndótur (i,e) mb. dirty, soiled, unclean, polluted
ndreq kal., ~a,~ur. 1. repair, fix; 2. mend; 3. correct
ndriç/ój kal.,~óva, ~úar. 1. lighten; 2. **fig.** illuminate; 3. **fig.** elucidate
ndrit (ndris) jokal., ~a, ~ur. shine, glitter, sparkle
ndrítsh/ëm (i), ~me (e) mb. bright, radiant, luminous, dazzling
ndrítur (i,e) mb. bright
ndrydh kal., ~a, ~ur. 1. sprain; 2. suppress, repress, subdue
ndrydhur (i,e) mb. reticent, reserved, restrained; suppressed
ndryshe ndajf. otherwise, differently; or else
ndrysh/ëm (i), ~me (e) mb. 1. different, dissimilar, distinct; 2. various
ndryshím, ~i m. sh. ~e, ~et. change, alteration, modification
ndryshk, ~u m. rust
ndryshk kal., ~a, ~ur. rust
ndryshkur (i,e) mb. 1. rusty; 2. **fig.** rusty
ndrysh/ój kal., ~óva, ~úar. change, alter, modify; **ndryshoj drejtim** change direction
ndryshúesh/ëm (i), ~me(e) mb. changeable, alterable, modifiable
ndyrë (i,e) mb. 1. dirty, filthy; 2. **fig.** filthy, dirty; 3. foul; 4. despicable
ne vetor. we
negatív, ~e mb. negative

negativísht ndajf. negatively
nen, ~i m. sh. ~e, ~et. article, item
neón, ~i m. neon; llambë me neon a neon lamp
nepërk/ë, ~a f. sh. ~a, ~at. viper
nerv, ~i m. sh. ~a, ~at. 1. anat. nerve; 2. nerves
nervór, ~e mb. anat. nervous; sistemi nervor the nervous
system
nervóz, ~e mb. nervous, tense
nésër ndajf. tomorrow
néto mb. net; pesha neto net weight; fitimi neto net profit
neutrál, ~e mb. neutral
nevój/ë, ~ f. sh. ~a, ~at. need, want, necessity
nevojít/em vetv., ~a(u), ~ur. be necessary, be needed
nevójsh/ëm (i), ~me (e) mb. necessary, needful; ështe e
nevojshme it is necessary
nevojtár, ~e mb. needy
nevrikósur (i,e) mb. hot-tempered, hotheaded, hot
në parafj. in; on; at; into
nën parafj. under; beneath
nënçm/ój kal., ~óva, ~úar. undervalue, underestimate,
underrate
nëndhésh/ëm (i) me (e) mb. underground, subterranean
nën/ë, ~a f. sh. ~a, ~at. mother
nënkuptím, ~i m. ~e, ~et. implication
nënkupt/ój kal., ~óva, ~úar. imply
nënndárj/e, ~a f. sh. ~e, ~et. subdivision
nënshkr/úaj kal., ~óva, ~úar. sign
nënshtr/ój kal., ~óva, ~úar. subdue, subjugate
nëntë num. them. nine
nëntëmbëdhjétë num. them. nineteen
nëntëqind num. them. nine hundred
nëntokësór, ~e mb. subterranean, underground; tunel
nëntokesor a subterranean tunnel
nënviz/ój kal., ~óva, ~úar. 1. underline; 2. fig. underline,
emphasize
nënvlerës/ój kal., ~óva, ~úar. underestimate, undervalue
nëpër parafj. through
nëpërmés ndajf. through, across
nëpërmjét parafj. by means of, through
nëpúnës, ~i m. sh. ~, ~it. employee
nësé lidh. if, whether
nga ndajf. from; of; out of
ngacm/ój kal., ~óva, ~úar. 1. excite; 2. incite, provoke; 3.
tease
ngacmúes, ~e mb. annoying; provoking; exciting
ngadálë ndajf. slowly
ngadalës/ój kal., ~óva, ~úar. slow up (down)
ngadálsh/ëm (i), ~me (e) mb. slow
ngado ndajf. wherever; everywhere
ngadhënjimtár, ~e mb. triumphant
ngadonjëhérë ndajf. sometimes
ngarkés/ë, ~a f. sh. ~a, ~at. cargo, load
ngark/ój kal., ~óva, ~úar. 1. load; 2. charge, entrust; 3.
delegate, assign, authorize
nga/s kal., ~va, ~rë. 1. touch; 2. tease; 3. ride; drive;
steer; pilot

ngáthët (i,e) mb. clumsy, awkward, inept; **njeri i ngathët** an awkward man

ngathtësí, ~a f. clumsiness, awkwardness

nge, ~ja f. leisure; **më nge** at leisure

ngec jokal., ~a, ~ur. stick; **autobuzi ngeci në baltë** the bus stuck in the mud

ngel jokal., ~a, ~ur. 1. stick; 2. remain; 3. fail

ngr/e kal., ~íta, ~ítur. 1. raise, elevate, lift (up); 2. hoist; 3. hold up; 4. raise, build, erect (a monument, statue etc); 5. put forward; 6. put up, erect; 7 rouse; 8 create, found

ngreh kal., ~a, ~ur. 1. wind up; 2. pitch (a tent); 3. set

ngrënsh/ëm (i), ~me (e) mb. edible, eatable

ngríc/ë, ~a f. sh. ~a, ~at. frost

ngríhem vetv. 1. get up; 2. stand up; 3. rise, ascend, soar; 4. rise, rebel

ngri/j jokal., ~va, ~rë. 1. freeze; freeze up; 2. be, feel cold; chill; 3. **fig.** freeze; **ngriu nga tmerri** froze with terror; 4. freeze (wages, prices etc)

ngrírë (i,e) mb. frozen

ngrírj/e, ~a f. freeze; freezing; **pika e ngrirjes** the freezing point **ngrítj/e, ~a f.** 1. rise; 2. increase; boost; 3. uplift; 4. hoist; 5. lift, lifting

ngroh kal., ~a, ~ur. 1. warm; heat; 2. warm up

ngróhës, ~i m. sh ~, ~it. heater

ngróhj/e, ~a f. 1. heating; 2. warm

ngróhtë (i,e) mb. 1. warm; 2. **fig.** warm

ngrohtësísht ndaj. warmly

ngul kal., ~a, ~ur. 1. drive (in); 2. thrust; 3. stare at, fix one's eyes on; 4. inculcate, fix in mind

ngulm, ~i m. persistence, perseverance

ngulm/ój jokal., ~óva, ~úar. insist, persist, persevere

ngur/ój kal., ~óva, ~úar. hesitate

ngúrtë (i,e) mb. 1. solid; 2. **fig.** rigid, stiff

ngushëllím, ~i m. sh ~e, ~et. 1. condolence; 2. comfort, consolation

ngushëll/ój kal., ~óva, ~úar. condole; console

ngúshtë (i,e) mb. 1. narrow; 2. tight, strait; 3. intimate, close; **mik i ngushtë** a close friend

ngusht/ój kal., ~óva, ~úar. narrow

ngut, ~i m. haste, hurry; **me ngut** in haste

ngja/j jokal., ~va, ~rë. resemble, look like

ngjál/ë, ~ f. sh. ~a, ~at. zool. heel

ngjall kal., ~a, ~ur. 1. bring to life; 2. evoke

ngjárj/e, ~a f. sh. ~e, ~et. event, circumstance, happening, incident

ngjásh/ëm (i), ~me (e) mb. similar

ngjashmërí, ~a f. sh. ~, ~të. similarity, resemblance, likeness

ngjírur (i,e) mb. hoarse

ngjit (ngjis) kal., ~a, ~ur. 1. stick, glue, paste; 2. transmit (a malady, a disease); 3. **fig.** impute, attribute

ngjítem vetv. go up, climb up, ascend

ngjítës, ~i m. sh. ~, ~it. glue, gum, paste

ngjyr/ë, ~a f. sh. ~a, ~at. color, hue
ngjyrím, ~i m. sh. ~e, ~et. coloring
ngjyr/ój kal., ~óva, ~úar. dye, color, tint
ngjyrúes, ~i m. sh. ~, ~it. color, pigment
níkel, ~i m. kim. nickel
nikotín/ë f. nicotine
nip, ~i m. sh. ~a, ~at dhe ~ër, ~ërit. nephew
nis kal., ~a, ~ur. 1. begin, start, commence; 2. send; **nis një letër** send a letter
nísem vetv. 1. set off, start out; **nisem për udhëtim** set off on a journey; 2. leave, depart
nísj/e, ~a f. 1. departure; 2. start; 3. beginning
nísm/ë, ~ f. sh. ~a, ~at. initiative
nishán, ~i m. sh. ~e, ~et. 1. aim; **marr nishan** take aim; 2. birthmark, mole
nivél, ~i m. sh. ~e, ~et. 1. level; **mbi nivelin e detit** above the sea level; 2. fig. level
nivel/ój kal., ~óva, ~úar. 1. level; 2. fig. level
nocíon, ~i m. sh. ~e, ~et. notion
nófk/ë, ~a f. sh. ~a, ~at. nickname
normál, ~e mb. 1. normal; **gjendje normale** normal state; 2. sane, sound
normalísht ndajf. normally
normaliz/ój kal., ~óva, ~úar. normalize
normatív, ~e mb. normative; **gramatikë normative** a normative grammar
nórm/ë, ~ f. sh. ~a, ~at. 1. norm, rule, standard; 2. norm; **plotësoj normën** fulfill the norm; **normë prodhimi** production norm
not, ~i m. swim
notár, ~i m. sh. ~ë, ~ët. swimmer
notér, ~i m. sh ~ë, ~ët. notary, notary public
nót/ë, ~a f. sh. ~a, ~at. 1. muz. note; 2. fig. note; **nota optimiste** optimistic note
nót/ë f. sh. ~a, ~at. mark
nót/ë, ~a f. sh. ~a, ~at. dipl. note
notím, ~i m. swimming
not/ój jokal., ~óva, ~úar. swim
novél/ë, ~a f. sh. ~a, ~at. novel
novelíst, ~i m. sh. ~ë, ~ët. novelist
nuhát (nuhás) kal., ~a, ~ur. smell, sniff, scent
numerík, ~e mb. numerical
núm/ër, ~ri m. sh. ~ra, ~rat. number
numër/ój kal., ~óva, ~úar. count, number, enumerate
nús/e, ~ja f. sh. ~e, ~et. bride
nxeh kal., ~a, ~ur. 1. heat; 2. fig. anger, enrage, infuriate
nxëhtë (i,e) mb. 1. hot; 2. intense; fiery; passionate; 3. ardent
nxehtësí, ~a f. heat
nxë kal., nxúri, nxënë. hold, contain, accommodate, have a capacity for
nxënës, ~i m. sh. ~, ~it. 1. pupil; 2. disciple
nxi/j kal., ~va, ~rë. 1. blacken; 2. tan
nxit (nxis) kal., ~a, ~ur. 1. promote, stimulate, encourage; 2. incite, instigate; 3. arouse, rouse, inspire

nxítës, ~**i m. sh.** ~, ~**it.** 1. instigator, incitor, incentor; 2. incentive; 3. stimulus

nxitím, ~**i m.** haste, hurry

nxit/ój kal., ~**óva,** ~**úar.** hurry, hasten, hustle

nxitúar (i,e) mb. hasty, rushing, hurried

nxjerr kal., nxórra, nxjérrë. 1. take out; 2. pull out; 3. put out; 4. unearth; 5. bring out, let out

nyj/ë, ~**a f. sh.** ~**a,** ~**at.** 1. knot; 2. **gjuh.** article

NJ

njerëzím, ~i m. mankind, humanity
njerëzísht ndajf. humanely
njerëzór, ~ e mb. 1. human; 2. humane
njerí, ~u m. sh. **njérëz**, **njérëzit**. man, human being; **origjina e njeriut** the origin of man
njerk, ~u m. kryes. nj. sh. ~ë, ~ët. stepfather
njérk/ë, ~a f. kryes. nj. sh. ~a, ~at. stepmother
një num. them. 1. one; 2. a, an
njëánsh/ëm (i), ~me (e) mb. 1. one-sided; 2. partial, biased
njëhérazi ndajf. 1. at the same time; 2. simultaneously
njëhérë ndajf. once, at one time; **na ishte njëherë ...** once upon a time ...
njëhérësh ndajf. at the same time, simultaneously
njëhérsh/ëm (i), ~me (e) mb. simultaneous, instantaneous
njëjës mb. gjuh. singular
njëjtë (i,e) mb. identical, similar, same; **pikëpamje të njejta** identical views
njëkohësísht ndajf. simultaneously, instantaneously
njëkóhsh/ëm (i), ~me (e) mb. instantaneous; simultaneous
njëllójtë (i,e) mb. identical, similar, same
njëmbëdhjétë num. them. eleven
njëmbëdhjetëmétërsh, ~i m. sh. ~a, ~at sport. penalty
njëpasnjësh/ëm (i), ~me (e) mb. successive, consecutive
njëqínd num. them. one hundred; a hundred
njëqindvjetór, ~i m. centenary
njëri, **njëra** pakuf. one; **njeri nga të dy** one of the two
njësí, ~a f. sh. ~, ~të. 1. unit; **njësi monetare** a monetary unit; 2. usht. unit
njësím, ~i m. unification
njës/ój kal., ~óva, ~úar. unify; **njësoj çmimet** unify the prices
njësój ndajf. alike
njësúar (i,e) mb. unified
njëtrájtsh/ëm (i), ~me (e) mb. uniform
njëzét num. them. twenty
njëzëri ndajf. unanimously, with one voice
njíhem vetv. 1. be known; 2. get known; 3. acquaint oneself with; **njihem me hollësitë** acquaint oneself with the details
njoftím, ~i m. sh. ~e, ~et. notice, information, notification
njoft/ój kal., ~óva, ~úar. inform, notify
njoh kal., ~a, ~ur. know; recognize
njóhj/e, ~a f. 1. acquaintance; 2. acknowledgment, recognition; 3. cognition
njóhur (i,e) mb. 1. known, familiar; 2. celebrated, noted
njohurí, ~a f. kryes. sh. ~, ~të. knowledge; **kam njohuri të kufizuara për kompjuterat** I have a limited knowledge of computers
njóll/ë, ~a f. sh. ~a, ~at. 1. stain, blot, spot; **njolla boje** ink stains; 2. fig. stain, moral blemish; **pa asnjë njollë në karakterin e tij** without a stain on his character
njollós kal., ~a, ~ur. 1. blot, spot, stain, speck; 2. fig. sully; **njollos emrin** sully one's name
njollósur (i,e) mb soiled, sullied, smirched, spotted, stained

njom kal.., ~a, ~ur. wet, soak, moisten; njom rrobat në ujë
soak the clothes in water
njómë (i,e) mb. 1. wet, damp, moistened; 2. fresh, tender
njómur (i,e) mb. moist, soaked

O

obelísk, ~u m. sh. ~ë, ~ët. obelisk
objékt, ~i m. sh. ~e, ~et. object
objektív, ~i m. sh. ~a, ~at. objective, object, purpose
objektív, ~i m. sh. ~a, ~at. object glass, object lens
objektív, ~e mb. 1. **filoz.** objective; **realiteti objektiv** the objective reality; 2. **fig.** objective; **vlerësim objektiv** an objective assessment
objektivísht ndajf. objectively; **gjykoj objektivisht** judge objectively
objektivitét, ~i m. objectivity
obórr, ~i m. sh. ~e, ~et. yard, courtyard
ofensív/ë, ~a f. sh. ~a, ~at. offensive; **kaloj në ofensivë** go on (take) the offensive
ofért/ë, ~a f. sh. ~a, ~at. 1. offer; **bëj një ofertë** make an offer; 2. **ek.** supply; **kërkesa dhe oferta** supply and demand
oficér, ~i m. sh. ~ë, ~ët. officer
ogúr, ~i m. sh ~e, ~et. omen
oksíd, ~i m. sh. ~e, ~et. oxide
oksigjén, ~i m. kim. oxygen
okulíst, ~i m. sh. ~ë, ~ët. oculist, eye doctor
olimpíad/ë, ~a f. sh. ~a, ~at. olympiad
olimpík, ~e mb. olympic; **Lojrat Olimpike** Olympic Games
ombréll/ë, ~a f. sh. ~a, ~at. 1. umbrella; 2. **fig.** umbrella
omëlét/ë, ~a f. sh. ~a, ~at. omelette, omelet
operació́n, ~i m. sh. ~e, ~et. 1. operation; **operacion shpëtimi** rescue operation; 2. **mjek.** operation; 3. **usht.** operation; 4. **fin.** operation
operatív, ~e mb. operational; operative
óper/ë, ~a f. sh. ~a, ~at. **muz.** opera
oper/ój kal., ~óva, ~úar. **mjek.** operate on smb (for smth)
opinión, ~i m. sh. ~e, ~et. opinion; **opinioni public (individual)** public (individual) opinion
opiúm, ~i m. opium
oponént, ~i m. sh. ~ë, ~ët. opponent
oportuníst, ~i m. sh. ~ë, ~ët. opportunist
oportuníst, ~e mb. opportunist
opozitár, ~ e mb. oppositional, opposing, oppositive
opozít/ë, ~a f. sh. ~a, ~at. opposition; **jam në opozitë me** be in opposition to
optík, ~e mb. optic; optical; **nervi optik** the optic nerve
optimál, ~e mb. optimum, optimal
optimíst, ~i m. sh. ~ë, ~ët. optimist
optimíst, ~e mb. optimistic
optimíz/ëm, ~mi m. optimism; **shikoj të ardhmen me optimizëm** look forward to the future with optimism
oqeán, ~iu m. h. ~e, ~et. ocean; **Oqeani Atlantik (Paqësor)** the Atlantic (Pacific) Ocean
oqeaník, ~e mb. oceanic
orár, ~i m. sh. ~ë, ~ët. 1. timetable; **orari i shkollës** school timetable; **orari i trenave** train timetable; 2. hours; **jashtë orarit** after hours
orbít/ë, ~a f. **astr.** orbit

oréks, ~i m. appetite; oreksi vjen me të ngrënë appetite
comes with eating
orendí, ~a f. kryes. sh. ~, ~të. furniture
ór/ë, ~a f. sh. ~ë, ~ët. 1. hour; një gjysmë (një çerek) ore
half (a quarter of) an hour; në çdo orë at any hour; 2. time;
3. watch; 4. period
orgán, ~i m. sh. ~e, ~et. organ
organík, ~e mb. organic; sëmundje organike organic diseases
organizát/ë, ~a f. sh. ~a, ~at. organization
organizatív, ~e mb. organizational
organíz/ëm, ~mi m. sh. ~ma, ~mat. organism
organizóhem vetv. get organized
organiz/ój kal., ~óva, ~úar. organize
organizúar (i,e) mb. organized; krimi i organizuar organized
crime
orientál, ~e mb. oriental
orient/ój kal., ~óva, ~úar. orientate, orient
origjinál, ~i m. sh. ~e, ~et. original; the original
origjinál, ~e mb. original
origjinalitét, ~i . libr. originality
origjín/ë, ~a f. sh. ~a, ~at. origin
oríz, ~i m. bot. rice
orkést/ër, ~ra f. sh. ~ra, ~rat. muz. orchestra
ortodóks, ~e mb. orthodox
orvát/em vetv., ~a (u), ~ur. try, attempt, endeavor
orvátje, ~a f. sh. ~e, ~et. attempt, endeavor
óse lidh. or
oxhá/k, ~ku m. sh. ~kë, ~kët dhe ~qe, ~qet. chimney
ozón, ~i m. kim. ozone; shtresë ozoni ozone layer

paáftë (i,e) mb. 1. unable, incapable; 2. unfit; **i paaftë për shërbimin ushtarak** unfit for military service
paaftësí, ~a f. sh. ~, ~të. incapability, inability; **paaftësi fizike** physical incapability
paánë (i,e) mb. infinite, boundless, endless, limitless
paanësí, ~a f. 1. impartiality; 2. infinity
paangazhúar (i,e) mb. libr. 1. disengaged; 2. non-aligned; **shtetet e pangazhuara** non-aligned nations
paánsh/ëm (i), ~me (e) mb. impartial, unbiased; **gjykatës i paanshëm** impartial judge
paarsyeshëm (i), ~me (e) mb. unreasonable, irrational, illogical; unsensible
paarrítsh/ëm (i), ~me (e) mb. 1. unattainable; 2. inaccesible, unapproachable, unreachable
pabanúar (i,e) mb. uninhabited, unpopulated, untenanted
pabarabártë (i,e) mb. unequal; **kushte të pabarabarta** unequal conditions
pabarazí, ~a f. sh. ~, ~të. inequality; disparity; **pabarazi shoqërore (politike)** social (political) inequality
pabésë (i,e) mb. faithless, disloyal, unfaithful; **mik i pabesë** a faithless friend
pabesí, ~a f. sh. ~, ~të. infidelity, faithlessness, disloyalty, unfaithfulness
pabesísht ndajf. unfaithfully
pabesúesh/ëm (i), ~me (e) mb. unbelievable, incredible
pabër/ë (i,e) mb. unripe
pabíndur (i,e) mb. 1. disobedient; **fëmijë i pabindur** a disobedient child; 2. unconvinced; 3. restive
pacaktúar (i,e) mb. indefinite, indeterminate; **kohë e pacaktuar** indefinite time
pacënúesh/ëm (i), ~me (e) mb. inviolable, inalienable, untouchable; invulnarable
pacifíst, ~i m. sh. ~ë, ~ët. pacifist
pacípë (i,e) mb. insolent, impertinent, impudent, shameless
paçmúesh/ëm (i)~me (e) mb. invaluable, precious, valuable, priceless, inestimably valuable
padáshur ndajf. unintentionally, involuntarily
padénjë (i,e) mb. unworthy; **sjellje e padenjë** unworthy conduct
padepërtúesh/ëm (i), ~me (e) mb. 1. impenetrable; 2. impermeable, tight, proof
padëgjúar (i,e) mb. unheard of
padëgjúesh/ëm (i), ~me (e) mb. 1. disobedient; **fëmijë i padëgjueshëm** a disobedient child; 2. inaudible
padëmtúar (i,e) mb. intact, undamaged, unimpaired
padëshirúesh/ëm (i), ~me (e) mb. 1. undesirable; 2. unwelcome, unwanted
padí, ~a f. sh. ~, ~të drejt. indictment, accusation, charge; **ngre padi kundër** bring in an indictment against smb
padíj/e, ~a f. ignorance; **nga padija** from (through) ignorance
padiskutúesh/ëm (i), ~me (e) mb. indisputable, unquestionable, incontestable

padít (padis) kal., ~a, ~ur. sue, bring suit, bring to court, indict

padobíshëm (i), ~me (e) mb. useless, ineffectual, ineffective

padréjtë (i,e) mb. unjust, unrightful; **vendim i padrejtë** unjust decision

padrejtësí, ~a f. sh. ~, ~të. injustice

padrejtësisht ndajf. unjustly

padúksh/ëm (i), ~me (e) mb. invisible; **njeri i padukshëm** invisible man

padurím, ~i m. impatience

padúruesh/ëm (i), ~me (e) mb. 1. impatient; 2. unbearable, intolerable

padyshímtë (i,e) mb. undoubted

padhunúesh/ëm (i), ~me (e) mb. inviolable

paedukátë (i,e) mb. uncivil, ill-mannered

paedukúar (i,e) mb. ill-bred, ill-educated

paépur (i,e) mb. 1. inflexible, unbendable, unyeilding; 2. undaunted, indomitable

pafájsh/ëm (i), ~me (e) mb. 1. innocent, guiltless; 2. naive, ingenuous

pafálsh/ëm (i) ~me (e) mb. unforgivable, inexcusable; **sjellje e pafalshme** inexcusable conduct

pafát (i,e) mb. unlucky, unfortunate, ill-starred

pafjálë (i,e) mb. wordless, speechless, mum

pafrýtsh/ëm (i), ~me (e) mb. fruitless, futile; **diskutim i pafrytshëm** a fruitless discussion

paftúar (i,e) mb. uninvited, unwelcome

pafúnd (i,e) mb. endless, infinite, limitless

pafuqísh/ëm (i), ~me (e) mb. 1. powerless, strengthless; 2. weak, feeble, infirm

pagabúesh/ëm (i), ~me (e) mb. infallible, unerring

pagán, ~i m. sh. ~ë, ~ët. pagan

pagán, ~e mb. pagan

pagés/ë, ~a f. sh. ~a, ~at. payment

pág/ë, ~a f. sh. ~a, ~at. wage, pay, salary; **rritje e pagës** a pay increase

pagëz/ój kal., ~óva, ~úar. baptize

pag/úaj kal., ~óva, ~úar. 1. pay; **paguaj taksa** pay taxes; 2. **fig.** pay for smth

pagúar (i,e) mb. paid

pagúes, ~i m. sh. ~, ~it. payer

pagúesh/ëm (i), ~me (e) mb. payable

pagjúmë (i,e) mb. sleepless, wakeful; **kaloj një natë të pagjumë** pass a sleepless night

paharrúesh/ëm (i), ~me (e) mb. unforgettable; **çast i paharrueshëm** an unforgettable moment

pahíjsh/ëm (i), ~e (e) mb. indecent, unbecoming

pajétë (i,e) mb. 1. lifeless, inanimate, non-living; 2. **fig.** languid, listless

páj/ë, ~a f. sh. ~a, ~at. dowry

pajím, ~i m. sh. ~e, ~et. 1. outfit, kit, set; 2. provision, providing, furnishing

pajís kal., ~a,~ur. supply, provide, equip, furnish
pajtím, ~i m. sh. ~e, ~et. 1. reconciliation; 2. accordance, conformity; **në pajtim me** in accordance with; 3. subscription
pajtimtár, ~i m. sh. ~ë, ~ët. subscriber
pajt/ój kal., ~óva, ~úar. reconcile, conciliate
pajt/ój kal., ~óva, ~úar. 1. employ; 2. subscribe
pajtúes, ~e mb. conciliatory
pak pakuf. few, a few, little, a little
pak ndajf. little
pakalúesh/ëm (i), ~me (e) mb. impassable; **rrugë të pakalueshme** impassable roads
pakapërcyesh/ëm (i), ~me (e) mb. insurmountable; **pengesa të pakapërcyeshme** insurmountable obstacles
pakét/ë, ~a f. sh. ~a, ~at. packet; **paketë cigaresh** a packet of cigarettes
paketím, ~i m. packing
paket/ój kal., ~óva,~úar. pack up, package
pakënaqësí,~a f. sh. ~, ~të. dissatisfaction; **shpreh pakënaqësinë** voice one's dissatisfaction
pakënáqsh/ëm (i), ~me (e) mb. unsatisfactory; **zgjidhje e pakënaqshme** unsatisfactory solution
pakënáqur (i,e) mb. discontented, dissatisfied; **klient i pakënaqur** a dissatisfied customer
pakëndsh/ëm (i), ~me (e) mb. unpleasant, disagreeable, distasteful, undesirable
pakës/ój kal., ~óva, ~úar. 1. lessen, cut back, decrease, reduce; 2. diminish, abate, ease
pakíc/ë, ~a f. sh. ~a, ~at. 1. minority, smaller part (number); 2. minority; **pakicat etnike** ethnic minorities
páko, ~ja f. sh. ~, ~t. parcel, package
pakrahasúesh/ëm (i), ~me (e) incomparable
pakryer (i,e) mb. unaccomplished, undone, uncompleted, unfinished
paksá ndajf. a little, a little bit
pakt, ~i m. sh. ~e, ~et. pact; **pakt mossulmimi** a non-agression pact
páktë (i,e) mb. little, small
páktën (të) ndajf. at least; **të paktën dy muaj** at least two months
pakufísh/ëm (i), ~me (e) mb. boundless, unlimited
pakfizúar (i,e) mb. unlimited, limitless
pakujdesí, ~a f. sh. ~, ~të. incaution, carelessness
pakujdéssh/ëm (i), ~me (e) mb. careless, negligent; **shofer i pakujdeshëm** a careless driver
pakuptímsh/ëm (i), ~me (e) mb. 1. senseless; **veprim i pakuptimshëm** a senseless action; 2. meaningless
pakuptúesh/ëm (i), ~me (e) mb. incomprehensible, unintelligible
pakursyer (i,e) mb. unsparing
pálc/ë, ~a f. marrow
palejúesh/ëm (i), ~me (e) mb. unallowable, inadmissible
palexúesh/ëm (i), ~me (e) mb. illegible
palezétsh/ëm (i), ~me (e) mb. unpleasant, disagreeable
pál/ë, ~a f. sh. ~a, ~at. pleat, fold
pál/ë, ~a f. sh. ~ë, ~ët. 1. pair; 2. pack; **një palë letra** a pack of cards; 3. **drejt.** party

palëkúndur (i,e) mb. unshakable; **besim i palëkundur** an unshakable faith
palëvízsh/ëm (i), ~me (e) mb. immovable, immobile, motionless
palígjsh/ëm (i), ~me (e) mb. 1. unlawful, illegal; 2. illegitimate; **fëmijë i paligjshëm** an illegitimate child
pálm/ë, ~a f. sh. ~a, ~at. bot. palm, palm-tree
palódhsh/ëm (i), ~me (e) mb. tireless, untiring
palódhur (i,e) mb. untiring, tireless
palogjíksh/ëm (i), ~me (e) mb. illogical, irrational
palós kal., ~a, ~ur. fold up; **palos letrën në dysh** fold the letter in two
palúajtsh/ëm (i), ~me (e) mb. 1. motionless, immobile; 2. immovable; **pasuri e paluajtshme** real estate, immovables, immovable property
pallát, ~i m. sh. ~e, ~et. 1. palace; 2. flat
pallogarítsh/ëm (i), ~me (e) mb. incalculable, inestimable; **dëm i pallogaritshëm** incalculable harm
pállto, ~ja f. sh. ~, ~t. overcoat
pall/úa, ~ói m. sh. ~ónj, ~ónjtë. zool. peacock
pamartúar (i,e) mb. unmarried
pamásë (i,e) mb. 1. immense, enormous; 2. boundless
pambarím (i,e) mb. endless
pambarúar (i,e) mb. 1. unfinished, unaccomplished; 2. endless
pambúk, ~u m. bot. cotton
pambúktë (i,e) mb. cotton; **veshje të pambukta** cotton clothes
paménd (i,e) mb. irrational, illogical, unsound
pamendúar (i,e) mb. unthinking, thoughtless
pamëshírsh/ëm (i), ~me (e) mb. merciless, pitiless, cruel, heartless
pamflét, ~i m. sh. ~e, ~et. pamphlet
pamjaftúesh/ëm (i), ~me (e) mb. inadequate, insufficient, deficient; **njohuri të pamjaftueshme** deficient knowledge
pámj/e, ~a f. sh. ~e, ~et. 1. view, sight; **pamje e mrekullueshme** a fine view; **në pamje të parë** at first sight; 2. look, aspect, appearance; 3. eyesight
pamorálsh/ëm (i), ~me (e) mb. immoral
pampóshtsh/ëm (i), ~me (e) mb. indomitable, unconquerable
pampóshtur (i,e) mb. invincible, dauntless
pamúndur (i,e) mb. 1. impossible; 2. unbearable; 3. unwell, under the weather
panaír, ~i m. sh. ~e, ~et. fair
pandálsh/ëm (i), ~me (e) mb. unceasing, incessant
pandárë (i,e) mb. inseparable; undividable; **shokë të pandarë** inseparable friends
pandásh/ëm (i), ~me (e) mb. indivisible, inseparable, undivided
pandérsh/ëm (i), ~me (e) mb. dishonest, unfair
pandërgjégjsh/ëm (i), ~me (e) mb. 1. unconscious; 2. unconscientious
pandërprérë (i) mb. ceaseless, incessant, unceasing, uninterrupted, continual
pandjésh/ëm (i), ~me (e) mb. insensible
pandréqsh/ëm (i), ~me (e) mb. 1. irreparable; 2. incorrigible
panevójsh/ëm (i), ~me (e) mb. unnecessary, needless; **shpenzim i panevojshëm** unnecessary expense

pangjárë (i,e) mb. unprecedented
pangjyrë (i,e) mb. colorless
paník, ~u m. panic
pankárt/ë f. sh. ~a, ~at. placard
panorám/ë, ~a f. sh. ~a, ~at. 1. panorama, view; 2. overview, survey
pantallóna, ~t f. vet. sh. trousers, pants
pantér/ë, ~a f. sh. ~a, ~at. zool. panther
panúmërt (i,e) mb. numberless, numerous, countless, innumerable
panxhár, ~i m. sh. ~ë, ~ët. bot. beet, beetroot
panjóhur (i,e) mb. unknown, unfamiliar
papagá/ll, ~lli m. sh. ~j, ~jt. zool. parrot
papajtúesh/ëm (i), ~me (e) mb. irreconciable, incompatible; **pikëpamje të papajtueshme** irreconciable views
paparashikúar (i,e) mb. unforeseen, unexpected, unanticipated; **vështirësi të paparashikuara** unforeseen difficulties
papárë (i,e) mb. unobserved, unnoticed, unnoted, unseen
papástër (i,e) mb. unclean; impure; mineral **(ajër) i papastër** impure metal (air)
papëlqyesh/ëm (i), ~me (e) mb. unpleasant, disagreeable; indecent; **shije e papëlqyeshme** unpleasant smell
papërcaktúar (i,e) mb. indefinite, undetermined
papërdórur (i,e) mb. unused; **pullë e papërdorur** an unused stamp
papërfíllsh/ëm (i), ~me (e) mb. inconsiderable
papërfundúar (i,e) mb. unfinished, uncompleted
papërgjégjsh/ëm (i), ~me (e) mb. drejt. irresponsible, unaccountable, unanswerable
papërkúlur (i,e) mb. 1. unbent, unbending; 2. invincible; undefeated
papërlígjsh/ëm (i), ~me (e) mb. unjustifiable; **vendim i papërligjshëm** an unjustifiable decision
papërpunúar (i,e) mb. raw, crude, unprocessed, unrefined
papërqendrúar (i,e) mb. disconcerted
papërshkúesh/ëm (i), ~me (e) mb. impermeable, impenetrable
papërshtátsh/ëm (i), ~me (e) mb. unfit, improper, unsuitable; unbecoming
papërtúesh/ëm (i), ~me (e) mb. untiring, indefatigable
papërvójë (i,e) mb. inexperienced, green
papërzíer (i,e) mb. unmixed, unmingled
papíjsh/ëm (i), ~me (e) mb. undrinkable; **ujë i papijshëm** undrinkable water
papjékur (i,e) mb. 1. unbaked; 2. unripe; 3. **fig.** immature; green, inexperienced
papjekurí, ~a f. immaturity
paplótë (i,e) mb. incomplete
paplotësúar (i,e) mb. unaccomplished; unfulfilled
papranúesh/ëm (i), ~me (e) mb. unacceptable; **kushte të papranueshme** unacceptable terms
papréksh/ëm (i), ~me (e) mb. inviolable, untouchable
paprítmas ndajf. unexpectedly, suddenly, all of a sudden
papritur (i,e) mb. sudden; **vdekje e papritur** sudden death
papritur ndajf. unexpectedly, all of a sudden
papúnë (i,e) mb. unemployed
papunësí, ~a f. unemployment; **ul papunësinë** reduce unemployment

paqártë (i,e) mb. unclear, indistinct, inexplicit, vague;
tingull i paqartë an indistinct sound
paqartësí, ~a f. unclarity, unclearness, vagueness
páq/e, ~ja f. peace; **paqe e qëndrueshme** lasting peace;
traktat i paqes peace treaty
paqedáshës, ~e mb. peace-loving; **popuj paqedashës** peace-
loving people
paqénë (i,e) mb. non-existing, inexistant
paqenësíshëm (i), ~me (e) mb. non-essential
paqétë (i) mb. unquiet, uneasy, restless **paqendrúesh/ëm (i),**
~me (e) mb. unstable; inconstant, changeable
paqëndrueshmërí, ~a f. instability
paqësísht ndajf. peacefully
paqësór, ~e mb. peaceful; **demostratë paqësore** a peaceful
demonstration
pará, ~ja f. sh. ~, ~të. money; **para të holla** small money;
para xhepi pocket money
pára ndajf. ahead; forward
pára parafj. before; in front of
paraárdhës, ~i m. sh. ~, ~it. forerunner, predecessor
paracakt/ój kal., ~óva, ~úar. predetermine
paracaktúar (i,e) mb. predetermined
parád/ë, ~a f. sh. ~a, ~at. parade; **paradë ushtarake** military
parade; **paradë mode** a fashion parade
paradóks, ~i m. sh. ~e, ~et. paradox
paradréke ndajf. before noon
parafabrikát, ~i m. sh. ~e, ~et. prefab; prefabrication
parafjál/ë, ~a f. sh. ~ë, ~ët. gjuh. preposition
paragráf, ~i m. sh. ~ë, ~ët. paragraph
paragjykím, ~i m. sh ~e, ~et. prejudice
paragjyk/ój kal., ~óva, ~úar. prejudice
parájs/ë, ~a f. sh. ~a, ~at. paradise
parakalím, ~i m. sh. ~e, ~et. march, parade
parakal/ój jokal., ~óva, ~úar. march
parakóhsh/ëm (i), ~me (e) mb. premature; **përfundim i**
parakohshëm a premature conclusion
paralajmërím, ~i m. sh. ~e, ~et. warning, admonition
paralajmër/ój kal., ~óva, ~úar. warn, admonish
paralajmërúes, ~e mb. premonitory, warning; **sinjal**
paralajmërues a warning signal
paralél, ~i m. sh. ~ë, ~ët. gjeogr. parallel
paralízë, ~a f. sh. ~a, ~at. paralysis (edhe **fig.**)
paraliz/ój kal., ~óva, ~úar. paralyze
paralizúar (i,e) mb. paralyzed
paramendím, ~i m. sh. ~e, ~et. premeditation
paramend/ój kal., ~óva, ~úar. premeditate
parandalím, ~i m. sh. ~e, ~et. prevention
parandal/ój kal., ~óva, ~úar. prevent
parandalúes, ~e mb. preventive; **masa parandaluese** preventive
measures
para/ndíej kal., ~ndjéva, ~ndíer. forebode
parandjénjë, ~a f. sh. ~a, ~at. presentment, foreboding

parapëlq/éj kal., ~éva, ~yer. prefer
parapëlqím, ~i m. sh. ~e, ~et. preference
parapërgatitór, ~e mb. preparatory; **masa përgatitore**
preparatory measures
paraprák, ~e mb. preliminary; **bisedime paraprake** preliminary
negotiations
paraprí/j kal., ~va, ~rë. precede, lead
paraqít kal., ~a, ~ur. 1. proffer; 2. present; 3. show,
exhibit, put on display, put on a show, make a production; 4.
introduce
paraqítem vetv. present oneself; **paraqitem në gjyq** present
oneself in court
paraqítsh/ëm (i), ~me (e) mb. presentable
pararój/ë, ~a f. sh. ~a, ~at. vanguard; **në pararojë të** in the
vanguard of
parashikím, ~i m. sh. ~e, ~et. prediction; forecast;
prognostication
parashik/ój kal., ~óva, ~úar. predict, forsee, foretell,
prophecy; forecast
parashikúes, ~e mb. predictive, foretelling, forecasting
parashikúesh/ëm (i), ~me (e) mb. predictable, foreseeable;
kohë e parashikueshme predictable weather
parashtés/ë, ~a f. sh. ~a, ~at. prefix
parashtr/ój kal., ~óva, ~úar. put forward, put forth, present
parashútë, ~a f. sh. ~a, ~at. parachute
parathëni/e, ~a f. sh. ~e, ~et. introduction, preface,
foreword
parazít, ~i m. sh. ~ë, ~ët. 1. biol. parasite; 2. fig.
parasite
pardjé ndajf. the day before yesterday
pár/e, ~ja f. kryes. sh. ~, ~et. bised. money
parehátsh/ëm (i), ~me (e) mb. bised. uncomfortable,
discomforting
párë, ~t (të) as. sight; vision, eyesight
párë (i,e) mb. first
párë ndajf. first; ago
parëndësísh/ëm (i), ~me (e) mb. unimportant, insignificant
parësór, ~e mb. primary, prime
parfúm, ~i m. sh. ~e, ~et. perfume
parfum/ój kal., ~óva, ~úar. perfume
pári (së) ndajf. firstly
parím, ~i m. sh. ~e, ~et. principle; **në parim** in principle
parimór, ~e mb. principled; **njeri parimor** a principled man;
kundërshtim parimor a principled objection
par/k, ~ku m. sh. ~qe, ~qet. 1. park; 2. car park
parlamént, ~i m. sh. ~e, ~et. parliament
parlamentár, ~e mb. parliamentary; **debatet parlamentare**
parliamentary debates
parmák, ~u m. sh. ~ë, ~ët. banisters, railing
partí, ~a f. sh. ~, ~të. party
partizán, ~i m. sh. ~ë, ~ët. partisan
partnér, ~i m. sh. ~ë, ~ët. partner
parúll/ë, ~a f. sh. ~a, ~at. 1. password; 2. slogan
parrégullt (i,e) mb. 1. untidy, disorderly; 2. irregular;
puls i parregullt an irregular pulse; 3. **gjuh.** irregular;
folje e parregullt irregular verb

parrezíksh/ëm (i), ~me (e) mb. harmless
pas ndajf. behind
pas, ~i m. sh. ~a, ~at sport. pass
pas parafj. 1. behind; 2. after; 3. with, through
pas ndajf. behind
pasagjér, ~i m. sh. ~ë, ~ët. passenger; **treni i pasagjerëve** a passenger train
pasáktë (i,e) mb. inexact, incorrect, imprecise, inaccurate; **përgjigje e pasaktë** an incorrect answer
pasaktësí, ~a f. inaccuracy, inexactness
pasaník, ~u m. sh. ~ë, ~ët. rich (wealthy) man; **pasanikët** the rich
pasapórt/ë, ~a f. sh. ~a, ~at. passport, identity card
pasárdhës, ~i m. sh. ~, ~it. descendant, offspring
pasárdhës, ~e mb. successive; succeeding
pasdít/e, ~ja f. sh. ~e, ~et. afternoon; **çdo pasdite** every afternoon
pasí lidh. after; since, as
pasigurí, ~a f. insecurity, uncertainty
pasígurt (i,e) mb. insecure, uncertain; **punë e pasigurt** an insecure job
pasinqértë (i,e) mb. insincere
pasión, ~i m. sh. ~e, ~et. passion; **kam pasion për** have a passion for something
pasív, ~e mb. passive, inactive
pasjéllshëm (i), ~me (e) mb. ill-behaved, impolite, ill-mannered, uncivil
pas/ój kal., ~óva, ~úar. follow, ensue
pas/ój kal., ~óva, ~úar. sport. pass; **pasoj topin** pass the ball
pasój/ë, ~a f. sh. ~a, ~at. consequence; **mbaj pasojat** bear the consequences
pasósur (i,e) mb. endless
pasqyr/ë, ~a f. sh. ~a, ~at. 1. mirror, looking-glass; 2. table; **pasqyra e lëndës** table of contents
pasqyr/ój kal., ~óva, ~úar. 1. reflect, mirror; 2. **fig.** mirror
pastáj ndajf. then; after; later; afterwards
pástër (i,e) mb. 1. clean, pure; **ajër i pastër** pure air; 2. chaste; virtuous; 3. tidy; 4. fair; **kopje e pastë** fair copy; 5. clear
pástër ndajf. cleanly, purely
pastrím, ~i m. sh ~e, ~et. cleaning
pastr/ój kal., ~óva, ~úar. 1. clean, cleanse; 2. scavenge, sweep; 3. purge; 4. clear; 5. purify
pasthírrm/ë, ~a f. sh. ~a, ~at. gjuh. interjection
pasúes, ~i m. sh. ~, ~it. follower, adherent
pásur (i,e) mb. 1. rich, wealthy, affluent, moneyed; 2. **fig.** rich
pasurí, ~a f. sh. ~, ~të. riches, affluence, wealth, fortune
pasur/ój kal., ~óva, ~úar. enrich, make rich
pashémbullt (i,e) mb. unprecedented, unparalleled
pásh/ëm (i), ~me (e) mb. good-looking, handsome
pashërúesh/ëm (i), ~me (e) mb. incurable; **sëmundje e pashërueshme** an incurable disease
páshk/ë, ~a f. sh. ~ë, ~ët. Easter
pashmángsh/ëm (i), ~me (e) mb. inevitable, unavoidable

pashpállur (i,e) mb. undeclared; **luftë e pashpallur** undeclared war
pashpírt (i,e) mb. 1. lifeless, dead; 2. inanimate; 3. cruel, heartless
pashpjegúesh/ëm (i), ~me (e) mb. inexplicable; **fenomen i pashpjegueshëm** an inexplicable phenomenon
pashprésë (i,e) mb. desperate, hopeless; **gjendje e pashpresë** a desperate situation
pashúar (i,e) mb. inextinguishable, unquenched; **dëshirë e pashuar** inextinguishable desire
patát/e, ~ja f. sh. ~e, ~et. bot. potato; **patate të skuqura** fried potatoes
patént/ë, ~a f. sh. ~a, ~at. 1. patent; 2. license
patéríc/ë, ~a f. sh. ~a, ~at. clutch
pát/ë, ~a f. sh. ~a, ~at. zool. goose
patëllxhán, ~i m. sh. ~ë, ~ët. bot. egg-plant
patinázh, ~i m. skating
patín/ë, ~a f. kryes. sh. ~a, ~at. skate, ice-skate
patjétër ndajf. necessarily; without fail, surely, without doubt
patjetërsúesh/ëm (i), ~me (e) mb. drejt. inalienable
patológ, ~u m. sh. ~ë, ~ët. pathologist
patregúesh/ëm (i), ~me (e) mb. inexpressible; **gëzim i patregueshëm** inexpressible joy
patriót, ~i m. sh. ~ë, ~ët. patriot
patriotík, ~e mb. patriotic; **këngë patriotike** patriotic songs
patúndsh/ëm (i), ~me (e) mb. 1. immovable, immobile; 2. **drejt.** immovable; **pasuri e patundshme** immovable property; 3. irrevocable, irreversible, irrefutable
patúndur (i,e) mb. firm, staunch, unshakeable; **besim i patundur** an unshakeable faith
patúrp (i,e) mb. shameless, insolent, impudent, unabashed, brazen; **sjellje e paturp** a shameless conduct
pathemëltë (i,e) mb. groundless, baseless, unfounded
pathyesh/ëm (i), ~me (e) mb. 1. unbreakable; 2. **fig.** invincible
páuz/ë, ~a f. sh. ~a, ~at. pause
pavarësí, ~a f. independence
pavarësísht ndajf. independent of
pavárur (i,e) mb. independent
pavdéksh/ëm (i), ~me (e) mb. immortal; **lavdi e pavdekshme** immortal glory
pavénd (i,e) mb. inopportune, untimely
pavendósur (i,e) mb. irresolute, uncertain, undecided, unresolved, vacillating
pavetëdíjsh/ëm (i), ~me (e) mb. unconscious
pavëméndsh/ëm (i), ~me (e) mb. inattentive, heedless, unmindful; **nxënës i pavëmendshëm** an inattentive pupil
pavërtétë (i,e) mb. untrue
pavléfsh/ëm (i), ~me (e) mb. worthless, useless; **kontratë e pavlefshme** a worthless contract
pavolítsh/ëm (i), ~me (e) mb. 1. inconvenient, inopportune; **kohë e pavolitshme** an inconvenient time; 2. unhandy
pavullnétsh/ëm (i), ~me (e) mb. involuntary; **lëvizje e pavullnetshme** involuntary movement

pazakónsh/ëm (i), **~me (e) mb.** uncommon, unusual
pazár, **~i m. sh. ~e**, **~et.** 1. market; 2. bargaining
pazëvendësúesh/ëm (i), **~me (e) mb.** irreplaceable
pazgjídhsh/ëm (i), **~me (e) mb.** 1. insoluble; **problem i pazgjithshëm** an insoluble problem; 2. inextricable
pazotësí, **~a f.** inability, disability, incapacity
pazóti (i), **pazónja (e) mb.** unable, incapable, inept
pazhvillúar (i,e) mb. undeveloped
pe, **~ri m. sh. ~nj**, **~njtë.** thread
pecét/ë, **~a f. sh. ~a**, **~at.** napkin
pedagóg, **~i m. sh. ~ë**, **~ët.** pedagogue
peizázh, **~i m. sh. ~e**, **~et.** landscape
pell/g, **~gu m. sh. ~gje**, **~gjet.** 1. pool; 2. gjeogr. basin
pém/ë, **~a f. sh. ~ë**, **~ët.** tree
penál, **~e mb. drejt.** penal; **kodi penal** penal code
pendés/ë, **~a f. sh. ~a**, **~at.** repentance, penitence
pénd/ë, **~a f. sh. ~ë**, **~ët.** feather; quill
pendím, **~i m.** repentance, contrition, remorse
pend/óhem vetv., **~óva (u)**, **~úar.** repent, regret, rue
pendúar (i,e) mb. repentant
pén/ë, **~a f. sh. ~a**, **~at.** pen
pen/g, **~gu m. sh. ~gje**, **~gjet.** 1. pawn; 2. hostage
pengés/ë, **~a f. sh. ~a**, **~at.** 1. obstacle, barrier, hindrance; 2. hurdle
peng/ój kal., **~óva**, **~úar.** hinder, frustrate, hamper, impede, obstruct
penicilín/ë, **~a f. sh. ~a**, **~at. farm.** penicillin
pensión, **~i m. sh. ~e**, **~et.** pension; **pension pleqërie** an old-age pension
pensioníst, **~i m. sh. ~ë**, **~ët.** pensioner
perandór, **~i m. sh. ~ë**, **~ët.** emperor
pérd/e, **~ja f. sh. ~e**, **~et.** curtain
perëndésh/ë, **~a f. sh. ~a**, **~at.** goddess
perëndí, **~a f. sh. ~**, **~të.** god
perëndím, **~i m.** 1. west; 2. sunset
perëndimór, **~e mb.** western
perím/e, **~ja f. sh. ~e**, **~et.** vegetables
periodík, **~e mb.** periodic(al)
periodikísht ndajf. periodically
periúdh/ë, **~a f. sh. ~a**, **~at.** period
persón, **~i m. sh. ~a**, **~at.** person
personál, **~e mb.** personal; **për përdorim** personal for personal use
personalísht ndajf. personally
personázh, **~i m. sh. ~e**, **~et.** character
personél, **~i m. përmb.** staff
perspektív/ë, **~a f. sh. ~a**, **~at.** perspective
pésë num. them. five
pesëdhjétë num. them. fifty
pesëmbëdhjétë num. them. fifteen
pesëqínd num. them. five hundred
pesimíst, **~i m. sh. ~ë**, **~ët.** pessimist
pesimíz/ëm, **~mi m.** pessimism

pésh/ë, ~a f. sh. ~a, ~at. 1. weight; **pesha neto (bruto)** net (gross) weight; 2. **fig.** weight
pesh/k, ~ku m. sh. ~q, ~qit. **zool.** fish; **zë peshk** catch fish; **peshk i tymosur** smoked fish
peshkaqén, ~i m. sh. ~ë, ~ët. **zool.** shark
peshkatár, ~i m. sh. ~ë, ~ët. fisherman
peshk/ój kal., ~óva, ~úar. fish
pesh/ój kal., ~óva, ~úar. 1. weigh; 2. **fig.** weigh, consider; 3. carry weight
peshór/e, ~ja f. sh. ~e, ~et. weighing-machine, scales, weigher, balance
peshqír, ~i m. sh. ~ë, ~ët. towel; **fshij duart me peshqir** dry one's hands with a towel
pétull, ~a f. sh. ~a, ~at. pancake
pëlcás jokal., plása (pëlcíta), plásur (pëlcítur). 1. blow up; 2. explode
pëlhúr/ë, ~a f. sh. ~a, ~at. fabric, cloth
pëlq/éj kal., éva, ~yer. 1. like, be fond of; **më pëlqen muzika** I am fond of music; 2. approve, assent
pëlqím, ~i m. assent, consent, approval
pëlqyesh/ëm (i), ~me (e) mb. agreeable
pëllëmb/ë, ~a f. sh. ~ë, ~ët. 1. palm; 2. slap
pëllúmb, ~i m. sh. ~a, ~at **zool.** dove, pigeon
për parafj. for
përáfërt (i,e) mb. approximate; **shifra të përafërta** approximate figures
përbállë ndajf. opposite
përbállë parafj. in front of, in face of, before
përball/ój kal., ~óva, ~úar. 1. stand up to, withstand, brave, face; 2. afford
përbáshkët (i,e) mb. common; joint; **nuk kam asgjë të përbashkët me** have nothing in common with
përbë/j kal., ~ra, ~rë. make up, constitute, compose, comprise, form
përbërë (i,e) mb. 1. composite, compound; 2. **gjuh.** compound
përbërës, ~e mb. component, constituent, composing, integral; **pjesët përbërëse** the integral parts
përbërj/e, ~a f. sh. ~e, ~et. composition, make-up; **përbërja e tokës** the composition of the soil
përbrí ndajf. next door; next door to
përbúz kal., ~a, ~ur. disdain, scorn, despise, look down upon, hold in contempt
përbúzës, ~e mb. contemptible, scornful, disdainful
përcaktím, ~i m. sh. ~e, ~et. determination, definition
përcakt/ój kal., ~óva, ~úar. define, delimit; determine
përcaktúar (i,e) mb. determined, settled, fixed, set
përcaktúes, ~e mb. determining, decisive; crucial
përc/jéll kal., ~ólla, ~jéllë. 1. see somebody off, show somebody out; 2. swallow; 3. **muz.** accompany
përçá/j kal., ~va, ~rë. divide
përçmím, ~i m. contempt, derision, disdain, scorn
përçm/ój kal., ~óva, ~úar. disdain, scorn, despise, contempt

përçmúes, ~e mb. scornful, contemptuous, derisive; **shikim përçmues** a scornful look

përdítë ndajf. every day

përdítsh/ëm (i), ~me (e) mb. daily; **gazetë e përditshme** a daily newspaper; **nevojat e përditshme** daily necessities (wants)

përdór kal., ~a, ~ur. use, employ, utilize, make use of; **përdor forcën** use force

përdorím, ~i m. sh. ~e, ~et. use, employment, usage, utilization, application; **është në përdorim** be in use; **del nga përdorimi** fall out of use

përdórsh/ëm (i), ~me (e) mb. usable

përdorúes, ~i m. sh. ~, ~it. user; **përdoruesit e drogës** drug-users

përdórur (i,e) mb. used

përdhun/ój kal., ~óva, ~úar. 1. violate; 2. rape

përém/ër, ~ri m. sh. ~ra, ~rat gjuh. pronoun

përfaqës/ój kal., ~óva, ~úar. represent; **përfaqëson vullnetin e popullit** represents the will of the people

përfaqësúes, ~i m. sh. ~, ~it. representative

përfaqësúes, ~e mb. representative; **organ përfaqësues** representative organ

përfitím, ~i m. sh. ~e, ~et. profit, benefit, advantage; **siguroj përfitim** ensure a profit

përfit/ój kal. dhe jokal., ~óva, ~úar. 1. profit, benefit; 2. exploit, take advantage of

për/flás kal., ~fóla, ~fólur. slander, calumniate, libel

përforc/ój kal., ~óva, ~úar. reinforce, bolster

përfshí/j kal., ~va, ~rë. 1. include; 2. embrace

përfundím, ~i m. sh. ~e, ~et. conclusion; **arrij në përfundim se** come to the conclusion that; **si përfundim** in conclusion

përfundimísht ndajf. definitively

përfundimtár, ~e mb. final, definitive, conclusive, ultimate

përfund/ój kal., ~óva, ~úar. 1. end, complete, finish, accomplish; 2. conclude, close

përfundúar (i,e) mb. finished, ended, completed, accomplished

përfytyrím, ~i m. sh. ~e, ~et. fancy, imagination

përfytyr/ój kal., ~óva, ~úar. imagine, envisage, image, picture

përgatít (përgatís) kal., ~a, ~ur. 1. prepare, make ready; 2. train; 3. prepare somebody for something; 4. hatch up

përgatítj/e, ~a f. sh. ~e, ~et. preparation

përgatitór, ~e mb. preparatory

përgëz/ój kal., ~óva, ~úar. congratulate, felicitate

përgjáksh/ëm (i), ~me (e) mb. bloody; **luftë e përgjakshme** a bloody war

përgjégjës, ~e mb. 1. accountable, responsible, answerable; 2. correspondent

përgjegjësí, ~a f. sh. ~, ~të. 1. responsibility; **mbaj përgjegjësi të plotë** bear full responsibility; 2. commitment, duty

përgjégjsh/ëm (i), ~me (e) mb. responsible

përgjígj/e, ~ja f. sh. ~e, ~et. answer, reply, response; **në përgjigje të** in reply to

përgjígj/em vetv., ~a (u), ~ur. 1. answer, reply; 2. respond; 3. correspond; 4. be responsible

përgjithësísht ndajf. generally
përgjithmónë ndajf. for ever, for good; **një herë e**
përgjithmonë once and for all
përgjíthsh/ëm (i), ~me (e) mb. general; **parim i përgjithshëm**
a general principle; **grevë e përgjithshme** a general strike
përgjúmur (i,e) mb. sleepy, drowsy
përháp kal., ~a, ~ur. 1. spread, scatter; 2. disseminate,
distribute, propogate; 3. communicate, pass on
përhérë ndajf. always
përhérsh/ëm (i), ~me (e) mb. 1. permanent; **përfaqësues i**
përhershëm permanent representative; 2. everlasting;
gjelbërim i përhershëm everlasting green
përjáshta ndajf. out
përjashtím, ~i m. sh. ~e, ~et. 1. exception; 2. exemption,
expulsion; **me përjashtim të** with the exception of, except
for; **pa përjashtim** without exception
përjasht/ój kal., ~óva, ~úar. 1. expel; 2. discharge,
dismiss; 3. exempt; 4. exclude
përjávsh/ëm (i), ~me (e) mb. weekly; **revistë e përjavshme** a
weekly magazine
përjetës/ój kal., ~óva, úar. perpetuate
përjet/ój kal., ~óva, ~úar. experience
përjétsh/ëm (i), ~me (e) mb. eternal, perpetual
përk/ás kal., ~íta, ~ítur. 1. touch lightly; 2. belong,
pertain; **për sa i përket** concerning, as regards, as far as
... is concerned
përkátës, ~e mb. respective
përkëdhél kal., ~a, ~ur. caress, fondle
përkëdhélës, ~e mb. caressing
përkohësísht ndajf. temporarily
përkóhsh/ëm (i), ~me (e) mb. 1. temporary, transient,
transitory; 2. passing; 3. interim, provisional; **qeveri e**
përkohshme a provisional government
përkráh kal., ~a, ~ur. support, back up
përkráhj/e, ~a f. sh. ~e, ~et. support
përkryer (i,e) mb. perfect
përkth/éj kal., ~éva, ~yer. translate
përkthím, ~i m. sh. ~e, ~et. translation
përkthyes, ~i m. sh. ~, ~it. translator
përkufizím, ~i m. sh. ~e, ~et. definition; **përkufizimi i**
fjalës word definition
përkufiz/ój kal., ~óva, ~úar. define
përkujdés/em vetv. ~a (u), ~ur. take care of, look after;
përkujdesem për fëmijët take care of the children
përkujt/ój kal., ~óva, ~úar. commemorate
përkúl kal., ~a, ~ur. 1. bend; 2. bow, stoop
përkúlsh/ëm (i), ~me (e) mb. flexible, pliant, pliable
përkúndrazi pj. on the contrary
përkundréjt ndajf. opposite, face to face, vis-a-vis
përlígj kal., ~a, ~ur. justify
përllogarít (përllogarís) kal., ~a, ~ur. calculate, compute,
reckon
përmbáj kal., ~ta, ~tur. 1. restrain, curb, repress; 2.
bridle, check; 3. contain, comprise

përmbájtj/e, **~a** f. 1. content; 2. restraint
përmbl/édh kal., **~ódha**, **~édhur**. 1. summarize, compress, condense; 2. collect, gather
përmbúsh kal., **~a**, **~ur**. fulfill, realize, accomplish, effect; **përmbush kushtet** fulfill the conditions
përmbys kal., **~a**, **~ur**. 1. upset, overturn; 2. overthrow, topple; 3. capsize; 4. turn upside-down
përmbys ndajf. upside-down; **kthej shtëpinë përmbys** turn the house upside-down
përmbysj/e, **~a** f. sh. **~e**, **~et**. 1. overturn, overthrow; 2. capsize
përmbyt (**përmbys**) kal., **~a**, **~ur**. flood, inundate
përménd kal., **~a**, **~ur**. mention
përméndem vetv. come round (to), regain consciousness
përméndsh ndajf. by heart; **mësoj përmendsh** learn by heart
përméndur (i,e) mb. noted, renowned
përmés ndajf. through, across
përmirësím, **~i** m. sh. **~e**, **~et**. improvement, amelioration
përmirës/ój kal., **~óva**, **~úar**. 1. improve, ameliorate, better; 2. improve on (upon) something
përmúajsh/ëm (i), **~me** (e) mb. monthly
përndryshe ndajf. otherwise
përpára ndajf. before; in front; ahead; first; onward; forward
përpárës/e,~ ja f. sh. **~e**, **~et**. apron, pinafore
përparím, **~i** m. sh. **~e**, **~et**. progress, advancement
përparimtár, **~e** mb. progressive
përpar/ój kal., **~óva**, **~úar**. advance, progress
përparúar (i,e) mb. advanced; **metoda (ide) të përparuara** advanced methods (ideas)
përpíktë (i,e) mb. 1. accurate, precise, exact, punctual; **llogaritje e përpiktë** accurate calculation; 2. meticulous
përpil/ój kal., **~óva**, **~úar**. 1. compile; 2. write something out; **përpiloj një raport** write out a report
përpíqem vetv. 1. try, attempt, endeavor, venture; 2. hit upon; run against
përpjékj/e, **~a** f. sh. **~e**, **~et**. 1. endeavor, effort, exertion; **bëj të gjitha përpjekjet** make every effort, exert every effort; 2. encounter, clash
përpjesëtím, **~i** m. sh. **~e**, **~et**. proportion; **në përpjestim me** in proportion to
përplás kal., **~a**, **~ur**. 1. bang, slam; 2. stamp
përpun/ój kal., **~óva**, **~úar**. 1. process, treat; 2. elaborate, work out
përpunúar (i,e) mb. 1. processed; 2. elaborate
përqafím, **~i** m. sh. **~e**, **~et**. hug, embrace
përqaf/ój kal., **~óva**, **~úar**. embrace, hug, cuddle
përqendrím, **~i** m. sh **~e**, **~et**. concentration; **përqendrimi i trupave** concentration of troops; **mungesë përqendrimimi** lack of concentration
pëqendr/ój kal., **~óva**, **~úar**. concentrate; **përqendroj vëmendjen** focus (concentrate) one's attention
përqendrúar (i,e) mb. concentrated; **zjarr i përqendruar** concentrated fire
përqíndj/e, **~a** f. sh. **~e**, **~et**. percentage

përréth ndajf. round
përréth prep. round
përsé ndajf. why; **Përse nuk erdhe?** Why didn't you come?; **s'ka përse** not at all
përserí ndajf. again, anew, over again
përserít (përsërís) kal., ~a, ~úr. 1. repeat; reiterate; 2. review
përsërítj/e, ~a f. sh. ~e, ~et. 1. repetition, reiteration; 2. review
përsós kal., ~a, ~ur. perfect
përsósur (i,e) mb. perfect
përsosurí, ~a f. perfection
përshëndét (përshëndés) kal., ~a, ~ur. greet, hail, salute
përshëndétj/e, ~a f. sh. ~e, ~et. greeting; **dërgoj përshëndetje** send greetings
përshk/ój kal., ~óva, ~úar. 1. penetrate; 2. traverse; cover
përshkrím, ~i m. sh. ~e, ~et. description, depiction; **jap një përshkrim të** give a description of
përshkr/úaj kal., ~óva, ~úar. describe, depict; **përshkruaj bukurinë e detit** describe the beauty of the sea
përshkrúes, ~e mb. descriptive
përshpejt/ój kal., ~óva, ~úar. accelerate
përshtát kal., ~a, ~ur. adapt; **përshtat për radio** adapt for radio
përshtátem vetv. adapt oneself; **i përshtatem klimës së re** adapt oneself to the new climate
përshtátsh/ëm (i), ~me (e) mb. suitable, appropriate; **moment i përshtatshëm** suitable moment
përshtypj/e, ~a f. sh. ~e, ~et. impression; **bëj (lë) përshtypje të mira (të këqia)** make good (bad) impression on
përtác, ~e mb. lazy, idle, indolent; **njeri përtac** a lazy man
përtací, ~a f. laziness, idleness, indolence
përtyp kal., ~a, ~ur. 1. chew, masticate; 2. **fig.** chew; **përtyp fjalët** chew the words
përúl kal., ~a, ~ur. humble, humiliate
përur/ój kal., ~óva, ~úar. inaugurate
përvéç parafj. besides, except, save
përvéçëm (i), ~me (e) mb. gjuh. proper; **emër i përveçëm** proper noun
përvésh kal., ~a, ~ur. turn up, roll up
përvetës/ój kal., ~óva, ~úar. 1. appropriate, peculate, embezzle; 2. assimilate
përvël/ój kal., ~óva, ~úar. scald
përvëlúes, ~e mb. scalding
përvítsh/ëm (i), ~me (e) mb. annual, yearly
përvjetór, ~i m. sh. ~ë, ~ët. anniversary
përvój/ë, ~a f. experience; **këmbej përvojë** exchange experience
pëzemërsí, ~a f. cordiality
përzemërsísht ndajf. cordially
përzémërt (i,e) mb. cordial, heart-felt, hearty; **pritje e përzemërt** cordial (hearty) welcome
për/zë kal., ~zúra, ~zënë. turn out, drive out, expel, dismiss
për/zgjedh kal., ~zgjódha, ~zgjédhur. choose, select
përz/íej kal., ~jéva, ~íer. 1. mingle, blend, mix; 2. stir, agitate; 3. shuffle (the cards)
përzíer (i,e) mb. 1. mixed; 2. implicated

përráll/ë, ~a f. sh. ~a, ~at. 1. tale, story, yarn; **përralla populore** folk-tales; 2. tale, lie, fib, cock-and-bull story
përr/úa, ~ói m. sh. ~énj ~énjtë. stream, brook, torrent
pës/ój kal., dhe jokal. ~óva, ~úar. undergo, suffer; **pësoj humbje** suffer losses
pëshpërít kal., dhe jokal. ~a, ~ur. 1. whisper; 2. rumor
pështy/j kal., ~va, ~rë. spit; **e pështyu në fytyrë** he spat him in the face
pështym/ë, ~a f. sh. ~a, ~at. spit, saliva, spittle
pi kal., ~va, ~rë. 1. drink; **pi ujë** drink water; 2. take alcohol; 3. smoke; 4. absorb
pianíst, ~i m. sh. ~ë, ~ët. pianist
piáno, ~ja f. sh. ~, ~t. muz. piano; **luaj në piano** play on the piano
pick/ój kal., ~óva, ~úar. pinch, nip; sting
píj/e, ~a f. sh. ~e, ~et. drink, beverage; **pije freskuese** refreshing drink
píjsh/ëm (i), ~me (e) mb. drinkable, potable; **ujë i pijshëm** drinkable water
pík/ë, ~a f. sh. ~a, ~at. 1. drop; **pika shiu** rain-drops; **pika djerse** drops of sweat; 2. spot, speck, speckle, blot, stain; 3. **gjuh.** full stop; **dy pika (:)** colon; 4. **sport.** point; 5. **gjeogr.** point; **pikat e orientimit** the cardinal points; 6. point; **pika e valimit (e ngrirjes, e shkrirjes)** boiling (freezing, melting) point; 7 instant, moment; 8 point, issue, question, subject
pikëçudítj/e, ~a f. sh. ~e, ~et. gjuh. exclamation mark
pikënísj/e, ~a f. sh. ~e, ~et. starting point
pikëpámje, ~a f. sh. ~e, ~et. view, point of view; **nga kjo pikëpamje** from this point of view
pikëprésj/e, ~a f. sh. ~e, ~et. gjuh. semi-colon
pikëpyetj/e, ~a f. sh. ~e, ~et. question mark
pikërísht pj. just, right, precisely
pikësëparí ndajf. first of all
pikësím, i m. gjuh. punctuation; **shenjat e pikësimit** punctuation marks
pikësyním, ~i m. gjuh. goal, aim, end, target, objective; **pikësynimi në jetë** one's goal in life
pikësyn/ój kal., ~óva, ~úar. aim at
pikník, ~u m. sh. ~e, ~et. picnic
piktór, ~i m. sh. ~ë, ~ët. painter
piktúr/ë, ~a f. sh. ~a, ~at. painting, picture
piktur/ój kal., dhe jokal. ~óva, ~úar. paint, portray
pilót, ~i m. sh. ~ë, ~ët. pilot, aviator
pilúl/ë, ~a f. sh. ~a, ~at. pill
pínc/ë, ~a f. sh. ~a, ~at. pincers
pipér, ~i m. bot. pepper; **piper i kuq (i zi)** red (black) pepper; **mulli piperi** pepper-mill
pipérk/ë, ~a f. sh. ~a, ~at. bot. pepper
píp/ë, ~a f. sh. ~a, ~at. pipe
piramíd/ë, ~a f. sh. ~a, ~at. 1. gjeom. pyramid; 2. hist. pyramid
pirát, ~i m. sh. ~ë, ~ët. pirate
pirún, ~i m. sh. ~ë, ~ët. fork

pistolét/ë, ~**a** f. sh. ~**a**, ~**at**. pistol
pistón, ~**i** m. sh. ~**a**, ~**at**. tek. piston
písh/ë, ~**a** f. sh. ~**a**, ~**at**. bot. pine, pine-tree; **halë pishe**
pine- needle; **boçe e pishës** pine-cone
pishín/ë, ~**a** f. sh. ~**a**, ~**at**. swimming-pool
pizháme, ~**t** f. vet. sh. pyjamas, pajamas
pját/ë, ~**a** f. sh. ~**a**, ~**at**. 1. plate; saucer; 2. dish, plate;
një pjatë supë a plate of soup
pjek kal., **póqa**, ~**pjékur**. 1. bake; 2. roast; 3. broil, grill,
toast; 4. ripen
pjek kal., **póqa**, **pjékur**. meet, encounter
pjékur (i,e) mb. 1. roasted, baked, grilled; 2. ripe; **rrush i**
pjekur ripe grapes; 3. mature
pjekurí, ~**a** f. maturity; **mosha e pjekurisë** age of maturity;
arrij pjekurinë reach maturity
pjell kal. dhe jokal., **pólla**, **pjéllë**. procreate; calve;
kitten; foal; lamb; cub
pjellór, ~**e mb.** fertile; **tokë pjellore** fertile soil; **fusha**
pjellore fertile plains
pjép/ër, ~**ri** m. sh. ~**ra**, ~**rat**. bot. melon
pjérrët (i,e) mb. slanting, sloping
pjésë, ~**a** f. sh. ~**ë**, ~**ët**. 1. part; 2. piece (component) of a
machine (structure); **pjesë këmbimi** spare parts; 3. share; 4.
muz. part, piece; **marr pjesë** take part in smth
pjesmárrës, ~**e mb.** participating; **vendet pjesëmarrëse**
participating countries
pjesëmárrj/e, ~**a** f. participation; **pjesëmarrje aktive** active
participation
pjesërísht ndajf. partly, in part; **jam pjesërisht përgjegjës**
për be partly responsible for
pjesëtár, ~**i** m. sh. ~**ë**, ~**ët**. 1. member; 2. associate,
partner; 3. associate member
pjesëtím, ~**i** m. sh. ~**e**, ~**et**. 1. apportion, allotment; 2. **mat.**
division
pjesët/ój kal., ~**óva**, ~**úar**. 1. divide out (up), share, allot;
2. **mat.** divide
pjéssh/ëm (i), ~**me (e) mb.** partial; **ndryshime të pjesshme**
partial modifications (changes)
pjéshk/ë, ~**a** f. sh. ~**ë**, ~**ët**. bot. peach; peach-tree
pláçk/ë, ~**a** f. sh. ~**a**, ~**at**. 1. belongings; 2. cloth, stuff;
3. plunder; 4. clothes
plaçkít kal., ~**a**, ~**ur**. plunder, pillage, ravage, loot,
ransack
plág/ë, ~**a** f. sh. ~**ë**, ~**ët**. 1. wound; **plagë plumbi** bullet
wound; 2. **fig.** wound
plagós kal., ~**a**, ~**ur**. 1. wound; 2. **fig.** hurt, wound; **plagos**
zemrën e wound the heart of
plagósem vetv. get wounded
plagósur (i,e) mb. wounded; **ushtarët e plagosur** the wounded
soldiers
plak, ~**u** m. sh. **pleq**, **pléqtë**. old man
plak, ~**ë mb.** old, aged, elderly
plákur (i,e) mb. aged

plan, ~i m. sh. ~e, ~et. 1. plan; 2. scheme; 3. plane, level
planét, ~i m. sh. ~ë, ~ët. **astr.** planet
planifikím. sh. ~e, ~et. planning; **planifikimi familjar** family planning
planifik/ój kal., ~óva, ~úar. plan
planifikúar (i,e) mb. planned; **ekonomi e planifikuar** a planned economy
plantación, ~i m. sh. ~e, ~et. plantation
plasarítj/e, ~a f. sh. ~e, ~et. 1. crack; 2. chap
plasarítur (i,e) mb. 1. cracked; 2. chapped; **lëkurë e plasaritur** chapped skin
plásj/e, ~a f. sh. ~e, ~et. 1. explosion; 2. outburst
plastík, ~e mb. 1. plastic; **këpucë plastike** plastic shoes; 2. **art.** plastic; **arti plastik** the plastic art; 3. **mjek.** plastic; **kirurgjia plastike** plastic surgery
platín, ~i m. **kim.** platinum
plazh, ~i m. sh. ~e, ~et. beach
pleh, ~u m. sh. ~ra, ~rat. manure; fertilizer
plep, ~i m. sh. ~a, ~at. **bot.** poplar
pleqërí, ~a f. old age
plevíc/ë, ~a f. sh. ~a, ~at. barn
plis, ~i m. sh. ~a, ~at. 1. sod; 2. clod
plógët (i,e) mb. languid, sluggard; **njeri i plogët** a sluggard man
plot ndajf. full
plótë (i,e) mb. full, complete, entire; **hënë e plotë** full moon
plotësím, ~i m. sh. ~e, ~et. 1. fulfilment; 2. accomplishment; 3. realization
plotësísht ndajf. completely, entirely, fully, wholly
plotës/ój kal., ~óva, ~úar. 1. meet, satisfy, fulfil, gratify; 2. fill out; 3. fill; complete
plotësúes, ~e mb. additional, supplementary
plotfuqísh/ëm (i), ~me (e) mb. all-powerful, omnipotent, almighty
plúhur, ~i m. sh. ~a, ~at. 1. dust; **re pluhuri** cloud of dust; 2. powder; **sheqer pluhur** powdered milk
plumb, ~i m. sh. ~a, ~at. 1. **kim.** lead; **laps plumbi** lead pencil; **helmim nga plumbi** lead-poisoning; **i rëndë plumb sa** heavy as lead; 2. bullet
pluralíz/ëm, ~mi m. pluralism
plus, ~i m. sh. ~e, ~et. **mat.** plus (+)
pllák/ë, ~a f. sh. ~a, ~at. slab; **pllakë guri** a stone slab
po lidh. but
poém/ë, ~a f. sh. ~a, ~at. poem; **shkruaj poema** write poems
poét, ~i m. sh. ~ë, ~ët. poet
poetík, ~e mb. poetic, poetical
poezí, ~a f. sh. ~, ~të. poetry; **poezi epike (lirike)** epic (lyric) poetry
poh/ój kal., ~óva, ~úar. 1. affirm; 2. avow, confess; **pohoj gabimin** confess one's fault
pol, ~i m. sh. ~e, ~et. 1. **gjeogr.** pole; **Poli i Veriut (i Jugut)** the North (South) Pole; 2. **fiz.** pole; **pol pozitiv (negativ)** the positive (negative) pole
polár, ~e mb. polar; **ylli polar** pole-star

políc, ~i m. sh. ~ë, ~ët. policeman, constable, cop
policí, ~a f. police; **qën policie** police dog; **rajon policie** police station
policór, ~e mb. keq. police; detective; **film policor** detective film
politekník, ~e mb. polytechnic; **arsim politeknik** polytechnic education
politík, ~e mb. political; **sistem politik** a political system
politikán, ~i m. sh. ~ë, ~ët. politician
politík/ë, ~a f. sh. ~a, ~at. 1. politics; **politikë partiake** party politics; 2. policy; **politika e jashtme** foreign policy
pomád/ë, ~a f. sh. ~a, ~at. pomade, ointment
pómp/ë, ~a f. sh. ~a, ~at. pump
pópu/ll, ~lli m. sh. ~j, ~jt. people; the Albanian people **populli shqiptar**
popullariz/ój kal., ~óva, ~úar. popularize; **popullarizoj përdorimin e kompjuterëve** popularize the use of computers
popullát/ë, ~a f. sh. ~óva, ~úar. population
popull/ój kal., ~óva, ~úar. populate
popullór, ~e mb. popular; **muzikë popullore** folk music
popullsí, ~a f. sh. ~, ~të. population
popullúar (i,e) mb. populated
porcelán, ~i m. porcelain
porosí, ~a f. sh. ~, ~të. 1. order; 2. commission; 3. instruction
porosít (porosís) kal., ~a, ~ur. 1. order; 2. instruct; 3. commission
porsé lidh. but
porsí lidh. as, like
port, ~i m. sh. ~e, ~et. port, seaport, harbor
portatív, ~e mb. portable; **televizor portativ** a portable television set
pórt/ë, ~a f. sh. ~a, ~at. 1. gate; portal; 2. **sport.** goal
portiér, ~i m. sh. ~ë, ~ët. 1. door-keeper, gate-keeper; 2. **sport.** goal-keeper
portofól, ~i m. sh. ~a, ~at. billfold, wallet
portoká/ll, ~lli m. sh. ~j, ~jtë dhe **portokáll/e**, ~ja f. sh. ~e, ~et. bot. orange, orange-tree
portrét, ~i m. sh. ~e, ~et. portrait
posáç/ëm (i), ~me (e) mb. special; **tren (aeroplan) i posaçëm** a special train (air-plane)
post, ~i m. sh. ~e, ~et. 1. post, position; 2. **usht.** post
postár, ~e mb. postal
póst/ë, ~a f. sh. ~a, ~at. 1. post, mail; **postë ajrore** air-mail; 2. the post, post-office
postiér, ~i m. sh. ~ë, ~ët. postman, mailman
póshtë ndajf. down, downward
póshtë parafj. under; down; **poshtë tryezës** under the table
póshtër (i,e) mb. mean, wicked, vicious; **njeri i poshtër** a wicked (vicious) man
poshtërím, ~i m. sh. ~e, ~et. humiliation; **poshtërim publik** public humiliation
poshtër/ój kal., ~óva, ~úar. humiliate, humble
potenciál, ~ mb. potential

pothúajse ndajf. almost, nearly
pozición, ~i m. sh. **~e, ~et.** 1. position; **pozicioni i anijes** a ship's position; 2. **usht.** position; 3. posture
pozít/ë, ~a f. sh. **~a, ~at.** position
pozitív, ~ mb. positive; **përgjigje pozitive** a positive answer; **rezultat pozitiv** a positive result; 2. **mat.** positive; 3. **fiz.** positive; 4. **mjek.** positive
pozitívsht ndajf. positively
pra ndajf. so; thus
pra/g, ~gu m. sh. **~gje, ~gjet.** 1. doorstep, threshold; 2. **fig** threshold; **në prag të** at the threshold of
praktík, ~e mb. practical; **njeri praktik** a practical man; **zgjidhje praktike** a practical solution
praktík/ë, ~a f. sh. **~a, ~at.** practice; **vë në praktikë** put into practice; 2. habit, custom; 3. practice (of law, medicine etc)
praktikísht ndajf. practically
praktik/ój kal., **~óva, ~úar.** practise, practice
prandáj lidh. therefore, hence
pránë ndajf. near; near by
pránë paraf. near; by
praní, ~a f. presence; **në prani të dikujt** in the presence of somebody (in somebody's presence)
pranísh/ëm (i) ~me (e) mb. present; **jam i pranishëm** be present
pran/ój kal., **~óva, ~úar.** 1. accept; **pranoj dhuratën** accept a gift; 2. be willing to agree to smth; 3. agree to; 4. admit
pranúesh/ëm (i), ~me (e) mb. acceptable; admissible; **zgjidhje e pranueshme** an acceptable solution
pranvér/ë, ~a f. sh. **~a, ~at.** spring; **në pranverë** in (the) spring; 2. **fig.** prime, spring
pranverór, ~e mb. spring; **lule pranverore** spring flowers
prápa ndajf. back, backward, behind
prápa parafj. behind; **prapa derës** behind the door
prapambétj/e, ~a f. sh. **~e, ~et.** backwardness
prapambétur (i,e) mb. backward
prapaník, ~e mb. backward, unprogressive
prapashtés/ë, ~a f. sh. **~a, ~at. gjuh.** suffix
prapavíj/ë f. sh. **~a, ~at.** rear
prápë (i,e) mb. naughty, wayward
prápë ndajf. 1. again; 2. back
prapëseprápë ndajf. yet; nevertheless
prapës/ój kal., **~óva, ~úar.** repulse, repel
prashít (prashís) kal., **~a, ~ur.** hoe
pre, ~ja f. 1. prey; 2. **fig.** prey, victim; **bie pre** fall prey to
predikím, ~i m. sh. **~e, ~et.** preaching, preachment
predik/ój jokal., **~óva, ~úar.** preach
prefékt, ~i m. sh. **~ë, ~ët.** prefect
prefektúr/ë, ~a f. sh. **~a, ~at.** prefecture
prefer/ój kal., **~óva, ~úar.** prefer
préh/ër, ~ri m. lap
prej parafj. from; of; out of
prejárdhj/e, ~a f. origin, descent, lineage
prejárdhur (i,e) mb. **gjuh.** derived

prek kal., ~a,~ur. 1.touch; 2.**fig.** touch, move; 3.affect, hit
prékem vetv. 1. be moved; 2. take offence; 3. be affected
prékës, ~e mb. touching, moving; **histori prekëse** a moving story
préksh/ëm (i), ~me (e) mb. 1. tangible, palpable, touchable; 2. vulnerable; 3. touchy; 4. touching
prékur (i,e) mb. 1. moved; 2. affected; 3. offended
premís/ë, ~a f. sh. ~a, ~at. premise, premiss
prémt/e, ~ja (e) f. Friday
premtím, ~i m. sh. ~e, ~et. promise, pledge; **mbaj premtimin** keep one's promise; **shkel premtimin** break one's promise
premt/ój kal., ~óva, ~úar. promise
premtúes, ~e mb. promising; **shenja premtuese** promising signs; **këngëtar premtues** a promising singer
prérë (i,e) mb. 1. cut; 2. set; 3. flat, categorical; 4. irreversible, irrevocable
prérës, ~e mb. cutting
prérj/e, ~a f. sh. ~e, ~et. cut
pre/s kal., ~va, ~rë. 1. cut; 2. cut, stop, give up; 3. cut away; cut off; 4. cut (the cards); 5. cut, intersect
pres kal., príta, prítur. 1. wait; 2. expect; 3. receive
président, ~i m. sh. ~ë, ~ët. president
presidiúm, ~i m. sh. ~e, ~et. presidium
presión, ~i m. sh. ~e, ~et. 1. pressure; **presioni i gjakut** blood pressure; **presion atmosferik** atmospheric pressure; 2. **fig.** pressure
présj/e, ~a f. sh. ~e, ~et gjuh. comma
prestígj, ~i m. sh. ~e, ~et libr. prestige; **gëzoj prestigj** enjoy prestige
presh, ~i m. sh. ~, ~të bot. leek
pretékst, ~i m. sh. ~e, ~et pretext, excuse; **me preteksin se** on (under) the pretext that
pretendím, ~i m. sh. ~e, ~et pretension
pretend/ój kal., ~óva, ~úar pretend
prift, ~i m. sh. ~ërínj, ~ërínjtë. priest
pri/j kal., dhe jokal., ~va, ~rë. lead, guide
prill, ~i m. April
primitív, ~ e mb. primitive; **zakone primitive** primitive customs
princ, ~i, m. sh. ~a, ~at dhe ~ër, ~ërit. prince
princésh/ë, ~a f. sh. ~a, ~at. princess
prind, ~i m. kryes. sh. ~ër, ~ërit. parent
prindërór, ~e mb. parental; **dashuria prindërore** parental love (affection)
prírem vetv. 1. incline towards smth; 2. **fig.** incline to (towards) smth, have a physical or mental tendency towards smth
prírj/e, ~a f. sh. ~e, ~et. inclination, bent, leaning, tendency
prish kal., ~a, ~ur. 1. destroy, demolish, tear down, break down; 2. ravage, ruin; 3. scratch; rub off (a word); 4. squander money, spend lavishly; 5. thwart (the plans); 6. break
prít/ë, ~a f. sh. ~a, ~at. embankment
prít/ë, ~a f. sh. ~a, ~at. ambush; **zë (rri) në pritë lie (wait) in ambush**
prítj/e, ~a f. sh. ~e, ~et. reception; **dhoma e pritjes** reception room; parlor; **jap një pritje** give a reception

privát, ~e mb. ek. private; **pronë private** private property;
vizitë private private visit; **jetë private** private life
privilégj, ~i m. sh. ~e, ~et. privilege
privilegjúar (i,e) mb. privileged; **jemi të privilegjuar të** we
are privileged to
príz/ë, ~a f. sh. ~a, ~at. plug
pro libr. ndajf. pro
pro fjalform. libr. pro- ¦
problém, ~i m. sh. ~e, ~et. problem; issue, question; **zgjidh
një** problem solve a problem; **problem për diskutim** a problem
for discussion
problematík, ~e mb. problematic(al)
problém/ë, ~a f. sh. ~a, ~at. mat. problem
proced/ój jokal., ~óva, ~úar 1. proceed, advance, go on; 2.
drejt. proceed, take legal action against; start a lawsuit
against somebody
procedúr/ë, ~a f. sh. ~a, ~at procedure; **proçedurë normale**
normal procedure
procés, ~i m. sh. ~e, ~et 1. process; **proces i vështirë** a
difficult process; 2. **drejt.** process, legal action, lawsuit
prodúkt, ~i m. sh. ~e, ~et. 1. product; **produkte farmaceutike**
pharmaceutical products; 2. **fig.** product, result, outcome
prodhím, ~i m. sh. ~e, ~et. production; **linjë prodhimi**
production line; **mjetet e prodhimit** means of production
prodhimtár, ~e mb. productive; **shkrimtar prodhimtar** a
productive writer
prodh/ój kal., ~óva, ~úar. produce, manufacture
prodhúes, ~i m. sh. ~, ~it. producer
prodhúes, ~e mb. 1. productive; **forcat prodhuese** productive
forces; 2. fertile, yielding; **tokë prodhuese** fertile land
prodhueshmërí. ~a f. productivity
profesión, ~i m. sh. ~e, ~et. profession; **me profesion** by
profession
profesionál, ~e mb. professional; **sëmundje profesionale**
professional illness
profesioníst, ~e mb. professional; **boksier profesionist** a
professional boxer
profesór, ~i m. sh. ~ë, ~ët. professor
profét, ~i m. sh. ~ë, ~ët prophet
profíl, ~i m. sh. ~e, ~et. profile; **në profil** in profile
prográm, ~i m. sh. ~e, ~et. program, programme
program/ój kal., ~óva, ~úar. program, programme
progrés, ~i m. progress
projékt, ~i m. sh. ~e, ~et. 1. design; 2. draft; 3. project
projektím, ~i m. sh. ~e, ~et. 1. projection; 2. designing
projekt/ój kal., ~óva, ~úar. design
prokúr/ë, ~a f. sh. ~a, ~at. proxy; **me prokurë** by proxy
prokurór, ~i m. sh. ~ë, ~ët drejt. public prosecutor
pronár, ~i m. sh. ~ë, ~ët. owner, proprietor; **pronar tokash**
landowner, landlord
prón/ë, ~a f. sh. ~a, ~at. property; **pronë private** private
property; **pronë vetjake** personal property

pronësí, ~a f. ownership
pronór, ~e mb. gjuh. possessive; **përemër pronor** possessive
pronoun
propagánd/ë, ~a f. sh. ~a, ~at. propaganda
propagand/ój kal., ~óva, ~úar. propagate
propozím, ~i m. sh. ~e, ~et. proposal, proposition; **bëj një**
propozín make a proposition
propoz/ój kal., ~óva, ~úar. propose
prostitút/ë, ~a f. sh. ~a, ~at. prostitute
proshút/ë, ~a f. ~a, ~at. ham, bacon
proteín/ë, ~a f. sh. ~a, ~at biokim. protein
protést/ë, ~a f. sh. ~a, ~at. protest; **organizoj një protestë**
kundër stage a protest against
protest/ój kal., ~óva, ~úar. protest; **protestoj fuqishëm**
protest strongly
protón, ~i m. sh. ~e, ~et. fiz. proton
provérb, ~i m. sh. ~a, ~at folk. proverb
próv/ë, ~a f. sh. ~a, ~at. 1. test, trial; **vë në provë** put
smb (smth) to the proof (test); 2. proof, evidence,
testimony; 3. rehearsal; 4. **mat.** proof
provím, ~i m. sh. ~e, ~et. examination; **jap provim sit** (take)
an examination; **mbetem në provim** fail an examination; **provim**
pranimi an entrance examination
provínc/ë, ~a f. sh. ~a, ~at. province
prov/ój kal., ~óva, ~úar. 1. prove; **provoj fajësinë e** prove
smb's guilt; 2. try; 3. put to the test; 4. try on; 5. taste
provok/ój kal., ~óva, ~úar. provoke
provokúes, ~e mb. provocative; provoking
proz/ë, ~a f. sh. ~a, ~at. prose
pse ndajf. why
psikík, ~e mb. psychic, psychical
psikológ, ~u m. sh. ~ë, ~ët. psychologist
psikologjí, ~a f. psychology
psikologjík, ~e mb. psychological; **metoda psikologjike**
psychological methods
psikopát, ~i m. sh. ~ë, ~ët. psychopath
psherëtí/j jokal., ~va, ~rë. sigh
psherëtím/ë, ~a f. sh. ~a, ~at. sigh
publík, ~u m. public; **në publik** in public
publík, ~e mb. public; **shërbimet publike** public services;
opinioni publik public opinion
púd/ër, ~ra f. sh. ~ra, ~rat. face-powder
púl/ë, ~a f. sh. ~a, ~at. 1. hen; chicken; **zog pule** chicken;
mish pule chicken
puls, ~i m. sh. ~e, ~et. pulse; **mat pulsin** feel (take) the
pulse; **puls i fortë (i dobët, i çrregullt)** a strong (weak,
irregular) pulse
púll/ë, ~a f. sh. ~a, ~at. 1. spot, speck; 2. button; 3.
stamp
pún/ë, ~a f. sh. ~ë, ~ët. 1. work, labor, toil; **punë e rëndë**
hard work; 2. work, job; 3. affair
punëdhënës, ~i m. sh. ~, ~it. employer
punës/ój kal., ~óva, ~úar. employ
punëtór, ~i m. sh. ~ë, ~ët. worker, workman, laborer, toiler

punëtór, ~e mb. 1. hard working, industrious, diligent; 2. working

pun/ój jokal., ~óva, ~úar. edhe **kal.** 1. work, labor, toil; 2. function

punónjës, ~i m. sh. ~, ~it. worker, workman; employee

púp/ël, ~la f. sh. ~la, ~lat. feather; **është i lehtë pupël** light as a feather

pus, ~i m. sh. ~e, ~et. 1. well; 2. **gjeol.** pit; **pus nafte** oil well

pushím, ~i m. sh. ~e, ~et. 1. break, recess, rest, repose; 2. respite; **pa pushim** without respite; 3. cessation, stoppage, arrest; 4. pause; 5. vacation

púshk/ë, ~a f. sh. ~ë, ~ët. rifle, gun, firearm

push/ój jokal., ~óva, ~úar. 1. cease, stop; 2. rest, repose; 3. dismiss, dicharge

pushtét, ~i m. sh. ~e, ~et. power

pushtím, ~i m. sh. ~e, ~et. occupation, invasion, conquest

pusht/ój kal., ~óva, ~úar. conquer, occupy

puth kal., ~a, ~ur. kiss

pye/s kal., ~ta, ~tur. 1. ask, query, question; 2. interrogate

pyetës, ~e mb. interrogative

pyetj/e, ~a f. sh. ~e, ~et. 1. question; 2. interrogation

py/ll, ~lli m. sh. ~je, ~jet. forest, wood, timberland

Q

qáf/ë, ~a f. sh. **~a, ~at.** 1. neck; **heq qafe** get rid of; 2. collar, neck (of a shirt); 3. neck (of a bottle); 4. **gjeog.** pass

qáhem vetv. bised. complain, grumble

qa/j jokal., ~va, ~rë. 1. cry, sob, weep, whimper, wail; shed tears; 2. lament, mourn, bewail

qar/k, ~ku m. sh. **~qe, ~qet.** 1. **gjeom.** circle; 2. **fiz.** circuit; 3. district

qark ndajf. round, around; **rreth e qark** round about

qarkullím, ~i m. sh. **~e, ~et.** 1. traffic; 2. circulation; **qarkullimi i mallrave** circulation of commodities; **qarkullimi i parasë** circulation of money; 3. rotation; **qarkullimi i bimëve** crop-rotation

qarkull/ój jokal., ~óva, ~úar. 1. circulate, flow; **qarkullon gjaku në trup** blood flows round the body; 2. rotate

qarkullúes, ~e mb. circulating; **kapital qarkullues** circulating capital

qártë (i,e) mb. 1. clear, lucid, transparent; 2. distinct, intelligible; 3. bright; 4. apparent, obvious, plain

qártë ndajf. 1. clearly, distinctly; 2. visibly; 3. explicitly, evidently, obviously

qartësí, ~a f. clarity, clearness

qartës/ój kal., ~óva, ~úar. 1. clarify, clear up, make clear; 2. make brighter, lighten

qejf, ~i m. sh. **~e, ~et bised.** 1. pleasure; **me gjithë qejf** with pleasure; 2. amusement, entertainment, fun; 3. desire; **bëj diçka me qejf** do smth willingly; **nuk kam qejf të** be unwilling to; 3. humor, temper; **jam në qejf** be in good humor

qelb, ~i m. pus

qélbur (i,e) mb. 1. dirty, filthy; 2. fetid, stinking

qelíz/ë, ~a f. sh. **~a, ~at biol.** cell

qelq, ~i m. glass; **fabrikë qelqi** a glass factory

qen , ~i m. sh. **~, ~të zool.** dog; **qen besnik** a faithful dog; **qen gjuetie** a hunting dog

qénd/ër, ~ra f. sh. **~ra, ~rat.** center, centre; **qendra e rrethit** the center of a circle; **qendra e vemendjes** the ceter of attention; **qendër tregëtare** a center of commerce; **qendra e gravitetit** center of gravity

qendrór, ~e mb central; **personazhi qendror** the central character; **çështja (idea) qëndrore** the central point (idea)

qenësish/ëm (i), ~me (e) mb essential; fundamental

qenësór, ~e mb essential

qengj, ~i m. sh. **~a, ~at.** lamb; **mish qengji** lamb

qéni/e, ~a f. sh. **~e, ~et.** 1. being, living creature; **qënie njerëzore** human being; 2. being, existence

qep kal., ~a, ~ur. sew; **qep me dorë** sew by hand

qepáll/ë, ~a f. sh. **~a, ~at.** eyelid

qép/ë, ~a f. sh. **~ë, ~ët bot.** onion; **qepë të njoma** fresh onions

qépsh/e, ~ja f. sh. **~e, ~et.** ladle

qerás kal., ~a, ~ur. treat smb to smth

qerpík, ~u m. sh. **~ë, ~ët.** eyelash

qershí, ~a f. sh. **~, ~të bot.** cherry; cherry-tree

qershór, ~i m. June
qërr/e, ~ja f. sh. ~e, ~et. cart, wagon
qés/e, ~ja f. sh. ~e, ~et. bag; wallet, purse
qesh jokal., ~a, ~ur. 1. laugh; 2. giggle; 3. mock;
qesharák, ~e mb. ridiculous, laughable; **gabim qesharak** a laughable mistake
qëshj/e, ~a f. sh. ~a, ~et. laugh, laughter
qëshur (i,e) mb. smiling, laughing; **fytyra të qeshura** laughing faces
qétë (i,e) mb. calm, still, quiet, tranquil, serene, placid, restful, peaceful
qétë ndajf. peacefully, quietly
qetësí, ~a f. 1. calm, stillness, quietness; 2. tranquility; 3. repose, rest, peace; 4. composure, self-possession; 5. silence
qetësísht ndajf. silently, tranquilly, quietly, peacefully
qetësóhem vetv. calm down
qetës/ój kal., ~óva, ~úar. 1. quiet, still, compose; 2. appease, soothe, assuage; 3. calm down, pacify, tranquilize
qetësúes, ~e mb. soothing, calming, comforting, pacifying, tranquilizing
qeth kal., ~a, ~ur. 1. cut the hair; 2. fleece, shear
qéthem vetv. have one's hair cut
qeverí, ~a f. sh. ~, ~të. government; **qeveri demokratike** democratic government
qeverís kal., ~a, ~ur. 1. govern, rule, reign; 2. keep (house); 3. run, manage
qeveritár, ~e mb. governmental; **institucione qeveritare** governmental institutions
që përem. that; who; whom
që lidh. that
që parafj. from; since
qëllím, ~i m. sh. ~e, ~et. purpose, aim, intention, intent, design, end; **me qëllim që ...** in order to, with a view to, intending to, with the intention of; **arrij qëllimin** reach (attain) one's aim; **me qëllim** on purpose
qëllimísht ndajf. purposely, intentionally, on purpose
qëllimór, ~e mb. purposeful, intentional
qëllímsh/ëm (i), ~me (e) mb. deliberate, intended, intentional, designed
qëll/ój kal., ~óva, ~úar. 1. hit, strike; 2. smack, slap, fist; 3. happen to be
qëndís kal., ~a, ~ur edhe jokal. embroider
qëndísj/e, ~a f. sh. ~e, ~et. embroidery
qëndísm/ë, ~a f. sh. ~a, ~at. kneedle-work, embroidery
qëndrés/ë, ~a f. sh. ~a, ~at. 1. stop; 2. resistance; **bëj qëndresë** offer resistance
qëndrím, ~i m. sh. ~e, ~et. 1. stand, halt; 2. stand, attitude; **mbaj qëndrim** take a (one's) stand on smth
qëndr/ój jokal., ~óva, ~úar. 1. stop, halt; 2. stand; qëndroj më këmbë stand on one's feet; 3. stay
qëndrúesh/ëm (i), ~me (e) mb. 1. resistant, resistible; 2. stable; 3. durable, enduring, lasting

qëndrueshmërí, ~a f. 1. **fiz.**, **tek.** resistance; 2. stability;
3. steadiness
qër/ój kal., ~óva, ~úar. 1. peel, pare, shell; 2. clean;
pick; 3. clear
qíe/ll, ~lli m. sh. ~j, ~jt. sky; heaven; **qiell i kaltër** a
blue sky; **ngre në qiell** loud (praise) to the skies
qiellgërvíshtës, ~i m. sh. ~, ~it. sky-scraper
qiellór, ~e mb. heavenly; **trupat qiellorë** heavenly bodies
qiéllz/ë, ~a f. sh. ~a, ~at. **anat.** palate
qilár, ~i m. sh. ~ë, ~ët. cellar
qilím, ~i m. sh. ~a, ~at. carpet
qím/e, ~ja f. sh. ~e, ~et. 1. hair; **shpëtoj për një qime**
escape by a hair's-breadth; 2. **tek.** hair-spring
qind, ~i m. hundred; **qind për qind** hundred per cent
qiparís, ~i m. sh. ~a, ~at. **bot.** cypress
qíq/ër, ~ra f. sh. ~ra, ~rat. **bot.** chick-pea; **kërkoj qiqra në**
hell cry for the moon
qirá, ~ja f. sh. ~, ~të. 1. rent; **qira e lartë (e ulët)** high
(low) rent; **paguaj qiranë** pay the rent; 2. lease
qiradhënës, ~i m. sh. ~, ~it. hirer
qiramárrës, ~i m. sh. ~, ~it. tenant, lessee, lodger
qirí, ~u dhe **qiri**, ~ri m. sh. ~nj, ~njtë. candle
qit (qis) kal., ~a, ~ur. 1. force out, drive out; 2. put out
(the tongue); 3. take out; 4. emit; 5. draw out; 6. lead to
qítës, ~i m. sh. ~, ~it. shooter, shot; **qitës i klasit të**
parë a first-class shot
qítro, ~ja f. sh. ~, ~t **bot.** lime
qortím, ~i m. sh. ~e, ~et. rebuke, reprimand, reproach,
reproof
qort/ój kal., ~óva, ~úar. rebuke, reprove, reproach,
reprimand
qortúes, ~e mb. reproachful
qorr, ~e mb. 1. blind, sightless; 2. concealed, hidden,
blicked
qósh/e, ~ja f. sh. ~e, ~et **bised.** corner
qúaj kal., ~ta, ~tur. 1. call, name; 2. consider, judge,
regard
qúhem vetv. be called; **unë quhem** my name is ...
qúmësht, ~i m. milk
qymyr, ~i m. sh. ~e, ~et. 1. coal; 2. charcoal
qyq/e, ~ja f. sh. ~e, ~et. **zool.** cuckoo
qysh ndajf. how; **qysh je?** how are you?
qytét, ~i m. sh. ~e, ~et. city; town
qytetár, ~i m. sh. ~ë, ~ët. citizen
qytetár, ~e mb. civic, civil
qytetarí, ~a f. citizenship
qytetërím, ~i m. sh. ~e, ~et. civilization
qytetër/ój kal., ~óva, ~úar. civilize
qytetërúar (i,e) mb. civilized
qytetór, ~e mb. urban

R

** rác/ë**, ~a f. sh. ~a, ~at. 1. race; 2. **zool.** breed, race
raciál, ~e mb. 1. racial; **tipar racial** a racial feature; 2.
keq. racial; **dallim racial** racial discrimination; **marrëdhënie raciale** race relations
ración, ~i m. sh. ~e, ~et. portion, ration, share; **racioni ditor** the daily ration
racionál, ~e mb. rational, sensible, reasonable; **zgjidhje racionale** a rational solution
racionaliz/ój kal., ~óva, ~úar. rationalize; **racionalizoj prodhimin** rationalize production
racioním, ~i m. rationing; **fus racionimin e benzinës** introduce petrol rationing
racion/ój kal., ~óva, ~úar. ration; ration smth out; **racionoj ujin e mbetur** ration the remaining water
racíst, ~i m. sh. ~ë, ~ët. racist, racialist
racíst, ~e mb. racist, racialist
racíz/ëm, ~mi m. racism, racialism
radár, ~i m. sh. ~ë, ~ët radar
radiatór, ~i m. sh. ~ë, ~ët tek. radiator
rádio, ~ja f. sh. ~, ~t. radio, radio set, wireless
radioaktív, ~e mb fiz. radioactive; **mbetje radioaktive** radioactive waste
radioaktivitét, ~i m. fiz. radioactivity
radiografí, ~a f. sh. ~, ~të. radiography
radiográm, ~i m. sh. ~e, ~et. radiogram
radiologjí, ~a f. radiology
radiostacion, ~i m. sh. ~e, ~et. radio station
radiúm, ~i m. kim. radium
rádh/ë, ~a f. sh. ~ë, ~ët. 1. line, row; **radhë pemësh** lines of trees; 2. queue; **qëndroj në radhë** stand in a queue; 3. rank; 4. turn; **me radhë** by turns; **e kështu me radhë** and so on; **në radhë të parë** first of all
radhít (radhis) kal., ~a, ~ur. 1. line up; 2. rank; 3. enumerate
rafinerí, ~a f. sh. ~, ~të. refinery
rafiním, ~i m. refinement
rafin/ój kal., ~óva, ~úar. refine; **rafinoj vajin (sheqerin)** refine oil (sugar)
rafinúar (i,e) mb. 1. refined; **vaj i rafinuar** refined oil; 2. **fig.** sly, foxy, crafty
raft, ~i m. sh. ~e, ~et. shelf; **raft librash** bookcase
rajón, ~i m. sh. ~e, ~et. region
rakét/ë, ~a f. sh. ~a, ~at usht. rocket, missile; **sulm me raketa** a rocket attack
rakét/ë, ~a f. sh. ~a, ~at. sport. racket, racquet
ran/g, ~gu m. sh. ~gje, ~gjet. rank, level; **në rang ambasadorësh** at ambassadorial level
rapórt, ~i m. sh. ~e, ~et. report; **bëj (hartoj) një raport** draw up a report
rapórt, ~i m. sh. ~e, ~et. ratio, proportion
raport/ój kal., dhe jokal., ~óva, ~úar. report
rás/ë, ~a f. sh. ~a, ~at gjuh. case; **rasa gjindore** possessive case

rast, ~i *m. sh.* ~e, ~et. 1. case; **në rast** in case of; **në çdo
rast** in any case; **në këtë rast** in this case; 2. occasion,
opportunity; **me rastin e** on the ocassion of; **përfitoj nga
rasti** take the opportunity to do something; 3. circumstance;
në asnjë rast in (under) no circumstances; 4. chance
rastësí, ~a *f. sh.* ~, ~të. accident, chance
rastësísh/ëm (i), ~me (e) *mb.* chance, accidental,casual,
haphazard, random, unintentional; **takim i rastësishëm an**
accidental meeting
rastësísht *ndajf.* accidentally, by accident, by chance; **gjej
rastësisht** find smth by chance
rastís *jokal.*, ~a, ~ur. chance, happen; **rastisa në shtëpi** I
chanced to be home
rástit (i,e) *mb.* chance, random
raúnd, ~i *m. sh.* ~e, ~et. 1. *sport.* round; 2. round
re, ~ja *f. sh.* ~, ~të. 1. cloud; **re të bardha (të zeza)** white
(black) clouds; 2. cloud; **re pluhuri** clouds of dust
re, ~ja (e) *f. sh.* ~ja, ~jat. news; **Ç'të reja kemi?** What is
the news?
reagím, ~i *m. sh.* ~e, ~et. reaction
reag/ój *jokal.*, ~óva, ~úar *biol.*, *fiziol.* react; **reagoj
pozitivisht (negativisht)** react positively (negatively)
reaksión, ~i *m. sh.* ~e, ~et. 1. reaction; 2. **kim.**, **fiz.**
reaction; **reaksion bërthamor** nuclear reaction; **reaksion
zinxhir** chain reaction
reaksión, ~i *m. sh.* ~e, ~et. reaction
reaksionár, ~e *mb.* reactionary
reaktív, ~e *mb.* **kim.** reactive
reaktór, ~i *m. sh.* ~ë, ~ët. reactor; **reaktor atomik** nuclear
reactor
reál, ~e *mb.* real, true, genuine; **jeta reale** real life; **fakt
real** a real fact
realíst, ~e *mb.* realistic; **qendrim realist** a realistic
attitude; **shkrimtar realist** a realistic writer
realitet, ~i *m.* reality; **në realitet** in reality; **bëhet
realitet** become a reality
realíz/ëm, ~mi *m.* realism
realiz/ój *kal.*, ~óva, ~úar. realize, effect, fulfill;
realizoj shpresat realize one's hopes
rebél, ~i *m. sh.* ~ë, ~ët. rebel
rebelím, ~i *m. sh.* ~e, ~et. rebellion
recensión, ~i *m. sh.* ~e, ~et. review
recens/ój *kal.*, ~óva, ~úar. review
recét/ë, ~a *f. sh.* ~a, ~at. 1. prescription; 2. recipe
reciprók, ~e *mb.* mutual, reciprocal; **ndihmë (tregëti)
reciproke** reciprocal help (trade)
recit/ój *kal.*, ~óva, ~úar. recite, declaim
reçel, ~i *m. sh.* ~e, ~et dhe ~ra, ~rat. jam
redakt/ój *kal.*, ~óva, ~úar. edit
redaktór, ~i *m. sh.* ~ë, ~ët. editor
referendúm, ~i *m. sh.* ~e, ~et. referendum
refléks, ~i *m. sh.* ~e, ~et *fiziol.* reflex, reflex action
reflektím, ~i *m. sh.* ~e, ~et reflection
reflekt/ój *kal.*, ~óva, ~úar reflect

refórm/ë, ~a f. sh. ~a, ~at. reform; **reforma arsimore** educational reform
reform/ój kal., ~óva, ~úar. reform
refugját, ~i m. sh. ~ë, ~ët. refugee
refuzím, ~i m. sh. ~e, ~et. refusal, rejection; **refuzim kategorik** a flat refusal; **refuzimi i ftesës** refusal of an invitation
refuz/ój kal. edhe jokal., ~óva, ~úar. refuse, reject, turn down; **refuzoj ndihmën** refuse one's help
regj kal., ~a, ~ur. 1. tan; 2. **fig.** harden
régjem vetv. harden
regjím, ~i m. sh. ~e, ~et. regime; **regjim demokratik** democratic regime; 2. regimen
regjimént, ~i m. sh. ~e, ~et usht. regiment
regjisór, ~i m. sh. ~ë, ~ët. producer
regjíst/ër, ~ri m. sh. ~ra, ~rat. register, ledger; record
regjistr/ój kal., ~óva, ~úar. 1. register; 2. enroll; 3. record
rehatí, ~a f. comfort
rehátsh/ëm (i), ~me (e) mb. comfortable; **shtrat i rehatshëm** a comfortable bed
reklám/ë, ~a f. sh. ~a, ~at. advertisment
reklam/ój kal., ~óva, ~úar. advertise
rekomandím, ~i m. sh. ~e, ~et. recommendation; **i jap një rekomandin dikujt** give smb a recommendation
rekomand/ój kal., ~óva, ~úar. recommend
rekórd, ~i m. sh. ~e, ~et sport. record; **thyej një rekord** break a record
rekrút, ~i m. sh. ~ë, ~ët. recruit
rekrut/ój kal., ~óva, ~úar recruit, enlist
rektór, ~i m. sh. ~ë, ~ët. rector
relatív, ~e mb. relative
relativísht ndajf. relatively
reliév, ~i m. sh. ~e, ~et gjeogr. relief; **harta e relievit** relief map
rend, ~i m. sh. ~e, ~et. 1. order; **rendi alfabetik** alphabetic order; 2. agenda; **rendi i ditës** order of the day; 3. turn
rend, ~i m. sh. ~e, ~et. order; **rendi politik** political order
rend jokal., ~a, ~ur. run
rendimént, ~i m. sh. ~e, ~et. productivity, output
rent/ë, ~a f. sh. ~a, ~at. ek. rent
republík/ë, ~a f. sh. ~a, ~at. republic
respékt, ~i m. respect, deference; **fitoj respektin e** win (earn) the respect of
respekt/ój kal., ~óva, ~úar. respect; **respektoj ndjenjat e dikujt** respect smb's feelings
restaur/ój kal., ~óva, ~úar. 1. restore; **restauroj kështjellën** restore a fort; 2. restore, bring back to power
restoránt, ~i m. sh. ~e, ~et. restaurant
reumatíz/ëm, ~mi m. sh. ~ma, ~mat mjek. rheumatism
revíst/ë, ~a f. sh. ~a, ~at. magazine, periodical
revokím, ~i m. sh. ~e, ~et. revocation
revok/ój kal., ~óva, ~úar. revoke
revól/e, ~ja f. sh. ~e, ~et revolver

revólt/ë, ~a f. sh. ~a, ~at. revolt; **mbys revoltën** quell (put down) the revolt
revoltóhem vetv. be revolted
revolt/ój kal., ~óva, ~úar. revolt
revolución, ~i m. sh. ~e, ~et. revolution
revolucionár, ~e mb. revolutionary
revolucionariz/ój kal., ~óva, ~úar. revolutionize
rezérv/ë, ~a f. sh. ~a, ~at. 1. reserve; 2. **usht.** the reserve; reserves; 3. reserve, reservation; **pa rezerva** without reservation
rezerv/ój kal., ~óva, ~úar 1. reserve, put aside; 2. reserve, book; **rezervoj bileta** reserve tickets; **reservoj një tavolinë** reserve a table
rezisténc/ë, ~a f. sh. ~a, ~at. resistance; **bëj rezistencë** put up a resistance
rezist/ój kal., ~óva, ~úar. resist
rezolút/ë, ~a f. sh. ~a, ~at. resolution
rezultát, ~i m. sh. ~e, ~et. 1. result, outcome; **si rezultat** as a result; **arrij rezultate** achieve results; **pa rezultat** without result; 2. **sport.** result; score
rëndë (i,e) mb. 1. heavy, weighty; 2. **usht.** heavy; **artileri e rëndë** heavy artillery; 3. serious, grave; 4. hard, difficult
rëndësí, ~a f. importance, significance; **i jap rëndësi** attach importance to
rëndësish/ëm (i), ~me (e) mb. important, significant; **vendim i rëndësishëm** important decision
rënd/ój kal., ~óva, ~úar. 1. burden; 2. overload; 3. worsen, aggravate
rëndómtë (i,e) mb. ordinary, common
rëni/e, ~a f. sh. ~e, ~et. 1. fall, drop; 2. decline
rënkím, ~i m. sh. ~e, ~et. groan, moan
rënk/ój jokal., ~óva, ~úar. groan, moan
rër/ë, ~a f. sh. ~a, ~at. sand
ri, ~u (i) m. sh. ~nj, ~njtë (të). the young; the youth
ri (i), re (e) mb. 1. young; 2. new
rifill/ój kal., ~óva, ~úar. recommence, start anew (afresh)
rím/ë, ~a f. sh. ~a, ~at. rhyme
rindërt/ój kal., ~óva, ~úar. reconstruct, rebuild
riní, ~a f. youth; **rinia e vendit** the youth of the country
riparím, ~i m. sh. ~e, ~et. repair; **në riparim** under repair
ripar/ój kal., ~óva, ~úar. repair, mend
riprodh/ój kal., ~óva, ~úar. reproduce
riprodhúes, ~e mb. reproductive
rishik/ój kal., ~óva, ~úar. review, reexamine
rit, ~i m. sh. ~e, ~et. rite
rít/ëm, ~mi m. sh. ~me, ~met. rhythm; **ritmi i zemrës** the rhythm of the heart
ritmík, ~e mb. rhythmic, rythmical; **frymarrje ritmike** rhythmic breathing
ritreg/ój kal., ~óva, ~úar. retell
rivál, ~i m. sh. ~ë, ~ët. rival
rivalitét, ~i m. sh. ~e, ~et. rivalry
rivaliz/ój jokal., ~óva, ~úar. rival, compete, vie
rivendós kal., ~a, ~ur. restore; **rivendos rendin** restore order

rivlerësím, ~i m. sh. ~e, ~et. revaluation
rivlerës/ój kal., ~óva, ~úar revalue
rob, ~i m. sh. ~ër, ~ërit hist. slave
robót, ~i m. sh. ~ë, ~ët. robot
rój/ë, ~a f. sh. ~a, ~at. watchman, guard; **roje nate** night
watchman
rol, ~i m. sh. ~e, ~et teatër. role; **luaj një rol të**
rëndësishëm play an important role
romantík, ~e mb. romantic
rós/ë, ~a f. sh. ~a, ~at zool. duck
rúaj kal., ~ta, ~tur. 1. guard, watch; 2. protect; 3.
preserve; 4. reserve
ryshfét, ~i m. sh. ~e, ~et. bribe, graft

rrafsh/ój kal., ~óva, úar. 1. level, even; 2. smooth over; iron out; 3. raze; **rrafshoj për tokë** raze to the ground

rrah kal., ~a, ~ur. 1. beat; 2. **fig.** thrash out; **rrah një problem** thrash out a problem; 3. hammer, beat (metal); 4. beat smth up; **rrah vezët** beat the eggs; 5. beat, pulsate; 6. beat smb at something; **më rrahu në shah** he beat me at chess; **rrah ujë në havan** beat the air

rráhur (i,e) mb. 1. beaten; 2. seasoned, experienced

rrállë (i,e) mb. 1. rare, infrequent, scarce, uncommon; 2. sparse; 3. thin

rrállë ndajf. seldom, infrequently, rarely, scarcely, occasionally

rall/ój kal., ~óva, ~úar. rarefy

rrap, ~i m. sh. ~e, ~et. bot. plane, plane-tree

rras kal., ~a, ~ur. ram smth in (into, on), pack in, push in, press in; **rras plaçkat në valixhe** cram the clothes into a suitcase; **rrasi kapelen** crammed the cap on his head

rraskapít kal., ~a, ~ur. exhaust, overtire

rraskapítem vetv. exhaust oneself, tire out

rraskapítur (i,e) mb. exhausted, tired out, dead tired, overtired

rrégull, ~i m. 1. rule; **regullat e lojës** the rules of the game; 2. practice, habit; 3. order; **vë në regull** put in order

rregullísht ndajf. regularly

rregull/ój kal., ~óva, ~úar. 1. tidy up; **regulloj dhomën** tidy up the room; 2. repair; **rregulloj biçikletën** repair the bicycle; 3. adjust; **rregulloj flokët** adjust the hair; 4. regulate; 5. arrange

rrégullt (i,e) mb. 1. regular; **frymarje e regullt** regular breathing; 2. proper; 3. normal, usual; 4. **usht.** regular; **ushtri e regullt** regular army

rregullúes, ~i m. sh. ~, ~it. regulator

rrej kal., ~ta, ~tur. lie, fib

rrém/ë, ~e (i,e) mb. false, sham

rrén/ë, ~a f. sh. ~a, ~at. lie, fib

rrép/ë, ~a f. sh. ~a, ~at. bot. turnip

rréptë (i,e) mb. strict, austere, rigid, severe, stern; rigorous; **rregull i rreptë** a strict rule

rreptësísht ndajf. strictly

rresht, ~i m. sh. ~a, ~at. rank, line; **vë në rresht** line up

rreth, ~i m. sh. rráthë, rráthët. 1. **gjeom.** circle; **vizatoj një rreth** draw a circle; 2. circle; **rreth letrar** literary circle; 3. district; 4. hoop

rreth ndajf. round, around, about

rreth parafj. round; **ulur rreth tavolinës** sitting round the table

rrethán/ë, ~a f. zakon. sh. ~a, ~at. circumstance; **rrethana rënduese (lehtësuese)** aggravating (mitigating) circumstances; **në këto rrethana** under the circumstances

rrethanór, ~e mb. circumstantial

rrethín/ë, ~a f. sh. ~a, ~at. outskirts, periphery; **në periferi të qytetit** on the periphery (outskirts) of the city

rreth/ój kal., ~óva, ~úar. 1. enclose, surround; 2. encircle; besiege

rrezatím, ~i m. sh. ~e, ~et. radiation; **nivel i lartë (i ulët) i rrezatimit** a high (low) level of radiation

rrezat/ój kal., ~óva, ~úar. 1. radiate; 2. **fig.** radiate

rrezatúes, ~e mb. radiant
rréz/e, ~ja f. sh. ~e, ~et. 1. ray, beam; **rrezet e diellit**
the ray of the sun; **rreze iks** X-rays; 2. **fig.** ray
rrezí/k, ~ku m. sh. ~qe, ~qet. danger, hazard, jeopardy,
peril, risk, threat; **në rrezik** in danger; **jashtë rrezikut** out
of danger
rrezik/ój kal., ~óva, ~úar. endanger, hazard, imperil,
jeopordize, risk, threaten
rrezíksh/ëm (i), ~me (e) mb. dangerous, hazardous, perilous,
precarious, risky
rrëf/éj kal., ~éva, ~yer. 1. tell, relate, narrate; 2. show,
tell; 3. disclose, divulge, spill, reveal
rrëfénj/e, ~a f. sh. ~a, ~at. tale, story
rrëfim, ~i m. sh. ~e, ~et. 1. confession; 2. story
rrëmb/éj kal., ~éva, ~yer. 1. snatch, grab; 2. kidnap; 3.
take up arms
rrëmbyer (i,e) mb. rash, impetuous
rrëm/ój kal., ~óva, ~yer. 1. dig up; 2. **fig.** grub; rummage,
ransack
rrëmúj/ë, ~a f. sh. ~a, ~at. disorder, disarray, mess; **në
rrëmujë** in disorder; **bëj rrëmujë** make a mess of
rrëním, ~i m. sh. ~e, ~et. ruin; demolition, destruction
rrën/ój kal., ~óva, ~úar. ruin, destroy, demolish
rrënj/ë, ~a f. sh. ~ë, ~ët. 1. root; **lëshon (nxjerr, zë)
rrënjë** strike (take) roots; 2. **fig.** root; 3. **gjuh.** root (of a
word); 4. **mat.** root
rrënjós kal., ~a, ~ur. 1. root, establish; 2. inculcate,
implant
rrëshq/ás jokal., ~íta, ~ítur. 1. slip, slide, glide; 2.
steal out
rrëzóhem vetv. fall down, tumble down; **rrëzohem nga shkallët
(nga biçikleta)** tumble down the stairs (off a bicycle)
rrëz/ój, ~óva, ~úar. 1. bring down, pull down; 2. knock down;
throw down; 3. cut down; 4. shoot down; 5. flunk
rri jokal., ndénja, ndénjur. 1. sit; 2. stand; 3. stay
rrip, ~i m. sh. ~a, ~at. belt, girdle
rrit (rris) kal., ~a, ~ur. 1. bring up; **rrit fëmijën** bring up
a child; 2. rear, breed; 3. grow; 4. increase, augment
rritem vetv. grow up
rrítës, ~i m. sh. ~, ~it. grower; breeder
rrítj/e, ~a f. sh. ~e, ~et. 1. increase, growth, raise, rise;
2. breeding; rearing
rrjedh jokal., kryes. veta III ródhi, rrjédhur. 1. flow; 2.
leak 3. come, derive; 4. result, ensue
rrjedhím, ~i m. sh. ~e, ~et. consequence; **si rrjedhim i** in
consequence of smth
rrjedhimísht fj. ndërm. consequently
rrjet, ~i m. network; **rrjeti hekurudhor** railway network
rrjet/ë, ~a f. sh. ~a, ~at. net; **rrjet peshkimi** fishing net
rrób//ë, ~a f. sh. ~a, ~at. clothes, garment; **rroba të
gatshme** ready-made clothes
rróg/ë, ~a f. sh. ~a, ~at. wage, salary, pay; **marr rrogën**
draw one's pay
rroj jokal., ~ta, ~tur. 1. live; 2. reside; 3. remain in
existence; survive; 4. wear well
rrókj/e, ~a f. sh. ~e, ~et. gjuh. syllable

rrót/ë, ~**a** f. sh. ~**a**, ~**at**. 1. wheel; 2. tire
rrótull ndajf. round
rrótull parafj. round
rrúaj kal., **rróva**, ~**rúar.** shave
rrúaz/ë, ~**a** f. sh. ~**a**, ~**at**. 1. bead, beading; 2. globule
rrúdhur (i,e) mb. wrinkled, creased
rrufé, ~**ja** f. sh. ~, ~**të**. thunder-bolt
rrúg/ë, ~**a** f. sh. ~**a**, ~**at**. 1. avenue, street, road, route; 2. way, method, style, manner; 3. means; 4. **fig.** path, road; **rruga drejt suksesit** the road (path) to success; 5. track
rrugíc/ë, ~**a** f. sh. ~**a**, ~**at**. lane, alley
rrumbullákët (i,e) mb. round
rrush, ~**i** m. bot. grape; **rrush i thatë** raisin; **lëng rrushi** grape juice
rrúzu/ll, ~**lli** m. sh. ~**j**, ~**jt**. globe
rrym/ë, ~**a** f. sh. ~**a**, ~**at**. current; **kundër rrymës** against the current

sa ndajf. how much, how many
sabotím, ~i m. sh. ~e, ~et. sabotage
sabot/ój kal., ~óva, ~úar. sabotage
sahán, ~i m. sh. ~ë, ~ët. bowl
sahát, ~i m. sh. ~e, ~et 1. watch, clock; **sahat dore** wrist-watch; **sahat muri** wall-clock; 2. **tek.** meter; **sahat elektriku** an electricity meter; **sahat uji** a water meter
saj(i,e) pron. sh. saj (e). her
saj/ój kal., ~óva, ~úar. 1. invent, concoct; 2. contrive; improvise
sakáq ndajf. bised. instantly, immediately, on the instant, in no time
sakát, ~e mb. disabled; **fëmijë sakat** a disabled child
sakrifíc/ë, ~a f. sh. ~a, ~at. sacrifice; **bëj sakrifica** make sacrifices
sakrifikohem vetv. sacrifice oneself
sakrifik/ój kal., ~óva, ~úar. sacrifice
saksí, ~a f. sh. ~, ~të. flower-pot
saksofón, ~i m. sh. ~a, ~at muz. saxophone
sáktë, (i,e) mb. 1. exact, accurate, precise; **peshore e saktë** accurate weighing machine; 2. sound; **njeri i saktë** a sound man **saktësí,** ~a f. accuracy, exactness, precision
sálc/ë, ~a f. sh. ~a, ~at sauce; **salcë domate** tomato sauce
saldím, ~i m. sh. ~e, ~et. tek. solder
sald/ój kal., ~óva, ~úar tek. weld, solder
salsíç/e, ~ja f. sh. ~e, ~et gjell. sausage
sallám, ~i m. sh. ~e, ~et. salami
sallát/ë, ~a f. sh. ~a, ~at bot. salad; **vaj sallate** salad-oil
sáll/ë, ~a f. sh. ~a, ~at. hall; **sallë mbledhjesh** meeting room; **sallë vallëzimi** dance hall
sallón, ~i m. sh. ~e, ~et. saloon
samár, ~i m. sh. ~ë, ~ët. saddle
sandál/e, ~ja f. kryes. sh. ~e, ~et. sandals
sanitár, ~e mb. sanitary
sanksión, ~i m. sh. ~e, ~et drejt. sanction; **zbatoj sanksione ekonomike kundër** apply economic sanctions against
sapó ndajf. just now, at this moment; right away; **e njoha sapo e pashë** I recognized him right away
sapún, ~i m. sh. ~ë, ~ët. soap; **një kallëp sapun** a bar of soap
sapunís kal., ~a, ~ur. soap
sardél/e, ~ja f. sh. ~e, ~et. sardine
sarkastík, ~e mb. sarcastic; **ton sarkastik** a sarcastic tone
sarkáz/ëm, ~mi m. sh. ~ma, ~mat. sarcasm
sasí, ~a f. sh. ~, ~të. quantity; **sasia dhe cilësia** quantity and quality; **në sasi të madhe** in large quantities
sasiór, ~e mb. quantitative
satelít, ~i m. sh. ~ë, ~ët. 1. satellite; **Hëna është satelit i Tokës** The moon is the Earth's satellite; 2. **fig.** satellite
satír/ë, ~a f. sh. ~a, ~at. satire
satirik, ~e mb. satiric, satirical; **poemë satirike** a satirical poem
satiriz/ój kal., ~óva, ~úar. satirize
se pyet. what

seánc/ë, ~a f. sh. ~a, ~at. session, sitting; **seancë plenare** plenary session

secíl/i, ~a pakuf. each

sekónd/ë, ~a f. sh. ~a, ~at. second

sekrét, ~i m. sh. ~e, ~et. secret; **ruaj sekretin** keep a secret; **nxjerr sekretin** reveal (disclose) a secret

sekrét, ~e mb. secret; **dokument (kalim) sekret** a secret document (passage)

sekretár, ~i m. sh. ~ë, ~ët. secretary; **sekretar shteti** secretary of state

seks, ~i m. sh. ~e, ~et. sex; **pa dallim seksi** regardless of sex

seksión, ~i m. sh. ~e, ~et. section

seksuál, ~e mb. sexual

sekt, ~i m. sh. ~e, ~et. sect

sektár, ~e mb. sectarian; **pikëpamje sektare** sectarian views

sektór, ~i m. sh. ~ë, ~ët gjeom. sector

seleksioním, ~i m. sh. ~e, ~et. selection

seleksion/ój kal., ~óva, ~úar. select, choose

seleksionúes, ~e mb. selective

selví, ~a f. sh. ~, ~të bot. cypress-tree

semafór, ~i m. sh. ~ë, ~ët. semaphore

semantík/ë, ~a f. gjuh. semantics

semést/ër, ~ri m. sh. ~ra, ~rat. semester

seminár, ~i m. sh. ~e, ~et. seminar

senát, ~i m. sh. ~e, ~et. senate

senatór, ~i m. sh. ~ë, ~ët. senator

send, ~i m. sh. ~e, ~et. object, thing

sensación, ~i m. sh. ~e, ~et. sensation

sensacional, ~e mb. sensational; **lajm sensacional** sensational news

sentimentál, ~e mb. sentimental

sepsé lidh. for, because, why

serí, ~a f. sh. ~, ~të. series

serióz, ~e mb. serious; **njeri serioz** a serious man

seriozísht ndajf. seriously; **flas seriozisht** speak seriously

seriozitét, ~i m. seriousness; **me gjithë seriozitetin** in all seriousness

serúm, ~i m. sh. ~e, ~et biol. mjek. serum

servíl, ~i m. sh. ~ë, ~ët. servile

sesá lidh. than

sesión, ~i m. sh. ~e, ~et. session, sitting

set, ~i m. sh. ~e, ~et sport. set

sëmúndj/e, ~a f. sh. ~e, ~et. illness, ailment, disease, malady, sickness

sëmúrem vetv. get sick, fall ill

sëmúr/ë, ~i (i) m. sh. ~ë, ~ët (të). the sick

sëmúrë (i,e) mb. ill, sick

sëpát/ë, ~a f. sh. ~a, ~at. ax, axe, hatchet

sërish ndajf. afresh, anew

sfér/ë, ~a f. sh. ~a, ~at 1. **mat.** sphere; 2. sphere, range, realm; **sfera e interesave** the sphere of interests

sferík, ~e mb. spherical; **objekt sferik** a spheric object

sfíd/ë, ~a f. sh. ~a, ~at challenge

sfond, ~i m. sh. ~e, ~et. background
sfungjér, ~i m. sh. ~ë, ~ët 1. **zool.** sponge; 2. sponge
si ndajf. 1. how; 2. what
siç lidh. as
sidomós pj. especially, particularly
sidoqoftë fj. ndërm. anyhow
sigurí, ~a f. sh. ~, ~të. security, safety
sigurím, ~i m. sh. ~e, ~et. 1. security; 2. insurance
sigurísht ndajf. surely, certainly
sigur/ój kal., ~óva, ~úar. 1. secure; **siguroj derën** secure
the door; 2. secure, obtain; 3. ensure; guarantee; 4. assure
sígurt (i,e) mb. 1. sure, certain; 2. safe, secure
sigurúar (i,e) mb. insured
sikúr lidh. as if
sikursé lidh. as
síllem vetv. 1. behave; 2. rotate, revolve
simból, ~i m. sh. ~e, ~et. symbol
simbolík, ~e mb. symbolic, symbolical
simetrí, ~a f. symmetry
simetrík, ~e mb. symmetric, symmetrical
simfoní, ~a f. sh. ~, ~të. **muz.** symphony
simfoník, ~e mb. symphonic
simpatí, ~a f. sh. ~, ~të. sympathy; **ndjej simpati për** feel
sympathy for; **shpreh simpati për** express sympathy for
simpatík, ~e mb. sympathetic
simpatiz/ój kal., ~óva, ~úar. sympathize
simpatizúes, ~i m. sh. ~, ~it. sympathizer
simpoziúm, ~i m. sh. ~e, ~et. symposium
simptóm/ë, ~a ~a, ~at. **mjek.** symptom
simul/ój jokal., ~óva, ~úar simulate
sindikalíst, ~i m. sh. ~ë, ~ët. syndicalist
sindikát/ë, ~a f. sh. ~a, ~at. syndicate
sinoním, ~i m. sh. ~e, ~et gjuh. synonym
sinqerísht ndajf. sincerely, frankly
sinqeritét, ~i m. sincerity, frankness
sinqértë (i,e) gjuh. sincere, candid, frank, ingenuous,
straightforward
sintáks/ë, ~a f. gjuh. syntax
sintetik, ~e mb. synthetic
sintéz/ë, ~a f. sh. ~a, ~at. synthesis
sinjál, ~i m. sh. ~e, ~et. signal; **sinjalet e trafikut**
traffic signals
sinjaliz/ój kal dhe jokal., ~óva, ~úar. 1. signal; 2. notify
sinjalizúes, ~i m. sh. ~, ~it. 1. signaller, signaler; 2.
signalman; 3. signal-box
sipás parafj. according to
sípër ndajf. above, high up, on the top, over
sípër parafj. on, upon, over, above
sipërfáq/e, ~ja f. sh. ~e, ~et. surface
sipërfaqësór, ~ e mb. 1. superficial; **plagë sipërfaqësore**
superficial wound; 2. **fig.** superficial
sipërfáqsh/ëm (i), ~me (e) mb. superficial (edhe **fig.**)

sípërm (i), ~e (e) mb. upper; **kati i sipërm** the upper floor
sipërmárrës, ~i m. sh. ~, ~it. undertaker
sipërmárrj/e, ~a f. sh. ~e, ~et. undertaking, enterprise
sipërór, ~e mb. gjuh. superlative; **shkalla sipërore** superlative degree
sirtár, ~i m. sh. ~ë, ~ët. drawer
sistém, ~i m. sh. ~e, ~et. system; **sistem demokratik** a democratic system
sistematík, ~e mb. systematic; **përpjekje sistematike** a systematic attempt
sistematiz/ój kal., ~óva, ~úar. systematize
sit (sis) kal., ~a, ~ur. sift, sieve
sít/ë, ~a f. sh. ~a, ~at. sieve
situát/ë, ~a f. sh. ~a, ~at. situation; **situatë e nderë (e vështirë)** a tense (difficult) situation; **dal nga situata** get out of a situation
sivjét ndajf. this year
sjell kal., ~sólla, sjéllë. 1. bring; 2. produce; 3. cause
sjéllj/e, ~a f. sh. ~e, ~et. behavior, conduct
sjéllsh/ëm (i), ~me (e) mb. well-behaved, well-mannered, good- mannered
skaj, ~i m. sh. ~e, ~et. extreme, extremity, end
skajór, ~e mb. extreme, remote
skájsh/ëm (i), ~me (e) mb. extreme, remote
skalít (skalis) kal., ~a, ~ur. 1. carve, chisel; 2. engrave; 3. fig. etch
skámj/e, ~a f. poverty; **jetoj në varfëri** live in poverty
skandál, ~i m. sh. ~e, ~et. scandal; **shkaktoj skandal** cause a scandal
skandalóz, ~e mb.scandalous; **sjellje skandaloze** scandalous behavior
skár/ë, ~a f. sh. ~a, ~at. 1. gridiron, grill; 2. saddle
skedár, ~i m. sh. ~ë, ~ët. card index
skelét, ~i m. sh. ~e, ~et. 1. skeleton; 2. framework
skél/ë, ~a f. sh. ~a, ~at. wharf
ském/ë, ~a f. sh. ~a, ~at. design
skén/ë, ~a f. sh. ~a, ~at. 1. stage; **vë në skenë** stage, present on a stage; 2. fig. stage, scene
skeptík, ~u m. sh. ~ë, ~ët. skeptic, sceptic
ski, ~të f. vet. sh. ski; **një palë ski** a pair of skis
skíc/ë, ~a f. sh. ~a, ~at. sketch; outline
skic/ój kal., ~óva, ~úar. 1. sketch; 2. outline
skllav, ~i m. sh. skllévër, skllévërit. slave; **trajtoj dikë si skllav** treat smb like a slave
skllavër/ój kal., ~óva, ~úar. enslave
skuád/ër, ~ra f. sh. ~ra, ~rat. 1. squad; 2. team
skulptór, ~i m. sh. ~ë, ~ët. sculptor
skulptúrë, ~a f. sh. ~a, ~at. sculpture
skuq kal., ~a, ~ur. 1. redden; 2. fry; **skuq vezë** fry eggs
skúqem vetv. 1. blush, flush; 2. redden
slogán, ~i m. sh. ~e, ~et. slogan
sociál, ~e mb. social; **probleme sociale** social problems

socialíst mb. socialist
sốd/ë, ~a f. soda; **soda kaustike** caustic soda; **sodë rrobash** washing soda
sodít (sodís) kal., ~a, ~ur. contemplate; **sodit bukuritë e natyrës** contemplate the beauties of nature
sodítj/e, ~a f. sh. ~e, ~et. contemplation
soj, ~i m. sh. ~e, ~et. 1. kin, relative; 2. kind, sort
sój/ë, ~a f. sh. ~a, ~at. bot. soya bean, soy bean; **vaj soje** soya oil
solémn, ~e mb. solemn; **premtim solemn** a solemn promise
solíst, ~i m. sh. ~ë, ~ët. soloist
sólo, ~ja f.. sh. ~, ~t. muz.solo; **solo për violinë** a violin solo
sonát/ë, ~a f. sh. ~a, ~at. muz. sonata
sốnte ndajf. tonight
sopráno, ~ja f. sh. ~, ~t. muz. soprano
sot ndajf. today
sốt/ëm (i), ~me (e) mb. 1. today's; **gazeta e sotme** today's paper; 2. present, present-day
sovrán, ~e mb. sovereign; **shtet sovran** a sovereign state
sovranitét, ~i m. sovereignty
spángo, ~ja f. sh. ~, ~t. twine, string
spastr/ój kal., ~óva, ~úar. 1. **fig.** cleanse, purge; 2. clean smth up
spec, ~i m. sh. ~a, ~at bot. pepper; **speca të mbushura me mish e oriz** peppers stuffed with meat and rice
speciál, ~e mb. special; **trajtim special** special treatment
specialíst, ~i m. sh. ~ë, ~ët. expert, specialist
specialitét, ~i m. sh. ~e, ~et. speciality
specializóhem vetv. be (get) specialized
specializ/ój kal., ~óva, ~úar. specialize
specifík, ~e mb. specific
specifikím, ~i m. sh. ~e, ~et. specification
specifik/ój kal., ~óva, ~úar specify
spektatór, ~i m. sh. ~ë, ~ët. 1. spectator; 2. bystander, onlooker
spekul/ój jokal., ~óva, ~úar. 1. speculate; 2. exploit, take advantage of
spërkát (spërkás) kal., ~a, ~ur. 1. sprinkle; 2. spray; 3. splash, spatter
spíker, ~i m. sh. ~, ~ët. speaker
spináq, ~i m. bot. spinach
spín/ë, ~a f. sh. ~a, ~at elektr. plug; **vë spinën në prizë** put the plug in the socket
spiránc/ë, ~a f. sh. ~a, ~at det. anchor; **hedh spirancën** cast anchor
spitál, ~i m. sh. ~e, ~et. hospital; **shtrohem në spital** be admitted (be taken) to hospital
spiún, ~i m. sh. ~ë, ~ët. spy
spiun/ój kal., ~óva, ~úar. spy
spontán, ~e mb spontaneous
spontaнísht ndajf. spontaneously
sport, ~i m. sh. ~e, ~et. sport; **merrem me sport** go in for sport; **më pëlqen sporti** be fond of sport
sportíst, ~i m. sh. ~ë, ~ët. sportsman

sportív, ~e mb. sporty
spraps kal., ~a, ~ur. repulse, repel, drive back, beat back, put (push) back
sprápsem vetv. 1. retreat; 2. flinch from
spróv/ë, ~a f. sh. ~a, ~at. trial, test, trial period, testing period
spróv/ój kal., ~óva, ~úar. try, put through a trial, give a trial
sprovúar (i,e) mb. tried, tested, time-tested, proved
sqarím, ~i m. sh. ~e, ~et. clarification, elucidation
sqar/ój kal., ~óva, ~úar. clarify, elucidate; **sqaroj një problem** elucidate a problem
sqep, ~i m. sh. ~a, ~at. beak, bill
stabilitét, ~i m. stability
stabiliz/ój kal., ~óva, ~úar. stabilize
stación, ~i m. sh. ~e, ~et. station; **stacion autobusësh** a bus station; **stacion i trenit** railway station
stad, ~i m. sh. ~e, ~et phase, stage
stadium, ~i m. sh. ~e, ~et. stadium
stafét/ë, ~a f. sh. ~a, ~at sport. relay, relay race
standárd, ~i m. sh. ~e, ~et. standard; **poshtë standardit** below the standard
standárd, ~e mb. standard
standardiz/ój kal., ~óva, ~úar. standardize
start, ~i m. sh. ~e, ~et sport. start
statík, ~e mb fiz. static
statistík/ë, ~a f. sh. ~a, ~at. statistics
statistikór, ~e mb. statistical
statúj/ë, ~a f. sh. ~a, ~at. statue
statút, ~i m. sh. ~e, ~et. statute
stém/ë, ~a f. sh. ~a, ~at. 1. emblem; 2. badge
steríl, ~e mb mjek. sterile
stetoskóp, ~i m. sh. ~ë, ~ët mjek. stethoscope
stërvít kal., ~a, ~ur. 1. train; 2. exercise, practice
stërvitj/e, ~a f. sh. ~e, ~et. training
stërvítur (i,e) mb. trained; **qën i stërvitur** a trained dog
stil, ~i m. sh. ~e, ~et art. style
stilistík, ~e mb gjuh., let. stylistic; **mjetet stilistike** stylistic means
stímu/l, ~li m. sh. ~j, ~jt incentive, stimulus; **stimul moral (material)** moral (material) incentive
stimul/ój kal., ~óva, ~úar arouse, stimulate
stín/ë, ~a f. sh. ~ë, ~ët. 1. season; 2. period, time; **stina teatrale** the theatre season
stol, ~i m. sh. ~a, ~at. stool
stolí, ~a f. sh. ~, ~të. ornament, trinket
stolís kal., ~a, ~ur. ornament, decorate, adorn, deck
stomák, ~u m. sh. ~ë, ~ët anat. stomach; **çregullim (prishje) të stomakut** a stomach upset (disorder); **dhembje stomaku** stomach-ache
stomatológ, ~u m. sh. ~ë, ~ët mjek. dentist
strategjík, ~e mb usht. strategic
stréh/ë, ~a f. sh. ~ë, ~ët. 1. eaves; 2. edge; visor; 3. shelter; **gjej streh** seek (take) shelter; 4. lodging

strehím, ~i m. sh. ~e, ~et. 1. housing, accommodation;
strehim i përkohshëm temporary accommodation; 2. refuge; 3.
asylum; **strehim politik** political asylum
strehóhem vetv. 1. put up at; 2. take shelter; take refuge
streh/ój kal., ~óva, ~úar. accommodate, lodge, house
struktúr/ë, ~a f. sh. ~a, ~at. structure
strukturór, ~e mb structural
studént, ~i m. sh. ~ë, ~ët. student
studím, ~i m. sh. ~e, ~et. study
stúdio, ~ja f. sh. ~, ~t. studio
studi/ój kal., ~óva, ~úar. study
studiúes, ~i m. sh. ~, ~it. scholar; student; researcher,
research worker
stúf/ë, ~a f. sh. ~a, ~at. stove
stuhí, ~a f. sh. ~, ~të. storm
stuhísh/ëm (i), ~me (e) mb. 1. stormy; **mot i stuhishëm** stormy
weather; 2. **fig.** stormy
subjékt, ~i m. sh. ~e, ~et subject
subjektív, ~e mb subjective
subjektivísht ndajf. subjectively
substánc/ë, ~a f. sh. ~a, ~at. substance
sugjerím, ~i m. sh. ~e, ~et. suggestion
sugjer/ój kal., ~óva, ~úar. suggest
suksés, ~i m. sh. ~e, ~et. success; **arrij suksese** achieve
successes
sukséssh/ëm (i), ~me (e) mb. successful
súl/em vetv. ~a (u), ~ur. rush, dash
sulm, ~i m. sh. ~e, ~et 1. **usht.** attack, assault; 2. **fig.**
onslaught; 3. **sport.** attack
sulm/ój kal., ~óva, ~úar usht. assail, attack, sally
sulmúes, ~i m. sh. ~, ~it. assailant, assaulter; attacker
sundím, ~i m. sh. ~e, ~et. rule, reign
sundimtár, ~i m. sh. ~ë, ~ët. ruler
sund/ój kal., ~óva, ~úar. 1. rule, govern; 2. dominate; 3.
dominate, overlook
sup, ~i m. sh. ~e, ~et. shoulder; **mbledh (ngre, rruth) supet**
shrug one's shoulders
superstruktúr/ë, ~a f. sh. ~a, ~at. superstructure
súp/ë, ~a f. sh. ~a, ~at. soup; **supë pule** chicken soup; **supë
me zarzavate** vegetable soup
suplementár, ~e mb supplementary; **pagesë suplementare** a
supplementary payment
supozím, ~i m. supposition, conjecture, guess, surmise
supoz/ój kal.dhe jokal., ~óva, ~úar. suppose, conjecture,
guess, surmise
suprém, ~e mb. supreme
surpríz/ë, ~a f. sh. ~a, ~at. surprise
súst/ë, ~a f. sh. ~a, ~at. spring
sy, ~ri m. sh. ~, ~të. 1. eye; **bebja e syrit** the pupil of the
eye; **hap (mbyll) sytë** open (close) one's eyes; **mbyll sytë
para** shut (close) one's eyes to smth; **përpara syve të** in the
eyes of smb (in smb's eyes); 2. power of seeing; observation;
kam sy të mprehtë have sharp eyes

syním, ~i m. sh. ~e, ~et. intention, design, intent
syn/ój kal., ~óva, ~úar. intend, aim
syth, ~i m. sh. ~a, ~at. 1. bud; 2. mesh
syze, ~t f. vet. sh. spectacles, glasses

SH

shah, ~u m. 1. chess; **gur shahu** chessman; **fushë shahu** chessboard; luaj shah play chess; 2. check
shahíst, ~i m. sh. ~ë, ~ët. chess-player
sha/j kal., ~va, ~rë. 1. call smb names; 2. scold, chide
shaká, ~ja f. sh. ~, ~të dhe ~ra, ~rat. joke; jest; **bëj shaka** crack jokes
shakatár, ~e mb. jokey, joking
shál/ë, ~a f. sh. ~a, ~at. saddle
shalqí, ~ri m. sh. ~nj, ~njtë bot. water-melon
shall, ~i m. sh. ~e, ~et. shawl; scarf; neckerchief
shamát/ë, ~a f. sh. ~a, ~at. racket, commotion, din, noise
shamí, ~a f. sh. ~, ~të. handkerchief; kerchief; scarf; tie
shampánj/ë, ~a f. champagne
shantázh, ~i m. sh. ~e, ~et. blackmail; **bëj shantazh** blackmail
shápk/ë, ~a f. sh. ~a, ~at. slipper; **një palë shapka** a pair of slippers
shart/ój kal., ~óva, ~úar bujq. graft
shárr/ë, ~a f. sh. ~a, ~at. saw; **sharrë dore** a handsaw
sharr/ój kal., ~óva, ~úar. saw
shastís kal., ~a, ~ur. 1. stun; 2. **fig.** stun, daze, shock
shat, ~i m. sh. ~a, ~at dhe **shát/ë,** ~a f. sh. ~a, ~at. hoe
shatërván, ~i m. sh. ~ë, ~ët. fountain
shef, ~i m. sh. ~a, ~at. chief; **shefi i policisë** a chief of police
shég/ë, ~a f. sh. ~ë, ~ët bot. pomegranate
shéku/ll, ~lli m. sh. ~j, ~jt. century; **shekulli i njëzetë** the 20th century
shel/g, ~gu, m. sh. ~gje, ~gjet bot. willow; **shelg lotues** a weeping willow
shemb kal., ~a, ~ur. 1. demolish, raze, tear down, break down, throw down, pull down; 2. overthrow
shémbj/e, ~a f. sh. ~e, ~et. 1. demolition, tearing down, pulling down, bringing down; 2. downfall
shémbu/ll, ~lli m. sh. ~j, ~jt. example; **për shembull** for example; **e bëj shembull** make an example of smb; **ndjek shembullin e** follow smb's example
shembullór, ~e mb. exemplary, model
shénj/ë, ~a f. sh. ~a, ~at. 1. sign, mark; 2. scar; 3. trace, track; 4. token; 5. omen; 6. cue, gesture, signal; **shenjat e pikësimit** punctuation marks; **shenjat matematike** mathematical signs
shenjt, ~i m. sh. ~ër, ~ërit. saint
shénjt (i,e) mb. holy, sacred; **shkrimet e shenjta** the Holy Scriptures
sheqér, ~i m. sugar; **sheqer pluhur** granulated sugar; **panxhar sheqeri** sugar-beet; **kallam sheqeri** sugar-cane
sheqérk/ë, ~a f. sh. ~a, ~at. sweet, candy
sheríf, ~i m. sh. ~ë, ~ët. sheriff
sherr, ~i m. sh. ~e, ~et. quarrel, squabble, wrangle; **mollë sherri** an apple of discord
shes kalim., shíta, shítur. sell; **shes me pakicë** retail; **shes me shumicë** sell wholesale; **shes në ankand** sell by auction; **shes me humbje** sell at a loss

shesh, ~i m. sh. ~e, ~et. square
sheshít ndajf. openly; evidently
shesh/ój kal., ~óva, ~úar. 1. level; 2. **fig.** smooth over
shéshtë (i,e) mb. level, flat
shëmbëll/éj jokal., ~éva, ~yer. resemble, look like
shëmbëllím, ~i m. sh. ~e, ~et. 1. **resemblance**; 2. image
shëmbëlltyr/ë, ~a f. sh. ~a, ~at. image
shëmtúar (i,e) mb. 1. ugly; **njeri i shëmtuar** an ugly man; 2.
fig. ugly, horrible, hideous
shëndét, ~i m. health; **gëzoj shëndet të mirë** enjoy good
health
shëndetësí, ~a f. public health
shëndetësór, ~e mb. medical, health; **shërbimi shëndetësor**
health service
shëndetlíg, ~ë mb. sickly, unhealthy
shëndétsh/ëm (i), ~me (e) mb. healthy, sound, fit; **klimë e
shëndetshme** healthy climate
shëndósh kal., ~a, ~ur. 1. heal, cure; 2. fatten
shëndóshem vetv. 1. be healed; 2. grow fat; 3. get stronger
shëndósh (i,e) mb. 1. healthy, sound; **mendje e shëndoshë** a
sound mind; 2. fat, plump; 3. strong, stout
shëním, ~i m. sh. ~e, ~et. 1. note; **mbaj shënime** take down
notes; 2. annotation
shën/ój kal., ~óva, ~úar. 1. put down, note down, write down;
2. mark; 3. score
shënúar (i,e) mb. 1. noted, celebrated; 2. marked; 3.
memorable; **ngjarje e shënuar** memorable event
shënúes, ~i m. sh. ~, ~it sport. scorer
shërb/éj jokal., ~éva, ~yer. 1. serve, wait on, minister to;
2. performs the duties of, function as, be of use; **kjo
shërben për** it is used for
shërbëtór, ~i m. sh. ~ë, ~ët. servant
shërbím, ~i m. sh. ~e, ~et. 1. service; **shërbim ushtarak**
military service; 2. duty; **jam me shërbim** be on duty; 3.
favor, service; 4. **sport.** service
shërbyes, ~e mb. 1. service; 2. **gjuh.** functional
shërím, ~i m. recovery, recuperation
shërohem vetv. recover, recuperate
shër/ój kal., ~óva, ~úar. cure, heal
shëtít (shëtís) jokal., ~a, ~ur. walk, amble, saunter,
stroll, promenade
shëtítës, ~e mb. walking, mobile, ambulatory
shëtítj/e, ~a f. sh. ~e, ~et. walk, stroll, saunter,
promenade
shëtitór/e, ~ja f. sh. ~e, ~et. avenue, boulevard
shfaq kal., ~a, ~ur. 1. display, show, exhibit; 2. manifest;
3. perform; 4. express
shfáqem vetv. appear, show up
shfáqj/e, ~a f. sh. ~e, ~et. 1. show, performance; 2.
display, manifestation
shfarós kal., ~a, ~ur. wipe out, exterminate
shflet/ój kal., ~óva, ~úar. thumb, turn over the pages
shfrej jokal., shfréva, shfryer. wreak, unleash
shfrenúar (i,e) mb. unrestrained, unbridled, unchecked

shfryj jokal., **shfryva, shfryrë.** 1. puff, blow, pant; 2. deflate; 3. blow (the nose)
shfrytëzim, ~i m. 1. exploitation; 2. utilization
shfrytëz/ój kal., ~óva, ~úar. make use of, exploit, utilize
shfrytëzúar (i,e) mb. exploited
shfrytëzúes, ~i m. sh. ~, ~it. exploiter
shi, ~u m. sh. ~ra, ~rat. rain; **bie shi** it rains; **pika shiu** raindrop; **stina e shirave** the rains
shíf/ër, ~ra f. sh. ~ra, ~rat. cipher
shigjét/ë, ~a f. sh. ~a, ~at. arrow
shíhem vetv. 1. meet; 2. look at; 3. be examined (by a doctor); 4. be seen; 5. look like, seem
shíj/e, ~a f. sh. ~e, ~et. 1. taste, flavor, savor; 2. relish; **ha me shije të madhe** eat with great relish; 3. liking, taste
shij/ój kal., ~óva, ~úar. 1. taste, savor; 2. relish, enjoy; 3. **fig.** appreciate, enjoy
shíjsh/ëm (i), ~me (e) mb. tasty, savory, delicious
shikím, ~i m. sh. ~e, ~et. look, gaze, glance, stare
shikóhem vetv. 1. meet; 2. look at
shik/ój kal., ~óva, ~úar. 1. see, look; 2. notice, observe; 3. look upon, examine; 4. watch, view; 5. consider, think; 6. look after, watch over
shikúes, ~i m. sh. ~, ~it. seer, observer, onlooker; watcher, viewer, spectator
shilárës, ~i m. sh. ~, ~it. see-saw, swing
shiríng/ë, ~a f. sh. ~a, ~at. mjek. syringe
shirít, ~i m. sh. ~a, ~at. 1. ribbon, band, strip; 2. tape
shísh/e, ~ja f. sh. ~e, ~et. bottle
shítës, ~i m. sh. ~, ~it. seller, salesman; vendor, peddler
shítës/e, ~ja, f. sh. ~e, ~et. salewoman, salesgirl, shopgirl, saleslady
shitj/e, ~ f. sh. ~, ~et. sale, selling; **vë (nxjerr) në shitje** put up for sale
shkáb/ë, ~a f. sh. ~a, ~at zool. eagle
shka/k, ~ku m. sh. ~qe, ~qet. cause, motive, reason; **nga shkaku i** because of
shkaktár, ~i m. sh. ~ë, ~ët. cause
shkakt/ój kal., ~óva, ~úar. 1. cause, effect, bring about, produce; 2. inflict
shkáll/ë, ~a f. sh. ~ë, ~ët. 1. staircase, stairway; 2. stair, step; 3. ladder; 4. scale
shkállë-shkállë ndajf. gradually, by degrees, step by step
shkallëzim, ~i m. sh. ~e, ~et. 1. gradation; 2. escalation
shkallëz/oj kal., ~óva, ~úar. 1. graduate; 2. scale; 3. escalate
shkallm/ój kal., ~óva, ~úar. 1. break; 2. crush, smash
shkárazi dhe **shkáras** ndajf. cursorily
shkárj/e, ~a f. sh. slide; **shkarje e tokës** a landslide
shkarkím, ~i m. sh. ~e, ~et. 1. unloading; 2. dismissal; 3. discharge
shkark/ój kal., ~óva, ~úar. 1. unload, unlade, unburden; 2. dicharge; 3. disencumber
shkas, ~i m. sh. ~e, ~et. grounds, cause, reason
shka/s jokal., ~va, ~rë. slip, glide, slide

shkatërrim, ~i m. sh. ~e, ~et. demolition, devastation, ruin, destruction

shkatërr/ój kal., ~óva, ~úar. ruin, demolish, destroy

shkatërrues, ~e mb. destructive, ruinous

shkáthët (i,e) mb. deft, adroit, dexterous, skillful

shkathtësí, ~a f. dexterity, agility, deftness, adroitness

shkel kal., ~a, ~ur. 1. step; 2. crush; 3. press (the button); 4. violate, break

shkélës, ~i m. sh. ~, ~it. violator, transgressor, breaker, offender

shkélj/e, ~a f. sh. ~e, ~et. 1. violation, transgression, infringement; 2. breach

shkelm, ~i m. sh. ~e, ~et. kick

shkelm/ój kal., ~óva, ~úar. kick

shkénc/ë, ~a f. sh. ~a, ~at. science

shkencërísht ndajf. scientifically

shkencëtár, ~i m. sh. ~ë, ~ët. scientist

shkencór, ~e mb. scientific

shkëlq/éj jokal., ~éva, ~yer. 1. shine, glitter, glow, sparkle; 2. brighten; 3. polish

shkëlqím, ~i m. sh. ~e, ~et. 1. glitter, shining, sparkling, glow, radiance; 2. splendor

shkëlqyer (i,e) mb. 1. bright, brilliant; **nxënës i shkëlqyer** a brilliant pupil; 2. shining

shkëlqyéshëm ndajf. perfectly; brilliantly

shkëmb, ~i m. sh. ~ínj, ~ínjtë. rock, boulder

shkëmb/éj kal., ~éva, ~yer. exchange, swap, substitute

shkëmbím, ~i m. sh. ~e, ~et. exchange, swap, substitution; **në shkëmbim të** in exchange for

shkëmbór, ~e mb. rocky

shkëndíj/ë, ~a f. sh. ~a, ~at. spark

shkëpút (shkëpús) kal., ~a, ~ur. 1. detach, disconnect, uncouple, disjoin, unfasten; 2. disassociate

shkëpútur (i,e) mb. detached, separated

shkoj jokal., shkóva, shkúar. 1. go; **shkoj në shkollë** go to school; 2. fare, get on, progress; 3. elapse, pass; 4. function, operate, work; 5. harmonize, go together

shkóll/ë, ~a f. sh. ~a, ~at. school; **shkollë fillore** primary school; **shkollë e mesme** secondary school; **shkollë profesionale** vocational school; **shkollë e lartë** high school; **ndjek shkollën** attend school

shkoll/ój kal., ~óva, ~úar. school; give education (schooling) to

shkollór, ~e mb. school; **viti shkollor** school year; **mosha shkollore** school age

shkop, ~i m. sh. ~ínj, ~ínjtë. stick, cane, staff

shkopsít (shkopsís) kal., ~a, ~ur. unbutton; **shkopsit xhaketën** unbutton one's jacket

shkoqít (shkoqís) kal., ~a, ~ur. explain, clear up

shkrétë (i,e) mb. 1. desolate, deserted; 2. barren, bleak, bare; 3. poor; **i shkreti djalë!** poor boy!

shkretëtír/ë, ~a f. sh. ~a, ~at. desert

shkret/ój kal., ~óva, ~úar. devastate, desolate, ruin

shkri/j kal., ~va, ~rë. 1. melt, dissolve, thaw; 2. fuse, merge; 3. **fig.** melt

shkrim, ~i m. sh. ~e, ~et. writing; **letër shkrimi** writing paper; **me shkrim** in writing

shkrimtár, ~i m. sh. ~ë, ~ët. writer

shkrírë (i,e) mb. melted, molten

shkrónj/ë, ~a f. sh. ~a, ~at. letter, character

shkr/úaj kal., ~óva, ~úar. write

shkrúar (i,e) mb. written; **fjalë e shkruar** written word

shkrúes, ~i m. sh. ~, ~it. writer; **shkruesi i letrës** the writer of the letter

shkúar, ~a (e) f. sh. ~a, ~at (të). 1. past; **të shkuara të harruara** let bygones be bygones; 2. past tense

shkúar (i,e) mb. past, gone; **në kohët e shkuara** in times past

shkujdésj/e, ~a f. sh. ~e, ~et. carelessness

shkujdésur (i,e) mb. care-free, free and easy **shkul kal., ~a, ~ur.** 1. uproot, pull out by the roots, root out; 2. extract; 3. unearth, dig up; 4. dislodge, displace

shkúm/ë, ~a f. sh. ~a, ~at. lather, froth, foam, spume

shkúmës, ~i m. sh. ~a, ~at. chalk

shkund kal., ~a, ~ur. shake; shake out

shkurt, ~i m February **shkurt ndajf.** shortly, briefly

shkúrtër (i,e) mb. short

shkurtimísht ndajf. shortly, briefly

shkurt/ój kal., ~óva, ~úar. 1. shorten; 2. cut short; 3. reduce, cut down; 4. abridge; 5. abbreviate

shlyej kal., shléva, shlyer. 1. efface, rub out, erase; 2. pay off, square, clear, settle, liquidate; 3. expiate (one's sin, guilt etc.)

shmang kal., ~a, ~ur. 1. deviate, stray; 2. avoid, evade, dodge, avert, elude

shmángem vetv. shun, avoid, shirk

shmángi/e, ~a f. sh. ~e, ~et. 1. avoidance, elusion, evasion, dodging, shunning; 2. deviation, digression

shndërrim, ~i m. sh. ~e, ~et. transformation

shndërrohem vetv. be transformed

shndërr/ój kal., ~óva, ~úar. transform

shndrit (shndris) jokal., ~a, ~ur. shine; glitter

shndrítsh/ëm (i), ~me (e) shiny, bright, glittering, gleaming

shofér, ~i m. sh. ~ë, ~ët. driver; shofer autobusi busdriver; **shofer taksie** taxi-driver, cabdriver, cabman; **shofer kamioni** truck driver

shoh kal., páshë, párë. 1. see, behold, notice, observe; 2. examine; 3. regard; 4. see, consult (a doctor); 5. meet smb

shok, ~u m. sh. ~ë, ~ët. fellow, companion, comrade, friend; **shok i ngushtë** a close friend

shoq, ~i m. husband

shoqát/ë, ~a f. sh. ~a, ~at. association

shoqërí, ~a f. sh. ~, ~të. 1. society, community; 2. company, firm; 3. company, fellowship, companionship

shoqërísht ndajf. socially

shoqër/ój kal., ~óva, ~úar. accompany, escort, keep (bear) company

shoqëror, ~e mb. social; **rend (sistem) shoqëror** social order (system); **probleme shoqërore** social problems
shoqërúar (i,e) mb. sociable
shoqërúes, ~i m. sh. ~, ~it. attendant; escort
shoqërúes, ~e mb. attendant, accompanying
shoqërúesh/ëm (i), ~me (e) mb. sociable
short, ~i m. lot; **hedh short** draw lots
shósh/ë, ~a f. sh. ~a, ~at. screen, sieve
shoviníst, ~e mb. chauvinistic, chauvinist
shoviníz/ëm, ~mi m. chauvinism
shpagím, ~i m. sh. ~e, ~et. revenge, vengeance, retaliation
shpag/úaj kal., ~óva, ~úar. avenge, revenge
shpalós kal., ~a, ~ur. 1. unfold, unfurl, unroll; 2. spread out
shpall kal., ~a, ~ur. announce, declare, proclaim, publish, promulgate
shpállj/e, ~a f. sh. ~e, ~et. announcement, declaration, proclamation
shpartall/ój kal., ~óva, ~úar. defeat, rout
shpat, ~i m. sh. ~e, ~et. slope
shpát/ë, ~a f. sh. ~a, ~at. sword, scimitar, saber
shpátull/, ~a f. sh. ~a, ~at. shoulder
shpejt ndajf. 1. quickly, swiftly, speedily, rapidly, fast; 2. immediately, instantaneously
shpéjtë (i,e) mb. quick, fast, rapid, swift.
shpejtësí, ~a f. sh. ~, ~të. speed, quickness, rapidity, swiftness, velocity; **me shpejtësi prej** at a speed of
shpejt/ój kal., ~óva, ~úar. hasten, speed up, accelerate
shpejtúar (i,e) mb. hasty, hurried
shpend, ~i m. sh. ~ë, ~ët. zool. fowl
shpenzím, ~i m. sh. ~e, ~et. expenditure, expense; **shpenzime udhëtimi** traveling expenses; **përballoj shpenzimet** meet the expenses; **ul shpenzimet** reduce the expenses
shpenz/ój kal., ~óva, ~úar. spend, expend, disburse; **shpenzoi gjithë paratë** spent all his money
shpesh ndajf. often, frequently
shpeshhérë ndajf. often; now and again, time and again
shpéshtë (i,e) mb. 1. frequent; 2. dense
shpeshtësí, ~a f. frequency
shpëlá/j kal., ~va, ~rë. rinse; **shpëlaj duart** rinse one's hands
shpërbl/éj kal., ~éva, ~yer. reward, remunerate
shpërbë/j kal., ~ra, ~rë. break up, disintegrate
shpërbl/éj kal., ~éva, ~yer. reward, remunerate
shpërblím, ~i m. sh. ~e, ~et. reward, remuneration
shpërdor/ój kal., ~óva, ~úar. misuse, abuse, ill-use, wrong
shpërndá/j kal., ~va, ~rë. 1. disperse, break up, disband, scatter; 2. dispel, dissipate; 3. distribute
shpërndárë (i,e) mb. 1. scattered; 2. distracted
shpërndárj/e, ~a f. sh. ~e, ~et. 1. distribution; 2. dispersion, dissipation; 3. dissolution
shpërth/éj kal., ~éva, ~úar. 1. break down; **shpërthej derën** break the door down; 2. break into; 3. break out, burst; 4. explode; 5. erupt

shpëtím, ~i m. 1. rescue, salvation; **gomë shpëtimi** lifebelt, lifebuoy; **barkë shpëtimi** lifeboat; 2. salvage
shpëtimtár, i m. sh. ~ë, ~ët. saver, rescuer, deliverer
shpët/ój kal., ~óva, ~úar. save, deliver, rescue
shpíe kal., **shpúra**, **shpënë**. 1. carry, bear, convey; 2. lead to
shpif kal., ~a, ~ur. slander, culminate, libel
shpífës, ~i m. sh. ~, ~it. slanderer
shpífj/e, ~a f. sh. ~e, ~et. slander, calumny, libel
shpi/j kal., ~va, ~rë. loosen up, relax, stretch one's limbs
shpik kal., ~a, ~ur. 1. invent, contrive; 2. concoct, fabricate, make up
shpíkës, ~i m. sh. ~, ~it. inventor
shpíkj/e, ~a f. sh. ~e, ~et. invention
shpín/ë, ~a f. sh. ~a, ~at. 1. anat. back; 2. back; **shpina e dorës** the back of one's hand
shpirt, ~i m. sh. ~ra, ~rat. spirit; soul
shpirtërór, ~e mb. spiritual
shpirtkéq, ~e mb. malevolent
shpirtmírë mb. benevolent, good-hearted
shpjegím, ~i m. sh. ~e, ~et. explanation
shpjeg/ój., ~óva, ~úar. explain; **shpjegoj kuptimin e fjalëve** explain the meaning of words
shpjegúes mb. explanatory; **shënime shpjeguese** explanatory notes
shpleks kal., ~a, ~ur. unravel, unsnarl, untangle
shpóhem vetv. prick oneself
shp/ój kal., ~óva, ~úar. 1. pierce; 2. bore, drill; 3. pick
shpopull/ój kal., ~óva, ~úar. depopulate
shpórt/ë, ~a f. sh. ~a, ~at. basket
shpreh kal., ~a, ~ur. express, utter, voice; **shpreh ndjenjat** express one's feelings
shpréhës, ~e mb. expressive
shprehí, ~a f. sh. ~, ~të. habit
shpréhj/e, ~a f. sh. ~e, ~et. 1. expression, utterance; 2. gjuh. expression, phrase, idiom
shprés/ë, ~a f. sh. ~a, ~at. hope, expectation; **me shpresë se** in the hope of smth; **kam shpresë** have a hope of doing smth
shpres/ój kal., ~óva, ~úar. hope, expect
shprétk/ë, ~a f. sh. ~a, ~at. anat. spleen
shpronës/ój kal., ~óva, ~úar. expropriate
shpyllëzím, ~i m. sh. ~e, ~et. deforestation
shpyllëz/ój kal., ~óva, ~úar. deforest, disafforest
shqetësím, ~i m. sh. ~e, ~et. 1. trouble, annoyance; 2. concern, worry; 3. uneasiness
shqetësóhem vetv. trouble about, worry oneself about
shqetës/ój kal., ~óva, ~úar. trouble, disturb, worry smb
shqetësúar (i,e) mb. troubled, worried, disturbed
shqetësúes, ~e mb. worrisome, troublesome
shqip, ~e mb. Albanian; **gjuha shqipe** the Albanian language; **flas shqip** speak Albanian
shqipër/ój kal., ~óva, ~úar. render (translate) into Albanian
shqipónj/ë, ~a f. sh. ~a, ~at. zool. eagle
shqiptár, ~i m. sh. ~ë, ~ët. Albanian

shqiptár *mb.* Albanian; **populli shqiptar** the Albanian people
shqiptím, ~i *m. sh.* ~e, ~et. pronunciation
shqipt/ój *kal.*, ~óva, ~úar. pronounce
shqís/ë, ~a *f. sh.* ~a, ~at. sense; **pesë shqisat** the five senses
shqit (shqis) *kal.*, ~a, ~ur. 1. detach, uncouple, disjoin; 2. disassociate
shqítem *vetv.* 1. come off; 2. tear oneself from
shqúaj *kal.*, ~shqóva, shqúar. 1. distinguish, discern, notice; 2. characterize
shqúar (i,e) *mb.* noted, celebrated, renowned, distinguished, illustrious, remarkable
shqúes, ~e *mb.* characteristic; **tiparet shquese** characteristic features
shqúhem *vetv.* 1. be discerned (distinguished); 2. distinguish oneself
shqyrtím, ~i *m. sh.* ~e, ~et. examination
shqyrt/ój *kal.*, ~óva, ~úar. examine
shtang *jokal.*, ~a, ~ur. stun, daze, petrify
shtángem *vetv.* get stunned, get petrified
shtat, ~i. *m.* stature, height
shtátë *num. them.* seven
shtatëdhjétë *num. them.* seventy
shtatëmbëdhjétë *num. them.* seventeen
shtatëqínd *num. them.* seven hundred
shtatór, ~i. September
shtatzënë *mb.* pregnant
shtazarák, ~e *mb.* bestial, beastly, brutish
shtáz/ë, ~a *f. sh.* ~ë, ~ët. beast; animal
shtegtár, ~e *mb.* migrant, migratory; **zog shtegëtar** migratory bird
shtegt/ój *kal.*, ~óva, ~úar. migrate
shter *jokal.*, ~a, ~ur. dry up, run dry
shtéret *vetv.* dry up, run dry
shterp, ~ë *mb.* 1. barren, infertile, sterile; 2. arid, unproductive
shtet, ~i *m. sh.* ~e, ~et. state
shtétas, ~i *m. sh.* ~, ~it. citizen
shtetërór, ~e *mb.* state; national
shtetëzím, ~i *m. sh.* ~e, ~et. nationalization
shtetëz/ój *kal.*, ~óva, ~úar. nationalize
shtën/ë, ~a (e) *f. sh.* ~a, ~at. shot
shtëpí, ~a *f. sh.* ~, ~të. house, home; **në shtëpi** at home
shtëpiák, ~e *mb.* domestic, household; **kafshë shtëpiake** domestic animals
shtíe *kal.*, ~shtíva, ~shtënë. 1. pour; 2. put
shtír/em *vetv.*, ~a (u), ~ur. feign
shtjell/ój *kal.*, ~óva, ~úar. expand, develop, enlarge on, expound (on, upon)
sht/ój *kal.*, ~óva, ~úar. 1. increase, augment, enlarge, expand; 2. raise, elevate; 3. add
shtojc/ë, ~a *f. sh.* ~a, ~at. 1. appendix; 2. supplement; 3. extension
shtrat, ~i *m. sh.* ~shtrétër, ~shtretërit. bed
shtrémbër (i,e) *mb.* 1. crooked; 2. **fig.** wrong, unjust; 3. deformed, distorted
shtrémbër *ndajf.* awry, askew; **shikoj shtrembër** look askew

shtrénjtë (i,e) mb. 1. dear, costly, expensive; 2. dear, sweet

shtrénjtë ndajf. dearly, expensively; **paguaj shtrenjtë për** pay dearly for

shtrés/ë, ~a f. sh. ~a, ~at. 1. layer; 2. stratum

shtrëngát/ë, ~a f. sh. ~a, ~at. gale, hurricane, storm

shtrëngës/ë, ~a f. sh. ~a, ~at. constraint

shtrëng/ój kal., ~óva, ~úar. 1. tighten; 2. shake, clasp; 3. force, constrain, compel

shtrëngúar (i,e) mb. 1. tight; 2. tight-fisted; 3. clenched; 4. constrained

shtrëngúes, ~e mb. coercive; **metoda (masa) shtrënguese** coercive methods (measures)

shtríhem vetv. 1. lie; 2. lie, extend, be situated

shtri/j kal., ~va, ~rë. 1. lay, lay down; 2. extend, expand, stretch

shtróhem vetv. get down to

shtr/ój kal., ~óva, ~úar. 1. lay; **shtroj tavolinën** lay the table; **shtroj qilimin** lay the carpet; 2. lay, cover, coat; 3. pave; **shtroj rrugën** pave the path; 4. lay smth down; 5. put forward (for discussion)

shtruar ndajf. easy; **merre shtruar** take it easy

shtrydh kal., ~a, ~ur. press, squeeze; **shtrydh ullinjtë** press olives; **shtrydh rrushin** press grapes

shtún/ë, ~a f. sh. ~a, ~at (të). Saturday; **të shtunën** on Saturday

shty/j kal., ~va, ~rë. 1. push; 2. put off, postpone; 3. shove, jostle; 4. urge, incite, instigate

shtyll/ë, ~a f. sh. ~a, ~at. 1. pillar, column, colonnade, post; 2. **fig.** backbone

shtyp, ~i m. 1. press; 2. newspapers; **konferencë shtypi** press conference

shtyp kal., ~a, ~ur. 1. crush, squash; 2. quell, put down; **shtyp një kryengritje** quell (put down) a revolt; 3. press; **shtyp sustën** press the button; 4. oppress, suppress, repress, subdue; **shtyp popullin** oppress the people; 5. print; type

shtypës, ~e mb. oppressive

shtypshkrím, ~i m. sh. ~e, ~et. printing

shtypur (i,e) mb. 1. pressed, crushed, squashed; 2. oppressed

shtyrj/e, ~a f. sh. ~e, ~et. 1. push, shove; 2. postponement; 3. incitement, instigation

shuaj kal., ~shóva, ~shúar. 1. put off; 2. put out, extinguish; 3. blow out; 4. quench; **shuaj etjen** quench the thirst; 5. erase, efface

shumánsh/ëm (i), ~me (e) mb. many-sided, multi-faceted

shúm/ë, ~a f. sh. ~a, ~at. sum

shúmë pakuf. many; much; very; very much; **faleminderit shumë** thank you very much

shumëfishím, ~i m. sh. ~e, ~et. multiplication

shumëfish/ój kal., ~óva, ~úar. multiply

shumëllójsh/ëm (i), ~me (e) mb. varied, diverse, multifarious

shumllojshmërí, ~a f. variety, diversity

shumëngjyrësh, ~e mb. multicolored

shúmës mb. gjuh. plural

shumëzím, ~i m. sh. ~e, ~et. mat. multiplication

shumëz/ój kal., ~**óva,** ~**úar.** multiply
shumíc/ë, ~**a f. sh.** ~**a,** ~**at.** 1. multitude; 2. abundance, plenty; 3. majority
shúmtë (i,e) mb. numerous, abundant
shuplák/ë, ~**a f. sh.** ~**a,** ~**at.** 1. palm; 2. slap
shurdh, ~**e mb.** deaf
shurúp, ~**i m. sh.** ~**e,** ~**et.** syrup

tabaká, ~ja f. sh. ~, ~të. tray; **tabaka çaji** tea-tray
tabél/ë, ~a f. sh. ~a, ~at. 1. table; **tabela e shumëzimit**
multiplication table; 2. board; 3. target
tabló, ~ja f. sh. ~, ~të. 1. painting, picture; 2. tableau
takím, ~i m. sh. ~e, ~et. meeting, appointment, date; **lë
takim me** make (fix) an appoinment with smb; **kam takim me** have
an appoinment with smb
takóhem vetv. meet, encounter
tak/ój kal., ~óva, ~úar. 1. meet, encounter, come upon, come
across; 2. 'run into'; 3. happen
taksapagúes, ~i m. sh. ~, ~it. taxpayer
táks/ë, ~a f. sh. ~a, ~at. tax, duty; **taksë doganore** custom
duty; **taksë mbi të ardhurat** income tax
taksí, ~a m. sh. ~, ~të. taxi, taxi-cab, cab; **marr një taksi**
take a taxi
taksój kal., ~óva, ~úar. tax, impose a tax on smb (smth)
takt, ~i m. tact
taktík, ~e mb. tactical; **gabim taktik** a tactical error;
lëvizje taktike a tactical move
taktík/ë, ~a f. sh. ~a, ~at. tactic; tactics
talént, ~i m. sh. ~e, ~et. talent, gift; **talent për muzikë**
talent for music
talentúar (i,e) mb. talented, gifted; **piktor i talentuar** a
talented painter
tall kal., ~a, ~ur. make fun of, deride, scoff at, mock,
jeer, ridicule
tállem vetv. make sport of, laugh at, make a fool out of
tállj/e, ~a f. sh. ~e, ~et. ridicule, mockery, kidding,
teasing
tamám ndajf. exactly, precisely, accurately
tángo, ~ja f. sh. ~, ~t. tango; **kërcej tango** dance the tango
taní ndajf. now, at present, at this time; **deri tani** up to
now; **tani për tani** for the time being
taním/ëm (i), ~me (e) mb. present, actual; **koha e tanishme**
present tense
táp/ë, ~a f. sh. ~a, ~at. cork; **heq tapën** draw the cork
tárg/ë, ~a f. sh. ~a, ~at. number-plate, license plate
taríf/ë, ~a f. sh. ~a, ~at. tariff
tas, ~i m. sh. ~e, ~et. bowl
tashmë ndajf. now, already
tashtí ndajf. now
tatím, ~i m. sh. ~e, ~et. tax, duty
taván, ~i m. sh. ~e, ~et. ceiling
tavolín/ë, ~a f. sh. ~a, ~at. table; desk; **shtoj tavolinën**
lay the table; **ngre tavolinën** clear the table
táze mb. bised. fresh
te dhe **tek ndajf.** at; to
teát/ër, ~ri m. sh. ~ra, ~rat dhe ~ro, ~rot. theater; **teatër
veror** an open-air theater
tejdúksh/ëm (i), ~me (e) mb. transparent
tejkal/ój kal., ~óva, ~úar. overfulfil
tek, ~e mb. odd, uneven; **numër tek** odd number

teknik, ~u m. sh. ~ë, ~ët. technician
teknik, ~e mb. technical; **shkollë teknike** a technical school; **term teknik** a technical term
teknik/ë, ~a f. technique
teknikísht ndajf. technically
teknologjí, ~a f. technology; **teknologji e avancuar** an advanced technology
teknologjík, ~e mb. technological
teksá lidh. while; as
tekst, ~i m. sh. ~e, ~et. 1. text; 2. textbook
tekstíl, ~e mb. textile; **industria tekstile** the textile industry
tel, ~i m. sh. ~a, ~at. 1. wire; 2. **muz.** chord, string
telefón, ~i m. sh. ~a, ~at. telephone, phone; **libër telefoni** telephone book, telephone directory; **numër telefoni** phone number
telefon/ój kal., ~óva, ~úar. ring up, call up, phone, telephone
telegráf, ~i m. sh. ~ë, ~ët. telegraph
telegrám, ~i m. sh. ~a, ~at. telegram; **telegram urimi** a telegram of congratulations
telekomunikacíon, ~i m. sh. ~e, ~et. telecommunication
teleskóp, ~i m. sh. ~ë, ~ët. telescope
televizión, ~i m. television, TV
televizór, ~i m. sh. ~ë, ~ët. television, television set; **televizor bardh e zi (me ngjyra)** a black-and-white (color) television
tém/ë, ~a f. sh. ~a, ~at. topic, subject, theme, point
temp, ~i m. sh. ~e, ~et. rhythm
temperamént, ~i m. sh. ~e, ~et. temperament; **njeri me temperament** a man with temperament
temperatúr/ë, ~a f. sh. ~a, ~at. temperature; **kam temperaturë** have (run) a temperature
témpu/ll, ~lli m. sh. ~j, ~jt. temple
tendénc/ë, ~a f. sh. ~a, ~at. tendency, trend
tendecióz, ~e mb. tendentious
ténd/ë, ~a f. sh. ~a, ~at. tent
tenís, ~i m. **sport.** tennis; **fushë tenisi** tennis court
tenór, ~i m. sh. ~ë, ~ët. **muz.** tenor
tensión, ~i m. sh. ~e, ~et. tension
tenxhér/e, ~ja f. sh. ~e, ~et. casserole; pressure-cooker; saucepan
teorí, ~a f. sh. ~, ~të. theory
teorík, ~e mb. theoretical
teorikísht ndajf. theoretically
tépër. ndajf. 1. too, too much; 2. so much; 3. much more
tépërt (i,e) mb. superfluous, excessive, extra
term, ~i m. sh. ~a, ~at. term; **term shkencor (teknik)** scientific (technical) term
terror, ~i m. terror
terroríst, ~i m. sh. ~ë, ~ët. terrorist
terroríst, ~e mb. terrorist
tétë num. them. eight
tetëdhjétë num. them. eighty
tetëmbëdhjétë num. them. eighteen
tetëqínd num. them. eight hundred
tetór, ~i m. October

tërbúar (i,e) mb. furious, enraged, raging, infuriated
tërësísht ndajf. wholly, entirely, completely, totally, fully; as a whole, all in all
tërësór, ~e mb. thorough, entire, complete
tërfíl, ~i m. bot. clover
tër/heq kal., ~hóqa, ~héqur. 1. pull; 2. attract; 3. draw, draught, haul; 4. drag, lug; 5. inhale; 6. retreat; 7 extract
tërhíqem vetv. 1. withdraw, draw back; 2. retreat
tërmét, ~i m. sh. ~e, ~et. earthquake
tërshër/ë, ~a f. sh. ~a, ~at. bot. oat
tërthórazi dhe tërthóras ndajf. indirectly, in a roundabout way
tifóz, ~i m. sh. ~ë, ~ët. fan
tigán, ~i m. sh. ~ë, ~ët. pan, frying-pan
tig/ër, ~ri m. sh. ~ra, ~rat. zool. tiger
tij (i,e) pron. sh. tij (e, të) his
tíllë (i,e) dëft. such, like
tim, ~e përem. pron. my
timón, ~i m. sh. ~ë, ~ët. helm; steering-wheel; handle-bar
tingëllím, ~i m. sh. ~e, ~et. ring
tingëll/ón jokal., ~ói, ~úar. sound, ring
tíngu/ll, ~lli m. sh. ~j, ~jt. sound, ring
tip, ~i m. sh. ~a, ~at. type
tipár, ~i m. sh. ~e, ~et. feature
tipík, ~e mb. typical; **shembull tipik** a typical example; **gabime tipike** typical mistakes
títu/ll, ~lli m. sh. ~j, ~jt. title
tjégull, ~a f. sh. ~a, ~at. tile
tjétër pakuf. sh. tjérë (të), tjéra (të). 1. other, another; 2. next
tmerr, ~i m. sh. ~e, ~et. horror
tmérrsh/ëm (i), ~me (e) mb. horrible, terrible, horrifying, horrid
to/g, ~gu m. sh. ~gje, ~gjet. heap, pile, mass
tók/ë, ~a f. sh. ~a, ~at. 1. earth; 2. land, soil; 3. ground
ton, ~i m. sh. ~e, ~et. 1. tone; 2. **muz.** tone
top, ~i m. sh. ~a, ~at 1. **usht.** cannon; 2. ball; **top futbolli** football; 3. roll
tórno, ~ja f. sh. ~, ~t tek. lathe
tortúr/ë, ~a f. sh. ~a, ~at. torture
tortur/ój kal., ~óva, ~úar. torture
totál, ~e mb. total; **shuma totale** total sum
tradicionál, ~e mb. traditional; **veshje tradicionale** traditional costumes
tradít/ë, ~a f. sh. ~a, ~at. tradition
tradhtár, ~e mb. treacherous, traitorous
tradhtí, ~a f. treason, betrayal, treachery
tradht/ój kal., ~óva, ~úar. betray
trafík, ~u m. traffic
tragjedí, ~a f. sh. ~, ~të. 1. **let.** tragedy; 2. **fig.** tragedy
tragjík, ~e mb. 1. **let.** tragic; 2. tragic; **aksident tragjik** a tragic accident
trájt/ë, ~a f. sh. ~a, ~at. 1. shape; 2. **gjuh.** form
trajt/ój kal., ~óva, ~úar. 1. treat, deal with, handle; 2. attend, doctor, medicate

traktór, ~i m. sh. ~ë, ~ët. tractor
trángu/ll, ~lli m. sh. ~j, ~jt bot. cucumber
transistór, ~i m. sh. ~ë, ~ët fiz., elektr. transistor
transít, ~i m. sh. ~e, ~et. transit
transmet/ój kal., ~óva, ~úar 1. broadcast, transmit; 2. tek.
transmit
transpórt, ~i m. sh. ~e, ~et. transport, transportation;
transporti tokësor road transport
transport/ój kal., ~óva, ~úar. transport, carry, convey
tráshë (i,e) mb. 1. thick; 2. dull, dull-witted, thick-
witted, fat- witted
trashëgím, ~i m. sh. ~e, ~et. inheritance, heritage
trashëgimtár, ~i m. sh. ~ë, ~ët. heir, inheritor
trashëg/ój kal., ~óva, ~úar. inherit, be willed, be
bequeathed, become heir to
traz/ój kal., ~óva, ~úar. 1. stir, mix; 2. poke (the fire);
3. tease
tre/g, ~gu m. sh. ~gje, ~gjet. market; tregu i lirë free
market; tregu i zi black market
tregím, ~i m. sh. ~e, ~et. 1. story, narrative; 2. narration
tregimtár, ~i m. sh. ~ë, ~ët. narrator
tregimtár, ~e mb. narrative
tregóhem vetv. show oneself to be
treg/ój kal., ~óva, ~úar. 1. tell, narrate; 2. show,
indicate; 3. display, exhibit
tregtár, ~i m. sh. ~ë, ~ët. trader, businessman, dealer,
merchant, salesman
tregtár, ~e mb. commercial, business, mercantile, sales,
trade
tregtí, ~a f. trade, commerce
tregt/ój kal. dhe jokal., ~óva, ~úar. trade
tregúes, ~i m. sh. ~, ~it. index
tregúes, ~e mb. index; gishti tregues index finger
trekëndësh, ~i m. sh. ~a, ~at. gjeom. triangle
tremb kal., ~a, ~ur. frighten, scare
trembëdhjétë num. them. thirteen
tren, ~i m. sh. ~a, ~at. train; tren udhëtarësh (mallrash)
passenger (goods, freight) train; tren ekspres express train
treqínd num. them. three hundred
tret (tres) kal., ~a, ~ur. 1. melt, dissolve, thaw; 2. digest
trëndafíl, ~i m. sh. ~a, ~at. bot. rose
trill/ój kal., ~óva, ~úar. invent, concoct
trim, ~i m. sh. ~a, ~at. brave man
trim, ~e mb. brave, courageous, valiant
trimërí, ~a f. sh. ~, ~të. bravery, valour
trimërísht ndajf. bravely, valiantly
triúmf, ~i m. triumph
triumf/ój jokal., ~óva, ~úar. triumph
trok/ás jokal., ~íta, ~ítur. knock
trokítj/e, ~a f. sh. ~e, ~et. knock
trondít kal., ~a, ~ur. 1. shake; 2. shake smb up, shock
tropikál, ~e mb. tropical; klimë tropikale a tropical climate
tru, ~ri m. sh. ~, ~të anat. brain; me tru brainy; pa tru
brainless
trun/g, ~gu m. sh. ~gje, ~gjet. trunk
trup, ~i m. sh. ~a, ~at fiz. 1. body; 2. corps

tryéz/ë, ~a f. sh. ~a, ~at. 1. table; 2. desk
trysní, ~a fiz. pressure; **trysnia e gjakut** blood pressure
tu (e) pron. your
túll/ë, ~a f. sh. ~a, ~at. brick
túf/ë, ~a f. sh. ~, ~at. bunch
tumór, ~i m. sh. ~e, ~et. tumor
tund kal., ~a, ~ur. 1. shake; 2. rock; 3. churn
tunél, ~i m. sh. ~e, ~et. tunnel
túrbullt (i,e) mb. 1. turbid, muddy; 2. **fig.** turbid
turíst, ~i m. sh. ~ë, ~ët. tourist
túrm/ë, ~a f. sh. ~a, ~at. crowd, mob
turp, ~i m. sh. ~e, ~et. shame
túrpsh/ëm (i), ~me (e) **mb.** 1. timid, bashful, shy; 2. shameful
túrr/ë, ~a f. sh. ~a, ~at. pile, heap
tútje ndajf. far away; farther
tym, ~i m. sh. ra, rat. smoke

TH

tháhem vetv. 1. dry, dry up; 2. run dry, go dry
tha/j kal., ~va, ~rë. 1. dry, dry out; 2. drain
thárë (i,e) mb. dry, dried, dried up
thártë (i,e) mb. sour, tart, acid; **kumbulla të tharta** sour plums
thátë (i,e) mb. dry, arid; **mot i thatë** a dry climate
thatësír/ë, ~a f. drought, aridity
thék/ër, ~ra f. sh. ~ra, ~rat. bot. rye
theks, ~i m. sh. ~a, ~at. gjuh. stress, accent
theks/ój kal., ~óva, ~úar. stress, emphasize, lay stress on, underline
theksúar (i,e) mb. stressed
thel/b, ~bi m. sh. ~pínj, ~pínjtë. 1. kernel; 2. fig. gist, core, essence, inner core, heart of the matter
thelbësór, ~e mb. essential
thél/ë, ~a f. sh. ~a, ~at. slice, piece
théllë (i,e) mb. deep; **det i thellë** a deep sea; 2. fig. deep, profound
théllë ndajf. deep, deeply
thellësí, ~a f. sh. ~, ~të. depth
thellësísht ndajf. deeply
them kal., tháshë, thënë. 1. say; 2. utter; 3. tell
thémb/ër, ~ra f. sh. ~ra, ~rat. heel; **Thembra e Akilit** Achilles' heel
themél, ~i m. sh. ~e, ~et. 1. base, foundation, groundwork; 2. fig. foundation, basis
themelím, ~i foundation, founding, establishment
themel/ój kal., ~óva, ~úar. found, establish
themelór, ~e mb. fundamental, basic
themelúes, ~i m. sh. ~, ~it. founder
ther kal., ~a, ~ur. butcher, slaughter
thérës, ~e mb. 1. sharp; 2. fig. biting, cutting, stinging, pungent
thes, ~i m. sh. thásë, thásët. sack, bag
thesár, ~i m. sh. ~e, ~et. treasure
thëni/e, ~a f. sh. ~e, ~et. saying
thërr/és (thërrás kal., ~íta, ~ítur **dhe thírra, thírrur.** 1. call; 2. summon, call for; 3. shout
thík/ë, ~a f. sh. ~a, ~at. knife
thírrj/e, ~a f. sh. ~e, ~et. call; summons
thith kal., ~a, ~ur. 1. inhale; 2. suck; 3. fig. take in
thjéshtë (i,e) mb. 1. pure; 2. simple; 3. easy; 4. common
thjesht ndajf. 1. purely; 2. merely; 3. simply, modestly
thjeshtësí, ~a f. simplicity
thónjëza, ~t f. vet. sh. inverted commas
thúa, thói m. sh. thonj, thónjtë. nail
thúajse pj. almost, nearly
thur kal., ~a, ~ur. 1. knit, purl; 2. interlace, intertwine; 3. plait
thyej kal., théva, thyer. 1. break; 2. bend
thyer (i,e) mb. broken

U

údh/ë, ~a f. sh. **~ë, ~ët.** path, track, road, way
udhëq/éq kal., ~óqa, ~équr. lead, guide
udhëhéqës, ~i m. sh. **~, ~it.** 1. leader; 2. guide
udhëhéqës, ~e mb. leading
udhëhéqj/e, ~a f. leadership, direction, guidance,
instruction
udhëhíqem vetv. be led (guided)
udhërrëfyes, ~i m. sh. **~, ~it.** guide
udhëtár, ~i m. sh. **~ë, ~ët.** traveler
udhëtím, ~i m. sh. **~e, ~et.** travel, journey, voyage, trip
udhët/ój jokal., ~óva, ~úar. travel, tour, voyage
udhëzím, ~i m. sh. **~e, ~et.** instruction
udhëz/ój kal., ~óva, ~úar. instruct
udhëzúes, ~ mb. instructive, instructional
új/ë, ~ i m. sh. **~ëra, ~ërat.** water; **ujë i pijshëm** drinking
water; **ujë mineral** mineral water; **ujë i rrjedhshëm** running
water
ujít (ujís) kal., ~a, ~ur. 1. water; 2. irrigate
ujk, ~u m. sh. **~ujq, újqit dhe újqër, újqërit.** zool. wolf
ul kal., ~a, ~ur. 1. lower, let down, drop; 2. reduce
úlem vetv. sit, seat oneself, sit down
ulërí/j jokal., ~ta, ~tur. 1. shriek, scream; 2. howl
ulërím/ë, ~a f. sh. **~a, ~at.** 1. shriek, scream; 2. howl
úlët (i,e) mb. 1. low; **temperaturë e ulët** low temperature;
presion i ulët low pressure; 2. **fig.** low, base, mean, vile;
3. vulgar, coarse; 4. low, depressed, feeble
úlj/e, ~a f. sh. **~e, ~et.** 1. descent; 2. reduction
ullí, ~ri m. sh. **~nj, ~njtë.** olive; olive-tree
unanimísht ndajf. unanimously
unáz/ë, ~a f. sh. **~a, ~at.** ring
únë (mua, tr. e shkurt. më; méje) vetor. I; me
ungjí/ll, ~lli m. sh. **~j, ~jtë.** gospel
unifikím, ~i m. sh. **~e, ~et.** unification
unifik/ój kal., ~óva, ~úar. unify
unifórm, ~e mb. uniform, unvarying
unifórm/ë, ~a f. sh. **~a, ~at.** uniform; **uniformë shkollore**
school uniform
uník, ~e mb. 1. unique, sole, single; 2. unparalleled
unitét, ~i m. unity; **uniteti kombëtar** national unity
universál, ~e mb. universal; **ligj universal** universal law
universitét, ~i m. sh. **~e, ~et.** university
uraniúm, ~i m. kim. uranium
úrdh/ër, ~ri m. sh. **~ra, ~rat.** order, command
urdhër/ój kal., ~óva, ~úar. order, command
urdhërór, ~e mb. gjuh. imperative
úr/ë, ~a f. sh. **~a, ~at.** 1. bridge; 2. **fig.** bridge
urgjénc/ë, ~a f. sh. **~a, ~at.** urgency
urgjént, ~e mb. urgent, pressing; **mesazh urgjent** an urgent
message
urí, ~a f. hunger; **grevë urie** hunger strike
urím, ~i m. sh. **~e, ~et.** wishes; congratulations
urítur (i,e) mb. hungry, starving
ur/ój kal., ~óva, ~úar. 1. wish; 2. congratulate
úrtë (i,e) mb. 1. quiet, silent; 2. wise, sage

urtësí, ~a f. 1. wisdom; 2. prudence
urr/éj kal., ~éva, ~yer. hate, abhor
urréjtj/e, ~a f. hate, hatred, abhorrence
urryer (i,e) mb. hateful, abhorrent
ushqéhem vetv. feed on smth; be nourished **ushq/ej kal., ~éva, ~yer.** feed, nourish
ushqím, ~i m. sh. ~e, ~et. food, nourishment, nutrition
ushqímór, ~e mb. grocery; **dyqan ushqimor** a grocery store
ushqyes, ~e mb. nutritious, nutritive, nourishing
ushqyesh/ëm (i), ~me (e) mb. nourishing, nutritious
ushtár, ~i m. sh. ~ë, ~ët. soldier
ushtarák, ~e mb. military; **shërbim ushtarak** military service
ushtrí, ~a f. sh. ~, ~të. army
ushtrím, ~i m. sh. ~e, ~et. exercise, drill, practice
ushtr/ój kal., ~óva, ~úar. exercise, practice, drill
utopík, ~e mb. utopic
úthull, ~a f. vinegar
uzín/ë, ~a f. sh. ~a, ~at. plant, works

V

vagón, ~i m. sh. ~ë, ~ët. carriage, coach, car; **vagon udhëtarësh** passenger car (coach); **vagon mallrash** freight car, goods wagon

vaj, ~i m. oil; **vaj ulliri** olive oil; **val luledielli** sunflower oil; **vaj sallate** salad oil

vaj/ój kal., ~óva, ~úar. oil, lubricate

vajt/ój kal., ~óva, ~úar. mourn, lament

vájz/ë, ~a f. sh. ~a, ~at. girl, lass

vákët (i,e) mb. tepid, lukewarm; **ujë i vakur** tepid (lukewarm) water

vaksín/ë, ~a f. sh. ~a, ~at. mjek. vaccine

vaksiním, ~i m. sh. ~e, ~et. mjek. vaccination

vaksin/ój kal., ~óva, ~úar. mjek.vaccinate

vál/ë, ~a f. sh. ~a, ~at. 1. wave; 2. **fig.** wave, surge; 3. **fiz.** wave

válë (i,e) mb. hot, boiling

valíxh/e, ~ja f. sh. ~e, ~et. suitcase, valise

vals, ~i m. muz. vals

valút/ë, ~a f. foreign currency

váll/e, ~ja f. sh. ~e, ~et. dance

vallëzím, ~i m. sh. ~e, ~et. dancing

vallëz/ój jakal., ~óva, ~úar. dance

vallëzúes, ~i m. sh. ~, ~it. dancer

váp/ë, ~a f. heat, hotness; **është vapë** it is hot; **kam vapë** be (feel) hot

vapór, ~i m. sh. ~ë, ~ët. ship, steamer

var kal., ~a, ~ur. hang, suspend

várem vetv. 1. hang oneself; 2. be dependent on (upon)

várës, ~ja m. sh. ~e, ~et. hanger, clothes-hanger

varësí, ~a f. dependence

várfër (i,e) mb. 1. poor, destitute; 2. meager

varfërí, ~a f. poverty

varfëróhem vetv. grow poor

varfër//ój kal., ~óva, ~úar. impoverish, reduce to poverty

var/g, ~gu m. sh. ~gje, ~gjet. 1. string; **varg qepësh** a string of onions; 2. row, range; 3. verse

variación, ~i m. sh. ~e, ~et. 1. variation, alteration, change; 2. **muz.** variation

variánt, ~i m. sh. ~e, ~et. variant

várk/ë, ~ f. sh. ~a, ~at. boat

varr, ~i m. sh. ~e, ~et. grave, tomb

varréz/ë, ~a f. sh. ~a, ~at. cemetery, graveyard, burial ground

varrós kal., ~a, ~ur. bury

vath, ~i m. sh. ~ë, ~ët. earring

vázo, ~ja f. sh. ~, ~t. vase

vazhdím, ~i m. sh. ~e, ~et. 1. continuation, continuance; 3. succession

vazhdimësí, ~a f. continuity, progression

vazhdimísht ndajf. continually, continuously, non-stop

vazhd/oj kal., ~óva, ~úar. 1. continue, go on with, keep on; 2. pursue

vazhdúes, ~i m. sh. ~, ~it. follower, adherent

vazhdúes, ~e mb. consecutive, successive

vazhdúesh/ëm (i), ~me (e) mb. continuous, continual

vdékj/e, ~a f. sh. ~e, ~et. death
vdekjeprúrës, ~e mb. mortal, deadly, lethal, fatal; **plagë vdekjeprurëse** a mortal wound
vdéksh/ëm (i), ~me (e) mb. mortal; **njeriu është i vdekshëm** man is mortal
vdékur (i,e) mb. 1. dead; 2. **fig.** dead, lifeless
vdes jokal., ~vdíqa, ~vdékur. die, depart, expire, pass away, perish
veç. ndajf. separately, singly
veçanërísht ndajf. especially
veçántë (i,e) mb. 1. special, specific; **rast i veçantë** a special occasion; 2. peculiar
veçorí, ~a f. sh. ~, ~të. peculiarity; particularity
veç/ój kal., ~óva, ~úar. separate, isolate, seclude
veçorí, ~a f. sh. ~, ~të. peculiarity, characteristic, feature, distinction
veçsé lidh. but; only
vég/ël, ~la f. sh. ~la, ~lat. 1. tool, appliance, device, implement, instrument; 2. **fig.** tool, instrument
vel, ~i m. sh. ~a, ~at. sail
vend, ~i m. sh. ~e, ~et. 1. place; 2. seat; **vend i zënë (i lirë)** an occupied (free) seat; 3. room, space; 4. country, land, home; 5. post, position; 6. spot, place
vendburím, ~ m. sh. ~e, ~et. source
véndës, ~i m. sh. ~, 'it. native
véndës, ~e mb. native
vendím, ~i m. sh. ~e, ~et. 1. decision; 2. decree, verdict, sentence
vendimtár, ~e mb. decisive; **moment vendimtar** a decisive moment
vendlíndj/e, ~a f. birthplace
vendós kal., ~a, ~ur. 1. decide, make up one's mind, make a decision; 2. establish; 3. fix; 4. place; 5. set
vendosmërí, ~a f. resolution, determination
vendósur (i,e) mb. firm, resolute, resolved, determined
vén/ë, ~a f. sh. ~a, ~at. anat. vein
venít (venís) kal., ~a, ~ur. 1. dwindle; **venit shpresat** dwindle the hopes; 2. wane; 3. fade away; 4. pale
ventilatór, ~i m. sh. ~ë, ~ët. fan, ventilator
vép/ër, ~ra f. sh. ~ra, ~rat. 1. deed, act, exploit; 2. work; **vepër arti** work of art
veprím, ~i m. sh. ~e, ~et. 1. act, action; 2. **kim.** action; 3. **mek.** motion, movement; 4. operation
veprimtár, ~i m. sh. ~ë, ~ët. activist
veprimtarí, ~a f. sh. ~, ~të. activity
vepr/ój jokal., ~óva, ~úar. act, operate
veprúes, ~e mb. active
vérbër (i,e) mb. blind, sightless
verbërísht ndajf. blindly
verbóhem vetv. be blinded (dazzled)
verb/ój kal., ~óva, ~úar. 1. blind, dazzle; 2. **fig.** blind smb to smth
vérdhë (i,e) mb. yellow
vérdhëz, ~a. mjek. jaundice
vér/ë, ~a f. sh. ~a, ~at. Summer; **pushimet e verës** summer vacations

vér/ë, ~a f. wine; **verë e bardhë (e kuqe)** white (red) wine; **verë e ëmbël** sweet wine

verí, ~u m. 1. north; the north; 2. north wind

vertifikím, ~i m. sh. ~e, ~et. verification

verifik/ój kal., ~óva, ~úar. verify

veriór, ~e mb. northern

verór, ~e mb. summer; **rroba veriore** summer clothes

ves, ~i m. sh. ~e, ~et. vice

vés/ë, ~a f. dew

vesh, ~i m. sh. ~ë, ~ët. 1. ear; **ka vesh të mirë për muzikë** has a good ear for music; 2. bunch

vesh kal., ~a, ~ur. 1. put on; 2. dress, clothe; 3. attribute; 4. invest

véshj/e, ~a f. sh. ~e, ~et. clothes, clothing, garments, wear

véshk/ë, ~a f. sh. ~a, ~at. anat. kidney

vet (i,e) pron. vetv. sh. ~(të), ~a (të). 1. own; 2. his, her; its

vét/ë, ~ja f. self, oneself

véte jokal., ~vájta, vájtur. 1. go; 2. go together

veterán, ~i m. sh. ~ë, ~ët. veteran

veterinár, ~e mb. veterinary

vét/ë, ~a f. sh. ~a, ~at. gjuh. person

vétë përem.pron. oneself, myself, yourself, himself, herself, ourselves, yourselves, themselves

vetëbesim, ~i m. self-confidence, self-assurance

vetëdíj/e, ~a f. awareness, consciousness

vetëdíjsh/ëm (i), ~me (e) mb. conscious, aware

vetëkënaqësí, ~ a f. self-satisfaction, self-content

vét/ëm (i), ~me (e) mb. only, sole, single

vëtëm ndajf. 1. alone; 2. only, just, simply, merely

vetëpërmbájtj/e, ~a f. self-restrained, self-control

vetëshërbim, ~i m. self-service

vetëtím/ë, ~a f. sh. ~a, ~at. lightning

vetëtímthi ndajf. like lightning, like a shot

vetëtí/n jokal., ~u, ~rë. 1. it lightens; 2. lighten, brighten; 3. gleam, shine

vetëveprúes, ~e mb. self-acting, self-moving, automatic

vetí, ~a f. sh. ~, ~të. feature

vetják, ~e mb. personal, individual; **pronë vetjake** personal property

vetmí, ~a f. solitude, solitariness, loneliness

vetmitár, ~e mb. lonely, solitary, lonesome

véto, ~ja f. sh. ~, ~t. veto; **e drejta e vetos** the right of veto; **vë veton** veto

vétull, ~a f. sh. ~a, ~at. eye-brow

vetúr/ë, ~a f. sh. ~a, ~at. car, motorcar

véz/ë, ~a f. sh. ~ë, ~ët. egg

vezull/ón jokal., ~ói, ~úar. twinkle, glimmer, glitter

vë kal., vúra, vënë. 1. put; 2. set; 3. place

vëllá, ~i m. sh. ~vëllézër, vëllézërit. brother

vëllim, ~i m. sh. ~e, ~et. 1. gjeom. volume; 2. volume

vëméndj/e, ~a f. attention, heed; **i kushtoj vëmendje** pay attention to; **tërheq vëmendjen e** attract (draw) smb's attention to

vëmendsh/ëm (i), ~me (e) mb. attentive, heedful, watchful
vëréj kal., ~ta, ~tur. 1. observe; 2. notice, regard, watch;
3. remark
vërejtj/e, ~a f. sh. ~e, ~et. 1. remark, observation; 2.
attention
vërsh/ój kal., ~óva, ~úar. 1. overflow; 2. flood, inundate;
3. gush out; **vërshoi nafta nga pusi** oil gushing out from the
well
vërtét ndajf. really, truly, indeed
vërtét/ë, ~a (e) f. sh. ~a, ~at (të). truth, reality; **të them
(themi) të vërtetën** to tell the truth
vërtétë (i,e) mb. true, real; **është e vërtetë** it is true;
dashuri e vërtetë true love
vërtetësí, ~a f. veracity, verity, truthfulness
vërtet/ój kal., ~óva, ~úar. 1. attest, certify, verify,
confirm; 2. mat. prove
vërtítem vetv. revolve, spin, turn round
vështírë (i,e) mb. hard, difficult; **gjuhë e vështirë** a hard
language; **detyrë e vështirë** a hard task
vështírë ndajf. hard
vështirësí, ~a f. sh. ~, ~të. difficulty
vështrím, ~i m. sh. ~e, ~et. look, glance
vështr/ój kal., ~óva, ~úar. 1. look, see; 2. watch; 3. view,
regard
vëzhgím, ~i m. sh. ~e, ~et. observation
vëzhg/ój kal., ~óva, ~úar. observe
vëzhgúes, ~i m. sh. ~, ~it. observer
vëzhgúes, ~e mb. observant; observation; **pikë vëzhguese**
observation post
viç, ~i m. sh. ~a, ~at. calf
vídh/ë, ~a f. sh. ~a, ~at. screw; **ka një vidhë mangut** have a
screw loose
vidhós kal., ~a, ~ur. screw
vigjilénc/ë, ~a f. vigilance, alertness, watchfulness
vigjilént, ~e mb. vigilant, watchful, alert
vigjílj/e, ~a f. eve; **në vigjilje të** on the eve of
víhem vetv. 1. place oneself; 2. devote, dedicate oneself to
vij jokal., érdha, ~árdhur. 1. come; 2. occur; 3. derive
víj/ë, ~a f. sh. ~a, ~at. 1. gjeom. line; 2. sport. the line;
3. usht. line; 4. fig. line
vij/ój kal., ~óva, ~úar. 1. go on, continue, proceed; 2.
follow; 3. go on with, proceed with smth
viktím/ë, ~a f. sh. ~a, ~at. 1. victim; 2. fig. victim
víl/ë, ~a f. sh. ~a, ~at. villa
vinç, ~i m. sh. ~a, ~at. tek. crane
violín/ë, ~a f. sh. ~a, ~at. violin
violiníst, ~i m. sh. ~ë, ~ët. violinist **violonçél**, ~i m. sh.
~a, ~at. cello **virtyt**, ~i m. sh. ~e, ~et. virtue
virtytsh/ëm (i), ~me (e) mb. virtuous
vírus, ~i m. sh. ~e, ~et. mjek. virus
víshem vetv. dress
vit, ~i m. sh. ~e, ~et. year; **vit kalendarik** calendar year;
vit akademik the academic year; **gjatë gjithë vitit** all the
year round; **vit për vit** year after year
vitamín/ë, ~a f. sh. ~a, ~at. vitamin

vitrín/ë, ~a f. sh. ~a, ~at. window
vizatím, ~i m. sh. ~e, ~et. drawing
vizat/ój kal., ~óva, ~úar. 1. draw; 2. outline
víz/ë, ~a f. sh. ~a, ~at. dash
víz/ë, ~a f. sh. ~a, ~at. visa
vizít/ë, ~a f. sh. ~a, ~at. visit; bëj një vizitë pay a visit to
vizit/ój kal., ~óva, ~úar. visit
vizitór, ~i m. sh. ~ë, ~ët. visitor; libri i vizitorëve visitors' book
vizór/e, ~ja f. sh. ~e, ~et. ruler
vjedh kal., vódha, vjédhur. steal, rob, pilfer, purloin
vjédhj/e, ~a f. sh. ~e, ~et. stealing, theft, robbery
vjel kal., vóla, vjélë. 1. pick up, gather, collect; 2. fig. cull smth from smth
vjell kal., vólla, vjéllë. 1. vomit, disgorge; 2. fig. vomit
vjérsh/ë, ~a f. sh. ~a, ~at. verse
vjeshták, ~e mb. autumnal
vjesht/ë, ~a f. sh. ~a, ~at. autumn, fall
vjetár, ~i m. sh. ~ë, ~ët. year-book
vjétër (i,e) mb. 1. old; 2. aged, elderly; 3. ancient, antique, archaic; 4. outmoded
vjetór, ~e mb. annual, yearly; prodhimi vjetor an annual production
vjóllc/ë, ~a f. sh. ~a, ~at. bot. violet
vléfsh/ëm (i), ~me (e) mb. 1. valuable, precious; 2. valid
vlej jokal., ta, ~tur. be worth
vlér/ë, ~a f. sh. ~a, ~at. value, worth
vlerësím, ~i m. sh. ~e, ~et. estimation, appraisal, evaluation
vlerës/ój kal., ~óva, ~úar. value, appraise, assess, estimate, evaluate
vódk/ë, ~a f. vodka
vógël (i,e) mb. 1. little, small, paltry; 2. petty, slight, unimportant, trivial
vokál, ~e mb. vocal
volejbóll, ~i m. volley-ball
volítsh/ëm (i), ~me (e) mb. 1. convenient; 2. handy
volt, ~i m. sh. ~, ~ët. fiz. volt
vónë (i,e) mb. late, tardy, delayed
vónë ndajf. late; më vonë later on; jam vonë be late; herët a vonë sooner or later; më mirë vonë se kurrë better late than never
vonóhem vetv. be late
von/ój kal., ~óva, ~úar. delay, retard
vót/ë, ~a f. sh. ~a, ~at. vote, ballot
votëbesím, ~i m. vote of confidence
votím, ~i m. sh. ~e, ~et. suffrage, franchise, ballot
vot/ój kal., ~óva, ~úar. vote
votúes, ~i m. sh. ~, ~it. voter
vóz/ë, ~a f. sh. ~a, ~at. barrel
vozít (vozís) jokal., ~a, ~ur. row
vrap, ~i m. run; ia dha vrapit he broke into a run
vrapím, ~i m. sh. ~e, ~et. running
vrap/ój jokal., ~óva, ~úar. run, dash, dart, bolt
vrapúes, ~i m. sh. ~, ~it. runner; racer, sprinter

vra/s kal., ~**va**, ~**rë**. 1. kill, murder, assassinate; 2. poniard, stab, slay; 3. hurt, injure

vrásës, ~**i m. sh.** ~, ~**it**. killer, murderer, assassin

vrásj/e, ~**a f**. killing, assassination

vrázhdë (i,e) mb. rough, harsh, coarse, rude

vrénjtur (i,e) mb. 1. cloudy, nebulous; 2. sullen, gloomy

vresht, ~**i m. sh.** ~**a**, ~**at**. vineyard

vrím/ë, ~**a f. sh.** ~**a**, ~**at**. hole, perforation, puncture; **vrima e çelësit** key-hole; **vrima e këmishës** button-hole; **vrimat e hundës** nostrils

vrítem vetv. be killed

vrojtím, ~**i m. sh.** ~**e**, ~**et**. observation

vrojt/ój kal., ~**óva**, ~**úar**. observe

vrull, ~**i m. sh.** ~**e**, ~**et**. impetus, vigor

vúaj jokal., ~**ta**, ~**tur**. suffer

vúajtj/e, ~**a f. sh.** ~**e**, ~**et**. suffering

vúl/ë, ~**a f. sh.** ~**a**, ~**at**. stamp, seal

vulós kal., ~**a**, ~**ur**. seal, stamp

vullkán, ~**i m. sh.** ~**e**, ~**et. gjeogr. gjeol**. volcano

vullkaník, ~**e mb**. volcanic

vullnét, ~**i m. sh.** ~**e**, ~**et**. will; **vullnet i lirë** free will; **vullnet i fortë** a strong will

vullnetár, ~**i m. sh.** ~**ë**, ~**ët**. volunteer

vullnetár, ~**e mb**. voluntary

vullnetarísht ndajf. voluntarily

vullnetsh/ëm (i), ~**me (e) mb**. willing, willful

vyer (i,e) mb. precious, valuable

X

xíx/ë, ~a f. sh. ~a, ~at. spark
xixëllím/ë, ~a f. sh. ~a, ~at. sparkling, sparkle, glint,
twinkle, scintillation
xixëll/ón jokal., ~ói, ~úar. sparkle, twinkle, scintillate,
glitter
xixëllónj/ë, ~a f. sh. ~a, ~at zool. fire-fly
xixëllúes, ~e mb. sparkling

XH

xhakét/ë, ~a f. sh. ~a, ~at. jacket
xham, ~i m. sh. ~a, ~at. dhe ~e, ~et. glass
xhamí, ~a f. sh. ~, ~të. mosque
xhámtë (i,e) mb. glassy (edhe **fig.**)
xhaz, ~i m. sh. ~e, ~et. jazz
xheloz, ~e mb. jealous
xhelozí, ~a f. jealousy
xhep, ~i m. sh. ~a, ~at. pocket; **fjalor xhepi** a pocket
dictionary
xhevahír, ~i m. sh. ~e, ~et. jewel
xhúng/ël, ~la f. sh. ~la, ~lat. jungle

ylbér, ~i m. sh. ~e, ~et. rain-bow
yll ~i m. sh. yje, yjet dhe yj, yjtë. star
yndyr/ë, ~a f. sh. ~a, ~at. grease
ynë pron. (gjin., dhan., kallëz., tónë) sh. tánë our; vendi
ynë our country
yt pron. (gjin., dhan., kallëz., rrjedh. tënd) your; babai yt
your father
yzengji, ~a f. sh. ~, ~të. stirrup

Z

zakon, ~i m. sh. ~e, ~et. custom, habit, practice
zakonísht ndajf. usually, habitually, customarily
zakónsh/ëm (i), ~me (e) mb. usual, habitual, customary
zakóntë (i,e) mb. usual
zambák, ~u m. sh. ~ë, ~ët bot. lily
zámk/ë, ~a f. glue
zanát, ~i m. sh. ~e, ~et. profession, occupation, craft, trade
zán/ë, ~a f. sh. ~a, ~at mit. fairy
zanór, ~e mb. vocal
zapt/ój kal., ~óva, ~úar. occupy, invade, conquer
zar, ~i m. sh. ~e, ~et. dice; **hedh zaret** cast the dice
zarf, ~i m. sh. ~e, ~et. envelope
zarzavát/e, ~ja f. ~e, ~et. vegetables, greens
zbardh kal., ~a, ~ur. 1. whiten, bleach; 2. go white, grow pale; 3. dawn; 4. wash out
zbatím, ~i m. sh. ~e, ~et. 1. application; 2. execution; observation
zbat/ój kal., ~óva, ~úar. 1. apply, implement; 2. execute; 3. observe
zbatúar (i,e) mb. applied; **gjuhësia e zbatuar** applied linguistics
zbatúesh/ëm (i), ~me (e) mb. applicable
zbath kal., ~a, ~ur. take off
zbáthur (i,e) mb. barefoot, barefooted
zbavít kal., ~a, ~ur. amuse, divert, entertain
zbavitém vetv. bised. amuse oneself, entertain oneself
zbavítës, ~e mb. amusing, diverting, entertaining; **një film shumë zbavitës** a very entertaining film
zbavitj/e, ~a f. sh. ~e, ~et. amusement, entertainment
zbéhem vetv. 1. pale, go (turn) pale; 2. wane
zbéhtë (i,e) mb. pale, pallid, wan, ashen
zbërth/éj kal., ~éva, ~yer. 1. unbutton, untie, unfasten; 2. resolve, break up; 3. analyse
zbraz kal., ~a, ~ur. 1. empty; 2. pour out; 3. evacuate
zbrázët (i,e) mb. empty, void, vacant
zbres jokal., zbríta, zbrítur. 1. descend, come down, go down, climb down; 2. dismount, light, get down; 3. derive, be the descendant of; 4. lower
zbukurím, ~i m. sh. ~e, ~et. 1. ornamentation, adornment, embellishment, decoration; 2. ornament
zbukuróhem vetv. embellish oneself
zbukur/ój kal., ~óva, ~úar. 1. beautify, prettify; 2. adorn, decorate, embellish
zbukurúes, ~e mb. ornamental, decorative, decorating, embellishing
zbulím, ~i m. sh. ~e, ~et. 1. discovery; 2. innovation, invention; 3. **usht.** intelligence
zbul/ój kal., ~óva, ~úar. 1. discover; 2. uncover; 3. reveal; 4. find out; 5. invent
zbut (zbus) kal., ~a, ~ur. 1. soften; 2. tame; 3. mitigate, alleviate; 4. pacify, calm, soothe
zéb/ër, ~ra f. sh. ~ra, ~rat zool. zebra
zéj/e, ~a f. sh. ~e, ~et. craft, handicraft
zekth, ~i m. sh. ~a, ~at. zool. gadfly
zell, ~i m. zeal, ardor

zéllsh/ëm (i), **~me (e) mb.** zealous **zém/ër**, **~ra f. sh. ~ra,**
~rat 1. **anat.** heart; 2. courage; 3. **fig.** heart; 4. center,
core; **me gjithë zemër** with all one's heart; **i hap zemrën**
dikujt open (pour out) one's heart to smb; **marr zemër** take
heart
zemërím, **~i m. sh. ~e, ~et.** anger, wrath, indignation
zemërmírë mb. good-hearted
zemër/ój kal., **~óva, ~úar.** anger, incense, vex, annoy, peeve
zenít, **~i m.** 1. **astr.** zenith; 2. **fig.** zenith, peak
zéro, **~ja f. sh. ~, ~t. mat.** zero
zezák, **~e mb.** negro
zéz/ë, **~a (e) f. sh. ~a, ~at (të).** black
zë, **~ri m. sh. ~ra, ~rat.** 1. voice, sound; 2. say; **me zë të**
lartë in a loud voice; **ngre (ul) zërin** raise (lower) one's
voice; **ngre zërin kundër** raise one's voice against
zëvendësím, **~i m. sh. ~e, ~et.** replacement, substitution
zëvendës/ój kal., **~óva, ~úar.** replace, substitute
zëvendësúesh/ëm (i), **~me (e) mb.** replaceable
zgalem, **~i m. sh. ~a, ~at zool.** petrel
zgjat (zgjas) kal., **~a, ~ur.** 1. lengthen, extend; 2. prolong;
3. stretch out, spread out
zgjedh kal., **zgjódha, zgjédhur.** 1. choose, cull, pick,
select; 2. elect
zgjédhës, **~i m. sh. ~, ~it.** elector
zgjédhj/e, **~a m. sh. ~e, ~et.** 1. election; 2. choice, option,
selection
zgjédhur (i,e) mb. 1. selected; 2. elect
zgjer/ój kal., **~óva, ~úar.** broaden, widen, enlarge, expand
zgjidh kal., **~a, ~ur.** 1. untie, unfasten, undo; 2. unleash,
unbind; 3. solve, resolve
zgjídhj/e, **~a f. sh. ~e, ~et.** solution
zgjóhem vetv. wake up
zgjoj kal., **zgjóva, zgjúar.** awake, wake smb up, awaken
zgjúar (i,e) mb. 1. clever, intelligent, smart; 2. awake
zi (i), **zezë (e) mb.** 1. black; 2. **fig.** black
zíej kal., **zjéva, zíer.** 1. boil; 2. **fig.** seethe **zihem vetv.**
1. quarrel; 2. catch hold of
zíl/e, **~ja f. sh. ~e, ~et.** bell; **zile biçiklete** a bicycle
bell; **I bie ziles** ring the bell
zilí, **~ f.** envy, covetousness
ziliqár, **~e mb.** envious, covetous
zinxhír, **~i m. sh. ~ë, ~ët.** 1. chain; 2. zip, zip-fastener,
zipper
zjarr, **~i m. sh. ~e, ~et.** fire, blaze; **bëj një zjarr** make
(build) a fire; 2. **usht.** fire; 3. **fig.** ardor, fervor
zjarrdurúes, **~e mb.** fireproof; fire (flame) resistant
zjarrfíkës/e, **~ja f. sh. ~e, ~et.** fire-engine; fire
extinguisher, extinguisher
zmadh/ój kal., **~óva, ~úar.** enlarge, expand, augment, magnify
zmbraps kal., **~a, ~ur.** repel, repulse, drive back, push back
zmbrápsem vetv. withdraw, recede, recoil, retreat
zo/g, **~gu m. sh. ~gj, ~gjtë zool.** bird
zonál, **~e mb.** zonal

zón/ë, ~a f. sh. ~a, ~at gjeogr. zone; **zonë industriale** industrial zone
zoologjí, ~a f. zoology
zot, ~i m. sh. ~a, ~at. God
zotërí, ~a m. sh. ~nj, ~njtë. mister, gentleman, sir
zotër/ój kal., ~óva, ~úar. possess, own
zotërúes, ~i m. sh. ~, ~it. possessor, owner, proprietor
zotësí, ~a f. ability, capability
zóti (i), zónja (e) mb. able, capable
zotím, ~i m. sh. ~e, ~et. pledge
zot/óhem vetv. ~óva (u), ~úar. pledge oneself
zvogël/ój kal., ~óva, ~úar. 1. decrease, deplete, dwindle, diminish, lessen; 2. belittle
zymtë (i,e) mb. gloomy
zyr/ë, ~a f. sh. ~a, ~at. office
zyrtár, ~e mb. official
zyrtarísht ndajf. officially

ZH

zháb/ë, ~a f. sh. **~a, ~at** zool. toad
zhavórr, ~i m. sh. **~e, ~et.** gravel
zhbë/j kal., ~ra, ~rë. undo
zhdërvjéllët (i,e) mb. agile, nimble
zhdréjtë (i,e) mb. indirect; **kundrinor i zhdrejtë** indirect object
zhduk kal., ~a, ~ur. wipe out, do away with, eliminate
zhdúkem vetv. disappear, vanish, fade
zhgënjéhem vetv. be disillusioned
zhgënj/éj kal., ~éva, ~yer. disillusion, disappoint
zhgënjím, ~i m. sh. **~e, ~et.** disillusionment, disillusion
zhúrm/ë, ~a f. sh. **~a, ~at.** noise, row, ado
zhúrmët (i,e) mb. noisy
zhúrmsh/ëm (i), ~me (e) mb. boisterous
zhvendós kal., ~a, ~ur. 1. displace, dislodge, shift; 2. dislocate
zhvesh kal., ~a, ~ur. undress, strip
zhvillím, ~i m. sh. **~e, ~et.** development
zhvillimór, ~e mb. developmental
zhvillóhem vetv. 1. develop, grow; mature; 2. advance, progress; 3. take place, happen, occur
zhvill/ój kal., ~óva, ~úar. 1. develop; 2. treat; 3. conduct
zhvillúar (i,e) mb. developed
zhvíshem vetv. undress, strip
zhvleftësím, ~i m. sh. **~e, ~et.** devaluation
zhvlerës/ój kal., ~óva, ~úar. devalue
zhyt (zhys) kal., ~a, ~ur. dip, immerse
zhytem vetv. 1. sink; 2. immerse oneself in; 3. dive

GEOGRAPHICAL NAMES
(Emrat Gjeografikë)

ALBANIAN - ENGLISH

A

Abu Dabi/ Abu Dabhi
Adis Abebë/ Addis Ababa
Afganistan/ Afghanistan
Afrikë/ Africa
Akrë/ Accra
Alabamë/ Alabama
Alaskë/ Alaska
Algjeri/ Algeria
Algjer/ Algiers
Alma-Atë/ Alma Ata
Alpe/ Alps
Altaj/ Altai
Aman/ Amman
Amazonë/ Amazon
Amerikë/ America
Amerika Qëndrore/ Central America
Amerika e Veriut/ North America
Amsterdam/ Amsterdam
Ande/ Andes
Andorrë/ Andorra
Angli/ England
Angolë/ Angola
Ankara/ Ankara
Anktarktikë/ Antarctic Continent
Apalashe/ Appalachian Mountains, Appalachian
Apenine/ Apennines
Arabia Saudite/ Saudi Arabia
Argjentinë/ Argentina
Arizonë/ Arizona
Arkanzas/ Arkansas
Arhangelsk/ Arkhangelsk
Armeni/ Armenia
Asuncion/ Asunción
Ashkabad/ Ashkhabad
Athinë/ Athens
Atlantë/ Atlanta
Australi/ Australia
Austria/ Austria
Azerbajxhan/ Azerbaijan
Azi/ Asia
Azi e Vogël/ Asia Minor

B

Bab-el-Mandeb/ Bab el Mandeb
Bagdad/ Bag(h)dad
Bahrejn/ Bahrain, Bahrein
Bajkal/ Baikal
Baku/ Baku

Baltimorë/ Baltimore
Bamako/ Bamako
Bangkok/ Bangkok
Bangladesh/ Bangladesh
Bejrut/ Beirut
Belfast/ Belfast
Belgjikë/ Belgium
Benin/ Benin
Beograd/ Belgrade
Berlin/ Berlin
Bishkek/ Bishkek
Bogotë/ Bogota
Bolivi/ Bolivia
Bombej/ Bombay
Bon/ Bonn
Borneo/ Borneo
Boston/ Boston
Botsvanë/ Botswana
Brazil/ Brazil
Brazavil/ Brazzaville
Britani/ Britain
Bregu i Fildishtë/ Cote d'Ivoire
Brunei/ Brunei
Bruksel/ Brussels
Bukuresht/ Bucharest
Budapest/ Budapest
Buenos Ajres/ Buenos Aires
Bullgari/ Bulgaria
Burundi/ Burundi
Bjellorusi/ Byelorussia

Ç

Çad/ Chad
Çikago/ Chicago
Çeki/ Czech Republic

D

Dakar/ Dakar
Dakë/ Dacca
Damask/ Damascus
Danimarkë/ Denmark
Danub/ Danube
Dardanele/ Dardanelles
Dar-es-Salam/ Dar es Salaam
Delhi/ Delhi
Deti Adriatik/ Adriatic Sea
Deti Arabik/ Arabian Sea
Deti i Azovit/ Azov, Sea of
Deti Balltik/ Baltic Sea
Deti Barenc/ Barents Sea
Deti Bering/ Bering Sea
Deti i Karaibeve/ Caribbean Sea
Deti Kaspik/ Caspian Sea
Deti i Kuq/ Red Sea

Deti Mesdhe/ Mediterranean Sea
Deti i Verdhë/ Yellow Sea
Deti i Veriut/ North Sea
Deti i Zi/ Black Sea
Dniepër/ Dnieper
Dniestër/ Dniester
Don/ Don
Dublin/ Dublin

E

Edinburg/ Edinburgh
Egjipt/ Egypt
Ekuador/ Ecuador
Elbë/ Elbe
Elbrus/ Elbrus, Elbruz
Emiratet e Bashkuara Arabe/ United Arab Emirates
Estoni/ Estonia
Etiopi/ Ethiopia
Eufrat/ Euphrates
Everest/ Everest
Evropë/ Europe

F

Filadelfia/ Philadelphia
Filipine/ Philippines
Finlandë/ Finland
Firence/ Florence
Floridë/ Florida
Francë/ France

G

Gabon/ Gabon, Gaboon
Gadishulli i Ballkanit/ Balkan Peninsula
Gambia/ Gambia
Ganë/ Ghana
Gang/ Ganges
Glasgou/ Glasgow
Gobi/ Gobi, the
Greqi/ Greece
Groenlandë/ Greenland
Guadalupë/ Guadeloupe
Guajanë/ Guyana
Guatemalë/ Guatemala
Guine/ Guinea
Guineja Ekuatoriale/ Equatorial Guinea
Guineja e Re/ New Guinea

GJ

Gjenevë/ Geneva
Gjenovë/ Genoa

Gjeorgji/ Georgia
Gjermani/ Germany
Gjibraltar/ Gibraltar
Gjiri i Biskajës/ Biscay, Bay of
Gjiri i Bengalit/ Bengal, Bay of
Gjiri i Hudsonit/ Hudson Bay
Gjiri Persik/ Persian Gulf

H

Hagë/ Hague, The
Haiti/ Haiti
Hamburg/ Hamburg
Hanoi/ Hanoi
Havai/ Hawaii
Havanë/ Havana
Havër/ Havre
Helsinki/ Helsinki
Himalajë/ Himalaya(s), the
Hindustan/ Hindustan
Hiroshimë/ Hiroshima
Ho Shi Min/ Ho Chi Minh
Hollandë/ Holland, Netherlands
Hollivud/ Hollywood
Honduras/ Honduras
Hong Kong/ Hong Kong
Hungari/ Hungary

I

Ilinois/ Illinois
Indi/ India
Indianë/ Indiana
Indonezi/ Indonesia
Iran/ Iran
Irak/ Iraq
Irlandë/ Ireland
Islandë/ Iceland
Ishujt Bermude/ Bermuda Islands, Bermudas
Ishujt Falkland/ Falkland Islands
Ishujt Kurile/ Kuril(e) Islands
Ishujt e Kepit të Gjelbër/ Cape Verde Islands
Itali/ Italy
Izrael/ Israel

J

Jafë/ Jaffa
Japoni/ Japan
Javë/ Java
Jemen/ Yemen
Jeruzalem/ Jerusalem
Johanesburg/ Johannesburg
Jordan/ Jordan
Jugosllavi/ Yugoslavia

Kabul/ Kabul
Kaliforni/ California
Kalkutë/ Calcutta
Kajro/ Cairo
Kamçatkë/ Kamchatka
Kamerun/ Cameroon
Kanada/ Canada
Kanali i Panamasë/ Panama Canal
Kanali i Suezit/ Suez Canal
Kanberrë/ Canberra
Kanzas/ Kansas
Karaçi/ Karachi
Karakas/ Caracas
Karolina e Veriut/ North Carolina
Karolina e Jugut/ South Carolina
Karpate/ Carpathian Mountains, Carpathians
Kategat/ Kattegat
Katmandu/ Katmandu
Kaukaz/ Caucasus, the
Kazakistan/ Kazakhstan
Kejptaun/ Cape Town, Capetown
Kembrixh/ Cambridge
Kenia/ Kenya
Kepi Horn/ Horn, Cape
Kepi i Shpresës së Mirë/ Cape of Good Hope
Kiev/ Kiev
Kili/ Chile
Kilimanxharo/ Kilimanjaro
Kinë/ China
Kinshasë/ Kinshasa
Kioto/ Kyoto
Kirxhikistan/ Kirghizstan
Kishinev/ Kishinev
Kolombo/ Colombo
Kolorado/ Colorado
Kolumbi/ Colombia
Kolumbia/ Columbia
Konakri/ Conakry
Kongo/ Congo, the
Kopenhagen/ Copenhagen
Kore/ Korea
Kore e Jugut/ South Korea
Korsikë/ Corsica
Kosta Rikë/ Costa Rica
Kretë/ Crete
Krime/ Crimea, the
Kubë/ Cuba
Kuvajt/ Kuwait

Lajpcig/ Leipzig
Lahorë/ Lahore
Laos/ Laos

Leningrad/ Leningrad
Lesoto/ Lesotho
Letoni/ Latvia
Lhasë/ Lhasa
Liban/ Lebanon
Liberi/ Liberia
Libi/ Libya
Lihtenshtajn/ Liechtenstein
Limë/ Lima
Lisbonë/ Lisbon
Lituani/ Lithuania
Liverpul/ Liverpool
Londër/ London
Los Anxheles/ Los Angeles
Luandë/ Luanda
Luizianë/ Louisiana
Luksemburg/ Luxembourg
Lusakë/ Lusaka

M

Madagaskar/ Madagascar
Madrid/ Madrid
Malajzi/ Malaysia
Malet Shkëmbore/ Rocky Mountains
Maltë/ Malta
Majami/ Miami
Managua/ Managua
Mançester/ Manchester
Manhatan/ Manhattan
Manilë/ Manila
Marok/ Morocco
Marsejë/ Marseilles
Martinikë/ Martinique
Masaçusets/ Massachusetts
Mauricius/ Mauritius
Mauritani/ Mauritania
Mbretëria e Bashkuar e Britanisë së Madhe dhe Irlandës së
Veriut/ United Kingdom of Great Britain and Northern Ireland
Mekë/ Mecca
Melanezi/ Melanesia
Meksikë/ Mexico
Merilend/ Maryland
Miçigan/ Michigan
Milano/ Milan
Minesotë/ Minnesota
Minsk/ Minsk
Misisipi/ Mississippi
Misuri/ Missouri
Moldavi/ Moldova
Monako/ Monaco
Mongoli/ Mongolia
Monreal/ Montreal
Moskë/ Moscow
Mozambik/ Mozambique
Mynih/ Munich

N

Najrobi/ Nairobi
Namibi/ Namibia
Napoli/ Naples
Nebraskë/ Nebraska
Nepal/ Nepal
Nevadë/ Nevada
Nevë/ Neva
Niagarë/ Niagara
Nicë/ Nice
Nigeri/ Nigeria
Nil/ Nile
Nikaragua/ Nicaragua
Ngushtica e Magelanit/ Magellan, Strait of
Norvegji/ Norway
Nuremberg/ Nuremberg, Nurnberg

NJ

Nju-Jork/ New York
Nju-Orleans/ New Orleans

O

Oklahomë/ Oklahoma
Oksford/ Oxford
Oman/ Oman
Oqeani/ Oceania
Oqeani Arktik/ Arctic Ocean
Oqeani Atlantic/ Atlantic Ocean
Oqeani Indian/ Indian Ocean
Oqeani Paqësor/ Pacific Ocean
Oregonë/ Oregon
Oslo/ Oslo

P

Palestinë/ Palestine
Pakistan/ Pakistan
Panama/ Panama
Paraguai/ Paraguay
Paris/ Paris
Pekin/ Peking
Pensilvani/ Pennsylvania
Peru/ Peru
Phenian/ Pyongyang
Pirenej/ Pyrenees
Poli i Jugut/ South Pole
Poli i Veriut/ North Pole
Poloni/ Poland
Portugali/ Portugal
Porto Riko/ Puerto Rico
Pragë/ Prague
Pretorie/ Pretoria

Q

Qipro/ Cyprus

R

Rekjavik/ Reykjavik
Ren/ Rhine
Republika e Afrikës së Jugut/ Republic of South Africa
Republika e Afrikës Qëndrore/ Central African Republic
Republika Federale Gjermane/ Federal Republic of Germany
Rio de Zhaneiro/ Rio de Janeiro
Romë/ Rome
Rumani/ Romania
Rusi/ Russia

S

Sahalin/ Sakhalin
Saharë/ Sahara
San Francisko/ San Francisco
San Paolo/ Sao Paulo
San Salvador/ San Salvador
Santiago/ Santiago
Santo-Domingo/ Santo Domingo
Sao-Tome-e-Principe/ Sao Tomé and Principe
Senegal/ Senegal
Senë/ Seine
Seul/ Seoul
Sevastopol/ Sevastopol
Siberi/ Siberia
Sicili/ Sicily
Sidnei/ Sydney
Singapor/ Singapore
Siri/ Syria
Skoci/ Scotland
Sllovaki/ Slovakia
Sofje/ Sofia
Somali/ Somalia
Spanjë/ Spain
Sri-Lankë/ Sri Lanka
Stamboll/ Istanbul
Stokholm/ Stockholm
Suazilend/ Swaziland
Sudan/ Sudan, the
Suedi/ Sweden

SH

Shangai/ Shanghai
Shtetet e Bashkuara të Amerikës/ United States of America,
USA

Tailandë/ Thailand
Tajvan/ Taiwan
Tanzani/ Tanzania
Tashkent/ Tashkent
Taxhikistan/ Tadjikistan
Tbilis/ Tbilisi
Teheran/ Teh(e)ran
Tel-Aviv/ Tel Aviv
Teksas/ Texas
Tibet/ Tibet
Tokio/ Tokyo
Toronto/ Toronto
Trinidad dhe Tobago/ Trinidad and Tobago
Tuniz/ Tunis
Tunizi/ Tunisia
Turkmenistan/ Turkmenistan
Turqi/ Turkey

Uashington/ Washington
Uells/ Wales
Ugandë/ Uganda
Ukrahinë/ Ukraine, the
Ulan-Bator/ Ulan Bator
Ulster/ Ulster
Ural/ Urals, the
Uruguai/ Uruguay
Uzbekistan/ Uzbekistan

Varshavë/ Warsaw
Vatikan/ Vatican
Venezuelë/ Venezuela
Venecie/ Venice
Vermont/ Vermont
Viktoria/ Victoria
Virgjinia/ Virginia
Viskonsin/ Wisconsin
Vistulë/ Vistula
Vjetnam/ Vietnam
Vladivostok/ Vladivostok
Vollgë/ Volga

Zaire/ Zaire
Zambia/ Zambia
Zanzibar/ Zanzibar
Zelanda e Re/ New Zealand

Zimbabve/ Zimbabwe
Zvicër/ Switzerland
Zyrih/ Zurich

XH

Xhakartë/ Jakarta
Xhamajkë/ Jamaica
Xhibuti/ Jibuti
Xhomolungmë/ Chomolungma
Xhorxhtaun/ Georgetown

ENGLISH-ALBANIAN
(Fjalor Anglisht-Shqip)

LIST OF ABBREVIATIONS

adj.	adjective
adv.	adverb
conj.	conjunction
def art.	definite article
demonstr.	demonstrative
imp.	imperative
impers.	impersonal
indef. art.	indefinite article
int.	interjection
interr.	interrogative
masc.	masculine
neg.	negative
num.	numeral
part. adj.	participial adjective
pers. pron.	personal pronoun
pl.	plural
poss.	possessive
pp.	past participle
pref.	prefix
prep.	preposition
pron.	pronoun
reflex.	reflexive
rel.	relative
smb.	somebody
smth.	something
suff.	suffix
superl.	superlative
vi.	verb intransitive
vt.	verb transitive
vti.	verb transitive and intransitive

PREFACE

This bilingual Albanian-English/English-Albanian Practical Dictionary will be useful for English speaking travelers, businesspersons, and students, as well as for native Albanian speakers learning English. It contains over 20,000 entries, alphabetically arranged and supplied with basic grammatical information and simple pronunciation. The headwords, which include all the important words needed in everyday life, are in bold type. Compound words appear as headwords. Derivatives of the headword are also found in bold type. Every entry is followed by its phonetic transliteration and stress mark, its part of speech, and if it is a verb, whether it is transitive or intransitive. Idioms are also given in bold type. If an idiom has more than one meaning, its definitions are divided by a semicolon. If the idiom contains both a noun and a verb, it is entered according to its verb.

A

A, a /ei/ 1. shkronja e parë e alfabetit anglez; **from A to Z** nga fillimi në fund; **A 1.** i dorës së parë, i klasit të parë, i mrekullueshëm, i shkëlqyeshëm; 2. nota më e mirë
a /ei,ë/ **an** / ën/ **indef.art.** një
aback /ë'bek/ **adv. taken aback** zihem befas, befasohem
abandon /ë'bendën/ **v.t.** 1. braktis; 2. heq dorë
abate /ë'beit/ **v.t. & i.** 1. ul, pakësoj; 2. zbret, bie
abbey /'ebi/ **n.** manastir, abaci
abbot /'ebët/ **n.** abat, murg
abbreviation /ë'bri:vi'eishën/ **n.** shkurtim
abdomen /'ebdëmën/ **n.** bark
abduct /ëb'dakt/ **v.t.** rrëmbej
ability /ë'bilëti/ **n.** 1. aftësi; 2. zgjuarsi, dhunti
able /'eibl/ **adj.** i aftë, i zoti; **be able to do something** jam në gjendje të bëj diçka
aboard /ë'bo:rd/ **adv.** në bord (të anijes, aeroplanit etj.)
abolish /ë'bolish/ **vt.** heq, anuloj; zhduk
abortion /ë'bo:rshën/ **n.** dështim
abortive /ë'bo:rtiv/ **adj.** i dështuar
abound /ë'baund/ **v.** ka me shumicë, me bollëk
about /ë'baut/ **prep.** rreth, nëpër; **adv.** rreth, afro; rrotull
above /ë'bav/ **prep.** mbi, përmbi; lart, sipër
abridge /ë'brixh/ **vt.** shkurtoj
abroad /ë'bro:d/ **adv.** jashtë shtetit
abrupt /ë'brapt/ **adj.** 1. i papritur, i menjëhershëm; 2. i vrazhdë, i rreptë
absent /'ebsënt/ **adj.** i papranishëm, mungues
absent-minded /'ebsent'maindid/ **adj.** i hutuar
absolute /'ebsëlu:t/ **adj.** absolut
absorb /ëb'so:rb/ **vt.** 1. thith; 2. përpij, përvetësoj
abstain /ëb'stein/ **vi.** 1. përmbahem; 2. jam i përkorë; 3. abstenoj
abstract /'ebstrekt/ **adj.** abstrakt
absurd /ëb'së:rd/ **adj.** absurd
abundant /ë'bandënt/ **adj.** i bollshëm
abuse /ë'bju:z/ **n.** abuzim, shpërdorim
academic /,ekë'demik/ **adj.** akademik
academy /ë'kedemi/ **n.** akademi
accelerate /ëk'selëreit/ **vt.** përshpejtoj, shpejtoj
accent /'eksënt/ **n.** 1. theks; 2. shqiptim
accept /ëk'sept/ **vt.** pranoj
acceptable /ëk'septëbl/ **adj.** i pranueshëm
accessible /ëk'sesëbl/ **adj.** i arritshëm
accident /'eksidënt/ **n.** 1. aksident; 2. rastësi
acclaim /ë'kleim/ **vt.** brohoras, pres me duartrokitje
accomodation /ë,komë'deishn/ **n.** 1. përshtatje; 2. strehim, vend në hotel
accompany /ë'kampëni/ **vt.** shoqëroj
accomplish /ë'kamplish/ **vt.** kryej, përmbush
accordingly /ë'ko:rdinli/ **adv.** 1. në pajtim; 2. në këtë mënyrë; për këtë arsye
according to /ë'kordin tu:/ **prep.** sipas, në përputhje me

account /ë'kaunt/ **n.** 1. llogari; **settle accounts with** qëroj, laj hesapet me; 2. raport, llogari; **call (bring) to account** thërres në raport; 3. vlerësim; **take into account** marr parasysh
accountant /ë'kauntënt/ **n.** llogaritar
accredited /ë'kreditid/ **adj.** i akredituar
accumulate /ë'kju:mjuleit/ **vt.** akumuloj; grumbulloj
accurate /'ekjërët/ **adj.** 1. i përpiktë, i saktë; 2. i kujdesshëm
accuse /ë'kju:z/ **vt.** akuzoj, padit, fajësoj
accustomed /ë'kastëmd/ **adj.** i zakonshëm
ace /eis/ 1. as (në letra); 2. njëshi (në zare, në domino)
achieve /ë'çi:v/ **vt.** 1. arrij; 2. kryej, përfundoj
achievement /ë'çivmënt/ **n.** 1. arritje; 2. kryerje, plotësim
acid /'esid/ **adj.** i thartë; **n.** acid
acknowledge /ëk'nolixh/ **vt.** 1. njoh, pranoj; 2. vërtetoj marrjen (e një letre etj.)
acoustic /ë'ku:stik/ **adj.** akustik
acquaintance /ë'kveintëns/ **n.** 1. njohje; 2. i njohur
acquire /ë'kvaië(r)/ **vt.** 1. fitoj, përftoj; 2. siguroj
acquit /ë'kwit/ **vt.** 1. shfajësoj, fal; 2. sillem
acquittance /ë'kvitëns/ **n.** çlirim (nga detyrimet); shlyerje (e borxhit)
acre /eikë(r)/ **n.** akër
across /ë'kro:s/ **adv.** tërthor, mes për mes; **prep.** nëpër, përmes
act /ekt/ **n.** 1. veprim; 2. akt, dekret; 3. akt; **vt.** 1. veproj; 2. luaj, interpretoj
action /'ekshn/ **n.** 1. veprim; 2. veprimtari, aktivitet
activity /ek'tivëti/ **n.** aktivitet, veprimtari
actor /'ektë(r)/ **n.** aktor
actual /'ekçjuël/ **adj.** aktual, i sotëm
actually /'ekçjuëli/ **adv.** faktikisht, realisht, aktualisht
acute /ë'kju:t/ **adj.** 1. i mprehtë; 2. **fig.** i mprehtë; 3. therës
adapt /ë'dept/ **vt.** përshtas
add /ed/ **vt.** 1. shtoj, plotësoj; 2. **mat.** mbledh
addendum /ë'dendëm/ **n.** shtesë (në libër etj.)
addict /'edikt/ **n.** narkoman
additional /ë'dishënl/ **adj.** plotësues, shtesë
address /ë'dres/ **n.** 1. adresë; 2. fjalim, ligjëratë; **vt.** adresoj, dërgoj; 2. i drejtohem
addressee /,edre'si:/ **n.** marrës (i letrës)
adequate /'edikwët/ **adj.** i mjaftueshëm; adekuat
adhere /ëd'hië(r)/ **vi.** 1. ngjitet; 2. i përmbahem me vendosmëri (parimit etj.)
adjective /'exhiktiv/ **n.** **gram.** mbiemër
adjourn /ë'xhë:rn/ **vt.** 1. shtyj; 2. kaloj nga një vend te tjetri
adjust /ë'xhast/ **vt.** rregulloj; përshtas
administration /ëd,mini'streishn/ **n.** drejtim, qeverisje, administrim
admirable /'edmërëbl/ **adj.** i admirueshëm
admiral /'edmërël/ **n.** admiral
admire /ëd'maië(r)/ **vt.** admiroj
admission /ëd'mishn/ **n.** 1. lejim, hyrje; 2. pranim
admit /ëd'mit/ **vt.** 1. lejoj, lë të hyjë; 2. pranoj

adolescent /,edë'lesnt/ **adj.** adolishent
adopt /ë'dopt/ **vt.** 1. birësoj, adoptoj; 2. përvetësoj; 3. miratoj, pranoj (një vendim)
adorable /ë'do:rëbl/ **adj.** i adhurueshëm
adorn /ë'do:rn/ **vt.** zbukuroj, stolis
adult /ë'dalt/ **adj. n.** i rritur
advance /ëd'vens/ **n.** 1. përparim; 2. parapagim; paradhënie; 3. rritje **vt.** 1. përparoj; 2. parapaguaj; jap paradhënie; 3. rritem
advanced /ëd'venst/ **adj.** i përparuar, i avancuar
advantage /ëd'ventixh/ **n.** 1. dobi, përfitim; 2. epërsi, avantazh
adventure /ëd'vençë(r)/ **n.** aventurë
adverb /'edvë:b/ **n. gram.** ndajfolje
advertisement /ëd'vë:rtismënt/ **n.** 1. shpallje; 2. reklamë
advice /ëd'vais/ **n.** këshillë
advise /ëd'vaiz/ **vt.** këshilloj
advocate /'edvëkët/ **n.** avokat; mbrojtës **vt.** /'edvëkeit/ mbroj, përkrah
aeroplane /'erëplein/ **n.** aeroplan
aesthetics /i:s'thetiks **n.** estetikë
affair /ë'feë(r)/ **n.** punë, çështje; **love affair** punë dashurie
affect /ë'fekt/ **vt.**1 ndikoj, veproj; 2. prek, mallëngjej; 3. infektoj
affiliate /ë'filieit/ **vt.** 1. futem (në një shoqëri); 2. bashkoj si filiale; 3. bashkohem
affirm /ë'fë:rm/ **vt.** 1. pohoj; 2. konfirmoj
afford /ë'fo:rd/ **vt.** 1. jam në gjendje, kam mundësi (të paguaj etj.); 2. jap
afraid /ë'freid/ **adj. pred.** i frikësuar
after /'a:ftë; 'eftë(r)/ **prep.** pas, mbas; **adv.** pastaj; pas, më vonë; nga prapa; **after all** në fund të fundit
afternoon /'a:ftë'nu:n; 'eftë'nu:n/ **n.** pasdreke, pasdite
afterwards /'a:ftë'vëdz; 'eftë'vëdz/ **adv.** paskëtaj, më pas, pastaj
again /ë'gen; ë'gein/ **adv.** përsëri, sërish, prapë
against /ë'geinst; ë'genst/ **prep.** kundër
age /eixh/ **n.** 1. moshë; 2. kohë, epokë
aged /eixhd/ **adj.** i moshuar, i thyer nga mosha
agency /'eixhënsi/ **n.** 1. agjensi; 2. mjet; 3. veprim
agent /'eixhënt/ **n.** agjent
aggravate /'egrëveit/ **vt.** 1. rëndoj, keqësoj; 2. acaroj; 3. ngacmoj
aggressive /ë'gresiv/ **adj.** agresiv
ago /ë'gou/ **adv.** para, më parë; **long ago** shumë kohë më parë
agony /'egëni/ **n.** agoni, dhembje shumë e fortë
agree /ë'gri/ **vt.** jam i një mendje me, jam dakord me; **vi.** i përgjigjet, i përshtatet
agreement /ë'gri:mënt/ **n.** 1. pajtim; 2. marrëveshje
agriculture/'egrikalçë(r)/ **n.** bujqësi
ahead /ë'hed/ **adv.** përpara, para
aid /eid/ **n.** 1. ndihmë; 2. mjet
ailment /'eilmënt/ **n.** sëmundje
aim /eim/ **n.** 1. qëllim; 2. shenjë
air /eë(r)/ **n.** ajër; atmosferë; **adj.** ajror
air-conditioning /'eë(r)kën'dishënin/ **n.** ajër i kondicionuar

airline /'eë(r)lain/ **n.** linjë ajrore
airmail /'eë(r)meil/ **n.** postë ajrore
alarm /ë'la:rm/ **n.** 1. alarm; 2. panik, rrëmujë
alarm clock /ë'la:rm klok/ **n.** sahat me zile
alas /ë'les/ **inter.** medet! eh! mjerisht!
Albania /al'benië/ **n.** Shqipëri
Albanian /al'benien/ **adj.** 1. shqiptar; 2. shqip
album /'elbëm/ **n.** album
alcohol /'elkëho:l/ **n.** alkool
alert /ë'lë:rt/ **adj.** vigjilent, syhapët
algebra /'elxhibrë/ **n.** algjebër
alibi /'elibai/ **n. drej.** alibi
alien /'eilien/ **adj.** i huaj; **n.** i huaj
alike /ë'laik/ **adj.** i ngjashëm, i njëjtë; **adv.** njëlloj
alimony /'elimëni/ **n.** detyrim, kompensim (i burrit për gruan para ose pas ndarjes)
alive /ë'laiv/ **adj.** 1. i gjallë; 2. i hedhur
all /o:l/ **adj.** gjithë, tërë; i gjithë; **all the same** njëlloj; **all right** mirë, në rregull; **pron.** të gjithë, çdokush; **not at all** aspak; **adv.** tërësisht, plotësisht
allergic /ë'lë:rxhik/ **adj.** alergjik
alliance /ë'laiëns/ **n.** 1. bashkim; 2. lidhje, aleancë
allotment /ë'lotmënt/ **n.** 1. ndarje, shpërndarje; 2. pjesë; 3. parcelë, copë
allow /ë'lau/ **vt.** 1. lejoj; 2. jap; 3. lë
allowance /ë'lauëns/ **n.** 1. leje, lejim; 2. fond; racion; 3. zbritje; 4. lëshime
ally /'elai/ **n.** aleat
almost /'o:lmëost/ **adv.** thuajse, gati
alone / ë'lëun/ **adj.** i vetëm; **adv.** vetëm
along /ë'lon/ **prep.** gjatë, nëpër; **along the road** gjatë rrugës; **adv.** përpara; me vete
aloud /ë'laud/ **adv.** me zë të lartë
alphabet /'elfëbet/ **n.** alfabet
already /o:l'redi/ **adv.** tashmë, tanimë
also /'o:lsëo/ **adv.** edhe, gjithashtu
alter /'o:ltë(r)/ **vt.** ndryshoj, ndërroj
alternative /o:l'të:nëtiv/ **n.** alternativë
although /o:l'dhou/ **conj.** megjithëse, sadoqë
altogether /,o:ltë'gedhë(r)/ **adv.** plotësisht, krejt, gjithsej
always /'o:lweiz/ **adv.** gjithmonë, përherë
ambassador /em'besëdë(r)/ **n.** ambasador
ambiguous /em'bigjuës/ **adj.** i dykuptimshëm
ambition /em'bishn/ **n.** ambicie, pikësynim, dëshirë
ambulance /'embjulëns/ **n.** autoambulancë
amiable /'eimiëbl/ **adj.** i dashur, i sjellshëm, i përzemërt
among /ë'man/ **prep.** ndërmjet, midis
amount /ë'maunt/ **n.** 1. sasi; 2. shumë; 3. vlerë
amplifier /'emplifaië/ **n.** përforcues, amplifikator
amusing /ë'mju:zin/ **adj.** dëfryes, zbavitës
analyze /'enëlaiz/ **vt.** analizoj, shqyrtoj
analysis /ë'nelësis/ **n.** analizë

anatomy /ë'netëmi/ n. anatomi
ancestor /'ensestë(r)/ n. stërgjysh
anchovy /'ençëvi/ n. sardele
ancient /'einshënt/ adj. i moçëm, i lashtë, antik
and /end/ conj. edhe, dhe , e
angel /'einxhël/ n. engjëll
anger /'engë/ n. zemërim, inat; vt. zemëroj, inatos
angle /engl/ n. kënd
angry /'engri/ adj. i zemëruar, i inatosur
animal /'eniml/ n. kafshë
animated /'enimeitid/ adj. i gjallë, i gjallëruar; animated
cartoon(s) film vizatimor
ankle /'enkl/ n. nyjë e këmbës
anniversary /,eni'vë:sëri/ n. përvjetor
announce /ë'nauns/ vt. njoftoj, shpall, lajmëroj
annoy /ë'noi/ vt. 1. mërzis, zemëroj; 2. ngacmoj, shqetësoj
annual /'enjuël/ adj. vjetor, i përvitshëm
anonymous /ë'nonimës/ adj. anonim
another /e'nëdhë(r)/ adj. tjetër, edhe një
answer /'ensër/ ; 'ensër/ n. përgjigje; vt. përgjigjem
ant /ent/ n. milingonë, mizë dheu
ante meridiem /'entimë'ridiëm/ adv. para dreke
antibiotic /,entibai'otik/ n. antibiotik
anticipate /en'tisipeit/ vt. 1. parashikoj; 2. parandiej
antidote /'entidout/ n. kundërhelm
antiquity /en'tikwëti/ n. antikitet, lashtësi
antiseptic /,enti'septik/ n. antiseptik; adj. antiseptik
anus /einës/ n. anat. pasdalje, anus
anxious /'enkshës/ adj. i shqetësuar, i merakosur; be anxious
jam i shqetësuar; dëshiroj shumë
any /'eni/ adj. pron. ndonjë; çfarëdo
anybody, anyone /'enibëdi, 'enivën/ pron. kushdo, cilido;
dikush
anyhow /'enihau/ adv. në një mënyrë ose në një tjetër;
dosido; sidoqoftë
anything /'enithin/ pron. 1. diçka; 2. gjithçka
anyway /'enivei/ adv. në çdo rast
apart /ë'p:art/ adv. mënjanë, veç e veç
apartment /ë'pa:rtment/ n. apartament; hyrje; dhomë
ape /eip/ n. majmun; vt. imitoj, bëj si majmuni
apologize /ë'polëxhaiz/ vt. shfajësohem, kërkoj ndjesë
appalling /ë'polin/ adj. i tmerrshëm, i frikshëm
apparatus /,epë'reitës; ,epë'retës/ n. aparat, mjet
apparent /ë'perënt/ adj. i dukshëm, i qartë
appeal /ë'pi:l/ n. apelim, thirrje; vi..1. apeloj, bëj thirrje
2. tërheq, bëj për vete
appear /ë'pië(r)/ vi. dukem, shfaqem
appearance /ë'piërëns/ n. shfaqje, dukje, pamje e jashtme
appendicitis /ë'pendi'saitis/ n. mjek. apendicit
appetite /'epitait/ n. 1. oreks; 2. dëshirë, etje, qejf
applaud /ë'plo:d/ vt. duartrokas
apple /'epl/ n. mollë
applicant /'eplikënt/ n. kërkues; kandidat

application /,epli'keishn/ **n. 1.** zbatim; **2.** kërkesë, lutje
apply /ë'plai/ **vt. 1.** zbatoj, vë në zbatim; **2.** i drejtohem;
apply oneself to jepem pas; i kushtohem
appointment /ë'pointmënt/ **n. 1.** emërim; **2.** takim
appraisal /ë'preizl/ **n.** vlerësim
appreciate /ë'pri:shieit/ **vt.** çmoj, vlerësoj
approach /ë'prouç/ **vi. 1.** afrohem; **2.** i drejtohem; **n. 1.**
afrim; **2.** hyrje; **3.** këndvështrim; trajtim
appropriate /ë'propriët/ **adj.** i përshtatshëm; **vt.**
/ë'proprieit/ **1.** përvetësoj; **2.** caktoj
approve /ë'pru:v/ **vt.** miratoj, aprovoj
approximate /ë'proksimët/ **adj.** i përafërt
apricot /'eiprikot/ **n.** kajsi; zerdeli
April /'eiprl/ **n.** prill
apt /ept/ **adj. 1.** i aftë; **2.** i prirur
aquarium /ë'kveëriëm/ **n.** akuarium
Arabic /'erëbik/ **adj.** arabik; **n.** arabishte
arable /'erëbl/ **adj.** i lërueshëm, i punueshëm
arbiter /'a:rbitë(r)/ **n.** arbitër, gjyqtar
arc /a:rk/ **n.** hark, qemer
archaeology /,a:ki'olëgji/ **n.** arkeologji
archaic /a:'keik/ **adj.** arkaik, i vjetëruar
archbishop /'a:ç'bishëp/ **n.** kryepeshkop
archipelago /,a:rki'pelëgou/ **n.** arkipelag
architecture /'a:kitekçë(r)/ **n.** arkitekturë
ardent /'a:rdent/ **adj.** i flaktë, i zjarrtë; i zellshëm
area /'eërië/ **n. 1.** hapësirë e lirë; **2.** sipërfaqe; **3.** zonë,
krahinë
argue /'a:gju:/ **vt. 1.** argumentoj, sjell prova; **2.** debatoj,
zihem me fjalë
argument /'a:gjumënt/ **n. 1.** argument; **2.** diskutim, debat
arise /ë'raiz/ **vi. 1.** ngrihet, del; **2.** rrjedh, rezulton
aristocratic /,eristë'kretik/ **adj.** aristokrat, aristokratik
arithmetic /ë'rithmetik/ **adj.** aritmetik
arm /a:rm/ **n. 1.** krah; **2.** armë; **vt.** armatos
armament /'a:rmëmënt/ **n.** armatim; armatosje
armchair /'a:rm'çeë/ **n.** kolltuk
armpit /'a:rmpit/ **n.** sqetull
army /'a:rmi/ **n.** ushtri; **join the army** shkoj ushtar
around /ë'raund/ **prep.** rreth, përreth; **adv.** përreth
arrange /ë'reinxh/ **vt. 1.** rregulloj, vë në rregull; **2.**
organizoj, parapërgatis; **3.** përshtas
arrest /ë'rest/ **n.** arrestim; **vt.** arrestoj
arrival /ë'raivël/ **n.** arritje, ardhje
arrive /ë'raiv/ **vi.** arrij, mbrrij
arrogant /'erëgënt/ **adj.** arrogant
arsenic /'a:snik/ **n.** arsenik
arson /'a:rson/ **n.** zjarrvënie
art /a:rt/ **n.** art
article /'a:rtikl/ **n. 1.** artikull; **2.** artikull, send; **3.**
gram. nyjë
artificial /,a:rti'fishl/ **adj.** artificial
artillery /a:r'tileri/ **n.** artileri
artist /'a:rtist/ **n.** artist

as /ez/ **adv.** si, në cilësinë e; **as a rule** zakonisht, si
rregull; **as if** sikur
ascend /ë'send/ **vi.** ngjitem, ngrihem
ash /esh/ **n.** 1. hi; 2. ah, frashër
ashamed /ë'sheimd/ **adj.** i turpëruar
ashore /ë'sho:(r)/ **adv.** në breg
ash-tray /'eshçrei/ **n.** tavllë, taketuke
Asian /'eishën; 'eizhn/ **adj.** aziatik; **n.** aziatik
ask /a:sk/ **vt.** 1. pyes; 2. kërkoj; 3. ftoj, thërres; **ask a
question** bëj një pyetje
asleep /ë'sli:p/ **adv.** në gjumë; **be asleep** jam në gjumë; **fall
asleep** bie në gjumë
asparagus /ë'sperëgës/ **n. bot.** shparg, shpargull
aspect /'espekt/ **n.** 1. aspekt; 2. dukë, pamje; 3. pikëpamje
aspiration /'espë'reishn/ **n.** 1. aspirim, aspiratë 2.
frymëmarrje
aspirin /'espërin; 'esprin/ **n.** aspirinë
ass /es/ **n.** gomar
assassin /ë'ses(i)n/ **n.** vrasës
assault /ë'so:lt/ **n.** sulm; **vt.** sulmoj
assemble /ë'sembl/ **vt.** 1. mbledh; 2. montoj
assent /ë'sent/ **n.** pëlqim, miratim; **vi.** miratoj, jap pëlqimin
assert /ë'së:rt/ **vt.** 1. pohoj, shpall; 2. mbroj
assess /ë'ses/ **vt.** 1. vlerësoj; 2. çmoj
assets /esets/ **n. pl.** 1. pronë, pasuri; 2. **fin.** aktivi
assignment /ë'sainmënt/ **n.** 1. caktim, ngarkim; 2. detyrë
assimilate /ë'simëleit/ **vt.** asimiloj; përvetësoj
assistance /ë'sistëns/ **n.** ndihmë
association /ë'sousi'eishn/ **n.** 1. shoqëri; 2. shoqatë
assortment /ë'so:rtmënt/ **n.** asortiment, lloj
assume /ë'sju:m/ **vt.** 1. marr përsipër; 2. pranoj si të
vërtetë
assure /ë'shuë/ **vt.** siguroj; garantoj
asthma /'esmë; 'ezmë/ **n.** astmë
astonish /ë'stonish/ **vt.** habit, mahnit
astrology /ë'strologji/ **n.** astrologji
astronomy /ë'stronëmi/ **n.** astronomi
asylum /ë'sailëm/ **n.** 1. strehim; 2. azil
at /et/ **prep.** në; **at first** në fillim; **at last** së fundi, më në
fund; **at least** së paku, të paktën; **at once** menjëherë; **at home**
në shtëpi; **at night** natën
athlete /'ethli:t/ **n.** atlet
atmosphere /'etmësfië/ **n.** atmosferë; mjedis
atom /'etëm/ **n.** atom
attach /ë'teç/ **vt.** 1. ngjis, bashkoj; 2. jap
attack /ë'tek/ **n.** 1. sulm; 2. atak; **vt.** sulmoj
attain /ë'tein/ **vt.** arrij; përmbush
attempt /ë'tempt/ **n.** orvajtje, përpjekje; **vt.** orvatem,
përpiqem
attend /ë'tend/ **n.** merrem, ndjek; 2. shërbej, kujdesem
attention /ë'tenshn/ **n.** vëmendje; kujdes
attitude /'etitu:d/ **n.** 1. qëndrim; 2. pikëpamje
attract /ë'trekt/ **vt.** tërheq, bëj për vete
attractive /ë'trektiv/ **adj.** tërheqës
attribute /'etribju:t/ **n.** atribut, veti, tipar; **vt.** i
atribuoj

auction /'o:kshn/ **n.** ankand; **vt.** shes në ankand
audience /'o:diëns/ **n.** audiencë; auditor
audit /'o:dit/ **n.** revizion; **vt.** revizionoj
auditor /'o:ditë/ **n.** 1. dëgjues; 2. revizor
augment /o:g'ment/ **vt.** shtoj, rrit, zmadhoj
August /'o:gëst/ **n.** gusht
aunt /a:nt; ent/ **n.** teze, hallë
Australian /o:'streiliën/ **adj.** australian; **n.** australian
author /'o:thë(r)/ **n.** autor
authority /o:'thorëti/ **n.** autoritet; **pl.** pushtet
automatic /,o:të'metik/ **adj.** automatik
autonomy /o:'tonëmi/ **n.** autonomi, vetëqeverisje
autumn /'o:tëm/ **n.** vjeshtë
auxiliary /o:g'ziliëri/ **adj.** ndihmës, ndihmëtar
available /ë'veilëbl/ **adj.** 1. i disponueshëm; 2. i arritshëm,
i realizueshëm; 3. i vlefshëm
avenue /'evënju:; 'evënu:/ **n.** shëtitore
average /'evërixh/ **adj.** mesatar, i mesëm
aviation /,eivi'eishn/ **n.** aviacion
avoid /ë'void/ **vt.** shmang, largoj; anuloj
awake /ë'veik/ **adj.** 1. i zgjuar; 2. syçelur, syhapur
award /ë'vo:rd/ **n.** 1. çmim; dekorim; dhënie çmimi; 2. vendim
gjyqi
aware /ë'veë(r)/ **adj.** i vetëdijshëm; **be aware of** jam i
vetëdijshëm për
away /ë'vei/ **adj.** i largët; **adv.** tutje, larg; **far away** larg
awful /'o:fl/ **adj.** i tmerrshëm; i frikshëm
awkward /'o:kvërd/ **adj.** 1. pavolitshëm; 2. i ngathët, kaba
axe /eks/ **n.** sëpatë

B

babble /'bebël/ **v.** 1. belbëzoj; 2. llomotis, dërdëllis; **n** 1.
gugatje; 2. murmurimë; 3. llomotitje
baby /'beibi/ **n.** 1. foshnjë; 2. e dashur
baby-sitter /'beibi sitë(r)/ **n.** dado
bachelor /'beçëlë(r)/ **n.** beqar
back /bek/ **n.** 1. shpinë, kurriz; 2. shpinore; 3. anë e
prapme; **adj.** i prapmë, i pasmë; **adv.** prapa, pas; **vti.** 1.
mbështes, përkrah; 2. prapsohem
background /'bekgraund/ **n.** 1. sfond; 2. hije; **be (keep,stay)
in the background** rri, qëndroj në hije
backward /'bekvërd/ **adj.** 1. i prapambetur; 2. i kundërt; **adv.**
prapa, praptazi
bacon /'beikën/ **n.** proshutë; pastërma derri; **save one's back**
shpëtoj lëkurën
bad /bed/ **adj.** 1. i keq; 2. i pakëndshëm; 3. i dëmshëm
badge /bexh/ **n.** 1. distinktiv; 2. shenjë dalluese
bag /beg/ **n.** 1. thes; 2. trastë; çantë
baggage /'begixh/ **n.** bagazh
bake /beik/ **vti.** 1. pjek; 2. piqem
baker's shop /'beikërs'shop/ **n.** furrë, dyqan buke
balance /'belëns/ **n.** 1. peshore; 2. drejtpeshim; 3. **ek.**
bilanc; **vti.** 1. peshoj; 2. drejtpeshoj; 3. **ek.** balancoj
balcony /'belkëni/ **n.** ballkon
bald /bo:ld/ **adj.** 1. tullac; 2. i zhveshur
ball /bo:l/ **n.** 1. top; 2. sferë; 3. lëmsh; 4. gjyle
ballet /'belei/ **n.** balet
balloon /bë'lu:n/ **n.** balonë; aerostat
ballot /'belët/ **n.** 1. votim; 2. fletë votimi; **vi.** votoj
ballot-paper /'belët'peipë/ **n.** fletë votimi
ban /ben/ **vt.** ndaloj; **n.** ndalim
banana /bë'nenë/ **n.** banane
banal /'bë'na:l; 'beinl/ **adj.** 1. banal; 2. vulgar
band /bend/ **n.** 1. bandë muzikore; 2. shirit kordele; 3. bandë
bandage /'bendixh/ **n.** fashë; **vt.** fashoj, lidh me fashë
bang /ben/ **n.** goditje; përplasje e derës; **vti.** 1. godas; 2.
përplas derën
banish /'benish/ **vt.** dëboj, syrgjynos
bank /benk/ **n.** 1. breg; ledh; 2. bankë
bankrupt /'benkrëpt/ **n.** njeri i falimentuar; **adj.** i
falimentuar; **vt.** falimentoj; **go bankrupt** falimentoj
banquet /'benkwit/ **n.** banket, gosti; **vti.** shtroj banket,
gosti
bar /b:a(r)/ **n.** 1. shufër hekuri; 2. copë; kallëp; 3. lloz;
4. bar, bufe; 4. avokaturë
barber /'ba:bë(r)/ **n.** berber
bare /beë(r)/ **adj.** i zhveshur; **vt.** 1. zhvesh; 2. nxjerr në
shesh
bargain /'ba:rgin/ **n.** marrëveshje, ujdi; **strike a bargain**
arrij marrëveshje; **into the bargain** përveç kësaj, për më
tepër; **vti.** 1. tregtoj; 2. bie në ujdi
barley /'ba:rli/ **n.** elb
barrier /'berië/ **n.** pengesë
barter /'ba:rtë/ **n.** trambë, tregti me këmbim; **vti.** këmbej,
shkëmbej
base /beis/ **n.** 1. bazë, themel; 2. pikënisje; 3. bazë
(ushtarake)

213

baseball /'beisbɔ:l/ **n.** bejsboll
basement /'beismёnt/ **n.** 1. bodrum; qilar; 2. themel
basic /'beisik/ **adj.** themelor, bazal
basin /'beisin/ **n.** 1. legen; 2. tas, sahan
basis /'beisis/ **n.** 1. bazë, themel; 2. pikënisje; **on the basis of** në bazë të
basket /'beskit/ **n.** shportë; kosh
bastard /'bestёrd/ **n.** 1. bastard; 2. kopil, doç; **adj.** 1. bastard; 2. i jashtëligjshëm
bath /beth; b:ath/ **n.** 1. banjë; 2. banjë, dush; 3. larje në det
bathe /beith/ **vit.** laj; lahem; **n.** larje; banjë
battery /'betёri/ **n.** bateri
battle /'betl/ **n.** betejë, luftim; **vi.** luftoj, përleshem
bay /bei/ **n.** gji, liman
bazaar /bё'za:r/ **n.** pazar
be /bi:, bi/ **vi. jam; how are you?** si jeni?; **how much is it?** sa kushton kjo?; **be off** nisem, shkoj
beach /bi:ç/ **n.** plazh; bregdet
bean /bi:n/ **n.** bathë
bear /beё(r)/ **n.** ari
bear /beё(r)/ **vti.** 1. mbaj; 2. duroj; 3. lind; 4. prodhon, jep; **bear in mind** mbaj ndër mend
beard /biёd/ **n.** mjekёr
beast /bi:st/ **n.** bishё, egёrsirё
beat /bi:t/ **vt.** 1. rrah, godas; 2. mund
beautiful /'bju:tiful/ **adj.** i bukur
beauty /'bju:ti/ **n.** bukuri
because /bi'kɔ:z/ **conj.** sepse, për arsye se; **because of** për shkak të, për arsye të
become /bi'kam/ **vi.** 1. bёhem; 2. ndodh, ngjan, ngjet, bёhet
bed /bed/ **n.** krevat, shtrat; **go to bed** bie tё fle
bedroom /'bedru:m/ **n.** dhomë gjumi
bee /bi:/ **n.** bletё
beef /bi:f/ **n.** mish lope, viçi
beefsteak /'bi:fsteik/ **n.** biftek
beer /biё(r)/ **n.** birrё
beetroot /'bi:tru:t/ **n.** kokёrr e panxharit
before /bi:fɔ:(r)/ **adv.** mё parё, përpara; **long before** shumё kohё mё parё; **prep.** para, pёrpara; **the day before** dje
beg /beg/ **vti.** lyp; kёrkoj lёmoshё
beggar /'begё(r)/ **n.** lypёs
begin /bi'gin/ **vti.** 1. fillon; 2. filloj
beginning /bi'ginin/ **n.** fillim; **at the beginning** në fillim
behave /bi'heiv/ **vi.** sillem
behavior /bi'heivjё(r)/ **n.** sjellje
behind /bi'haind/ **adv.** prapa; **prep.** pas, prapa
being /'bi:in/ **n.** 1. qenie; 2. ekzistencё; 3. krijesё e gjallё; **human being** njeri; **for the time being** tani për tani; për ca kohё
belief /bi'li:f/ **n.** besim
believe /bi'li:v/ **vti.** besoj
bell /bel/ **n.** 1. kambanё; 2. zile
belong /bi'lɔ:n/ **vi.** i përkas, i takoj

belongings /bi'lonins/ n. pl. plaçka, tesha vetjake
below /bi'lou/ prep. nën, poshtë; adv. poshtë, përposh
belt /belt/ n. brez, rrip
bench /benç/ n. fron, stol
beneath /bi'ni:th/ adv. poshtë, përposh; prep. nën, poshtë
benefit /'benifit/ n. dobi, përfitim; vti. përfitoj; sjell
dobi, përfitim
bent /bent/ adj. i pandershëm, i korruptuar; n. prirje
berry /'beri/ n. bot. rrushk
beside /bi'said/ prep. pranë
besides /bi'saidz/ adv. përveç kësaj, për më tepër
best /best/ adj. më i miri
bestseller /'best'seller/ n. libër, etj. që shitet më shumë
bet /bet/ n. bast; **make a bet** vë bast; vti. vë bast
betray /bi'trei/ vt. 1. tradhtoj; 2. nxjerr në shesh
better //betë/ adj. më i mirë; adv. më mirë; më shumë; **be
better off** jam i pasur, jam në gjendje të mirë
between /bi'twi:n/ prep. midis, ndërmjet; adv. në mes; ndër
kohë
beware /bi'veë(r)/ vit. ruhem, hap sytë; **beware of trains!**
kujdes nga trenat!
beyond /bi'jond/ prep. përtej, tej, matanë; **beyond all doubt**
jashtë çdo dyshimi; adv. përtej, tutje
bias /'baiës/ n. 1. prirje; anësi; 2. paragjykim
Bible /'baibël/ n. bibël
bicycle /'baisikl/ n. biçikletë; vi. ngas biçikletën
bid /bid/ n. 1. urdhër; 2. ofertë, propozim për çmimin; **make
a bid** bëj një ofertë; vti. 1. urdhëroj; 2. jap, propozoj
çmimin
big /big/ adj. i madh; i rëndësishëm
bike /baik/ n. biçikletë
bill /bill/ n. 1. faturë; llogari; 2. bankënotë; **10 dollar
bill** bankënotë 10 dollarshe; 3. afishe, pllakatë
billion /'biliën/ n. miliard
bin /bin/ n. kovë, arkë plehërash
bind /baind/ vt. lidh; **bind hand and foot** lidh këmbë e duar
biography /bai'ogrëfi/ n. biografi
biology /bai'olëxhi/ n. biologji
birch /bë:rç/ n. mështenkë
bird /bë:rd/ n. zog
birth /bë:rth/ n. lindje; **birth certificate** çertifikatë
lindje; **birth control** kontroll i lindjeve; **give birth to** lind
birthday /'bë:rthdei/ n. ditëlindje; **Happy birthday!** Gëzuar
ditëlindjen!
biscuit /'biskit/ n. biskotë
bit /bit/ n. copë, grimë; **a bit** pak, paksa; **not a bit** aspak;
bit by bit dalëngadalë; **every bit** krejt
bitch /biç/ n. 1. bushtër; 2. kurvë
bite /bait/ n. 1. kafshatë; 2. kafshim; **have a bite** ha një
kafshatë bukë; vti. 1. kafshoj; 2. pickoj
bitter /'bitë(r)/ adj. 1. i hidhur; **a bitter taste** shije e
hidhur; 2. fig. i hidhur; **bitter words** fjalë të hidhura
black /blek/ adj. 1. i zi; 2. i errët; 3. i zymtë; n. ngjyrë
e zezë
blackmail /'blekmeil/ n. kërcënim, shantazh; vt. kërcënoj

bladder /'bledë(r)/ **n.** fshikëz
blade /'bleid/ **n.** teh brisku etj.
blame /bleim/ **n.** faj, fajësim; **vt.** fajësoj
blanket /'blenkit/ **n.** batanije; **vt.** mbuloj me batanije
blast /bla:st/ **n.** shkulm ere; rrymë ajri e fortë; **vt.** hedh në
erë, shpërthej
blazer /'bleizë(r)/ **n.** xhaketë sportive
bleach /bli:ç/ **vti.** zbardh, zbardhoj
blend /blend/ **n.** përzierje; **vt.** përziej; bashkoj, kombinoj
bless /bles/ **vt.** bekoj
blind /blaind/ **adj.** 1. i verbër; 2. i paarsyeshëm; **vt.** 1.
verboj; 2. errësoj
block /blok/ **n.** bllok banesash etj.; **vt.** bllokoj
blond(e) /blond/ **n.** bjond(e)
blood /blad/ **n.** gjak; **blood pressure tension** i gjakut; **blood
donor** dhurues gjaku
blouse /blauz/ **n.** bluzë
blow /blou/ **n.** 1. goditje; 2. fryrje; **vti.** fryj; fryn
blue /blu:/ **adj.** i kaltër; **once in a blue moon** rrallëherë,
një herë në mot
blunder /'blandë(r)/ **n.** gabim trashanik; **vit.** bëj gabim
trashanik
blunt /blant/ **vti.** çmpreh; topit; **adj.** i paprehur; i topitur
blush /blash/ **n.** skuqje, turpërim; **vi.** skuqem, turpërohem
board /bo:rd/ **n.** 1. dërrasë; 2. kuvertë e anijes; **on board** në
bordin e anijes; 3. bord, këshill drejtues; **vti.** hipi në
anije, në tren **boarding** /'bo:rdin/ **n.** pension, internat
boast /boust/ **n.** lavdërim, mburrje; **vti.** lëvdoj, lëvdohem
boat /bout/ **n.** varkë, barkë, lundër
bobsleigh /'bobslei/ **n.** bob, bobsled, slitë garash
body /'bodi/ **n.** 1. trup; 2. trung, skelet; 3. grumbull
njerëzish; 4. korporatë
boil /boil/ **n.** pikë vlimi; **vti.** valoj, ziej; zien, valon
boiled /boild/ **adj.** i zier
bold /bould/ **adj.** 1. guximtar, i guximshëm; 2. i paturpshëm
bolt /boult/ **n.** shul dere; **vti.** i vë shulin, mbyll me shul
bomb /bom/ **n.** bombë; **the bomb** bombë atomike; **vt.** bombardoj
bond /bond/ **n.** 1. lidhje; 2. marrëveshje, kontratë; 3.
obligacion
bone /boun/ **n.** 1. kockë; 2. halë peshku
bonus /'bounës/ **n.** shtesë, mbishtesë **(page)**
book /buk/ **n.** libër; **vt.** porosis një biletë
booking-office /'bukin'ofis/ **n.** biletari
book-keeper /'buk,ki:pë(r)/ **n.** llogaritar
boom /bu:m/ **n.** bum
boot /bu:t/ **n.** 1. këpucë me qafa; shoshone; **high boots** çizme
border /'bo:dë(r)/ **n.** 1. kufi; 2. buzë, skaj, anë
boredom /'bo:rdëm/ **n.** mërzitje, mërzi
born /'bo:rn/ **adj.** i lindur; **be born** lind
borrow /'borou/ **vti.** marr hua, huaj
bosom /'buzëm/ **n.** 1. kraharor, gjoks; 2. gji
boss /bos/ **n.** bos
botany /'botëni/ **n.** botanikë
both /bouth/ **adj. pron.** të dy

bother /'bodhë(r)/ **n.** shqetësim, bezdisje; **vti.** shqetësoj,
mërzis; shqetësohem
bottle /'botl/ **n.** shishe; **vt.** fus në shishe
bottom /'botëm/ **n.** 1. fund; 2. pjesë e poshtme; 3. shtrat,
bazë
bound /baund/ **n.** cak, kufi; **vt.** kufizohem, kam kufi; **adj.**
gati për; **the ship is bound for** anija është gati të niset
për; **bound up with** i lidhur ngushtë me
boundary /'baundri/ **n.** kufi; **beyond the boundaries** jashtë
kufijve
bow /bou/ **n.** 1. hark; 2. hark lahute, violine; **vt.** 1. i bie
violinës; 2. harkoj, i jap trajtën e harkut
bow /bau/ **n.** 1. përkulje për të përshëndetur; 2. kiç i
anijes; **vi.** 1. përkulem; 2. përkul, lakoj
bowels /bauëlz/ **n.pl.** të brendshmet; **move the bowels** dal
jashtë, bëj nevojën
bowl /boul/ **n.** 1. tas; 2. rruzull; top druri për lojë
box /boks/ **n.** 1. kuti, arkë; **vt.** fut në kuti, arkë
box /boks/ **n.** shuplakë; boks; **vti.** godas me pëllëmbë; bëj
boks, merrem me boks
box-office /'boks'ofis/ **n.** arkë, biletari
boxer /'boksë/ **n.** boksier
boy /boi/ **n.** djalë; bir, çun
brain /brein/ **n.** 1. tru; 2. arsye, mendje; **beat (rack) one's**
brains vras mendjen
brain-drain 'breindrein/ **n.** humbje e trurit (nga emigracioni)
brainwash /'breivosh/ **n.** "shpëlarje e trurit" (për ndërrimin
e mendimeve të vjetra)
brake /breik/ **n.** frenë; **put on (apply) the brakes** mbaj frenat
vti. frenoj
branch /bra:nç; brenç/ **n.** 1. degë (peme); 2. filial; 3. degë,
fushë
brand /brend/ **n.** 1. damkë; 2. **fig.** damkë, njollë; 3. markë
brandy /'brendi/ **n.** konjak, brandi
brass /bra:s/ **n.** 1. tunxh; 2. **gj.fl.** para; **top brass** officer,
zyrtar i lartë
brassiere /'bresië(r)/ **n.** sutiena
brave /breiv/ **adj.** trim, i guximshëm; **vt.** përballoj me guxim
breach /bri:ç/ **n.** 1. e çarë; 2. prishje e marrëdhënieve; 3.
shkelje (e ligjit, betimit etj.)
bread /bred/ **n.** bukë; **earn one's daily bread** fitoj bukën e
gojës
bread-winner /'bredwinë(r)/ **n.** mbajtësi i familjes me bukë
break /breik/ **n.** 1. pushim; **without a break** pa pushim; 2.
çarje, thyerje; **vt.** thyej
breakfast /'brekfëst/ **n.** mëngjes; **vi.** ha mëngjes
breast /brest/ **n.** 1. kraharor; 2. gji, sisë
breath /breth/ **n.** frymëmarrje
breathe /bri:dh/ **vit.** marr frymë
bribe /braib/ **n.** rryshfet, mitë; **vt.** mitos, jap mitë
brick /brik/ **n.** tullë
bride /braid/ **n.** nuse
bridegroom /'braidgrum/ **n.** dhëndër
bridge /brixh/ **n.** 1. urë; 2. urë e anijes; **vt.** lidh me urë
brief /bri:f/ **adj.** i shkurtër, i përmbledhur; **n.** përmbledhje;
vt. përmbledh

brigade /bri'geid/ **n.** brigadë; **fire brigade** skuadër
zjarrfikësish
bright /'brait/ **adj.** 1. i ndritshëm; 2. i shkëlqyeshëm; 3.
mendjemprehtë
brilliant /'briliënt/ **adj.** 1. i ndritshëm; 2. madhështor; 3.
mendjemprehtë
bring /brin/ **vti.** sjell, bije; **bring to life** kthej në jetë;
bring up 1. rrit; edukoj; 2. ngre, paraqes; 3. nxjerr, vjell
ushqimin
British /british/ **adj.** britanik, anglez
broad /bro:d/ **adj.** i gjerë
broadcast /'bro:dka:st/ **n.** transmetim; **vti.** transmetoj (me
radio, në televizion)
broiler /'broilë/ **n.** skarë
broken /broukën/ **adj.** 1. i thyer; 2. i ndërprerë; 3. i vrarë
(shpirtërisht)
broker /'broukë(r)/ **n.** 1. aksionar; 2. komisioner
bronchitis /bron'kaitis/ **n.** bronkit
bronze /bronz/ **n.** 1. bronz; 2. ngjyrë bronzi
brooch /brouç/ **n.** karficë
broth /broth/ **n.** lëng mishi; supë
brother /'bradhë(r)/ **n.** vëlla
brother-in-law /'bradhër in lo:/ **n.** kunat **brow** /brau/ **n.** 1.
vetull; 2. ballë
brown /braun/ **adj.** 1. bojë kafe, i kafenjtë; 2. i zeshkët,
zeshkan
brush /brash/ **n.** 1. furçë; 2. penel, furçë; **vt.** 1. pastroj me
furçë; 2. kreh flokët; 3. laj dhëmbët
bucket /'bakit/ **n.** kovë
bud /bad/ **n.** syth, burbuqe; **in the bud** në embrion
budget /'baxhit/ **n.** buxhet; **vi.** parashikoj, fus në buxhet
buffet /'bafit/ **n.** shpullë, shuplakë; **vt.** godas me pëllëmbë
bug /bag/ **n.** çimkë, tartabiq
build /bild/ **vt.** ndërtoj; ngre
building /'bildin/ **n.** ndërtesë
bulb /balb/ **n.** 1. kokë, bulb; 2. poç
bulk /balk/ **n.** sasi, masë, vëllim; **sell in bulk** shes me
shumicë
bull-dog /'bëlldog/ **n.** zagar
bullet /'bulit/ **n.** plumb
bulletin /'bulëtin/ **n.** buletin
bunch /banç/ **n.** 1. tufë; 2. vandak; 3. vile
burden /'bë:rdn/ **n.** barrë, ngarkesë; **vt.** ngarkoj; rëndoj
bureau /bjuë'rou/ **n.** 1. zyrë; 2. tryezë shkrimi
bureaucratic /,bjuërë'kretik/ **adj.** burokratik
burglary /'bë:rglëri/ **n.** thyerje, vjedhje shtëpish
burn /bë:rn/ **vti.** djeg, i vë zjarrin; 2. djeg, përvëloj,
përcëlloj; 3.ciknos, shkrumboj; **n.** djegie, plagë (nga djegia)
burst /bë:rst/ **n.** shpërthim, plasje; **vit.** pëlcet, shpërthen
bury /'beri/ **vt.** 1. varros; 2. gropos
bus /bas/ **n.** autobus; **go by bus** shkoj me autobus
bush /bush/ **n.** shkurre, kaçube
business /'biznis/ **n.** biznes; tregti
businessman /'biznismen/ **n.** biznesmen, afarist, tregtar
bust /bast/ **n.** bust
busy /'bizi/ **adj.** 1. i zënë; 2. i gjallë

but /bët; bat/ **prep.** veç, përveç; **conj.** po, por; **adv.** vetëm
butcher /'buçë(r)/ **n.** kasap
butter /'batë(r)/ **n.** gjalpë; **vt.** lyej me gjalpë; skuq, gatuaj
me gjalpë
butterfly /'batërflai/ **n.** flutur
buttock /'batëk/ **n.** mollaqe; të ndenjurat
button /'batn/ **n.** kopsë; **vti.** kopsit
buy /bai/ **vti.** blej
buyer /baië(r)/ **n.** blerës
by /bai/ **prep.** tek, pranë, rreth, gjatë; me anën e; **by**
airmail me postë ajrore; **by the river** anës lumit; **by no means**
me çdo kusht; **by the way** me që ra fjala; **by 5. o'clock** rreth
orës pesë; **by and by** gradualisht; **adv.** pranë; ngjitur; **stand**
by qëndroj pranë
by-election /'baiilekshn/ **n.** zgjedhje plotësuese
by-pass /'baipas; 'baipes/ **n.** rrugë anësore; **vt.** kaloj në
rrugë anësore

C

cab /keb/ **n.** 1. karrocë; 2. taksi; 3. kabinë (e shoferit etj.)
cabbage /'kebixh/ **n.** lakër
cabin /kebin/ **n.** 1. kasolle; 2. kabinë
cabinet /'kebinit/ **n.** 1. kabinet; 2. këshilli i ministrave; 3. dollap, bufe
cable /'keibl/ **n.** 1. kabllo; 2. telegraf; **vti.** telegrafoj
cabman /'kebmen/ **n.** shofer taksie
café /'kefei; ke'fei/ **n.** 1. kafene; 2. pijetore; gjellëtore
cafeteria /,kefë'tiërië/ **n.** mensë; gjellëtore
cage /keixh/ **n.** 1. kafaz; 2. burg; 3. ashensor miniere; **vt.** vë, mbyll, mbaj në kafaz; izoloj
cake /keik/ **n.** kek; tortë
calculate /'kelkjuleit/ **vt.** llogarit
calculating /'kelkjuletin/ **adj.** llogaritës; **calculating machine** makinë llogaritëse
calendar /'kelindë(r)/ **n.** kalendar
calf /ka:lf; kef/ **n.** viç
call /ko:ll/ **vti.** 1. thërras; bërtas; 2. quaj; 3. kërkoj; **call for** shkoj të marr dikë; kërkoj; meriton; **call off** shtyj; largoj vëmendjen; **call on** shkoj për vizitë; **n.** 1. britmë, thirrje; 2. kërkesë, thirrje; 3. vizitë e shkurtër
calm /ka:m; ka:lm/ **adj.** i qetë; **be calm!** qetësi! **vti.** qetësoj; **calm down** qetësohem
camel /'keml/ **n.** deve, gamile
camera /'kemërë/ **n.** aparat fotografik; kamera
camp /kemp/ **n.** 1. kamp; 2. fushim, kampim; **vi.** fushoj; **camp out** fushoj
campaign /kem'pein/ **n.** fushatë; **vi.** bëj fushatë; marr pjesë në një fushatë
can /ken/ **n.** 1. bidon; 2. kuti konservash; **vt.** konservoj
can /ken/ **aux. v.** mund, mundem
Canadian /kë'neidiën/ **n.** kanadez; **adj.** kanadez
canal /kë'nell/ **n.** kanal; **the Suez Canal** Kanali i Suezit
cancel /'kensl/ **vt.** 1. fshij, eliminoj; shuaj; 2. anuloj
cancer /'kensë(r)/ **n.** kancer
candid /'kendid/ **adj.** i hapët, i sinqertë
candidate /'kendideit/ **n.** kandidat
candle /'kendl/ **n.** qiri; **candle light** dritë qiriri
cane /kein/ **n.** 1. kallam; 2. thupër
cap /kep/ **n.** 1. kasketë, shapkë; 2. skufje; 3. kapak; **vt.** i vë kapakun
capable /'keipëbl/ **adj.** i aftë, i zoti
capacity /kë'pesiti/ **n.** 1. aftësi, fuqi; cilësi; 2. nxënësi, kapacitet; **filled to capacity** i mbushur plot
capital /'kepitl/ **n.** 1. kapital; **circulating (floating) capital** kapital qarkullues; 2. kryeqytet; **adj.** 1. kapital; **capital punishment** dënim kapital; 2. themelor; 3. e madhe (shkronja); **capital letter** shkronjë e madhe
capitalism /'kepitëlizëm/ **n.** kapitalizëm
captain /'keptin/ **n.** kapiten
capture /'kepçë(r)/ **vt.** 1. zë, kap rob; 2. fitoj, bëj për vete; **n.** 1. zënia e robit; 2. pushtim i territorit; 3. plaçkë e kapur
car /ka:(r)/ **n.** veturë, makinë; vagon

card /ka:rd/ **n.** 1. kartë; 2. skedë; 3. kartelë; 4. teserë
(anëtarësie)
care /keë(r)/ **n.** 1. kujdes; përkujdesje; **take care of**
kujdesem për; **vi.** 1. kujdesem; 2. dua, pëlqej; 3.
shqetësohem, pyes, përfill; **i don't care** se çaj kokën
career /kë'rië(r)/ **n.** 1. karrierë; 2. vrapim i shpejtë
careful /'keëful/ **adj.** i kujdesshëm; i vëmendshëm
careless /'keërlis/ **adj.** i shkujdesur, i pakujdesshëm
carpet /'ka:rpit/ **n.** qilim
carriage /'kerixh/ **n.** 1. karrocë; 2. vagon; 3. pagesë për
dërgesë **carrot** /'kerët/ **n.** karrotë
carry /'keri/ **vt.** 1. bart, mbaj, transportoj; 2. çoj, shpie;
carry on vazhdoj; kryej; **carry out** kryej, zbatoj; **carry
through** kryej, zbatoj, çoj deri në fund; **carry off** marr,
fitoj; kaloj me sukses
cartoon /ka:'tu:n/ **n.** 1. karikaturë; 2. film multiplikativ,
vizatimor
carve /ka:rv/ **vti.** 1. skalis, gdhend; 2. pres
case /keis/ **n.** 1. rast; **in any case** në çdo rast; **in no case**
në asnjë rast; **in this case** në këtë rast; **a case in point** një
rast në fjalë
cash /kesh/ **n.** monedha, para; **cash on delivery, cash down** me
para në dorë; **vt.** marr para me çek
cassette /kë'set/ **n.** kasetë; **video cassette** vidiokasetë
cast /ka:st/ **vti.** hedh, flak; **n.** 1. hedhje, flakje; 2. formë
për derdhje; 3. personazhet (në një dramë a film); 4. model;
5. lloj, tip
castle /'ka:sl; 'kesl/ **n.** kështjellë; **castles in the air**
kështjella në erë; **castles in Spain** ëndrra në diell
casual /'kezjuël/ **adj.** 1. rastësishëm, i rastit; 2. i
shkujdesur
cat /ket/ **n.** mace; **let the cat out of the bag** nxjerr të
fshehtën në shesh
catarrh /kë:ta:(r)/ **n.** rrufë
catastrophe /kë'testrëfi/ **n.** katastrofë
catch /keç/ **vti.** 1. kap, zë; 2. kuptoj, nxjerr (kuptimin);
catch cold ftohem; **catch hold of** kapem pas; **catch fire** merr
zjarr
category /'ketëgo:ri/ **n.** kategori
cater /'keitë(r)/ **vi.** 1. furnizoj me ushqime; 2. plotësoj
kërkesat, nevojat
Catholic /'kethëlik/ **adj.** katolik
cattle /'ketl/ **n.** gjedhë, bagëti e trashë
cauliflower /'ko:li,flauë(r)/ **n.** lule lakër
cause /ko:z/ **n.** 1. shkak; 2. arsye; 3. çështje; **vt.** shkaktoj;
krijoj, ngjall, sjell
cautious /'ko:shës/ **adj.** i kujdesshëm
caviar /'kevia:(r)/ **n.** havjar, vezë peshku
cavity /'kevëti/ **n.** gropë, zgavër
cease /si:s/ **vti.** i jap fund, ndërpres; **n.** ndërprerje;
without cease pa ndërprerje
ceiling /si:lin/ **n.** tavan
celebrate /'selibreit/ **vt.** festoj, kremtoj
celery /'selëri/ **n. bot.** selino
cell /sel/ **n.** 1. qeli; 2. **bot.** qelizë; 3. celulë
cemetery /'semëtri; 'semëteri/ **n.** varrezë
cent /sent/ **n.** 1. cent; 2. qindarkë
central /'sentrël/ **adj.** qendror

center (centre) /'sentë(r)/ **n.** qendër; **center of gravity** qendra e rëndesës; **vti.** 1. përqëndroj; 2. qendërzoj
century /'sençëri/ **n.** shekull
cereal /'siëriël/ **n.** 1. drithëra; 2. bollgur
certain /'së:rtn/ **adj.** i sigurt; be certain jam i sigurtë
certainly /'së:tënli/ **adv.** natyrisht, pa dyshim
certificate /së'tifikët/ **n.** dëshmi, certifikatë; **certificate of health** certifikatë shendetsore
chain /çein/ **n.** 1. zinxhir, vargua, prangë; 2. varg, vargëzim; **vt.** lidh me zinxhir
chair /çeë(r)/ **n.** 1. karrike; 2. katedër; 3. kryesi; **take the chair** kryesoj, drejtoj; **vt.** kryesoj, drejtoj
chairman /'çeë(r)mën/ **n.** kryetar
challenge /'çelinxh/ **n.** sfidë; **vt.** 1. sfidoj; 2. thërras në duel
chamber /'çeimbë(r)/ **n.** dhomë; **chamber music** muzikë dhome
champagne /shem'pein/ **n.** shampanjë
champion /'çempiën/ **n.** kampion
chance /ça:ns; çens/ **n.** 1. rast; **by chance** rastësisht; 2. mundësi; **stand a good (fair) chance** kam shpresë; 3. sukses; **take a chance** rrezikoj; **vit.** rastis, ndodh, ngjan rastësisht
change /çeinxh/ **n.** 1. ndryshim; 2. ndërrim, këmbim; **make a change** bëj një ndryshim; 3. zëvendësim; 4. shkëmbim; 5. të holla; kusur; **here is your change** merrni kusurin; **vti.** 1. ndryshoj; **change one's mind** ndërroj mendje; 2. këmbej, shkëmbej
channel /'çenl/ **n.** 1. **gjeogr.** ngushticë; kanal; 2. **rad. telev.** kanal
chapter /'çeptë(r)/ **n.** kapitull
character /'kerëktë(r)/ **n.** 1. karakter; 2. veti, veçori dalluese; 3. shkronjë; 4. personazh
charge /ça:rxh/ **n.** 1. akuzë, fajësim, padi; **bring a charge against smb** ngre një padi kundër; 2. çmim; pagesë; **free of charge** pa pagesë; 3. urdhër, porosi; 4. detyrë, përgjegjësi; 5. **pl.** shpenzime; **vti.** 1. akuzoj, fajësoj; 2. caktoj, vë çmimin; 3. ngarkoj me detyrë; 4. urdhëroj, porosit
charity /'çerëti/ **n.** mirëbërësi, bamirësi
charming /'ça:rmin/ **adj.** tërheqës; mahnitës
charter /ça:rtë(r)/ **n.** kartë; **the Charter of the United Nations** Karta e OKB-së
chat /çet/ **vi.** bisedoj; **n.** bisedë
chatter /'çetë(r)/ **vi.** 1. llomotis; 2. kërcëllij dhëmbët
chauffeur /shou'fë:r/ **n.** shofer
cheap /çi:p/ **adj.** i lirë
cheat /çi:t/ **n.** mashtrim; mashtrues; **vti.** mashtroj; bëj hile
check /çek/ **n.** 1. kontroll; 2. kufizim; 3. ndalesë; **vt.** kontrolloj, verifikoj; ndaloj, ndërpres; **check in** regjistrohem në hotel
cheek /çi:k/ **n.** 1. faqe; 2. paturpësi; **have the cheek to** ka paturpësinë të; **vt.** flas me paturpësi
cheer /çië(r)/ **vt.** 1. mbush me gëzim, gëzoj; **cheer up** çelem, më shndrit fytyra 2. nxit, inkurajoj; 3. duartrokas; **n.** 1. brohoritje; 2. gëzim; 3. inkurajim
cheerful /'çiëful/ **adj.** i gëzueshëm; gëzimprurës
cheese /çi:z/ **n.** djathë
chemical /'kemikl/ **adj.** kimik; **chemical agent** agjent kimik

chemist /'kemist/ n. kimist; farmacist
cheque /çek/ n. çek
chess /çes/ n. shah; **play chess** luaj shah
chest /çest/ n. 1. arkë, sëndyk; 2. kraharor
chewing-gum /'çu:ingam/ n. çamçakëz
chicken /'çikn/ n. 1. zog pule; 2. mish pule; **count one's chickens before they are hatched** bëj hesapet pa hanxhinë
chief /çi:f/ n. kryetar, shef; adj. kryesor
child /çaild/ n. fëmijë
children /'çildrën/ n. pl. fëmijë
chilly /'çili/ adj. 1. i ftohtë; 2. fig. i ftohtë
chin /çin/ n. mjekër; **keep one's chin up** mbaj ballin lart
china /'çainë/ n. farfuri; porcelan; enë porcelani
Chinese /çai'ni:z/ n. kinez; gjuhë kineze; adj. kinez
chocolate /'çokëlit/ n. çokollatë
choice /çois/ n. zgjedhje; alternativë; **take one's choice** zgjedh
choose /çu:z/ vt. 1. zgjedh; 2. vendos
chop /çop/ n. 1. goditje; 2. kotëletë; bërxollë; vti. pres; copëtoj
chorus /'ko:rës/ n. kor; **in chorus** në kor
Christ /kraist/ n. Krishti
Christian /'kristiën/ adj. kristian; n. kristian, i krishterë
Christmas /'krismës/ n. Krishlindje; **Merry Christmas!** Gëzuar Krishlindjet!; **Christmas tree** pema e Krishlindjeve
chronic /'kronik/ adj. 1. kronik; 2. i vazhdueshëm, i përhershëm
chuck /çak/ vt. hedh, flak
church /çë:rç/ n. kishë
cigar /si'ga:(r)/ n. puro
cigarette /,sigë'ret/ n. cigare
cinema /'sinëmë; 'sinëma:/ n. kinema
cinnamon /'sinëmën/ n. kanellë
circle /'së:rkl/ n. 1. rreth; 2. qark, mjedis
circulate /'së:kjuleit/ vi. qarkulloj; vë në qarkullim
circumstance /'së:këmstëns/ n. 1. rrethanë; **under the circumstances** në këto kushte; 2. hollësira; 3. pl. gjendje financiare
circus /'së:kës/ n. 1. cirk; 2. amfiteatër
cite /sait/ vt. 1. citoj; 2. thërres në gjyq
citizen /'sitizn/ n. qytetar
citizenship /'sitiznship/ n. qytetari
city /'siti/ n. qytet
civil /'sivil/ adj. civil, qytetar
civilization /,sivëlai'zeishn/ n. qytetërim
claim /kleim/ n. 1. kërkesë; 2. pretendim; vt. 1. kërkoj; 2. pretendoj
clan /klen/ n. klan
clap /klep/ n. 1. gjëmim; 2. duartrokitje; vti. 1. duartrokas; 2. i bie dikujt krahëve
clarify /'klerifai/ vt. 1. sqaroj; 2. pastroj; kulloj një lëng
clash /klesh/ n. 1. përplasje; 2. mospajtim; kundërti; vit. 1. përplas; 2. ndesh; ndeshem; 3. përplasen
clasp /kla:sp; klesp/ n. rrokje duarsh; përqafim; vt. 1. rrok, shtërngoj; 2. mbërthej
class /kla:s; kles/ n. 1. klasë; 2. klasë, lloj, kategori; 3. mësim; klasë, grup nxënësish

classical /'klesikl/ **adj.** klasik
clause /klo:z/ **n.** 1. **gram.** fjali; 2. nen, artikull
clay /klei/ **n.** argjilë, deltinë
clean /kli:n/ **adj.** 1. i pastër; **keep clean** mbaj të pastër; 2.
i papërdorur, i pavënë; 3. i dlirë; **vti.** pastroj; pastrohem
clear /klië(r)/ **adj.** 1. i kthjellët, i qartë, i tejdukshëm;
2. i paturbulluar; 3. i panjollë, i pastër; 4. i kuptueshëm;
vt. 1. qëroj, heq, pastroj; 2. përligj, shfajësoj; 3. sqaroj;
shpjegoj; **adv.** 1. shkoqur, qartë; 2. krejt, tërësisht
clerk /kla:k; klë:rk/ **n.** 1. nëpunës; 2. shitës
clever /'klevë(r)/ **adj.** 1. i mençur, i zgjuar; 2. i aftë; i
shkathët
client /'klaiënt/ **n.** klient, myshteri; blerës
climate /'klaimit/ **n.** 1. klimë; 2. **fig.** klimë, atmosferë
climb /klaim/ **vti.** 1. ngjitem, kacavirrem;. 2. ngjitet; **n.**
ngjitje, kacavarje
clinic /'klinik/ **n.** klinikë
clip /klip/ **n.** kapëse; **vt.** mbërthej; kap me kapëse
cloak-room /'kloukru:m/ **n.** gardërobë
clock /klok/ **n.** orë (muri, tavoline); **at five o'clock** në orën
pesë
close /klous/ **adj.** 1. i afërt; **a close friend** mik i afërt; 2.
i ngjeshur, i dendur; 3. i fshehtë; **vti.** 1. mbyll; 2. mbuloj;
3. përfundoj; **adv.** nga afër, së afërmi
clothes /kloudhz; klëuz/ **n. pl.** rroba, veshje
cloud /klaud/ **n.** 1. re; 2. shtëllungë; 3. hije e zezë; **vit.**
mjegullohet; turbullohet
clown /klaun/ **n.** palaço, gaztor, kloun
club /klab/ **n.** klub
clue /klu:/ **n.** fill drejtues
clumsy /'klamzi/ **adj.** 1. i ngathët, i plogët; 2. kaba
cluster /'klastë(r)/ **n.** 1. vile, tufëz; 2. grumbull, tog;
vit. mblidhet tufë, grumbullohet
clutch /klaç/ **n.** kapje, shtërngim; **vti.** kap, rrok mbërthej;
shtrëngoj
coach /kouç/ **n.** 1. karrocë; 2. trainer; 3. autobus; **vti.** 1.
stërvis; 2. konsultoj
coal /koul/ **n.** qymyr
coarse /ko:s/ **adj.** 1. i trashë; 2. i papunuar; 3. i rëndomtë
coast /koust/ **n.** bregdet
coat /kout/ **n.** pallto; xhaketë; **vt.** mbuloj
cock /kok/ **n.** 1. gjel, këndes; 2. çark pushke
cockroach /'kokrouç/ **n.** kacabu, furrtare e zezë
cocktail /'kokteil/ **n.** koktej
cocoa /'koukou/ **n.** kakao (druri); kakao
cod /kod/ **n.** merluc
code /koud/ **n.** kod; shifër
coercion /kou'ë:shën; kou'ë:zhn/ **n.** shtrëngim, detyrim
coffee /'ko:fi/ **n.** kafe
coffee-pot /'kofipot/ **n.** ibrik kafeje
coffin /'kofin/ **n.** arkivol, qivur
coil /koil/ **n.** 1. dredhë; 2. unazë; spirë; 2. **el.** bobinë
coin /koin/ **n.** monedhë; **pay one back in his own coin** e
shpërblej me të njëjtën monedhë; **vt.** 1. pres monedha; 2.
krijoj fjalë të reja

coincidence /kou'insidëns/ **n.** përkim, koincidencë
coke /kouk/ **n.** 1. koks; 2. koka-kola
cold /kould/ **adj.** i ftohtë; **I am cold** kam ftohtë; **n.** 1. të
ftohtë; 2. rrufë; **catch cold** ftohem, marr të ftohtë
collaborate /kë'lëbëreit/ **vi.** bashkëpunoj
collapse /kë'leps/ **n.** 1. rrënim, shkatërrim; 2. shembje,
katastrofë; **vi.** 1. rrënoj; 2. prish
collar /'kolë(r)/ **n.** 1. qafore, jakë; 2. kular; 3. zgjedhë
(edhe **fig.**); **vt.** kap për jake; mbërthej për gryke
colleague /'koli:g/ **n.** bashkëpunëtor, koleg
collect /kë'lekt/ **vti.** 1. mbledh; 2. koleksionoj
college /'kolixh/ **n.** kolegj; **amer.** universitet
colloquial /kë'loukwiël/ **adj.** bisedor
colonel /'kë:nl/ **n.** kolonel
color (colour) /'kalë(r)/ **n.** 1. ngjyrë; 2. çehre; 3. bojë; 4.
kolorit; 5. **pl.** flamur; **be off color** jam i zbehtë,
nuk ndjehem mirë; **come off with flying colors** dal faqebardhë;
show one's true colors tregoj fytyrën e vërtetë; **vti.** ngjyej,
lyej me bojë
colorful /'kalërful/ **adj.** 1. gjithë ngjyra; i larmishëm; 2. i
gjallë, i gëzueshëm
column /'kolëm/ **n.** 1. kolonë; shtyllë; 2. rubrikë; 3. varg
columnist /'kolëmnist/ **n.** gazetar, reporter (për rubrika të
veçanta)
comb /koum/ **n.** 1. krehër; 2. makinë krehje; **vti.** kreh
(flokët); kreh (leshin, pambukun)
combine /këm'bain/ **vti.** 1. kombinoj, kombinohem; 2. bashkoj,
bashkohem
combustible /këm'bastibl/ **adj.** i djegshëm **come** /kam/ **vi.** 1.
vij, arrij; 2. ndodh, ngjan; **come back** kthehem; sjell ndër
mend; **come in** 1. hyj, futem; 2. vjen, arrin treni etj; 3. hyn
në përdorim, në modë; 4. piqet, është gati për treg; **come off**
1. këputet (kopsa); 2. bie; 3. dal me sukses; 4. zhvillohet;
come to vij në vete; **come what may** të bëhet ç'të bëhet
comedy /'komëdi/ **n.** komedi
comet /'komit/ **n.** kometë
comfortable /'kamfërtëbl/ **adj.** i rehatshëm
comic /'komik/ **adj.** komik; qesharak
coming /kamin/ **adj.** i ardhshëm
comma /'komë/ **n.** presje
command /kë'mand; kë'mend/ **n.** urdhër, komandë, komandim; **vti.**
urdhëroj; komandoj
commander /kë'ma:ndë(r); kë'mendë(r)/ **n.** komandant **commend**
/kë'mend/ **vt.** lavdëroj, lëvdoj
commentary /'komëntri; 'komënteri/ **n.** koment
commerce /'komë:rs/ **n.** tregti
commercial /kë'më:rshël/ **adj.** tregtar
commission /kë'mishn/ **n.** komision
commit /kë'mit/ **vt.** 1. bëj, kryej një krim; 2. i besoj dikujt
diçka
commitment /kë'mitmënt/ **n.** 1. angazhim; 2. kryerje (e krimit
etj.)
committee /kë'miti/ **n.** komitet
commodity /kë'moditi/ **n.** mall, artikull
common /'komën/ **adj.** 1. i përbashkët; 2. i zakonshëm; 3. i
rëndomtë

commonplace /'komënpleis/ **n.** gjë e zakonshme; **adj.** i
rëndomtë, i zakonshëm
commonwealth /'komënwelth/ **n.** shtet; republikë; federatë
communication /kë,mju:ni'keishn/ **n.** 1. komunikim; 2. kumtim;
3. mjete komunikimi
communism /'komju:nizëm/ **n.** komunizëm
community /kë'mjuniti/ **n.** bashkësi, komunitet
companion /këm'peniën/ **n.** 1. shok; 2. bashkudhëtar
company /'kampëni/ **n.** 1. shoqëri; **keep company** shoqërohem me;
part company prishem me dikë; **a man is known by the company
he keeps** thuaj me kë rri, të të them se cili je; 2. kompani,
shoqëri **compare** /këm'peë(r)/ **n.** krahasim; **beyond compare** s'ka
të krahasuar; **vt.** krahasoj, përqas
comparison /këm'perisn/ **n.** krahasim; **in comparison with** në
krahasim me; **make a comparison between** bëj krahasim mes
compartment /këm'pa:rtmënt/ **n.** 1. kupe; 2. e ndarë; 3.
kompartament
compassion /këm'peshn/ **n.** dhembshuri; mëshirë
compatible /këm'petëbl/ **adj.** i pajtueshëm
compatriot /këm'petriët; këm'peitriët/ **n.** bashkatdhetar
compel /këm'pel/ **vt.** detyroj, shtrëngoj
compensate /'kompenseit/ **vt.** shpërblej; kompensoj
compete /këm'pi:t/ **vt.** konkuroj, hyj në konkurrencë
competent /'kompitënt/ **adj.** kompetent
competition /,kompë'tishn/ **n.** 1. konkurrencë; 2. garë,
ndeshje
competitive /këm'petëtiv/ **adj.** konkurrues
competitor /këm'petitë(r)/ **n.** konkurrent
compile /këm'pail/ **vt.** 1. mbledh, grumbulloj; 2. hartoj,
përpiloj
complain /këm'plein/ **vi.** ankohem, shfaq pakënaqësi, qahem
complete /këm'pli:t/ **adj.** i plotë; i përfunduar; **vt.**
përfundoj, kryej, plotësoj
completely /këm'pli:tli/ **adv.** tërësisht, plotësisht **complex**
/këm'pleks/ **adj.** kompleks, i ndërlikuar; **n.** kompleks
complicated /'kompliketid/ **adj.** i komplikuar, i ndërlikuar, i
ngatërruar
complicity /këm'plisëti/ **n.** pjesëmarrje (në krim etj.);
bashkëfajësi
compliment /'komplimënt/ **n.** 1. kompliment; 2. **pl.** urime; **vt.**
1. përshëndes, 2. uroj; 3. bëj komplimente
comply /këm'plai/ **vi.** plotësoj, zbatoj, veproj
component /këm'pounënt/ **n.** komponent; **adj.** përbërës
compose /këm'pouz/ **vti.** 1. përbëj; 2. hartoj, kompozoj; 3.
qetësoj, përmbaj; **compose one's thoughts** sistemoj mendimet;
compose oneself qetësohem
composer /këm'pouzë/ **n.** kompozitor
composition /,kompë'zishn/ **n.** 1. përbërje; 2. hartim; 3.
vepër (letrare, muzikore); 4. marrëveshje
compound /'kompaund/ **adj.** i përzier, i përbërë; **n.** përzierje,
përbërje; **vti.** bashkoj; përziej
comprehend /,kompri'hend/ **vt.** 1. kuptoj; 2. përfshij
compress /këm'pres/ **vt.** 1. ngjesh; 2. përmbledh
comprise /këm'praiz/ **vt.** përfshij, përmbaj
compulsory /këm'palsëri/ **adj.** i detyrueshëm

computer /këm'pju:të(r)/ n. kompjuter
conceal /kën'si:l/ vt. fsheh, mbaj të fshehtë; **conceal the truth** fsheh të vërtetën
concentrate /'konsntreit/ vti. përqëndroj, përqëndrohem; **concentrate one's attention** përqëndroj vëmendjen
concept /konsept/ n. koncept
concern /kën'së:rn/ n. 1. përkujdesje, shqetësim, kujdes; 2. interes; **it is no concern of mine** kjo nuk më përket mua; vt. 1. më përket, më intereson; 2. shqetësohem
concerning /kën:së:rnin/ prep. në lidhje me, për sa i përket
concert /'konsët/ n. 1. koncert; 2. ujdi, marrëveshje; harmoni; vt. bashkërendoj, merrem vesh
concession /kën'seshn/ n. lëshim; koncesion; **make a concession** bëj lëshim
concise /kën'sais/ adj. i përmbledhur, i ngjeshur, konçiz
conclude /kën'klu:d/ vti. 1. përfundoj; mbyll; nxjerr përfundim; 2. vendos, zgjidh
conclusion /kën'klu:zhn/ n. përfundim; **in conclusion** si përfundim; **bring to a conclusion** mbyll, i jap fund; **draw a conclusion** nxjerr një përfundim
concrete /'konkri:t/ adj. 1. konkret, real; 2. i betontë; n. beton; vt. betonoj, çimentoj
condemn /kën'dem/ vt. 1. dënoj; 2. shpall të pavlefshëm
condition /kën'dishn/ 1. kusht; **on condition that** me kusht që; **on no condition** në asnjë mënyrë; 2. gjendje; 3. pl. rrethana
conduct /kën'dakt/ vti. 1. çoj, drejtoj; 2. sillem; /'kondakt/ n. 1. sjellje; 2. drejtim
confectioner /kën'fekshnë(r)/ n. pastiçer; **confectioner's shop** pastiçeri
confederacy /kën'fedërësi/ n. konfederatë
confer /kën'fë:r/ vt. 1. akordoj; 2. këshillohem; 3. krahasoj
conference /'konfërëns/ n. konferencë
confess /kën'fes/ vti. 1. pranoj; pohoj; 2. rrëfej; rrëfehem
confidence /'konfidëns/ n. mirëbesim; **in strict confidence** në mirëbesim të plotë
confinment /kën'fainmënt/ n. 1. mbyllje, izolim, burgosje; 2. kufizim; 3. lindje, lehoni
confirm /kën'fë:rm/ vt. 1. përforcoj; 2. pohoj, vërtetoj; 3. verifikoj
confiscate /'konfiskeit/ vt. konfiskoj
conflict /'konflikt/ n. 1. përleshje; 2. konflikt; mosmarrëveshje; /kën'flikt/ vi. 1. ndeshem, luftoj; 2. bie ndesh
confront /kën'frant/ vt. 1. ballësoj; 2. ballafaqoj, krahasoj
confuse /kën'fju:z/ vt. 1. ngatërroj, pështjelloj; 2. i prish mendjen
confusion /kën'fju:zhn/ n. 1. ngatërrim; 2. çrregullim; 3. hutim, pështjellim
congratulate /kën'gretjuleit/ vt. uroj
congratulation /kën,gretju'leishn/ n. urim **congress** /'kongres; 'kongrës/ n. kongres
conjecture /kën'xhekçë(r)/ n. hamendje, supozim **connect** /kë'nekt/ vti. lidh; bashkoj
connection, connexion /kë'nekshn/ n. lidhje
conquer /'konkë(r)/ vt. 1. pushtoj; 2. mund, mposht

conscience /'konshëns/ n. ndërgjegje, vetëdije
conscious /'konshës/ adj. i vetëdijshëm; be conscious of jam
i vetëdijshëm për
conscription /kën'skripshn/ n. rekrutim, thirrje nën armë
consensus /kën'sensës/ n. konsensus; marrëveshje
consent /kën'sent/ n. pëlqim, miratim; with one's consent
njëzëri; vi. miratoj, jap pëlqimin
consequence /'konsikvens/ n. 1. rrjedhim, pasojë; in
consequence of si rrjedhim i; 2. kuptim, rëndësi; of no
consequence i parëndësishëm
conservative /kën'së:vëtiv/ adj. konservator, i prapambetur;
n. konservator
consider /kën'sidë(r)/ vt. 1. konsideroj, quaj, marr
parasysh; 2. mendoj
considerable /kën'sidërëbl/ adj. i konsiderueshëm
consideration /kën,sidë'reishn/ n. 1. konsideratë; 2. mendim,
gjykim; shqyrtim; take into consideration marr parasysh
consign /kën'sain/ vt. 1. besoj, ia lë në ngarkim; 2. dërgoj
consignee /,konsai'ni:/ n. marrës i ngarkesës
consist /kën'sist/ vi. 1. përbëhet nga; 2. qëndron në
consistent /kën'sistënt/ adj. i qëndrueshëm, konsekuent
console /kën'soul/ vt. ngushëlloj
constant /'konstënt/ adj. 1. i qëndrueshëm; 2. i përhershëm;
3. i pandryshueshëm
constituency /kën'stitjuënsi/ n. zonë elektorale
constitution /,konsti'tu:shn/ n. 1. ndërtim, organizim; 2.
kushtetutë 3. ndërtim i trupit, shtat
construction /kën'strakshën/ n. 1. ndërtim; under
construction në ndërtim e sipër; 2. godinë, ndërtesë
consul /'konsël/ n. konsull
consult /kën'salt/ vt. 1. këshillohem (me mjekun); 2. marr
parasysh; 3. konsultohem, diskutoj me
consume /kën'sju:m; kën'su:m/ vti. harxhoj; konsumoj
consumer /kën'sju:më(r)/ n. konsumator, përdorues
consumption /kën'sampshn/ n. harxhim, konsumim, shpenzim;
consumption goods artikuj të konsumit të gjerë
contact /'kontekt/ n. 1. takim, prekje; 2. kontakt; come into
contact with marr kontakt me; /kën'tekt/ vt. takoj, marr
kontakt
contain /kën'tein/ vt. përmbaj, mbaj, nxë
contemporary /kën'tempëreri/ adj. bashkëkohor, bashkëkohës;
n. bashkëkohës
contempt /kën'tempt/ n. përbuzje; mospërfillje; hold in
contempt përbuz, përçmoj; show contempt for tregoj, shpreh
përbuzje
content /kën'tent/ adj. 1. i kënaqur; 2. i gatshëm; vt.
kënaq; kënaqem; n. 1. kënaqësi; 2. brendi, përmbajtje; 3.
pasqyra e lëndës
contest /'kontest/ n. 1. garë; konkurs; 2. luftë; vti.
/kën'test/ 1. kundërshtoj; 2. diskutoj; 3. marr pjesë (në
garë, konkurs etj.)
continent /'kontinënt/ n. kontinent
continue /'kën'tinju:/ vit. 1. vazhdoj; 2. zgjatet, shtrihet;
3. vijon
contraceptive /,kontrë'septiv/ n. mjete kontraseptive
contract /'kontrekt/ n. kontratë, marrëveshje; /kën'trekt/
vti. 1. kontraktoj, bëj kontratë; 2. tkurret, mblidhet

contradiction /,kontrë'dikshn/ **n.** 1. kundërshtim; 2. kontradiktë; kundërti; 3. mospajtim, mospërputhje
contrary /'kontreri; 'kontrëri/ **adj.** 1. i kundërt; 2. i disfavorshëm; **n.** kundërti, e kundërta; **on the contrary** përkundrazi
contrast /'kontra:st; 'kontrest/ **n.** kontrast, kundërshtim; dallim i theksuar; /kën'tra:st; kën'trest/ **v.** kundërvë, ballafaqoj
contribute /'kën'tribju:t/ **vti.** 1. ndihmoj; kontribuoj; 2. jap, fal; jap ndihmesë
control /kën'troul/ **n.** 1. kontroll; **out of control** jashtë kontrollit; 2. rregullim, mbarështrim; **vt.** kontrolloj; verifikoj
controversial /,kontrë'vë:rshël/ **adj.** i diskutueshëm
convalescent /,konvë'lesnt/ **adj.** që është duke rimarrë veten, konvaleshent
convenience /kën'vi:niëns/ **n.** lehtësi, voli, kollajllëk
convenient /kën'viniënt/ **adj.** i volitshëm; i përshtatshëm
convention /kën'venshn/ **n.** 1. kuvend; kongres; 2. marrëveshje, konventë; 3. traditë, zakon
conventional /kën'venshënl/ **adj.** konvencional; tradicional
conversation /,konvë'seishn/ **n.** bisedë
convertible /kën'vë:rtbl/ **adj.** i këmbyeshëm
conviction /kën'vikshn/ **n.** 1. bindje; 2. dënim
convince /kën'vins/ **vt.** bind; i mbush mendjen
convoke /kën'vouk/ **vt.** thërres, mbledh
cook /kuk/ **n.** kuxhinier, gjellëbërës; **too many cooks spoil the broth** shumë mami e mbysin fëmijën; **vti.** gatuaj; **cook up** sajoj, trilloj
cool /ku:l/ **adj.** 1. i freskët; 2. i qetë, gjakftohtë; 3. i ftohtë; **vti.** 1. freskoj; 2. qetësoj; **n.** 1. freski; 2. qetësi
co-operate /kou'opëreit/ **vi.** kooperoj; bashkëpunoj; bashkëveproj
co-operative /kou'opërëtiv/ **adj.** 1. kooperues; 2. i përbashkët, i bashkuar
cope /koup/ **vi.** përballoj, i bëj ballë
copper /'kopë(r)/ **n.** 1. bakër; 2. monedhë bakri
copy /'kopi/ **vti.** 1. kopjoj; 2. imitoj; **n.** kopje; ekzemplar
copyright /'kopirait/ **n.** e drejtë e autorit; **vt.** siguroj të drejtën e autorit
cordial /'ko:rdiël; 'ko:rxhël/ **adj.** i përzemërt **corduroy** /'ko:dëroi/ **n.** kadife
cork /ko:k/ **n.** 1. tapë; 2. dru tape; **vt.** mbyll me tapë, tapos
corkscrew /'ko:k,skrju:/ **n.** hapëse tapash
corn /ko:rn/ **n.** drithë; **amer.** misër
corn-flour /ko:rnflauë/ **n.** mjell misri
corned beef /'ko:rndbi:f/ **n.** pastërma lope, viçi
corner /'ko:rnë(r)/ **n.** 1. kënd, qoshe; 2. goditje këndi; 3. skutë; skaj
corporation ,ko:pë'reishn/ **n.** korporatë; shoqëri aksionare
corps /ko:/ **n.** 1. **usht.** korpus; 2. trup; **the Diplomatic Corps** trupi diplomatik
correct /kë'rekt/ **adj.** i drejtë, i saktë; i rregullt; **vt.** ndreq **correspondence** /,ko:ri'spondëns/ **n.** 1. përputhje; ngjashmëri; 2. korrespondencë, letërkëmbim
corridor /'ko:rido:(r)/ **n.** korridor

corrupt /kë'rapt/ **adj.** i prishur, i korruptuar; i shitur;
vti. prish, korruptoj
cosmetics /koz'metiks/ **n.** kozmetikë
cosmic /'kozmik/ **adj.** kozmik
cost /kost/ **n.** 1. çmim, kosto; **the cost of living** kostoja e
jetesës; 2. **pl.** shpenzime; **at all costs** me çdo kusht; **vi.**
kushton
costume /'kostju:m; 'kostu:m/ **n.** kostum
cottage /'kotixh/ **n.** 1. kasolle, shtëpizë fshati; 2. kabinë
cotton /'kotn/ **n.** pambuk; pëlhurë, pe pambuku
cough /ko:f/ **n.** kollë; **vit.** kollitem
council /'kaunsl/ **n.** këshillë
count /kaunt/ **vt.** 1. numëroj; 2. njehsoj; 3. nxjerr
përfundimin; 4. llogaris; 5. quaj, konsideroj; **n.** 1.
llogaritje; 2. numërim
counter /'kauntë(r)/ **n.** 1. tezgë; 2. banak; **under the counter**
nën banak
counterfeit /'kauntëfit/ **adj.** i falsifikuar; **n.** falsifikim;
vt. falsifikoj
countless /'kauntlis/ **adj.** i panumërt
country /'kantri/ **n.** 1. vend; 2. atdhe; 3. fshat
countryman 'kantrimën/ **n.** fshatar
county /'kaunti/ **n.** qark
couple /'kapl/ **n.** 1. çift, dyshe; 2. çift; **married couple**
çift i martuar; **vti.** bashkoj, lidh; çiftohem
courage /'karixh/ **n.** kurajë, zemër, guxim
courageous /kë'reixhës/ **adj.** kurajoz, guximtar, trim
course /ko:s/ **n.** 1. kurs; 2. zhvillim; 3. kurs (leksionesh);
4. gjellë; **in the course of** gjatë; **of course** natyrisht; **in
due course** në kohën e duhur
court /ko:rt/ **n.** 1. gjykatë; gjyq; trupi gjykues; 2. fushë
sportive; 3. oborr
cousin /'kazn/ kushëri, kushërirë
cover /'kavë(r)/ **n.** 1. mbulesë; 2. kapak; 3. strehë, strehim;
vt. 1. mbuloj; 2. fsheh; 3. përshkoj një largësi
cow /kau/ **n.** lopë
coward /'kauërd/ **adj.** frikacak
cowboy /'kauboi/ **n.** lopar; **amer.** kauboi
crab /kreb/ **n.** gaforre
crack /krek/ **n.** 1. kërcitje, krismë; 2. plasë, plasaritje;
vti. 1. kris; 2. pëlcet; 3. plasaritet; **crack a joke** bëj
shaka
crackle /'krekl/ **n.** kërcitje, kërcëllimë; **vi.** kërcet,
kërcëllen
cradle /'kredl/ **n.** djep (edhe **fig.**)
craft /kra:ft/ **n.** 1. zanat, zeje; 2. shoqëri (zejtarësh)
craftsman /'kra:ftsmën/ **n.** zejtar, zanatçi
cramp /kremp/ **n.** 1. ngërç; 2. **tek.** kllapë; zhabicë
cranberry /'krenbëri; 'krenberi/ **n.** boronicë e kuqe
crane /krein/ **n.** 1. lejlek; 2. **tek.** vinç
crash /kresh/ **vti.** 1. bie, rrëzohem me krismë; 2. rrëzohet,
përplaset (aeroplani); 3. shkatërrohem, falimentoj; **n.** 1.
krismë, kërcitje; 2. avari; 3. falimentim
crawl /kro:l/ **vit.** zvarritem, tërhiqem zvarrë; **n.** zvarritje
crazy /'kreizi/ **adj.** i çmendur, i krisur; maniak (për diçka)
creak /kri:k/ **n.** kërcitje; **vi.** kërcet

cream /kri:m/ **n.** 1. ajkë qumështi; kajmak; 2. krem
cream-cheese /'kri:mçi:z/ **n.** djathë i bardhë i kremuar
crease /kri:s/ **n.** zhubër, rrudhë; **vti.** zhubros, rrudhos
create /kri:'eit/ **vt.** 1. krijoj; 2. shkaktoj, ngjall
creation /kri:'eishn/ **n.** 1. krijesë; 2. krijim, vepër
creature /'kri:çë(r)/ **n.** krijesë, qënie e gjallë
credit /'kredit/ **n.** 1. kredi, besim; 2. nder, nderim; 3.
kredi, kredit; **vt.** 1. besoj; 2. jap me kredi
creeper /'kri:pë(r)/ **n.** bimë zvarritëse
crime /kraim/ **n.** krim
criminal /'kriminl/ **adj.** kriminal; **n.** kriminel
cripple /'kripl/ **n.** sakat, ulok; **vt.** sakatoj; gjymtoj, cungoj
crisis /'kraisis/ **n.** 1. **ek.** krizë; **economic crisis** krizë
ekonomike; 2. **mjek.** krizë
crisp /krisp/ **adj.** 1. i thyeshëm; 2. i acartë; 3. gjallërues
critical /kritikl/ **adj.** 1. kritik; 2. vendimtar; 3. **fiz.**
kritik
crocodile /'krokëdail/ **n.** krokodil; **crocodile tears** lotë
krokodili
crook /kruk/ **n.** 1. kërrabë; 2. kthesë; 3. **gj. fl.** mashtrues,
hajdut; **by hook or by crook** me të gjitha mjetet
crop /krop/ **n.** prodhim; të korra; të lashta
cross /kros/ **n.** 1. kryq; 2. kryqëzim; 3. hibrid; **vti.** 1.
kaloj, kapërcej; 2. kryqëzoj; i vë kryq; **cross out** fshij, i
vë kryq; **cross one's path** has, ndesh; **cross one's mind** më
shkon nder mend
crossing /'kro:sin/ **n.** kryqëzim, udhëkryq
cross-road /'kro:sroud/ **n.** udhëkryq; **at the cross-road** në
udhëkryq
crow /krou/ **n.** sorrë
crowd /kraud/ **n.** 1. turmë; 2. grumbull, kapicë; **vti.**
mblidhen, grumbullohen
crown /kraun/ **n.** 1. kurorë; 2. koronë (monedhë); 3.
kurorëzim; **vt.** kurorëzoj
crucial /'kru:shl/ **adj.** vendimtar, kritik
crude /kru:d/ **adj.** 1. i papërpunuar, i papastruar; 2. i
vrazhdë, i ashpër
cruel /kruël/ **adj.** i egër, mizor
cruise /kru:z/ **n.** lundrim
cruiser /'kru:zë(r)/ **n.** kryqëzor
crumb /kram/ **n.** thërrime
crush /krash/ **vti.** 1. shtyp; 2. dërrmoj; mposht; 3. shtrydh;
n. 1. shtypje; 2. dërrmim, mposhtje; 3. shtrydhje
crust /krast/ **n.** 1. kore; 2. sipërfaqe e fortë
cry /krai/ **n.** 1. britmë; 2. vajtim; **vti.** 1. thërras, bërtas;
2. qaj
crystal /'kristl/ **n.** kristal; **adj.** i kristaltë
cube /kju:b/ **n.** kub
cucumber /'kju:kambë(r)/ **n.** trangull
cuddle /'kadl/ **n.** përqafim; **vi.** përqafoj e ledhatoj
cue /kju:/ **n.** 1. replikë; kundërpërgjigje; 2. sugjerim; 3.
stekë bilardoje
cuff-link /'këflink/ **n.** kopsë, buton mansheti
culinary /'kalinëri; 'kalineri/ **adj.** i kuzhinës, i gatimit
cultivate /'kaltiveit/ **vt.** 1. lëroj, kultivoj; 2. **fig.**
kultivoj
culture /'kalçë(r)/ **n.** 1. kulturë; 2. rritje, kultivim
cunning /'kanin/ **adj.** dinak, dhelpërak

cup /kap/ **n.** 1. kupë, gotë; 2. **sport.** kupë
cupboard /'kabërd/ **n.** bufe, dollap
curb /kë:rb/ **n.** fre (edhe **fig.**); **vt.** mbaj nën fre
curd /kë:rd/ **n.** gjizë
cure /kjuë(r)/ **n.** mjekim, kurim; **vti.** mjekoj, kuroj, shëroj
curious /'kjuëriës/ **adj.** kureshtar
curl /kë:rl/ **n.** 1. kaçurrela; 2. spirale; dredhë; **vti.**
dridhet, përdridhet; 2. bëj kaçurrela
currant /'karënt/ **n.** stafidhe
currency /'karënsi/ **n.** 1. qarkullim; 2. monedhë; valutë
current /'karënt/ **adj.** 1. vazhdues; 2. qarkullues; 3. i
ditës, aktual; **current affairs** çështje, probleme të ditës; **n.**
rrymë
curriculum /kë'rikjulëm/ **n.** program mësimor
curse /kë:rs/ **n.** mallkim; **vti.** mallkoj, shaj
curt /kë:rt/ **adj.** 1. i shkurtër, konçiz; 2. i prerë
curtail /kë:r'teil/ **vt.** shkurtoj, zvogëloj
curtain /'kë:rtn/ **n.** perde
curve /kë:rv/ **n.** 1. lakore; 2. kthesë, lakim rruge; **vti.**
lakoj, përkul
cushion /'kushn/ **n.** jastëk (divani)
custom /'kastëm/ **n.** 1. zakon; 2. klientelë
customer /'kastëmë(r)/ **n.** blerës, klient
customs /'kastëms/ **n.** taksë doganore
cut /kat/ **vti.** pres; **n.** prerje
cute /kju:t/ **adj.** 1. mendjemprehtë; 2. **amer.** tërheqës
cutlery /'këtlëri/ **n.** takëm (me thika, lugë apo pirunë)
cutlet /'këtlit/ **n.** kotoletë
cycle /'saikl/ **n.** 1. cikël; rreth; 2. biçikletë
cynical /'sinikl/ **adj.** cinik
cyst /sist/ **n.** **mjek.** cist

dab /deb/ **n.** 1. prekje, cekje; 2. njollë (boje etj.); **vti.** 1. lag, njom pak; 2. stërkit; spërkat; 3. lyej

dad(dy) /'ded(i)/ **n.** baba; **fëm.** babi

dagger /'degë(r)/ **n.** kamë **daily** /'deili/ **adj.** i përditshëm, i ditëpërditshëm; **daily wants** nevojat e përditshme; **adv.** përditë; **n.** e përditshme (gazetë)

dairy /'deëri/ **n.** 1. bazho qumështi; 2. bulmetore

daisy /'deizi/ **n.** lule shqerrë

dam /dem/ **n.** sfrat, digë

damage /'demixh/ **n.** 1. dëmtim; 2. dëm; 3. dëmshpërblim; **vt.** dëmtoj

damn /dem/ **vt.** mallkoj; nëm

damp /demp/ **vt.** 1. lag, njom; 2. shkurajoj; **n.** 1. lagështi; 2. dëshpërim; **adj.** i lagësht

dance /da:ns; dens/ **n.** 1. vallëzim; 2. mbrëmje vallëzimi; **vit.** 1. vallëzoj; 2. kërcej, hidhem

danger /'deinxhë(r)/ **n.** rrezik; **in danger** në rrezik; **out of danger** jashtë rrezikut

dangerous /'deinxhërës/ **adj.** i rrezikshëm

dangle /'dengl/ **vt.** lëkund, kolavit

dare /deë(r)/ **vt.** 1. guxoj; 2. përballoj

dark /da:k/ **adj.** 1. i errët; 2. i mbyllur; 3. i zymtë; 4. i fshehtë; **keep it dark** mbaj të fshehtë; **n.** 1. terr, errësirë; 2. paqartësi

darling /'da:rlin/ **n.** i dashur, i shtrenjtë

dart /da:rt/ **vit.** turrem, derdhem

dash /desh/ **n.** 1. hov, vrull, 2. sulm; 3. përplasje, goditje; 4. përzierje; **vti.** 1. hedh, flak; 2. holloj, përziej; 3. spërkat; 4. hidhem, vërvitem, sulem

data /'deitë; da:të; detë/ **n.** të dhëna, fakte

date /deit/ **n.** 1. datë; 2. afat; 3. **amer.** takim; 4. kohë, epokë; **out of date** i vjetëruar, i dalë mode; **up to date** i kohës, bashkëkohor; **vti.** 1. datoj; datohet; 2. vjetërohet

daughter /'do:të(r)/ **n.** bijë, vajzë

daughter-in-law /'do:tër in lo:/ **n.** e re, nusja e djalit

dawn /do:n/ **n.** 1. agim; 2. **fig.** fillim, lindje; **vi.** 1. agon; 2. shfaqet; 3. qartësohet

day /dei/ **n.** ditë; **all day long** gjithë ditën; **day off** ditë pushimi; **by day** ditën; **one day** një ditë; **some day** në njërën prej ditëve më të afërme; **the day after tomorrow** pasnesër; **the day before yesterday** pardje

daylight /'deilait/ **n.** dritë e diellit; **in broad daylight** në dritën e diellit

day-time /'deitaim/ **n.** ditë; gjatë ditës; **in the day-time** ditën

dazzle /'dezl/ **vt.** verbohem (nga drita, shkëlqimi etj.)

dead /ded/ **adj.** 1. i vdekur; 2. i mpirë; **dead silence** heshtje e plotë; **a dead language** gjuhë e vdekur

dead-end /'dedend/ **n.** rrugë pa krye, qorrsokak

deaf /def/ **adj.** i shurdhër; **turn a deaf ear to** bëj veshin e shurdhër

deal /di:l/ **n.** 1. pjesë, sasi; **a good (great) deal** shumë, një pjesë e madhe; 2. marrëveshje, ujdi; **make a deal** arrij marrëveshje; **vti.** 1. ndaj, jap; 2. merrem; kam të bëj; 3. trajtoj; 4. tregtoj

dealer /'di:lë(r)/ **n.** tregtar

dear /dië(r)/ **adj.** 1. i shtrenjtë, i dashur; 2. i çmueshëm;
n. i dashur, e dashur; **adv.** shtrenjt
death /deth/ **n.** vdekje; **to the death** deri në vdekje; **put to
death** vras; ekzekutoj
death-rate /'dethreit/ **n.** vdekshmëri; **low (high) death-rate**
vdekshmëri e ulët (e lartë)
debate /di'beit/ **n.** debat, diskutim, rrahje mendimesh; **vti.**
debatoj, diskutoj
debit /'debit/ **n.** treg. debit, borxh
debt /det/ **n.** borxh; **get (run) into debt** kridhem në borxhe;
settle (pay off) a debt shlyej, paguaj një borxh
debtor /'detë(r)/ **n.** debitor, borxhli
decade /'dekeid/ **n.** dekadë
decadent /'dekëdënt/ **adj.** dekadent; **n.** dekadent
decay /di'kei/ **n.** 1. kalbje; 2. rënie, shkatërrim; **vi.** 1.
kalbet; 2. shpërbëhet; 3. merr të tatëpjetën
deceitful /di'sitful/ **adj.** mashtrues
deceive /di'si:v/ **vt.** gënjej, mashtroj
December /di'sembë(r)/ **n.** dhjetor
decent /di'snt/ **adj.** 1. i denjë, i përshtatshëm; 2. i
hijshëm, i thjeshtë
deceptive /di'septiv/ **adj.** mashtrues, gënjeshtar
decide /di'said/ **vti.** 1. vendos; 2. zgjidh
decision /di'sizhn/ **n.** vendim
decisive /di'saisiv/ **adj.** vendimtar; i vendosur
declare /di'kleë(r)/ **vti.** 1. njoftoj, shpall botërisht; 2.
deklaroj, bëj deklaratë; 3. shprehem
decline /di'klain/ **n.** 1. zvogëlim; 2. rënie, keqësim; 3.
perëndim; **vti.** 1. refuzoj, kundërshtoj; 2. keqësohet;
rrënohet; 3. perëndon
decorate /'dekëreit/ **vt.** 1. zbukuroj, stolis; 2. dekoroj
decrease /'di:kri:s/ **n.** pakësim, ulje, rënie; **vti.** ul,
pakësoj, zvogëloj
dedicate /'dedikeit/ **vt.** 1. kushtoj, bëj fli; 2. i kushtoj
(një vepër)
deed /di:d/ **n.** 1. veprim, 2. punë; 3. vepër, bëmë
deem /di:m/ **vt.** mendoj, gjykoj, quaj
deep /di:p/ **adj.** i thellë (edhe **fig.**); **adv.** thellë; **n.**
thellësi, vend i thellë
deer /dië(r)/ **n.** dre
defeat /di'fi:t/ **n.** 1. disfatë; 2. shpartallim; 3. mundje;
vt. 1. mund, shpartalloj; 2. ndaloj, prish
defect /di'fekt/ **n.** 1. defekt, e metë, mungesë; 2. cen
defend /di'fend/ **vt.** mbroj; mbrohem
defensive /di'fensiv/ **adj.** mbrojtës; **n.** mbrojtje **defiant**
/di'faiënt/ **adj.** 1. mospërfillës, kundërshtues; 2. nxitës,
provokues
deficiency /di'fishënsi/ **n.** 1. mungesë; 2. mangësi, zbrazëti
deficit /'defisit/ **n.** deficit
define /di'fain/ **vt.** 1. përcaktoj; 2. përkufizoj; 3. shpjegoj
definition /,defi'nishn/ **n.** 1. përkufizim; 2. përcaktim
deflate /di'flate/ **vt.** 1. shfryj (gomën, ballonin); 2. **fig.**
ul; 3. bëj deflacion

defy /di'fai/ *vt.* 1 sfidoj, nuk përfill; 2 kundërshtoj

degree /di'gri:/ *n.* 1 shkallë, gradë; **by degrees** shkallë-shkallë, gradualisht; **to a high degree** në shkallë të lartë; **to what degree** në çfarë shkalle; 2 titull, gradë shkencore

delay /di'lei/ *n.* vonesë; shtyrje; *vit.* vonoj; shtyj

delegation /,deli'geishn. *n.* delegacion

delivery /di'livëri/ *n.* 1 shpërndarje; 2 dërgim

demand /'di:mand; di'mend/ *n.* kërkesë; *vt.* kërkoj, kam nevojë

democracy /di'mokrësi/ *n.* demokraci

demonstration /,demën'streishn/ *n.* 1 demonstrim; 2 provë; 3 demonstratë

dental /'dentl/ *adj.* dental, dhëmbor

dentist /'dentist/ *n.* dentist

deny /di'nai/ *vt.* 1 mohoj; 2 kundërshtoj, hedh poshtë

department /di'pa:rtmënt/ *n.* degë, departament

departure /di'pa:çë(r)/ *n.* nisje, ikje; **take one's departure** iki, nisem

depend /di'pend/ *vi.* 1 varem, jam i varur; është në varësi; 2 var shpresat; **it depends** varet nga

deportation /,di:po:rteishn/ n. syrgjynosje

deposit /di'pozit/ *n.* 1 depozitë; 2 *fin.* depozitë; 3 fundërri; depozitim, shtresë; *vt.* 1 vë, vendos; 2 *fin.* vë, depozitoj në bankë; 3 precipiton, fundërron

depression /di'preshn/ *n.* 1 depresion, gjendje e keqe shpirtërore; 2 *ekon.* depresion, rënie; 3 rënie e trysnisë atmosferike

deputy /'depjuti/ *n.* 1 deputet; delegat; 2 zëvëndës

descent /di'sent/ *n.* 1 zbritje; 2 prejardhje, origjinë; 3 trashëgim; brezni

describe /dis'kraib/ *vt.* 1 përshkruaj; 2 vizatoj; 3 paraqes, quaj

description /dis'kripshn/ *n.* përshkrim

desert /'dezërt/ *n.* shkretëtirë; *adj.* i shkretë; i pabanuar; *vi.* / di'zë:rt/ 1 braktis; 2 dezertoj

deserve /di'zë:rv/ *vti.* meritoj

design /di'zain/ *vti.* 1 bëj skicën, vizatimin, projektin; 2 synoj, kam për qëllim; *n.* projekt, vizatim; 2 dizenjo; 3 qëllim, synim

desk /desk/ n. tavolinë, tryezë

desperate /'despërit/ *adj.* i dëshpëruar, i pashpresë

dessert /di'zë:rt/ *n.* ëmbëlsirë (në fund të ngrënies)

destination /,desti'neishn/ *n.* destinacion, vendmbërritje

destroy /di'stroi/ *vt.* 1 prish, thyej, shkatërroj; 2 dërrmoj, shpartalloj, asgjësoj

detach /di'teç/ *vt.* 1 shkëput, ndaj; 2 dërgoj

detail /'di:teil/ *n.* hollësi, imtësi; *vt.* jap hollësira, tregoj me hollësi; hyj në hollësira

detain /di'tein/ *vt.* 1 vonoj, pengoj; 2 mbaj; 3 mbaj nën arrest

detect /di'tekt/ *vt.* diktoj, zbuloj

detective /di'tektiv/ *adj.* zbulues, detektiv; *n.* detektiv

deteriorate /di'tiëriëreit/ *vti.* 1 keqësoj; 2 prish, dëmtoj

determination /di,të:mi'neishn/ *n.* 1 përkufizim, përcaktim; 2 vendosmëri, ngulmim

determine /di'të:rmin/ *vti.* 1 përcaktoj; 2 vendos; 3 llogaris; 4 kushtëzoj

detest /di'test/ *vt.* urrej, ndiej neveri

devaluation /,di:velju'eishn/ *n.* zhvleftësim

develop /di'velëp/ *vti.* 1 zhvilloj; 2 shtjelloj, trajtoj; 3 shfaq

development /di'velëpmënt/ *n.* zhvillim; ecuri

device /di'vais/ *n.* 1 plan, sajim, shpikje; 2 mjet; 3 mekanizëm, aparat, pajisje

devil /'devl/ *n.* djall; **go to the devil** shkoj në djall

devise /di'vaiz/ **vt.** mendoj, trilloj
devoid /di'void/ **adj.** pa; **devoid of sense** pa kuptim
devote /di'vout/ **vt.** i kushtohem, i jepem
devoted /di'voutid/ **adj.** i devotshëm, besnik
dew /dju:/ **n.** vesë
diabetes /ˌdaië'bi:ti:z/ **n.** diabet, sëmundje e sheqerit
diagnosis /ˌdaiëg'nëusis/ **n.** diagnozë; diagnostikim
dial /'daiël/ **n.** 1. fushë sahati; 2. rrethi me numra telefoni; 3. orë diellore; **vt.** telefonoj
dialect /'daiëlekt/ **n.** dialekt
dialogue /'daiëlo:g/ **n.** dialog, bashkëbisedim
diameter /dai'emitë(r)/ **n.** diametër
diamond /'daimënd/ **n.** 1. diamant, xhevahir; 2. diamant, elmaz; 3. karo (në letra)
diarrhoea (diarrhea) /ˌdaië'rië/ **n.** diare, heqje barku
diary /'daiëri/ **n.** ditar; **keep a diary** mbaj ditar
dictate /dik'teit; 'dikteit/ **vti.** 1. diktoj; 2. urdhëroj, diktoj, **dictatorship** /dik'teitëship/ **n.** diktaturë
dictionary /'dikshëneri/ **n.** fjalor
die /dai/ **vi.** 1. vdes; 2. thahet, vyshket; 3. kam shumë dëshirë për, digjem për
diet /'daiët/ **n.** dietë, pehriz; **be on a diet** mbaj dietë
differ /'difë(r)/ **vi.** 1. ndryshoj, dallohem; 2. kam tjetër mendim
difference /'difrëns/ **n.** ndryshim; mosmarrëveshje, divergjencë
difficult /'difikëlt/ **adj.** i vështirë
difficulty /'difikëlti/ **n.** vështirësi; **with (without) difficulty** me (pa) vështirësi; **be in difficulties** jam në vështirësi, në hall
diffident /'difidënt/ **adj.** i druajtur
dig /dig/ **vti.** gërmoj, rrëmih
digest /dai'xhest/ **vti.** 1. tres, bluaj (ushqimin); 2. përvetësoj, thith, bluaj një mendim
dignity /'digniti/ **n.** dinjitet
dilapidated /di'lepideitid/ **adj.** i shpartalluar, i shkatërruar
dilemma /di'lemë; dai'lemë/ **n.** mëdyshje; **be in a dilemma** jam në dilemë, mëdyshje
diligent /'dilixhënt/ **adj.** i zellshëm, punëtor
dimension /di'menshn; dei'menshn/ **n.** dimension, përmasë, madhësi
diminish /di'minish/ **vti.** 1. zvogëloj, pakësoj, ul; 2. zvogëlohem
dine /dain/ **vi.** ha darkë
dinner /'dinë(r)/ **n.** ngrënie kryesore e ditës (drekë ose darkë)
diphtheria /dif'thiërië/ **n.** difteri
diploma /di'ploumë/ **n.** diplomë
diplomat /'diplomet/ **n.** diplomat
direct /di'rekt; dai'rekt/ **adj.** 1. i drejtë; 2. i drejtpërdrejtë; i çiltër, i hapur; **vti.** 1. drejtoj, tregoj rrugën; 2. nis, dërgoj, adresoj; 3. drejtoj, udhëheq
direction /di'rekshn; dai'rekshn/ **n.** 1. drejtim; 2. udhëzim; 3. urdhra **dirt** /dë:rt/ **n.** papastërti, pisllëk
dirty /'dë:rti/ **adj.** 1. i ndotur, i pistë; 2. i ndyrë, i pacipë
disabled /dis'eibld/ **adj.** i gjymtë, sakat, i paaftë
disaccord /ˌdisë'ko:rd/ **n.** mospërputhje
disadvantage /ˌdisëd'ventixh/ **n.** disfavor, disavantazh

disagree /ˌdisëˈgriː/ **vi.** 1. nuk pajtohem, nuk merrem vesh; zihem, grindem; 2. nuk më përshtatet (klima etj.)
disagreable /ˌdisëˈgriːëbl/ **adj.** i papëlqyeshëm, i pakëndshëm
disagreement /ˌdisëˈgriːmënt/ **n.** mospajtim; mosmarrëveshje
disappear /ˌdisëˈpië(r)/ **vi.** 1. zhdukem; fshihem; 2. shuhem, humb
disappoint /ˌdisëˈpoint/ **vt.** 1. zhgënjej; 2. prish, nuk e lë të kryhet
disappointment /ˌdisëˈpointmënt/ **n.** zhgënjim; mërzitje
disapproval /ˌdisëˈpruːvl/ **n.** mospëlqim, mospranim
disapprove /ˌdisëˈpruːv/ **v.** nuk miratoj
disarmament /disˈaːmëmënt/ **n.** çarmatosje; çarmatim
disaster /diˈzaːstë(r); diˈzestë(r)/ **n.** fatkeqësi, katastrofë
disastrous /diˈzaːstrës/ **adj.** shkatërrimtar, shkatërrues
disband /disˈbend/ **vt.** shpërndaj
disbelief /ˈdisbiˈliːf/ **n.** mosbesim, dyshim
discard /disˈkaːrd/ **vt.** hedh, flak tej; **n.** hedhje, flakje
discern /diˈsë:rn/ **vti.** dalloj, shquaj
discharge /disˈçaːrxh/ **vt.** 1. shkarkoj; 2. pushoj nga puna; 3. liroj; 4. plotësoj detyrat; **n.** 1. shkarkim; 2. lirim; 3. pushim; 4. kryerje e detyrave
disciple /diˈsaipl/ **n.** ndjekës, nxënës, dishepull
discipline /ˈdisiplin/ **n.** disiplinë; **vt.** disiplinoj
disclose /disˈklouz/ **vt.** hap, zbuloj, nxjerr në dritë
disconnect /ˌdiskëˈnekt/ **vt.** shkëpus lidhjen; ndaj, veçoj
discontent /ˌdiskënˈtent/ **n.** pakënaqësi; **vt.** lë, bëj të pakënaqur; **adj.** i pakënaqur
discord /ˈdiskoːrd/ **n.** 1. mosmarrëveshje; 2. grindje
discount /ˈdiskaunt/ **n.** zbritje; **vt.** bëj zbritje
discover /disˈkavë(r)/ **vt.** zbuloj; marr vesh
discovery /disˈkavëri/ **n.** zbulim
discreet /diˈskriːt/ **adj.** i matur, i arsyeshëm; i përmbajtur; fjalëpakë
discrimination /diˌskrimiˈneishn/ **n.** diskriminim; dallim
discuss /diˌskas/ **vt.** shqyrtoj, diskutoj
disdain /disˈdein/ **n.** mospërfillje, përbuzje; **vt.** përçmoj, përbuz
disease /diˈziːz/ **n.** sëmundje
disentangle /ˌdisinˈtengl/ **vt.** shpengoj, liroj, zgjidh; shkoklavit **disfigure** /disˈfigë(r); disˈfigjër/ **vt.** shëmtoj, shfytyroj
disgrace /disˈgreis/ **n.** dalje nga hiri; rënie në sy të keq; **vt.** marr me sy të keq
disguise /disˈgaiz/ **n.** maskim; paraqitje e gënjeshtërt; **vt.** maskoj; fsheh, mbuloj
disgust /disˈgast/ **n.** neveritje, të pështirë; **vt.** shkaktoj neveritje, pakënaqësi; neveris, pështiros
dish /dish/ 1. pjatë; 2. gjellë; 3. **pl.** enët
dishwasher /ˈdishwoshë(r)/ **n.** pjatalarës; makinë pjatalarëse
dishonest /disˈonist/ **adj.** i pandershëm
dishonor (dishonour) /disˈonë(r)/ **n.** turpërim, çnderim, turp; **vt.** çnderoj, turpëroj
disillusion /ˌdisiˈluːzhn/ **n.** zhgënjim
disinherit /ˌdisinˈherit/ **vt.** e lë pa trashëgim; i heq të drejtën e trashëgimisë

disintegrate /dis'intigreit/ **vti.** zbërthej, shpërbëj
disintegration /dis,inti'greishn/ **n.** disintegrim, shpërbërje
disinterested /dis'intrëstid/ **adj.** i painteres
disk /disk/ **n.** disk manjetik, disketë
dislike /dis'laik/ **n.** mospëlqim, antipati; **vt.** nuk pëlqej
dismal /'dizmël/ **adj.** i vrenjtur, i ngrysur, i zymtë
dismantle /dis'mentl/ **vt.** çmontoj, zbërthej
dismiss /dis'mis/ **vt.** 1. pushoj, dëboj nga puna; 2. shpërndaj; 3. heq, largoj nga mendja
dismissal /dis'misl/ **n.** 1. pushim nga puna; 2. shpërndarje
disobedient /,disë'bi:diënt/ **adj.** i pabindur
disobey /'disë'bei/ **vt.** nuk bindem
disorder /dis'o:dë(r)/ **n.** çrregullim, rrëmujë, pështjellim; **vt.** çrregulloj; sjell pështjellim
disordered /dis'o:rdëd/ **adj.** 1. i çrregullt; 2. i prishur (stomaku)
disorganize /,dis'o:gënaiz/ **vt.** shthur, çorganizoj
dispassionate /dis'peshënit/ **adj.** 1. i paanshëm; 2. gjakftohtë, i matur
dispatch (despatch) /di'speç/ **vt.** 1. dërgoj, nis; 2. kryej, mbaroj shpejt; **n.** nisje, dërgim; shpejtësi (e kryerjes së diçkaje)
dispel /di'spel/ **vt.** shpërndaj, përhap, largoj
dispense /di'spëns/ **vti.** 1. shpërndaj; 2. përgatis; **dispense with** bëj pa, ia dal pa
disperse /di'spë:rs/ **vti.** shpërndaj, përhap
displace /dis'pleis/ **vt.** 1. zhvendos, shpërngul; 2. largoj, heq, zëvendësoj
display /di'splei/ **n.** 1. ekspozitë; 2. demonstrim; 3. shfaqje, manifestim; **vt.** 1. paraqes, tregoj; 2. ekspozoj
disposable /di'spozëbl/ **adj.** i disponueshëm
disposal /di'spouzl/ **n.** 1. dispozicion; **at one's disposal** në dispozicion të; 2. prirje; 3. dhënie, dorëzim
dispute /di'spju:t/ **n.** debat; kundërshtim, konflikt; **beyond dispute** pa dyshim
disqualify /dis'kwolifai/ **vt.** shkualifikoj
disregard /,disri'ga:rd/ **n.** mospërfillje; **vt.** shpërfill
dissatisfaction /,di,setis'fekshn/ **n.** pakënaqësi
dissatisfied /di'setisfaid/ **adj.** i pakënaqur
disseminate /di'semineit/ **vt.** 1. përhap; 2. mbjell, propagandoj
dissertation /,disë'teishn/ **n.** dezertacion
dissipate /'disipeit/ **vti.** 1. largoj, davaris; 2. harxhoj kot (kohën etj.)
dissolve /di'zolv/ **vti.** 1. tres; 2. shpërbëj, dekompozoj; 3. prish, zgjidh (një kontratë); 4. shpërndaj
distance /'distëns/ **n.** 1. distancë; **at a distance** në distancë; 2. interval
distant /'distënt/ **adj.** i largët
distil (distill) /di'stil/ **vt.** 1. pikon, rrjedh pikë-pikë; 2. distiloj
distinct /di'stinkt/ **adj.** 1. i qartë; 2. i dallueshëm; 3. i dalluar, i veçantë
distinction /di'stinkshn/ **n.** ndryshim; dallim; veti dalluese
distinguish /di'stinguish/ **vti.** dalloj; shquaj

distinguished /di'stinguisht/ **adj.** i shquar
distort /di'sto:rt/ **vt.** shtrembëroj; shfytyroj
distortion /di'sto:rshn/ **n.** shtrembërim; shfytyrim
distress /di'stres/ **n.** 1. brengë, hidhërim, pikëllim; 2.
mjerim; 3. vuajtje; 4. e keqe; **vt.** mjeroj; pikëlloj
distribute /di'stribju:t/ **vt.** shpërndaj; ndaj
distribution /,distri'bju:shn/ **n.** shpërndarje; ndarje
district /'distrikt/ **n.** rajon; qark; krahinë
distrust /dis'trast/ **n.** mosbesim; **vt.** nuk besoj
disturb /di'stë:rb/ **vt.** shqetësoj; prish qetësinë
disturbance /di'stë:rbëns/ **n.** 1. shqetësim; 2. çrregullim; 3.
prishje (e rregullit etj.)
dive /daiv/ **vi.** zhytem, kridhem; **n.** zhytje
diverse /dai'vë:rs/ **adj.** i ndryshëm, i shumëllojshëm
divert /dai'vë:rt/ **vt.** 1. devijoj, kthej drejtimin; 2.
argëtoj; 3. largoj vëmendjen
divide /di'vaid/ **vti.** 1. ndaj, pjesëtoj; 2. shpërndaj; 3.
veçoj; 4. përçaj, ndaj
dividend /'dividend/ **n.** dividend
divine /di'vain/ 1. hyjnor; 2. **gj. fl.** i mrekullueshëm
division /di'vizhn/ **n.** 1. ndarje; 2. pjesëtim; 3. divizion;
4. pjesëtim
divorce /di'vo:rs/ **n.** divorc; ndarje; **vt.** divorcoj, ndaj
dizzy /'dizi/ **adj.** që i merren mendtë
do /du:/ **vti.** 1. bëj, 2. veproj, 3. kryej; 4. pastroj,
rregulloj; **do a room** rregulloj dhomën; **do away with** i jap
fund, zhduk; **how do you do?** si jeni?; **do without** bëj pa
dockyard /'dokja:rd/ **n.** kantier (detar)
doctor /'doktë(r)/ **n.** 1. mjek, doktor; 2. doktor (titull
shkencor)
document /'dokjumënt/ **n.** dokument; dëshmi; **vt.** dokumentoj
dog /dog/ **n.** qen; **go to the dogs** shkatërrohem, marr të
tatëpjetën; **vt.** ndjek këmba-këmbës
dole /doul/ **n.** lëmoshë, ndihmë për të papunët
doll /do:l/ **n.** kukull
dollar /'dolë(r)/ **n.** dollar
domestic /dë'mestik/ **adj.** 1. shtëpiak; 2. i zbutur; 3. i
brendshëm, vendas
donate /dou'neit/ **vt.** dhuroj
donation /dou'neishn/ **n.** dhurim
done /dan/ **adj.** i bërë
donkey /'donki/ **n.** gomar
doom /du:m/ **n.** 1. vdekje; 2. rrënim, shkatërrim
door /do:(r)/ **n.** derë; **show smb the door** i tregoj dikujt
derën
doorway /'do:(r)wei/ **n.** hyrje
dose /dous/ **n.** dozë, sasi, masë
dot /dot/ **n.** pikë; **vt.** vë pikë
double /'dabl/ **adj.** dyfish, i dyfishtë, dysh; **double room**
dhomë dyshe; **double bed** krevat dopio; **n.** dyfish; dyshe; **vti.**
dyfishoj; bëj dysh
double-dealing /'dabl'di:lin/ **n.** hipokrizi, dyfaqësi
doubt /daut/ **n.** dyshim; **no doubt** pa dyshim; **in doubt** në
dyshim; **vti.** dyshoj, kam dyshim

doubtful /'dautful/ **adj.** i dyshimtë
doubtless /'dautlis/ **adj.** i padyshimtë, i sigurt
dough /dou/ **n.** brumë
doughnut /'dounat/ **n.** petull
dove /dav/ **n.** pëllumb
down /daun/ **adv.** poshtë, përposh; **prep.** poshtë, teposhtë
downfall /'daunfo:l/ **n.** 1. rënie; 2. **fig.** tatëpjetë, shkatërrim
downstairs /,daun'steëz/ **adv.** poshtë shkallëve; në katin poshtë
dozen /'dazn/ **n.** duzinë; **dozens of** shumë
draft /dra:ft; dreft/ **n.** 1. vizatim, plan, skicë; projekt; 2. çek; **vt.** 1. bëj projektin, skicën e; 2. rekrutoj
drag /dreg/ **vti.** 1. tërheq zvarrë; 2. zvarritem, tërhiqem
dragon /'dregën/ **n.** dragua
drain /drein/ **vt.** thaj, drenazhoj, kulloj; 2. thaj, pi deri në fund; **n.** drenë, drenazhim
drainpipe /'dreinpaip/ **n.** drenë
dramatic /drë'metik/ **adj.** dramatik
drastic /'drestik/ **adj.** 1. vrullshëm; 2. i prerë, i rreptë, i ashpër; 3. radikal
draught /dra:ft; dreft/ **n.** 1. rrymë ajri; 2. heqje, tërheqje; 3. gllënjkë, kurbë
draw /dro:/ **n.** 1. tërheqje; 2. hedhje e shortit; llotari; 3. barazim; **vti.** 1. tërheq; 2. nxjerr, heq; 3. barazoj; 4. skicoj, vizatoj
drawback /'dro:bek/ **n.** e metë, mangësi
drawer /dro:(r)/ **n.** 1. sirtar; 2. vizatues; 3. **pl.** të mbathura, brekë **dreadful** /'dredful/ **adj.** i tmerrshëm
dream /dri:m/ **n.** ëndërr; vegim; **vit.** ëndërroj, shoh në ëndërr; parafytyroj
dress /dres/ **n.** 1. veshje, rroba; 2. fustan; **vti.** vesh, vishem, stolisem; 2. përgatis, gatuaj; 3. kreh, rregulloj
dressing /'dresin/ **n.** 1. veshje; 2. lidhje, fashim i plagës; materialet për lidhjen e plagëve
dress rehearsal /'dresri'hë:rsël/ **n.** provë gjenerale
dried /draid/ **adj.** i tharë
drift /drift/ **n.** rrjedhë, rrymë; **vi.** e merr rryma; **fig.** shkon mbas rrymës
drink /drink/ **n.** 1. pirje; 2. gotë (pije); **soft drinks** pije freskuese; **vti.** 1. pi; 2. pi pije alkoolike
drip /drip/ **n.** pikim; **vti.** pikon, rrjedh pika-pika
drive /draiv/ **n.** 1. udhëtim, shëtitje me makinë; 2. energji, vrull; 3. fushatë; 4. **tek.** transmision; **vti.** 1. ngas (makinën); 2. çoj (me makinë) 3. vë në lëvizje; 4. shtyj; përplas; **drive at** bëj aluzion, hedh fjalën; **drive home** sqaroj, bëj të qartë
driver /'draivë(r)/ **n.** shofer
driving /'draivin/ **n.** ngarje, drejtim i makinës; **driving license** patentë e makinës
drizzle /'drizl/ **n.** vesë shiu, shi i imët; **vi.** veson, bie shi i imët
drop /drop/ **n.** 1. pikë; 2. gllënjkë, hurbë, gërrqe; 3. rënie; **vit.** 1. pikon; 2. bie; 3. ndaloj, ndërpres; 4. rrëzoj, lëshoj; **drop in** shkoj, kaloj për vizitë
drought /draut/ **n.** thatësirë

drown /draun/ **vti.** mbyt, mbytem
drug /drag/ **n.** 1. bar, ilaç; 2. narkotik, drogë; **drug addict**
narkoman
drugstore /'dragsto:(r)/ **n.** farmaci
drunk /drank/ **adj.** i pirë, i dehur
dry /drai/ **adj.** 1. i thatë; 2. i mërzitshëm; 3. jo e ëmbël
(vera); 4. i etur; **vti.** thaj, thahem
dry-cleaning /'draikli:nin/ **n.** pastrim kimik
dual /'dju:ël/ **adj.** i dyfishtë
dubious /'dju:bjës; du:biës/ **adj.** i dyshimtë; dyshues
duck /dak/ **n.** rosë; **vti.** zhytem, kridhem
due /dju:; du:/ **adj.** i duhur, i përshtatshëm; i detyrueshëm;
i përcaktuar; **due to** për shkak të, në sajë të; **in due course**
(time) në kohën e duhur; **n.** 1. ajo që i takon; **give the devil
his due** jepi atë që i takon; 2. **pl.** taksa, tatime; kuotë
antarsie
duet /dju:'et; du:'et/ **n.** duet
dull /dal/ **adj.** 1. i turbullt; 2. i trashë; i ngathët; 3. i
pamprehur, i mpirë; 4. monoton, i mërzitshëm
dumb /dam/ **adj.** memec, pa gojë
dummy /'dami/ **n.** 1. manekin; 2. **fig.** vegël, mashë; **adj.** fals,
kallp
dump /damp/ **n.** grumbull hedhurinash; plehërishtë; **vt.** zbras,
derdh, shkarkoj (plehrat)
dumping /'damping/ **n. ek.** dumping
dupe /dju:p; du:p / **n.** njeri dede, leshko; **vt.** vë në lojë; ia
hedh
duplicate /'du:plëkeit/ **adj.** i dyfishtë; i dyzuar; **n.**
duplikatë
durable /'djërëbl/ **adj.** i qëndrueshëm; i rrojtshëm, i
durueshëm
during /'djuërin/ **prep.** gjatë
dusk /dask/ **n.** muzg i mbrëmjes, mugëtirë
dust /dast/ **n.** 1. pluhur; 2. plehra; 3. rrëmujë; **vt.**
pluhuroj; pluhuros; fshij pluhurin
dustbin /'dastbin/ **n.** kosh për plehra
Dutch /daç/ **adj.** holandez; **n.** holandishte
duty /'dju:ti; 'du:ti/ **n.** 1. detyrë; **do one's duty** bëj
detyrën; 2. shërbim, punë; **on duty** në punë, në shërbim; 3.
taksë doganore
dwell /dwel/ **vi.** jetoj, banoj; **dwell on (upon)** trajtoj me
hollësi
dwelling /'dwelin/ **n.** shtëpi, banesë; vendbanim
dye /dai/ **n.** bojë; ngjyrë; **vt.** ngjyej, ngjyros
dynamic /dai'nemik/ **adj.** dinamik
dysentery /'disëntri; 'disënteri/ **n.** dizenteri

E

each /i:ç/ **adj. pron.** çdo; secili; **each other** njëri-tjetrin; **each time** çdo herë, sa herë

eager /'i:gë(r)/ **adj.** i etshëm, i etur, i paduruar, që mezi pret

eagle /'i:gl/ **n.** shqiponjë

ear /ië(r)/ **n.** 1. vesh; **be all ears** jam gjithë sy e veshë; **up to the ears** deri në grykë; 2. dëgjim

early /'ë:rli/ **adj.** i hershëm; **adv.** herët

earn /ë:rn/ **vt.** fitoj; meritoj; **earn one's living** siguroj, fitoj jetesën

earnest /'ë:rnist/ **adj.** 1. serioz; 2. i vendosur; i zellshëm; **in earnest** seriozisht

earnings /ë:rninz/ **n.** rrogë; fitime

earring /'iërin/ **n.** vëth

earth /ë:rth/ **n.** 1. tokë; 2. rruzul i dheut; 3. dhe; **vt.** 1. mbuloj me dhe; 2. tokëzoj

earthquake /'ë:rthkweik/ **n.** tërmet

ease /i:z/ **n.** 1. qetësi; 2. lehtësi; 3. shpengim; shkujdesje

easily /'i:zili/ **adv.** lehtë, lirshëm **east** /i:st/ **n.** lindje

Easter /'i:stë(r)/ **n.** pashkë

eastern /'i:stën/ **adj.** lindor

easy /'i:zi/ **adj.** 1. i lehtë; 2. i shkujdesur, i qetë; 3. i lirshëm, i natyrshëm; **adv.** lehtë

easy-going /,i:zi'goin/ **adj.** i shkujdesur

eat /i:t/ **vit.** 1. ha; 2. brej; 3. prish, shpenzoj

eau-de-Cologne /'oudëkë'loun/ **n.** kolonjë

echo /'ekou/ **n.** jehonë; **vit.** jehon, ushton

ecology /i:'kolëxhi/ **n.** ekologji

economic /,i:kë'nomik; ,ekë'nomik/ **adj.** ekonomik

economy /i'konëmi/ **n.** ekonomi

edge /exh/ **n.** 1. teh; presë; 2. anë, cep, kënd; 3. buzë

edible /'edibl/ **adj.** i ngrënshëm

edit /'edit/ **vt.** botoj; redaktoj

edition /i'dishn/ **n.** botim

editorial /,edi'to:riël/ **n.** kryeartikull; **adj.** redaksional

education /,edju:'keishn/ **n.** 1. arsim; **higher education** arsim i lartë; **compulsory education** arsim i detyruar; 2. edukatë

effect /i'fekt/ **n.** 1. veprim; 2. pasojë, rezultat, efekt; 3. kuptim

effective /i'fektiv/ **adj.** 1. efektiv, i efektshëm; 2. efektiv, real, konkret

efficient /i'fishnt/ **adj.** 1. veprues, efektiv; frytdhënës; 2. i zoti, i aftë

e.g. /,i:'xhi:/ **abbr.** p.sh.

egg /eg/ **n.** 1. vezë; 2. **biol.** vezë; **fried eggs** vezë të skuqura

egoism /'egouizëm/ **n.** egoizëm

eight /eit/ **n.** tetë

eighteen /'ei'ti:n/ **n.** tetëmbëdhjetë

eighty /'eiti/ **n.** tetëdhjetë

either /'aidhë(r); 'i:dhë(r)/ **adj.,pron.** një nga të dy, njëri ose tjetri; cilido, kushdo; **conj.** ose

elaborate /i'lebërit/ **adj.** i përpunuar, i punuar me kujdes; i stërholluar; **vt.**/i'lebëreit/ përpunoj; shtjelloj

elastic /i'lestik/ **adj.** elastik
elbow /'elbou/ **n.** 1. bërryl; 2. **tek.** bërryl; 3. kthesë rruge
ose lumi; **at one's elbow** pranë, ngjitur; **vt.** shtyj me bërryl;
elbow one's way hap rrugën me bërryla
elder /'eldë(r)/ **adj.** më i madh, më i moshuar; **n.** plak
elderly /'eldërli/ **adj.** i thyer, i shkuar nga mosha
eldest /'eldist/ **adj.** më plaku, më i madhi
elect /i'lekt/ **vt.** zgjedh me votim
election /i'lekshn/ **n.** zgjedhje; **election campaign** fushatë e
zgjedhjeve
electoral /i'lektërël/ **adj.** elektoral
electorate /i:'lektërët/ **n.** elektorati, zgjedhësit
electric /i'lektrik/ **adj.** elektrik; **electric current** rrymë
elektrike
electricity /i,lek'trisëti/ **n.** elektricitet
electron /i'lektron/ **n.** elektron
elegant /'eligënt/ **adj.** elegant
element /'elimënt/ **n.** 1. element; 2. **kim.** element
elementary /,eli'mentri/ **adj.** i thjeshtë, elementar;
fillestar; fillor
elephant /'elifënt/ **n.** elefant
elevate /'eliveit/ **vt.** ngre, lartësoj; **elevate the voice** ngre
zërin; nge moralisht
eleven /i'leven/ **num.** njëmbëdhjetë
eliminate /i'limineit/ **vt.** eleminoj, zhduk
elite /ei'li:t/ **n.** elitë, ajkë
eloquent /'elëkvënt/ **adj.** gojëtar, i gojës
else /els/ **adv.** ende, përveç; ndryshe, për ndryshe; **pron.**
tjetër
emancipate /i'mensipeit/ **vt.** emancipoj, çliroj
embankment /im'benkmënt/ **n.** 1. pendë; sfrat; 2. breg, trase e
veshur
embark /im'ba:rk/ **vti.** 1. ngarkoj në anije; 2. hipi në anije;
3. i hyj një pune
embarras /im'berës/ **vt.** 1. zë ngushtë, vë në pozitë të
vështirë; 2. pengoj, ngatërroj
embassy /'embësi/ **n.** ambasadë
emblem /'emblëm/ **n.** stemë, emblemë
embodiment /im'bodimënt/ **n.** mishërim, personifikim, trupëzim
embody /im'bodi/ **vt.** mishëroj, personifikoj, trupëzoj
embrace /im'breis/ **n.** përqafim; **vt.** 1. përqafoj; 2. bëj
timen, pranoj, përqafoj
embroidery /im'broidëri/ **n.** qëndisje; qëndismë; qëndistari
emerald /'emërëld/ **n.** smerald
emerge /i'më:rxh/ **vi.** dal, shfaqem
emergence i'më:rxhëns/ **n.** dalje, shfaqje
emergency /i'më:rxhënsi/ **n.** urgjencë; **in case of emergency** në
rast urgjence; **emergency exit** dalje për raste emergjente
emigrant /'emigrënt/ **n.** emigrant; **economic (political)**
emigrant emigrant ekonomik (politik); **adj.** emigrues
emigrate /'emigreit/ **vi.** emigroj, mërgohem
emigration /,emi'greishn/ **n.** emigrim, mërgim
eminent /'eminënt/ **adj.** i shquar, i famshëm; eminent
emit /i'mit/ **vt.** 1. emeton, lëshon, përhap; 2. emetoj, nxjerr
para

emotion /i'moushn/ **n.** 1. ndjenjë, emocion; 2. mallëngjim
emotional /i'moushënl/ **adj.** i prekshëm, i ndjeshëm, emocional
emphasis /'emfësis/ **n.** theksim, theks, emfazë
emphasize /'emfësaiz/ **vt.** theksoj
emphatic /im'fetik/ **adj.** emfatik
empire /'empaië(r)/ **n.** perandori
employ /im'ploi/ **n.** punë, zënie në punë; **vt.** 1. pajtoj, marr
në punë, punësoj; 2. përdor, shfrytëzoj
employee /,emplo'i:; im'ploi:/ **n.** nëpunës
employer /im'ploië(r)/ **n.** punëdhënës
employment /im'ploimënt/ **n.** 1. punë, pajtim në punë; 2. punë,
zanat, profesion
emporium /im'po:riëm/ **n.** qendër tregëtare; treg; mapo
universale
empty /'empti/ **adj.** 1. i zbrazët, bosh; 2. i lirë, i pazënë;
vti. zbras, boshatis; derdhet
enable /i'neibl/ **vt.** mundësoj
enchanting /in'çantin/ **adj.** magjepës
enclose /in'klëuz/ **vt.** 1. mbyll; 2. paketoj; vë, fut; 3.
rrethoj
encounter /in'kauntë(r)/ **n.** ndeshje, përpjekje, përleshje;
vt. 1. takoj, ndesh (befas) 2. ndesh (vështirësi etj.); 3.
hyj në luftë me, përleshem
encourage /in'karixh/ **vt.** nxit, i jap zemër, inkurajoj
encouragement /in'karixhmënt/ **n.** inkurajim, nxitje
encouraging /in'karixhin/ **adj.** inkurajues
encroach /in'krouç/ **vi.** shkel, cënoj, marr nëpër këmbë
encyclopedia /in'saiklë'pi:dië/ **n.** enciklopedi
end /end/ **n.** 1. fund; **in the end** në fund, më në fund; **make
both ends meet** jetoj me të keq, mezi mbaj frymën ngjallë; 2.
bisht, mbetje; 3. vdekje; 4. qëllim; **gain one's end** ia arrij
qëllimit; **vti.** mbaroj, përfundoj; përfundon
endanger /in'deinxhë(r)/ **vt.** rrezikoj, vë në rrezik
endless /'endlis/ **adj.** i pambarim, i pafund
endure /in'djuë(r); in'duër/ **vt.** duroj, qëndroj
enema /'enimë/ **n.** klizmë
enemy /'enimi/ **n.** armik; kundërshtar
energy /'enëxhi/ **n.** energji
engage /in'geixh/ **vt.** 1. punësoj; 2. zë me punë; 3. fejohem
engaged /in'geixhd/ **adj.** 1. i zënë me punë; 2. i fejuar; 3. i
pajtuar
engender /in'xhendë(r)/ **vt.** lind, sjell
engine /'enxhin/ **n.** 1. motor; 2. lokomotivë; 3. makinë
engineer /,enxhi'nië(r)/ **n.** inxhinier
English /'inglish/ **n.** gjuha angleze, anglishtja; **adj.** anglez
engrave /in'greiv/ **vt.** gdhend; skalis
engraving /in'greivin/ **n.** gdhendje; skalitje
enhance /in'ha:ns; in'hens/ **vt.** ngre, shtoj, rrit, zmadhoj
enjoy /in'xhoi/ **vt.** 1. kënaqem, gjej kënaqësi; 2. gëzoj, kam
enjoyment /in'xhoimënt/ **n.** 1. kënaqësi, gëzim; argëtim; 2.
pasje, zotërim
enlarge /in'la:rxh/ **vti.** zmadhoj, zgjeroj; zgjerohem
enlist /in'list/ **vti.** 1. rekrutoj; 2. bëj për vete
enmity /'enmëti/ **n.** armiqësi
enormous /i'no:mës/ **adj.** gjigand, shumë i madh

enough /i'naf/ **adj.** i mjaftueshëm; **adv.** mjaft
enrich /in'riç/ **vt.** pasuroj
enrol(l) /in'roul/ **vt.** 1. regjistroj; 2. bëhem anëtar
e(i)nsure /in'shuě(r)/ **vt.** 1. siguroj; 2. garantoj
entail /in'teil/ **vt.** 1. kërkoj; 2. lë trashëgim
entangle /in'tengl/ **vt.** 1. ngec; 2. nuk ia dal dot; 3.
ngatërrohem, përzihem keq
enter /'entě(r)/ **vti.** 1. hyj,futem; 2. shënoj në listë; 3.
përçoj, depërtoj; 4. nis, filloj
enterprise /'entěpraiz/ **n.** 1. ndërmarrje; 2. iniciativě,
vetëveprim; 3. sipërmarrje
entertain /,entě'tein/ **vti.** 1. argětoj, zbavit; 2. pres miq;
3. ushqej, kam shpresě
entertainment /,entě'teinmënt/ **n.** 1. zbavitje, argětim; 2.
shfaqje
enthusiasm /in'thu:ziezěm/ **n.** entuziazěm
enthusiastic /in,thu:zi'estik/ **adj.** i entuziazmuar
entire /in'taiě(r)/ **adj.** i těrě, i gjithě; **n.** těrësi
entitle /in/taitl/ **vt.** 1. titulloj; 2. i jap tě drejtě
entrance /'entrěns/ **n.** 1. hyrje; derě; 2. e drejtě e hyrjes
entrust /in'trast/ **vt.** i besoj, ia lë në dorë
entry /'entri/ **n.** 1. hyrje; 2. shěnim, regjistrim; 3. derě,
portě
enumerate /i'nju:měreit; i'nu:měreit/ **vt.** 1. numěroj; 2.
emërtoj
envelope /,envěloup/ **n.** 1. zarf; 2. mbështjellě
envious /'enviěs/ **adj.** ziliqar, lakmitar, lakmues
environment /in,vaiěrěnmënt/ **n.** mjedis, ambient
envy /'envi/ **n.** zili, smirě; **vt.** kam zili, zilepsem
epidemic /,epi'demik/ **adj.** epidemik; **n.** epidemi
episode /'episoud/ **n.** episod, ngjarje
epoch /'i:pok; 'epěk/ **n.** epokě
equal /'i:kwěl/ **adj.** i njějtě, i barabartě; **vt.** barazoj;
rrafshoj
equality /i':kwoliti/ **n.** barazi
equator /i'kweitě(r)/ **n.** ekuator
equip /i'kwip/ **vt.** pajis
equipment /i'kwipměnt/ **n.** pajisje; pajim
equivalent /i'kwivělěnt/ **adj.** ekuivalent, i barazvlefshěm; **n.**
barasvlerěs
era /'iěrě/ **n.** erě, epokě
erect /i'rekt/ **adj.** drejt, pingul; **vt.** 1. ngre, ndërtoj; 2.
drejtoj lart
erosion /i'rouzhn/ **n.** gěrryerje; erozion
erotic /i'rotik/ **adj.** erotik, dashuror
erroneous /i'rouniěs/ i gabuar
error /'erě/ **n.** gabim; **make (commit) an error** běj një gabim
eruption /i'rapshěn/ **n.** shpěrthim, nxjerrje, derdhje
escape /is'keip/ **n.** 1. shpětim; 2. rredhje, dalje, nxjerrje;
vit. 1. shpětoj; 2. iki, arratisem; 3. del; rrjedh
especial /i'speshl/ **adj.** i veçantě, i posaçěm
especially /is'peshěli/ **adv.** sidomos, veçaněrisht
essay /e'sei/ **n.** 1. ese; 2. prově
essence /'esens/ **n.** thelb, esencě
essential /i'senshěl/ **adj.** thelbësor, i qeněsishěm; i
domosdoshěm
establish /i'steblish/ **vt.** 1. themeloj, krijoj; 2. vendosem

establishment /i'steblishmënt/ **n.** 1. themelim, krijim; 2. ndërmarrje, institucion; 3. ekonomi (shtëpiake)
estate /i'steit/ **n.** 1. çiflig; pronë; 2. pasuri; **personal estate** pasuri e tundshme; **real estate** pasuri e patundshme
estimate /'estimët/ **n.** 1. vlerësim; 2. preventiv; /'estimeit/ **vti.** 1. vlerësoj, çmoj; 2. përgatis, hartoj një preventiv
et cetera, etc. /it'setërë/ e të tjera; etj.
eternal /i'të:rnl/ **adj.** i përjetshëm; i përhershëm, i pafund
ethics /'ethiks/ **n.** etikë
ethnic /'ethnik/ **adj.** etnik
Europian /,juërë'piën/ **adj.** evropian
evacuate /i'vekjueit/ **vt.** evakuoj, shpërngul
evade /i'veid/ **vt.** 1. shmang; 2. i dredhoj
evaluate /i'veljueit/ **vt.** 1. vlerësoj; 2. llogarit, numëroj
evasive /i'veisiv/ **adj.** evaziv
eve /i:v/ **n.** vigjilje, prag; **on the eve of** në vigjilje të
even /i:vn/ **adj.** 1. i rrafshtë, i sheshtë; 2. i njëtrajtshëm; 3. i barabartë; 4. çift (për numrat); **adv.** madje, edhe; **even if** edhe sikur; **vti.** rrafshoj; sheshoj; barazoj; njëjtësoj
evening /'i:vnin/ **n.** 1. mbrëmje; 2. mbrëmje muzikore, letrare etj.
event /i'vent/ **n.** 1. ndodhi, ngjarje; 2. rast; **at all events** në çdo rast; **in the event of** në rast se; **in any event** sidoqoftë
ever /'evë(r)/ **adv.** gjithmonë; **for ever** përgjithmonë; **ever since** qyshkur
every /'evri/ **adj.** çdo; **every now and then** herë pas here; kohë pas kohe; **every other day** një herë në dy ditë
everybody /'evribodi/ **pron.** kushdo, secili, cilido
everyday /'evridei/ **adj.** i përditshëm
everyone /'evriwan/ **pron.** çdo kush, secili
everything /'evrithin/ **pron.** çdo gjë; gjithçka
everywhere /'evriweër/ **adv.** kudo, në çdo vend
evict /i:'vikt/ **vt.** dëboj, përzë; shpërngul
evidence /'evidëns/ **n.** provë, dëshmi; **give evidence** dëshmoj
evident /'evidënt/ **adj.** i dukshëm, i qartë
evidently /'evidëntli/ **adv.** dukshëm, qartë
evil /'i:vl/ **n.** e keqe; **adj.** 1. i keq, i lig, i poshtër; 2. i dëmshëm
evolution /,i:vë'lu:shn/ ,evë'lu:shn/ **n.** zhvillim, evolucion
evolve /i'volv/ **vti.** 1. evoluon; 2. zhvilloj, shtjelloj
exact /ig'zekt/ **adj.** i saktë, i përpiktë; **vt.** kërkoj; zhvat (para)
exactly /ig'zektli/ **adv.** saktësisht; pikërisht
exaggerate /ig'zexhëreit/ **vti.** tepëroj, ekzagjeroj, zmadhoj
examination /ig'zemi'neishn/ **n.** 1. shqyrtim, ekzaminim; 2. provim; **take an examination** jap provim; **pass one's examination** kaloj provimin; **fail in an examination** mbetem në provim
examine /ig'zemin/ **vt.** 1. shqyrtoj; 2. marr në provim
example /ig'za:mpl/ ig'zempl/ **n.** shembull; **for example** për shembull; **follow smb's example** ndjek shembullin e; **set an example to** bëhem shembull për
exceed /ik'si:d/ **vt.** kaloj, tejkaloj, kapërcej
excellent /'eksëlënt/ **adj.** i shkëlqyeshëm, i shkëlqyer
except /ik'sept/ **prep.** me përjashtim, përveç; **vt.** përjashtoj; kundërshtoj

exception /ik'sepshn/ **n.** 1. përjashtim; **with the exception of** me përjashtim të; **make an exception** bëj përjashtim; **without exception** pa përjashtim; 2. kundërshtim

exceptional /ik'sepshënl/ **adj.** i veçantë, i jashtëzakonshëm

excerpt /'eksë:pt/ **n.** pjesë, fragment; **vt.** nxjerr, shkëpus një fragment

excess /ik'ses/ **n.** tepri; teprim; **adj.** i tepërt

excessive /ik'sesiv/ **adj.** i tepërt

exchange /iks'çeinxh/ **n.** 1. shkëmbim; këmbim; **exchange rate** kursi i këmbimit 2. bursë; **vti.** këmbej; ndërroj

excite ik'sait/ **vt.** 1. ngacmoj, eksitoj; 2. gjallëroj, ngjall; 3. nxit

exciting /ik'satin/ **adj.** 1. ngacmues, eksitues; 2. emocionues

exclaim /ik,skleim/ **vi.** thërras (me habi, gëzim etj.)

exclude /ik'sklu:d/ **vt.** përjashtoj; lë jashtë

exclusive /ik'sklu:siv/ **adj.** i veçantë

excursion /ik'skë:shn/ **n.** ekskursion

excuse /ik'skju:s/ **n.** falje; shfajësim; **vt.** shfajësoj, fal; **excuse me!** më falni!

execute /'eksikju:t/ **vt.** 1. zbatoj, përmush; 2. ekzekutoj

executive /ig'zekjutiv/ **adj.** ekzekutiv; ekzekutues, zbatues; **n.** 1. pushtet ekzekutiv; 2. zbatues

exempt /ig'zempt/ **adj.** i përjashtuar; **vt.** përjashtoj

exercise /'eksësaiz/ **n.** ushtrim; praktikë, stërvitje; **vti.** 1. ushtroj; 2. përdor

exert ig'zë:rt/ **vt.** 1. përpiqem, mundohem; 2. ushtroj; **exert one's influence** ushtroj ndikimin

exhale /eks'heil/ **vti.** nxjerr (frymë, avull etj.)

exhausted /ig'zo:stid/ **adj.** i rraskapitur, i këputur

exhibit /ig'zibit/ **vt.** 1. ekspozoj; 2. tregoj, shfaq; **n.** eksponat

exhibition /,eksi'bishn/ **n.** 1. ekspozitë; 2. paraqitje; shfaqje

exile /'eksail/ **n.** mërgim; **vt.** mërgoj

exist /ig'zist/ **vi.** ekzistoj, jetoj

existence /ig'zistëns/ **n.** jetesë; ekzistencë, qenie

exit /'eksit; 'egzit/ **n.** dalje

expand /ik'spend/ **vti.** 1. zgjeroj, zmadhoj, shtrij; 2. bymehet; 3. hap, shpalos

expanse /ik'spens/ **n.** shtrirje; hapësirë

expect /ik'spekt/ **vt.** 1. pres, shpresoj; 2. parashikoj

expedient /ik'spi:diënt/ **adj.** 1. i përshtatshëm; 2. i këshillueshëm

expel /ik'spel/ **vt.** dëboj, nxjerr jashtë, përjashtoj

expenditure /ik'spendiçë(r)/ **n.** harxhim, shpenzim

expense /ik'spens/ **n.** shpenzim; **at our expense** për llogari tonë

expensive /ik'spensiv/ **adj.** i shtrenjtë

experience /ik'spiëriëns/ **n.** përvojë; ndjenjë e provuar; **vt.** 1. provoj; 2. përjetoj; 3. ndiej

experiment /ik'sperimënt/ **n.** eksperiment, provë; **vi.** eksperimentoj, bëj provë

expert /'ekspë:rt/ **n.** ekspert, specialist

expire /ik'spaië(r)/ **vi.** 1. vdes; 2. mbaron, kalon (afati)

explain /ik'splein/ **vt.** 1. shpjegoj, sqaroj; 2. shtjelloj

explanation /,eksplë'neishn/ **n.** shpjegim; sqarim

explode /ik'sploud/ **vti.** shpërthej; shpërthejnë

exploit /'eksploit/ **n.** bëmë; **vt.** /ik'sploit/ 1. shfrytëzoj, vë në shfrytëzim; 2. përfitoj, nxjerr përfitime

explore /ik'splo:(r)/ **vt.** 1. hetoj, shqyrtoj; 2. gjurmoj, kërkoj; 3. eksploroj, bëj ekspeditë kërkimore

explosion /ik'splouzhn/ **n.** shpërthim, plasje, eksplozion

export /'ekspo:rt/ **n.** eksport; eksportim; **vt.** /ik'spo:rt/ eksportoj

exporter /ek'spo:rtë(r)/ **n.** eksportues

expose /ik'spouz/ **vt.** 1. ekspozoj; lë të ekspozuar; 2. nxjerr në shesh, nxjerr në dritë

express /ik'spres/ **n.** ekspres (tren, aeroplan etj.); **adj.** ekspres; **vt.** 1. shpreh; 2. dërgoj ekspres

expression /ik'spreshn/ **n.** 1. shprehje; 2. **gjuh.** shprehje, lokucion, frazeologji; 3. shprehësi

extend /ik'stend/ **vti.** shtrij, zgjat, zgjeroj

extension /ik'stenshn/ **n.** 1. shtrirje, zgjerim; 2. shtojcë, shtesë

extensive /ik,stensiv/ **adj.** 1. i gjerë, i shtrirë; 2. ekstensiv

extent /ik'stent/ **n.** shtrirje, gjerësi; shkallë, masë; **to a certain extent (degree)** në një farë shkalle

external /ik'stë:rnl/ **adj.** i jashtëm; **n. pl.** anët e jashtme

extinguish /ik'stingwish/ **vt.** 1. shuaj, fik; 2. shkatërroj, zhduk

extinguisher /ik'stingwishë(r)/ **n.** zjarrfikëse; fikës

extra /'ekstrë/ **adj.** plotësues, suplementar; **adv.** tepër

extract /ik'strekt/ **vt.** 1. heq, nxjerr; shkul; 2. shtrydh; **n.** /'ekstrekt/ ekstrakt

extradition /,ikstrë'dishn/ **n.** ekstradim

extraordinary /ik'stro:dëneri/ **adj.** i jashtëzakonshëm

extravagant /ik'strevëgënt/ **adj.** 1. ekstravagant; 2. dorëlëshuar

extreme /ik'stri:m/ **adj.** ekstrem, i skajshëm; **n.** skaj, ekstrem; **go to extreme** shkoj në ekstrem

extremely /ik'stri:mli/ **adv.** tepër, jashtëzakonisht

eye /ai/ **n.** 1. sy; 2. vrimë gjilpëre; 3. filiqe; 4. shikim, vështrim; **keep an eye on** kujdesem; **vt.** shikoj, vështroj

eyebrow /'aibrau/ **n.** vetull

eyesight /'aisait/ **n.** shikim

eyewitness /ai'witnis/ **n.** dëshmitar okular

F

fable /'feibl/ **n.** fabul
fabric /'febrik/ **n.** 1. pëlhurë; 2. strukturë
fabricate /'febrikeit/ **vt.** 1. shpik, trilloj; falsifikoj 2.
fabrikoj, prodhoj
face /feis/ **n.** 1. fytyrë; 2. çehre; **in the face of** përballë;
face to face ballë për ballë; 3. paturpësi; **have the face** kam
paturpësinë; 4. faqe, fasadë; 5. fushë sahati; **vti.** 1. jam
përballë; 2. ndesh ballë për ballë; 3. i bëj ballë
facilitate /fë'siliteit/ **vt.** lehtësoj; ndihmoj
facility /fë'silëti/ **n.** lehtësi
fact /fekt/ **n.** fakt; **in fact** në fakt; **as a matter of fact** në
të vërtetë; **in point of fact** faktikisht
factor /'fektë(r)/ **n.** faktor
factory /'fektëri/ **n.** fabrikë, uzinë
factual /'fekçjuël/ **adj.** faktik
faculty /'feklti/ **n.** 1. aftësi, zotësi; **the mental faculties**
aftësi mendore; 2. fakultet
fade /feid/ **vti.** 1. fishk; 2. venis; 3. zbeh, del ngjyra
fail /feil/ **vit.** 1. dështoj, nuk arrij; 2. rrëzohem, ngelem
në provim **failure** /'feiljë(r)/ **n.** 1. dështim; 2. falimentim;
3. rrëzim; 4. mungesë, pamjaftueshmëri
faint /feint/ **adj.** 1. i dobët, i ligur; 2. i zbehtë, i dobët,
i pafuqishëm; **n.** të fikët, zali; **vi.** më bie të fikët
fair /feë(r)/ **n.** panair; **adj.** 1. i ndershëm, i drejtë; 2.
mjaft i mirë; 3. e mirë, e kthjellët (koha)
fairly /'feërli/ **adv.** ndershmërisht, drejt; mjaft
fairy /'feëri/ **n.** zanë; **adj.** përrallor, magjik
faith /feith/ **n.** 1. besim; 2. fe; 3. premtim; besnikëri,
mirëbesim; **by my faith** për fjalën e nderit; **in good faith**
ndershmërisht
faithful /'feithful/ **adj.** besnik, besëtar
faithfully /'feithfuli/ **adv.** besnikërisht
faithless /'feithlis/ **adj.** i pabesë
fake /feik/ **adj.** i falsifikuar, i rremë; **n.** vepër e
falsifikuar
fall /fo:l/ **n.** 1. rënie; 2. ulje; 3. rreshje; 4. ujëvarë; **vi.**
1. bie; rrëzohem; 2. ulet, zbret; 3. varet; 4. bie, rastis;
5. zbret, shkon teposhtë; **fall behind** mbetem prapa; **fall
asleep** bie në gjumë; **fall sick** sëmurem; **fall in love with** bie
në dashuri me
false /fo:ls/ **adj.** fals, i rremë
falsify /'fo:lsifai/ **vt.** falsifikoj, shtrembëroj
fame /feim/ **n.** nam, famë, emër
familiar /fë'milië(r)/ **adj.** 1. i familjarizuar; 2. i afërm,
intim; 3. i njohur, i ditur; 4. i zakonshëm
family /'femëli/ **n.** 1. familje; 2. **biol. gjuh.** familje
famous /'feimës/ **adj.** i famshëm, i njohur
fan /fen/ **n.** ventilator; freskore; **vti.** bëj fresk
fancy /'fensi/ **n.** 1. imagjinatë, fantazi; 2. trill, kapriço;
3. qejf, dëshirë; **have a fancy for** më pëlqen të; **vt.**
përfytyroj, marr me mend; pëlqej
fantastic /fen'testik/ **adj.** fantastik
fantasy /'fentësi/ **n.** fantazi, imagjinatë
far /fa:(r)/ **adv.** larg; **far and wide** gjithandej; **adj.** i
largët
fare /feë(r)/ **n.** pagesë, tarifë udhëtimi

farewell /ˌfeə'wel/ **n.** ndarje, lamtumirë; **bid farewell to** i lë lamtumirën
farm /fa:m/ **n.** fermë
farmer /'fa:më(r)/ **n.** fermer
farther /'fa:dhë(r)/ **adv.** më larg, më tej; **adj.** më i largët, më tej
fascinate 'fesineit/ **vt.** magjeps, josh
fascinating /'fesinetin/ **adj.** tërheqës, joshës
fascism /'feshizëm/ **n.** fashizëm
fascist /'feshist/ **adj.** fashist
fashion /'feshn/ **n.** 1. modë; 2. model; 3. stil, mënyrë; **out of fashion** i dalë nga moda, i vjetëruar; **in fashion** në modë
fashionable /'feshnëbl/ **adj.** i modës, elegant
fast /fa:st/ **adj.** 1. i shpejtë; 2. i qëndrueshëm; **adv.** 1. fort; 2. shpejt; **vi.** mbaj kreshmë
fasten /'fa:sn; fesn / **vti.** 1. lidh, bashkoj; 2. mbyll, siguroj; 3. mbërthej, përqëndroj (shikimin)
fat /fet/ **adj.** 1. i majmë; 2. i shëndoshë; **n.** 1. dhjamë, sallo; 2. majmëri
fatal /'feitl/ **adj.** fatal
fate /feit/ **n.** fat
father /'fa:dhë(r)/ **n.** 1. baba, atë; 2. krijues, themelues
father-in-law /'fa:dhë(r) in lo:/ **n.** vjehërr
fatherland /'fa:dhë(r)lend/ **n.** atdhe
fatherless /'fa:dhë(r)lis/ **adj.** i pababë
fatigue /fë'ti:g/ **n.** lodhje; **vt.** lodh
fault /fo:lt/ **n.** e metë, gabim; **find fault with** grindem; gjej kleçka
favor (favour) /'feivë(r)/ **n.** 1. favor; 2. simpati, dashamirësi; **in favor of** në favor të, në të mirë të; **do smb a favor** i bëj dikujt një nder; **vt.** favorizoj
favorable (favourable) /'feivërëbl/ **adj.** i favorshëm, i volitshëm
favo(u)rite /'feivërit/ **adj.** i preferuar, i parapëlqyer; **n.** favorit
fear /fië(r)/ **n.** frikë; **for fear of** nga frika se; **vt.** 1. kam frikë, frikësohem; 2. druaj
feasible /'fi:zëbl/ **adj.** 1. i mundshëm; 2. i arsyeshëm, i besueshëm
feast /fi:st/ **n.** gosti, banket; **vti.** 1. bëj, shtroj gosti; 2. festoj, marr pjesë në gosti
feather /'fedhë(r)/ **n.** pupël, pendë; **as light as a feather** i lehtë pupël; **in high feather** në humor të mirë
feature /'fi:çë(r)/ **n.** 1. tipar fytyre; 2. veçori, tipar; 3. **amer.** film; feature film film artistik
February /'februëri/ **n.** shkurt
federal /'fedërël/ **adj.** federal
fee /fi:/ **n.** 1. kuotizacion; 2. honorar, shpërblim; 3. kuotë, pagesë (hyrjeje)
feeble /'fi:bl/ **adj.** i dobët; shëndetlig
feed /fi:d/ **vit.** ushqej, i jap ushqim; **be fed up** jam i ngopur deri në grykë; 2. kullot; **feed on** ushqehem me; **n.** ushqim
feel /fi:l/ **n.** 1. ndijim; 2. prekje; **vti.** ndiej, ndijoj; i feel like sleeping më vjen si për gjumë; i feel cold kam ftohtë
feeling /'fi:lin/ **n.** 1. ndjenjë; 2. ndijim; 3. parandjenjë
fellow /'felou/ **n.** 1. shok; 2. djalë; 3. njeri

fellow-countryman /'felou'kantrimen/ **n.** bashkatdhetar
female /'fi:meil/ **n.** femër
fence /fens/ **n.** 1. gardh; 2. rrethojë; **vit.** gardhoj, rrethoj me gardh
ferment /'fë:ment/ **n.** ferment, tharm, maja
ferocious /fë'roushës/ **adj.** i egër; mizor
ferry /'feri/ **n.** lundër; trap
fertile /'fë:rtail/ **adj.** pjellor; prodhues; prodhimtar
fertilizer /'fë:tilaizë(r)/ **n.** pleh kimik
fervent /'fë:rvënt/ **adj.** i flaktë; i zjarrtë
festival /'festëvël/ **n.** festival
fetch /feç/ **vti.** shkoj të marr, të sjell
fetters /'fetë(r)z/ **n. pl.** pranga
feudal /'fju:dl/ **adj.** feudal
fever /'fi:vë(r)/ **n.** ethe; zjarrmi
few /fju:/ **adj.** pak, i pakët; **a few** ca
fiancé /,fia:n'sei/ **n.** i fejuar
fiancée /,fia:n'sei/ **n.** e fejuar **fiction** /'fikshn/ **n.** 1. trillim; 2. letërsi artistike, prozë letrare
fidgety /'fixhiti/ **adj.** nervoz, i paqetë
field /fi:ld/ **n.** fushë; sferë; lëmë
fierce /fiës/ **adj.** i ashpër, i rreptë, i egër
fiery /'faiëri/ **adj.** 1. i zjarrtë, i flaktë; 2. i përflakur, flakërues; 3. i rrëmbyer, i hovshëm, i flaktë
fifteen /,fif'ti:n/ **num.** pesëmbëdhjetë
fifty /'fifti/ **num.** pesëdhjetë; **go fifty-fifty** ndaj barabar
fig fig/ **n.** fik; **I don't care a fig** se çaj kokën fare
fight /fait/ **n.** 1. betejë, luftim; 2. rrahje, përleshje; **vit.** 1. luftoj; 2. përleshem, zihem
fighter /'faitë(r)/ **n.** 1. luftëtar; 2. aeroplan gjuajtës
figure /'figë(r)/ **n.** 1. shifër; numër; 2. figurë; 3. njeri i njohur, personalitet
file /fail/ **n.** 1. radhë, rrjesht; 2. varg, kolonë; 3. dosje; 4. kartotekë; 5. limë
fill /fil/ **vit.** mbush; **fill in** mbush, plotësoj (një anketë, formular etj.)
film /film/ **n.** film (fotografik, artistik)
filthy /'filthi/ **adj.** 1. i fëlliqur, i ndyrë; 2. i poshtër
final /'fainl/ **adj.** i fundit, përfundimtar; **n.** 1. finale; 2. provim i fundit
finance /fai'nens/ **n.** 1. financë; 2. **pl.** financat; **vt.** financoj
find /faind/ **vt.** gjej; zbuloj; **find out** zbuloj, mësoj
fine /fain/ **adj.** 1. i shkëlqyer, i mrekullueshëm; 2. i hollë, delikat; 3. i imët; 4. i bukur, elegant; **fine arts** artet e bukura; **that's fine!** shkëlqyeshëm; **n.** gjobë; **vt.** gjobit
finger /'fingë(r)/ **n.** gisht; **lay a finger on** vë dorë mbi; **have a finger in the pie** kam gisht në
fingerprint /'fingë(r)print/ **n.** shenjë e gishtave
finish /'finish/ **n.** fund; mbarim, përfundim; **vti.** mbaroj, përfundoj; përmbush; **finish off** mbaroj; **finish up with** mbaroj me
fir /fë:(r)/ **n.** bredh
fire /'faië(r)/ **n.** zjarr; **catch (take) fire** merr flakë; **set on fire** i vë zjarrin; 2. dëshirë e fuqishme; **vti.** 1. ndez, djeg; 2. entuziazmoj

fire alarm /'faië(r) ë'la:rm/ **n.** alarm zjarri
fireproof /'faië(r)pru:f/ **n.** i padjegshëm, kundër zjarrit
firm /fë:rm/ **adj.** i fortë; i qëndrueshëm
first /fë:rst/ **adj.** i parë; **adv.** së pari, në radhë të parë;
first of all pikësëpari, para së gjithash; **n.** i parë; **at**
first fillimisht; **from the first** nga fillimi
first aid /,fë:rst'eid/ **n.** ndihma e shpejtë
first floor /,fë:rst'flo:(r)/ **n.** kati i parë
first-hand /,fë:rst'hend/ **adj.** i drejtpërdrejtë; **adv.**
drejtpërsëdrejti
first-rate /,fë:rstreit/ **adj.** i dorës së parë, i klasit të
parë
fiscal /'fiskl/ **adj.** financiar; fiskal
fish /fish/ **n.** peshk; **hæ other fish to fry** kam punë tjetër
për të bërë; **vi.** peshkoj, zë peshk; **fish in troubled waters**
peshkoj në ujë të turbulit
fisherman /'fishëmën/ **n.** peshkatar **fishing** /'fishin/ **n.**
peshkim
fist /fist/ **n.** grusht
fit /fit/ **n.** 1. goditje, krizë; 2. shpërthim, shkulm; 3.
gjendje shpirtërore; **adj.** 1. i përshtatshëm; 2. i aftë
(fizikisht); **vit.** 1. jam i përshtatshëm; 2. përshtat,
rregulloj; 3. pajis
fitness /'fitnis/ **n.** 1. përshtatshmëri; 2. gatishmëri; 3.
aftësi (fizike)
five /faiv/ **num.** pesë
fix /fiks/ **vti.** 1. fiksoj; 2. ngulit (në kujtesë, në mendje);
3. rregulloj, vë në rregull; **n.** mëdyshje, dilemë; gjendje e
vështirë; **be in a fix** jam në hall
fixed /fikst/ **adj.** 1. i fiksuar, i ngulitur; 2. i
palëvizshëm; 3. i caktuar, i përcaktuar
flag /fleg/ **n.** flamur
flake /fleik/ **n.** 1. cifël, leskër; 2. **pl.** flokë (dëbore)
flame /fleim/ **n.** 1. flakë; 2. flakërimë; 3. zjarr, pasion;
vi. digjet, lëshon flakë; përflaket
flare /fleë(r)/ **vi.** 1. ndizet, flakëron; 2. merr zjarr; **n.** 1.
shkrepëtimë, flakërimë; 2. shpërthim i ndjenjave
flash /flesh/ **n.** 1. shkrepëtimë, flakërimë; **in a flash** në
çast; 2. lajm i shkurtër, lajm telegrafik; **vit.** 1. shkreptin,
flakëron; 2. shkreptin (një mendim)
flat /flet/ **adj.** i sheshtë, i rrafshtë; **n.** apartament, hyrje;
block of flats bllok apartamentesh
flatter /'fletë(r)/ **vt.** lajkatoj, mikloj
flavor (flavour) /'fleivë/ **n.** shije e këndshme, aromë; **vt.** i
jap shije, aromë
flaw /flo:/ **n.** 1. e çarë, plasë; 2. e metë, cen
flea fli:/ **n.** plesht
flee /fli:/ **vti.** iki me të katra, ua mbath këmbëve
fleet /fli:t/ **n.** flotë
flesh /flesh/ **n.** 1. mish; 2. tul, mish i fryteve; **put on**
flesh shëndoshem
flexibility ,fleksë'bilëti/ **n.** përkuelshmëri, lakueshmëri
flexible /'fleksëbl/ **adj.** 1. i lakueshëm, i epshëm; 2. i
paqëndrueshëm

flight /flait/ **n.** 1. fluturim; 2. tufë; 3. udhëtim, fluturim; 4. ikje, arrati
fling /flin/ **vti.** hedh, flak
float /flout/ **vit.** pluskon
flock /flok/ **n.** 1. tufë, kope; 2. turmë
flog /flog/ **vt.** rrah, fshikulloj
flood /flad/ **n.** 1. përmbytje; 2. rrëke, përrua; 3. **fig.** lumë, det; **vti.** vërshon, përmbyt
floor /flo:(r)/ **n.** 1. dysheme; 2. kat; **ground floor** kati i parë
flora /'flo:rë/ **n.** florë
flour /'flauë(r)/ **n.** miell
flourish /'flarish/ **vit.** lulëzoj,përparoj; **n.** lulëzim
flow /flou/ **vi.** 1. rrjedh (lumi); 2. zbraz; 3. rrjedhin (fjalët, mendimet); **n.** 1. rrjedhë; 2. rrymë; 3. rrëke
flower /'flauë(r)/ **n.** lule; **vi.** 1. lulëzon; 2. zbukuroj me lule
fluent /'flu:ënt/ **adj.** i lirshëm, i rrjedhshëm
fluid /'flu:id/ **adj.** 1. i rrjedhshëm; 2. i paqëndrueshëm
fly /flai/ **n.** mizë; **vit.** 1. fluturoj; 2. valëvit
foam /foum/ **n.** shkumë; **vi.** shkumëzoj
fodder /'fodë(r)/ **n.** tagji, ushqim (për kafshë)
fog /fog/ **n.** mjegull; **vti.** mbështjell në mjegull, mjegulloj
fold /fould/ **vti.** 1. palos; 2. përqafoj, pushtoj; **n.** 1. palë; 2. vathë
folk /fouk/ **n.** 1. popull; 2. njerëz; 3. farefis
follow /'folou/ **vti.** 1. ndjek, i shkoj pas; 2. vijon, vjen pas; **as follows** si vijon; 3. veproj sipas; 4. ndjek, kuptoj
following /'folouin/ **adj.** vijues, pasues
fond /fond/ **adj.** i dashur; **be fond of** dua, pëlqej, kam qejf
food /fu:d/ **n.** 1. ushqim; 2. **fig.** ushqim (shpirtëror)
foodstuffs /'fu:dstafs/ **n. pl.** produkte ushqimore
fool /fu:l/ **n.** budalla, i trashë; **make a fool of smb** e bëj budalla
foolish /'fu:lish/ **adj.** i marrë
foot /fut/ **n.** 1. këmbë; **on foot** në këmbë; **from head to foot** nga koka te këmbët; 2. hap; 3. rrëzë, këmbë; **at the foot of the mountain** në rrëzë të malit; 4. këmbë, fut
football /'futbo:l/ **n.** futboll
footwear /'futweë(r)/ **n.** këpucë, çizme etj.
for /fo:/ **prep.** për; **as for me** për mua; **for good** përgjithmonë; **for all I know** me sa di unë; **conj.** mbasi, sepse
forbid /fë'bid/ **vt.** ndaloj, nuk lejoj
force /fo:rs/ **n.** 1. forcë, fuqi; **by force** me forcë; 2. **pl.** usht. forcat ushtarake; **vt.** 1. detyroj; 2. bëj me forcë; **force open a door** hap një derë me forcë
forecast /'fo:ka:st/ 'fo:kest/ **vt.** 1. parashikoj; 2. parathem; **n.** parashikim; **weather forecast** parashikimi i motit
forehead /'forid/ **n.** ballë
foreign /'fo:rin/ **adj.** i jashtëm, i huaj; **foreign policy** politikë e jashtme; **foreign trade** tregti e jashtme
foreigner /'forinë/ **n.** i huaj
foreman /'fo:mën/ **n.** kryepunëtor, mbikqyrës
forest /'forist/ **n.** pyll
foretell /fo:'tell/ **vt.** 1. parathem; 2. profetizoj
foreword /'fo:wë:rd/ **n.** parathënie

forge /fo:rzh/ **n.** farkëtari; farkë; **vt.** farkëtoj (edhe **fig.**)
forget /fë'get/ **vti.** 1. harroj; 2. heq nga mendja
forgetful /fë'getful/ **adj.** 1. harraq; 2. i shkujdesur
forgive /fë'giv/ **vti.** 1. fal; 2. liroj nga detyrimi; **forgive me** më falni
fork /fo:rk/ **n.** 1. pirun; 2. sfurk
form /fo:rm/ **n.** 1. trajtë, pamje e jashtme; 2. formë; 3. formular; 4. klasë (nxënësish); 5. gjendje fizike e shpirtërore; **vti.** 1. formoj, i jap formë; 2. formoj, krijoj; 3. merr formë
formal /'fo:rml/ **adj.** formal
former /'fo:më/ **adj.** i mëparshëm
formula /'fo:mjulë/ **n.** formulë
forsake /fë'seik/ **vt.** 1. heq dorë; 2. lë, braktis
forth /fo:rth/ **adv.** përpara; jashtë; tutje; **and so forth** e të tjera
fortify /'fo:rtifai/ **vt.** fortifikoj
fortnight /'fo:tnait/ **n.** dy javë
fortress /'fo:tris/ **n.** kala, fortesë
fortunate /'fo:çënët/ **adj.** fatbardhë, fatmirë
fortune /'fo:çju:n/ **n.** fat; pasuri; **make a fortune** pasurohem
forty /'fo:ti/ **num.** dyzet
forward /'fo:wërd/ **adj.** i përparmë; **n.** sulmues; **vt.** 1. çoj më përpara, avancoj; 2. dërgoj, nis; 3. përcjell, dorëzoj; **adv.** përpara
foul /faul/ **adj.** 1. i keq, i qelbur; 2. i ulët, i ndyrë; **n.** faull
found /faund/ **vt.** 1. themeloj; 2. ngre, krijoj, formoj
foundation /faun'deishn/ **n.** 1. themelim; krijim; 2. themel, bazë
fountain /'fauntin/ **n.** 1. burim (uji); 2. shatërvan
fountain-pen /'fauntinpen/ **n.** stilograf
four /fo:(r)/ **num.** katër
fourteen /,fo'ti:n/ **num.** katërmbëdhjetë
fowl /faul/ **n.** 1. shpend; 2. shpesë shtëpiake
fox /foks/ **n.** dhelpër
foxy /'foksi/ **adj.** dhelparak, dinak
fraction /'frekshn/ **n.** 1. thyesë; 2. thërrmijë, grimcë, fragment
fragile /'frexhail/ **adj.** i brishtë, i thyeshëm; i dobët, delikat
fragment /'fregmënt/ **n.** 1. copë, cifël; 2. fragment, pjesë
fragrant /'freigrënt/ **adj.** aromatik, kundërmues
frail /freil/ **adj.** i thyeshëm, i brishtë; i dobët, delikat
frame /freim/ **n.** 1. kornizë; 2. skelet; 3. strukturë; **vti.** 1. ndërtoj, ngre; 2. vë në kornizë
framework /'freimwë:rk/ **n.** 1. skelet, karkasë; 2. kornizë; 3. konstruksion; **within the framework of** në kuadrin e
franchise /'frençaiz/ **n.** e drejtë e votimit
frank /frenk/ **adj.** i singertë, zemërhapur, i çiltër
fraternal /frë'të:rnl/ **adj.** vëllazëror
fraud /fro:d/ **n.** 1. mashtrim; 2. mashtrues
freckle /'frekl/ **n.** prenkë, pikë
free /fri:/ **adj.** 1. i lirë; 2. i pazënë, i lirë; 3. falas, pa pagesë; 4. i çlirët, i shpenguar; **vt.** 1. liroj; 2. çliroj
freedom /'fri:dëm/ **n.** liri; **freedom of speech** liri e fjalës
freedom-loving /,fri:dëm'lavin/ **adj.** liridashës
freeze /fri:z/ **vti.** 1. ngrin; 2. ngrij; 3. mbetem i shtangur
freezer /'fri:zë(r)/ **n.** ftohës; frigorifer

freight /freit/ **n.** 1. transport, mbartje e mallrave; 2. mall,
ngarkesë
French /frenç/ **adj.** francez; **n.** frëngjishte
frenzy /'frenzi/ **n** tërbim
frequent /'fri:kwënt **adj.** i shpejshtë; **vt.** /fri:'kvent/
frekuentoj
fresh /fresh/ **adj.** 1. i freskët (moti); 2. i freskët, i njomë
(mishi); 3. i ri, i papërvojë; 4. freskues; 5. i ri, i fundit
(lajmi)
friction /'frikshn/ **n.** 1. fërkim; 2. **fig.** mosmarrëveshje,
grindje
Friday /'fraidi/ **n.** e premte
friend /frend/ **n.** mik, mikeshë; **make friends with** miqësohem me
friendly /'frendli/ **adj.** miqësor
friendship /'frendship/ **n.** 1. miqësi; 2. dashamirësi
frighten /'fraitn/ **vt.** frikësoj, lemeris, i fut frikën
frigid /'frixhid/ **adj.** 1. i ftohët; 2. **fig.** i ftohët,
mospërfillës
fringe /frinxh/ **n.** 1. thekë; 2. anë, skaj, cep; 3. balluke
frog /frog/ **n.** bretkosë
from /from/ **prep.** prej, nga; **from above** nga sipër; **from
behind** nga prapa; **from now on** që tani e tutje
front /frant/ **n.** 1. ballë, anë e përparme; **in front of** para,
përpara; 2. **usht.** front; **adj.** i përparmë
frontal /'frantl/ **adj.** frontal, ballësor
frontier /'frantië(r)/ frant'tiër/ **n.** kufi
frost /fro:st/ **n.** ngricë; brymë
frosty /'frosti/ **adj.** 1. i ftohtë, i akullt; 2. **fig.** i
ftohtë, mospërfillës
frown /fraun/ **n.** rrudhje (e vetullave, e ballit); 2. **vi.**
vrenjtem, rrudh vetullat
frozen /'frouzn/ **adj.** 1. i ngrirë; 2. **fig.** i ftohtë
frugal /'fru:xhl/ **adj.** 1. kursimtar; 2. i lirë
fruit /fru:t/ **n.** 1. frutë; 2. **fig.** rezultat, fryt
fruitful /'fru:tful/ **adj.** 1. pjellor; 2. **fig.** frytdhënës, i
frytshëm
fruitless /'fru:tlis/ **adj.** 1. i pafryt; 2. **fig.** i pafrytshëm,
i padobishëm
frustrate /'frastreit/ fra'streit/ **vt.** pengoj, prish (planet etj.)
frustration /fra'streishn/ **n.** prishje, pengim
fry /frai/ **vti.** tiganis, fërgoj
frying pan /'frainpen/ **n.** tigan
fuel /fju:ël/ **n.** lëndë djegëse, karburant; **add fuel to the
flames** i hedh benzinë zjarrit
fulfil (fulfill) /ful'fil/ **vt.** kryej, përmbush, plotësoj
fulfilment /ful'filmënt/ **n.** kryerje, plotësim
full /ful/ **adj.** 1. i mbushur plot; 2. i plotë; 3. i zënë; **in
full** tërësisht, plotësisht
full stop /,ful'stop/ **n.** pikë
full time /,ful'taim/ **adv.** me orar të plotë
fully /fuli/ **adv.** tërësisht, plotësisht
fume /fju:m/ **n.** 1. tym; 2. **fig.** turbullim, errësim i mendjes
fun /fan/ **n.** shaka, dëfrim, zbavitje, gallatë; **have fun**
zbavitem, dëfrehem; **make fun of** vë në lojë; **in/for fun** me
shaka, për shaka
function /'fankshën/ **vi.** punoj, veproj, funksionoj; **n.**
funksion; detyrë
functionary /'fankshënëri/ **n.** funksionar

fund /fand/ **n.** 1. fond; kapitl; 2. **pl.** mjete financiare; **vt.** financoj; investoj
fundamental /,fandë'mentl/ **adj.** themelor, bazal
funeral /'fju:nërël/ **n.** funeral, varrim; funeral service shërbimi funeral
funny /'fani/ **adj.** 1. qesharak; 2. zbavitës; 3. i çuditshëm
fur /fë:r/ **n.** 1. qime (e maces, e qenit, etj.); 2. gëzof
furious /'fjuëriës/ **adj.** i egër, i tërbuar, i xhindosur
furnace /'fë:rnis/ **n.** 1. furrë; 2. ngrohtore
furnish /'fë:rnish/ **vt.** 1. furnizoj; 2. mobiloj; pajis
furniture /'fë:rniçë(r)/ **n.** mobilje, orendi shtëpiake
further /'fë:rdhë(r)/ **adv.** më tutje, më tej; **adj.** i mëtejshëm; tjetër
furthermore /'fë:rdhë'mo:(r)/ **adv.** përveç kësaj
fury /'fjuëri/ **n.** 1. tërbim,; zemërim i madh; 2. furi, shpërthim
fuse /fju:z/ **n.** 1. shkrirje e metaleve; 2. siguresë; **vti.** shkrij, ngjit, saldoj metalet
fuss /fas/ **n.** 1. shqetësim, trazim; 2. zhurmë, rrëmujë; **make a fuss about** bëj zhurmë rreth
futile /'fju:tail; 'fju:tl/ **adj.** i kotë, i pavlerë, i padobi
future /'fju:çë(r)/ **n.** e ardhme, ardhmëni

G

gab /geb/ **n.** llomotitje
gadget /'gexhit/ **n.** vegël e vogël
gaily /'geili/ **adv.** gëzueshëm
gain /gein/ **vti.** 1. fitoj, marr; **gain time** fitoj kohë; 2. shtoj; **gain in weight** shtoj në peshë; 3. arrij; **n.** 1. fitim, përfitim; 2. **pl.** të ardhura; 3. zmadhim, rritje, shtesë
gainful /'geinful/ **adj.** fitimprurës
gala /'ga:lë; 'geilë/ **n.** festim, kremtim
galaxy /'gelëksi/ **n.** 1. udha e qumështit; 2. **fig.** plejadë
gale /geil/ **n.** tufan, stuhi
gall /go:l/ **n.** 1. plagë; 2. ngacmim, acarim
gallery /'gelëri/ **n.** galeri
gallon /'gelën/ **n.** gallon (= 4.54 l.)
gallop /'gelëp/ **n.** galop; **vti.** eci me galop
game /geim/ **n.** 1. lojë, lodër; 2. hile, dredhi; **give the game away** nxjerr një të fshehtë
gang /gen/ **n.** 1. bandë; 2. tufë, grup (njerëzish)
gap /gep/ **n.** e çarë; hendek; **bridge a gap** mbyll një të çarë; **narrow the gap** ngushtoj ndryshimin
garage /'gera:zh; gë'ra:zh/ **n.** garazh
garbage /'ga:rbixh/ **n.** 1. mbeturina; 2. plehra
garden /'ga:dn/ **n.** kopsht
garlic /'ga:rlik/ **n.** hudhër
gas /ges/ **n.** 1. gaz; 2. **amer.** benzinë, karburant
gas cooker /'ges ku:kë(r)/ **n.** sobë, furnelë me gaz
gas meter /ge'smi:të(r)/ **n.** gazmatës
gasolene /'gesëlin/ **n.** gazolinë
gasp /ga:sp/ **vit.** gulçoj, më zihet fryma; **n.** gulçim, frymëmarrje e vështirë
gastric /'gestrik/ **adj.** gastrik
gate /geit/ **n.** portë
gather /'gedhë(r)/ **vti.** 1. mbledh; mblidhemi; 2. grumbulloj; 3. kuptoj; 4. arrij në përfundim
gathering /'gedhërin/ **n.** 1. mbledhje; 2. grumbullim
gauge (gage) /geixh/ **n.** 1. kalibër; 2. matës; **vt.** 1. mat me saktësi; 2. vlerësoj
gay /gei/ **adj.** i gëzuar, gazmor
gaze /geiz/ **vi.** vështroj, shikoj me ngulm; **n.** shikim ngulmues
gear /gië(r)/ **n.** 1. mekanizëm; 2. ingranazh; 3. marsh
general /'xhenrël/ **adj.** 1. i përgjithshëm; **in general** përgjithësisht; 2. i zakonshëm
generation /,xhenë'reishn/ **n.** 1. brez, gjeneratë; 2. prodhim
generator /'xhenëreitë(r)/ **n.** gjenerator
generosity /,xhenë'rosëti/ **n.** bujari, shpirtmadhësi
generous /'xhenërës/ **adj.** bujar, shpirtmadh
genius /'xhi:niës/ **n.** gjeni
gentle /'xhentl/ **adj.** 1. butë, i urtë; 2. fisnik, bujar
gentleman /'xhentlmën/ **n.** zotni; fisnik, bujar
gently /'xhentli/ **adv.** 1. butësisht; 2. me delikatesë
genuine /'xhenjuin/ **adj.** i vërtetë
geography /xhi'ogrëfi/ **n.** gjeografi
geology /xhi'olëxhi/ **n.** gjeologji

geometry /xhi'omëtri/ **n.** gjeometri
germ /xhë:rm/ **n.** 1. mikrob; 2. embrion, zanafillë
German /'xhë:rmën/ **adj.** gjerman; **n.** 1. gjerman; 2. gjuhë
gjermane
gesture /'xhesçë(r)/ **n.** gjest, shenjë
get /get/ **vti.** 1. marr, 2. gjej; 3. bëj, përgatit; 4. bind;
5. kam; 6. bëhem; 7 kuptoj; **get married** martohem; **get on** 1.
kaloj, çoj; 2. hipi; 3. vesh; **get out of order** prishet;
çrregullohet; **get ready** bëhem gati; **get rid of** zhduk, heq
qafe; **get up** ngrihem; çohem
ghost /goust/ **n.** fantazëm, lugat
giant /'xhaiënt/ **adj.** gjigant
giddy /'gidi/ **adj.** marramendës, që ka maramenth
gift /gift/ **n.** 1. dhuratë; 2. talent, prirje; 3. dhurëti
gifted /'giftid/ **adj.** i talentuar
gigantic /xhai'gentik/ **adj.** gjigant
gin /xhin/ **n.** xhin
ginger /'xhinxhë(r)/ **n.** 1. xhenxhefil; 2. gjallëri; shtytje,
frymëzim
gipsy /'zhipsi/ **n.** cigan; arixhi; **adj.** cigane, arixhiu
girl /gë:rl/ **n.** vajzë, çupë, gocë
gist /xhist/ **n.** thelb, esencë
give /giv/ **vti.** 1. jap; 2. dorëzoj; 3. nxjerr, prodhoj; 4.
fal, dhuroj; 5. ia kushtoj; 6. lëshoj; **give away** tregoj;
zbuloj; **give birth** lind; **give in** lëshoj pe, hap rrugë; **give
up** 1. lë, heq dorë; 2. dorëzohem
glad /gled/ **adj.** i kënaqur, i gëzuar; **be glad to** jam i gëzuar të
glance /gla:ns; glens/ **n.** shikim i shpejtë; **at a glance** me
një shikim; **at first glance** në shikimin e parë; **vti.** shikoj
(shpejt); **glance one's eyes over** hedh një shikim të shpejtë
gland /glend/ **n.** gjendër; **sweat glands** gjendrat e djersës
glare /gleë(r)/ **vt.** 1. shkëlqen në mënyrë verbuese; 2. shikoj
me ngulm, me inat; **n.** 1. shikim i rreptë; 2. shkëlqim verbues
glass /gla:s/ **n.** 1. xham, qelq; 2. gotë, kupë; 3. pasqyrë; 4.
pl. syze
gleam /gli:m/ **vi.** feks, shkëlqen
glide /glaid/ **vi.** 1. rrëshqas, shkas; 2. rrëshqet; **n.**
rrëshqitje
glimmer /'glimë(r)/ **vi.** regëtin, vezullon dobët; **n.** regëtinë,
vezullim i dobët
glimpse /glimps/ **n.** shikim i shpejtë; **at a glimpse** në
shikimin e parë; **get (catch) a glimpse** shikoj fluturimthi;
vt. shikoj fluturimthi
glitter /'gli:të(r)/ **vi.** xixëllon, vezullon; **n.** xixëllim, vezullim
globe /gloub/ **n.** 1. glob, lëmshi i dheut; 2. rruzull
gloom /'glu:m/ **n.** 1. gjysmëerrësirë; terr; 2. trishtim
gloomy /'glu:mi/ **adj.** 1. i errët; 2. i trishtuar
glorious /'glo:riës **adj.** 1. i lavdishëm; 2. i shkëlqyer, i
mrekullueshëm
glory /'glo:ri/ **n.** lavdi, madhështi
glossary /'glosëri/ **n.** fjalorth
glove /glav/ **n.** dorashkë, dorezë; **a pair of gloves** një palë
doreza
glow /glou/ **n.** 1. zjarr, flakë; 2. shkëlqim; 3. përflakje; 4.
skuqje; **vi.** 1. skuq, digjet prush; 2. kuqëlon
glue /glu:/ **n.** 1. tutkall; 2. çiriç; 3. ngjitës; **vt.** ngjit
gnat /net/ **n.** harrje
gnaw /no:/ **vti.** brej, gërryej

go /gou/ **vi.** 1. eci, shkoj; 2. udhëtoj, endem; 3. iki; kaloj; 4. punon, funksionon; **go ahead** 1. përparoj; 2. vazhdoj; **go away** iki, largohem; **go back** kthehem; **go on** 1. vazhdoj; 2. kalon; 3. ndodh
goad /goud/ **n.** hosten
goal /goul/ **n.** 1. synim, qëllim; 2. **sport.** portë; 3. gol
goal-keeper /'goul,ki:pë(r)/ **n.** portier
goat /gout/ **n.** dhi
go-between /'gou bi,twi:n/ **n.** 1. ndërmjetës; 2. shkues; 3. lajmës
god /god/ **n.** zot, perëndi; **thank God!** lavdi Zotit!
godchild /'godçaild/ **n.** famull
godfather /'god,fa:dhë(r)/ **n.** nun
godmother /'god,mëdhë(r)/ **n.** ndrikull
gold /gould/ **n.** ar, flori
golden /'gouldën/ **adj.** 1. i artë, i prarur me flori; 2. **fig.** i artë
goldsmith /'gouldsmith/ **n.** arpunues; argjendar
golf /golf/ **n.** golf
good /gud/ **adj.** i mirë; **good for** i mirë për; **n.** e mirë; **do good** bëj të mirë; **for your own good** për të mirën tuaj; **for good** përgjithmonë
goods /gudz/ **n.** 1. **pl.** mallra; 2. ngarkesë; 3. plaçka
goose /'gu:s/ **n.** patë; mish pate
gorgeous /'go:xhës/ **adj.** madhështor; i madhërishëm
gospel /'gospl/ **n.** ungjill
gossip /'gosip/ **vi.** përgojoj, marr nëpër gojë; **n.** thashetheme, përgojosje
govern /'gavërn/ **vti.** 1. qeveris; 2. drejtoj
government /'gavënmënt/ **n.** 1. qeveri; 2. qeverim, drejtim
governor /'gavënë(r)/ **n.** guvernator
grab /greb/ **vti.** rrëmbej, mbërthej; **n.** rrëmbim, grabitje
grace /greis/ **vt.** hijeshoj, i jap hir
graceful /'greisful/ **adj.** i hijshëm, hirmadh
gracious /'greishës/ **adj.** 1. i hirshëm; i këndshëm; 2. i mëshirshëm
grade /greid/ **n.** 1. shkallë; kategori; 2. rend; gradë; 3. **amer.** klasë (shkolle); **vt.** ndaj, klasifikoj
gradual /'gredjuël/ **adj.** gradual; i shkallëzuar
graduate /'gredjueit/ **vti.** diplomoj; diplomohem, mbaroj shkollën; /'gredjuët/ **n.** diplomant, i diplomuar
grain /grein/ **n.** 1. drithë; 2. kokërr, grimcë; 3. figuracion
gram(me) /grem/ **n.** gram
grammar /'gremë(r)/ **n.** gramatikë
grandchild /'grend,çaild/ **n.** nip, mbesë
grandfather /'grend,fa:dhë(r)/ **n.** gjysh
grandmother /'grend,mëdhë(r)/ **n.** gjyshe
granny /'greni/ **n. gj. fl.** gjyshe
grant /gra:nt/ **vt.** 1. jap (borxh, kredi etj.); 2. pohoj, pranoj; 3. dhuroj; **n.** dhuratë; ndihmë; pëlqim
grape /greip/ **n.** rrush
grapefruit /'greipfru:t/ **n.** qitro
graphic /'grefik/ **adj.** grafik
grasp /gra:sp/ **n.** 1. kapje; 2. shtrëngim; 3. mbërthim; 4. shtënie në dorë; 3. rrokje, kapje; **vti.** 1. rrok, kap, mbërthej, shtrëngoj; 2. kuptoj, marr vesh

grass /gra:s; gres/ **n.** bar
grate /greit/ **n.** skarë; **vti.** grij
grateful /'greitfl/ **adj.** mirënjohës
grater /'greitë(r)/ **n.** grirëse, rende
gratis /'gretis/ **adv.** falas
gratitude /'gretitju:d; 'gretitu:d/ **n.** mirënjohje
gratuity /grë't(j)u:ëti/ **n.** ndihmë në të holla; shpërblim
grave /greiv/ **adj.** 1. serioz; 2. i rëndë; 3. i errët, i zymtë; **n.** varr
gravel /'grevl/ **n.** zhavorr; **vt.** shtroj me zhavorr
gravity /'grevëti/ **n.** 1. gravitet, rëndesë; 2. seriozitet; **specific gravity** pesha specifike
grease /gri:s/ **vt.** 1. lubrikoj, lyrësoj, vajoj; 2. **fig.** jap ryshfet, mitos; **grease sb's palm (hand)** mitos, jap ryshfet; **n.** 1. lyrë, dhjamë, yndyrë, sallo; 2. graso; lubrifikues
great /greit/ **adj.** 1. i madh; 2. i rëndësishëm; 3. i shquar; **a great many** shumë
greatcoat /'greit,kout/ **n.** 1. pallto e madhe; 2. kapotë
greed, greediness /gri:d, 'gri:dinis/ **n.** makutëri, lakmi
greedy /'gri:di/ **adj.** lakmues, makut, lakmitar
Greek /gri:k/ **adj.** grek; **n.** 1. grek; 2. gjuha greke, greqishtja
green /gri:n/ **adj.** 1. i gjelbër; 2. i papjekur, i papërvojë; **n.** 1. jeshile, ngjyrë jeshile; 2. vend i gjelbëruar
greengrocer /gri:n,grousë(r)/ **n.** perimeshitës; pemëshitës
greenhouse /'gri:n,haus/ **n.** serrë
greet /gri:t/ **vt.** përshëndet
greeting /'gri:tin/ **n.** përshëndetje
grey /grei/ **adj.** 1. i përhimtë, bojë hiri, gri; 2. i thinjur
grief /gri:f/ **n.** 1. hidhërim, pikëllim; 2. fatkeqësi, mjerim
grieve /gri:v/ **vti.** 1. helmoj, hidhëroj, pikëlloj; 2. hidhërohem, brengosem
grill gril/ **n.** 1. skarë; 2. mish, qofte të skarës
grim /grim/ **adj.** 1. i zymtë; 2. i ashpër, i rreptë, i pamëshirshëm
grin /grin/ **vit.** 1. zgërdhij, zbardh dhëmbët; 2. vë buzën në gaz; **n.** zgërdheshje, zbardhja e dhëmbëve
grip /grip/ **n.** shtrëngim, kapje; **vti.** shtrëngoj, mbërthej, kap
groan /groun/ **n.** 1. rënkim; 2. kuisje; **vit.** 1. rënkoj; 2. kuis
grocer /'grousë(r)/ **n.** bakall; shitës ushqimesh
grocery /'grousëri/ **n.** 1. ushqimore; 2. mallra ushqimore
groin /groin/ **n.** ijë
grope /group/ **vi.** eci, gjej rrugën (me të prekur)
gross /grous/ **adj.** 1. i madh, i vëllimshëm; 2. trashanik; flagrant; 3. bruto
ground /graund/ **n.** 1. tokë; 2. truall, tokë; 3. fushë; 4. arsye; **vti.** 1. cek, ulet; 2. ndesh në cektësirë (vapori)
ground floor /'graund'flo:/ **n.** kati përdhes
groundless /'graundlis/ **adj.** i pashkak; i pabazuar, i pathemeltë
group /gru:p/ **n.** grup; **vti.** 1. mbledh, mblidhem në grupe; 2. klasifikoj, grupoj
grow /grou/ **vti.** 1. rrit, kultivoj; 2. rritem; rritet, zmadhohet, ngrihet 3. bëhem, shndërrohem; **grow out of** s'më bëjnë rrobat, këpucët etj; **grow up** rritem, hedh shtat
grown-up /'groun,ëp/ **adj.** i rritur; **n.** i rritur, i madh

growth /grouth/ *n.* 1 rritje; 2 zmadhim, shtim, zgjerim; 3 zhvillim, ngritje

grumble /'grambl/ *vit.* grindem, qahem, ankohem; *n.* ankim, qarje

guarantee /,gerën'ti:/ *vt.* garantoj; *n.* garanci

guarantor /,gerën'to:(r)/ *n.* garant, dorëzanës

guard /ga:rd/ *n.* 1 roje; **on guard** në gatishmëri; **stand guard** qëndroj, bëj roje; 2 vigjilencë; syhaptësi; 3 ruajtje, mbrojtje; *vti.* 1 ruaj; 2 mbroj; 3 bëj roje

guess /ges/ *vti.* marr me mend; gjej me hamendje; supozoj, pandeh; *n.* pandehje, hamendje, supozim

guesswork /'geswë:rk/ *n.* pandehje, hamendje, supozim

guest /gest/ *n.* mik; mysafir, i ftuar

guidance /'gaidns/ *n.* 1 udhëheqje, drejtim; 2 parim drejtues

guide /gaid/ *n.* 1 shoqërues, ciceron; 2 drejtim, udhëheqje; 3 udhëzues; *vt.* udhëheq, prij, drejtoj

guidebook /'gaidbuk/ *n.* libër udhëzues

guilt /gilt/ *n.* faj

guilty /'gilti/ *adj.* fajtor

guise /gaiz/ *n.* 1 dukje, pamje; 2 veshje, petk; **under the guise of** nën maskën e

guitar /gi'ta:/ *n.* kitarë

gulf /galf/ *n.* 1 gji; 2 humnerë

gull /gal/ *n.* çafkë, pulëbardhë

gulp /galp/ *vti.* gëlltit; *n.* gllënjkë; **at one gulp** me një gllënjkë

gum /gam/ *n.* 1 gomë, llastik, kauçuk; 2 ngjitës, rrëshirë; 3 mish i dhëmbëve; *vt.* ngjit

gun /gan/ *n.* 1 armë, pushkë; 2 *amer. gj. fl.* pistoletë

gunpowder /'gënpaudë(r)/ *n.* barut

gurgle /'gë:rgl/ *n.* 1 gurgullimë; 2 llokoçitje; 3 gërgëritje

gust /gast/ *n.* 1 shpërthim; 2 furi, vrull

gut /gat/ *n.* 1 zorrë; 2 *pl.* të brendshme; 3 *pl.* kurajë, guxim

guy /gai/ *n.* djalë, djalosh

gymnastics /xhim'nestiks/ *n. pl.* gjimnastikë

gynecologist /'gainë'kolëxhist/ *n.* gjinekolog

haberdasher /'hebĕdeshĕ(r)/ n. shitës kinkalerie; çikërrimtar
haberdashery /'hebĕdeshĕri/ n. 1. kinkaleri; 2. galanteri; 3.
dyqan me veshje burrash
habit /'hebit/ n. 1. rregull, normë; 2. zakon; 2. shprehi; **be
in the habit of** e kam zakon të; **make a habit of** e bëj zakon;
fall (get) out of a habit heq (pres) një zakon
habitable /'hebitĕbl/ adj. i banueshëm
habitation /,hebi'teishn/ n. 1. vendbanim; 2. banesë; 3.
banim
habitual /hĕ'biçjuĕl/ adj. i zakonshëm
hack /hek/ vti. pres
hackneyed /'heknid/ adj. bajat, i rëndomtë, banal
hail /heil/ n. 1. breshër; 2. breshëri
hair /heĕ(r)/ n. 1. flok; 2. qime; 3. lesh; **not turn a hair**
si bën tërr syri; **make one's hair stand on end** iu ngjitën
qimet e kokës përpjetë; **lose one's hair** 1. më bien flokët; 2.
nxehem, inatosem
haircut /'heĕ(r)kat/ n. 1. qethje e flokëve; 2. stil, formë
qethjeje
hairdo /'heĕ(r)du:/ n. 1. krehje e flokëve; 2. bërje e
flokëve me forma
hairdresser /'heĕ(r)dresĕ(r)/ n. floktar, floktare
hair-drier /'heĕ(r)'draiĕ(r)/ n. tharëse flokësh
half /ha:f/ n. gjysmë; adj. i gjysmuar, gjysmak; adv.
përgjysmë; **go halves with smb** ndaj përgjysmë; **do something by
halves** bëj shkel e shko
halfway /,ha:f'wei/ adv. në gjysmë të rrugës; **meet smb
halfway** bëj lëshime, lëshoj pe
hall /ho:l/ n. 1. sallë; 2. sallon; paradhomë
hallo /hĕ'lou/ interj. hej! tungjatjeta!
halt /ho:lt/ n. ndalim, qëndrim; **come to a halt** ndaloj
ham /hem/ n. proshutë
hammer /'hemĕ(r)/ n. çekiç
hamper /'hempĕ(r)/ vt. pengoj, ndaloj
hand /hend/ n. 1. dorë; 2. akrep (sahati); 3. punëtor; **at
hand** pranë, afër; gati; **by hand** me dorë; **hand in hand** dorë
për dore; **on hand** në dispozicion; **hands off!** larg duart!;
hands up! duart lart!; **get the upper hand** fitoj epërsi mbi;
bëj zap; **lend a hand** ndihmoj; **have one's hands full** jam i
zënë; **get out of hand** del nga kontrolli; **shake hands with**
shtrëngoj duart me; **have a free hand** kam dorë të lirë; vt.
dorëzoj; **hand in** dorëzoj; **hand over** dorëzoj; **hand down** kaloj
brez pas brezi
handbag /'hendbeg/ n. 1. kuletë, çantë grash; 2. çantë dore
handful /'hendful/ n. një grusht, një dorë
handicap /'hendikep/ n. pengesë; vt. pengoj
handicraft /'hendikra:ft/ n. 1. zeje; 2. punë dore
handkerchief /'henkĕçi:f/ n. shami dore
handle /'hendl/ n. 1. dorezë, dorëz; 2. vegjë, bisht; vti. 1.
prek, zë me dorë; 2. trajtoj; sillem
handmade /'hend'meid/ adj. i punuar me dorë
handshake /'hendsheik/ n. rrokje, shtrëngim duarsh; toka
handsome /'hendsĕm/ adj. i bukur, i pashëm
handwriting /'hend,ratin/ n. dorëshkrim
hang /hen/ vti. var, varem; **hang about** sorrolatem, sillem kot

haphazard /'hep'hezërd/ **n.** rastësi; **adj.** i rastësishëm; **adv.** rastësisht, aksidentalisht

happen /'hepën/ **vi.** 1. ndodh, ngjet, rastis; 2. gjendem rastësisht; **whatever happens** si do që ndodhë; **as it happens** rastësisht

happening /'hepenin/ **n.** ngjarje, ndodhi

happily /'hepili/ **n.** lumturisht, fatmirësisht

happiness /'hepinis/ **n.** lumturi; fatbardhësi

happy /'hepi/ **adj.** i lumtur, fatbardhë

harass /'herës/ **hë'res/ vt.** shqetësoj, ngacmoj

harbor (harbour) /'ha:rbë(r)/ **n.** port, skelë, liman

hard /ha:rd/ **adj.** 1. i fortë; 2. i vështirë, i rëndë; 3. i ashpër; 4. i rreptë, i pashpirt; **be hard on smb** sillem ashpër me dikë; **be hard up** jam ngushtë për para; **hard cash** të holla në dorë; **adv.** 1. fort; **work hard** punoj shumë; 2. ashpër, rëndë

hard-boiled /,ha:rd'boild/ **adj.** 1. e zierë shumë (veza); 2. **amer.** i regjur

hardly /'ha:rdli/ **adv.** 1. zor, vështirë; 2. thuajse, pothuajse

hardship /'ha:rdship/ **n.** vuajtje; mundim

hardware /'ha:rdweë(r)/ **n.** 1. hekurishte; 2. artikuj metalikë

hare /heë(r)/ **n.** lepur

harm /ha:rm/ **n.** dëmtim, dëm; **vt.** dëmtoj; cënoj

harmful 'ha:rmfl/ **adj.** i dëmshëm

harmless /'ha:rmlis/ **adj.** i padëmshëm

harmony /'ha:rmëni/ **n.** harmoni; **in harmony with** në përputhje me, në harmoni me

harsh /ha:rsh/ **adj.** i ashpër, i egër

harvest /'ha:rvist/ **n.** të korra; **vt.** korr, vjel, mbledh prodhimin

haste /heist/ **n.** nxitim, ngutje; **make haste** nxitoj, ngutem; **in haste** me ngut

hasten /'heisen/ **vti.** 1. përshpejtoj, nxitoj, ngutem; 2. nxit

hastily /'heistili/ **adv.** me ngut, me nxitim

hasty /'heisti/ **adj.** i shpejtuar, i ngutur, i nxituar

hat /het/ **n.** kapele

hate /heit/ **n.** urrejtje; **vt.** urrej, kam urrejtje

hatred /'heitrid/ **n.** urrejtje

haughty /'ho:ti/ **adj.** mendjemadh, kryelartë

have /hev/ **vt.** 1. kam; 2. marr; 3. ka, ndodhet; 4. bëj; **will not have** s'do lejoj; **have to** duhet të; **have smb do something** ngarkoj dikë të kryejë një punë; **have something done** kryej, përfundoj, bëj; **had better** më mirë do ishte

hay /hei/ **n.** bar i thatë, sanë

hazard /'hezërd/ **n.** rrezik

hazardous /'hezëdës/ **adj.** i rrezikshëm

he /hi:/ **pron.** ai

head /hed/ **n.** 1. kokë; 2. tru, kokë, arsye; 3. kreu, maja; 4. kreu, drejtues, udhëheqës; 5. kapitull, krye; **at the head of** në krye të; **keep one's head** ruaj gjakftohtësinë; **lose one's head** humb toruan; **put heads together** vrasim mendjen, këshillohemi, mblidhemi kokë më kokë; **vti.** 1. kryesoj, drejtoj; 2. drejtohem, shkoj drejt

headache /'hedeik/ **n.** dhembje koke

heading /'hedin/ **n.** titull

headline /'hedlain/ **n.** titull (gazete)

headphones /'hedfounz/ **n. pl.** kufje
headquarters /,hed'kwo:tërz/ **n. pl.** shtab
heal /hi:l/ **vti.** 1. shëroj, mjekoj; 2. mbyllet, përthahet plaga
health /helth/ **n.** shëndet; **drink a health to** ngre një shëndet për; **to your health!** shëndeti juaj!
healthy /'helthi/ **adj.** i shëndoshë, i shëndetshëm
heap /hi:p/ **n.** pirg, grumbull, turrë, stivë; **vt.** 1. bëj kapicë, grumbulloj; 2. mbush me majë
hear /hiё(r)/ **vti.** dëgjoj; **hear from** marr lajme, letra nga; **hear of** di, kam dijeni; **hear about something** mësoj, marr vesh
hearing /'hiёrin/ **n.** dëgjim
heart /ha:rt/ **n.** 1. zemër; 2. **fig.** zemër, guxim; 3. mes; 4. zemër, bërthamë; **break sb's heart** i thyej zemrёn dikujt; **by heart** përmendsh; **take to heart** prekem thellë; **heart and soul** me gjithë shpirt; **cry one's heart out** ngashërehem, prekem; **have one's heart in one's mouth** më gjak të ngrirë; **loose heart** humbas kurajon; **set one's heart upon something** më digjet zemra për, dua me gjithë shpirt; **take heart** marr zemër; **with a heavy heart** me zemër të lënduar; **with all one's heart** me gjithë shpirt
heartbroken /'ha:rtbroukën/ **adj.** zemërplasur, zemërthyer
hearth /ha:th/ **n.** vatër; oxhak
hearty /'ha:rti/ **adj.** i përzemërt, i sinqertë
heat /hi:t/ **n.** 1. nxehtësi; 2. zjarrmi, zjarr; 3. vapë; 4. ngrohje;
5 zemërim, pezmatim; **vti.** ngroh; ngrohem
heater 'hi:të(r)/ **n.** sobë (elektrike, me gaz etj.)
heating /'hi:tin/ **n.** ngrohje; **central heating** ngrohje qëndrore
heaven /'hevn/ **n.** qiell
heavy /'hevi/ **adj.** 1. i rëndë; 2. **usht.** i rëndë; 3. i rëndë, i patretshëm; 4. i stuhishëm (deti); i fortë (shi, etj.)
hectare /'hekta:(r); 'hekteё(r)/ **n.** hektar
hedge /hexh/ **n.** gardh
hedgehog /'hexhho:g/ **n.** iriq **heed** /hi:d/ **n.** vëmendje, kujdes; **give (pay) heed to** i kushtoj vëmendje; **vt.** i kushtoj vëmendje
heedless /'hi:dlis/ **adj.** i pavëmendshëm
heel /hi:l/ **n.** 1. thembër; 2. takë; **at (on) one's heels** në gjurmët e; **take to one's heels** ua mbath këmbëve; **Achille's heel** thembra e Akilit **height** /hait/ **n.** lartësi
heighten /'haitn/ **vt.** 1. ngre; 2. zmadhoj; 3. rrit
heir /eё(r)/ **n.** trashëgimtar
helicopter /'helikoptё(r)/ **n.** helikopter
hell /hel/ **n.** ferr, skëterrë; **go to hell!** shko në djall!
help /help/ **n.** 1. ndihmë, mbështetje, përkrahje; 2. ndihmës; **vti.** 1. ndihmoj; 2. gostit; **help someone to something** i ofroj dikujt diçka; **help yourself** merrni
helpful /'helful/ **adj.** 1. i dobishëm; 2. ndihmues
helpless /'helplis/ **adj.** i papërkrahje
hemisphere /'hemisfiё(r)/ **n.** hemisferë
hemorrhage /'hemёrixh/ **n. hemoragji**
hen /hen/ **n.** pulë
her /hë:(r)/ **pron.** i saj **herb** /hë:rb/ **n.** bar, bimë

herd /hë:rd/ **n.** 1. kope; 2. tufë, turmë
here /hië(r)/ **adv.** këtu; **here is to** për shëndetin e; **here and there** andej këndej
heredity /hi'rediti/ **n.** trashëgimi
heritage /'heritixh/ **n.** trashëgim
hero /'hiërou/ **n.** hero
heroic /hi'roik/ **adj.** heroik
heroine /'herouin/ **n.** heroinë
herring /'herin/ **n.** harengë
hers /hë:z/ **pron.** i saj
herself /hë:'self/ **pron.** veten; vetë
hesitate /'heziteit/ **vi.** hezitoj, ngurroj
hi /hai/ **interj.** hej! tungjatjeta!
hiccup /'hikap/ **n.** lemzë
hide /haid/ **vti.** fsheh; fshihem
high /hai/ **adj.** 1. i lartë; 2. i madh; 3. i lartë, i rëndësishëm; **adv.** lart; **high and low** gjithandej
highway /'haiwei/ **n.** rrugë kryesore, autostradë
hijack /'haixhek/ **vt.** rrëmbej; grabit
hill /hil/ **n.** kodër
him /him/ **pron.** atë; atij
himself /him'self/ **pron.** vetë; veten
hinder /'hindë(r)/ **vt.** pengoj
hint /hint/ **n.** aluzion; **give a hint** aludoj, i hedh fjalën; **vti.** aludoj, hedh fjalën; **hint at** bëj aluzion
hip /hip/ **n.** kofshë; vithe
hire /'haië(r)/ **n.** 1. qira; 2. mëditje; **vt.** 1. pajtoj në punë; 2. jap (marr) me qira
his /his/ **pron.** itij, i veti
historic(al) /hi'storik(l)/ **adj.** historik
history /'histri/ **n.** histori
hit /hit/ **n.** 1. goditje; 2. sukses i madh; **song hits** këngët më të suksesshme; **vti.** godas, qëlloj
hitch /hiç/ **vti.** 1. hipi, udhëtoj në makinën e tjetrit; 2. ngre; 3. lidh, ngec
hitchhike /'hiçhaik/ **vi.** udhëtoj duke hipur në makinën e tjetrit
hive /haiv/ **n.** zgjua, koshere
hoarse /ho:rs/ **adj.** i ngjirur
hobby /'hobi/ **n.** gjë që pëlqej të bëj në kohën e lirë, hobi
hockey /'hoki/ **n.** **sport.** hokej
hoe /hou/ **n.** shat **hoist** /hoist/ **vt.** ngre
hold /hould/ **vti.** 1. mbaj; 2. kap, mbërthej, shtrëngoj; 3. nxë, mban, merr; 4. bëj; 5. zotëroj, kam; 6. i mbahem, i përmbahem; **hold on** mbahem, kapem; **hold one's tongue** mbaj gjuhën, hesht; **hold up** vonoj, ndaloj; **n.** 1. kapje; 2. mbajtje
holding /'houldin/ **n.** 1. pronë; 2. aksion
hole /houl/ **n.** 1. vrimë; 2. zgavër; 3. gropë; 4. strofull
holiday /'holidei/ **n.** 1. ditë pushimi; 2. **pl.** pushime
hollow /'holou/ **n. adj.** i zbrazët; bosh
holy /'houli/ **adj.** i shenjtë
homage /'homixh/ **n.** homazh; **do (pay) homage to** bëj homazhe, nderoj

home /houm/ n. shtëpi; **at home** në shtëpi; **adj.** 1. shtëpiak;
2. i lindjes; 3. i brendshëm; **adv.** në shtëpi; **go home** shkoj
në shtëpi
homeland /'houmlend/ n. atdhe
homeless /'houmlis/ **adj.** i pashtëpi
home-made /,houm'meid/ **adj.** i gatuar, i prodhuar në shtëpi
homesick /'houmsik/ **adj.** i malluar për shtëpi, për atdhe
homework /'houmwë:rk/ n. detyrë shtëpie
honest /'onist/ **adj.** i ndershëm
honesty /'onisti/ n. ndershmëri
honey /'hani/ n. mjaltë
honeymoon /'hanimu:n/ n. muaj i mjaltit
honor (honour) /'onë(r)/ n. 1. nder; 2. **pl.** nderime; **have the
honor of (to)** kam nderin të; **in honor of** për nder të; **do smb
honor (do honor) to smb** i bëj nder dikujt; **on (upon) one's
honor** për fjalën e nderit; **do the honors** nderoj miqtë; bëj
nderimet e rastit
hook /huk/ n. kanxhë, çengel; grep; **by hook or by crook** me
çdo mjet
hop /hop/ n. kërcim, hop; **vi.** kërcej, hov
hope /houp/ n. shpresë; **in the hope of** me shpresë se; **past
(beyond) hope** jashtë çdo shprese; **vti.** shpresoj, kam shpresë
hopeful /'houpful/ **adj.** shpresëplotë, shpresëdhënës
hopeless /'houplis/ **adj.** i pashpresë
horizon /hë'raizën/ n. horizont
horn /ho:rn/ n. 1. bri; 2. bori
horoscope /'ho:rëskop/ n. horoskop
horrible /'ho:rëbl/ **adj.** i tmerrshëm, i frikshëm; i keq (moti)
horror /'horë/ n. tmerr, frikë e madhe
horse /ho:s/ n. 1. kalë; 2. **shah.** kalë; **flog a dead horse**
rrah ujë në havan
horse-power /'ho:spauë(r)/ n. kalë-fuqi
horse-race /'ho:sreis/ n. garë me kuaj
horseshoe /'ho:sshu:/ n. patkua
hosiery /'houzëri/ n. trikotazhe; çorape
hospitable /ho'spitëbl; 'hospitëbl/ **adj.** mikpritës
hospital /'hospitl/ n. spital; **go to the hospital** shtrohem në
spital
hospitality /,hospi'teliti/ n. mikpritje
host /houst/ n. 1. mikpritës; 2. hanxhi, pronar, i zoti (i
pijetores etj.); **reckon without one's host** bëj hesapet pa
hanxhinë
hostage /'hostixh/ n. peng; **take smb hostage** marr, mbaj peng
hostess /'hostis/ n. 1. zonjë shtëpije; 2. hanxheshë
hostile /'hostail/ **adj.** armiqësor
hostility /ho'stiliti/ n. armiqësi
hot /hot/ **adj.** 1. i nxehtë; 2. djegës; 3. i flaktë; i zjarrtë
hotel /hou'tel/ n. hotel; **put up at a hotel** zë vend në hotel
hour /'auë(r)/ n. 1. orë; 2. orar; 3. kohë, çast
house /haus/ n. 1. shtëpi; 2. dhomë; 3. dinasti; **keep house**
mbaj, qeveris shtëpinë
household /'hauzhold/ n. njerëzit e shtëpisë; ekonomi
shtëpiake
housewife /'hauzwaif/ n. amvisë, grua shtëpiake
housework /'hauzwë:rk/ n. punë shtëpiake
housing /'hauzin/ n. strehim
how /hau/ **adv.** si, në ç'mënyrë; **how do you do?** tungjatjeta!
how are you? si jeni? **how much (many)** sa

however /hau'evë(r)/ **conj.** por, megjithatë, sidoqoftë; **adv.** sado

howl /haul/ **n.** 1. ulërimë; 2. hungërimë; **vti.** 1. ulërij; 2. hungëroj

hue /hju:/ **n.** nuancë; ngjyrim

hug /hag/ **vt.** përqafoj; **n.** përqafim

huge /hju:xh/ **adj.** i madh, vigan

hull /hal/ **n.** trup anije, tanku etj.

human /'hju:mën/ **adj.** njerëzor

humane /hju:'mein/ **adj.** i njerëzishëm, humanitar, shoqëror

humanitarian /hju:,meni'teriën/ **adj.** humanitar

humanity /hju:'menëti/ **n.** 1. njerëzim; 2. njerëzi; 3. natyrë njerëzore; 4. sjellje e njerëzishme

humble /'hambl/ **adj.** 1. i përulur, kokëulur; 2. i përvuajtur; **vt.** përul, poshtëroj

humid /'hju:mid/ **adj.** i lagësht

humidity /hju:'midëti/ **n.** lagështi

humiliate /hju:'milieit/ **vt.** poshtëroj

humorous /'hju:mërës/ **adj.** humoristik, shakatar

humor (humour) /'hju:më(r)/ **n.** 1. humor; 2. gjendje shpirtërore; **have a sense of humor** kam sensin e humorit

hundred /'hanxhrëd/ **n.** qind

hunger /'hangë(r)/ **n.** uri; **hunger strike** grevë urie

hungry /'hangri/ **adj.** 1. i uritur; 2. i etur

hunt /hant/ **vit.** 1. gjuaj; 2. kërkoj; **n.** gjueti; gjah

hurrah /hu'ra:/ **interj.** urra

hurricane /'harikein/ **n.** tufan, stuhi, furtunë

hurry /'hari/ **vti.** nxitoj; nxitohem; **n.** nxitim, ngutje; **in a hurry** me nxitim

hurt /hë:rt/ **vti.** 1. vritem; 2. lëndoj, plagos; 3. më dhemb; **n.** 1. dhembje; vuajtje; 2. dëmtim, plagë, e vrarë

hurtful /'hë:rtful/ **adj.** 1. i dëmshëm; 2. lëndues

husband /'hazbënd/ **n.** burrë, bashkëshort

hush /hash/ **n.** qetësi; heshtje; **vti.** hesht, qetësoj, pushoj

husk /hask/ **vit.** zhvesh, pastroj nga lëvorja; **n.** lëvore; cipë

hustle /'hasl/ **vti.** shtyj, shtyhem

hydrogen /'haidrëxhën/ **n.** hidrogjen

hygiene /'haixhin/ **n.** higjienë

hymn /him/ **n.** himn

hypocrisy /hi'pokrësi/ **n.** hipokrizi

hypodermic /,haipou'dë:rmik/ **adj.** hipodermik

hysterical /hi'sterikl/ **adj.** histerik

I /ai/ **pron.** unë
ice /ais/ **n.** 1. akull; 2. akullore, kasatë; **break the ice**
thyej akullin
iceberg /'aisbë:rg/ **n.** ajsberg
ice-cream /,ais'kri:m/ **n.** akullore
icicle /'aisikl/ **n.** hell akulli
icon (ikon) /'aikon/ **n.** ikonë
idea /ai'dië/ **n.** 1. ide, mendim; 2. qëllim; 3. njohuri,
dijeni; **bright idea** ide e shkëlqyer; **have an idea of** kam
dijeni për
ideal /ai'diël/ **n.** ideal
identical /ai'dentikl/ **adj.** identik, i njëjtë
identification /ai,dentifi'keshn/ **n.** identifikim
identify /ai'dentifai/ **vt.** identifikoj; njëjtësoj
identity /ai'dentiti/ **n.** identitet; njëjtësi
ideology /,aidi'olëxhi/ **n.** ideologji
idiocy /'idiësi/ **n.** 1. idiotësi; 2. marrëzi, budallallëk
idiom /'idiëm/ **n.** idiomë; shprehje fraziologjike
idle /'aidl/ **adj.** 1. i pazënë, i papunë; 2. i padobishëm, i
kotë; **vit.** rri kot, pa punë; **idle away one's time** kaloj kohën
kot
idol /'aidl/ **n.** idhull
if /if/ **conj.** në se, në qoftë se; **as if** sikur; **even if** edhe
sikur
ignition /ig'nishn/ **n.** ndezje
ignorance /'ignërëns/ **n.** padituri, injorancë
ignorant /'ignërënt/ **adj.** i paditur, injorant
ignore /ig'no:(r)/ **vt.** injoroj, nuk përfill
ill /il/ **adj.** 1. i sëmurë; **fall ill, be taken ill** sëmurem; 2.
i keq; **adv.** keq; **speak ill of smb** flas keq për dikë
illegal /i'li:gl/ **adj.** ilegal, i paligjshëm
illegible /i'lexhëbl/ **adj.** i palexueshëm
illegitimate /,ili'xhitimët/ **adj.** i paligjshëm
illiterate /i'litërët/ **adj.** analfabet
illness /'ilnis/ **n.** sëmundje
illuminate /i'lu:mineit/ **vt.** ndriçoj; hedh dritë mbi
illusion /'i'lu:zhn/ **n.** iluzion **illustrate** /'ilëstreit/ **vt.**
ilustroj
illustration /,ilë'streishn/ **n.** ilustrim
image /'imixh/ **n.** shëmbëlltyrë, imazh, përfytyrim; **vt.**
përfytyroj, imagjinoj
imagination /i,mexhi'neishn/ **n.** 1. përfytyrim, imagjinatë; 2.
fantazi
imagine /i'mexhin/ **vt.** 1. përfytyroj, imagjinoj; 2. mendoj
sikur
imitate /'imiteit/ **vt.** imitoj
imitation /,imi'teishn/ **n.** imitim
immature /,imë'tjuë(r)/ **adj.** i papjekur
immediate /i'mi:diët/ **adj.** 1. i menjëhershëm; 2. i afërm; i
ngutshëm
immediately /i'mi:diëtli/ **adv.** menjëherë, sakaq
immense /i'mens/ **adj.** 1. i pamasë; 2. vigan, shumë i madh
immigrant /'imigrënt/ **n.** imigrant
immigrate /'imigreit/ **vi.** imigroj
immobile /i'moubail/ **adj.** i palëvizshëm
immoral /i'mo:rël/ **adj.** imoral, i pandershëm
immortal /i'mo:rtl/ **adj.** i pavdekshëm; i përjetshëm

immovable /i'mu:vëbl/ **adj.** 1. i palëvishëm; 2. i patundshëm
immune /i'mju:n/ **adj.** i imunizuar
immunity /i'mju:niti/ **n.** imunitet; paprekshmëri; **diplomatic immunity** imunitet diplomatik
impact /'impekt/ **n.** 1. ndeshje, përpjekje, përplasje; 2. ndikim
impair /im'peë(r)/ **vt.** dëmtoj
impartial /im'pa:rshl/ **adj.** i paanshëm
impatient /im'peishnt/ **adj.** i padurueshëm, i paduruar
impeachment /im'pi:çmënt/ **n.** 1. vënie në dyshim; 2. paditje; nxjerrje para gjyqit
impede /im'pi:d/ **vt.** ndaloj, pengoj
impel /im'pel/ **vt.** 1. detyroj; 2. nxit, vë në lëvizje
impending /im'pendin/ **adj.** i afërm, i afërt
imperative /im'perëtiv/ **adj.** imperativ; urgjent
imperialism /im'piëriëlizëm/ **n.** imperializëm
impersonal /im'pë:rsënl/ **adj.** pavetor
implement /'implimënt/ **vt.** kryej, përmbush, zbatoj
implementation /,implimen'teishn/ **n.** zbatim, përmbushje
implore /im'plo:/ **vt.** lus
imply /im'plai/ **vt.** aludoj; nënkuptoj
impolite /,impë'lait/ **adj.** i pasjellshëm; i panjerëzishëm
import /im'po:rt/ **vt.** importoj; **n.** /'impo:rt/ 1. importim; 2. pl. mallra të importuara
importance /im'po:rtns/ **n.** rëndësi
important /im'po:rtënt/ **adj.** i rëndësishëm
impossible /im'posibl/ **adj.** 1. i pamundur; **do the immpossible** bëj të pamundurën; 2. i padurueshëm
impotent /'impëtënt/ **adj.** 1. i pafuqishëm; 2. impotent
impoverish /im'povërish/ **vt.** varfëroj
impress im'pres/ **vt.** 1. stampoj; 2. lë gjurmë, mbresë; 3. fiksoj, ngulit në mendje
impression /im'preshn/ **n.** 1. përshtypje; mbresë; **make an impression** lë, bëj përshtypje; **be under the impression that** kam përshtypjen se; 2. shtypje, botim; 3. shenjë, gjurmë, tragë
impressive /im'presiv/ **adj.** përshtypjelënës, mbresëlënës
imprint /im'print/ **n.** gjurmë; shenjë; **vt.** 1. lë mbresë, tragë; 2. ngul, fiksoj (në mendje)
imprison /im'prizn/ **vt.** burgos
improbable /im'probëbl/ **adj.** i pamundshëm, i pamundur
improve /im'pru:v/ **vti.** përmirësoj; përmirësohem
improvement /im'pru:vmënt/ **n.** përmirësim
impudent /'impju:dënt/ **adj.** i paturpshëm, i pacipë
impudence /'impju:dëns/ **n.** paturpësi
impulse /'impals/ **n.** 1. shtytje, nxitje; 2. impuls
impulsive /im'palsiv/ **adj.** impulsiv
impunity /im'pju:nëti/ **n.** pandëshkueshmëri
in /in/ **prep.** në; gjatë; **adv.** brenda, përbrenda
inability /,inë'biliti/ **n.** 1. paaftësi; 2. pamundësi
inaccessible /,inek'sesibl/ **adj.** 1. i paarritshëm; 2. i pakapshëm
inaccurate /in'ekjërët/ **adj.** i pasaktë, i papërpiktë
inactive in'ektiv/ **adj.** mosveprues, i plogësht; i fjetur, i mefshtë
inadequate /in'edikvit/ **adj.** 1. i pamjaftueshëm; 2. i pakënaqshëm

inasmuch as /ˌinəz'maç ëz/ **conj.** duke marrë parasysh; meqenëse
inattentive /inë'tentiv/ **adj.** i pavëmendshëm; i papërqëndruar
incalculable /in'kelkjulëbl/ **adj.** i pallogaritshëm
incapable /in'keipëbl/ **adj.** i paaftë, i pazoti
incentive /in'sentiv/ **n.** stimul; nxitje **incessant**
/in'sesnt/**adj.** i parreshtur, i vazhdueshëm, i pandërprerë
inch /inç/ **n.** inç (= 2.5 cm.)
incident /'insidënt/ **n.** 1. incident; 2. ndodhi, ngjarje e
papritur
incidental /ˌinsi'dentl/ **adj.** i rastësishëm, i rastit
inclination /ˌinkli'neishn/ **n.** 1. pjerrësi, pjerrje; 2.
prirje, anim
inclined /in'klaind/ **adj.** 1. i prirët, i pjerrët; 2. i prirur
include /in'klu:d/ **vt.** 1. përfshij; 2. fut
including /in'klu:din/ **prep.** përfshirë
income /'inkëm/ **n.** e ardhur; **income tax** tatim fitimi
incompatible /ˌinkëm'petëbl/ **adj.** i papajtueshëm; që nuk
shkon bashkë
incompetent /in'kompitënt/ **adj.** i paaftë, jo kompetent
incomplete /ˌinkëm'pli:t/ **adj.** 1. i paplotë; 2. i
papërfunduar
inconsistent /ˌinkën'sistënt/ **adj.** 1. i papajtueshëm; 2.
jokonsekuent; 3. kontradiktor, i paqëndrueshëm
inconvenient /ˌinkën'vi:niënt/ **adj.** i pavolitshëm, i
papërshtatshëm
incorrect /ˌinkë'rekt/ **adj.** i pasaktë, i gabuar
increase /in'kri:s/ **vti.** rrit, shtoj, zmadhoj; **n.** 1. rritje,
shtim; 2. ngritje; **on the increase** në rritje
incredible /in'kredëbl/ **adj.** i pabesueshëm
increment /'inkrëmënt/ **n.** 1. shtesë, rritje; 2. fitim
incur /in'kë:(r)/ **vt.** 1. shkaktoj, ngjall; 2. marr mbi vete;
incur losses pësoj humbje
indebted /in'detid/ **adj.** i detyruar, borxhli
indecent /in'di:snt/ **adj.** i pahijshëm
indecisive /ˌindi'saisiv/ **adj.** 1. i pavendosur; 2. i
papërcaktuar
indeed /in'di:d/ **adv.** në të vërtetë, realisht, vërtet
indefinite /in'definët/ **adj.** 1. i pacaktuar, i papërcaktuar;
2. e pashquar (nyja)
indemnity /in'demnëti/ **n.** 1. zhdëmtim, dëmshpërblim; 2.
garanci, siguri (nga humbjet)
independence /ˌindi'pendëns/ **n.** pavarësi
independent /ˌindi'pendënt/ **n.** 1. i pavarur; 2. i
mëvetësishëm
index /'indeks/ **n.** indeks, tregues
Indian /'indiën/ **adj.** indian; **n.** indian; **Indian summer**
vjeshtë me kohë të mirë
indicate /'indikeit/ **vt.** tregoj, dëftej
indication /ˌindi'keishn/ **n.** 1. tregues; 2. shenjë
indicative /in'dikëtiv/ **adj.** 1. tregues; 2. dëftor;
indicative mood mënyra dëftore
indicator /'indikeitë(r)/ **n.** 1. indikator; 2. tregues
indictment /in'daitmënt/ **n.** padi, akt padi
indifferent /in'difrënt/ **adj.** 1. indiferent, moskokëçarës; 2.
i rëndomtë; i parëndësishëm
indigestion /ˌindi'xhesçën/ **n.** mostretje; kapsllëk
indignant /in'dignënt/ **adj.** i zëmëruar, i indinjuar
indignation /ˌindig'neishn/ **n.** indinjatë, zemëratë

indirect /,indi'rekt/ **adj.** 1. i tërthortë; 2. i zhdrejtë;
indirect object kundrinë e zhdrejtë
indispensable /,indi'spensëbl/ **adj.** i domosdoshëm, esencial
indisputable /,indi'spju:tëbl/ **adj.** i padiskutueshëm, i
pakundërshtueshëm
indissoluble /,indi'soljubl/ **adj.** i patretshëm; i
pazbërthyeshëm
indistinct /,indis'tinkt/ **adj.** i padallueshëm; i paqartë
individual /,indi'vidjuël/ **adj.** 1. vetjak, personal,
individual; 2. i veçantë; **n.** 1. individ; 2. qënie
indivisible /,indi'vizëbl/ **adj.** 1. i pandashëm, i
pazbërthyeshëm; 2. i papjesëtueshëm
Indo-European /'indou'juërë'pi:ën/ **adj.** indo-evropian
indomitable /in'domitëbl/ **adj.** i pamposhtshëm, i pathyeshëm
indoor /'indo:/ **adj.** i mbyllur, që zhvillohet brenda
indoors /in'do:rz/ **adv.** brenda; **keep indoors** mbaj brenda;
stay indoors qëndroj brenda (në shtëpi)
induce /in'dju:s; in'du:s/ **vt.** 1. nxit, shtyj; 2. shkaktoj
indulge /in'dalxh/ **vti.** 1. i plotësoj dëshirën, kënaq, i bëj
qejfin; 2. jepem pas, kënaqem me
industrial /in'dastriël/ **adj.** industrial; **industrial goods**
artikuj industrialë; **industrial school** shkollë industriale
industrious /in'dastriës/ **adj.** punëtor, i zellshëm, i
palodhur
industry /'indëstri/ **n.** industri; **light (heavy) industry**
industri e lehtë (e rëndë)
ineffective /,ini'fektiv/ **adj.** i paefektshëm, i pafrytshëm
inefficiency /,ini'fishnsi/ **n.** paaftësi, pazotësi
inefficient /,ini'fishnt/ **adj.** i paaftë, i pazoti; i
pafrytshëm
inequality /,ini'kwolëti/ **n.** pabarazi
inevitable /in'evitëbl/ **adj.** i pashmangshëm, i paevitueshëm
inexact /,inig'zekt/ **adj.** i pasaktë
inexcusable /,inik'skju:zëbl/ **adj.** i pafalshëm
inexhaustible /,inig'zo:stëbl/ **adj.** i pashtershëm, i
pashteruesheëm
inexpensive /,inik'spensiv/ **adj.** i lirë
inexperience /,inik'spiëriëns/ **n.** papërvojë, mungesë përvoje
inexperienced /,inik'spiëriënsd/ **adj.** i papërvojë
inexplicit /,inik'splisit/ **adj.** i paqartë
infallible /in'felëbl/ **adj.** i pagabueshëm
infamous /'infëmës/ **adj.** famëkeq; i ulët, i poshtër, i
turpshëm
infant /'infënt/ **n.** foshnjë, fëmijë; **adj.** foshnjor, fëminor
infantry /'infëntri/ **n. usht.** këmbësori
infect /in'fekt/ **vt.** moleps, infekton
infection /in'fekshn/ **n.** 1. infektim; infeksion; 2. ndikim,
përhapje
infectious /'in'fekshës/ **adj.** infektiv, ngjitës
infer /in'fë:(r)/ **vt.** nxjerr përfundim
inferior /in'fiërië(r)/ **adj.** inferior; **n.** vartës
inferiority /in,fiëri'orëti/ **n.** 1. inferioritet; 2. vartësi;
inferiority complex kompleksi i inferioritetit
infertile /in'fë:tail/ **adj.** 1. shterp; 2. jopjellor, joprodhues
infidel /'infidël/ **n.** njeri i pafe, femohues
infinite /'infinët/ **adj.** i pakufishëm; i pafund
infirm /in'fë:rm/ **adj.** 1. i dobët, shëndetlig; 2. i pavendosur
inflame /in'fleim/ **vt.** ndez, i vë flakën; 2. **fig.** ndez, nxis

inflate /in'fleit/ **vt.** 1. fryj (me ajër, me gaz etj); 2. **ek.** krijoj inflacion

inflation /in'fleishn/ **n.** 1. fryrje (me ajër, gaz etj.) 2. **ek.** inflacion

inflexible /in'fleksëbl/ **adj.** 1. i papërthyeshëm, i papërkulshëm; 2. **fig.** i paepur, i palëkundshëm

inflict /in'flikt/ **vt.** 1. i jap (një dackë, goditje etj.); 2. shkaktoj

influence /'influëns/ **vt.** ndikoj, ushtroj ndikim; **n.** ndikim

influential /,influ'enshl/ **adj.** ndikues; me influencë

influenza /,influ'enzë/ **n. mjek.** grip

inform /in'fo:rm/ **vti.** 1. njoftoj; 2. informoj; **inform against** padit

informal /in'fo:rml/ **adj.** jozyrtar, joformal; bisedor

information /,infë'meishn/ **n.** 1. informim; 2. informatë; informacion

infringe /in'frinxh/ **vt.** shkel, cënoj (ligjin etj.); **infringe sb's rights** shkel të drejtat e dikujt

infringement /in'frinxhmënt/ **n.** shkelje; dhunim

infuriate /in'fjuëriet/ **vt.** egërsoj, tërboj

ingenious /in'xhi:niës/ **adj.** 1. mendjemprehtë; 2. i çiltër, zemërhapur; i padjallëzuar

inglorious /in'glo:riës/ **adj.** i palavdishëm, i turpshëm

inhabit /in'hebit/ **vt.** jetoj, banoj

inhabitable /in'hebitëbl/ **adj.** i banueshëm

inhabitant /in'hebitënt/ **n.** banor

inhale /in'heil/ **vti.** marr, thith frymë

inherit /in'herit/ **vti.** trashëgoj

inheritance /in'heritëns/ **n.** 1. trashëgimi; 2. trashëgim

inhibit /in'hibit/ **vt.** ndaloj, pengoj, frenoj **inhuman** /in'hju:mën/ **adj.** çnjerëzor; mizor, i egër

initial /i'nishl/ **adj.** 1. fillestar; 2. i parë

initially /i'nishëli/ **adv.** fillimisht

initiate /i'nishieit/ **vt.** 1. nis, filloj; inicioj; 2. pranoj, fut

initiative /i'nishëtiv/ **n.** nismë, iniciativë, vetëveprim

inject /in'xhekt/ **vt.** injektoj

injection /in'xhekshn/ **n.** 1. injektim; 2. injeksion

injury /'inxhë(r)/ **vt.** 1. dëmtoj; 2. cënoj

injury /'inxhëri/ **n.** 1. dëmtim; dëm; 2. cënim

injustice /in'xhastis/ **n.** padrejtësi; **do smb an injustice** i bëj dikujt një padrejtësi

ink /ink/ **n.** bojë shkrimi; **printer's ink** bojë tipografike

ink-stand /'inkstend/ **n.** 1. shishe boje; 2. mbajtëse boje

inmate /'inmeit/ **n.** bashkëbanor; bujtës

inn /in/ **n.** han; bujtinë

inner /'inë(r)/ **adj.** i brendshëm

innocence /'inësns/ **n.** 1. pafajësi; 2. çiltërsi

innocent /'inësnt/ **adj.** 1. i pafajshëm; njeri i pafajshëm **an innocent man**; 2. i çiltër, i padjallëzuar

innovate /'inëveit/ **vi.** 1. fus të renë; 2. shpik, racionalizoj

innovation /,inë'veishn/ **n.** novacion, novatorizëm, risi

innumerable /i'nju:mërëbl/ **adj.** i panumurueshëm; i panumurt

inoculate /i'nokjuleit/ **vt.** 1. shartoj; 2. i fus në kokë mendime; 3. vaksinoj

in-patient /'in peshnt/ **n.** pacient i shtruar në spital
inquest /'inkwest/ **n.** 1. hetim; 2. hetuesi
inquire /in'kvaië(r)/ **vt.** 1. pyes; 2. kërkoj të dhëna; 3. shqyrtoj, hetoj; 4. pyes, interesohem për shëndetin e dikujt
inquiry /in'kwaiëri/ **n.** 1. informatë; 2. pyetje; 3. hetim;
hold an inquiry into something bëj hetime për diçka
insane /in'sein/ **adj.** i çmendur
insanity /in'senëti/ **n.** marrëzi, çmenduri
insect /'insekt/ **n.** insekt, kandërr
insecure /,insi'kjuë(r)/ **adj.** i pasigurt **insensible**
/in'sensëbl/ **adj.** 1. i pandjenja; 2. i pavetëdijshëm
inseparable /in'seprëbl/ **adj.** i pandashëm
insert /in'së:rt/ **vt.** 1. fut; 2. përfshij; 3. ndërfut
inside /in'said/ **n.** ana e brendshme; **adj.** i brendshëm; **adv.**
brenda; **inside out** së prapthi
insignificant /,insig'nifikënt/ **adj.** i parëndësishëm
insincere /,insin'sië(r)/ **adj.** i pansinqertë
insist /in'sist/ **vti.** këmbëngul, insistoj
insistent /in'sistënt/ **adj.** këmbëngulës, ngulmues
insolent /'insëlënt/ **adj.** i pacipë, i pafytyrë
insoluble /in'soljubl/ **adj.** 1. i patretshëm; 2. i
pazbërthyeshëm; 3. i pazgjithshëm
insomnia /in'somnië/ **n.** pagjumësi
inspect /in'spekt/ **vt.** 1. inspektoj; 2. shqyrtoj
inspector /in'spektë(r)/ **n.** 1. kontrollor; 2. inspektor
inspiration /,inspë'reishn/ **n.** 1. frymëzim; 2. burim
frymëzimi
inspire in'spaië(r)/ **vt.** frymëzoj, mbush me frymëzim
instability /,instë'biliti/ **n.** 1. paqëndrueshmëri; 2.
pavendosmëri
install (instal) /in'sto:l/ **vt.** 1. vendos (në një detyrë); 2.
instaloj, montoj; 3. pajis
installation /,instë'leishn/ **n.** 1. vendosje; 2. rregullim; 3.
instalim; montim
instalment (installment) /in'sto:lmënt/ **n.** 1. këst; **pay by
instalments** paguaj me këste; 2. pjesë e një (vepre, tregimi
etj.)
instance /'instëns/ **n.** 1. shëmbull; **for instance** për
shembull; 2. kërkesë; **at the instance of** me kërkesë të; 3.
rast; **in this instance** në këtë rast
instant /'instënt/ **adj.** 1. i ngutshëm, urgjent; 2. i
menjëhershëm; 3. ekspres; **instant coffee** kafe ekspres; **n.**
çast; **on the instant** në çast; **this instant** tani, këtë çast
instantly /'instëntli/ **adv.** menjëherë
instead /in'sted/ **adv.** në vend të
instead of /in'sted ov/ **prep.** në vend të
instigate /'instigeit/ **vt.** shtyj, nxit
instinct /'instikt/ **n.** instikt; **by instinct** me instinkt
instinctive in'stinktiv/ **adj.** instiktiv
institute /'institju:t; 'institu:t/ **n.** institut; **vt.** 1.
krijoj, themeloj; 2. nis, filloj, ndërmarr
institution /,insti't(j)u:shn/ **n.** 1. institucion, organizëm
(shtetëror, shoqëror); 2. vendosje
instruct /in'strëkt/ **vt.** 1. mësoj, udhëzoj, instruktoj; 2.
njoftoj **instruction** /in'strakshn/ **n.** 1. mësim, stërvitje; 2.
udhëzim

instructive /in'straktiv/ **adj.** udhëzues
instructor /in'straktë(r)/ **n.** instruktor; trainer
instrument /'instrumënt/ **n.** vegël, instrument, aparat
insufficient /,insë'fishnt/ **adj.** i pamjaftueshëm
insulin /'insjulin; 'insëlën/ **n.** insulinë
insult /in'salt/ **vt.** shaj, fyej; **n.** fyerje
insurance /in'shuërëns/ **n.** 1. sigurim; 2. siguracion
insure /in'shuë(r)/ **vt.** 1. siguroj (shtëpinë etj.); 2.
siguroj
integral /'intigrël/ **adj.** përbërës, integral
integrate /'intigreit/ **vt.** integroj
integrity /in'tegrëti/ **n.** integritet, tërësi
intellect /'intëlekt/ **n.** intelekt, aftësi mendore
intellectual /,inti'lekçuël/ **n.** intelektual; **adj.**
intelektual, mendor
intelligence /in'telixhëns/ **n.** intelekt, mënçuri, zgjuarsi
intelligent /in'telixhënt/ **adj.** i zgjuar, i mençur,
mendjemprehtë **intend** /in'tend/ **vt.** 1. kam ndërmend, kam në
plan; 2. paracaktoj, destinoj
intended /in'tendid/ **adj.** i parashikuar, i destinuar
intense /in'tens/ **adj.** 1. i fortë, i madh, i fuqishëm; 2. i
tendosur, i nderë
intensify /in'tensifai/ **vti.** intensifikoj
intensity /in'tensiti/ **n.** intensitet
intensive /in'tensiv/ **adj.** intensiv
intent /in'tent/ **n.** qëllim, synim
intention /in'tenshn/ **n.** qëllim, synim; plan; **with the
intention of** me qëllim të
intentionally /in'tenshënëli/ **adv.** qëllimisht
interact /,intër'ekt/ **vi.** bashkëveproj
interchange /,intë'çeinxh/ **vt.** 1. ndërkëmbej, shkëmbej; 2.
zëvendësoj, alternoj
interchangeable /,intë'çeinxhëbl/ **n.** i ndërkëmbyeshëm, i
shkëmbyeshëm
intercommunicate /,intë'komju:nikeit/ **vi.** komunikoj, merrem
vesh
intercontinental /,intë,konti'nentl/ **adj.** ndërkontinental
intercourse /'intëko:rs/ **n.** 1. shkëmbim; 2. marrëdhënie,
lidhje; 3. marrëdhënie seksuale
interdependence /,intëdi'pendëns/ **n.** ndërvarësi
interdependent /,intëdi'pendent/ **adj.** i ndërvarur
interest /'intrëst/ **n.** 1. interes; 2. rëndësi; 3. dobi, e
mirë; 4. **fin.** përqindje interesi; **take an interest in** tregoj
interes për; **in the interest of** në interes të; **rate of
interest** përqindja e interesit; **lose interest** humb interesin;
vt. 1. tërheq, ngjall interesin e dikujt; 2. interesohem
interested /'intrëstid/ **adj.** i interesuar
interesting /'intrëstin/ **adj.** interesant, tërheqës
interfere /,intë'fië(r)/ **vi.** 1. ndërhyj, përzihem; 2. trazoj;
3. pengoj; **interfere with smb** pengoj dikë
interference /,intë'fiërëns/ **n.** interferencë, ndërhyrje;
përzierje **interior** /in'tiërië(r)/ **adj.** i brendshëm; **n.** 1.
brendësi; pjesë e brendshme; 2. krahinat (punët) e brendshme
të një vendi **interjection** /,intë'xhekshn/ **n. gram.** pasthirrmë

intermediate /ˌintë'mi:diët/ **adj.** i ndërmjetëm
intern /in'të:rn/ **vt.** internoj
internal /in'të:rnl/ **adj.** i brendshëm
international /ˌintë'neshnël/ **adj.** ndërkombëtar,
internacional
interpret /in'të:prit/ **vti.** 1. interpretoj; 2. luaj
interpretation /in,të:pri'teishn/ **n.** interpretim
interpreter /in'të:pritë(r)/ **n.** interpretues
interrogate /in'terëgeit/ **vt.** pyes, marr në pyetje
interrogation /in,terë'geishn/ **n.** pyetje, marrje në pyetje
interrupt /ˌintë'rapt/ **vti.** 1. ndërpres; 2. pengoj, ndaloj
interruption /ˌintë'rapshn/ **n.** 1. ndërprerje; 2. ndalim,
ndalesë; 3. interval
interval /'intëvl/ **n.** 1. interval; **at intevals** në interval;
2. pushim (midis dy akteve të dramës)
intervene /ˌintë'vi:n/ **vi.** 1. ndërhyj; 2. pengoj **interview**
/'intërvju:/ **n.** intervistë; **vt.** intervistoj
intestine /in'testin/ **n.** zorrë; **small (large) intestine** zorra
e hollë (e trashë)
intimate /'intimët/ **adj.** intim, i afërm, i afërt
into /'intu:; 'intë/ **prep.** në, brenda në
intolerable /in'tolërëbl/ **adj.** i padurueshëm; **intolerable
heat** vapë e padurueshme
intolerance /in'tolërëns/ **n.** intolerancë
intolerant /in'tolërënt/ **adj.** jotolerues **intoxicate**
/in'toksikeit/ **vt.** 1. intoksikoj; 2. deh
intricate /'intrikët/ **adj.** i ngatërruar, i ndërlikuar, i
koklavitur
introduce /ˌintrë'd(j)u:s/ **vt.** 1. paraqes, njoh me; 2.
parashtroj; 3. fut për herë të parë
introduction /ˌintrë'dakshn/ **n.** 1. hyrje, parathënie; 2.
paraqitje
intrude /in'tru:d/ **vti.** fut(em), ndërhyj **intuition**
/ˌint(j)u:ishn/ **n.** intuitë
invade /in'veid/ **vt.** 1. pushtoj; 2. ndërhyj; 3. shkel
invalid /in'velid/ **adj.** i pavlefshëm, i pavlerë
invalid /'invëli:d/ **adj.** i sëmurë, i paaftë për punë; **n.**
invalid
invaluable /in'veljuëbl/ **adj.** i paçmueshëm, i vyer
invariable /in'veëriëbl/ **adj.** i pandryshueshëm, konstant
invasion /in'veizhn/ **n.** pushtim, invazion
invention /in'venshn/ **n.** 1. shpikje; 2. trillim
inventory /'invëntri; 'invënto:ri/ **n.** inventar
invest /in'vest/ **vti.** 1. investoj (kapital etj.); 2. vesh (me
pushtet)
investigate /in'vestigeit/ **vt.** 1. hetoj; 2. gjurmoj; 3.
shqyrtoj
investigation /in,vesti'geishn/ **n.** 1. shqyrtim; 2. gjurmim;
3. hetim; 4. ndjekje (gjyqësore)
investment /in'vestmënt/ **n.** 1. investim (i kapitalit); 2.
kapital i investuar
investor /in'vestë(r)/ **n.** investues
invincible /in'vinsëbl/ **adj.** i pathyeshëm, i pamposhtur
invisible /in'vizëbl/ **adj.** i padukshëm
invitation /ˌinvi'teishn/ **n.** ftesë
invite /in'vait/ **vt.** 1. ftoj; i bëj ftesë; 2. tërheq, josh,
gris
invoice /'invois/ **n.** faturë, kuitancë

invoke /in'vëuk/ **vt.** 1. thërras (në ndihmë); 2. **fet.** lut, i drejtoj një lutje; 3. i drejtohem
involuntary /in'volëntri; in'volënteri/ **adv.** pa vullnet, pa dashje
involve /in'volv/ **vt.** 1. presupozon, nënkupton; 2. ndërlikoj, komplikoj, ngatërroj; 3. sjell, shkakton; 4. ngatërrohem
inward /'inwëd/ **adj.** 1. i brendshëm; 2. mendor; shpirtëror
iodine /'aiëdi:n; 'aiëdain/ **n.** jod
IOU /,ai ëu 'ju:/ **n.** (= I owe you) dëftesë borxhi
Irish /'aiërish/ **adj.** irlandez; **n.** 1. irlandez; 2. irlandishte
iron /'aiën; 'aiërn/ **n.** 1. hekur; 2. hekur (për të hekurosur); **vti.** 1. hekuros; 2. sheshoj; **iron out** sheshoj, zhduk (një keqkuptim, mosmarrëveshje etj.); **adj.** i hekurt, prej hekuri
ironic(al) /ai'ronik(l)/ **adj.** ironik
ironing /'aiërnin/ **n.** hekurosje
irony /'aiërëni/ **n.** ironi
irrational /i'reshënl/ **adj.** i paarsyeshëm, irracional
irregular /i'regjulë(r)/ **adj.** i parregullt, i çrregullt
irrelevant /i'relëvënt/ **adj.** që s'ka lidhje me , që s'ka të bëjë me
irrespective /,iri'spektiv/ **adj.** pavarësisht
irresponsible /,iri'sponsëbl/ **adj.** i papërgjegjshëm
irrigate /'irigeit/ **vt.** ujit, vadit
irrigation /,iri'geishn/ **n.** ujitje, vaditje
irritable /'iritëbl/ **adj.** 1. zemërak, idhnak; 2. i acaruar, i pezmatuar
irritate /'iriteit/ **vt.** irritoj, ngacmoj, acaroj, pezmatoj
irritation /,iri'teishn/ **n.** acarim, ngacmim
Islam /iz'la:m; 'isla:m/ **n.** 1. islam; 2. islamizëm; 3. myslimanët
island /'aiëlënd/ **n.** ishull
isolate 'aisëleit/ **vt.** veçoj, izoloj
isolation /,aisë'leishn/ **n.** veçim, izolim
Israelite /'izriëlait/ **adj.** izraelit; **n.** izraelit
issue /'isju:/ **n.** 1. dalje; 2. rrjedhje; 3. botim; 4. emetim, nxjerrje e parasë; 5. problem, çështje; **vit.** 1. del, rrjedh; 2. nxjerr, vë në qarkullim; 3. shpërndaj
it /it/ **pron.** ai, ajo; ky, kjo
Italian /i'teliën/ **adj.** italian; **n.** 1. italishte; 2. italian
item /'aitëm/ **n.** 1. pikë; 2. paragraf, nen; 3. artikull, send; 4. çështje
its /its/ **poss. pron.** i saj; i vet; e vetja
itself /it'self/ **reflex. pron.** veten; vetë
ivory /'aivëri/ **n.** 1. fildish; 2. dhëmb elefanti

J

jab /xheb/ **vti.** ngul, godit, shpoj (me thikë etj.); **n.** goditje; shpim
jack xhek/ **n.** krik; **vt.** ngre me krik
jacket /'xhekit/ **n.** 1. xhaketë; 2. lëkurë, cipë
jail /xheil/ **n.** burg
jailer 'xheilë(r)/ **n.** rojtar burgu, gardian
jam /xhem/ **n.** 1. ngecje, mosfunksionim (i një aparati etj.); 2. bllokim (i rrjetit të qarkullimit); 2. hall; **be in a jam** jam në pozitë të vështirë; **vt.** 1. shtyp, shtrëngoj; 2. fut, rras, ngjesh; 3. mbush plot e përplot; 4. zë (kalimin)
jam /xhem/ **n.** reçel
January /'xhenjuëri/ **n.** janar
Japanese /,xhepë'ni:z/ **adj.** japonez; **n.** 1. japonishte; 2. japonez
jar /xha:r/ **n.** 1. kavanoz; 2. qyp; poçe
jaundice /'xho:ndis/ **n.** 1. **mjek.** verdhëz, të verdhët; 2. smirë, zili
jaw /xho:/ **n.** nofull
jazz /xhez/ **n.** xhaz
jealous /'xhelës/ **adj.** xheloz
jealousy /'xhelësi/ **n.** xhelozi; zili
jeans /xhi:nz/ **n.** pantallona xhinse
jeep /xhi:p/ **n.** xhips
jelly /'xheli/ **n.** 1. pelte; 2. xhelatinë
jerk /xhë:rk/ **n.** shtytje, tërheqje, ndalim i papritur
jersey /'xhë:zi/ **n.** fanellë, triko leshi
jest /xhest/ **n.** shaka; **in jest** me shaka; **vi.** bëj shaka
jet /xhet/ **n.** çurg, curril
Jesus /'xhi:zës/ **n.** Jezu
Jew /xhu:/ **adj.** izraelit; **n.** izraelit
jewel /'xhu:ël/ **n.** xhevahir, diamant; gur i çmuar
jewellery /'xhu:ëlri/ **n.** 1. xhevahire; 2. argjendari
Jewish /'xhu:ish/ **adj.** izraelit
jingle /'xhingl/ **n.** tringëllimë; **vti.** tringëlloj; tringëllon
job /xhob/ **n.** punë; **odd jobs** punë të rastit; **out of a job** pa punë; **on the job** në punë; **be paid by the job** paguhem sipas punës që bëj; **a good job** gjë e mirë, fat i madh; **just the job** tamam ajo që duhet
jobless /'xhoblis/ **adj.** i papunë
jog /xhog/ **vti.** 1. godas, shtyj lehtë; 2. troshitem; 3. tundem; 4. përparoj ngadalë; 5. vrapoj ngadalë
join /xhoin/ **vti.** 1. bashkoj, lidh; 2. bashkohem, bëhem anëtar; 3. marr pjesë; **join forces** bashkoj forcat; **join in** marr pjesë, futem; **n.** 1. bashkim; 2. pikë bashkimi, lidhjeje
joint /xhoint/ **n.** 1. pikë, vend bashkimi; 2. **anat.** kyç, nyjë; 3 kofshë, shpatull (mishi); **adj.** i bashkuar, i përbashkët; **joint- stock company** shoqëri aksionare; **joint efforts** përpjekje të përbashkëta; **vt.** bashkoj, lidh **joke** /xhouk/ **n.** shaka; **crack jokes** bëj shaka; **it is no joke** s'bëhet shaka; **make a joke about smb** tallem me
jolly /'xholi/ **adj.** i gëzueshëm, i gjallë
jolt /xhoult/ **n.** tronditje; troshitje
journal /'xhë:rnl/ **n.** revistë; gazetë
journalist /'xhë:rnëlist/ **n.** gazetar

journey /'xhë:rni/ **n.** udhëtim
jowl /xhaul/ **n.** nofull
joy /xhoi/ **n.** gëzim i madh, gjendje e gëzueshme
joyful /'xhoiful/ **adj.** i gëzuar, gëzimplotë, i gëzueshëm
jubilee /'xhu:bili:/ **n.** jubile, përvjetor
judge /xhaxh/ **n.** gjykatës; gjyqtar; **vti.** 1. gjykoj; 2. arbitroj; 3. vlerësoj
judgement /'xhaxhmënt/ **n.** 1. vendim gjyqi; 2. dënim, ndëshkim; 3. gjykim, mendim
jug /xhag/ **n.** brokë; kanë
juice /xhu:s/ **n.** lëng
juicy /'xhu:si/ **adj.** lëngës, me lëng, i lëngshëm
July /xhu:'lai/ **n.** korrik; **adj.** i korrikut
jump /xhamp/ **vti.** 1. kërcej, hidhem; 2. kapërcej; 3. hidhem, kërcej (nga frika, habia etj.); **n.** kërcim
jumper /'xhampë(r)/ **n.** 1. pulover; 2. xhup
junction /'xhankshn/ **n.** 1. bashkim, pikë takimi; 2. gjendje, kushte, rrethana; **at a critical junction** në gjendje kritike
June /xhu:n/ **n.** qershor
junior /'xhu:nië(r)/ **adj.** më i ri; i ri
juridical /xhuë'ridikl/ **adj.** juridik; ligjor
jurisprudence /,xhuëris'pru:dns/ **n.** jurisprudencë
jurist /'xhuërist/ **n.** jurist
jury /'xhuëri/ **n.** 1. juri; 2. trup gjukues
just /xhast/ **adj.** i drejtë; i arsyeshëm; **adv.** sapo, posa; pikërisht, tamam; **just about** sapo
justice /'xhastis/ **n.** drejtësi
justify /'xhastifai/ **vt.** përligj, justifikoj, arsyetoj
justly /'xhastli/ **adv.** drejtësisht
juvenile /'xhu:vënail/ **n.** djalosh; **adj.** djaloshar, rinor

K

kangaroo /,kengë'ru:/ **n.** kangur
keen /ki:n/ **adj.** 1. i mprehtë; 2. therës; keen sarcasm
sarkazmë therëse; 3. i hollë, i mprehtë; 4. i madh, i
fuqishëm, i fortë; **be keen on** pëlqej, jepem pas
keep /ki:p/ **vti.** 1. mbaj; ruaj; **keep silence** mbaj qetësi;
keep smb waiting lë dikë të presë; **keep a secret** e ruaj të
fshehtë; **keep up** vazhdoj; ruaj; mirëmbaj; mbaj lart; **keep
well** mbahem mirë; **keep one's word** mbaj fjalën; 2. qëndroj;
keep still qëndroj pa lëvizur; 3. vazhdoj (të bëj diçka);
keep at vazhdoj të bëj diçka; **keep going** vazhdoj; 4. pengoj,
vonoj, ndaloj; 5. respektoj (ligjin, rregullin etj.); **n.** 1.
shpenzimet e mbajtjes; 2. kullë (kështjelle)
keeping /'ki:pin/ **n.** 1. kujdes; 2. ruajtje; **in safe keeping**
në duar të sigurta; 3. pajtim; **in keeping with** në pajtim me
keepsake /'ki:pseik/ **n.** dhuratë (për kujtim), kujtim
kennel /'kenl/ **n.** stelë, kolibe (qeni)
kerb /kë:rb/ **n.** 1. anë rruge; 2. buzë trotuari
kerchief /'kë:rçif/ **n.** shami (koke)
kernel /'kë:rnl/ **n.** 1. thelb (arre etj.); 2. **fig.** thelb i një
çështjeje
kerosene /'kerësi:n/ **n.** vajguri; **a kerosene lamp** llampë
vajguri
kettle /'ketl/ **n.** ibrik, çajnik
key /ki:/ **n.** 1. çelës; 2. çelës (kurdisje); 3. tast; 4. **muz.**
çelës; 5. **fig.** çelës
keyboard /'ki:bo:rd/ **n.** tastierë
keyhole /'ki:houl/ **n.** vrimë çelësi
kick /kik/ **n.** 1. shqelmim; 2. zmbrapsje e armës; 3. kënaqësi;
vti. 1. shqelmoj; 2. zmbrapset arma
kid /kid/ **n.** 1. kec; 2. kalama, fëmijë; **vt.** mashtroj
kidnap /'kidnep/ **vt.** rrëmbej (një fëmijë etj.)
kidney /'kidni/ **n. anat.** veshkë
kill /kil/ **vti.** 1. vras; 2. ther (bagëtinë); 3. prish,
shkatërroj; 4. zhduk, shfaros; **kill the time** vras kohën
killer /'kilë(r)/ **n.** vrasës
kilo /'ki:lou/ **n.** kilogram
kilogram(me) /'kilëgrem/ **n.** kilogram
kin /kin/ **n.** 1. gjini, familje; 2. fis, farefis
kind /kaind/ **adj.** 1. i mirë, i dashur, i përzëmërt; 2. i
sjellshëm; **kind regards** të fala të përzëmërta; **n.** lloj, soj;
a kind of një lloj; **all kinds of** lloj-lloj
kindergarten /'kindëga:rtn/ **n.** kopsht fëmijësh
kind-hearted /,kaind'ha:rtid/ **adj.** zemërbutë, zemërdhembshur
kindle /'kindl/ **vti.** 1. ndez; 2. digjet, merr flakë
kindness /'kaindnis/ **n.** mirësi, dashamirësi
king /kin/ **n.** mbret
kingdom /'kindëm/ **n.** mbretëri
kiss /kis/ **vti.** puth; **n.** puthje
kit /kit/ **n.** 1. pajime
kitchen /'kiçin/ **n.** kuzhinë
kit-bag 'kitbeg/ **n.** çantë (ushtarake, sportive etj.)
kitchenette /,kiçi'net/ **n.** aneks
kite /kait/ **n.** balonë

kitten /'kitn/ **n.** kotele
knapsack /'nepsek/ **n.** çantë shpine
knead /ni:d/ **vt.** bëj, përgatis brumë
knee /ni:/ **n.** gju; **bring smb to his knees** gjunjëzoj dikë; **go down to one's knees** bie në gjunjë; **vi.** 1. gjunjëzoj; 2. shtyj, hap me gjunjë
knee-cap /'ni:kep/ **n.** 1. kupë e gjurit; 2. gjunjëse
kneel /ni:l/ **vi.** përgjunjem, gjunjëzohem, bie në gjunjë
knife /naif/ **n.** thikë; **vt.** pres, godas me thikë
knight /nait/ **n.** kalorës
knit /nit/ **vti.** 1. thur; 2. vrenjt (vetullat); 3. bashkoj; 4. lidh
knitting /'nitin/ **n.** 1. thurje; 2. thurimë
knock /nok/ **vt.** 1. trokas (në derë); 2. qëlloj, godit; 3. kritikoj; 4. kërcet, bën zhurmë; **knock down** hedh, rrëzoj për tokë; zbërthej, çmontoj; **knock smb out** e nxjerr jashtë luftimit (në boks)
knot /not/ **n.** 1. nyje, lidhje; **2. det.** nyje
know /nou/ **vti.** 1. di, jam në dijeni; 2. njoh, dalloj, shquaj; **n.** dijeni; **in the know** jam në brendësi të çështjes
know-how /'nouhao/ **n.** njohuri, shprehi, shkathtësi praktike
knowledge /'nolixh/ **n.** njohje, dituri, dije; **to my knowledge** me sa di unë; **with (without) one's knowledge** me (pa) dijeninë e
known /noun/ **adj.** i njohur

L

label /'leibl/ **n.** etiketë; **vt.** vë etiketën
laboratory /lë'borëtri; 'lebrëto:ri/ **n.** laborator
laborious /lë'boriës/ **adj.** 1. i vështirë; 2. i lodhshëm; 3. i
zellshëm **labor (labour)** /'leibë(r)/ **n.** punë; **vti.** 1. punoj;
2. lodhem, mundohem
labourer (laborer) /'leibërë(r)/ **n.** 1. punëtor; 2. argat
lace /leis/ **n.** 1. lidhëse; 2. dantellë; **vti.** 1. lidh me
lidhëse; 2. zbukuroj me dantella
lack /lek/ **n.** mungesë; **for lack of** për mungesë të; **vti.** i
mungon, ka mungesë
lad /led/ **n.** çun, djalë
ladder /'ledë(r)/ **n.** 1. shkallë; 2. syth i dalë, i ikur
ladle /'leidl/ **n.** sapllak, garuzhdë
lady /'leidi/ **n.** zonjë
lag /leg/ **n.** 1. prapambetje; 2. vonim; **vi.** mbetem prapa,
vonohem
lake /leik/ **n.** liqen
lamb /lem/ **n.** 1. qengj; 2. mish qengji
lame /leim/ **adj.** 1. i çalë; 2. që s'të bind, i pabesueshëm
lament /lë'ment/ **n.** vajtim; vaje, vaj, ligje; **vti.** 1. vajtoj,
qaj; 2. qahem, ankohem
lamentable /'lemëntëbl/ **adj.** 1. i vajshëm; 2. i vajtueshëm
lamp /lemp/ **n.** llambë
lampoon /lem'pu:n/ **n.** pamflet satirik
lamp-shade /'lempsheid/ **n.** abazhur
land /lend/ **n.** 1. tokë; 2. atdhe; 3. tokë, truall; 4. pronë
toke; **vti.** 1. zbres (në breg); 2. ul në tokë
landing /'lendin/ **n.** 1. zbritje; 2. ulje
landlady /''lenleidi/ **n.** pronare (shtëpish, hotelesh etj.)
landlord /'lendlo:rd/ **n.** 1. pronar (banesash, hotelesh); 2.
çifligar
landscape /'lendskeip/ **n.** peisazh, pamje
lane /lein/ **n.** 1. rrugicë; 2. shteg
language /'lengwixh/ **n.** gjuhë; **foreign language** gjuhë e huaj
lantern /'lentën/ **n.** fener (edhe **fig.**)
lap /lep/ **n.** prehër, pëqi
lapel /lë'pel/ **n.** jakë e xhaketës
lapse /leps/ **n.** 1. gabim, shkarje; 2. kalim i kohës; **vi.** 1.
bie (në koma etj); 2. kalon (koha); 3. kalon, skadon afati
lard /la:rd/ **n.** dhjamë (derri)
larder /la:dë(r)/ **n.** qilar
large /la:rxh/ **adj.** i madh; **at large** i lirë; gjerësisht,
hollësisht; **by and large** përgjithësisht, në tërësi
largely /'la:rzhli/ **adv.** 1. kryesisht; 2. në shkallë të madhe
lash /lesh/ **n.** fshikull, kamxhik, frushkull
last /la:st/ **adj.** 1. i fundit; 2. i kaluar; **last but one** i
parafundit; **n.** 1. mbarim, fund; 2. përfundim; **at long last** më
në fund; **to (till) the last** deri në fund; **vi.** 1. vazhdon; 2.
mjafton
lasting /'la:stin/ **adj.** i qëndrueshëm
lastly /'la:stli/ **adv.** më në fund, si përfundim
late /leit/ **adj.** i vonë, i vonshëm; i kohës së fundit; **adv.**
vonë; **later on** më vonë; **sooner or later** herët a vonë
lately /'leitli/ **adv.** 1. para pak kohe; 2. kohët e fundit

lateral /'letërël/ **adj.** anësor
lathe /leidh/ **n.** torno
lather /'la:dhë(r); 'ledhë(r)/ **n.** shkumë sapuni; **vti.** 1.
sapunis; 2. shkumëzoj **Latin** /'letin; 'letn/ **n.** latinishte;
adj. latin
latter /'letë(r)/ **adj.** i fundit (nga të dy)
lattice /'letis/ **n.** kangjelë, parmak
laud /lo:d/ **vt.** lavdëroj, mburr, lëvdoj
laugh /la:f/ **n.** e qeshur, qeshje; **break into a laugh** ia plas
të qeshurit; **vi.** qesh; **laugh off** kaloj me të qeshur; **laugh at**
qesh; tallem me
laughing /'la:fin; 'lefin/ **adj.** 1. i qeshur; 2. qesharak;
laughing-stock gaz i botës
laughter /'la:ftë(r); 'leftë(r)/ **n.** e qeshur; **burst into**
laughter ia jap të qeshurit
launch /lo:nç/ **vt.** 1. lëshoj; 2. hedh; 3. filloj, ndërmarr;
4. hidhem, lëshohem
laundry /lo:ndri/ **n.** 1. pastërti; 2. rroba për t'u larë
laurel /'lo:rël/ **n.** dafinë; **rest on one's laurels** fle mbi
dafina
lavatory /'levëtri; 'levëto:ri/ **n.** 1. lajtore; 2. banjë
lavish /'levish/ **adj.** bujar, dorëlëshuar, i pakursyer; **vt.**
shpenzoj pa kursim, pa hesap
law /lo:/ **n.** 1. ligj; 2. normë, rregull 3. e drejtë; 4.
drejtësi; 5. proces gjyqësor; **go to law against smb** hedh dikë
në gjyq; **lay down the law** bëj ligjin
law-court /'lo:ko:rt/ **n.** gjykatë
lawful /'lo:ful/ **adj.** i ligjshëm
lawless /'lo:lis/ **adj.** i paligjshëm
lawn /lo:n/ **n.** lëndinë
lawn-mower /'lo:nmouë(r)/ **n.** korrëse bari
lawsuit /'lo:sju:t/ **n.** padi
lawyer /'lo:jë(r)/ **n.** 1. jurist; 2. avokat
lay /lei/ **vti.** vë, vendos; 2. shtroj (tavolinën etj.); 3. bën
vezë (pula); 4. parashtroj; 5. ngarkoj, fajësoj; **lay off**
pushoj nga puna; pushoj, çlodhem; **lay on** furnizoj; **lay out**
shtroj, rregulloj, sistemoj; lë pa ndjenja (nga goditja)
layette /lai'et/ **n.** pelena
laziness /'leizinis/ **n.** përtaci, dembeli, përtesë
lazy /'leizi/ **adj.** dembel, përtac
lead /li:d/ **n.** 1. udhëheqje, drejtim; **take the lead** marr
drejtimin; 2. shembull; **follow sb's lead** ndjek shembullin e
dikujt; 3. roli kryesor; 4. krye, vend i parë; **vti.** 1. shpie,
çoj, shoqëroj; 2. prij, udhëheq; 3. kryesoj; 4. bëj, jetoj;
lead to çon në
leader /'li:dë(r)/ **n.** 1. udhëheqës; 2. kryeartikull
leadership /'li:dë(r)ship/ **n.** udhëheqje
leading /'li:din/ **adj.** 1. udhëheqës; 2. kryesor
leaf /li:f/ **n.** gjethe; **turn over a new leaf** filloj një jetë
të re **leaflet** /'li:flit/ **n.** 1. trakt; 2. fletushkë; 3. gjethe
e re, e njomë
league /li:g/ **n.** bashkim, lidhje, ligë; **the League of Nations**
Lidhja e Kombeve
leak /li:k/ **n.** 1. pikë; 2. pikim; 3. çurgë
leakage /'li:kixh/ **n.** 1. pikim; 2. dalje, përhapje e një të
fshehte

lean /li:n/ **adj.** 1. i dobët (mishi); 2. i hollë; **vti.** 1. prirem, anohem; 2. pjerr, përkul; 3. mbështetem
leap /li:p/ **n.** 1. kërcim; 2. hap; **vit.** 1. kërcej, hidhem; 2. kapërcej
leap-year /'li:pjiё(r)/ **n.** vit i brishtë
learn /lë:rn/ **vti.** 1. mësoj; 2. mësoj, marr vesh, marr njoftim; 3. nxjerr mësim; **learn by heart** mësoj përmendsh
lease /li:s/ **n.** 1. qiradhënie; 2. qira; **vt.** jap, marr me qira
leaseholder /'li:shouldë(r)/ **n.** qiradhënës
leash /li:sh/ **n.** 1. rrip (për të lidhur qenin); 2. **fig.** fre, kontroll
least /li:st/ **n.** sasia më e pakët; **at least** së paku; **not in the least** aspak; **adv.** më pak se; **adj.** më i vogli
leather /'ledhë(r)/ **n.** 1. lëkurë; 2. artikuj (lëkure)
leave /li:v/ **vti.** 1. iki, shkoj; 2. lë; 3. mbetet; 4. lë trashëgim; 5. ia besoj, ia dorëzoj; **leave someone alone** lë të qetë; **leave something alone** nuk trazoj; **leave behind** harroj; **leave for** nisem për; **leave go** lëshoj; **leave off** ndal, pushon; **leave out** lë jashtë, nuk përfshij; **leave something to someone** i lë trashëgim; **leave word** lë fjalë; **n.** 1. leje; **by (with) your leave** me lejen tuaj; 2. leje (e zakonshme); **on leave** me leje të zakonshme; 3. nisje, largim; **take leave of smb** ndahem me
lecture /'lekçë(r)/ **n.** 1. leksion; 2. qortim; **give smb a lecture** qortoj dikë; **vi.** 1. jap leksion; 2. qortoj
lecturer /'lekçërë(r)/ **n.** lektor
leek /li:k/ **n.** presh
left /left/ **adj.** i majtë; **n.** e majtë; **on the left** në të majtë
left-handed /,left'hendid/ **adj.** mëngjarash
leg /leg/ **n.** 1. këmbë; 2. këmbë (karrigeje, etj.)
legacy /'legësi/ **n.** 1. trashëgim; 2. trashëgimi
legal /'li:gl/ **adj.** ligjor; legal
legend /'lexhend/ **n.** legjendë
legible /'lexhëbl/ **adj.** i lexueshëm
legislate /'lexhisleit/ **vi.** nxjerr ligje
legislation /,lexhis'leishn/ **n.** legjislacion
legitimate /li'xhitimët/ **adj.** 1. ligjor, i ligjshëm; 2. i arsyeshëm
leisure /'lezhё(r)/ **n.** pushim, kohë e lirë, nge; **at one's leisure** në kohën e lirë
lemon /'lemën/ **n.** limon **lemonade** /,lemë'neid/ **n.** limonadë
lend /lend/ **vt.** 1. huaj, jap hua; 2. jap; **lend a hand** ndihmoj
length /length/ **n.** 1. gjatësi; **at length** më në fund; gjerësisht, hollësisht; 2. shkallë; 3. koha (për kryerjen e një pune)
lengthen /'lengthën/ **vti.** 1. zgjat, zgjatoj; 2. zgjatohem
lengthy /'lengthi/ **adj.** i gjatë
lenient /'li:niënt/ **adj.** i butë
lens /lenz/ **n. pl.** thjerrë, thjerrëz
leopard /'lepërd/ **n. zool.** leopard
less /les/ **adv.** më pak; **more or less** pak a shumë
lessen /'lesn/ **vti.** 1. ul, pakësoj, zvogëloj; 2. pakësohet
lesson /'lesn/ **n.** mësim
let /let/ **vti.** 1. lejoj; 2. lë; 3. le të; **let's/let us** le të; 4. jap me qira; **let smb alone** lë të qetë; **let go of** lëshoj; **let down** lë në baltë; ul, lëshoj poshtë; **let out** lëshoj; zgjeroj (fustanin etj)

letter /'letë(r)/ **n.** 1. shkronjë; 2. letër
letter-box /'letëboks/ **n.** kuti postare
lettuce /'letis/ **n.** sallatë e njomë, marule
level /'levl/ **n.** 1. nivel; 2. lartësi; 3. rrafshinë; 4.
nivelues; **vti.** 1. sheshoj; 2. rrafshoj; **adj.** i rrafshtë
lever /'li:vë(r); 'levër/ **n.** 1. levë; **2. fig.** levë; **vt.** ngre
me levë **liability** /,laië'bilëti/ **n.** 1. detyrim; përgjegjësi;
2. prirje; 3. pengesë; 4. **pl.** borxhe
liable /'laiëbl/ **adj.** 1. përgjegjës; 2. i prirur ndaj
liar /'laië(r)/ **n.** gënjeshtar
libel /'laibl/ **n.** shpifje
liberal /'libërël/ **adj.** 1. liberal; 2. dorëlëshuar, bujar; **n.**
liberal
liberate /'libëreit/ **vt.** çliroj
liberation /,libë'reishn/ **n.** çlirim
liberty /'libërti/ **n.** liri; **at liberty** i lirë
library /'laibrëri; 'laibreri/ **n.** bibliotekë
license (licence) /'laisëns/ **n.** 1. liçencë; 2. patentë;
driver's license patentë e shoferit; 3. dëshmi; 4. lejë
lick /lik/ **vt.** 1. lëpij; **lick one's lips** lëpij buzët; **lick
sb's boots** i puth këmbët dikujt
lid /lid/ **n.** 1. kapak; 2. qepallë
lie /lai/ **n.** gënjeshtër, mashtrim; **give the lie to something**
nxjerr gënjeshtrën në shesh; **vi.** gënjej
lie /lai/ **vi.** 1. shtrihem; 2. shtrihet, ndodhet; 3. qëndron;
lie down shtrihem; **lie in wait** rri në pritje
life /'laif/ **n.** 1. jetë; 2. mënyrë jetese; 3. jetëshkrim; 4.
gjallëri; **lead a life** jetoj, bëj një jetë; **run for your life**
ia mbath nga frika; **take sb's life** vras dikë; **spare sb's life**
i kursej jetën dikujt
life-belt /'laifbelt/ **n.** brez shpëtimi
life-boat /'laifbout/ **n.** varkë shpëtimi
life-insurance /'laif inshurëns/ **n.** sigurimi i jetës
lifeless /'laiflis/ **adj.** i pajetë; jofrymor
lifelike /'laiflaik/ **adj.** si i gjallë
lifetime /'laiftaim/ **n.** jetë, koha e jetës
lifelong /'laiflon/ **adj.** i përjetshëm
lift /lift/ **n.** 1. ashensor; 2. udhëtim falas në makinën e
tjetrit; **vti.** 1. ngre; ngrihet; 2. largohet
light /lait/ **n.** 1. dritë; 2. ndriçim; burim ndriçimi; 3.
zjarr; 4. ndezje; **in the light of** në dritën e; **bring
something to light** zbuloj, nxjerr në shesh; **cast (shed,
throw) light on something** hedh dritë mbi; **come to light** del
në dritë; **adj.** i lehtë; i butë; **vti.** 1. ndriçoj; 2. ndez; 3.
çelem në fytyrë
lighten /'laitn/ **vti.** 1. ndriçoj; 2. lehtësoj
lighter /'laitë(r)/ **n.** çakmak
lighthouse /'lait hauz/ **n.** far, fener
lightning /'laitnin/ **n.** vetëtimë, shkrepëtimë, rrufe
like /laik/ **vt.** pëlqej; **adj.** i ngjashëm; i njëjtë; **prep.** si
likely /'laikli/ **adj.** 1. i mundshëm, i ngjashëm; 2. i
besueshëm; 3. i përshtatshëm; **adv.** ka të ngjarë
likeness /'laiknis/ **n.** 1. ngjasim, ngjashmëri; 2. përngjasim
likewise /'laikvaiz/ **conj.** gjithashtu; **adv.** në të njëjtën
mënyrë

liking /'laikin/ **n.** pëlqim; dëshirë; **have a liking for** pëlqej; **to one's liking** sipas dëshirës të
lily /'lili/ **n. bot.** zambak
limb /lim/ **n.** gjymtyrë
lime /laim/ **n.** gëlqere; **vt.** gëlqeroj (tokën)
lime /laim/ **n. bot.** qitro
limit /'limit/ **n.** kufi, cak; **within limits** brenda mundësive, brenda caqeve **vt.** kufizoj, vë kufirin
limitation /,limi'teishn/ **n.** 1. kufizim; 2. mangësi
limited /'limitid/ **adj.** i kufizuar
limitless /'limitlis/ **adj.** 1. i pakufi; 2. i pakufishëm
limp /limp/ **vi.** çaloj; **n.** çalim
line /lain/ **n.** 1. vijë; 2. fill, tel, spango; 3. radhë, rresht; 4. vijë hekurudhore; 5. vijë (kufizuese); **read between the lines** lexoj mes rreshtave; **vti.** 1. vijëzoj, heq vija; 2. rreshtoj; radhitem; **line up** vihem në radhë
linen /'linin/ **n.** 1. pëlhurë e linjtë; 2. të linjtat; ndërresat
liner /'lainë(r)/ **n.** 1. transoqeanik; 2. avion pasagjerësh
linesman /'lainzmën/ **n.** vijërojtës
linguist /'lingwist/ **n.** gjuhëtar, linguist
linguistic /lin'gwistik/ **adj.** gjuhësor
lining /'lainin/ **n.** astar
link /link/ **n.** 1. hallkë (zinxhiri); 2. lidhje; **vti.** lidh, bashkoj
lion /'laiën/ **n.** luan
lioness /'laiënis/ **n.** luaneshë
lip /lip/ **n.** 1. buzë; 2. skaj, buzë; **the lip of a cup** buza e gotës; **bite one's lip** kafshoj buzët
lipstick /'lipstik/ **n.** të kuq buzësh
liquid /'likwid/ **n.** lëng; **adj.** i lëngshëm
liquor /'likë(r)/ **n.** 1. pije alkolike; 2. lëng
list /list/ **n.** listë; **vt.** 1. vë, shënoj (në listë); 2. hartoj një listë
listen /'lisn/ **vi.** 1. dëgjoj, kap me vesh; 2. i vë veshin; **listen to** dëgjoj
listener /'lisnë(r)/ **n.** dëgjues
literacy /'litërësi/ **n.** shkrim e këndim
literal /'litërël/ **adj.** i fjalëpërfjalshëm; **a literal translation** përkthim fjalë për fjalë
literate /'litërët/ **adj.** i mësuar, i kënduar
literature /'litrëçë(r)/ **n.** letërsi
litre (liter) /'li:të(r)/ **n.** litër
litter /'litë(r)/ **n.** hedhurina; mbeturina
little /'litl/ **adj.** 1. i vogël; 2. i paktë; **n.** një çikë; pak; **little by little** pak nga pak, gradualisht; **after a little** pas pak; **a little** pak
live /liv/ **vit.** 1. jetoj; 2. jam gjallë; 3. banoj; 4. kaloj jetën; **live on** jetoj me
live /laiv/ **adj.** 1. i gjallë; 2. direkt, i drejpërdrejtë
livelihood /'laivlihud/ **n.** jetesë, bukë e gojës; **earn (gain) one's livelihood** siguroj jetesën
lively /'laivli/ **adj.** 1. aktiv, i gjallë; 2. i gëzueshëm
liver /'livë(r)/ **n.** mëlçi

livestock /'laivstok/ **n.** 1. bagëti; 2. gjë e gjallë
living /'livin/ **n.** jetesë; **means of living** mjete jetese; **adj.** i gjallë
living-room /'livinru:m/ **n.** dhomë ndenjeje
load /loud/ **n.** ngarkesë; barrë; **vti.** 1. ngarkoj; 2. mbush
loaf /louf/ **n.** çyrek, franxhollë, pllakë (buke)
loan /loun/ **n.** 1. hua; 2. huadhënie, huamarrje; **vt.** jap hua
lobby /'lobi/ **n.** 1. holl; 2. hajat; korridor, paradhomë; 3. lobi
local /'loukl/ **adj.** 1. lokal, krahinor; 2. lokal, i pjesshëm; **n.** banor i një krahine
locality /lou'keliti/ **n.** 1. vend; 2. lokalitet
lock /lok/ **n.** 1. kyç; 2. portë; **vti.** 1. mbyll (dikë në shtëpi etj.); 2. kyç derën etj.; 3. kyçet, mbyllet; **lock smb in** mbyll dikë brenda; **lock up** mbyll me çelës
locksmith /'loksmith/ **n.** bravapunues, çelsabërës
lodge /loxh/ **vti.** 1. strehoj; 2. banoj, jetoj (si qirazhi); 3. ngulet; 4. bëj, paraqes; **lodge a complaint** bëj, paraqes një ankesë
lodger /'loxhë(r)/ **n.** qiraxhi
lodging /'loxhin/ **n.** 1. dhomë me qira; 2. fjetje
lofty /'lofti/ **adj.** 1. i lartë; 2. krenar, kryelartë
log /log/ **n.** kërcu
logical /'loxhikl/ **adj.** logjik **lollipop** /'lolipop/ **n.** gjel sheqeri
lonely /'lounli/ **adj.** 1. i vetëm; 2. i vetmuar; 3. i shkretë
long /lon/ **adj.** i gjatë; **in the long run** në fund të fundit; **for a long time** për një kohë të gjatë; **adv.** 1. gjatë, për një kohë të gjatë; 3. qëkur, prej kohësh; **long ago** shumë kohë më parë; **all day long** gjithë ditën; **so long!** mirëupafshim; **n.** kohë e gjatë; **before long** shpejt; **the long and the short of it** shkurt; **vi.** dëshirohem, digjem nga dëshira, nga malli
longing /'lonin/ **n.** mall
longitude /'lonxhitju:d; 'lonxhitu:d/ **n. gjeogr.** gjatësi
look /luk/ **vti.** 1. shikoj, hedh vështrimin; 2. dukem; 3. kërkoj; **look after** kujdesem; **look as if/look as though** duket sikur; **look at** shqyrtoj; konsideroj; shikoj; **look for** kërkoj; **look forward to** pres me padurim; **look into** shqyrtoj; studioj; **look on (upon)** vështroj; quaj, konsideroj; **look out!** kujdes!; **look over** shqyrtoj; **look round** shikoj përreth; **look through** shikoj, studioj me kujdes; **look up** ngre sytë; shikoj një fjalë në fjalor; **look like** duket si; **look up to smb** admiroj, respektoj dikë; **n.** 1. vështrim, shikim; 2. pamje; **have (take) a look at** shikoj; **good looks** pamje tërheqëse
looker-on /'lukër'on/ **n.** shikues
looking-glass /'lukingla:s/ **n.** pasqyrë
look-out /'luk aut/ **n.** 1. syhaptësi, vigjilencë; **be on the look-out for** i mbaj sytë hapur; 2. pikë vëzhgimi
loom /lu:m/ **n.** avlëmend, tezgjah, vegjë
loop /lu:p/ **n.** lak, nyjë
loose /lu:s/ **adj.** 1. i lirë, i çlirët; 2. i gjerë; 3. i shthurur; **break (get) loose** lëshohem, lirohem; **come loose** lirohet, zgjidhet (nyja); **let smb (sth) loose** lë të lirë; **lead a loose life** bëj jetë të shthurur; **vt.** liroj, çliroj, zgjidh
lorry /'lori/ **n.** kamion

lose /lu:z/ **vti. 1.** humb, humbas; **lose one's way** humb rrugën; **lose one's head** humb toruan; **lose heart** shkurajohem; **lose a chance (opportunity)** humb rastin; **lose one's balance** humb drejtpeshimin; **lose sight of** humb nga sytë; **lose (waste) no time in doing something** veproj pa humbur kohë; **2.** pësoj humbje; **3.** mbetet prapa (ora)

loser /'lu:zë(r)/ **n.** humbës

loss /los/ **n. 1.** humbje; **2.** dëm; **be at a loss** jam tym, s'di nga t'ia mbaj

lost /lost/ **adj.** i humbur; **be lost in something** humbas i tëri në, zhytem në

lot /lot/ **n. 1.** fat, kismet; **2.** llotari, short; **draw (cast) lots** hedh short

lot /lot/ **adv.** shumë; **a lot, lots** shumë

loud /laud/ **adj.** i lartë, i fortë, i zhurmshëm; **adv.** fort, me zë të lartë

loudspeaker /'laudspikë(r)/ **n.** altoparlant

love /lav/ **n. 1.** dashuri; **fall in love** bie në dashuri; **be in love with** dashuroj dikë; **make love** bëj dashuri; **2.** dëshirë, dashuri; **3.** i dashur, e dashur; **4.** përshëndetje, të fala; **give (send) smb one's love** përshëndet, i dërgoj të fala dikujt; **vt. 1.** dua, dashuroj; **2.** pëlqej

lovely /'lavli/ **adj. 1.** i bukur, tërheqës, i mrekullueshëm; **2.** i dashur

lover /'lavë(r)/ **n. 1.** dashnor; **2.** dashurues

loving /'lavin/ **adj.** i dashur

low /lou/ **adj. 1.** i ulët; **2.** i dobët; **3.** i trishtuar; **4.** i rëndomtë, vulgar; **adv.** poshtë

loyal /'loiël/ **adj.** besnik

loyalty /'loiëlti/ **n.** besnikëri

lubricate /'lu:brikeit/ **vt.** lubrifikoj, vajos

luck /lak/ **n. 1.** fat; **2.** fatbardhësi, lumturi; **as fate would have it** fatmirësisht; **in luck** fatlum, fatbardhë; **out of luck** fatkeq; **try one's luck** provoj fatin; **hard luck** fat i keq; **for luck** për fat

luckily /'lakili/ **adv.** fatmirësisht

lucky /'laki/ **adj.** me fat, fatlum, fatbardhë

luggage /'lagixh/ **n.** bagazh, plaçka udhëtimi

lukewarm /'lu:kwo:m/ **adj.** i vakët

lumber /'lambë(r)/ **n. 1.** lëndë drusore; **2.** rrangulla; rraqe

lump /lamp/ **n. 1.** copë (qymyri, dheu etj.); **2.** kokërr (sheqeri)

lunch /lanç/ **n.** drekë

lung /lan/ **n.** mushkëri

lurch /lë:rç/ **vi.** eci duke u lëkundur

lurk /lë:rk/ **vi.** rri në pritë, përgjoj

luxurious /lag'zhjuëriës/ **adj.** luksoz

luxury /'lakshëri/ **n.** luks

M

ma /ma:/ **n.** ma, nënë
macaroni /mekë'rouni/ **n.** makarona
machine /më'shi:n/ **n.** 1. makinë, mekanizëm, aparat; 2. **fig.** makinë
machinery /më'shi:nëri/ **n.** 1. makineri; 2. mekanizëm
mackintosh /'mekintosh/ **n.** mushama (shiu)
mad /med/ **adj.** 1. i çmendur, i marrë, i marrosur; 2. i tërbuar; **go mad** çmendem; **like mad** si i çmendur; **drive smb mad** e luaj dikë nga mendtë; **mad about** çmendem pas
made /meid/ **adj.** i prodhuar; **made in USA** prodhuar në SHBA
made-up /'meid'ap/ **adj.** 1. i sajuar; 2. i grimuar
madhouse /'medhauz/ **n.** çmendinë
madman /'medmën/ **n.** i çmendur, i marrë
madness /'mednis/ **n.** çmenduri
magazine /,megë'zi:n; 'megëzi:n/ **n.** 1. revistë; 2. depo (armësh)
magic /'mexhik/ **adj.** magjik
magician /më'xhishn/ **n.** magjistar
magistrate /'mexhistreit/ **n.** 1. gjykatës; 2. magjistrat
magnet /'megnit/ **n.** magnet
magnificent /meg'nifisnt/ **adj.** madhështor, i madhërishëm
maid /meid/ **n.** 1. vajzë, vashë; 2. shërbëtore
mail /meil/ **n.** 1. postë; 2. letra, pako, posta; **vt.** dërgoj me postë
mail-box /'meilboks/ **n.** kuti postare
mailman /'meilmen/ **n.** postier
maim /meim/ **n.** gjymtim, sakatim; **vt.** gjymtoj, sakatoj
main /mein/ **adj.** kryesor; **the main thing** gjëja kryesore; **n.pl.** 1. tubacioni kryesor i ujit, gazit etj; 2. linja qëndrore e energjisë elektrike; **in the main** kryesisht; **with might and main** me të gjitha forcat
mainly /'meinli/ **adv.** kryesisht; në pjesën më të madhe
maintain /men'tain/ **vt.** 1. mbaj, ruaj; 2. mirëmbaj; 3. mbaj (financiarisht); 4. pohoj
maintenance /'meintënëns/ **n.** 1. mbajtje; 2. mirëmbajtje; 3. mjete jetese
maize /meiz/ **n.** misër
majestic /më'xhestik/ **adj.** madhështor, i madhërishëm
major /'meixhë(r)/ **adj.** 1. kryesor; 2. më i rëndësishëm; 3. më i madh; **n.** major
majority /më'xho:riti/ **n.** shumicë; **gain (carry) the majority** fitoj shumicën
make /meik/ **vti.** 1. bëj; 2. prodhoj; 3. përgatit; 4. përfitoj; 5. detyroj; 6. bëhem; **make do** mbaroj punë me; **make for** shkoj drejt; sulem, turrem; **make off** ia mbath; **make out** kuptoj; shquaj, dalloj; plotësoj, mbush, përpiloj; **make sure (certain)** sigurohem; **make up** kompensoj; grimoj; shpik, trilloj; **make as if** bëj sikur; **make after smb** ndjek dikë; **make a bed** rregulloj shtratin; **make inquires** bëj hetime; **make up one's mind** vendos; **make money** bëj, fitoj para; **make use of** përdor, shfrytëzoj; **n.** markë, model, prodhim
maker /'meikë(r)/ **n.** krijues, bërës
malady /'melëdi/ **n.** sëmundje
male /meil/ **n.** mashkull; **adj.** mashkullor
malice /'melis/ **n.** shpirtligësi, ligësi, keqdashje
malicious /më'lishës/ **adj.** i keq, i lig
malign /më'lain/ **adj.** 1. i dëmshëm, i rrezikshëm; 2. shpirtkeq, keqdashës

malignant /më'lignënt/ **adj.** 1. shpirtlig, zemërkeq; 2. **mjek.** i keq

malnutrition /'meln(j)u:'trishn/ **n.** të ushqyerit keq

malt /mo:lt/ **n.** malt, maja (birre)

maltreat /mel'tri:t/ **vt.** keqtrajtoj, keqpërdor

maltreatment /mel'tri:tmënt/ **n.** keqtrajtim

man /men/ **n.** 1. njeri; 2. burrë; 3. mashkull; 4. punëtor; 5. gur (shahu); 6. bashkëshort; **man in the street** njeri i zakonshëm; **vt.** plotësoj me njerëz

manage /'menixh/ **vti.** 1. qeveris, drejtoj; 2. ia dal mbanë

management /'menixhmënt/ **n.** 1. drejtim, qeverisje; 2. përdorim; 3. aftësi; 4. udhëheqje, administratë; drejtori

manager /'menixhë(r)/ **n.** 1. drejtues, administrator; 2. manazher

manhood /'menhu:d/ **n.** 1. burrëri; 2. burrërim

maniac /'meiniek/ **adj.** maniak; **n.** maniak

manifest /'menifest/ **vti.** 1. tregoj qartë; 2. shfaq; **adj.** i qartë

manifestation /,menife'steishn/ **n.** 1. shfaqje; 2. manifestim

manifold /'menifould/ **adj.** 1. i shumëfishtë; 2. i shumanshëm; 3. i shumëllojshëm

manipulate /më'nipjuleit/ **vt.** manipuloj

manipulation /më'nipju'leishn/ **n.** manipulim

mankind /,men'kaind/ **n.** njerëzim

manlike /'menlaik/ **adj.** burrëror

manly /'menli/ **adj.** burrëror

manner /'menë(r)/ **n.** 1. mënyrë, formë, rrugë; 2. **pl.** sjellje; **all manner of** lloj-lloj; **in a manner** në një farë mënyre

mantlepiece /'mentlpi:s/ **n.** 1. buhari e oxhakut; 2. raft mbi oxhak

manual /'menjuël/ **adj.** krahu; **n.** manual, doracak

manufacture /,menju'fekçë(r)/ **vt.** prodhoj; fabrikoj; **n.** prodhim

manufacturer /,menju'fekçërë/ **n.** 1. prodhues; 2. fabrikant

manure /më'njuë(r)/ **n.** pleh organik

manuscript /'menjuskript/ **n.** dorëshkrim

many /'meni/ **adj.** shumë; **a good many** shumë; **how many?** sa?; **many a time** shpesh

map /mep/ **n.** hartë; **on the map** i famshëm, i rëndësishëm

marble /'ma:rbl/ **n.** mermer

march /ma:rç/ **n.** 1. marshim; **on the march** në marshim; 2. rrjedhë, zhvillim i ngjarjeve; 3. **muz.** marsh

March /ma:rç/ **n.** mars

mare /meë(r)/ **n.** pelë

margarine /,ma:xhë'rin; 'ma:rxhërin/ **n.** margërinë **marine** /më'ri:n/ **n.** 1. flotë; **merchant (mercantile) marine** flotë tregëtare; 2. marinar; 3. marinës; **adj.** detar

mariner /më'ri:në(r)/ **n.** marinar

marital /'meritl/ **adj.** bashkëshortor

mark /ma:rk/ **n.** 1. shenjë; 2. njollë; 3. shenjë, nishan; 4. tregues; 5. simbol; 5. notë; 6. markë (monedhë); **up to the mark** në lartësinë e duhur; **vt.** 1. shënoj; 2. vë një shënim a shenjë; 3. vërej; 4. vlerësoj me notë; **mark time** bëj në vend numëro

market /'ma:rkit/ **n.** 1. treg, pazar; **put something on the market** nxjerr në pazar; 2. tregti; **on the market** në treg; **vit.** tregtoj

marketing /'ma:rketin/ **n.** marketing

marmalade /'ma:mëleid/ **n.** marmelatë

marriage /'merixh/ **n.** martesë
married /'merid/ **adj.** i martuar, bashkëshortor; **get married**
martohem; **newly-married couple** çift i martuar rishtas
marry /'meri/ **vti.** martoj; martohem
marsh /ma:rsh/ **n.** kënetë
martial /'ma:rshl/ **adj.** 1. ushtarak; 2. luftarak
martyr /'ma:të(r)/ **n.** martir, dëshmor
marvel /'ma:rvël/ **n.** çudi, habi, mrekulli; **vi.** habitem,
mahnitem, mrekullohem
marvelous /'ma:vëlës/ **adj.** mahnitës; i mrekullueshëm
masculine /'meskjulin/ **adj.** mashkullor; **n.** 1. gjini
mashkullore; 2. mashkull
mash /mesh/ **n.** pure
mask /mesk/ **n.** maskë (edhe **fig.**); **vt.** 1. maskoj, maskohem; 2.
fig. maskoj
mason /'meisn/ **n.** 1. murator; 2. gurlatues; 3. mason **mass**
/mes/ **n.** 1. masë; 2. grumbull; 3. shumicë; **mass production**
prodhimi në seri; **in the mass** në masë
mass /mes/ **n. fet.** meshë
massacre /'mesëkë(r)/ **n.** masakër; **vt.** masakroj
massage /'mesa:zh/ më'sa:zh/ **n.** masazh; **vt.** bëj masazh
massive /'mesiv/ **adj.** 1. masiv; 2. i madh; 3. i rëndë
master /'ma:stë(r)/ 'mestë(r)/ **n.** 1. pronar; 2. mësues; 3.
kryefamiljar; 4. mjeshtër; **vt.** 1. zotëroj; 2. përmbaj, mposht
master-key /'ma:stëki:/ **n.** çelës kopil
mastermind /'ma:stëmaind/ **n.** mjeshtër i organizimit,
planifikimit
masterpiece /'ma:stëpi:s/ **n.** kryevepër
mat /met/ **n.** 1. hasër; 2. rrogoz; 3. udhëz
match /meç/ **n.** 1. shkrepëse; 2. ndeshje; 3. rival; 4. shok;
meet your match gjej shokun; **vti.** 1. ndeshem, bëj garë; 2.
shkon, përshtatet, harmonizohet; 3. krahasohet
match-box /'meçboks/ **n.** kuti shkrepësesh
mate /meit/ **n.** 1. shok; 2. bashkëshort(e)
material /më'tiëriël/ **n.** 1. material, lëndë; 2. stof; **adj.**
material, lëndor
maternity /më'të:rnëti/ **n.** amësi; **maternity home** maternitet,
shtëpi lindjeje
mathematics /,methë'metiks/ **n.** matematikë
matrimony /'metrimëni/ **n.** martesë
matter /'metë(r)/ **n.** 1. lëndë, substancë; 2. çështje; 3.
materie; 4. rëndësi; **no matter** s'ka rëndësi; **a matter of
course** një çështje e natyrshme; **What is the matter?** Si është
puna? **as a matter of fact** faktikisht, në të vërtetë; **no
matter** pavarësisht se si; **vi.** ka rëndësi; **it doesn't
matter** s'ka rëndësi
matter-of-course /'metë(r) ëv'ko:z/ **adj.** i natyrshëm
mature /më'tjuë(r)/ **adj.** 1. i pjekur, i arrirë; 2. i maturuar
maturity /më'tjuëriti/ **n.** pjekuri
maximum /'meksimëm/ **n.** maksimum
May /mei/ **n.** maj
may /mei/ **v. aux.** mund, mundem, ka mundësi
maybe /'meibi/ **adv.** ndoshta, mbase
mayor /meë(r)/ 'meiër/ **n.** kryetar bashkie

me /mi:/ **pron.** mua
meadow /'medou/ **n.** livadh
meager (meagre) /'mi:gë(r)/ **adj.** 1. i dobët, thatanik; 2. i
varfër, i pamjaftueshëm
meal /mi:l/ **n.** 1. vakt ushqimi; 2. ushqim
mealtime /'mi:ltaim/ **n.** koha e ngrënies
mean /mi:n/ **vt.** 1. kam si qëllim; 2. do të thotë, ka
kuptimin; 3. nënkupton; 4. ka rëndësi; **adj.** 1. i poshtër, i
keq, i ulët; 2. mediokër, i rëndomtë; **n.** mjet
meaning /'mi:nin/ **n.** kuptim
means /mi:nz/ **n.** 1. rrugë, mënyrë, mjet; **by all means** me të
gjitha mjetet; **by means of** me anë të; **by no means** në asnjë
mënyrë; **by some means or other** në një mënyrë a në një tjetër;
2. para, pasuri; **a man of means** njeri i pasur
measure /'mexhë(r)/ n. masë; përmasë; **take measures** marr masa
measurement /'mexhëmënt/ **n.** matje; përmasë
meat /mi:t/ **n.** mish
mechanic /mi'kenik/ **n.** mekanik
mechanic(al) /mi'kenik(l)/ **adj.** 1. mekanik; 2. automatik
medal /'medl/ **n.** dekoratë, medalje
meddle /'medl/ **vi.** ndërhyj, përzihem
mediation /,mi:di'eishn/ **n.** ndërmjetësim
medical /'medikl/ **adj.** mjekësor
medicine /'medsin; 'medisin/ **n.** 1. mjekësi; 2. ilaç
medium /'mi:diëm/ **n.** 1. mjet; 2. mënyrë; 3. mjedis; **adj.**
mesatar
meek /mi:k/ **adj.** i bindur, i urtë, i butë **meet** /mi:t/ **vti.** 1.
takoj; takohem; 2. plotësoj (një dëshirë); 3. njihem,
prezantohem; **meet a bill** paguaj llogarinë
meeting /'mi:tin/ **n.** mbledhje
megaphone /'megëfoun/ **n.** megafon
melody /'melëdi/ **n.** melodi
melon /'melën/ **n.** pjepër
melt /melt/ **vti.** 1. shkrij, shkrihet; 2. zhduket
member /'membë(r)/ **n.** anëtar
membership /'membëship/ **n.** anëtarësi
memorize /'memëraiz/ **vt.** memorizoj, mbaj mend
memory /'memëri/ **n.** 1. kujtesë; 2. kujtim; **in memory of** në
kujtim të; **to the best of my memory** me sa më kujtohet; **commit
something to memory** fiksoj në kujtesë
menace /'menës/ **n.** 1. kërcënim; 2. rrezik
mend /mend/ **vti.** 1. ndreq, riparoj, meremetoj; 2. përmirësoj;
rregulloj; 3. përmirësohem, e marr veten
mending /'mendin/ **n.** ndreqje, rregullim, riparim
mental /'mentl/ **adj.** mendor, psikik; mental patient i sëmurë
psikik
mention /'menshën/ **vt.** përmend, zë në gojë; **don't mention it**
s'ka përse; **not to mention** pa përmendur; **n.** përmendje
menu /'menju:/ **n.** menu, listë gjellësh
merchandise /'më:rçëndaiz/ **n.** mallra
merchant /'më:çënt/ **n.** tregtar; **adj.** tregtar
merciful /'më:siful/ **adj.** i mëshirshëm
merciless /'më:silis/ **adj.** i pamëshirshëm
mercy /'më:si/ **n.** mëshirë; **at the mercy of** në mëshirë të

mere /mië(r)/ **adj.** i thjeshtë
merely /'mië(r)li/ **adv.** thjesht, vetëm
merge /më:rxh/ **vti.** 1. shkrij, bashkoj; 2. shkrihem
merger /'më:rxhë(r)/ **n.** shkrirje, bashkim
merit /'merit/ **n.** meritë; **vt.** meritoj
merriment /'merimënt/ **n.** gëzim, gazmend
merry /'meri/ **adj.** i gëzuar, i gëzueshëm; **make merry**
zbavitem, dëfrehem, festoj
merry-go-round /'merigou,raund/ **n.** karusel, rrotullame
mess /mes/ **n.** rrëmujë; **in a mess** rrëmujë
message /'mesixh/ **n.** njoftim, lajm, mesazh
messenger /'mesinxhë(r)/ **n.** lajmëtar, lajmës, kasnec
metal /'metl/ **n.** metal
metallurgy /me'telëxhi/ **n.** metalurgji
metaphor /'metëfë(r)/ **n.** metaforë
meter /'mi:të(r)/ **n.** kontator, sahat
method /'methëd/ **n.** 1. metodë; 2. mënyrë veprimi
meter (metre) /'mi:të/ **n.** metër
metric /'metrik/ **adj.** metrik; the metric system sistemi
metrik
metropolis /më'tropëlis/ **n.** 1. kryeqytet; 2. metropol
metropolitan /,metrë'politën/ **adj.** kryeqytetas, i kryeqytetit
mew /mju:/ **vi.** mjaullin (macja); **n.** mjaullimë
microbe /'maikroub/ **n.** mikrob
microphone /'maikrëfoun/ **n.** mikrofon
microscope /'maikrëskoup/ **n.** mikroskop
mid /mid/ **adj.** i mesit
midday /,mid'dei/ **n.** mesditë
middle /'midl/ **adj.** i mesëm; **n.** mes
middle-aged /,midl'eixhd/ **adj.** me moshë mesatare
midnight /'midnait/ **n.** mesnatë
midwife /'midwaif/ **n.** mami
might /mait/ **n.** fuqi, forcë; **with might and main** me të gjitha
forcat; **with all one's might** me gjithë fuqinë
mighty /'maiti/ **adj.** 1. i fuqishëm; 2. i madh
migrant /'maigrënt/ **n.** shtegtar
migrate /mai'greit/ **vi.** shtegtoj
migration /mai'greishn/ **n.** shtegtim
mild /maild/ **adj.** i butë
mile /mail/ **n.** milje
milestone /'mailstoun/ **n.** gur kilometrazhi
militant /'militënt/ **adj.** militant, luftarak; **n.** militant
military /'militëri/ **adj.** ushtarak
milk /milk/ **n.** qumësht; **vt.** mjel
milky /'milki/ **adj.** 1. qumështor; 2. i bardhë si qumësht; **the
Milky Way** Udha e Qumështit
mill /mil/ **n.** 1. mulli (drithi); 2. fabrikë, uzinë
miller /'milë(r)/ **n.** mullis
milliard /'milia:rd/ **n.** miliard
million /'miljën/ **n.** milion
millionaire /,miljë'neë(r)/ **n.** milioner
mimosa /mi'mouzë/ **n.** mimozë
mince /mins/ **vti.** grij (mishin); **n.** mish i grirë

mind /maind/ n. 1. mendje; **keep (bear) in mind** ruaj në
mendje; **bring (call) something to mind** sjell ndër mend; **be
out of one's mind** e ka lënë mendja; **be of one mind** jam i një
mendjeje; **be in two minds about something** jam me dy mendje;
take one's mind off something heq mendjen nga diçka; 2.
mendim; **make up one's mind** vendos; **to my mind** sipas mendimit
tim; 2. mend, kujtesë; 3. qëllim, synim; **vti.** 1. tregoj, bëj
kujdes; **mind! mind out!** kujdes!; 2. kundërshtoj, jam kundër;
never mind s'ka gjë, nuk prish punë
mine /main/ **poss. pron.** imi, imja, të mitë, të miat
mine /main/ n. 1. minierë; 2. minë
miner /'mainë(r)/ n. minator
mineral /'minërël/ n. mineral; **adj.** mineral
minister /'ministë(r)/ n. 1. ministër; 2. meshtar
ministry /'ministri/ n. 1. ministri, kabinet; 2. shërbim, shërbesë
minor /'mainë(r)/ **adj.** 1. më i vogël; më i ri; 2. i
parëndësishëm, i dorës së dytë; 3. **muz.** minor
minority /mai'norëti/ n. 1. pakicë; 2. minoritet
mint /mint/ n. **bot.** nenexhik, mendër
minus /'mainës/ **prep.** minus, pa
minute /'minit/ n. 1. minutë; çast; **in a minute** në çast; **just
a minute!** një minutë!; **the minute that** sapo; 2. **pl.**
protokoll, proçesverbal
minute /mai'n(j)u:t/ **adj.** 1. i imët, i vogël; 2. i hollësishëm
minute-hand /'minithend/ n. akrepi i minutave
miracle /'mirëkl/ n. mrekulli, çudi; **work miracles** bëj
çudira; **by a miracle** nga një mrekulli
miraculous /mi'rekjulës/ **adj.** 1. i mrekullueshëm; 2.
çudibërës **mire** /'maië(r)/ n. 1. baltë, lluçë; 2. **fig.** batak
mirror /'mirë(r)/ n. pasqyrë; **vt.** pasqyroj
mirth /më:rth/ n. gaz, gëzim
misbehave /'misbi'heiv/ **vi.** sillem keq
miscarriage /mis'kerixh; 'miskerixh/ n. 1. dështim; 2. **mjek.**
dështim
miscarry /mis'keri/ **vi.** 1. dështoj, nuk arrij; 2. **mjek.** dështoj
mischief /'misçif/ n. 1. djallëzi; 2. qëllim i keq; 3.
shejtanllëk, çapkanllëk
mischievous /'misçivës/ **adj.** 1. i dëmshëm; 2. i mbrapshtë; 3.
çapkën, trazovaç
miser /'maizë(r)/ n. koprac, kurnac
miserable /'mizrëbl/ **adj.** 1. i mjerë, fatkeq; 2. i keq, i
mjerueshëm
misery /'mizëri/ n. 1. mjerim, varfëri; **live in misery** jetoj
në mjerim; 2. mizerje
misfortune /mis'fo:çju:n/ n. 1. fat i keq; 2. fatkeqësi, e keqe
misgiving /mis'givin/ n. 1. dyshim; 2. ndjenjë druajtjeje,
shqetësimi
mishap /'mishep/ n. 1. aksident fatkeq; 2. fat i keq
mislead /mis'li:d/ **vt.** 1. çorientoj; 2. fut në rrugë të
shtrembër
misleading /mis'li:din/ **adj.** çorientues, keqorientues
misprint /mis'print/ n. gabim shtypi; **vt.** shtyp me gabime
Miss /mis/ n. zonjushe
miss /mis/ **vti.** 1. nuk qëlloj në shenjë; 2. nuk arrij, më
ikën, më lë (treni etj.); 3. më merr malli, ndiej mungesën
missile /'misail/ n. raketë; **guided missile** raketë e
telekomanduar
mission /'mishn/ n. mision, detyrë

missionary /'mishënri; 'mishëneri/ **n.** misionar
mist /mist/ **n.** mjegull
mistake /mis'teik/ **n.** gabim; keqkuptim; **by mistake** gabimisht;
vti. gaboj; gabohem; **be mistaken** jam gabim; **mistake smb (sth)**
for smb (sth) ngatërroj me
mistaken /mis'teikën/ **adj.** i gabuar
mister /'mistë(r)/ **n.** zotëri
mistress /'mistris/ **n.** zonjë shtëpie, amvisë
mistrust /mis'trast/ **n.** mosbesim; **vt.** nuk i besoj
misunderstand /,mis,andë'stand/ **vt.** keqkuptoj
misunderstanding /,mis,andë'stendin/ **n.** keqkuptim
misuse /mis'ju:z/ **vt.** shpërdoroj, përdor gabim; **n.**
/,mis'ju:s/ shpërdorim; përdorim i gabuar
mitten /'mitn/ **n.** dorezë (me një gisht)
mix /miks/ **vti.** 1. përziej; 2. përzihem; **mix up** përziej;
ngatërroj
mixed /mikst/ **adj.** i përzier
mixture /'miksçë(r)/ **n.** përzierje
moan /moun/ **n.** 1. rënkim; 2. uturimë; **vi.** 1. rënkoj; 2.
ankohem
mob /mob/ **n.** turmë
mobile /'moubail/ **adj.** 1. i lëvizshëm, lëvizës; 2. i
ndryshueshëm
mobility /mou'bilëti/ **n.** lëvizshmëri
mock /mok/ **n.** tallje, qesëndi; **vti.** tall, vë në lojë
mocking /'mokin/ **adj.** tallës, qesëndisës
mode /moud/ **n.** 1. mënyrë (veprimi); 2. modë; 3. zakon; 4.
gjuh. mënyrë
model /moudl/ **n.** 1. model, mostër; 2. **art.** model, pozues; 3.
model, maket; 4. manekin; **vti.** modeloj; **adj.** shembullor
moderate /'modërët/ **adj.** i matur, i përkorë, i përmbajtur;
vti. /'modëreit/ ul, zbut
moderation /,modë'reishn/ **n.** moderim; përmbajtje; përkore;
zbutje
modern /'modën/ **n.** i kohës, bashkëkohor, modern; **modern**
languages gjuhët moderne
modest /'modist/ **adj.** modest, i thjeshtë; i përmbajtur, i
përkorë
modesty /'modisti/ **n.** modesti, thjeshtësi
modify /'modifai/ **vt.** 1. modifikoj; 2. ul, zbut
moist /moist/ **adj.** i njomur, i lagët
moisture /'moisçë(r)/ **n.** lagështirë
mole /moul/ **n.** urith
moment /'moumënt/ **n.** moment, çast; **at the moment** tani; **in a**
moment në çast; **this moment** këtë çast
momentary /'moumënteri/ **adj.** i çastit, i çastshëm
momentous /mou'mentës/ **adj.** i rëndësishëm
Monday /'mandi/ **n.** e hënë
monetary /'maniteri/ **adj.** monetar; monetary unit njësi monetare
money /'mani/ **n.** para, të holla; **make money** fitoj para
money-changer /'mani,çeinxhë(r)/ **n.** kambist
money order /'mani,ordë(r)/ **n.** mandat pagese
money-lender /'mani,lendë(r)/ **n.** fajdexhi
monk /mank/ **n.** murg
monkey /'manki/ **n.** majmun
monopoly /më'nopëli/ **n.** monopol
monotonous /më'notënës/ **adj.** monoton
monotony /më'notëni/ **n.** monotoni

monstrous /'monstrës/ **adj.** 1. i përbindshëm, monstruoz; 2. i
llahtarshëm; 3. i tmerrshëm
month /manth/ **n.** muaj
monthly /'manthli/ **adj.** mujor, i përmuajshëm; **n.** e
përmuajshme; **adv.** çdo muaj
monument /'monjumënt/ **n.** monument, përmendore
mood /mu:d/ **n.** 1. gjendje shpirtërore; **be in the mood for** kam
qejf të, jam i prirur të; 2. **gjuh.** mënyrë
moon /mu:n/ **n.** hënë; **once in a blue moon** një herë në hënë;
full moon hënë e plotë; **cry for the moon** kërkoj të pamundurën
moonlight /'mu:nlait/ **n.** dritë e hënës
mop /mop/ **n.** shtupë, sukull, leckë; **vt.** laj me leckë
moral /'mo:rël/ **adj.** moral, i moralshëm; i moralit; **n.** 1.
moral; 2. pl. sjellje morale
morale /më'ra:l/ **n.** moral, gjendje e lartë morale
morbid /'mo:bid/ **adj.** i sëmurë
more /mo:(r)/ **adj.** më, më i madh; **adv.** më, më shumë; **once
more** edhe një herë; **more or less** pak a shumë **moreover**
/mo:'rovë(r)/ **adv.** përveç kësaj, për më tepër
morning /'mo:nin/ **n.** mëngjes; **adj.** mëngjesor
morsel /'mo:sl/ **n.** kafshatë
mortal /'mo:rtl/ **adj.** 1. i vdekshëm; 2. vdekjeprurës; **mortal
wound** plagë vdekjeprurëse; 3. i betuar
mortality /mo:'teliti/ **n.** mortalitet, vdekshmëri
mortgage /'mo:gixh/ **n.** 1. peng, rehen; 2. hipotekë; **vt.** lë
peng
mosque /mosk/ **n.** xhami
mosquito /mës'ki:tou/ **n.** mushkonjë
moss /mos/ **n.** myshk
most /moust/ **adj.** shumica e; **most people** shumica e njerëzve;
n. pjesa më e madhe; **adv.** më
mostly /'moustli/ **adv.** në pjesën më të madhe, kryesisht
mother /'madhë(r)/ **n.** nënë
motherhood /'madhë(r)hu:d/ **n.** amësi
mother-in-law /'madhë(r) in lo:/ **n.** vjehërr
motherland /'madhë(r)lend/ **n.** mëmëdhe, atdhe
motherless /'madhë(r)lis/ **adj.** i panënë
motion /'moushn/ **n.** 1. lëvizje; **put something in motion** vë
diçka në lëvizje; 2. gjest; 3. propozim
motionless /'moushnlis/ **adj.** i palëvizur
motivate /'moutiveit/ **vt.** shtyj, nxis; motivoj
motivation /,mouti'veishn/ **n.** nxitje, motivim
motive /'moutiv/ **n.** motiv; **adj.** lëvizës; **motive force** forcë
lëvizëse
motor /'moutë(r)/ **n.** 1. motor; 2. **fig.** motor, forcë lëvizëse;
motor bike motoçikletë; **motor car** veturë; **motor boat**
motobarkë
motorist /'moutërist/ **n.** shofer, ngarës (i makinës)
mould /mould/ **n.** myk; **vi.** zë myk
mountain /'mauntin/ **n.** mal
mountaineer /,maunti'niё(r)/ **n.** alpinist
mountaineering /,maunti'niёrin/ **n.** alpinizëm
mountainous /'mauntinёs/ **adj.** malor
mournful /'mo:rnful/ **adj.** 1. i trishtuar, i pikëlluar; 2.
zije

mouse /maus/ n. (pl. mice) mi
mousetrap /'maustrep/ n. çark (minjsh)
moustache (mustache) /mës'ta:sh/ n. mustaqe
mouth /mauth/ n. 1. gojë; 2. grykë (lumi)
movable /'mu:vëbl/ adj. 1. i lëvizshëm, i luajtshëm; 2. i
tundshëm
move /mu:v/ vti. 1. lëviz, zhvendos, luaj; 2. prek,
mallëngjej; 3. futem në shtëpi të re; n. 1. zhvendosje,
lëvizje; 2. veprim; 3. ndërrim banese; move house ndërroj
shtëpi; 4. hap, veprim; be on the move jam në lëvizje; get a
move on shpejtoj
movement /'mu:vmënt/ n. lëvizje
movie /'mu:vi/ n. film (kinematografik); the movies kinema;
industria e prodhimit të filmave
moving /'mu:vin/ adj. 1. prekës, mallëngjyes; 2. lëvizës;
moving picture film; moving staircase shkallë lëvizëse
much /maç/ adj. i shumtë; adv. shumë; how much? sa?; n. shumë
mud /mad/ n. baltë; throw (fling,sling) mud at smb hedh baltë
mbi
muffler /'maflë(r)/ n. 1. shall; 2. zhurmëmbytës
mug /mag/ n. 1. gotë; 2. krikëll mule /mju:l/ n. mushkë; as
obstinate as a mule kokëfortë si mushka
multicolored /,malti'këlërd/ adj. shumëngjyrësh
multi-lingual /'malti'lingwël/ adj. shumëgjuhësh
multi-millionaire /,maltimiljë'neë(r)/ n. multimilioner
multiple /'maltipl/ adj. i shumëfishtë; n. mat. shumëfish
multiplication /,maltipli'keishn/ n. shumëzim; multiplication
table tabelë shumëzimi
multiply /'maltiplai/ vti. 1. shumëzoj; shumëfishoj; 2. rrit,
shumoj
multitude /'maltit(j)u:d/ n. grumbull, masë, mori, mizëri
(njerëzish, etj.)
municipal /mju:'nsipl/ adj. bashkiak
murder /'më:dë(r)/ n. vrasje; commit murder kryej një vrasje
murderer /'më:dërë(r)/ n. vrasës
murderous /'më:dërës/ adj. vrasës
murk /më:rk/ n. 1. errësirë; 2. zymtësi
murmur /'më:rmë(r)/ n. murmuritje, murmurimë; gurgullimë;
shushurimë
muscle /'masl/ n. muskul
muscular /'maskjulë(r)/ adj. muskulor
museum /mju:'ziëm/ n. muzeum
mushroom /'mashrum/ n. kërpudhë; vi. rritet, shfaqet shpejt
music /'mju:zik/ n. 1. muzikë; 2. muz. partiturë
musical /'mju:zikl/ adj. muzikor; n. komedi, film muzikor
music-hall /'mju:zikhol/ n. teatër variete
musician /mju:'zishn/ n. muzikant
mussel /'masl/ n. midhje
must /mëst; mast/ aux. v. duhet
mustard /'mastërd/ n. mustardë
mutable /'mjutëbl/ adj. i ndryshueshëm
mute /mju:t/ adj. 1. memec; 2. i heshtur; 3. i pazëshëm n.
memec
mutilate /'mju:tileit/ vt. gjymtoj, sakatoj
mutiny /'mjutini/ n. kryengritje, revoltë; vi. ngre krye
mutton /'matn/ n. mish deleje, dashi
mutual /'mju:çuël/ adj. reciprok, i ndërsjellë

mutually /'mju:çuëli/ **adv.** reciprokisht
my /mai/ **poss. pron.** imi, imja; të mitë, të miat
myself /mai'self/ **refl. pron.** vetë, veten; **by myself** vetëm
mysterious /mi'stiëriës/ **adj.** misterioz, i mistershëm
mystery /'mistëri/ **n.** fshehtësi, mister
myth /mith/ **n.** mit
mythology /mi'tholëxhi/ **n.** mitologji

nail /neil/ **n.** 1. gozhdë; **hit the right nail on the head** qëlloj në shenjë; 2. thua; **fight tooth and nail** luftoj me mish e me shpirt; 3. kthetër, çapua

naive /na'i:v/ **adj.** naiv, i patëkeq

naked /'neikid/ **adj.** lakuriq, i zhveshur; **the naked truth** e vërteta lakuriq; **see with the naked eye** shoh me sy (pa mjete optike)

name /neim/ **n.** 1. emër; **in the name of** në emër të; **call smb names** shaj dikë; 2. emër, famë, nam; **make a name for oneself** bëj emër, bëhem i dëgjuar; **vt.** 1. i vë emrin; 2. emëroj, përmend me emër

nameless /'neimlis/ **adj.** 1. i paemër; 2. i paparë, i padëgjuar

namely /'neimli/ **adv.** domethënë

nap /nep/ **n.** dremitje, dremkë; **take a nap** marr një sy gjumë; **vi.** dremit, kotem

napkin /'nepkin/ **n.** 1. pecetë; 2. pelenë

nappy /nepi/ **n.** pelenë

narcotic /na:'kotik/ **adj.** narkotik; **n.** narkotik

narrate /në'reit; 'nereit/ **vt.** rrëfej, tregoj

narrative /'nerëtiv/ **adj.** narrativ; **n.** tregim, rrëfenjë

narrow /'nerou/ **adj.** i ngushtë; **have a narrow escape** shpëtoj për qime

narrow-minded /,nerou'maindid/ **adj.** mendjengushtë

nasty /'na:sti; 'nesti/ **adj.** 1. i keq, i ndyrë; 2. i ulët, i poshtër; 3. i rrezikshëm

nation /'neishn/ **n.** 1. komb; 2. shtet; 3. vend

national /'neshnël/ **adj.** 1. kombëtar; **national hymn** himn kombëtar; 2. shtetëror

nationalism /'neshnëlizëm/ **n.** nacionalizëm

nationalist /'neshnëlist/ **n.** nacionalist; **adj.** nacionalist

nationality /,neshë'neliti/ **n.** 1. kombësi; 2. shtetësi

nationalize /'neshnëlaiz/ **vt.** 1. shtetëzoj; 2. jap shtetësinë

native /'neitiv/ **adj.** 1. vendës; 2. i lindjes; 3. i lindur, i natyrshëm; 4. amtar; **n.** vendës

natural /'neçrël/ **adj.** 1. i natyrshëm, natyror; 2. i lindur; 3. normal; 4. i thjeshtë, i çiltër

naturalization /,neçrëlai'zeishn/ **n.** natyralizim

naturally /'neçrëli/ **adv.** 1. natyrisht; 2. natyrshëm

nature /'neiçë(r)/ **n.** 1. natyrë; 2. natyrë, karakter; 3. lloj

naught /no:t/ **n.** asgjë

naughty /'no:ti/ **adj.** 1. i pabindur, i padëgjueshëm; 2. i mbrapshtë, i prapë; **a naughty child** fëmijë i prapë

naval /'neivl/ **adj.** detar, i flotës ushtarako-detare

navigation /,nevi'geishn/ **n.** lundrim

navy /'nevi/ **n.** flotë ushtarako-detare

near /nië(r)/ **adj.** i afërm, i afërt; **prep.** 1. afër, pranë; 2. rreth; **adv.** pranë, rreth; **near at hand** pranë, afër; **near by** afër, ngjitur

nearby /'nië(r)bai/ **adj.** i afërm; **adv.** pranë

nearly /'niëli/ **adv.** 1. afërsisht; 2. gati, pothuaj

near-sighted /,nië(r)'saitid/ **adj.** miop, dritëshkurtër

neat /ni:t/ **adj.** 1. i pastër; 2. i rregullt; 3. i thjeshtë; 4. i goditur; 5. shqeto, i papërzier; 6. i paholluar

necessarily /,nesë'sërili/ **adv.** doemos, domosdo

necessary /'nesësëri; 'nesëseri/ **adj.** 1. i nevojshëm; 2. i domosdoshëm; **n.** gjë e domosdoshme
necessity /ni'sesëti/ **n.** 1. nevojë; 2. domosdoshmëri; **in case of necessity** në rast nevoje
neck /nek/ **n.** 1. qafë; **break one's neck** thyej qafën; **neck and neck** hap më hap, barabar; **save one's neck** shpëtoj kokën; 2. grykë shisheje
necklace /'neklis/ **n.** gjerdan
necktie /'nektai/ **n.** gravatë
need /ni:d/ **n.** nevojë; **be in need of** kam nevojë për; **if need be** në rast nevoje; **vt.** 1. kam nevojë; 2. duhet, nevojitet
needful /'ni:dful/ **adj.** i nevojshëm
needle /ni:dl/ 1. gjilpërë (për të qepur); 2. gjilpërë, shigjetë, akrep; 3. grep (për të thurur)
needless /ni:dlis/ **adj.** i panevojshëm, i tepërt; **needless to say** është e tepërt të themi
needlework /'ni:dlwë:k/ **n.** 1. qepje; 2. qëndisje
needy /'ni:di/ **adj.** nevojtar
negative /'negëtiv/ **n.** 1. mohim; 2. **fot.** negativ; **adj.** negativ, mohues
neglect /ni'glekt/ **n.** pakujdesi, mospërfillje; **vt.** 1. lë pas dore; 2. braktis; 3. neglizhoj
negligence /'neglixhëns/ **n.** neglizhencë, shkujdesje, moskokëçarje
negligent /'neglixhënt/ **adj.** neglizhent, i pakujdesshëm, mospërfillës
negotiable /ni'goushiëbl/ **adj.** 1. i bisedueshëm; 2. i kalueshëm; 3. i këmbyeshëm
negotiate /ni'goshieit/ **vti.** 1. zhvilloj bisedime; 2. arrij marrëveshje (nëpërmjet bisedimeve); 3. kapërcej, kaloj
negotiation /ni,goushi'eishn/ **n.** bisedime; **enter into negotiations** hyj në bisedime; **conduct negotiations** bëj bisedime
Negro /ni'grou/ **n.** zezak
neigh /nei/ **n.** hingëllimë
neighbor (neighbour) /'neibë/ **n.** fqinj
neighbo(u)rhood /'neibëhud/ **n.** 1. fqinjësi; fqinjëri; 2. afërsi; **in the neighborhood of** në afërsi të
neighbo(u)ring /'neibërin/ **adj.** fqinj; kufitar
neither /'naidhë(r); 'ni:dhë(r)/ **adj.** asnjë prej; **conj.** as; **neither...nor** as...as
neon /'ni:on/ **n.** neon
nephew /'nefju:/ **n.** nip
nerve /në:v/ **n.** 1. **anat.** nerv; 2. vetëpërmbajtje, gjakftohtësi; **strain every nerve** tendos nervat; 3. forcë vullneti, energji; 4. paturpësi; **have the nerve to do something** ka paturpësinë të; 5. **pl.** nervozizëm; **get on sb's nerves** i acaroj nervat dikujt
nervous /'në:vës/ **adj.** 1. nervor; 2. nervoz
nest /nest/ **n.** 1. fole; 2. **fig.** strehë, fole; **vi.** ndërtoj fole
net /net/ 1. rrjetë; 2. kurth, grackë; 3. **sport.** rrjetë; **adj.** neto; **net cost** kostoja neto; **net profit (weight)** fitimi (pesha) neto;
network /'netwë:k/ **n.** rrjet (televiziv, hekurudhor etj.)
neuter /'nju:të/ **n. gjuh.** gjini asnjanëse; **adj.** asnjanës
neutral /'nju:trël/ **adj.** neutral, asnjanës

neutron /'n(j)u:tron/ **n.** neutron
never /'nevë(r)/ **adv.** kurrë; **never mind** s'ka gjë; as mos e përmend
nevertheless /,nevëdhë'les/ **adv.** megjithatë, prapëseprapë **new** /nju:; nu:/ **adj.** 1. i ri ; 2. i freskët
new-born /'nju:bo:rn/ **adj.** i porsalindur
newcomer /'nju:kamë(r)/ **n.** i ardhur rishtas
newly /'nju:li/ **adv.** 1. rishtas; 2. para pak kohe
news /nju:z/ **n.** lajm; të reja; **break the news** jap lajmin e keq
news agent /'nju:z,eixhënt/ **n.** gazetashitës
newspaper /'nju:speipë(r); 'nu:zpeipë(r)/ **n.** gazetë
news-stand /'nju:zstend/ **n.** qoshk gazetash
next /nekst/ **adj.** 1. vijues, pasues; 2. i ardhshëm; **next to nothing** thuajse asgjë; **adv.** pastaj, pas kësaj
next-door /,nekst'do:(r)/ **adv.** 1. ngjitur; 2. përballë
nib /nib/ **n.** majë pene
nice /nais/ **adj.** 1. i këndshëm; 2. i dashur; 3. delikat; 4. i hollë
nicety /'naisiti/ **n.** saktësi, përpikëri; **to a nicety** me përpikëri
nickel /'nikl/ **n.** 1. nikel; 2. **amer.** monedhë (pesë qindarkëshe)
nickname /'nikneim/ **n.** nofkë
niece /ni:s/ **n.** mbesë
night /nait/ **n.** natë; **good night!** natën e mirë!; **night and day** ditë e natë; **all night** gjithë natën; **at night** në mbrëmje; **in the dead of night** në mes të natës
nightclub /'naitklab/ **n.** klub nate
nightdress /'naitdres/ **n.** këmishë nate
nightingale /'naitingeil/ **n. zool.** bilbil
nightly /'naitli/ **adj.** 1. i natës; 2. i përnatshëm; **adv.** për natë, natë për natë
nightmare /'naitmeë(r)/ **n.** ankth, makth
nightwatchman /,nait'woçmën/ **n.** roje nate
nil /nil/ **n.** zero
nine /nain/ **n.** nëntë
nineteen /,nain'ti:n/ **n.** nëntëmbëdhjetë
nineteenth /,nain'ti:nth/ **adj.** i nëntëmbëdhjetë; **n.** i nëntëmbëdhjeti
ninetieth /'naintiëth/ **adj.** i nëntëdhjetë; **n.** i nëntëdhjeti
ninety /'nainti/ **n.** nëntëdhjetë
ninth /nainth/ **adj.** i nëntë; **n.** i nënti
nip /nip/ **vti.** 1. pickoj, cimbis; 2. prish, dëmton (ngrica); **nip in the bud** asgjësoj që në embrion; 3. shpejtoj; **n.** pickim; kafshim
no /nou/ **adv.** 1. jo, kurrsesi; 2. aspak; **adj.** 1. asnjë; 2. kurrfarë; **no admittance** ndalohet hyrja; **no doubt** pa dyshim; **no one** askush; **no smoking!** ndalohet duhani!
noble /'noubl/ **adj.** 1. fisnik, bujar; 2. **hist.** fisnik; 3. madhështor; **n.** fisnik
nobleman /'noublmën/ **n.** fisnik
nobly /'noubli/ **adv.** fisnikërisht
nobody /'noubëdi/ **pron.** askush; **n.** hiç; **he's a nobody** ai është një hiç
nod /nod/ **n.** përshëndetje me kokë
noise /noiz/ **n.** zhurmë, potere; **noiseless** /'noizlis/ **adj.** i pazhurmë

noisily /'noizili/ **adv.** me zhurmë
noisy /'noizi/ **adj.** i zhurmshëm; zhurmëmadh
nominate /'nomineit/ **vt.** 1. vë kandidaturën; 2. emëroj si kandidat; 3. emëroj
nominee /,nomi'ni:/ **n.** kandidat
non- /non/ **prefix** jo-; pa-
nonaligned /,nonë'laind/ **adj.** i paangazhuar
none /nan/ **pron.** askush, asnjë; **adv.** aspak
non-existent /,nonig'zistnt/ **adj.** që nuk ekziston, joekzistues
non-payment /,non'peimënt/ **n.** mospagim
nonsense /'nonsens/ **n.** marrëzi, budallallëk, gjepura
noon /nu:n/ **n.** mesditë
nor /no:(r)/ **conj.** as
norm /no:rm/ **n.** normë
normal /'no:rml/ **adj.** normal, i zakonshëm
north /no:rdh/ **n.** veri; **adj.** në veri; **adj.** verior
northern /'no:rdhën/ **adj.** verior
nose /nouz/ **n.** 1. hundë; 2. nuhatje; **blow one's nose** shfryj hundët; **lead smb by the nose** tërheq për hunde; **under one's nose** para hundës së dikujt; **have a good nose** kam nuhatje të mirë; **vti.** 1. nuhas; 2. ecën, çan përpara
nostril /'nostrël/ **n.** vrimë e hundës
not /not/ **adv.** nuk; jo; mos; **not at all** aspak, fare; s'ka për se
notable /'noutëbl/ **adj.** i shquar, i dalluar
notary /'noutëri/ **n.** noter
note /nout/ **n.** 1. shënim, pusullë; 2. **pl.** shënime; **take down notes** mbaj shënime; 3. **muz.** notë; 4. vëmendje; **take note of** dëgjoj me vëmendje; 5. ton; **change one's note** ndërroj ton; 6. notë; **vt.** 1. mbaj shënim; 2. vërej, i vë mendjen
note-book /'noutbuk/ **n.** fletore shënimesh
noted /'noutid/ **adj.** i njohur, i përmendur
noteworthy /'noutwë:rdhi/ **adj.** i shquar, që meriton vëmendje
nothing /'nathin/ **n.** asgjë; hiç; **come to nothing** dështon; **for nothing** falas; kot; **have nothing to do with smb** s'kam të bëj me dikë; **mean nothing to** s'ka kuptim për
notice /'noutis/ **n.** 1. shpallje, lajmërim; **put up a notice** vë një shpallje; 2. paralajmërim; 3. vrojtim, mbikqyrje; 4. vëmendje; **come to sb's notice** i bie në sy; **take no notice of** nuk i kushtoj vëmendje; **give notice** vë në dijeni; **vti.** vërej, vë re
noticeable /'noutisëbl/ **adj.** i dallueshëm
notice-board /'notisbo:d/ **n.** stendë (për njoftime)
notification /,noutifi'keishn/ **n.** 1. njoftim, lajmërim; 2. shpallje
notify /'noutifai/ **vt.** njoftoj, lajmëroj
notion /'noushn/ **n.** nocion, mendim, ide
notorious /nou'to:riës/ **adj.** famëkeq
nought /not/ **n.** 1. asgjë; 2. zero
noun /naun/ **n.** emër
nourish /'narish/ **vt.** ushqej (edhe **fig.**)
nourishing /'narishin/ **adj.** ushqyes
nourishment /'narishmënt/ **n.** ushqim
novel /'novl/ **n.** roman; **adj.** 1. i ri; 2. i çuditshëm
novelist /'novëlist/ **n.** romancier

November /nou'vembë(r)/ **n.** nëntor; **adj.** i nëntorit
now /nau/ **adv.** 1. tani, tashti; **just now** sapo; **till (up) to
now** deri tani; **from now on** tani e tutje; **now or never** o tani
o kurrë; 2. menjëherë; **n.** këtë çast; **conj.** tani që
nowadays /'nauëdeiz/ **adv.** sot, tani, në ditët tona
nowhere /'nouweë(r)/ **adv.** asgjëkundi, në asnjë vend
nuclear /'nju:klië(r)/ **adj.** nuklear, bërthamor; **nuclear
energy** energji bërthamore
nucleus /'n(j)u:kliës/ **n.** 1. bërthamë; 2. bërthamë (e atomit,
molekulës etj.)
nude /n(j)u:d/ **adj.** i zhveshur; lakuriq
nudge /naxh/ **vt.** cek, shtyj lehtë me bërryl
nuisance /'n(j)u:sns/ **n.** 1. bezdi; 2. mërzi; 3. njeri i
bezdisshëm
null /nal/ **adj.** i paefektshëm; i pafuqishëm; **null and void** i
pavlefshëm
numb /nam/ **adj.** i mpirë
number /'nambë(r)/ **n.** 1. numër; 2. numër, sasi; **a number of**
një sasi; 3. numër (i revistës etj.); **vt.** 1. numëroj; 2.
arrin numrin
numeral /'n(j)u:mërël/ **n.** 1. numur, shifër; 2. **gjuh.** numëror
numerous /'n(j)u:mërës/ **adj.** i shumtë
nun /nan/ **n.** murgeshë
nurse /në:rs/ **n.** 1. infermiere; 2. kujdestare fëmijësh; 3.
dado
nursery /'në:sëri/ **n.** 1. dhomë (fëmijësh); 2. çerdhe; 3.
fidanishte
nut /nat/ **n.** 1. arrë; **a hard nut to crack** çështje e vështirë;
2. **tek.** dado
nutrition /n(j)u:trishn/ **n.** ushqim
nutritious /n(j)u:'trishës/ **adj.** i ushqyeshëm
nylon /'nailën/ **n.** najlon

O

oak /ouk/ **n.** lis, dushk

oar /o:(r)/ **n.** lopatë, rrem

oath /outh/ **n.** be, betim; **make (take, swear) an oath** bëj betimin; **on my oath** për besë

oats /outs/ **n. pl.** tërshërë

oatmeal /'outmi:l/ **n.** miell (qull, bollgur) tërshëre

obedience /ë'bi:diëns/ **n.** bindje

obedient /ë'bi:diënt/ **adj.** i bindur, i dëgjueshëm; an obedient child fëmijë i dëgjueshëm

obey /ë'bei/ **vti.** dëgjoj, bindem

obituary /ë'bitjuëri/ **n.** nekrologji

object /'obxhikt/ **n.** 1. objekt, send; 2. synim, qëllim; 3. **gram.** kundrinë; /ëb'xhekt/ **vit.** 1. kundërshtoj; 2. protestoj

objection /ëb'xhekshn/ **n.** kundërshtim; **have an objection to** jam kundër

objective /ëb'xhektiv/ **adj.** 1. objektiv; 2. i paanshëm; **n.** qëllim, pikësynim, objektiv

objectively /ëb'xhektivli/ **adv.** objektivisht

obligate /'obligeit/ **vt.** detyroj, i vë detyrim

obligation /,obli'geishn/ **n.** 1. detyrim; 2. zotim; **fulfil an obligation** përmbush një detyrim

obligatory /o'bligëtri; 'ë'bligëto:ri/ **adj.** i detyrueshëm

oblige /ë'blaixh/ **vt.** 1. detyroj; shtrëngoj; **be obliged to do something** jam i detyruar të; 2. i bëj nder

obliging /ë'blaixhin/ **adj.** i gjindshëm, nderbërës

obscene /ëb'si:n/ **adj.** 1. i pahijshëm; 2. i turpshëm

obscure /ëb'skjuë(r)/ **adj.** 1. i errët, i turbullt; 2. i panjohur; 3. i pakuptueshëm, i paqartë; **vt.** 1. errësoj; 2. fsheh, mbuloj

observation /,obzë'veishn/ **n.** 1. vrojtim, vëzhgim; 2. mbikqyrje; **be under observation** jam nën mbikqyrje; **keep smb under observation** mbaj nën mbikqyrje

observe /ëb'zë:v/ **vti.** 1. respektoj; 2. mbaj; 3. vërej, vëzhgoj, vrojtoj

observer /ëb'zëvë(r)/ **n.** vrojtues; vëzhgues

obsolete /'obsëli:t/ **adj.** i vjetëruar; i dalë jashtë përdorimit

obstacle /'obstëkl/ **n.** pengesë; **overcome (surmount) obstacles** kapërcej pengesat

obstinate /'obstënët/ **adj.** kokëfortë, kokëngjeshur; **as obstinate as a mule** ngul këmbë si mushka

obstruct /ëb'strakt/ **vt.** 1. bllokoj; 2. pengoj

obtain /ëb'tein/ **vti.** 1. marr, fitoj, siguroj; 2. përdoret, është në veprim

obvious /'obviës/ **adj.** 1. i qartë, i dukshëm; 2. i kuptueshëm

occasion /ë'keizhn/ **n.** 1. rast; **on the occasion of** me rastin e; **take the occasion** përfitoj nga rasti; 2. ngjarje; **vt.** jap shkas për

occasional /ë'keizhënl/ **adj.** i rastësishëm, rastësor

occupation /,okju'peishn/ **n.** 1. punë, detyrë; 2. pushtim, okupacion; 3. zënie

occupational ,okju'peshënl/ **adj.** profesional

occupy /'okjupai/ **vt.** 1. jetoj, banoj; 2. zë; 3. pushtoj (një vend)

occur /ë'kë(r)/ **vti.** 1. ndodh, ngjan; 2. më bie ndër mend; 3. ndeshet, haset

ocean /'oushn/ **n.** oqean
o'clock /ë'klok/ **adv.** në orën; **at six o'clock** në orën gjashtë
October /ok'toubë(r)/ **n.** tetor
odd /od/ **adj.** 1. i çuditshëm; 2. **mat.** tek; 3. i tepërt; 4. i
rastit
odds /odz/ **n. pl.** gjasa, shanse, mundësi
odor (odour) /'oudë(r)/ **n.** erë, aromë, kundërmim
of /ov; ëv/ **prep.** i, e, të; prej; për; **of course** natyrisht
off /o:f/ **prep.** prej, nga; larg; **adv.** larg,; jashtë; **on and
off** kohë pas kohe; **badly off** i varfër; **well off** i pasur
offense (offence) /ë'fens/ **n.** 1. shkelje, kundërvajtje; 2.
fyerje; **take offence** fyhem, prekem, zemërohem; 3. bezdi,
shqetësim; 4. **usht.** sulm
offend /ë'fend/ **vti.** 1. shkel (ligjin); 2. fyej; 3. ngacmon,
vret (veshin)
offender /ë'fendë(r)/ **n.** 1. fyes; 2. kundërvajtës, shkelës
offensive /ë'fensiv/ **adj.** 1. ofendues, fyes; 2. i pakëndshëm,
i neveritshëm; 3. sulmues; **n.** ofensivë, mësymje; **take the
offensive** kaloj në mësymje
offer /'o:fë(r)/ **vt.** 1. ofroj; 2. paraqes; **n.** ofertë;
propozim; **on offer** për shitje
office /'o:fis/ **n.** zyrë; 2. ministri, dikaster; 3. nëpunësi;
ofiq; detyrë
officer /'ofisë(r)/ **n.** 1. oficer; 2. nëpunës
official /ë'fishël/ **adj.** zyrtar; official report raport
zyrtar; **n.** zyrtar
offspring /'o:fsprin/ **n.** 1. pasardhës; 2. pinjoll; 3. pjellë
often /'o:fn/ **adv.** shpesh; **how often?** sa herë?
oil /oil/ **n.** 1. vaj; 2. naftë; **strike oil** gjej, zbuloj naftë;
3. bojëra vaji; **vt.** vajoj, lyej me vaj
oil-color /'oil,këlër(r)/ **n.** bojë vaji
oil-painting /'oilpeintin/ **n.** pikturë në vaj
oil-tanker /'oiltenkë(r)/ **n.** anije çisternë; autobot
oilwell /'oilwel/ **n.** pus nafte
oily /'oili/ **adj.** vajor; i vajosur
ointment /'ointmënt/ **n.** melhem; pomadë
old /ould/ **adj.** 1. plak, i moshuar; **grow old** plakem; **how old
are you?** sa vjeç jeni?; **old age** pleqëri; 2. i vjetër; 3. i
lashtë, i kohës së shkuar; **an old friend of mine** një shoku im
i vjetër
old-fashioned /,ould'feshnd/ **adj.** i vjetëruar, i modës së
vjetër
olive /'oliv/ **n.** ulli; **olive oil** vaj ulliri
omelette /'omlit/ **n.** omëletë
omen /'oumën/ **n.** shenjë, ogur
omit /ou'mit/ **vt.** 1. lë jashtë; 2. lë pas dore
on /on/ **prep.** në, mbi; **adv.** më tutje, më tej; **from now on** që
tani e tutje; **and so on** e të tjera; **go on** vazhdoj; **on and on**
pa pushim; **later on** më vonë
once /wans/ **adv.** njëherë, dikur; **once more** edhe një herë;
once in a while nganjëherë; **once and for all** një herë e
përgjithmonë; **at once** menjëherë; **all at once** befas, papritur;
menjëherë; **once upon a time** një herë e një kohë
one /wan/ **num.** një; **one by one** një nga një; **adj.** i njëjtë;
pron. dikush; **one another** njëri tjetrin

oneself /wan'self/ **pron.** veten; vetë; **by oneself** vetëm; **be oneself** jam në vete; **come to oneself** vij në vete
one-way /'wanwei/ **adj.** i njëkahshëm (trafiku)
onion /'aniën/ **n.** qepë
onlooker /'onlukë(r)/ **n.** spektator, shikues, soditës
only /'ounli/ **adv.** vetëm; **if only** sikur; **adj.** i vetëm; **an only child** fëmijë i vetëm; **conj.** po, mirëpo, vetëm, veç
onrush /'onrash/ **n.** 1. sulm; 2. vërshim
onward(s) /'onwëd(z)/ **adv.** përpara
open /'oupën/ **adj.** 1. i hapur; 2. i zbuluar, i hapur; 3. **fig.** i hapur, i sinqertë, i çiltër; 4. i pazgjidhur; **vti.** 1. hap, çel; 2. hapet
opener /'oupnë(r)/ **n.** hapëse (shishesh, konservash etj.)
opening /'oupnin/ **n.** 1. e çarë, brimë; 2. fillim, hyrje; 3. hapje, çelje
openly /'oupnli/ **adv.** 1. hapur, haptas; 2. çiltas
opera /'op(ë)rë/ **n.** opera
opera-house /'op(ë)rëhaus/ **n.** teatri i operas
operate /'opëreit/ **vti.** 1. veproj, vë në veprim; 2. punon, funksionon; 3. **mjek.** operoj
operation /,opë'reishn/ **n.** 1. veprim, punë; **put into operation** vë në veprim; 2. **mjek.** operacion
operator /'opëreitë(r)/ **n.** 1. operator; centralist, telegrafist; 2. kirurg
opinion /ë'piniën/ **n.** mendim, opinion; **in my opinion** sipas mendimit tim; **be of the opinion that** kam mendimin se; **have a good opinion of smb** kam mendim të mirë për dikë; **share sb's opinion** jam i një mendimi me
opium /'oupiëm/ **n.** opium
opponent /ë'pounënt/ **n.** kundërshtar, oponent; **adj.** kundërshtar
opportunity /,opë't(j)u:nëti/ **n.** mundësi, rast; **take the opportunity** shfrytëzoj rastin
oppose /ë'pouz/ **vt.** 1. kundërvë, ballafaqoj; 2. kundërshtoj
opposite /'opëzit/ **adj.** i kundërt; **adv.** kundër, përballë, përkundrjet; **prep.** përkundrejt
opposition /,opë'zishn/ **n.** 1. opozitë, kundërshtim; **be in opposition to** jam në opozitë me; 2. rezistencë, qëndresë
oppress /ë'pres/ **vt.** shtyp, nënshtroj
oppression /ë'preshn/ **n.** shtypje, nënshtrim
oppressive /ë'presiv/ **adj.** shtypës
oppressor /ë'presë(r)/ **n.** shtypës
optical /'optikl/ **adj.** optik, pamor; **optical illusion** iluzion optik **optician** /op'tishn/ **n.** okulist
optimist 'optimist/ **n.** optimist
optimistic /,opti'mistik/ **adj.** optimist
option /'opshn/ **n.** opsion, mundësi zgjedhjeje, alternativë
optional /'opshnl/ **adj.** fakultativ, i padetyrueshëm
or /o:(r)/ **conj.** apo; ose; **or else** për ndryshe
oral /'o:rël/ **adj.** gojor
orally 'o:rëli/ **adv.** gojarisht
orange /'orinxh/ **n.** portokall; ngjyrë portokalli; **adj.** i portokalltë
orator /'o:rëtë(r)/ **n.** orator

orbit /'o:rbit/ **n.** orbitë
orchard /'o:çëd/ **n.** kopsht
orchestra /'o:kistrë/ **n.** orkestër
orchestral /o:'kestrël/ **adj.** orkestral
ordeal /o:'di:l/ **n.** provë e rëndë
order /'o:dë(r)/ **n.** 1. renditje; **alphabetical (chronological)
order** renditje alfabetike (kronologjike); 2. rregull; **in
order** në rregull; **out of order** i prishur; 3. rend; **keep order**
ruaj rendin; **restore order** vendos rendin; 4. urdhër; **give
orders** jap urdhra; **by order of** me urdhër të; **on sb's order**
sipas urdhrit të dikujt; **in order to (that)** me qëllim që; 5.
porosi; **made to order** bërë me porosi; **vt.** 1. urdhëroj; 2.
porosit; 3. rregulloj, vë në rregull
orderly /'o:dëli/ **adj.** 1. i rregullt, i pastërt; 2. i
disiplinuar; **n.** 1. ordinancë; 2. sanitar
ordinary /'o:dënri; 'o:rdëneri/ **adj.** i zakonshëm, i rëndomtë;
out of the ordinary i jashtëzakonshëm, i pazakontë
ore /o:(r)/ **n.** mineral, xeheror
organ /'o:gën/ **n.** 1. organ (i trupit); 2. organ (i shtypit
etj.); 3. **muz.** organo
organic /o:'genik/ **adj.** organik
organism /'o:gënizëm/ **n.** organizëm
organization /,o:gënai'zeishn/ **n.** 1. organizim; 2. organizëm
organize /'o:gënaiz/ **vt.** organizoj
organizer 'o:gënaizë(r)/ **n.** organizues, organizator
oriental ,o:ri'entl/ **adj.** oriental
orientation /,o:rien'teishn/ **n.** orientim
origin /'orixhin/ **n.** origjinë, burim, zanafillë
original /ë'rixhënl/ **adj.** 1. origjinal; 2. fillestar; **n.**
origjinal; **in the original** në origjinal
originally /ë'rixhënëli/ **adv.** 1. fillimisht, në fillim; 2. në
mënyrë origjinale
ornament /'o:nëmënt/ **n.** ornament, zbukurim, stoli
orphan /'o:fn/ **n.** jetim; **adj.** jetim
ostrich /'ostriç/ **n. zool.** struc
other /'adhë(r)/ **adj.** tjetër; **the other day** para disa ditësh;
every other day një ditë po, një ditë jo
otherwise /'adhëwaiz/ **adv.** ndryshe; **conj.** për ndryshe
ought /o:t/ **v. aux.** duhet
ounce /auns/ **n.** ons (= 28.3 gr.)
our /'auë(r)/ **poss. pron.** yni, jona; tonë, tanë **ours** /'auëz/
poss. pron. yni, jona
ourselves /,auë'selvz/ **refl. pron.** vetë, veten; **all by
ourselves** vetëm
out /aut/ **adv.** jashtë, përjashta; **go out** dal jashtë; **prep.**
prej; jashtë; me
outbreak /'autbreik/ **n.** 1. shpërthim; 2. plasje; 3. fillim
outburst /'autbë:rst/ **n.** shpërthim, plasje
outcome /'autkam/ **n.** rezultat, përfundim
outdoors /'aut'do:z/ **adv.** jashtë, në ajër të pastër
outer /'autë(r)/ **adj.** i jashtëm
outfit /'autfit/ **n.** 1. pajime; 2. pajisje
outing /'autin/ **n.** 1. shëtitje; 2. ekskursion

outlaw /'autlo:/ **n.** njeri i nxjerrë jashtë ligjit
outline /'autlain/ **n.** 1. skicë, përvijim; 2. përmbledhje; **vt.**
1. skicoj, përvijoj; 2. përmbledh
outlook /'autluk/ **n.** 1. pamje; 2. pikëpamje; 3. perspektivë
outnumber /aut'nambë(r)/ **vt.** ia kaloj në numër
out-patient /'autpeishnt/ **n.** pacient i jashtëm
output /'autput/ **n.** 1. prodhim; 2. prodhueshmëri
outrageous /aut'reixhës/ **adj.** 1. i tërbuar; i egër; 2. fyes,
i pacipë, imoral
outright /aut'rait/ **adv.** 1. plotësisht, tërësisht; 2. haptas;
3. me një herë; **adj.** i plotë, i tërë; 2. i shpallur, me damkë
outset /'autset/ **n.** nisje, fillim; **at the outset** në fillim;
from the outset që nga fillimi
outside /aut'said/ **n.** 1. anë, faqe e jashtme; 2. pamje e
jashtme; **from the outside** nga pamja e jashtme; **adj.** i
jashtëm; **outside repairs** riparime të jashtme; **adv.** jashtë,
nga jashtë; **prep.** jashtë; përveç
outskirts /'autskë:ts/ **n. pl.** rrethina; **at the outskirts of**
në rrethinat e
outspoken /aut'spoken/ **adj.** i hapur, i çiltër, zemërhapur
outstanding /aut'stendin/ **adj.** 1. i shquar; 2. i spikatshëm;
3. i pakryer; 4. i pazgjidhur; 5. i papaguar
outward /'autwëd/ **adj.** 1. i jashtëm; 2. i dukshëm; **adv.** nga
jashtë
outwardly /'autwëdli/ **adv.** nga jashtë, nga pamja e jashtme
oval 'ouvl/ **adj.** vezak
oven /'avn/ **n.** furrë
over /'ouvë(r)/ **prep.** mbi, përmbi; përtej; më shumë se; **adv.**
përmbys; tërësisht; përsëri; krejtësisht; **all over** në gjithë;
all over again sërisht, nga e para; **over and over again**
shpesh; **be all over** ka mbaruar; **pref.** mbi-, tej-
overall /,ouvër'o:l/ **adj.** i plotë, i tërë, i përgjithshëm; **n.**
pl. kominoshe
overcharge /,ouvë'ça:rxh/ **n.** mbingarkesë; **vti.** 1. mbingarkoj;
2. kërkoj çmim tepër të lartë
overcoat /'ouvëkout/ **n.** pallto e madhe
overcome /,ouvë'kam/ **vt.** 1. mund, mposht; 2. kapërcej
overdo /,ouvë'du:/ **vt.** 1. e teproj; 2. e tejpjek
overdraw /'ouvë'dro:/ **vti.** 1. ekzagjeroj; 2. tërheq më shumë
të holla se depozita
overdue /,ouvë'dju:/ **adj.** 1. i vonuar; 2. që i ka kaluar
afati
overestimate /,ouvër'estimit/ **vt.** mbivlerësoj, mbiçmoj
overgrown /,ouvë'groun/ **adj.** 1. i rritur shpejt; 2. i mbuluar
(me barëra etj.)
overhaul /,ouvë'ho:l/ **vt.** fut në remont kapital (makinën)
overhead /'ouvëhed/ **adv.** sipër; **adj.** i sipërm, mbitokësor
overhear /,ouvë'hië(r)/ **vt.** më kap veshi
overheat /'ouvë'hi:t/ **vti.** tejnxeh; tejnxehet
overjoyed /,ouvë'xhoid/ **adj.** tepër i gëzuar
overlook /,ouvë'luk/ **vt.** 1. nuk vë re; 2. vështroj, sodit; 3.
fal; lë pa ndëshkuar
overnight /,ouvë'nait/ **adv.** 1. natën, gjatë natës; 2. një
natë më parë; **adj.** natën

overpay /,ouvë'pei/ **vt.** paguaj më shumë se sa duhet
overpower /,ouvë'pauë(r)/ **vt.** 1. mposht; 2. mund
oversee /,ouvë'si:/ **vt.** survejoj, mbikqyr, kontrolloj
overseer /'ouvësië(r)/ **n.** mbikqyrës
oversleep /,ouvë'sli:p/ **vti.** ngrihem vonë (nga gjumi)
overthrow /,ouvë'throu/ **vt.** 1. përmbys; 2. rrëzoj
overtime /'ouvëtaim/ **adv.** jashtë orarit; **adj.** që kryhet
jashtë orarit (të punës)
overturn /,ouvë'të:rn/ **vti.** përmbys; përmbyset
overwork /,ouvë'wë:k/ **vit.** rraskapit, stërmundoj; rraskapitem
owe /ou/ **vti.** 1. i kam borxh; 2. i detyrohem, i jam
mirënjohës dikujt
own /oun/ **adj.** i veti, i tij; **vti.** 1. zotëroj; 2. pranoj; 3.
pohoj
owner /'ounë(r)/ **n.** pronar, zotërues
ownership /'ounëship/ **n.** 1. e drejtë e pronësisë; 2. pronësi
ox /oks/ **n.** ka; dem
oxygen /'oksixhën/ **n.** oksigjen

P

pace /peis/ **n.** 1. hap; 2. ritëm, shpejtësi; **keep pace with** mbaj hapin me
pacific /pë'sifik/ **adj.** paqësor; **the Pacific Ocean** Oqeani Paqësor
pack /pek/ **n.** 1. dëng; 2. pako, paketë; 3. tufë, kope; 4. palë (letra etj.); **vti.** 1. paketoj, ambalazhoj; 2. mbush; 3. ngjesh, rras **package** /'pekixh/ **n.** 1. pako; 2. deng; 3. dërgesë
packed /pekt/ **adj.** 1. i mbushur plot; 2. i paketuar
packer /'pekë(r)/ **n.** paketues
packet /'pekit/ **n.** pako; paketë; **a packet of cigarettes** paketë cigaresh
packing /'pekin/ **n.** 1. paketim; 2. ambalazhim
packing-case /'pekinkeis/ **n.** kuti ambalazhi
pact /pekt/ **n.** pakt
pad /ped/ **n.** 1. mbushje; 2. vatë; **vt.** mbush (me pambuk); i vë vatë
padding /pedin/ **n.** 1. mbushje; 2. material për mbushje
paddle /'pedl/ **n.** lopatë, rrem
padlock /'pedlok/ **n.** dry
page /peixh/ **n.** faqe (libri); **vt.** numëroj (faqet)
pail /peil/ **n.** kovë
pain /pein/ **n.** dhembje; **vt.** 1. dhemb; 2. shkaktoj dhembje
painful /'peinful/ **adj.** 1. i dhembshëm; 2. i mundimshëm
painstaking /'peinztekin/ **adj.** 1. i kujdesshëm; 2. i zellshëm
paint /peint/ **n.** bojë; **vti.** 2. pikturoj (me bojëra); 2. lyej me bojë
painter /'peintë(r)/ **n.** 1. piktor; 2. bojaxhi
painting /'peintin/ **n.** 1. pikturë; 2. bojatisje
pair /peë(r)/ **n.** 1. çift; 2. palë; **a pair of shoes** një palë këpucë
pal /pel/ **n.** mik; shok
palace /'pelis/ **n.** pallat
pale /peil/ **adj.** 1. i zbehtë, i zbehur; 2. e dobët (drita)
palm /pa:m/ **n.** pëllëmbë
pan /pen/ **n.** tavë; **frying pan** tigan; **broiler pan** skarë
pancake /'penkeik/ **n.** petull
pane /pein/ **n.** xham dritareje
panel /'penl/ **n.** panel (dërrase, metali)
panic /'penik/ **n.** panik; **vit.** 1. më zë paniku; 2. bëj panik
panic-stricken /'penikstrikn/ **adj.** i pushtuar nga paniku
pant /pent/ **n.** gulçimë; **vi.** gulçoj
pantomime /'pentëmaim/ **n.** pantomimë
pants /pents/ **n.** 1. pantallona; 2. mbathje
papa /pë'pa:/ **n. fëm.** babi, ba
paper /'peipë/ **n.** 1. letër; 2. **pl.** dokumente; 3. gazetë; **vt.** vesh me letër
paper-mill /'peipëmil/ **n.** fabrikë letre
parachute /'perëshu:t/ **n.** parashutë
parade /pë'reid/ **n.** paradë
paradise /'perëdais/ **n.** parajsë
paragraph /'perëgra:f/ **n.** paragraf
paralyze /'perëlaiz/ **vt.** paralizoj
paralysis /pë'relësis/ **n.** paralizë
parcel /'pa:sl/ **n.** 1. pako; 2. pjesë; **vt.** ndaj në pjesë
pardon /'pa:dn/ **n.** falje; ndjesë; **vt.** fal, ndjej

parent /'peërënt/ **n.** prind
parish /'perish/ **n.** famulli
park /pa:k/ **n.** 1. park; 2. vend parkimi (për makina)
parking /'pa:rkin/ **n.** 1. parkim; 2. vend parkimi
parliament /'pa:lëmënt/ **n.** parlament
parlor (parlour) /'pa:lë(r)/ **n.** dhomë pritjeje
parrot /'perët/ **n.** papagall
parson /'pa:sn/ **n.** prift, famulltar
part /pa:rt/ **n.** 1. pjesë; **in part** pjesërisht; **for the most part** në pjesën më të madhe; 2. pjesëmarrje; **take part in** marr pjesë në; 3. anë; **take the part of** marr anën e; **for my part** nga ana ime; **on the part of** nga ana e; 4. rol, pjesë; **play a part** luaj një rol; **vti.** 1. ndahem; 2. ndaj, shpërndaj; **part company with smb** ndahem me dikë; **part with** ndahem nga
partial /'pa:shl/ **adj.** i pjesshëm
participant /pa:'tisipënt/ **n.** pjesëmarrës
participate /pa:'tisipeit/ **vi.** marr pjesë
participation /pa:,tisi'peishn/ **n.** pjesëmarrje
particle /'pa:rtikl/ **n.** grimcë
particular /pë'tikjulë(r)/ **adj.** i veçantë; i posaçëm; **in particular** në veçanti, veçanërisht; 2. zgjedhës, që s'kënaqet lehtë; **n.** hollësirë; e dhënë, fakt; **go into particulars** hyj në hollësira
particularly /pë'tikjulëli/ **adv.** sidomos, posaçërisht, veçanërisht
parting /'pa:tin/ **n.** 1. nisje; ndarje; 2. vijë e ndarjes (së flokëve)
partition /pa:'tishn/ **n.** 1. ndarje; 2. mur ndarës
partly /'pa:tli/ **adv.** pjesërisht
partner /'pa:tnë(r)/ **n.** partner
part-owner /'pa:tounë(r)/ **n.** bashkëpronar
part-time /'pa:t taim/ **adj.** i pjesshëm, jo i plotë; **a part-time job** punë me orar jo të plotë
party /'pa:rti/ **n.** 1. parti; 2. mbrëmje (argëtimi); 3. grup; ekip; 4. palë, anë
pass /pa:s/ **n.** 1. kalim (i klasës etj.); 2. shteg; qafë mali; 3. lejekalim; 4. pasim (i topit); **vti.** 1. kaloj, kapërcej; 2. shkon, kalon (koha); 3. kaloj, jap, pasoj; 4. kaloj (provimin); 5. jap, miratoj (një vendim etj); **pass on** njoftoj, transmetoj (një mesazh etj.); **pass out** humb ndjenjat; **pass over** lë në heshtje; **pass away** zhduket, kalon; mbaron, vdes
passage /'pesixh/ **n.** 1. rrugë, kalim, shteg; 2. korridor; 3. fragment, pasazh; 4. kalim (i kohës etj.)
passenger /'pesinxhë(r)/ **n.** pasagjer, udhëtar
passer-by /,pa:së'bai/ **n.** kalimtar
passing /'pa:sin/ **n.** kalim; **in passing** kalimthi; **adj.** kalimtar, i çastit
passion /'peshn/ **n.** 1. pasion; 2. zjarr, dashuri; dëshirë; 3. zemërim **passionate** /'peshënët/ **adj.** 1. i pasionuar; 2. i rrëmbyer
passive /'pesiv/ **adj.** pasiv; **n. gjuh.** trajtë pësore
passport /'pa:spo:rt/ /'pespo:rt/ **n.** pasaportë
password /'pa:swë:rd/ **n.** parrullë; fjalëkalim
past /pa:st/ **adj.** i kaluar, i shkuar; **n.** e shkuara, koha e kaluar; **prep.** pas; mbi; tej, tutje; **adv.** përtej, matanë
paste /peist/ **n.** 1. brumë; 2. ngjitës; qiriç; 3. pastë (dhëmbësh)

pastime /'pa:staim/ **n.** dëfrim, zbavitje
pastor /'pa:stë(r)/ **n.** pastor, meshtar
pastry /'peistri/ **n.** pastë; ëmbëlsirë
pastry-cook /'peistrikuk/ **n.** pastiçier
pat /pet/ **n.** goditje e lehtë
patch /peç/ **n.** arnë; mballomë; 2. pullë; 3. copë (toke); **vt.**
arnoj; **patch something up** riparoj, ndreq; **patch things up**
(patch up a quarrel) mbyll, sheshoj një grindje
patent /'peitnt/ **n.** patentë; **adj.** 1. i qartë, i dukshëm; 2. i
pajisur me patentë
path /pa:th; peth/ **n.** rrugë (për këmbësorë)
patience /'peishns/ **n.** 1. durim; 2. këmbëngulje; **lose**
patience with (be out of patience with) humb durimin
patient /'peishnt/ **adj.** i duruar, i durueshëm
patient /'peishnt/ **n.** pacient
patriot /'petriët/ **n.** atdhetar, patriot
patrol /pë'çroul/ **n.** 1. patrullë; 2. patrullim; **vti.**
patrulloj
patron /'peiçrën/ **n.** patron, mbrojtës
patronage /'petrënixh/ **n.** patronazh, kujdestari
patronize /'peçrënaiz/ **vt.** 1. frekuentoj rregullisht (një
dyqan); 2. sillem si patron me dikë; 3. mbroj, përkrah; 4.
begenis
patter /'petë(r)/ **n.** trokitje (e pikave të shiut etj.); **vi.**
troket (shiu etj.)
pattern /'petn/ **n.** 1. mostër, shabllon, model, formë; 2.
dizenjo, vizatim; 3. shembull; **vt.** modeloj
pattern-maker /'petnmeikë(r)/ **n.** modelist
pause /po:z/ **n.** pushim, pauz; **vi.** bëj një pushim, pauzë
pave /peiv/ **vt.** 1. shtroj (një rrugë); 2. **fig.** hap rrugën;
pave the way përgatit kushtet, terrenin për
pavement /'peivmënt/ **n.** trotuar
paw /po:/ **n.** putër; **vt.** prek, gërvisht me putër
pawn /po:n/ **n.** peng; **vt.** lë, jap peng
pawnshop /'po:nshop/ **n.** dyqan pengmarrës
pay /pei/ **n.** rrogë, pagë; **vti.** 1. paguaj; 2. shpërblej; 3. ka
leverdi; 4. i kushtoj (vëmendje); **pay back** shlyej borxhin;
pay for paguaj (të holla); **fig.** paguaj (një gabim, një faj
etj.); **pay something off** shlyej borxhet; **pay up** paguaj,
shlyej tërësisht
pay-day /'peidei/ **n.** ditë rrogash
payment /'peimënt/ **n.** 1. pagesë; 2. pagim
pay-office /'peiofis/ **n.** arkë
pay-roll /'peiroul/ **n.** bordero
pea /pi:/ **n.** bizele
peace /pi:s/ **n.** paqe; **make peace** bëj paqe; 2. qetësi; **leave**
smb in peace lë të qetë; **live in peace with** jetoj në paqe me;
keep the peace ruaj qetësinë, rendin
peaceful /'pi:sful/ **adj.** 1. paqësor; 2. i urtë, i qetë
peace-loving /'pi:slavin/ **adj.** paqedashës
peach /pi:ç/ **n.** pjeshkë
peacock /'pi:kok/ **n. zool.** pallua
peak /pi:k/ **n.** 1. majë (mali); 2. strehë (kapeleje)
peal /pi:l/ **n.** 1. tingëllim i kambanës; 2. kumbim, gjëmim
peanut /'pi:nat/ **n. bot.** kikirik

pear /peë(r)/ **n.** dardhë

pearl /'pë:rl/ **n.** perlë; **vi.** gjuaj perla

peasant /'peznt/ **n.** fshatar

pebble /'pebl/ **n.** haliç, guralec

peck /pek/ **n.** çukitje

peculiar /pi'kju:lië(r)/ **adj.** i veçantë, karakteristik

pedal /'pedl/ **n.** pedal

peddler /'pedlë(r)/ **n.** shitës ambulant

pedestal /'pedistl/ **n.** piedestal

pedestrian /pi'destriën/ **n.** këmbësor

pedigree /'pedigri/ **n.** gjenealogji

peel /pi:l/ **n.** lëkurë, lëvozhgë, lëvore; **vti.** 1. heq, qëroj lëkurën; 2. plasaritet lëkura

peep /pi:p/ **n.** 1. cicërimë; 2. piskamë; **vi.** 1. cicëron; 2. piskat

peep /pi:p/ **n.** 1. shikim vjedhurazi; 2. ag; **vi.** shikoj vjedhurazi

peg /peg/ **n.** 1. kunj; 2. kapëse (rrobash); 3. varëse (rrobash); **vti.** 1. kap me kapëse; 2. bllokoj çmimet etj.; 3. fiksoj, mbërthej me kunj **pen** /pen/ **n.** penë; **vt.** shkruaj

penal /'pi:nl/ **adj.** penal; **the penal code** kodi penal

penalize /'pi:nëlaiz/ **vt.** dënoj, ndëshkoj

penalty /'penlti/ **n.** 1. dënim, ndëshkim, gjobitje; 2. penallti

pencil /'pensl/ **n.** laps, kalem; **vt.** shkruaj, vizatoj me kalem

pendant /'pendënt/ **n.** varëse

penetrate /'penitreit/ **vti.** 1. depërtoj; 2. përshkoj

penetration /,peni'treishn/ **n.** depërtim

penguin /'pengwin/ **n. zool.** pinguin

penicillin /,peni'silin/ **n.** penicilinë **peninsula** /pë'ninsjulë/ **n. gjeogr.** gadishull

pen knife /'pennaif/ **n.** biçak, brisk

pen-name /'penneim/ **n.** pseudonim

penny /'peni/ **n.** peni, qindarkë

pension /'penshn/ **n.** pension; **retire on a pension** dal në pension

pensioner /'penshënë(r)/ **n.** pensionist

penthouse /'penthaus/ **n.** shtesë (shtëpie)

people /'pi:pl/ **n.** 1. popull; 2. njerëz; **vt.** populloj

pepper /'pepë(r)/ **n.** 1. piper; 2. spec

peppermint /'pepëmint/ **n. bot.** mendër, nenexhik

per /pë:/ **prep.** për, në; **per capita** për frymë; **per hour** në orë

perambulator /pë'rembjuleitë(r)/ **n.** karrocë fëmijësh

perception /pë'sepshn/ **n.** perceptim

perceptive /pë'septiv/ **adj.** i perceptueshëm, i kuptueshëm

perch /pë:rç/ **n.** degë (ku prehet zogu)

perfect /'pë:fikt/ **adj.** 1. i përsosur, i përkryer, i mrekullueshëm; 2. i patëmetë; 3. i plotë; **n. gram.** koha e kryer; **vti.** 1. përsos; 2. përkryej

perfectly /'pë:fiktli/ **adv.** 1. plotësisht; 2. përsosurisht, më së miri

perform /pë'fo:rm/ **vti.** 1. kryej, përfundoj; 2. luaj, ekzekutoj

performance /pë'fo:mëns/ **n.** 1. kryerje, ekzekutim; 2. shfaqje

performer /pë'fo:rmë(r)/ **n.** ekzekutues, interpretues

perfume /pë'fju:m; për'fju:m/ **n.** parfum; **vt.** parfumoj

perhaps /pë'heps/ **adv.** ndoshta, mbase

peril /'peril/ **n.** rrezik; **in peril** në rrezik
perilous /'perëlës/ **adj.** i rrezikshëm
period /'piëriëd/ **n.** 1. periudhë, kohë; 2. epokë; 3. pikë
periodical /,piëri'odikl/ **n.** revistë, gazetë periodike; **adj.** periodik
perishable /'perishëbl/ **adj.** që prishet shpejt; **n. pl.** prodhime, ushqime që prishen shpejt
permanent /'pë:mënënt/ **adj.** i përhershëm
permission /pë'mishn/ **n.** 1. lejim; 2. leje; **give smb permission to do something** lejoj dikë të bëj diçka
permit /pë'mit/ **vti.** lejoj; **smoking not permitted** ndalohet duhani; **n.** 1. lejim; 2. leje
perpetual /pë'peçjuël/ **adj.** 1. i përjetshëm; 2. i përhershëm; 3. i vazhdueshëm
perplex /pë'pleks/ **vt.** 1. hutoj; 2. shastis
perplexed /pë'plekst/ **adj.** i hutuar, i shastisur
persecute /'pë'sikjut/ **vt.** përndjek, persekutoj
persecution /,pë:sikju:shn/ **n.** përndjekje, persekutim
persist /pë'sist/ **vi.** 1ngul këmbë; 2. ngulmoj
persistent /pë'sistent/ **adj.** 1. këmbëngulës, ngulmues; 2. i qëndrueshëm
person /'pë:sn/ **n.** 1. person, njeri; 2. **gjuh.** vetë
personal /'pë:snl/ **adj.** 1. personal, vetjak; 2. privat
personality ,pe:së'neliti/ **n.** personalitet, njeri i shquar
personally /'pe:sënëli/ **adv.** personalisht
perspiration /,pë:spë'reishn/ **n.** 2. djersitje; 2. djersë
perspire /pë'spaië(r)/ **vi.** djersit, djersitem
persuade /pë'sweid/ **vt.** bind, i mbush mendjen
persuasion /pë'sweizhn/ **n.** bindje
persuasive /pë'sweisiv/ **adj.** bindës
pertinent /'pë:rtinënt; 'pë:rtënënt/ **adj.** i lidhur drejtpërdrejt
pessimist /'pesimist/ **n.** pesimist
pessimistic ,pesi'mistik/ **adj.** pesimist
pest /pest/ **n.** 1. dëmtues; 2. njeri i bezdisur
pester /'pestë(r)/ **vt.** mërzit
pet /pet/ **n.** 1. manar; 2. i përkëdhelur; **vt.** përkëdhel, llastoj
petition /pë'tishn/ **n.** peticion
petrol /'petrël/ **n.** 1. benzinë; 2. gazolinë
petroleum /pë'trouliëm/ **n.** naftë
petty /'peti/ **adj.** i vogël, i parëndësishëm
phantom /'fentëm/ **n.** fantazmë
pharmacy /'fa:mësi/ **n.** farmaci
phase /feiz/ **n.** fazë, shkallë
phenomenon /fi'nominën/ **n.** fenomen, dukuri
philosopher /fi'losëfë(r)/ **n.** filozof
philosophy /fi'losëfi/ **n.** filozofi
phone /foun/ **n. gj.fl.** telefon
phonetics /fë'netiks/ **n. gjuh.** fonetikë
phoney /'founi/ **adj.** kallp, i rremë, i gënjeshtërt
photo /'fëutou/ **n.** fotografi
photograph /'fëutëgra:f/ **n.** fotografi; **vt.** fotografoj
photographer /fë'tougrëfë(r)/ **n.** fotograf

phrase /'freiz/ **n.** 1. shprehje, frazë; 2. togfjalësh; **stock phrase** shprehje e ngurtësuar
physical /'fizikl/ **adj.** fizik; trupor; **physical education** edukim fizik
physician /fi'zishn/ **n.** mjek
physicist /'fizisist/ **n.** fizikan
physics /'fiziks/ **n.** fizikë
pianist /'piënist/ **n.** pianist
piano /pi'enou/ **n. muz.** piano
pick /pik/ **vti.** 1. mbledh, vjel, këput; 2. zgjedh; **pick out** zgjedh; shquaj, dalloj; kap, kuptoj; **pick up** marr, ngre nga toka; kap; zotëroj
pick /pik/ **n.** 1. kazmë; 2. kunj dhëmbësh
pick /pik/ **n.** 1. zgjedhje; 2. mbledhje, vjelje
picket /'pikit/ **n.** 1. piketë; 2. piketues
pickle /'pikl/ **n.** 1. turshi; 2. shëllirë; 3. fëmijë mistrec; **vt.** vë turshi
pickpocket /'pikpokit/ **n.** vjedhës xhepash
picnic /'piknik/ **n.** piknik; **go for a picnic** shkoj në piknik; **vi.** shkoj në piknik
pictorial /pik'to:riël/ **adj.** i ilustruar; **n.** revistë me piktura
picture /'pikçë(r)/ **n.** 1. kuadër, pikturë, tablo; 2. film; 3. fotografi; **take a picture** bëj një fotografi; 4. përshkrim; 5. përfytyrim mendor; **vt.** 1. pikturoj; 2. përfytyroj
picturesque /,pikçë'resk/ **adj.** piktoresk
pie /pai/ **n.** byrek; **have a finger in the pie** kam gisht në
piece /pi:s/ **n.** 1. copë; 2. pjesë, vepër muzikore etj.; 3. gur (shahu etj.); 4. monedhë; **take something to pieces** çmontoj; **break something to pieces** thyej copë-copë; **give smb a piece of one's mind** ia them troç mendimin që kam
piece-meal /'pi:smi:l/ **adv.** pjesë-pjesë
pig /pig/ **n.** derr (edhe **fig.**)
pigeon /'pixhin/ **n.** pëllumb
piglet /'piglit/ **n.** gic, derrkuc
pile /pail/ **n.** stivë, grumbull, turrë, pirg; **vti.** stivoj, vë grumbull; **pile up** grumbullohet, mblidhet (puna etj.)
pilgrim /'pilgrim/ **n.** 1. pelegrin, haxhi; 2. shtegtim
pilgrimage /'pilgrimixh/ **n.** 1. pelegrinazh, haxhillëk; 2. shtegtim
pill /pil/ **n.** pilulë, tabletë, hape
pillar box /'pilë(r)boks/ **n.** kuti postare
pillow /'pilou/ **n.** jastëk
pillow-case /'piloukeis/ **n.** këllëf jastëku
pilot /'pailët/ **n.** 1. pilot; 2. timonier; **vt.** pilotoj
pimple /'pimpl/ **n.** puçërr
pin /pin/ **n.** gjilpërë me kokë; **vt.** mbërthej, kap
pinafore /'pinëfo:(r)/ **n.** përparëse
pincers /'pinsëz/ **n.** darë
pinch /pinç/ **n.** 1. pickim, cimbisje; 2. një pulqer; **vti.** 1. pickoj; 2. shtrëngon (këpuca); 3. **gj. fl.** vjedh
pine /pain/ **n. bot.** pishë
pineapple /'painepl/ **n.** ananas
pink /pink/ **n.** 1. karafil; 2. ngjyrë rozë; **adj.** bojë trëndafili

pint /paint/ **n.** masë lëngjesh, pintë (= 0.57 l.)
pioneer /,paië'nië(r)/ **n.** 1. pioner; 2. nismëtar
pip /pip/ **n.** farë, bërthamë (molle, pjeshke etj.)
pipe /paip/ **n.** 1. çibuk; 2. tub, gyp; 3. **muz.** flaut; 4. fyell
pipe-line /'paiplain/ **n.** tubacion (uji, nafte etj.)
pistol /'pistl/ **n.** pistoletë
pit /pit/ **n.** gropë e thellë; 2. pus miniere; 3. minierë; 4. plate
pitch /piç/ **n.** 1. fushë (futbolli etj.); 2. lartësi (e tingullit); 3. hedhje; 4. shkallë intesiteti
pitiable /'pitiëbl/ **adj.** 1. i mjerë, i gjorë; 2. keqardhës
pitiful /'pitiful/ **adj.** keqardhës
pitiless /'pitilis/ **adj.** i pamëshirshëm
pity /'piti/ **n.** mëshirë, keqardhje; **take (have) pity on** tregoj mëshirë për dikë; **it's a pity** është për të ardhur keq; **what a pity!** sa keq!; **vt.** mëshiroj, tregoj keqardhje
placard /'pleka:d/ **n.** afishe, pllakat; **vt.** 1. afishoj; 2. vë, ngjit afishe
place /pleis/ **n.** vend; **in place** në vendin e duhur; **in place of** në vend të; **take place** ndodh, ngjan; **take the place of** zë vendin e; **from place to place** nga një vend në tjetrin; **out of place** i pavend, i papërshtatshëm; **take one's place** ulem; **vt.** vë, vendos
plague /pleig/ **n.** murtajë
plain /plein/ **adj.** 1. i qartë; 2. i dukshëm; 3. i thjeshtë, i zakonshëm; 3. i çiltër, i hapët; **in plain words** sinqerisht; **be plain with smb** i flas hapur dikujt; **in plain English** shkoqur, shqip; **adv.** qartë, hapur
plain /plein/ **n.** 1. fushë; 2. rrafshinë
plainly /'pleinli/ **adv.** qartë
plaint /pleint/ **n.** 1. akuzë; 2. ankesë
plaintiff /'pleintif/ **n.** paditës
plait /plet/ **n.** gërshetë; **vt.** gërshetoj, bëj gërshet
plan /plen/ **n.** 1. plan; 2. skicë, projekt; 3. vizatim, skemë; **vt.** 1. planifikoj; 2. hartoj një projekt
plane /plein/ **n.** 1. aeroplan; 2. rrafsh; 3. plan; 4. zdrukth; **vt.** 1. zdrukthoj; 2. rrafshoj; 3. lëmoj
planet /'plenit/ **n.** planet
plane-tree /'plein tri/ **n. bot.** rrap
plank /plenk/ **n.** dërrasë
plant /pla:nt/ **n.** 1. bimë; 2. uzinë; 3. makineri, pajisje, impiant; **vt.** mbjell
plantation /plen'teishn/ **n.** plantacion
plaster /'pla:stë(r)/ **n.** 1. jaki; 2. suva; 3. leukoplast; **plaster of Paris** allçi; **vt.** 1. vë në jaki, allçi; 2. suvatoj; 3. stukoj
plastic /'plestik/ **adj.** 1. plastik; 2. i përpunueshëm
plate /pleit/ **n.** 1. fletë (metali, xhami etj.); 2. pjatë
plate-rack /'pleit rek/ **n.** mbajtëse pjatash
platform /'pletfo:m/ **n.** 1. platformë; 2. peron; 3. podium
play /plei/ **n.** 1. lojë; 2. lodër; 3. dramë; 4. shaka; **vti.** 1. luaj; 2. qesëndis, tallem; 3. luaj, interpretoj, ekzekutoj
player /'pleië(r)/ **n.** 1. lojtar; 2. aktor; 3. instrumentist, muzikant
playful /'pleiful/ **adj.** i gjallë; lozonjar; shakatar; çamarrok
playground /'pleigraund/ **n.** shesh lojërash

playmate /'pleimeit/ **n.** shok loje
plea /pli:/ **n.** 1. shfajësim; 2. apel, lutje
plead /pli:d/ **vit.** 1. lutem, kërkoj; 2. mbroj një çështje
gjyqësore; 3. paraqet (si shfajësim apo arsye); 4. i
drejtohem gjyqit; **plead guilty** shpall fajëtor
pleasant /'pleznt/ **adj.** i këndshëm, i pëlqyeshëm
please /pli:z/ **vit.** 1. lutem; **two coffees, please** dy kafe ju
lutem; 2. kënaq, i bëj qejfin; 3. dëshiroj; **as you please** si
të dëshironi
pleased /pli:zd/ **adj.** i kënaqur, i gëzuar; **pleased to meet
you** gëzohem që u takuam
pleasing /'pli:zin/ **adj.** i këndshëm, i pëlqyeshëm
pleasure /'pleƶë(r)/ **n.** kënaqësi; ëndje; dëshirë; qejf; **with
pleasure** me kënaqësi; **take pleasure in** kënaqem, ndiej
kënaqësi; **I have the pleasure to** kam kënaqësinë të
pleat /pli:t/ **n.** palë (fustani etj.)
pledge /plexh/ **n.** 1. premtim, zotim; 2. garanci; 3. kapar; 4.
peng; **vt.** 1. lë peng; 2. zotohem; **pledge one's word** jap
fjalën
plentiful /'plentifl/ **adj.** i bollshëm
plenty /'plenti/ **n.** bollëk; **plenty of** shumë
pliers /'plaiëz/ **n. pl.** pinca; **a pair of pliers** një palë pinca
plight /plait/ **n.** gjendje e vështirë, hall
plot /plot/ **n.** 1. ngastër, truall; 2. subjekt, fabul; 3.
komplot; **vti.** 1. komplotoj; 2. ndërtoj subjektin (e një
tregimi etj.)
plug /plag/ **n.** 1. **el.** prizë; 2. tapë; 3. reklamë; **vti.** mbyll,
tapos; **plug in** vë në prizë
plum /plam/ **n.** kumbull
plumber /'plamë(r)/ **n.** hidraulik
plump /plamp/ **adj.** i mbushur, buçkan
plunder /'plandë(r)/ **n.** 1. plaçkitje; 2. plaçkë e vjedhur;
vti. plaçkit; grabit
plunge /planxh/ **vti.** 1. zhyt, kredh; 2. zhytem; **n.** zhytje,
kredhje
plural /'plurël/ **adj. gjuh.** shumës; **n. gjuh.** shumës, numri
shumës
plus /plas/ **prep.** plus, edhe; **n.** plus, shenja +
plush /plash/ **n.** kadife
pneumonia /n(j)u:'mounië/ **n. mjek.** pneumoni **pocket** /'pokit/
n. xhep; **pick someone's pocket** vjedh xhepat e dikujt; **adj.** i
xhepit, xhepi; **pocket-money** pare xhepi; **vt.** 1. fut në xhep;
2. përvetësoj
pocket-book /'pokitbuk/ **n.** 1. libër xhepi; 2. portofol
pod /pod/ **n.** bishtajë
poem /'pouim/ **n.** poemë
poet /'pouit/ **n.** poet
poetry /'pouitri/ **n.** poezi
point /point/ **n.** 1. pikë; **point of view** pikëpamje; 2. çast;
3. çështje, thelb; 4. pikë (në lojë); 5. arsye; qëllim; **miss
the point** nuk kap thelbin e çështjes; **on the point of** në
çastin kur; **there's no point in** s'ka kuptim të; **keep to the
point** i përmbahem temës; **beside the point** jashtë teme; **in
point of fact** në realitet; **up to a certain point** në një farë
mase; **vti.** 1. tregoj; 2. drejtoj; **point something at** i
drejtoj; **point out** vë në dukje
pointed /'pointid/ **adj.** majëmprehtë, me majë
pointless /'pointlis/ **adj.** i pakuptim

poison /'poizn/ n. helm; vt. helmoj (edhe **fig.**)
poisonous /'poizënës/ adj. helmues, i helmët
poker /'poukë(r)/ n. 1. mashë; 2. poker
polar /'poulë(r)/ adj. polar; **polar bear** ariu polar
pole /poul/ n. shtyllë (telefoni etj.) **pole** /poul/ n. pol;
the North, South Pole Poli i Veriut, i Jugut
police /pë'li:s/ n. polici
policeman /pë'li:smën/ n. polic
police-station /pë'li:ssteishn/ n. rajon i policisë
policy /'polisi/ n. politikë
polish /'polish/ n. 1. lustrim; 2. lustër, shkëlqim; vti. 1.
lustroj; 2. i jap shkëlqim
polite /pë'lait/ adj. 1. i sjellshëm; 2. i njerëzishëm
politeness /pë'laitnis/ n. mirësjellje
political /pë'litikl/ adj. politik
politically /pë'litikli/ adv. politikisht
politician /,poli'tishn/ n. politikan
politics /'politiks/ n. politikë
poll /poul/ n. votim; **go to the polls** shkoj në votime; vti.
votoj
polling-booth /'poulin bu:th/ n. kabinë votimi
polling-station /'poulin steishn/ n. qendër votimi
pollute /pë'lu:t/ vt. 1. ndot; 2. përdhos
pollution /pë'lu:shn/ n. 1. ndotje; 2. përdhosje, njollosje
polytechnic /,poli'teknik/ adj. politeknik; n. politeknikum
pond /pond/ n. pellg, hurdhë
ponder /'pondë(r)/ vti. mendoj, mendohem; **ponder on (over)**
something sjell në mend diçka
pool /pu:l/ n. 1. pellg (uji etj.); 2. pishinë
poor /puë(r)/ adj. 1. i varfër, i vobektë; 2. i mjerë, i
gjorë; 3. i dobët; i keq; **the poor** varfanjakët, të varfërit
poorly /'puërli/ adv. keq; varfërisht; **poorly off** ngushtë nga
paratë
pop /pop/ n. art. pop; **pop music** muzikë pop; **pop groups**
grupet pop
pop /pop/ n. 1. krismë (e hapjes së tapës së shishes); 2.
pije shkumëzuese
pop-corn /'popko:rn/ n. pufka
poplar /'poplë(r)/ n. bot. plep
poppy /'popi/ n. bot. lulëkuqe
popular /'popjulë(r)/ adj. popullor
populate /'popjuleit/ vt. populloj
population /,popju'leishn/ n. 1. popullsi; 2. popullim
porcelain /'po:sëlin/ n. 1. porcelan; 2. artikuj porcelani
porch /po:rç/ n. 1. hyrje; 2. **amer.** verandë
pork /po:rk/ n. mish derri; **a pork chop** bërzollë derri
porridge /'porixh/ n. bollgur tërshëre
port /po:rt/ n. 1. port, skelë; 2. qytet-port
portable /'po:rtëbl/ adj. portativ, i mbartshëm
porter /'po:rtë(r)/ n. 1. hamall; 2. birrë e zezë
portion /'po:rshn/ n. 1. pjesë, racion, porcion; 2. fat,
kismet
portrait /'po:tr(e)it/ n. portret
portray /po:'trei/ vt. 1. portretizoj; 2. përshkruaj
pose /pouz/ n. 1. pozë; 2. pozim; vti. 1. pozoj; 2. hiqem; 3.
paraqes **position** /pë'zishn/ n. 1. gjendje; 2. pozitë; 3.
detyrë; 4. pozicion

positive /'pozitiv/ **adj.** 1. pozitiv; 2. i prerë; 3. i sigurtë; 4. **mjek.** pozitiv
possess /pë'zes/ **vt.** 1. kam, zotëroj; 2. mbaj, vë nën kontroll
possession /pë'zeshn/ **n.** 1. zotërim; **in possession of something** në zotërim të; **take possession of something** vihem në zotërim të; 2. **pl.** pasuri; **lose all one's possessions** humb gjithë pasurinë
possessor /pë'zesë(r)/ **n.** 1. posedues, zotërues; 2. pronar
possibility /,posi'biliti/ **n.** mundësi; **within (beyond) the bounds of possibility** brenda (jashtë) kufijve të mundësive
possible /'posibl/ **adj.** i mundshëm; **as quickly as possible** sa më shpejt që të jetë e mundur
possibly /'posibli/ **adv.** 1. mundësisht; 2. ndoshta
post /poust/ **n.** shtyllë
post /poust/ **n.** postë; **by post** me postë; **vt.** postoj
post /poust/ **n.** 1. post, vendroje; 2. **usht.** postë roje; **vt.** vë roje
postage /'poustixh/ **n.** tarifë postare
postal /'poustl/ **adj.** postar; **postal order** mandapostë
postcard /'poustka:rd/ **n.** kartolinë
poster /'poustë(r)/ **n.** pllakat, afishe
postgraduate /,poust'gredjuët/ **n.** pasuniversitar
posthumous /'postjumës/ **adj.** i pasvdjekjes
postman /'poustmën/ **n.** postier
postmaster /'poustma:stë(r)/ **n.** përgjegjës poste
post meridiem, p.m. /'poustmë'ridiëm/ **adv.** pas dreke
post office /'poustofis/ **n.** postë, zyrë postare
postpone /pë'spoun/ **vt.** shtyj për më vonë
postponement /pë'spounmënt/ **n.** shtyrje (afati)
pot /pot/ **n.** 1. poçe, vorbë; 2. kavanoz; 3. kuti; 4. ibrik; 5. vazo (lulesh); 6. kusi, tenxhere
potato /pë'teitou/ **n.** patate
potent /'poutënt/ **adj.** i fuqishëm
potential /pou'tenshl/ **adj.** potencial, i mundshëm; **n.** 1. potencial, forcë, fuqi; 2. mundësi
potter /'potë(r)/ **n.** poçar, vorbar
pottery /'potëri/ **n.** poçeri; poçari
poultry /'poultri/ **n.** 1. shpendë shtëpiake; 2. mish shpendësh
pounce /pauns/ **vi.** 1. vërvitje, hedhje e befasishme; **vi.** 1. vërvitem; 2. sulem fluturimthi
pound /paund/ **n.** sterlinë; funt (= 453.6 gr.)
pour /po:(r)/ **vti.** 1. derdh, zbras; 2. derdhet; 3. bie rrëke (shiu)
poverty /'povërti/ **n.** varfëri, skamje; **live in poverty** jetoj në varfëri
powder /'paudë(r)/ **n.** 1. pluhur; 2. pudër; 3. barut; **keep one's powder dry** ruaj barutin e thatë; **vti.** 1. thërrmoj, bëj pluhur; 2. pudros
powdered /'paudërd/ **adj.** pluhur; **powdered milk (sugar)** qumësht (sheqer) pluhur
power /'pauë(r)/ **n.** 1. fuqi, forcë; 2. mundësi; **beyond my power** jashtë mundësive të mia; 3. energji; 4. pushtet; **in power** në pushtet
powerful /'pauërful/ **adj.** 1. i fuqishëm; 2. i plotfuqishëm
powerless /'pauërlis/ **adj.** i pafuqishëm **power-station** /'pauë(r)steishn/ **n.** central elektrik
practicable /'prektikëbl/ **adj.** 1. i realizueshëm; 2. i kalueshëm

practical /'prektikl/ **adj.** 1. praktik; 2. i dobishëm; 3. i volitshëm

practically /'prektikëli/ **adv.** 1. praktikisht; 2. thuajse

practice /'prektis/ **n.** praktikë; **in practice** në praktikë; 2. zakon, praktikë; **make a practice of something** e bëj zakon diçka; 3. praktikë, ushtrim; **be out of practice** jam i pastërvitur; **vti.** 1. praktikoj; 2. zbatoj në praktikë; 2. ushtroj një zanat; 3. stërvitem, praktikohem; 4. e bëj zakon

practitioner /prek'tishënë(r)/ **n.** 1. praktikant; 2. mjek, jurist praktikant

praise /preiz/ **n.** 1. lavdërim; 2. lartësim; **vt.** lavdëroj, lëvdoj, lartësoj

pram /prem/ **n.** karrocë fëmijësh

prattle /'pretl/ **vi.** 1. belbëzoj; 2. dërdëllit

pray /prei/ **vt.** 1. lutem, falem; 2. lus

prayer /preë(r)/ **n.** 1. lutës; 2. lutje

preacher /pri:çë(r)/ **n.** predikues

precaution /pri'ko:shn/ **n.** masë paraprake; **take precautions against** marr masa kundër

precede /pri'si:d/ **vti.** paraprij

precinct /'pri:sinkt/ **n.** 1. zonë e caktuar; **a pedestrian precinct** vetëm për këmbësorë; 2. rrethinë; 3. qark elektoral

precious /'preshës/ **adj.** 1. i çmueshëm, i çmuar; 2. i dashur, i shtrenjtë

precipice /'presipis/ **n.** humnerë, greminë, hon

precise /'prisais/ **adj.** 1. i saktë, i përpiktë; 2. i prerë

precisely /pri'saisli/ **adv.** 1. pikërisht; 2. saktësisht

precision /pri'sizhn/ **n.** preçizion, saktësi, përpikëri

precocious /pri'koushës/ **adj.** i parakohshëm

predict /pri'dikt/ **vt.** parashikoj, profetizoj

prediction /pri'dikshn/ **n.** 1. parashikim; 2. profeci

predictor pri'diktë(r)/ **n.** parashikues

predominant /pri:'dominënt/ **adj.** mbizotërues

predominate /pri:'domineit/ **vi.** mbizotëroj

preface /'prefis/ **n.** 1. parathënie; 2. hyrje; **vt.** bëj, shkruaj parathënien

prefer /pri'fë:(r)/ **vt.** preferoj, parapëlqej

preferable /'prefrëbl/ **adj.** i parapëlqyer, i preferuar

preference /'prefrëns/ **n.** parapëlqim, preferencë

prefix 'pri:fiks/ **n. gjuh.** parashtesë

pregnancy /'pregnënsi/ **n.** shtatzëni

pregnant /'pregnënt/ **adj.** 1. shtatzënë; 2. i mbarsur

prejudice /'prexhudis/ **n.** 1. paramendim; 2. paragjykim; **have a prejudice against** kam paragjykim kundër

preliminary /pri'liminëri/ **adj.** paraprak; **a preliminary examination** provim paraprak

premature /'premëtjuë(r)/ **adj.** i parakohshëm

premise /'premis/ **n.** 1. premisë, kusht paraprak; 2. **pl.** shtëpia tok me anekset e tokën përreth

premonition /,pri:më'nishn/ **n.** 1. parandjenjë; 2. paralajmërim

preoccupation /,pri:okju'peishn/ **n.** preokupim

preparation /,prepë'reishn/ **n.** 1. përgatitje; 2. preparat

preparatory /pri'perëtri; pri'perëtori/ **adj.** përgatitor

prepare /pri'peë(r)/ **vti.** 1. përgatit; 2. përgatitem
prepay /'pri:pei/ **vt.** parapaguaj
prescribe /pri'skraib/ **vti.** 1. lëshoj, jap (recetë ilaçesh); 2. parashkruaj, paracaktoj
prescription /pri'skripshn/ **n.** 1. recetë (mjeku); 2. ilaç, medikament
presence /'prezns/ **n.** prani; **in the presence of** në prani të
present /'preznt/ **adj.** 1. i pranishëm; **be present** jam i pranishëm; 2. i tanishëm; **at the present time** tani, në kohën e tanishme; 3. i dhënë; **in the present case** në rastin e dhënë; **n.** e tanishme; **at present** tani; **for the present** tani për tani
present /'presnt/ **n.** dhuratë; **make smb a present of something** i bëj dikujt një dhuratë
present /pri'zent/ **vt.** 1. paraqes; 2. dhuroj; 3. shfaq; 4. prezantoj
presentation /,prezn'teishn/ **n.** 1. paraqitje; 2. dhurim; 3. shfaqje, vënie në skenë
present-day /'prezntdei/ **adj.** i sotëm, i kohës
presently /'prezntli/ **adv.** së shpejti **preservation** /,prezë'veishn/ **n.** 1. ruajtje; 2. konservim
preservative /pri'zë:vëtiv/ **n.** mjet mbrojtës, ruajtës; **adj.** ruajtës, mbrojtës
preserve /pri'zë:v/ **vt.** 1. ruaj, mbroj; 2. mirëmbaj; 3. konservoj; **n.** 1. ushqim, frut i konservuar; 2. rezervat
preserved /pri'zë:vd/ **adj.** i konservuar
president 'prezidënt/ **n.** president
presidential /,prezi'denshl/ **adj.** presidencial
press /pres/ **n.** 1. shtypje; 2. shtyp; **freedom of the press** liri e shtypit; **in the press** në shtyp; **the press** shtypi; 3. tipografi; 4. presë; **vti.** 1. shtyp; **press the button** shtyp butonin; 2. shtrydh; 3. hekuros; 4. shtrëngoj, detyroj; 5. është urgjente; the matter is pressing çështja është urgjente; **press on** ngulmoj
pressman /'presmën/ **n.** gazetar
pressure /'preshë(r)/ **n.** 1. fiz. shtypje; presion; trysni; 2. **fig.** presion; **put pressure on smb to do something** ushtroj presion mbi dikë të bëjë diçka; **be under pressure to** jam nën presionin e
prestige /pres'ti:zh/ **n.** prestigj
presumably /pri'zju:mëbli/ **adv.** siç duket; nga sa mund të merret me mend
presume /pri'zju:m/ **vti.** 1. supozoj, marr me mend; 2. marr guximin
presumption /pri'zampshn/ 1. supozim; pandehje; hamendje; 2. mendjemadhësi, arrogancë
presuppose /,pri:së'pouz/ **vt.** presupozoj, marr me mend
pretence /pri'tens/ **n.** 1. shtirje, simulim; 2. pretekst, shkak; 3. kërkesë, pretendim
pretend /pri'tend/ **vti.** kërkoj, pretendoj; 2. shtirem, hiqem
pretext /'pri:tekst/ **n.** shkas, arsye, pretekst; **under the pretext of** me pretekstin e
pretty /'priti/ **adj.** 1. i bukur, i pashëm, tërheqës; 2. i mjaftë; **adv.** mjaft, në një farë mase
prevail /pri'veil/ **vi.** 1. dal fitimtar, triumfoj; 2. mbizotëroj
prevent /pri'vent/ **vt.** 1. pengoj; 2. parandaloj
prevention /pri'venshn/ **n.** 1. parandalim; 2. shmangie
preventive /pri'ventiv/ **adj.** 1. parandalues, preventiv; 2. paraprak

previous /'pri:viës/ **adj.** i mëparshëm
previously /'pri:viësli/ **adv.** më parë
prey /prei/ **n.** 1. pre, gjah; **fall prey to** bie pre i; 2. **fig.**
viktimë
price /prais/ **n.** çmim; **at any price** me çdo çmim; **vt.**
vlerësoj, çmoj
priceless /'praislis/ **adj.** i paçmueshëm
price-list /'praislist/ **n.** lista e çmimeve
prick /prik/ **n.** 1. shpim (me gjilpërë); 2. therje; 3. dhembje
prickle /'prikl/ **n.** gjemb
pride /praid/ **n.** 1. krenari, kryelartësi; 2. fodullëk,
mendjemadhësi
priest /pri:st/ **n.** prift
primary /'praimëri/ **adj.** 1. primar, parësor, themelor; 2.
fillor; **primary school** shkollë fillore
prime /praim/ **n.** lulëzim; **adj.** 1. kryesor, themelor; 2. i
shkëlqyer, i klasit të parë
primer /'praimë(r)/ **n.** abetare
primitive /'primitiv/ **adj.** primitiv
primrose /'primrouz/ **n. bot.** aguliçe
prince /prins/ **n.** princ
princess /prin'ses/ **n.** princeshë
principal /'prinsipl/ **adj.** kryesor
principal /'prinsipl/ **n.** 1. drejtor shkolle; 2. kryetar, krye
principally /'prinsipli/ **adv.** kryesisht
principle /'prinsipl/ **n.** parim; **in principle** në parim
print /print/ **n.** 1. gjurmë; 2. shtyp; **in print** botuar e vënë
në shitje; **out of print** mbaruar, shitur (për një botim); 3.
gravurë; **vti.** 1. shtyp; 2. stampoj
printer /'printë(r)/ **n.** 1. tipograf; 2. stampues; 3. printer
priority /prai'oriti/ **n.** prioritet, përparësi
prison /'prizn/ **n.** burg; **be released from prison** lirohem nga
burgu
prisoner /'priznë(r)/ **n.** i burgosur; rob; **take someone
prisoner** zë dikë rob
privacy /'praivësi/ **n.** 1. vetmi; qetësi; 2. jetë private,
intimitet; 3. fshehtësi
private /'praivit/ **adj.** 1. **ek.** privat; 2. personal, vetjak;
3. i fshehtë; 4. konfidencial; **n.** ushtar i thjeshtë; **in
private** privatisht, vetëm për vetëm
privation /prai'veishn/ **n.** privim, privacion
privilege /'privilixh/ **n.** privilegj
privileged /'privilixhd/ **adj.** i privilegjuar
prize /praiz/ **n.** çmim; **award a prize** jap, akordoj një çmim;
vt. çmoj, vlerësoj lart
probability /,probë'biliti/ **n.** ngjasë, mundësi, probabilitet;
in all probability ka shumë të ngjarë, sipas të gjitha
ngjasave
probable /'probëbl/ **adj.** i mundshëm
probably /'probëbli/ **adv.** ndoshta, ka të ngjarë
probation /prë'beishn/ **n.** 1. dënim me kusht; 2. provë; stazh
probationer /prë'beishënë(r)/ **n.** stazhier
problem /'problëm/ **n.** 1. problem, çështje; 2. **mat.** problem
procedure /prë'si:xhë(r)/ **n.** procedurë, ecuri
proceed /prë'si:d/ **vi.** 1. vazhdoj; 2. ngre padi kundër; 3.
buron
proceedings /prë'si:dinz/ **n. pl.** 1. padi; 2. punime; 3.
protokoll

proceeds /'prëusi:dz/ **n. pl.** fitime; të ardhura
process /'prouses/ **n.** 1. proces; **in the process of doing something** gjatë; 2. proces (teknologjik, gjyqësor etj.); **vt.** përpunoj; **process leather** përpunoj lëkurën
procession /prë'seshn/ **n.** procesion
proclaim /prë'kleim/ **vt.** 1. shpall; **proclaim a republic** shpall republikën; 2. tregon
proclamation /,proklë'meishn/ **n.** 1. shpallje; 2. njoftim, lajmërim
produce /prë'd(j)u:s/ **n.** 1. prodhim, produkt; 2. rezultat; **vti.** 1. prodhoj; 2. paraqes, sjell; 3. vë në skenë; 4. shkakton; 5. jep fryte, rezultate
producer /prë'd(j)u:së(r)/ **n.** 1. prodhues; 2. regjizor
product /'prodakt/ **n.** 1. prodhim, produkt; 2. rezultat
production /prë'dakshn/ **n.** 1. prodhim; **production line** linjë prodhimi; 2. prodhim (i një filmi, drame etj.)
productive /prë'daktiv/ **adj.** prodhues, prodhimtar
productivity /,prodak'tiviti/ **n.** prodhimtari, prodhueshmëri
profession /prë'feshn/ **n.** 1. profesion, zanat, mjeshtëri; **by profession** me profesion; 2. shpallje, shprehje e hapur
professional /prë'feshnl/ **adj.** profesional; profesionist; **n.** profesionist
professor /prë'fesë(r)/ **n.** profesor
proficient /prë'fishnt/ **adj.** i aftë, i zoti
profit /'profit/ **n.** fitim; **vti.** 1. përfitoj; 2. sjell fitim
profitable /'profitëbl/ **adj.** 1. fitimprurës; **profitable investments** investime fitimprurëse; 2. i dobishëm
profiteer /,profi'tië(r)/ **n.** spekulator; **vi.** fitoj me spekulime
profound /prë'faund/ **adj.** i thellë
profuse /prë'fju:s/ **adj.** i bollshëm, i shumtë
profusion /prë'fju:zhn/ **n.** bollëk; shumicë
programme (program) /'prougrem/ **n.** 1. program; 2. plan
progress /'prougres/ **n.** progres, përparim, zhvillim; **make progress** përparoj, bëj përparime; **vi.** përparoj
progressive /prë'gresiv/ **adj.** përparimtar, progresiv
prohibit /prë'hibit/ **vt.** ndaloj; **smoking prohibited** ndalohet duhani
prohibition /,prëuhi'bishn/ **n.** ndalim
prohibitive /prë'hibëtiv/ **adj.** ndalues, pengues
project /'proxhekt/ **n.** projekt; /prë'xhekt/ **vti.** 1. projektoj; 2. shfaq në ekran, projektoj; 3. hedh, lëshoj; 4. del, spikat
projector /prë'xhektë(r)/ **n.** projektor
promenade /,promë'na:d/ **n.** 1. shëtitje; 2. shëtitore; 3. mbrëmje vallëzimi
prominent /'prominënt/ **adj.** 1. i dalluar, i shquar; 2. i dukshëm, i spikatshëm; 3. i rëndësishëm
promise /'promis/ **n.** premtim; **keep a promise** mbaj premtimin; **break a promise** shkel premtimin; **make a promise** marr një premtim; **vt.** premtoj, jap fjalën; **promise well** duket premtuese
promising /'promisin/ **adj.** premtues
promote /prë'mout/ **vt.** 1. ngre në detyrë; 2. nxis, shtyj përpara
promotion /prë'moushn/ **n.** 1. ngritje në përgjegjësi, gradim; 2. shtytje, çuarje përpara
prompt /prompt/ **adj.** i shpejtë, i menjëhershëm

promptly /'promptli/ **adv.** atypëraty, menjëherë
pronoun /'prounaun/ **n. gjuh.** përemër
pronounce /prë'nauns/ **vti.** 1. shqiptoj; 2. shpall; 3. shprehem
pronunciation /prë,nansi'eishn/ **n.** shqiptim
proof /pru:f/ **n.** 1. provë; dëshmi; fakt; 2. bocë; 3. korrekturë
proof /pru:f/ **adj.** i papërshkrueshëm; **waterproof** i papërshkueshëm nga uji; **bullet proof** i papërshkueshëm nga plumbi
prop /prop/ **n.** 1. mbështetëse, mbajtëse; 2. mbështetje; **vt.** mbështetet
propaganda /,propë'gendë/ **n.** propagandë
propeller /prë'pelë(r)/ **n.** helikë (aeroplani, anije)
proper /'propë(r)/ **adj.** 1. i duhur, i saktë, i përshtatshëm; 2. i respektueshëm; 3. i vërtetë; 4. i përveçëm (emri)
properly /'propërli/ **adv.** siç duhet; siç ka hije; **properly speaking** në të vërtetë; në thelb
property /'propëti/ **n.** 1. veti, cilësi; 2. pronë; pasuri; 3. pronësi
prophecy /'profisi/ **n.** profeci
prophet /'profit/ **n.** profet
proportion /prë'po:shn/ **n.** 1. proporcion, përpjestim; 2. pjesë; 3. **pl.** madhësi; **vt.** përpjestoj
proportional /prë'po:shnl/ **adj.** proporcional, përpjestimor
proposal /prë'pouzl/ **n.** propozim; **make a proposal** bëj një propozim
propose /prë'pouz/ **vti.** 1. propozoj; 2. i kërkoj dorën, i propozoj (për martesë)
proposition /,propë'zishn/ **n.** 1. propozim; 2. çështje, problem; 3. deklaratë
proprietor /prë'praiëtë(r)/ **n.** pronar
prose /prouz/ **n.** prozë
prosecute /'prosikju:t/ **vt.** 1. ndjek, vazhdoj; 2. ndjek penalisht
prosecution /,prosi'kju:shn/ **n.** 1. **drejt.** ndjekje penale; 2. zbatim, kryerje, realizim
prosecutor /'prosikju:të(r)/ **n.** 1. paditës; 2. prokuror
prospect /'prospekt/ **n.** 1. pamje, panoramë; 2. perspektivë, mundësi; shpresë; 3. **gjeol.** kërkim; **vi.** bëj kërkime minerare
prosperity /pros'periti/ **n.** 1. lulëzim; 2. begati, mirëqënie
prosperous /'prospërës/ **adj.** i lulëzuar, i begatshëm
protect /prë'tekt/ **vt.** ruaj, mbroj
protection /prë'tekshn/ **n.** ruajtje, mbrojtje
protective /prë'tektiv/ **adj.** mbrojtës, ruajtës
protector /prë'tektë(r)/ **n.** ruajtës, mbrojtës
protest /prë'test/ **vti.** protestoj; **n.** /'proutest/ 1. protestë; 2. kundërshtim
protract /prë'trekt/ **vt.** zgjat, stërgjat
protrude /prë'tru:d/ **vti.** 1. del jashtë; 2. nxjerr jashtë
proud /praud/ **adj.** 1. krenar, kryelartë; 2. mendjemadh
proudly /'praudli/ **adv.** krenarisht, me krenari
prove /pru:v/ **vti.** 1. provoj, vë në provë; 2. del, rezulton; 3. **mat. drejt.** vërtetoj
proverb /'provë:b/ **n.** proverb, fjalë e urtë
provide /prë'vaid/ **vit.** 1. jap, siguroj, furnizoj; 2. marr masa; 3. parashikon
provided /prë'vaidid/ **conj.** me kusht që
provident /'providënt/ **adj.** 1. i kursyer; 2. parashikues

province /'provins/ **n.** provincë, krahinë
provision /prë'vizhn/ **n.** 1. furnizim; 2. **pl.** ushqime; 3.
rezerva ushqimore; 4. parapërgatitje
provisional /prë'vizhën̈l/ **adj.** provizor, i përkohshëm;
provisional government qeveri provizore
procative /prë'vokëtiv/ **adj.** ngacmues, provokues
provoke /prë'vouk/ **vt.** 1. zemëroj; 2. ngacmoj, provokoj; 3.
shkaktoj, nxit
proxy /'proksi/ **n.** 1. person i autorizuar; 2. prokurë
prudence /'pru:dns/ **n.** 1. urtësi; 2. maturi;
prudent /'pru:dnt/ **adj.** 1. i matur, i urtë; 2. kursimtar,
ekonomiqar
prune /pru:n/ **n.** kumbull e thatë
prune /pru:n/ **vt.** 1. krasit; 2. **fig.** qeth, shkurtoj
psalm /sa:m/ **n.** psalm
psychiatrist /sai'kaiëtrist/ **n.** psikiatër
psychic /'saikik/ **adj.** 1. psikik; 2. spiritulist
psycho-analysis /,saikouë'nelisis/ **n.** psikoanalizë
psycho-analyst /,saikou'enëlist/ **n.** psikoanalist
psychological /,saikë'loxhikl/ **adj.** psikologjik
psychology /sai'kolëxhi/ **n.** psikologji
pub /pab/ **n.** birrari, bar, pijetore
public /'pablik/ **adj.** 1. publik; **public house** pijetore;
public service shërbime publike; 2. komunal; 3. botor; 4.
popullor; **n.** publik; **in public** në publik
publication /,pabli'keishn/ **n.** 1. publikim, shpallje; 2.
botim
publicity /pab'lisiti/ **n.** publicitet
publicize /'pablisaiz/ **vt.** 1. i jap publicitet; 2. reklamoj
publish /'pablish/ **vt.** 1. botoj; 2. shpall, publikoj
publisher /'pablishë(r)/ **n.** botues
pudding /'pudin/ **n.** puding
puddle /'padl/ **n.** pellg (me ujë shiu)
puff /paf/ **n.** 1. shtëllungë (tymi, avulli etj.); 2. gulç ajri
(ere); 3. pufe (për pudër)
pull /pul/ **vti.** 1. tërheq; 2. heq, shkul, nxjerr; **pull down**
shemb, rrëzoj për tokë; **pull oneself together** e mbledh veten;
n. 1. tërheqje; 2. shkulje; 3. ndikim; 4. thithje (e duhanit
etj.)
pulse /pals/ **n.** puls; **feel the pulse** mat pulsin; **vi.** pulson,
rreh zemra
pump /pamp/ **n.** pompë
pumpkin /'pampkin/ **n. bot.** kungull
pun /pan/ **n.** kalambur, lojë fjalësh
punch /panç/ **vt.** 1. godit me grusht; 2. shpoj; **n.** shpues,
brimosëse
punctual /'pankçuël/ **adj.** i përpiktë, i saktë
punctuality /,pankçju'eliti/ **n.** përpikëri, saktësi
punctuate /'pankçjueit/ **vt.** 1. vë shenjat e pikësimit; 2.
ndërpres
punctuation /,pankçju'eishn/ **n.** pikësim
puncture /'pankçë(r)/ **n.** shpuarje (e gomës); **vti.** çaj, shpoj
punish /'panish/ **vt.** dënoj, ndëshkoj
punishment /'panishmënt/ **n.** dënim, ndëshkim
punitive /'pju:nëtiv/ **adj.** ndëshkimor; **a punitive expedition**
ekspeditë ndëshkimore
pupil /pju:pl/ **n.** nxënës shkolle

puppet /'papit/ **n.** kukull (edhe **fig.**)
puppy /'papi/ **n.** këlysh qeni
purchase /'pë:rçës/ **n.** blerje; **make a purchase** bëj blerje;
vt. blej
purchaser /'pë:rçësë(r)/ **n.** blerës
pure /pjuë(r)/ **adj.** 1. i pastër; 2. i dëlirë, i kulluar, i
çiltër; 3. i papërzier; 4. i pastër (shpirtërisht)
purify /'pjuërifai/ **vt.** pastroj, dëlir
purity /'pjuëriti/ **n.** pastërti, dëlirësi
purple /'pë:rpl/ **n.** ngjyrë e purpurt; **adj.** i purpurt
purpose /'pë:rpës/ **n.** qëllim, synim; **on purpose** me qëllim;
for the purpose of me qëllim që; **vt.** 1. kam qëllim; 2. kam
ndër mend
purposeful /'pë:rpësful/ **adj.** i qëllimshëm, qëllimor
purse /pë:rs/ **n.** kuletë
pursue /pë's(j)u:/ **vt.** 1. ndjek; 2. vazhdoj
pursuit /pë'sju:t/ **n.** 1. ndjekje; **in pursuit of** në ndjekje
të; 2. punë, aktivitet
push /push/ **n.** 1. shtytje; 2. sulm; 3. përpjekje e vrullshme;
give smb the push pushoj dikë nga puna; **vti.** 1. shtyj; 2.
shtrëngoj, detyroj
puss(y) /'pus(i)/ **n.** mace
put /put/ **vti.** vë, vendos; **put something away** vë, heq
mënjanë; **put something off** shtyj; mbyll (dritat etj.); **put
smb off (sth)** shqetësoj, zhvendos vëmendjen; i heq qejfin;
put something on vesh; **put on** ndez (dritën); **put out (a fire,
light)** shuaj zjarrin, dritën; **put something right** rregulloj,
ndreq; **put up** vendosem (në hotel etj.); **put smb up** strehoj;
put up with duroj
puzzle /'pazl/ **n.** 1. pasiguri, mëdyshje; 2. enigmë, rebus;
vti. vras mendjen
pyjamas (pajamas) /pë'xha:mëz/ **n.** pizhame
pyramid /'pirëmid/ **n.** piramidë

quack /kwek/ **n.** gagaritje
quake /kveik/ **vi.** dridhem; dridhet
qualification /,kwolifi'keishn/ **n.** kualifikim
qualified /'kwolifaid/ **adj.** i kualifikuar
qualify /'kwolifai/ **vti.** 1. kualifikoj; 2. moderoj, zbut
quality /'kwoliti/ **n.** cilësi
quantity /'kwontiti/ **n.** sasi
quarrel /'kworël/ **n.** grindje; **have a quarrel with smb** zihem
me dikë; **pick a quarrel with smb** gjej sebep për t'u grindur;
make up a quarrel pajtohem; **vi.** grindem
quarry /'kwo:ri/ **n.** gurore
quart /kwo:t/ **n.** masë lëngjesh (=1.14 l.)
quarter /'kwo:të(r)/ **n.** 1. çerek; 2. tremujor; 3. lagje
qyteti; 4. drejtim; 5. **amer.** monedhë (= 25 cent)
queen /kwi:n/ **n.** mbretëreshë
queer /kwië(r)/ **adj.** 1. i veçantë, i çuditshëm; 2. i paqejf,
i pamundur; 3. i dyshimtë
quench /kwenç/ **vt.** 1. shuaj; **quench one's thirst** shuaj etjen;
2. fik, shuaj (zjarrin)
query /'kwiëri/ **n.** 1. pyetje; 2. pikëpyetje; **vt.** 1. pyes; 2.
vë në dyshim
quest /kwest/ **n.** kërkim, ndjekje; **in quest of** në kërkim të
question /'kwesçën/ **n.** 1. pyetje; **put a question to smb** i bëj
dikujt një pyetje; 2. çështje, problem; 3. dyshim; **beyond**
question jashtë çdo dyshimi; **without question** pa dyshim; **call**
something in question vë në dyshim; **vt.** 1. bëj pyetje; 2.
marr në pyetje; 3. vë në dyshim
questionable /'kwesçënëbl/ **adj.** i dyshimtë
question-mark /'kwesçën ma:k/ **n.** pikëpyetje; (?)
questionnaire /'kwesçë'neë(r)/ **n.** pyetsor
queue /kju:/ **n.** radhë; **stand in a queue** qëndroj në radhë; **vi.**
rri në radhë; **queue up** rri, vihem në radhë
quick /kwik/ **adj.** 1. i shpejtë; 2. i gjallë, i zhdërvjelltë;
3. i mprehtë
quickly /'kwikli/ **adv.** shpejt
quick-tempered /,kwik'temperd/ **adj.** gjaknxehtë
quick-witted /,kwik'witid/ **adj.** mendjehollë, mendjemprehtë
quiet /'kwaiët/ **adj.** 1. i qetë; 2. i heshtur; **keep something**
quiet mbaj diçka të fshehtë; **n.** qetësi
quietly /'kwaiëtli/ **adv.** qetësisht
quilt /kwilt/ **n.** jorgan
quince kwins/ **n.** ftua
quinsy /'kwinsi/ **n. mjek.** bajame, angjinë
quit /kwit/ **vt.** 1. lë, largohem, braktis; 2. ndërpres,
pushoj, ndaloj; 3. çlirohem
quite /kwait/ **adv.** 1. tërësisht, plotësisht; 2. mjaft, goxha
quiz /kwiz/ **n.** 1. konkurs; 2. provim; 3. pyetje kontrolli
quotation /kwou'teishn/ **n.** 1. citat; 2. citim **quote** /kwout/
vt. citoj

rabbit /'rebit/ **n.** lepur
race /reis/ **n.** 1. racë; 2. **zool.** racë
race /reis/ **n.** 1. racë; run **a race** bëj garë; **arms race**
garë armatimi; 2. garë, rivalitet, konkurencë; 3. rrymë; **vit.**
1. vrapoj; 2. konkuroj; 3. nxitoj
race-course /'reisko:s/ **n.** hipodrom
racial /'reishl/ **adj.** racial
racism 'reisizm/ **n.** racizëm
rack /rek/ **n.** 1. varëse (rrobash); 2. mbajtëse (pjatash
etj.); 3. raft; 4. skarë (makine)
racket /'rekit/ **n. sport.** raketë (tenisi etj.)
racket /'rekit/ **n.** 1. zhurmë, shamatë; 2. fitim parash me
kërcënim apo mashtrim
radar /'reida:(r)/ **n.** radar
radiation /,reidi'eishn/ **n.** rrezatim
radiator /'redieitë(r)/ **n.** 1. radiator, ngrohës; 2. radiator
(i makinës)
radical /'redikl/ **adj.** rrënjësor, radikal; **radical changes**
ndryshime rrënjësore
radio /'reidiou/ **n.** 1. radio, aparat radioje; 2. radio,
qendër transmetimi
radioactive /'rediou'ektiv/ **adj.** radioaktiv
radish /'redish/ **n. bot.** rrepë, rrikë
raffle /'refl/ **n.** llotari
raft /ra:ft/ reft/ **n.** trap (lundrimi)
rag /reg/ **n.** leckë
rage /reixh/ **n.** 1. zemërim, tërbim, egërsim; **fly into a rage**
tërbohem; 2. modë; **be all the rage** janë në modë; **vi.** 1.
tërbohem; shpërthen, përhapet me shpejtësi (epidemia etj.)
ragged /'regid/ **adj.** 1. leckaman, i leckosur; 2. jouniform
raid /reid/ **n.** 1. sulm i befasishëm; 2. bastisje; **vti.**
sulmoj; bastis
rail /reil/ **n.** 1. parmak; 2. garth; 3. shinë; **by rail** me tren
railway /'reilwei/ **n.** hekurudhë; **railway station** stacion
hekurudhor **rain** /rein/ **n.** shi
raincoat /'reinkout/ **n.** mushama shiu
rainfall /'reinfo:l/ **n.** sasi e reshjeve
rainy /'reini/ **adj.** me shi; **a rainy day** ditë me shi
raise /reiz/ **vt.** 1. ngre; 2. shtoj, rrit (rrogën, çmimet
etj.); 3. rrit, mbaj, kultivoj; 4. ngre, ngjall (frikë,
dyshim etj.); 5. mbledh, grumbulloj (fonde etj.); 6. heq
(embargon etj.)
raisin /'reizn/ **n.** stafidhe, rrush i thatë
rake /reik/ **n.** rashqel, krehër, dhëmbës, proshajkë, capë
rally /'reli/ **n.** miting
ram /rem/ **n.** 1. dash; 2. **hist.** dash, tokmak; **vt.** 1. rrah; 2.
ngjesh
ramble /'rembl/ **n.** shëtitje; **vi.** 1. shëtis për qejf; 2. flas
degë më degë
ranch /ra:nç/ renç/ **n.** fermë
random /'rendëm/ **adj.** i rastësishëm; **at random** kuturu, në tym
range /reinxh/ **n.** 1. varg (malesh); 2. llojshmëri; 3. kufi;
4. **usht.** largësi qitjeje; 5. hapësirë, zonë; 6. sobë
ekonomike
rank /renk/ **n.** 1. varg, rrjesht; 2. rang; gradë; 3. shkallë,
kategori

ransom /'rensëm/ **n.** shpërblesë për lirim
rap /rep/ **n.** goditje e lehtë
rape /reip/ **n.** përdhunim; **vt.** përdhunoj
rapid /'repid/ **adj.** i shpejtë, i vrullshëm
rapidly /'repidli/ **adv.** shpejt
rare /reë(r) **adj.** 1. i rrallë; 2. i rralluar
rarely /'reë(r)li/ **adv.** rrallë
rascal /'ra:skl; 'reskl/ **n.** 1. maskara; 2. shejtan, çapkën
rash /resh/ **adj.** i ngutshëm, i nxituar
rash /resh/ **n.** njolla, puçra të kuqe
raspberry /'ra:zbri; 'rezberi/ **n.** bot. mjedër
rat /ret/ **n.** mi (gjirizesh)
rate /reit/ **n.** 1. shpejtësi; 2. klasë, kategori; 3. kurs
(këmbimi); **rate of exchange** kurs i këmbimit; 4. tarifë; 5.
ritëm, shpejtësi; 6. taksë, tatim; **at any rate** sidoqoftë; **vt.**
vlerësoj, çmoj
rather /'ra:dhë(r)/ **adv.** 1. mjaft; 2. më mirë; 3. thuajse,
gati
ratification /,retifi'keishn/ **n.** ratifikim
ratify /'retifai/ **vt.** ratifikoj
ratio /'reishiou/ **n.** përpjestim, raport
ration /'reshn/ **n.** racion
rational /'reshnl/ **adj.** racional, i arsyeshëm
rattle /'retl/ **n.** 1. raketake; 2. rrapamë, trokëllimë
ravenous /'revënës/ **adj.** 1. i pangopur, i uritur; 2.
grabitqar
raw /ro:/ **adj.** 1. i gjallë; **raw meat** mish i gjallë; 2. i
papërpunuar; 3. i papërvojë, i pastërvitur
ray /rei/ **n.** rreze; **a ray of hope** një rreze drite
razor /'reizë(r)/ **n.** brisk rroje; **razor blade** brisk (rroje);
safety razor makinë rroje
reach /ri:ç/ **n.** 1. shtrirje e dorës, krahut; 2. kufi i
arritjes, kapjes; **within reach** që arrihet, kapet me dorë; **out
of (beyond) reach** i pakapshëm, i paarritshëm me dorë etj.;
vti. 1. shtrij, zgjat dorën; 2. arrij; 3. shtrihet, arrin
react /ri'ekt/ **vti.** 1. reagoj; 2. kundërveproj; 3. **kim.**
reagon; **react on something** vepron
reaction /ri'ekshn/ **n.** 1. reagim, kundërveprim; 2. reaksion
reactor /ri'ektë(r)/ **n.** reaktor; **nuclear reactor** reaktor
bërthamor
read /ri:d/ **vti.** lexoj; **read through** lexoj me vëmendje deri
në fund; **read out** lexoj me zë
readable /'ri:dëbl/ **adj.** i lexueshëm
reader /'ri:dë(r)/ **n.** 1. lexues; 2. antologji, libër leximi;
3. lektor; 4. recesent
readily /'redili/ **adv.** 1. menjëherë, sakaq; 2. me kënaqësi,
me dëshirë
readiness /'redinis/ **n.** 1. gatishmëri; 2. shpejtësi; 3.
shkathtësi
reading /'ri:din/ **n.** 1. lexim; 2. deklamim; 3. lexim (i një
aparati etj.)
ready /'redi/ **adj.** 1. i gatshëm; 2. i menjëhershëm, i
atypëratyshëm; **get ready** përgatitem
ready-made /,redi'meid/ **adj.** i gatshëm
real /riël/ **adj.** real, i vërtetë
reality /ri'eliti/ **n.** realitet; **in reality** në të vërtetë
realization /,riëlai'zeishn/ **n.** realizim

realize /'riëlaiz/ **vt.** 1. kuptoj; 2. realizoj, vë në jetë
really /'riëli/ **adv.** realisht, në të vërtetë
reap /ri:p/ **vti.** korr
rear /rië/ **n.** 1. pjesa e prapme; 2. prapavijë; **adj.** i prapëm
rear /rië(r)/ **vti.** 1. ngre; 2. rrit; mbarështroj; 3. ngrihet qirithi (kali)
reason /'ri:zn/ **n.** 1. arsye, gjykim; 2. shkak, arsye; **by reason of** për arsye të, për shkak të; **vit.** arsyetoj
reasonable /'ri:znëbl/ **adj.** i arsyeshëm, i logjikshëm
reassure /,ri:ë'shuë(r)/ **vt.** siguroj
rebel /'rebl/ **n.** rebel, kryengritës; **vi.** /ri'bel/ ngre krye, rebeloj
rebellion /ri'beliën/ **n.** rebelim
rebellious /ri'beliës/ **adj.** rebel, kryengritës
rebuff /ri'baf/ **n.** kundërshtim; refuzim; **vt.** refuzoj, kundërshtoj
rebuke /ri'bju:k/ **n.** qortim; **vt.** qortoj
rebut /ri'bat/ **vt.** kundërshtoj, hedh poshtë
recall /ri'ko:l/ **n.** 1. kthim, tërheqje (e ambasadorit etj.); 2. kujtesë; **vt.** 1. kthej, tërheq (ambasadorin etj.); 2. kujtoj, sjell ndër mend
receipt /ri'si:t/ **n.** 1. faturë; 2. marrje
receive /ri'si:v/ **vti.** 1. marr; 2. pres (miq, vizitorë etj.)
receiver /ri'si:vë(r)/ **n.** 1. marrës; 2. **tek.** marrës; receptor; 3. radiomarrës, aparat tv
recent /'ri:snt/ **adj.** 1. i kohës së fundit; 2. i ri
recently /'ri:sentli/ **adv.** pak kohë më parë, kohët e fundit
reception /ri'sepshn/ **n.** 1. pritje (e miqve etj.); 2. marrje; 3. pritje; **give a reception** jap një pritje
receptionist /ri:sepshënist/ **n.** sportelist; pritës i klientëve
recess /ri'ses/ **n.** 1. pushim (gjatë orëve të punës, mësimit etj.); 2. vend i fshehtë, skutë
recipe /'resëpi/ **n.** 1. recetë (gatimi; 2. recetë, mënyrë (për të arritur diçka)
recipient /ri'sipiënt/ **n.** marrës
reciprocal /ri'siprëkl/ **adj.** reciprok, i ndërsjellë
reciprocate /ri'siprëkeit/ **vti.** këmbej, kthej, përgjigjem reciprokisht
reciprocity /,resi'prosëti/ **n.** reciprocitet
recital ri'saitl/ **n.** 1. recital; 2. recitim, deklamim; 3. rrëfim
recite /ri'sait/ **vti.** 1. recitoj, deklamoj; 2. emërtoj; 3. numëroj
reckless /'reklis/ **adj.** 1. shkujdesur; 2. i pavëmendshëm, i paarsyeshëm; 3. i papërmbajtur, i nxituar
reckon /'rekën/ **vti.** 1. konsideroj, quaj; 2. llogarit; 3. përfshij; **reckon something in** fus në llogari; **reckon something up** nxjerr shumën, totalin; **reckon with something (sb)** konsideroj, llogarit diçka (dikë)
reclaim /ri'kleim/ **vt.** 1. bonifikoj; 2. riformoj; 3. rikërkoj; 4. rifitoj; 5. rigjej
recline /ri'klain/ **vti.** mbështetem, rri gjysmë i shtrirë
recognition /,rekëg'nishn/ **n.** 1. njohje; **in recognition of** në njohje të; 2. miratim, pranim; 3. vëmendje
recognize /'rekëgnaiz/ **vt.** 1. njoh; 2. pranoj
recoil /ri'koil/ **n.** zmbrapsje; prapsje; **vi.** zbythem; zmbrapset arma

recollect /,rekë'lekt/ **vti.** kujtoj, sjell ndër mend
recollection /,rekë'lekshn/ **n.** 1. kujtim; 2. kujtesë
recommend /,rekë'mend/ **vt.** 1. rekomandoj; 2. sugjeroj
recommendation /,rekëmen'deishn/ **n.** rekomandim; **at (on) someone's recommendation** me rekomandimin e
recompense /'rekëmpens/ **n.** 1. shpërblim; 2. kompensim; **vt.** shpërblej; kompensoj
reconcile /'rekënsail/ **vt.** 1. pajtoj; 2. pajtohem
reconciliation /,rekënsili'eishn/ **n.** pajtim
reconnaissance /ri'konisëns/ **n.** zbulim
reconnoitre (reconnoiter) /,rekë'noitë(r)/ **vti.** 1. zbuloj; 2. diktoj
reconsider /,ri:kën'sidë(r)/ **vt.** rikonsideroj, rishqyrtoj
reconstruct /,ri:kën'strakt/ **vt.** 1. rindërtoj; 2. rikrijoj; rimontoj
reconstruction /'ri:kën'strakshn/ **n.** rindërtim
record /'reko:rd; 'rekërd/ **n.** 1. regjistrim; 2. dokumentim; 3. shënim; **keep a record of** regjistroj, mbaj shënim; 4. protokoll; 5. pllakë gramfoni; 6. **sport.** rekord; **break the record** thyej rekordin; 7 nam, famë; **vt.** /ri'ko:rd/ 1. regjistroj, shkruaj; 2. regjistroj (në shirit, disk etj); 3. fiksoj (në film)
recording /ri'ko:rdin/ **n.** regjistrim
recount /ri'kaunt/ **vt.** tregoj, rrëfej
recover /ri'kavë(r)/ **vti.** 1. rifitoj; 2. rigjej; 3. shërohem, marr veten
recovery /ri'kavëri/ **n.** 1. shërim; 2. rigjetje (e një sendi të humbur)
recreation /,rekri'eishn/ **n.** 1. çlodhje; 2. dëfrim
recruit /ri'kru:t/ **n.** rekrut; **vti.** rekrutoj
rectangle /'rektengl/ **n. gjeom.** katërkëndësh kënddrejtë
rector /'rektë(r)/ **n.** rektor
recuperate /ri'ku:përeit/ **vti.** përtërihem, marr veten (nga sëmundja, lodhja etj.)
recuperation /ri,ku:pë'reishn/ **n.** përtëritje; rigjenerim, rikuperim
red /red/ **adj.** 1. i kuq; 2. kuqalosh, kuqash; 3. i kuqërremë; **Red Cross** Kryqi i Kuq; **turn red in the face** skuqem në fytyrë
redeem /ri'di:m/ **vt.** 1. rifitoj; 2. rimarr; 3. paguaj, shlyej (një borxh etj.); 4. mbaj (premtimin etj.); 5. kompensoj; 6. liroj me shpërblesë; 7 shpengoj
red-head /'redhed/ **n.** kuqo
red-letter day /'red letë(r) dei/ **n.** ditë feste
red-tape /'redteip/ **n.** 1. burokraci; 2. metoda burokratike
reduce /ri'dju:s/ **vti.** 1. zvogëloj, ul, pakësoj; 2. sjell; 3. kthej; 4. katandis; 5. ul peshën (e trupit)
reduction /ri'dakshn/ **n.** 1. ulje, zvogëlim, pakësim; 2. **mat.** zbritje
reed /ri:d/ **n.** kallam
reel /ri:l/ **n.** 1. **tek.** rrotull; rrotkë; bobinë; 2. kasetë filmi; **vt.** mbështjell, mbledh në rrotull **refer** /ri'f:ë(r)/ **vti.** 1. përmend, bëj fjalë; 2. i referohem; 3. përcjell; 4. paraqes; 5. i drejtohem
referee /,refë'ri:/ **n.** 1. arbitër; 2. **sport.** gjyqtar
reference /'refrëns/ **n.** 1. referim; përmendje; aluzion; 2. rekomandim
refill /'ri:fil/ **vt.** rimbush; **n.** 1. rimbushje; 2. rezervë stilolapsi

refined /ri'faind/ **adj.** 1. i rafinuar (vaj etj.); 2. i hollë, i përpunuar
reflect /ri'flekt/ **vti.** 1. pasqyroj, reflektoj; 2. mendoj, reflektoj; 3. pasqyron
reflection /ri'flekshn/ **n.** 1. pasqyrim, reflektim; 2. mendim, refleksion
reflex /'ri:fleks/ **n.** refleks
reform /'ri:form/ **n.** reformë; **vti.** reformoj; reformohem
reformer /'ri:formë(r)/ **n.** reformator
refresh /ri'fresh/ **vt.** freskoj; freskohem; **refresh one's memory** freskoj kujtesën
refreshing /ri'freshin/ **adj.** freskues
refreshment /ri'freshmënt/ **n.** 1. freski; 2. freskim; 3. ushqim e pije freskuese
refrigerate /ri'frixhëreit/ **vt.** 1. ftoh, ngrij; 2. mbaj në frigorifer
refrigerator /ri'frixhëreitë(r)/ **n.** frigorifer
refuge /'refju:xh/ **n.** strehim
refugee /,refju'xhi:/ **n.** refugjat; **refugee camps** kampe për refugjatë
refusal /ri'fju:zl/ **n.** refuzim
refuse /ri'fju:z/ **vti.** refuzoj
refute /ri'fju:t/ **vt.** hedh poshtë, përgënjeshtroj
regain /ri'gein/ **vt.** rifitoj, rimarr
regard /ri'ga:rd/ **n.** 1. vlerësim, konsideratë, nderim; 2. **pl.** përshëndetje, të fala; 3. vëmendje, përkujdesje, përfillje; **in (with) regard to** në lidhje me; **vt.** 1. shikoj; 2. konsideroj, quaj; 3. tregoj vëmendje; **as regards** përsa i përket
regarding /ri'ga:rdin/ **prep.** lidhur me
regardless /ri'ga:rdlis/ **adv.** pavarësisht nga
regiment /'rexhimënt/ **n. usht.** regjiment
region /'rixhën/ **n.** krahinë, rajon
register /'rexhistë(r)/ **vti.** 1. regjistroj; regjistrohem; 2. regjistron, tregon; **n.** 1. regjistër; 2. **tek. muz. gjuh.** regjistër 3. **registered** /'rexhistërd/ **adj.** 1. i regjistruar; 2. rekomande
regret /ri'gret/ **n.** keqardhje; **vt.** më vjen keq, ndiej keqardhje
regular /'regjulë(r)/ **adj.** i rregullt
regularly /'regjulërli/ **adv.** rregullisht
regulate /'regjuleit/ **vt.** 1. rregulloj; 2. ndreq
regulation /,regju'leishn/ **n.** 1. rregullim; 2. rregull; **traffic regulations** rregullat e trafikut **rehabilitate** /,ri:ë'biliteit/ **vt.** rehabilitoj
rehabilitation /,ri:ë,bili'teishn/ **n.** rehabilitim
rehearsal /ri'hë:rsl/ **n.** prova (teatrale etj.)
reign /rein/ **n.** mbretërim, sundim; **vi.** 1. mbretëroj, sundoj; 2. mbretëron, sundon (qetësia etj.)
rein /rein/ **n.** kapistall, kapistër
reindeer /'reindië(r)/ **n.** dre polar
reinforce /,ri:in'fo:rs/ **vt.** përforcoj
reinforcement /,ri:in'fo:rsmënt/ **n.** 1. përfocim; 2. **pl.** përforcime
reject /ri'xhekt/ **vt.** 1. hedh poshtë; 2. hedh, flak
rejection /ri'xhekshn/ **n.** refuzim, mospranim
rejoice /ri'xhois/ **vti.** 1. gëzoj; 2. gëzohem

rejoicing /ri'xhoisin/ **n.** gëzim
relapse /ri'leps/ **n. mjek.** recidiv
relate /ri'leit/ **vti.** 1. lidh; 2. tregoj, rrëfej; **be related** kam lidhje familjare
related /ri'leitid/ **adj.** 1. i lidhur; 2. i afërm
relation /ri'leishn/ **n.** 1. lidhje (gjaku, farefisnie); 2. farefis; 3. lidhje, marrëdhënie; 4. rrëfim
relationship /ri'leishënship/ **n.** 1. marrëdhënie; 2. farefisni
relative /'relëtiv/ **n.** farefis; **adj.** relativ; **relative to** në krahasim me, në raport me
relatively /'relëtivli/ **adv.** relativisht
relax /ri'leks/ **vti.** 1. dobësoj, zbut, lehtësoj; 2. liroj, lëshoj; 3. çlodhem, qetësohem, shtendosem, relaksohem
relaxation /,ri:lek'seishn/ **n.** relaksim, çlodhje; 2. dobësim, zbutje
release /ri'li:s/ **vt.** 1. liroj, çliroj; 2. lëshoj; 3. vë në qarkullim (një film etj.); 4. liroj, shkarkoj; **n.** 1. lirim, çlirim; 2. shkarkim; 3. vënie në qarkullim
relevant /'relëvënt/ **adj.** i lidhur, përkatës
reliable /ri'laiëbl/ **adj.** i besueshëm
reliance /ri'laiëns/ **n.** besim, mbështetje
relic /'relik/ **n.** relikt
relief /ri'li:f/ **n.** 1. lehtësim, qetësim (i dhembjes etj.); 2. ndihmë; 3. zëvendësues, zëvendësim; 4. qetësues; 5. reliev
relieve /ri'li:v/ **vt.** 1. ul, heq (dhembjen); 2. qetësoj; lehtësoj; 3. ndihmoj; 4. çliroj (nga një detyrim, barrë etj.); 5. liroj, shkarkoj (nga një detyrë, përgjegjësi etj.); 5. i jap variacion
religion /ri'lixhën/ **n.** fe, besim fetar
religious /ri'lixhës/ **adj.** fetar; **religious belief** besimi fetar **reluctant** /ri'laktënt/ **adj.** mosdashës
reluctantly /ri'laktëntli/ **adv.** pa qejf, pa dëshirë, me zor
rely /ri'lai/ **vi.** mbështetem, bazohem, var shpresat
remain /ri'mein/ **vi.** 1. mbetem; 2. qëndroj; **n. pl.** 1. mbetje, mbeturina; 2. rrënoja, gërmadha
remainder /ri'meindë(r)/ **n.** pjesa tjetër, pjesa e mbetur
remark /ri'ma:rk/ **n.** vërejtje; **vti.** 1. vërej; 2. bëj vërejtje
remarkable /ri'ma:rkëbl/ **adj.** i shquar
remedy /'remëdi/ **n.** ilaç, mjet shërimi; **vt.** ndreq, rregulloj
remember /ri'membë(r)/ **vti.** 1. kujtoj, mbaj mend; 2. i jap të fala
remind /ri'maind/ **vt.** kujtoj, sjell ndër mend
remittance /ri'mitëns/ **n.** 1. dërgim të hollash me postë; 2. shuma e të hollave të dërguara
remnant /'remnënt/ **n.** 1. mbetje; 2. mbeturinë; 3. copë e mbetur
remodel /ri'modl/ **vt.** rimodeloj
remorse /ri'mo:rs/ **n.** 1. pendim; 2. brejtje e ndërgjegjes
remote /ri'mout/ **adj.** 1. i largët; 2. i thellë; 3. i vetmuar, i veçuar; 4. i largët (nga lidhjet familjare)
removal /ri'mu:vl/ **n.** 1. largim, heqje; 2. zhvendosje, spostim
remove /ri'mu:v/ **vti.** 1. largoj, heq; 2. shpërngulem; 3. heq, lëviz nga puna
remunerate /ri'mju:nëreit/ **vt.** 1. shpërblej; 2. paguaj
remuneration /ri,mnju:në'reishn/ **n.** 1. shpërblim; 2. pagesë

renaissance /'renësa:ns/ **n.** rilindje
render /'rendë(r)/ **vt.** 1. bëj; 2. jap, ofroj; 3. dorëzoj; 4.
interpretoj, ekzekutoj; 5. përkthej; **render account** jap
llogari
renew /ri'n(j)u:/ **vti.** 1. përtërij, ripërtërij; 2.
zëvendësoj; 3. rimarr; 4. rifilloj; 5. zgjat
renewal /ri'n(j)u:ël/ **n.** 1. përtëritje; 2. rifillim
rent /rent/ **n.** qira; **vti.** marr (jap) me qira
rental /'rentl/ **n.** pagesë qiraje
repair /ri'peë(r)/ **vt.** riparoj, ndreq, meremetoj; **n.** ndreqje,
riparim, rregullim, meremetim; **under repair** në riparim
repairable /ri'peërëbl/ **adj.** i riparueshëm; i ndreqshëm
repay /ri'pei/ **vti.** 1. kthej (borxhin etj.); 2. shpërblej
repayment /ri'peimënt/ **n.** 1. pagim (i borxhit); 2. shpërblim
repeal /ri'pi:l/ **n.** anulim, shfuqizim; **vt.** anuloj, shfuqizoj
repeat /ri'pi:t/ **vti.** përsërit; përsëritet; **n.** përsëritje
repeated /ri'pi:tid/ **adj.** i vazhdueshëm, i përsëritur
repeatedly /ri'pi:tidli/ **adv.** herë pas here, në mënyrë të
përsëritur
repel /ri'pel/ **vt.** 1. zmbraps; 2. ngjall neveri
repetition /,repi'tishn/ **n.** përsëritje
replace /ri'pleis/ **vt.** 1. rivendos, vë në vend; 2. zëvendësoj
replacement /ri'pleismënt/ **n.** zëvendësim, këmbim
reply /ri'plai/ **n.** përgjigje; **vti.** 1. përgjigjem; 2.
kundërpërgjigjem
report /ri'po:rt/ **n.** 1. raport; 2. referat; 3. fjalë, zëra,
thashetheme; **vti.** raportoj, referoj; 2. shpall, njoftoj; 3.
raportoj; 4. paraqitem; 5. raportoj, jap llogari
reporter /ri'po:rtë(r)/ **n.** korrespondent (gazete)
represent /,repri'zent/ **vt.** 1. përfaqësoj; 2. paraqit; 3.
përfaqëson, simbolizon
representative /,repri'zentëtiv/ **adj.** përfaqësues; **n.**
përfaqësues
repress /ri'pres/ **vt.** 1. mbaj, përmbaj, kontrolloj; 2. shtyp
(një revoltë etj.)
repressive /ri'presiv/ **adj.** shtypës
reprimand /'reprima:nd; 'reprimend/ **n.** qortim; vërejtje; **vt.**
1. qortoj; 2. heq vërejtje
reproach ri'prouç/ **n.** qortim; **vt.** 1. qortoj; 2. fajësoj
reproachful /ri'prouçful/ **adj.** qortues; **reproachful look**
vështrim qortues
reproduce /ri:prë'd(j)u:s/ **vti.** 1. riprodhoj; 2. shumëzoj
reproof /ri'pru:f/ **n.** 1. qortim; 2. vërejtje
reprove /ri'pru:v/ **vt.** 1. qortoj; 2. heq vërejtje
reptile /'reptail/ **n.** zvarranik
republic /ri'pablik/ **n.** republikë
repulse /ri'pals/ **vt.** 1. zmbraps (një sulm etj.); 2. refuzoj;
n. 1. zmbrapsje; 2. refuzim, kundërshtim
repulsive /ri'palsiv/ **adj.** 1. i neveritshëm; 2. shtytës
reputation /,repju:'teishn/ **n.** emër, nam, reputacion; **win
(gain) a reputation** fitoj emër
request /ri'kwest/ **vt.** kërkoj, bëj një kërkesë; **n.** lutje;
kërkesë **require** /ri'kwaië(r)/ **vt.** 1. kërkoj; 2. kërkohet
requirement /ri'kwaië(r)mënt/ **n.** kërkesë; nevojë; **meet sb's
requirements** plotësoj kërkesat e dikujt

rescue /'reskju:/ **n.** shpëtim; **come (go) to the rescue of** vij (shkoj) në ndihmë të dikujt; **vt.** shpëtoj
research /ri'së:rç/ **n.** punë kërkimore
resemblance /ri'zemblëns/ **n.** ngjashmëri, ngjasim, shëmbëllim
resemble /ri'zembl/ **vt.** shëmbëllej, ngjaj, përngjaj
resent /ri'zent/ **vt.** 1. lëndohem, prekem; 2. zemërohem, indinjohem
resentful /ri'zentful/ **adj.** 1. i fyer, i lënduar; 2. i inatosur, i zemëruar
resentment /ri'zentmënt/ **n.** 1. fyrje, lëndim; 2. zemërim, inatosje
reservation /,rezë'veishn/ **n.** 1. rezervë; 2. rezervim, vend i rezervuar (në hotel etj.); 3. rezervat
reserve /ri'zë:rv/ **n.** 1. rezervë; **a reserve of food** rezervë ushqimore; 2. **usht. pl.** forcat rezerviste; 3. lojtar rezervë; 4. rezervat; 5. rezervë, ngurrim; **vt.** 1. rezervoj, ruaj, vë mënjanë; 2. ruaj, rezervoj (të drejtën etj.);3 rezervoj (bileta, etj.)
reserved /ri'zë:vd/ **adj.** 1. i rezervuar (vendi etj.); 2. i përmbajtur
reservoir /'rezëvwa:(r)/ **n.** 1. rezervuar, ujëmbledhës; 2. fig. rezervuar
reside /ri'zaid/ **vi.** 1. banoj; 2. është, ekziston, qëndron
residence /'rezidëns/ **n.** vendbanim; seli, rezidencë
resident /'rezidënt/ **n.** banor i përhershëm
resign /ri'zain/ **vti.** 1. jap dorëheqjen; 2. nënshtrohem
resignation /,rezig'neishn/ **n.** 1. dorëheqje; **hand (send) in one's resignation** kërkoj dorëheqjen; 2. nënshtrim
resist /ri'zist/ **vti.** 1. rezistoj; 2. qëndroj; 3. duroj
resistance /ri'zistëns/ **n.** 1. rezistencë, qendresë; 2. qëndrueshmëri
resistant /ri'zistënt/ **adj.** rezistent, i qëndrueshëm
resolute /'rezëlu:t/ **adj.** i vendosur
resolution /,rezë'lu:shn/ **n.** 1. rezolutë; 2. vendim; **pass a resolution** miratoj një vendim; 3. vendosmëri; 4. zgjidhje
resolve /ri'zolv/ **vti.** 1. vendos, marr vendim; 2. zgjidh; 3. zbërthej; **n.** 1. vendim; **make a resolve** marr vendim; 2. vendosmëri
resolved /ri'zolvd/ **adj.** i vendosur
resort /ri'zo:rt/ **n.** 1. mjet; **the last resort** mjeti i fundit; 2. qendër klimaterike pushimi; **vi.** 1. i drejtohem; 2. frekuentoj
resource /ri'so:rs/ **n.** 1. **pl.** burime, pasuri (natyrore etj.); 2. mjet; 3. shkathtësi, mprehtësi mendore
resourceful /ri'so:rsful/ **adj.** mendjefemër, që i punon mendja
respect /ri'spekt/ **n.** 1. respekt, nderim; 2. konsideratë; 3. drejtim; 4. lidhje, marrëdhënie; **in respect of (with) to** përsa i përket; 5. **pl.** të fala; **vt.** nderoj, respektoj
respectable /ri'spektëbl/ **adj.** 1. i respektueshëm; 2. i mjaftë
respectful /ri'spektful/ **adj.** i respektueshëm
respective /ri'spektiv/ **adj.** përkatës
respiration /,respë'reishn/ **n.** frymëmarrje
respire /ri'spaië(r)/ **vi.** marr frymë
respite /'respait/ **n.** pushim; **work without a respite** punoj pa pushim
respond /ri'spond/ **vi.** 1. përgjigjem, jap përgjigje; 2. reagoj
response /ri'spons/ **n.** 1. përgjigje; **in response to** në përgjigje të; 2. reagim
responsibility /ri,sponsë'biliti/ **n.** përgjegjësi

responsible /ri'sponsëbl/ **adj.** 1. përgjegjës; **be responsible for** përgjigjem për; 2. i besueshëm
rest /rest/ **n.** 1. pushim; 2. çlodhje; **have (take) a rest** pushoj; 3. mbështetje; **vi.** 1. çlodhem, pushoj; 2. çlodh; 3. mbështes
restaurant /'restërënt/ **n.** restorant
restful /'restful/ **adj.** 1. qetësues; 2. çlodhës
restless /'restlis/ **adj.** 1. i paqetë; 2. i parreshtur; 3. i shqetësuar
restoration /,restë'reishn/ **n.** restaurim; përtëritje, ripërtëritje
restore /ris'to:(r)/ **vt.** 1. restauroj; 2. përtërij; 3. rikthej; 4. ringjall, rivendos
restrain /ri'strein/ **vti.** 1. mbaj, përmbaj; 2. mbaj nën kontroll
restrict /ri'strikt/ **vt.** kufizoj
restriction /ri'strikshn/ **n.** kufizim; **place (impose) a restriction** vendos një kufizim
result /ri'zalt/ **n.** përfundim, rezultat; **as a result of** si rezultat i; **vi.** 1. përfundon; 2. rrjedh, rezulton
resume /ri'z(j)u:m/ **vt.** 1. rifilloj; 2. marr, zë përsëri
resumption /ri'zampshn/ **n.** rifillim
retail /'ri:teil/ **n.** shitje me pakicë; **sell goods by retail** shes mallra me pakicë; **vti.** shes me pakicë
retailer /ri:'teilë(r)/ **n.** shitës me pakicë
retain /ri'tein/ **vt.** 1. mbaj; 2. ruaj
retard /ri'ta:rd/ **vt.** 1. vonoj; 2. ngadalësoj; 3. pengoj
retire /ri'taië(r)/ **vit.** 1. dal në pension; 2. jap dorëheqjen; 3. tërhiqem
retired /ri'taiërd/ **adj.** 1. pensionist; 2. i vetmuar
retirement /ri'taiëmënt/ **n.** 1. pension, dalje në pension; **retirement age** mosha e pensionit; 2. mënjanim, jetë e vetmuar
retreat /ri'tri:t/ **n.** tërheqje; **vi.** 1. tërhiqem, prapsem
return /ri'të:rn/ **n.** 1. kthim; **in return for** si shpërblim për; 2. raport zyrtar; 3. fitim; 4. përgjigje; **vti.** 1. kthej; kthehem; 2. përgjigjem; 3. sjell (të ardhura); 4. raportoj zyrtarisht
reunion /,ri:'ju:niën/ **n.** ribashkim
reveal /ri'vi:l/ **vt.** zbuloj, nxjerr në shesh
revenge ri'venxh/ **n.** hakmarrje; **take revenge on** hakmerrem, marr hak; **out of (in) revenge for** si hakmarrje për; **vt.** 1. hakmerrem; 2. shpaguhem; **revenge oneself on smb** marr hak
revengeful /ri'venxhful/ **adj.** hakmarrës
revenue /'reven(j)u:/ **n.** të ardhura
reverse ri'vë:rs/ **n.** e kundërt; anë e kundërt; **vti.** 1. lëviz në drejtim të kundërt; 2. kthej mbrapsht; 3. kthej në të kundërt; 4. përmbys
review /ri'vju:/ **n.** 1. rishikim, rishqyrtim; 2. pasqyrë; 3. recensë; 4. revistë periodike; 5. **usht.** revistë, parakalim; **vti.** 1. shoh në retrospektivë; 2. rishqyrtoj; 3. recensionoj; 4. përsërit
revise ri'vaiz/ **vt.** 1. rishikoj, rishqyrtoj; 2. rikaloj, ripërsëris
revival /ri'vaivl/ **n.** 1. ringjallje; 2. rimëkëmbje
revive /ri'vaiv/ **vti.** 1. sjell, vij në vete; 2. ringjall
revolt /ri'voult/ **n.** revoltë, kryengritje; **vti.** 1. ngre krye, bëj revoltë; 2. ngjall neveri
revolting /ri'voultin/ **adj.** 1. revoltues; 2. i neveritshëm
revolution /,revë'lu:shn/ **n.** 1. revolucion; 2. ndryshim rrënjësor

revolutionary /,revë'lu:shënëri/ **adj.** revolucionar
revolver /ri'volvë(r)/ **n.** revolver
reward /ri'wo:rd/ **n.** shpërblim; **vt.** shpërblej
rheumatism /'ru:mëtizëm/ **n.** reumatizëm
rhyme /raim/ **n.** let. rimë; **vti.** rimon
rhythm /'ridhëm/ **n.** ritëm
rib /rib/ **n. anat.** brinjë
ribbon /'ribën/ **n.** 1. shirit, kordele; 2. shirit (makine shkrimi)
rice /rais/ **n.** oriz
rich /riç/ **adj.** 1. i pasur; 2. i kushtueshëm; 3. i begatshëm, pjellor; i bollshëm; 4. i yndyrshëm; **n. the rich** të pasurit
riches /'riçiz/ **n. pl.** pasuri
rid /rid/ **vti.** 1. shpëtoj; 2. çliroj, heq qafe; **be (get) rid of** shpëtoj, heq qafe
riddle /'ridl/ **n.** 1. gjëzë; 2. enigmë
ride /raid/ **vit.** 1. ngas kalin, biçikletën etj.; 2. udhëtoj me autobuz etj.; 3. kalëroj, shëtis me kalë; **n.** udhëtim (me kalë, biçikletë, makinë etj.)
rider /'raidë(r)/ **n.** 1. kalorës; 2. shtesë; klauzolë
ridge /rixh/ **n.** 1. kreshtë (malesh); 2. kulm (çatie)
ridicule /'ridikju:l/ **n.** tallje; **vt.** tall, vë në lojë
ridiculous /ri'dikjulës/ **adj.** qesharak; absurd
rifle /'raifl/ **n.** pushkë
right /rait/ **adj.** 1. i drejtë; 2. i saktë, i përpiktë; 3. i duhur, i përshtatshëm; 4. i rregullt, normal; **all right** mirë, në rregull; dakord; **put (set) something right** rregulloj; **adv.** 1. drejt; 2. tamam, pikërisht; 3. saktë; **n.** e drejtë; **civil rights** të drejtat civile; **human rights** të drejtat e njeriut; **rights and duties** të drejtat dhe detyrat; **vt.** rregulloj, vë në rregull
right /rait/ **adj.** i djathtë; **adv.** djathtas; **n.** e djathta
rightful /'raitful/ **adj.** 1. i ligjshëm; 2. i drejtë
right-handed /,rait'hendid/ **adj.** djathtak
rightly /raitli/ **adv.** drejtësisht, me drejtësi
rigid /'rixhid/ **adj.** 1. i ashpër, i rreptë, i ngurtë; 2. i paepur, i papërkulshëm
rigidity /ri'xhiditi/ **n.** 1. rreptësi, ashpërsi; 2. ngurtësi; 3. papërkulshmëri
rim /rim/ **n.** 1. anë, buzë; 2. skelet (syzesh)
ring /rin/ **vti.** 1. bie, tingëllon (zilja, telefoni etj.); 2. i bie ziles; 3. telefonoj; 4. tingëllon, kumbon; **ring smb up** marr dikë në telefon; **ring off** mbaroj bisedën telefonike; **n.** 1. tingëllimë; 2. kumbim; 3. thirrje telefonike
ring /rin/ **n.** 1. unazë; 2. rreth; 3. rrjet, bandë; 4. arenë (cirku); ring (boksi); **vti.** rrethoj
ring-finger /'rinfingë(r)/ **n.** gishti i unazës
rink /rink/ **n.** fushë (patinazhi)
rinse /rins/ **vt.** shpëlaj (gojën, rrobat etj.); **rinse something down** shtyj ushqimin me pije; **n.** shpëlarje
riot /'raiët/ **n.** trazirë; rebelim; **vi.** 1. ngre krye; 2. bëj potere; 3. shkaktoj trazira
rip /rip/ **vti.** 1. gris; 2. çaj
ripe /raip/ **adj.** 1. i pjekur, i arrirë, i bërë; 2. **fig.** i pjekur

rise /raiz/ **vi.** 1. del, lind (dielli); 2. ngrihem, çohem; 3. shtohet, ngrihet (era etj.); 4. ngre krye; 5. hipi, ngrihem (në pozitë); **n.** 1. rritje, ngritje, hipje; 2. kodrinë; 3. lindje (e diellit); 4. prejardhje, fillim, zanafillë
risk /risk/ **n.** rrezik; **take a risk** rrezikoj; **at risk** në rrezik; **at the risk of** duke rrezikuar të; **vt.** rrezikoj; **risk one's neck** rrezikoj kokën
risky 'riski/ **adj.** i rrezikshëm
rival /'raivl/ **n.** rival; **vt.** rivalizoj
rivalry /'raivëlri/ **n.** rivalitet
river /'rivë(r)/ **n.** 1. lumë; 2. **fig.** lumë, rrjedhë (gjaku etj.)
riverside /'rivësaid/ **n.** anë, buzë, breg (lumi)
road /roud/ **n.** 1. rrugë, udhë; **by road** me makinë; **on the road** në udhëtim; **the road to** rruga drejt
road-map /'roudmep/ **n.** hartë e rrugëve automobilistike
roadside /'roudsaid/ **n.** buzë, anë e rrugës
roadway /'roudwei/ **n.** rrugë e makinave
roam roum/ **vti.** bredh, endem, sorollatem
roar /ro:(r)/ **n.** 1. hungërimë; 2. buçimë, oshëtimë; 3. gjëmim, shpërthim; **vti.** 1. ulërin; 2. hungëron; 3. buçet
roast /roust/ **vti.** 1. pjek (mish etj.); 2. piqem, thekem (në zjarr etj.)
rob /rob/ **vt.** grabit
robbery /'robëri/ **n.** grabitje, plaçkitje
robe /roub/ **n.** mantel
robin /'robin/ **n. zool.** gushëkuq
robust /rou'bast/ **adj.** i fuqishëm, i shëndoshë, i shëndetshëm
rock /rok/ **n.** lëkundje; **vti.** 1. lëkund, tund; 2. lëkundem
rock /rok/ **n.** shkëmb; gur; **as firm as a rock** i fortë si shkëmbi
rocket /'rokit/ **n.** raketë; **vi.** 1. ngrihet me shpejtësi; 2. lëviz me shpejtësi rakete
rocking-chair /'rokinçeë(r)/ **n.** karrike lëkundëse
rocky 'roki/ **adj.** 1. shkëmbor; 2. guror, me gurë; 3. i paqëndrueshëm, i lëkundshëm
rod /rod/ **n.** 1. shufër; 2. shkop; purtekë; 3. kallam
rogue /roug/ **n.** vagabond, batakçi, maskara
role /roul/ **n.** 1. **teat.** rol; 2. rol, funksion
roll /roul/ **n.** 1. rrotullare, cilindër, rrotull; 2. top (stofi); 3. lëkundje (e anijes etj.); 4. **pl.** simite; 5. listë; regjistër; **call the roll** bëj apelin; **vti.** 1. rrokullis, rrotulloj; 2. lëkundem; 3. shtroj, hap (petë etj.); 4. mbështjell (mbështillem); 5. gjëmon
roller-skate /'roulë skeit/ **n.** patina (me rrota)
rolling-pin 'roulin pin/ **n.** okllai, petës
Roman /'roumën/ **adj.** romak; **n.** romak
romance /'roumëns/ **n.** 1. romancë; 2. histori dashurie; 3. roman (kalorësie, aventurash); 4. romantikë
romantic /rou'mentik/ **adj.** romantik
roof /ru:f/ **n.** 1. çati; 2. pullaz; **vt.** i vë çatinë
room /rum/ **n.** 1. dhomë; 2. vend; **make room for** bëj vend për; 3. vend, mundësi; **room for improvement** vend për përmirësim
rooster /'ru:stë(r)/ **n.** këndez, kaposh
root /ru:t/ **n.** 1. rrënjë; 2. **gjuh.** rrënjë; 3. **mat.** rrënjë

rope /roup/ **n.** 1. litar, tërkuzë; 2. varg (me qepë etj.); **vt.** lidh me litar; **rope something off** rrethoj me litar

rose /rouz/ **n.** 1. bot. trëndafil; 2. ngjyrë trëndafili

rosy /'rouzi/ **adj.** 1. trëndafil; 2. i kuq; **rosy cheeks** faqe të kuqe

rot /rot/ **n.** 1. kalbje; 2. kalbëzim; **vit.** kalbet, prishet, dekompozohet

rotten /'rotn/ **adj.** 1. i kalbur, i prishur; 2. i keq, i qelbur

rouge /ru:zh/ **n.** të kuq (për fytyrë a buzë)

rough /raf/ **adj.** 1. i ashpër; 2. i egër, i vrazhdë; 3. i stuhishëm, i egërsuar (deti, moti); 4. i papërpunuar; 5. i përafërt; **n.** pikturë (skicë, projekt) i papërpunuar, në dorë të parë; **in rough** përafërsisht; **in the rough** në dorë të parë; **adv.** ashpër

roughly /'rafli/ **adv.** ashpër

round /raund/ **adj.** 1. i rrumbullakët; 2. i plotë; **adv.** përreth, përqark, rrotull; **n.** 1. rreth; 2. qark; 3. cikël; 4. **sport.** raund; **prep.** rreth, përreth; **vti.** 1. rrumbullakoj; 2. rrumbullakohet

roundabout /'raundëbaut/ **adj.** i tërthortë

route /ru:t/ **n.** udhë; **en route** në udhëtim

routine /ru:'ti:n/ **n.** rutinë

row /rau/ **n.** 1. zënie, grindje; 2. zhurmë, potere; **kick up a row** bëj potere

row /rou/ **n.** radhë, varg, rresht

row /rou/ **n.** 1. vozitje; 2. shëtitje me varkë; **vti.** vozis

rowdy /'raudi/ **adj.** i zhurmshëm, i potershëm

royal /'roiël/ **adj.** 1. mbretëror; 2. i shkëlqyeshëm, madhështor

royalty /'roiëlti/ **n.** 1. anëtar i familjes mbretërore; 2. honorar

rub /rab/ **vti.** 1. fshij; 2. fërkoj; fërkohet; **rub something out** heq, fshij (një njollë etj.); **n.** fërkim

rubber /'rabë(r)/ **n.** 1. kauçuk; 2. gomë (për të fshirë); 3. **pl.** galloshe

rubbish /'rabish/ **n.** 1. plehra, hedhurina; 2. dokrra, gjepura

rude /ru:d/ **adj.** 1. i pasjellshëm; 2. i pahijshëm; 3. primitiv; 4. i papërpunuar; 5. i pagdhendur

rudely /'ru:dli/ **adv.** ashpër; harbutçe; vrazhdë

rudiment /'ru:dimënt/ **n.** 1. **pl.** bazat, fillimet; 2. fillesë, zanafillë, formë fillestare

rudimentary /,ru:di'mentri/ **adj.** 1. fillestar; 2. rudimentar

rug /rag/ **n.** 1. sixhade; 2. tapet; 3. qilim

rugby /'ragbi/ **n. sport.** regbi

ruin /'ruin/ **n.** 1. rrënim, shkatërrim; 2. falimentim; 3. **pl.** rrënoja, gërmadha; **vt.** 1. prish, rrënoj, shkatërroj; 2. falimentoj

rule /ru:l/ **n.** 1. rregull; **obey (break) the rule** zbatoj (thyej) rregullin; 2. praktikë, zakon; **make it a rule** e bëj rregull; **as a rule** zakonisht; 3. sundim; **under the rule of** nën sundimin e; 4. vizore; **vti.** 1. sundoj; 2. drejtohem, dominohem; 3. vendos, dekreton, urdhëron; 4. heq një vijë (me vizore)

ruler /'ru:lë(r)/ **n.** 1. sundimtar; 2. vizore

ruling /'ru:lin/ **n.** 1. sundim; 2. vendim gjyqësor; **adj.** 1. sundues; 2. dominues

rum /ram/ **n.** rum

rumble /'rambl/ **n.** 1. gjëmim; 2. uturimë; **vti.** 1. gjëmon; 2. uturon

rumor /'ru:më(r)/ **n.** thashetheme, fjalë; **vt.** flitet, pëshpëritet

run /ran/ **vti.** 1. vrapoj; 2. mbuloj me vrap; 3. **sport.**
vrapoj, ushtroj vrapimin; marr pjesë në garën e vrapimit; 4.
nxitoj; 5. ecën, udhëton; 6. lëvizin, qarkullojnë (autobuzët,
trenat etj.); 7 shpie, çoj (me makinë); 8 kalon, shkon; 9 fus
(nxjerr) kontrabandë (armë etj.); 10 kalon, shtrihet; 11
rrjedh, derdhet; 12 drejtoj, organizoj, qeveris; 13 punon
(makina, motori); 14 ngas, drejtoj; 15 vë kandidaturën; 16
përplasem; **run after smb** ndjek, gjëmoj; shkoj pas dikujt; **run
away** iki, largohem; **run across (into)** has, takoj rastësisht;
run away with something shpenzoj, harxhoj; vjedh; **run down**
bie (bateria etj.); përplas; ndalet, mbetet (ora); **run smb
over** shtyp; **run over something** lexoj shpejt e shpejt; **run
through** hedh një sy, shikoj shpejt e shpejt; shpenzoj pa
hesap; **n.** 1. vrap; 2. vrapim; **at a run** me vrap; 3. shëtitje,
udhëtim, xhiro (me makinë etj); 4. drejtim, kurs; 5. rënie e
menjëhershme **runaway** /'rënëwei/ **n.** i ikur, i arratisur
rung /ran/ **n.** 1. këmbë shkalle; 2. **fig.** shkallë
runner /'ranë(r)/ **n.** vrapues
running /'ranin/ **n.** 1. vrapim; 2. qeverisje, drejtim,
manazhim; **adj.** 1. rrjedhës; 2. vazhdues; 3. vrapues **runway**
/'rënwei/ **n.** pistë aerodromi
rural /'ruërël/ **adj.** fshatar, fshatarak, rural
rush /rash/ **n.** 1. vërshim; 2. nxitim, ngutje; 3. sulm; 4.
vërshim; **rush hours** piku i qarkullimit; **vti.** 1. turrem,
sulem; 2. ngut; ngutem; 3. çoj me ngut
Russian /'rëshn/ **adj.** rus; **n.** 1. rus; 2. gjuha ruse
rust /rast/ **n.** ndryshk; **vti.** ndryshk, ndryshket
ruthless /'ru:thlis/ **adj.** i pamëshirshëm
rye /rai/ **n. bot.** thekër
rye-bread /'raibred/ **n.** bukë thekre

sable /'seibl/ n. zool. 1. shqarth; 2. kunadhe; 3. gëzof shqarthi

sabotage /'sebëta:zh/ n. sabotim; vt. sabotoj

sack /sek/ n. thes; **the sack** pushim nga puna; **give smb the sack** pushoj dikë nga puna; **get the sack** pushohem nga puna; vt. 1. pushoj nga puna; 2. vë, hedh në thes

sacred /'sekrid/ adj. i shenjtë; **sacred writings** shkrimet e shenjta

sacrifice /'sekrifais/ n. 1. fli, theror, flijim; 2. vetëmohim, sakrificë; vti. 1. fet. flijoj, bëj fli; 2. i sakrifikoj

sad /sed/ adj. 1. i trishtuar, i dëshpëruar, i brengosur; **be (feel) sad** jam (ndihem) i trishtuar; 2. i mjerë

sadden /'sedn/ vt. dëshpëroj, pikëlloj, brengos

saddle /'sedl/ n. shalë (kali, biçiklete); vt. i vë shalin (kalit etj.)

sadness /'sednis/ n. dëshpërim, brengosje, pikëllim

safe /'seif/ adj. i sigurt; **safe and sound** shëndoshë e mirë; n. kasafortë

safeguard /'seifga:rd/ n. ruajtje, mbrojtje; vt. ruaj, mbroj

safely /'seifli/ adv. me siguri

safety /'seifti/ n. siguri; adj. i sigurt; **safety belt** rrip sigurimi; **safety match** shkrepse; **safety pin** paraman, karficë; **safety razor** brisk rroje; **safety valve** valvulë sigurimi

sail /seil/ vti. 1. lundroj; 2. drejtoj anijen; 3. niset (anija); n. 1. vel; 2. anije (me vela); 3. udhëtim (në det)

sailor /'seilë/ n. detar

saint /'seint/ n. shenjt

sake /seik/ n. hir; **for the sake of** për hir të

salad /'selëd/ n. 1. sallatë; 2. bot. sallatë e njomë, marule

salary /'selëri/ n. pagë, rrogë

sale /'seil/ n. 1. shitje; **for sale** për shitje, shitet; **on sale** në shitje; 2. ankand

salesgirl /'seilzgë:rl/ n. shitëse

salesman /'seilzmën/ n. shitës

saleswoman /'seilzwumën/ n. shitëse

salmon /'semën/ n. zool. salmon

saloon /së'lu:n/ n. 1. sallon (pritjeje); 2. sallë (lojnash); 3. bar, birrari

salt /so:lt/ n. kripë; vt. krip, shtie në shëllirë; adj. i kripur

salt cellar /'so:ltselë(r)/ n. kripore, kripës

salty /'so:lti/ adj. i kripur

salutation /,selju:teishn/ n. salutim, përshëndetje

salute /së'lju:t/ n. përshëndetje; vt. 1. përshëndet; 2. nderoj

salvage /'selvixh/ n. 1. shpëtim (i anijes); 2. pasuri e shpëtuar; vt. shpëtoj (anijen, pasurinë etj.)

salvation /sel'veishn/ n. shpëtim (i mëkatarëve etj.)

same /seim/ adj. i njëjtë, i njëllojtë; **at the same time** në të njëjtën kohë, njëkohësisht; megjithatë; pron. i njëjtë; **all the same** njëlloj; **be all the same to** është njëlloj për

sample /'sa:mpl/ 'sempl/ n. 1. mostër, model; 2. shembull, ilustrim; vt. marr, provoj, analizoj (një mostër)

sanction /'senkshn/ n. 1. lejë; 2. miratim; 3. sanksion; **economic sanctions** sanksione ekonomike; vt. 1. miratoj; 2. drejt. sanksionoj

sand /send/ **n.** 1. rërë; 2. **pl.** ranishte; **vt.** mbuloj, pastroj
me rërë
sandal /'sendl/ **n.** sandale
sandbank /'sendbenk/ **n.** ranishte
sandpaper /'sendpeipë(r)/ **n.** zumpara, letër smerili
sandwich /'senwiç/ **n.** sanduiç
sandy /'sendi/ **adj.** ranor
sane /sein/ **adj.** 1. i shëndoshë (mendërisht); 2. i arsyeshëm
sanitary /'senitëri/ **adj.** sanitar, higjenik, shëndetsor
Santa Claus /'sentë klo:z/ **n.** Plaku i Vitit të Ri
sapling /'seplin/ **n.** fidan
sarcastic /sa:'kestik/ **adj.** sarkastik
sarcastically /sa:'kestikli/ **adv.** me sarkazëm
sardine /sa:'di:n/ **n.** sardele
sash /sesh/ **n.** kornizë (dritareje)
satchel /'seçël/ **n.** çantë (shkolle etj.)
satellite /'setëlait/ **n. astr.** satelit (edhe **fig.**)
satin /'setin; 'setn/ **n.** atlas
satire /'setaië(r)/ **n.** satirë
satirc(al) /së'tirik(l)/ **adj.** satirik
satirize /'setëraiz/ **vt.** satirizoj
satisfaction /,setis'fekshn/ **n.** 1. kënaqësi; 2. kënaqje,
përmbushje (e nevojave, dëshirave etj.)
satisfactory /,setis'fektëri/ **adj.** i kënaqshëm
satisfy /'setisfai/ **vt.** kënaq; plotësoj, përmbush (kërkesat
etj.)
satisfied /'setisfaid/ **adj.** i kënaqur
satisfying /'setisfaiin/ **adj.** i kënaqshëm
Saturday /'setëdi/ **n.** e shtunë
sauce /so:s/ **n.** salcë; **tomato sauce** salcë domate
saucepan /'so:spën; 'so:spen/ **n.** kusi, tenxhere me bisht
saucer /'so:së(r)/ **n.** pjatë filxhani
sausage /'sosixh/ **n.** suxhuk, salsiçe
savage /'sevixh/ **adj.** 1. i egër; 2. i vrazhdë, i rreptë; 3. i
paqytetëruar, primitiv
save /seiv/ **vti.** 1. shpëtoj; 2. ruaj; 3. kursej; **save the
situation** shpëtoj situatën; **save one's own hide (skin)**
shpëtoj lëkurën; **save one's breath** kursej frymën
saver /'seivë(r)/ **n.** kursimtar
saving /'seivin/ **n.** 1. kursim; 2. **pl.** kursime; **saving bank**
arkë, bankë kursimi
savior /'seivië(r)/ **n.** shpëtimtar
savor (savour) /'seivë(r)/ **n.** 1. shije; 2. aromë; 3. gusto;
vti. 1. shijoj; 2. ka shijen e
savory (savoury) /'seivëri/ **adj.** 1. i shijshëm; 2. pikant
saw /so:/ **n.** sharrë; **vti.** sharroj
sawdust /'so:dast/ **n.** tallash
saxophone /'seksëfoun/ **n. muz.** saksofon
say /sei/ **vti.** 1. them; 2. jap, shpreh mendim; **that is to say**
domethënë; **n.** mendim **saying** /'seiin/ **n.** fjalë e urtë
scab skeb/ **n.** 1. dregëz; 2. zgjebe; 3. grevëthyes
scaffolding /'skefëldin/ **n.** 1. skelë (ndërtimi); 2. material
skele
scald /sko:ld/ **vt.** 1. djeg, përvëloj; 2. digjem; 3. nxeh

scale /skeil/ **n.** 1. shkallë, shkallëzim (i vizores, termometrit etj.); 2. shkallë, madhësi, masë; 3. **muz.** shkallë; 4. **mat.** shkallë; **on a large scale** në shkallë të gjerë; 5. **gjeog.** shkallë (e hartës); **vt.** shkallëzoj (hartën etj.)

scale /skeil/ **n.** 1. pjatë e peshores; 2. **pl.** peshore; **vi.** peshoj

scandal /'skendl/ **n.** 1. skandal; 2. thashetheme, përfolje; 3. ngjarje, sjellje e pahijshme

scandalous /'skendëlës/ **adj.** 1. skandaloz; 2. shpifarak

scar /ska:(r)/ **n.** mbresë, vragë; shenjë plage; **vti.** 1. lë mbresë, vragë; 2. mbyllet (plaga)

scarce /skeës/ **adj.** 1. i pakët, i pamjaftueshëm; 2. i rrallë

scarcely /'skeësli/ **adv.** 1. mezi; 2. zor se; 3. sapo

scare /skeë(r)/ **n.** frikë, trembje; **vt.** frikësoj, fut frikën

scarecrow /'skeë(r)krou/ **n.** dordolec

scarf /ska:f/ **n.** 1. shall; 2. shami qafe

scarlet /'ska:lët/ **n.** ngjyrë e kuqe e ndezur; **adj.** i kuq i ndezur; **scarlet fever mjek.** skarlatinë

scary /'skeëri/ **adj.** i frikshëm

scatter /'sketë(r)/ **vti.** 1. shpërndaj; shpërndahem; 2. përhap, hedh andej-këndej

scattered /'sketërd/ **adj.** i shpërndarë, i përhapur

scene /si:n/ **n.** 1. skenë; 2. vend (i ngjarjes); 3. tablo, skenë; 4. **teatr.** dekor; 5. pamje, peizazh; **behind the scenes** prapa skene

scenery /'si:nëri/ **n.** 1. **teatr.** dekor; 2. pamje, peizazh

scent /sent/ **n.** 1. erë, kundërmim; 2. parfum; 3. nuhatje; 4. gjurmë; **on the scent of** në gjurmë të; **vt.** 1. nuhat, gjej me nuhatje; 2. kundërmon

schedule /'shedju:l/ **n.** 1. listë; 2. orar; 3. afat; **before the schedule** para afatit; 4. plan, program; **according to schedule** sipas planit; **on schedule** në afat; **vt.** 1. planifikoj; 2. përpiloj grafikun, orarin

scheme /ski:m/ **n.** 1. skemë; 2. plan; 3. intrigë; makinacion; **vti.** 1. intrigoj; 2. bëj plane të fshehta

scholar /'skolë(r)/ **n.** 1. shkollar; 2. student; 3. studiues, erudit, njeri i shkolluar

scholarship /'skolëship/ **n.** 1. dituri; 2. erudicion; 3. bursë

school /sku:l/ **n.** 1. shkollë; 2. mësim

school-book /'sku:lbuk/ **n.** libër shkollor

schoolboy /'sku:lboi/ **n.** nxënës

schoolfellow /'sku:lfelou/ **n.** shok shkolle

schoolgirl /'sku:lgë:rl/ **n.** nxënëse

schoolteacher /'sku:ltiçë(r)/ **n.** mësues shkolle

schoolmaster /'sku:lma:stë(r)/ **n.** mësues

schoolmistress /'sku:lmistris/ **n.** mësuese

science /'saiëns/ **n.** shkencë; 2. teknikë, mjeshtëri, art

scientific /,saiën'tifik/ **adj.** shkencor

scientist /'saiëntist/ **n.** shkencëtar

scissors /'sizëz/ **n. pl.** gërshërë

scold /skould/ **vti.** qortoj ashpër, shaj

scolding /'skouldin/ **n.** 1. sharje; 2. qortim i ashpër

scooter /'sku:të(r)/ **n.** motoçikletë

scope /skoup/ **n.** 1. mundësi; 2. fushë; 3. sferë

scorch /sko:rç/ **vti.** 1. djeg, përzhit; 2. përvëloj
scorching /'sko:rçin/ **adj.** përvëlues
score /sko:(r)/ **n.** 1. **sport.** pikaverazh; 2. rezultat; **keep the score** mbaj pikët, rezultatin; 3. e çarë, e prerë (në dru etj); 4. rruvijë; 5. **muz.** partiturë; 5. llogari; **vti.** 1. shënoj; 2. mbaj, shënoj pikët; 3. gërvisht
scorn /sko:rn/ **n.** përbuzje, përçmim; **vt.** përbuz, përçmoj
scornful /'sko:rnful/ **adj.** përbuzës, përçmues
Scotch /skoç/ **adj.** skocez; **n.** 1. skocez; 2. uiski skocez
scoundrel /'skaundrël/ **n.** maskara, i poshtër
scout /'skaut/ **n.** 1. zbulues; 2. anëtar i Shoqatës Skaut
scramble /'skrembl/ **vti.** 1. kacavarem; 2. kacafytem; 3. ngatërroj, bëj lëmsh; 4. skuq (vezë; **n.** 1. kacavarje; 2. kacafytje
scrap /skrep/ **n.** 1. copë; 2. **pl.** mbeturina; 3. grimë
scrape /skreip/ **n.** 1. gërvishtje; 2. situatë e vështirë; **vti.** 1. gërryej, kruaj; 2. gërvisht
scratch /skreç/ **vti.** 1. gërvisht, çjerr; 2. gërvishtem, çirrem; 3. gërvisht (pena); 4. tërhiqem nga një garë; 5. shkarravit, shkruaj nxitimthi; **n.** gërvishtje, çjerrje; **start from the scratch** filloj nga hiçi
scream /skri:m/ **n.** britmë, klithmë; ulërimë; **vit.** bërtas, ulërij
screen /skri:n/ **vt.** 1. mbuloj, fsheh, mbroj; 2. **mjek.** diagnostikoj, depistoj; 3. shfaq në ekran; 4. shoshis; **n.** 1. perde; 2. mburojë; 3. ekran; 4. rrjetë (teli); 5. shoshë
screw /skru:/ **n.** 1. vidhë, burmë; 2. vidhosje, shtrëngim (i vidhës); 3. elikë; **vti.** vidhos, shtrëngoj me vidhë
screwdriver /'skru:draivë(r)/ **n.** kaçavidë
scribble /'skribl/ **n.** shkarravinë; **vt.** shkarravit
script /skript/ **n.** 1. skenar; 2. dorëshkrim
scripture /'skripçë(r)/ **n.** shkrim i shenjtë; Bibla
scrub /skrab/ **n.** pastrim, fërkim, kruarje me furçë etj.; **vti.** 1. kashais; 2. kruaj, fërkoj me furçë
scrupulous /'skru:pjulës/ **adj.** skrupuloz
sculptor /'skalptë(r)/ **n.** skulptor
sculpture /'skalpçë(r)/ **n.** skulpturë; **vti.** gdhend, skalit, modeloj
scurry /'skari/ **vi.** vrapoj shpejt
sea /si:/ **n.** det; **sea of something** mori me; **at sea** në det; **by sea** me det, me anije; **be all at sea** s'di nga t'ia mbaj
seagull /'si:gal/ **n.** pulëbardhë
seal /si:l/ **n.** vulë; **vt.** 1. vulos; 2. plumbos
seal /si:l/ **n. zool.** fokë; **vi.** gjuaj foka
seam /si:m/ **n.** 1. tegel; 2. rrudhë; 3. shtresë (qymyri etj)
seaman /'si:mën/ **n.** detar
seamstress /'semsçris/ **n.** rrobaqepëse
sear /sië(r)/ **vt.** 1. djeg, përxhit; 2. përvëloj
search /së:rç/ **n.** 1. kërkim; **in search of** në kërkim të; 2. kontroll; **vti.** 1. kërkoj; 2. kontrolloj
searchlight /'së:rçlait/ **n.** projektor
seashore /'si:sho:(r)/ **n.** bregdet
seasick /'si:sik/ **adj.** që e zë deti
sea-sickness /'si:siknis/ **n.** sëmundje deti
seaside /'si:said/ **n.** bregdet

season /'si:zn/ n. stinë; sezon; **in (out) of season** në sezon (jashtë) sezonit; **vti.** 1. stazhionoj; 2. regj; 3. ndërtoj (sallatën, gjellën etj.)
seasonal /'si:znl/ adj. stinor, sezonal; **seasonal work** punë sezonale
seasoning /'si:zënin/ n. 1. ndërtim (i gjellës, sallatës etj.); 2. staxhionim (i verës); 3. regjje; 4. herza
seat /si:t/ n. 1. vend; **take a seat** ulem; 2. ndenjëse; 3. vend (në kinema etj.); 4. vend (në parlament etj.); **vt.** 1. ul, ulem; 2. nxë, ka vende për; **be seated** uluni; **seat yourself** ulem
seaweed /'si:wi:d/ n. leshterik
secluded /si'klu:did/ adj. i izoluar; i vetmuar
second /'sekënd/ adj. i dytë; n. i dytë
second /'sekënd/ n. sekondë; çast; **in a second** në çast
secondary /'sekëndri; 'sekënderi/ adj. 1. i dytë, dytësor; 2. anësor, ndihmës; **secondary school** shkollë e mesme
second-class /,sekënd'kla:s/ adj. i klasit të dytë
second-hand /,sekënd'hend/ adj. 1. i dorës së dytë; 2. i përdorur
secondly /'sekëndli/ adv. së dyti
second-rate /,sekënd'reit/ adj. i klasit të dytë
secrecy /'si:krisi/ n. fshehtësi; **in secrecy** fshehtas; **with the utmost secrecy** me fshehtësinë më të madhe
secret /'si:krit/ n. e fshehtë, sekret; **in secret** fshehtas; **keep a secret** mbaj, ruaj të fshehtën; **let someone into a secret** i tregoj një të fshehtë dikujt; adj. i fshehtë, sekret
secretarial /,sekrë'teëriël/ adj. sekretarie, i sekretarisë
secretary /'sekrëtri/ n. 1. sekretar; 2. sekretar, ministër; **Secretary of State** Sekretari i Shtetit (Ministri i Jashtëm)
secretive /'si:krëtiv/ adj. 1. i fshehtë; 2. i mbyllur
sect /sekt/ n. sekt
section /'sekshn/ n. 1. pjesë; 2. seksion; sektor; 3. paragraf; 4. lagje, rajon (qyteti)
secure /si'kjuë(r)/ adj. i sigurt; i siguruar; **vt.** siguroj; sigurohem; 2. arrij, siguroj; 3. gjej
security /si'kjuëriti/ n. 1. sigurim; **the Security Council** Këshilli i Sigurimit; 2. siguri, garanci
sedate /si'deit/ adj. i qetë, i përmbajtur
sedative /'sedëtiv/ n. bar qetësues; adj. qetësues
see /si:/ vti. 1. shoh, shikoj; 2. takoj; 3. vizitoj; 4. mësoj; 5. kuptoj, marr vesh; 6. përjetoj; 7 përcjell; 8 kujdesem; 9 vë re, shquaj, dalloj; **see someone off** përcjell dikë; **see to** merrem, kujdesem; **seeing that** meqenëse; **see through** kuptoj qartë; çoj deri në fund; **let me see** ta shoh
seed /si:d/ n. 1. farë; 2. **fig.** farë, rrënjë; **plant (sow) the seeds of** mbjell, hedh farën e; **vti.** mbjell farë
seek /si:k/ vt. 1. kërkoj; **seek help** kërkoj ndihmë; 2. përpiqem, orvatem; **seek one's fortune** kërkoj fatin
seem /si:m/ vi. duket, ngjan
seemingly /'si:minli/ adv. në dukje
seep /si:p/ vi. rrjedh, kullon
seesaw /'si:so:/ n. kolovajzë, shilarës; vi. kolovitem
seethe /si:dh/ vti. 1. valoj, ziej; 2. **fig.** ziej (nga inati etj.)

seize /si:z/ **vti.** 1. kap, mbërthej; 2. zë, marr, pushtoj; 3.
më kap, më zë; **seize on (upon) something** kap, shfrytëzoj
diçka; 4. konfiskoj
seldom /'seldëm/ **adv.** rrallë
select /si'lekt/ **vt.** zgjedh; **adj.** i zgjedhur
selection /si'lekshn/ **n.** 1. zgjedhje, përzgjedhje; 2.
seleksionim; 3. koleksion
selective /si'lektiv/ **adj.** seleksionues, zgjedhës
self /self/ **n.** 1. vetja; 2. uni; **pron.** vetë, veten
self-confidence /,self'konfidëns/ **n.** vetëbesim
self-conscious /,self'konshës/ **adj.** i vetëdijshëm
self-control /,self kën'troul/ **n.** vetëkontroll
selfish /'selfish/ **adj.** egoist
selfless /'selflis/ **adj.** vetëmohues
self-made /,self'meid/ **adj.** 1. që ka ecur, çarë vetë në jetë;
2. i bërë, i gatuar vetë
self-service /,self'së:rvis/ **n.** vetëshërbim
sell /sel/ **vti.** 1. shes; 2. shet (dyqani); 3. shitet; **sell
out** shes krejt; **fig.** shes, tradhtoj dikë
seller /'selë(r)/ **n.** 1. shitës; 2. mall etj. që shitet; a
good (bad) seller mall që shitet mirë (keq); **best seller**
libër, kasetë etj. që shitet shumë
semi- /'semi/ **pref.** gjysmë-
semicircle /'semisë:rkl/ **n.** gjysmërreth
semicolon /,semi'koulën/ **n. gjuh.** pikëpresje
semifinal /,semi'fainl/ **n.** gjysmëfinale
seminar /'semina:(r)/ **n.** seminar
semolina /,semë'li:në/ **n.** bollgur
senate /'senit/ **n.** senat
senator /'senëtë(r)/ **n.** senator
send /send/ **vti.** 1. nis, çoj, dërgoj; 2. jap, transmetoj;
send off nis, dërgoj; nxjerr nga loja; **send for** dërgoj për;
send out lëshon; **send word** dërgoj, çoj fjalë
senile /'si:nail/ **adj.** i pleqërisë
senior /'si:niё(r)/ **adj.** i madh, i vjetër, i moshuar; **n.** 1.
më i vjetër; 2. më i lartë (në pozitë); 3. student i vitit të
fundit
sensation /sen'seishn/ **n.** 1. **psikol.** ndijim; 2. ndjesi; 3.
bujë, sensacion
sensational /sen'seishënl/ **adj.** sensacional
sense /sens/ **n.** 1. shqisë; 2. ndjenjë; **a sense of duty**
ndjenja e detyrës; 3. arsye, vetëdije; 4. kuptim; **make sense**
ka kuptim, është e arsyeshme; **in a sense** në një kuptim;
common sense gjykim, mendim i shëndoshë; **vt.** 1. ndiej; 2.
ndijoj
senseless /'senslis/ **adj.** 1. i paarsyeshëm, i marrë, i
çmendur; 2. i pandjenja, i pavetëdije; 3. i pandjeshëm
sensibility /,sensë'biliti/ **n.** 1. ndjeshmëri; 2. ndjesi
sensible /'sensëbl/ **adj.** 1. i ndjeshëm; 2. i vetëdijshëm; 3.
i arsyeshëm; 4. i kuptueshëm
sensitive /'sensitiv/ **adj.** 1. i ndjeshëm; 2. i prekshëm
sensitivity /,sensë'tiviti/ **n.** ndjeshmëri
sentence /'sentëns/ **n.** 1. **gjuh.** fjali; 2. **drejt.** dënim; **pass
(pronounce) sentence** shpall vendimin; **serve a sentence** vuaj
vendimin; **vt.** dënoj

sentiment /'sentimënt/ **n.** ndjenjë, dhembshuri, sentiment; sentimentalizëm
sentimental /,senti'mentl/ **adj.** i ndjeshëm, sentimental
sentry /'sentri/ **n.** rojë; **sentry duty** shërbim i rojës
separable /'sepërëbl/ **adj.** i ndashëm
separate /'seprët/ **adj.** i ndarë, i veçantë, i veçuar, i mëvetësishëm; **vti.** /'sepëreit/ 1. ndaj, veçoj; 2. ndahem
separation /,sepë'reishn/ **n.** 1. ndarje, veçim; 2. **drejt.** ndarje (nga burri, gruaja)
September /sep'tembë(r)/ **n.** shtator
sergeant /'sa:xhënt/ **n. usht.** rreshter
serial /'siëriël/ **adj.** 1. rendor; 2. serial; **n.** film, roman (me pjesë)
series /'siëri:z/ **n.** 1. seri; 2. sërë; 3. varg; **in series** në seri
serious /'siëriës/ **adj.** 1. serioz; 2. i rëndë; **a serious accident** aksident i rëndë
seriously /'siëriësli/ **adv.** seriozisht
seriousness /'siëriësnis/ **n.** seriozitet; **in all seriousness** me gjithë seriozitetin
sermon /'së:mën/ **n.** 1. **fet.** predikim; 2. **fig.** moralizim
serpent /'së:pënt/ **n.** 1. **zool.** gjarpër; 2. **fig.** gjarpër
servant /'së:vënt/ **n.** shërbëtor; 2. nëpunës, punonjës
serve /së:v/ **vti.** 1. shërbej, punoj së hmeđu, bëj punën e; 2. shërbej (në ushtri etj.); 3. shërbej (ushqim etj.); 4. shërbej (në restorant etj.); 5. shërben, përdoret; 6. trajtoj, sillem me dikë; 7 **sport.** kryej shërbimin (e topit); **serve as** shërben si; **it serves him (her) right** mirë t'i bëhet
service /'së:rvis/ **n.** 1. shërbim; **at your service** në dispozicionin tuaj; 2. shërbim, ndihmë mjekësore; 3. shërbim (në restorant etj.); 4. shërbim (transporti); 5. **fet.** shërbesë; 6. **pl.** komplet, takëm (tavoline); 7 **sport.** shërbimi i (topit); 8 shërbimi (ushtarak)
serviette /,së:vi'et/ **n.** pecetë (tavoline)
servile /'së:vail/ **adj.** servil
session /'seshn/ **n.** 1. sesion; 2. seancë
set /set/ **vti.** 1. vë, vendos; 2. fiksoj; 3. caktoj; 4. përgatit; 5. rregulloj; 6. perëndon (dielli); 7 vë (një detyrë); 8 vendos në vend (një kockë të thyer); 9 filloj; **set about** nis, filloj; **set off (out)** nisem për udhëtim; **set fire to something (set something on fire)** ndez, i vë zjarrin; **set free** liroj, lë të lirë; **set up** ngre, ndërtoj; krijoj; **n.** 1. komplet, takëm; 2. aparat (radio, televizor); 3. perëndim (i diellit); 4. grup, rreth; **adj.** 1. i ngrirë, i palëvizur, i ngulitur; 2. i caktuar, i vendosur
set-back /'setbek/ **n.** 1. pengesë; 2. dështim
setee /se'ti:/ **n.** divan
settle /'setl/ **vti.** 1. ulem, qëndroj; 2. vendosem; 3. zgjidh; 4. vendos; 5. qetësoj; 6. shlyej (llogarinë); **settle down to something** i shtrohem, i jepem (punës); **settle smb down** qetësoj dikë
settled /'setld/ **adj.** 1. i vendosur; 2. i shlyer; 3. i pandryshueshëm
settlement /'setlmënt/ **n.** 1. koloni, vendbanim, ngulim; 2. zgjidhje (e një çështjeje etj.); 3. shlyerje (e borxhit etj.)
seven /'sevën/ **n.** shtatë
seventeen /'seventi:n/ **n.** shtatëmbëdhjetë

seventeenth /'seventi:nth/ **adj.** i shtatëmbëdhjetë
seventh /'seventh/ **adj.** i shtatë
seventieth /'seventith/ **adj.** i shtatëdhjetë
seventy /'seventi/ **n.** shtatëdhjetë
sever /'sevë(r)/ **vti.** 1. pres, ndërpres; 2. këputet (litari etj.)
several /'sevrël/ **adj.** disa; **pron.** ca, disa
severe /si'vië(r)/ **adj.** 1. i rreptë, i ashpër; 2. i fortë; 3. i egër
severely /si'vië̇rli/ **adv.** ashpër, rreptë
sew /sou/ **vti.** 1. qep; 2. mbyll, përfundoj
sewage /'su:ixh/ **n.** ujëra të zeza
sewer /'sjuë(r)/ **n.** tub, kanal i ujërave të zeza
sewerage /'sjuërixh/ **n.** kanalizim i ujërave të zeza
sewing /'souin/ **n.** qepje
sewing machine /'souin më'shi:n/ **n.** makinë qepëse
sex /seks/ **n.** 1. seks, gjini; 2. marrëdhënie seksuale
sexual /'seksjuël/ **adj.** seksual
sexy /'seksi/ **adj.** epshor; erotik
shabby /'shebi/ **adj.** 1. i leckosur; 2. i pandershëm; 3. i poshtër; 4. i turpshëm
shade /'sheid/ **n.** 1. hije; 2. nuancë, ngjyrim; 3. **art.** hijedritë, hije; 4. errësirë, mugëtirë; **vti.** 1. mbuloj; 2. hijesoj; 3. errësoj, terratis; 4. i bëj hijet (një vizatimi)
shadow /'shedou/ **n.** 1. hije; 2. hije, njollë (në fytyrë); 3. **art.** hije; 4. gjysmerrësirë, mugëtirë; 5. hije, fantazmë; **be afraid of one's own shadow** ka frikë nga hija e vet; **vt.** 1. bëj hije, hijesoj; 2. ndjek nga pas (si hije)
shady /'sheidi/ **adj.** 1. hijor, me hije; 2. **fig.** i errët, i dyshimtë
shake /sheik/ **vti.** 1. tund; 2. shkund; 3. trondit, lëkund; 4. dridhem; dridhet; **shake hands with smb** i shtrëngoj dorën dikujt; **shake smb up fig.** shkund, gjallëroj; **n.** tundje, lëkundje
shaky /'sheiki/ **adj.** 1. i lëkundshëm; 2. i pasigurt, i lëkundur, i paqëndrueshëm
shall /shel/ **aux. v.** 1. do të; 2. duhet, duhen
shallow /'shelou/ **adj.** 1. i cekët; 2. **fig.** i përciptë, i cekët
sham /shem/ **n.** 1. shtirje, shtirësi; 2. shtinjak, simulant; **adj.** i shtirë, shtinjak, i rremë
shame /sheim/ **n.** turp; **Shame on you!** Të kesh turp!; **bring shame on smb** turpëroj dikë; **vt.** turpëroj
shameful /'sheimfl/ **adj.** i turpshëm
shameless /'sheimlis/ **adj.** i paturpshëm, i paturp, i pacipë
shampoo /shem'pu:/ **n.** shampo; **vt.** laj me shampo
shape /sheip/ **n.** 1. formë, trajtë; 2. gjendje, formë; **in good shape** në formë të mirë; **take shape** merr formë; **vt.** 1. formoj; 2. modeloj
shapeless /'sheiplis/ **adj.** i paformë
share /sheë(r)/ **n.** 1. pjesë; 2. **fin.** aksion; **vti.** 1. ndaj, pjesëtoj; 2. kam, ndaj bashkë me; 3. kam pjesë
shareholder /'sheë(r)houldë(r)/ **n.** aksionar
shark /sha:rk/ **n.** peshkaqen
sharp /sha:rp/ **adj.** 1. i mprehtë; 2. majëmprehtë, majëhollë; 3. i vrazhdë, i ashpër; 4. therës; 5. i fortë, i menjëhershëm; **adv.** pikërisht, saktë
sharpen /'sha:rpën/ **vti.** 1. mpreh; 2. **fig.** mpreh

shatter /'shetë(r)/ **vti.** 1. thyej, copëtoj; 2. prish, shuaj, shkatërroj
shave /sheiv/ **n.** 1. rrojë; 2. rruarje; **a close (narrow) shave** shpëtim për qime; **vti.** 1. rruaj; 2. rruhem
shaver /'sheivë(r)/ **n.** makinë rroje
shawl /sho:l/ **n.** shall
she /shi:/ **pron.** ajo; **n.** femër
shear /shië(r)/ **vt.** 1. qeth (dhentë); 2. **fig.** rruaj nga paratë; **n. pl.** gërshërë të mëdha
shed /shed/ **n.** 1. barakë; 2. kasolle; 3. hangar; 4. plevicë; **vt.** 1. bien, rrëzohen (flokët etj.); 2. lëshoj, përhap; 3. derdh (lotë etj.)
sheep /shi:p/ **n.** dele
sheep-dog /'shi:pdog/ **n.** qen stani
sheep-fold /'shi:pfould/ **n.** vathë
sheepish /'shi:pish/ **adj.** i druajtur, i turpshëm
sheepskin /'shi:pskin/ **n.** lëkurë dhensh
sheer /shië(r)/ **adj.** 1. i pingultë, i pjerrët; 2. i plotë, i tërësishëm; 3. i hollë; 4. i tejdukshëm
sheet /shi:t/ **n.** 1. çarçaf; 2. fije, fletë (letre); 3. shtresë, mbulesë (akulli etj.)
shelf shelf/ **n.** raft
shell /shel/ **n.** 1. guaskë, guall; 2. lëvozhgë; 3. predhë; gëzhojë (fisheku); **vti.** 1. nxjerr nga guaska; 2. heq, qëroj lëvozhgën; 3. bombardoj me artileri
shellfish /'shelfish/ **n.** molusk
shelter /'sheltë(r)/ **n.** 1. strehë; 2. strehim; **vt.** 1. strehoj; 2. mbroj; 3. futem në strehim
shelve /shelv/ **vt.** 1. vë në raft (librat); 2. lë, shtyj
shepherd /'shepërd/ **n.** bari, çoban
sheriff /'sherif/ **n.** sherif
sherry /'sheri/ **n.** verë sherri
shield /shi:ld/ **n.** 1. mburojë, shqyt; 2. **fig.** mbrojtje; **vt.** mbroj, ruaj **shift** /shift/ **n.** 1. lëvizje; 2. shpërngulje; 3. zhvendosje; 4. ndërresë, turn; 5. dredhi, bishtnim; **vti.** 1. lëviz, zhvendos; 2. zhvendosem; 3. kaloj, spostoj; 4. lëviz këmbët, eci shpejt
shilling /'shilin/ **n.** shilingë
shin /shin/ **n.** kërci
shine /shain/ **n.** 1. ndriçim; 2. shkëlqim; 3. lustër; **vi.** 1. shkëlqen, ndriçon; 2. lustroj (këpucët etj.); 3. **fig.** shkëlqen, shquhet
shiny /'shaini/ **adj.** 1. i shndritshëm, shndritës; 2. shkëlqyes, i shkëlqyeshëm; 3. i lustruar
ship /ship/ **n.** 1. anije, vapor; 2. anije kozmike; **vt.** transportoj (me anije)
shipment /'shipmënt/ **n.** 1. transportim (me anije); 2. ngarkim; 3. ngarkesë
shipwreck /'shiprek/ **n.** anijethyerje; **vt.** mbytet, fundoset (anija)
shipyard /'shipja:rd/ **n.** kantier detar
shirt /shë:rt/ **n.** këmishë
shiver /'shivë(r)/ **vi.** dridhem, rrëqethem; **n.** dridhje, rrëqethje
shock /shok/ **n.** 1. goditje; 2. tronditje; **vt.** trondit, shtang

shocking /'shokin/ **adj.** 1. trondítës; 2. skandaloz; 3. i tmerrshëm
shoe /shu:/ **n.** 1. këpucë; **put on (take off) one's shoes** vesh (heq) këpucët; 2. potkua; **vt.** mbath me patkonj
shoeblack /'shu:blek/ **n.** lustraxhi
shoehorn /'shu:ho:rn/ **n.** lugë këpucësh
shoelace /'shu:leis/ **n.** lidhëse këpucësh
shoemaker /'shu:meikë(r)/ **n.** këpucar
shoeshine /'shu:shain/ **n.** 1. lustraxhi; 2. lustrim i këpucëve
shoot /shu:t/ **vti.** 1. qëlloj, shtie (me pushkë etj.); 2. vrapoj me shpejtësi; 3. vras, pushkatoj; 4. **sport.** gjuaj (topin); 5. fotografoj; marr në film, xhiroj film; 6. çel, nxjerr filiz; **n.** bisk, lastar, filiz
shooter /'shu:të(r)/ **n.** 1. qitës; 2. armë zjarri
shop /shop/ **n.** 1. dyqan; 2. punishte, repart; **vt.** psonis, bëj pazarin
shopkeeper /'shopki:pë(r)/ **n.** dyqanxhi
shoplifting /'shopliftin/ **n.** vjedhje e dyqaneve
shopper /'shopë(r)/ **n.** blerës
shopping /'shopin/ **n.** blerje, psonisje, pazar; **go shopping** shkoj për të bërë pazarin; **do shopping** bëj pazarin
shopwindow /'shop'windou/ **n.** vitrinë
shore /sho:(r)/ **n.** breg (deti, liqeni etj.)
short /sho:rt/ **adj.** 1. i shkurtër; 2. i rrallë; 3. i pamjaftueshëm, i pamjaftë; 4. mangut; **short of time** s'kam kohë; **adv.** befas, menjëherë; **stop short** ndaloj befas; **fall short of something** mungon, nuk mjafton; **run short of** mbaron
shortage /'sho:rtixh/ **n.** mungesë
shortcoming /,sho:rtkamin/ **n.** 1. shkelje; 2. gabim; 3. e metë
shorten /'sho:rtn/ **vti.** 1. shkurtoj; 2. shkurtohet
shorthand /'sho:rthend/ **n.** stenografi; **take something down in shorthand** marr me stenografi
shortly /'sho:rtli/ **adv.** 1. menjëherë; **shortly after** menjëherë pas; **shortly before** pak para se; 2. shkurt, shkurtimisht; 3. prerë, vrazhdë
shorts /sho:rts/ **n. pl.** 1. brekë, mbathje; 2. pantallona të shkurtra
shortsighted /,sho:rt'saitid/ **adj. mjek.** dritëshkurtër, miop
shot /shot/ **n.** 1. krismë, e shtënë; 2. përpjekje, orvatje; **have a shot at something** orvatem të bëj diçka; 3. **sport.** gjuajtje, goditje (topi); 4. qitës; 5. **sport.** gjyle; 6. fotografi; 7 **mjek.** injeksion
should /shud/ **aux. v.** duhet; duhej
shoulder /'shouldë(r)/ **n.** shpatull, sup; **shoulder to shoulder** sup më sup; **shift the blame to other shoulders** ia hedh fajin dikujt tjetër; **vt.** 1. hap rrugën me supe; 2. hedh në sup; 3. mbaj mbi vete (përgjegjësinë etj.)
shout /shaut/ **n.** britmë, thirrmë; **vit.** thërras, bërtas
shove /shav/ **vti.** shtyj; **n.** e shtyrë, shtyrje
shovel /'shavl/ **n.** lopatë; **vt.** heq, pastroj me lopatë
show /shou/ **n.** 1. ngritje (e dorës); 2. shfaqje, spektakël; 3. ekspozitë; 4. pamje e jashtme; dukje; **do something for show** bëj diçka për t'u dukur; **vt.** 1. tregoj, demonstroj; 2. shfaq; 3. shfaqem, dukem; **show someone round** shoqëroj të shikojë; **show someone to a place** çoj në; **show off** dukem, marr poza për t'u dukur; **show one's face** shfaqem; **show someone out** përcjell dikë

showcase /'shoukeis/ **n.** vitrinë
shower /'shauë(r)/ **n. 1.** shi i rrëmbyer, rrebesh; **2. fig.**
breshëri, mori; **a shower of blows** breshëri goditjesh; **3.**
dush; **4.** larje në dush; **take a shower** bëj dush
shred /shred/ **n.** copë; **tear something to shreds** bëj copa-copa
shrewd /shru:d/ **adj.** i mprehtë, mendjehollë
shriek /shri:k/ **n.** britmë, klithmë; **vti.** bërtas, këlthas
shrill /shril/ **adj.** i mprehtë, çjerrës
shrimp /shrimp/ **n.** karkalec deti
shrine /shrain/ **n. 1.** faltore; **2.** varr
shrink /shrink/ **vti. 1.** tkurrem, mblidhem; **2.** hyn në ujë (një
plaçkë); **3.** tërhiqem, prapsem; **4.** mënjanohem
shrivel /'shrivl/ **vti. 1.** fishkem, rrudhem; **2.** vyshkem; **3.**
mblidhem; gërmuqem
shrub /shrab/ **n. bot. 1.** shkurre; **2.** kaçube
shrubbery /'shrabëri/ **n.** shkurrajë, shkurrishte
shrug /shrag/ **vt.** ngre, mbledh supet; **n.** ngritje e supeve
shudder /'shadë(r)/ **vi.** dridhem, rrëqethem; **n.** dridhje,
rrëqethje
shuffle /'shafl/ **vti. 1.** tërheq këmbët zvarrë; **2.** përziej
(letrat); **3.** dredhoj
shut /shat/ **vti. 1.** mbyll; **2.** mbyllet; **shut down** mbyll (një
fabrikë, uzinë etj.); **shut smb (sth) in** kyç, mbyll brenda;
shut off mbyll (ujin, gazin etj.); **shut out** lë jashtë; **shut
up** mbyll; siguroj (shtëpinë); hesht, mbyll gojën
shut-down /'shatdaun/ **n.** mbyllje (e një fabrike, uzine)
shutter /'shatë(r)/ **n.** qepen; **put up the shutters** ngre
(mbyll) qepenat
shy /shai/ **adj.** i druajtur, i turpshëm; **vi.** frikësohet (kali)
shyness /'shainis/ **n.** druajtje
sick /sik/ **adj.** i sëmurë; **fall sick** sëmurem; **feel sick** më
vjen të vjellë; **be sick for** kam mall për; **n. 1.** e vjellë; **2.**
pl. të sëmurët
sicken /'sikn/ **vti. 1.** sëmurem; **2.** ngjall neveri; **3.**
neveritem; **sicken of something** më neveritet
sickening /'siknin/ **adj.** neveritës
sick leave /'sikli:v/ **n. 1.** raport (mjekësor); **2.** leje
shëndetësore
sickly /'sikli/ **adj. 1.** i sëmurë, shëndetlig; **2.** i zbehtë; **3.**
neveritës
sickness /'siknis/ **n. 1.** sëmundje; **2.** të pështirë
side /said/ **n. 1.** anë; **2.** anë, faqe; **3.** brinjë; **4.** anë,
anësi; **5.** anë, aspekt, drejtim; **by the side of** anës, në anë
të; **side by side** krah për krah; **on every side** gjithkund,
gjithandej; **put something on (to) one side** heq mënjanë; lë
për më vonë; **on the side of** në anën e; **take the side of**
someone marr anën e dikujt; **vi.** marr anën e dikujt
sideboard /'saidbo:rd/ **n.** bufe
sidewalk 'saidwo:k/ **n. amer.** trotuar
sideways /'saidweiz/ **adv. 1.** tërthor; **2.** anash, brinjazi
siege /si:xh/ **n.** rrethim; **lay seige to** rrethoj
sieve /siv/ **n. 1.** kullore, kullesë; **2.** shoshë; sitë; **vt. 1.**
kulloj; **2.** sit; shosh
sift /sift/ **vt. 1.** sit; shosh; **2. fig.** shoshit, shqyrtoj me
kujdes
sigh /sai/ **n.** psherëtimë, ofshamë; **utter (heave) a sigh**
nxjerr, lëshoj një psherëtimë; **vti. 1.** psherëtij; **2.**
dëshirohem; **3.** kam mall

sight /sait/ **n.** 1. shikim, të parët; **lose one's sight** humb
shikimin; 2. pamje; 3. fushëpamje; 4. **pl.** monumentet,
kuriozitetet, vendet me interes; **catch sight of** shoh; **at the
sight of** me të parë; **out of sight** jashtë fushës së shikimit;
at first sight në shikimin e parë; **lose sight of something**
humb nga sytë; **see the sights of** shoh vendet me interes të
qytetit etj.
sightseeing /'saitsi:in/ **n.** udhëtim turistik
sightseer /'saitsi:ë(r)/ **n.** vizitor, turist
sign /sain/ **n.** 1. shenjë, simbol (matematike); 2. tabelë; 3.
shenjë, sinjal; 4. dëshmi, tregues; 5. ogur; 6. gjurmë; **as a
sign of** si shenjë e; **vti.** 1. nënshkruaj; 2. bëj shenjë
signal /'signël/ **n.** sinjal; **vti.** sinjalizoj, bëj me shenjë;
adj. i shquar, i shënuar
signatory /'signëtri; 'signëto:ri/ **n.** nënshkrues; **adj.**
nënshkrues
signature /'signëçë(r)/ **n.** nënshkrim; firmë
significance /sig'nifikëns/ **n.** 1. rëndësi; 2. kuptim
significant /sig'nifikënt/ **adj.** i rëndësishëm
signify /'signifai/ **vti.** 1. nënkuptoj, ka kuptim, domethënie;
2. ka rëndësi
signpost /'sainpoust/ **n.** tabelë rrugore
silence /'sailëns/ **n.** heshtje, qetësi; **in silence** në qetësi;
keep silence mbaj qetësi; **break silence** thyej heshtjen; **put
(reduce) smb to silence** vendos qetësinë; **vt.** qetësoj, vendos
qetësinë
silencer /'sailënsë(r)/ **n.** zhurmëmbytës
silent /'sailënt/ **adj.** 1. i heshtur; 2. i qetë; **keep silent**
hesht; mbaj qetësi; 3. i pazëshëm
silk /silk/ **n.** mëndafsh; fije (pëlhurë) mëndafshi; **adj.**
mëndafshi
sill /sil/ **n.** pezul, prag (i derës, dritares)
silly /'sili/ **adj.** i pamend, mendjelehtë, budalla; **say silly
things** flas budallallëqe; **Don't be silly!** Mos u bëj budalla!
silver /'silvë(r)/ **n.** 1. **kim.** argjend; 2. **pl.** argjendurina;
adj. i argjendtë; i argjenduar; **vt.** argjendoj, laj me argjend
silversmith /'silvësmith/ **n.** argjendar
silverware /'silvëveë(r)/ **n.** argjendari
silvery /'silvëri/ **adj.** argjendor
similar /'similë(r)/ **adj.** i ngjashëm, i njëjtë
similarity /,simi'leriti/ **n.** ngjasim, ngjashmëri
simile /'simili/ **n. let.** krahasim
simmer /'simë(r)/ **vti.** 1. ziej ngadalë; 2. **fig.** vloj, ziej
përbrenda (nga inati etj.); 3. mbaj përbrenda
simple /'simpl/ **adj.** 1. i thjeshtë; 2. i padjallëzuar
simplification /,simplifi'keishn/ **n.** thjeshtësim, thjeshtim
simplify /'simplifai/ **vt.** thjeshtësoj
simply /'simpli/ **adv.** thjesht
simulate /'simjuleit/ **vt.** shtirem, simuloj
simultaneous /,siml'teiniës/ **adj.** i njëkohëshëm
sin /sin/ **n.** mëkat; gjynah; **it is a sin to** është mëkat të
since /sins/ **prep.** qysh, që nga; **conj.** që kur; që prej; **adv.**
që atëhere, qysh atëhere
sincere /sin'sië(r)/ **adj.** i çiltër, i sinqertë
sincerely /sin'siërli/ **adv.** sinqerisht
sincerity /sin'seriti/ **n.** çiltëri, sinqeritet

sinful /'sinful/ **adj.** mëkatar
sing /sin/ **vti.** këndoj
singe /sinxh/ **vt.** 1. përzhit, përcëlloj; 2. djeg; **n.**
përzhitje; djegie
singer /'sinë(r)/ **n.** këngëtar
single /'singl/ **adj.** 1. i vetëm; 2. i pamartuar; 3. tek;
single bed krevat tek
single-handed /,singl'hendid/ **adj.** i vetëm
singlet /'singlit/ **n.** 1. fanellë pa mëngë; 2. fanellë
sportive
singular /'singjulë(r)/ **adj.** 1. **gjuh.** njëjës; 2. i çuditshëm,
i veçantë; 3. i shquar; **n. gjuh.** njëjës
sinister /'sinistë(r)/ **adj.** 1. i lig, i poshtër; 2. ogurzi
sink /sink/ **n.** lavapjatë; lavaman
sink /sink/ **vti.** 1. fundos; 2. perëndon (dielli); 3. zhytem,
kridhem
sip /sip/ **n.** gllënjkë, hurbë; **vti.** pi me gllënjka
sir /së:(r)/ **n.** zotëri, sër
sirloin /'së:loin/ **n.** filetë
sister /'sistë(r)/ **n.** 1. motër; 2. infermiere; 3. murgeshë
sister-in-law /'sistë(r) in lo:/ **n.** kunatë
sit /sit/ **vti.** 1. ulem, rri ulur; 2. pozoj; 3. ul; **sit down**
ulem; **sit up** rri natën vonë
site /sait/ **n.** 1. vend, truall; 2. kantier
sitting-room /'sitinru:m/ **n.** dhomë pritjeje
situated /'sitjueitid/ **adj.** i vendosur
situation /,sitju'eishn/ **n.** 1. gjendje, kushte; 2. vendosje,
pozicion
six /siks/ **n.** gjashtë; **adj.** i gjashtë
sixteen /sik'sti:n/ **n.** gjashtëmbëdhjetë
sixteenth /sik'sti:nth/ **adj.** i gjashtëmbëdhjetë
sixth /siksth/ **adj.** i (e) gjashtë
sixtieth /'sikstith/ **adj.** i (e) gjashtëdhjetë
sixty /'siksti/ **n.** gjashtëdhjetë
size /saiz/ **n.** 1. numër; 2. masë; përmasë; madhësi; 3.
format; **vt.** ndaj, klasifikoj sipas përmasave; **size smb (sth)**
up mas, peshoj me sy
skate /skeit/ **n.** patinë; **vi.** rrëshqas me patina
skater /'skeitë(r)/ **n.** patinator
skating /'sketin/ **n.** patinazh
skating rink /'skeitin rink/ **n.** fushë patinazhi
skeleton /'skelitn/ **n.** skelet
sketch /skeç/ **n.** 1. skicë; 2. skeç
ski /ski:/ **n.** ski; **vi.** bëj, rrëshqas me ski
skid /skid/ **vi.** rrëshqet (makina etj.); **n.** 1. **tek.** takë e
frenit; 2. shkarje, rrëshqitje (e rrotave)
skillful /'skilful/ **adj.** i shkathët
skill /skil/ **n.** 1. aftësi; 2. mjeshtëri, art; 4. shkathtësi
skilled /skild/ **adj.** 1. i specializuar, i kualifikuar; 2. i
shkathët, me përvojë
skim /skim/ **vti.** 1. tund, rrah qumështin; 2. lexoj shkarazi;
3. rrëshqas, fluturoj mbi
skin /skin/ **n.** 1. lëkurë (njeriu, kafshe); 2. kacek, shakull;
3. lëkurë, lëvore; **soaked to the skin** i lagur deri në palcë;
vti. 1. rrjep (lëkurën); 2. **fig.** rrjep, rruaj (nga paret); 3.
zë cipë

skinny /skini/ **adj.** thatim, thatanik
skip /skip/ **n.** kërcim; **vit.** 1. kërcej, hidhem; 2. kaloj,
hidhem nga një temë në tjetrën, nga një vend në tjetrin; 3.
kërcej me litar
skipper /'skipë(r)/ **n.** 1. kapiten (i anijes tregëtare apo
peshkimit); 2. kapiten (i skuadrës së futbollit etj.)
skipping-rope /'skipinroup/ **n.** litar kërcimi
skirt /skë:rt/ **n.** fund
skull /skal/ **n.** kafkë
sky /skai/ **n.** qiell; **under the open sky** në qiell të hapur;
praise to the skies ngre në qiell
skyline /'skailain/ **n.** horizont
skyscraper /'skaiskreipë(r)/ **n.** qiellgërvishtës
slab /sleb/ **n.** 1. pllakë, plloçe; 2. copë, thelë
slack /slek/ **adj.** 1. i plogët, i mefshtë; 2. i lëshuar; 3. i
pangarkuar; 4. i lirshëm; 5. i amullt, i ndenjur; **n.** 1.
amulli; 2. plogështi; 3. përtaci; **vi.** 1. plogështohem; 2.
dembelosem; 3. ul ritmin, shpejtësinë
slam /slem/ **n.** përplasje e derës; **vt.** përplas (derën etj.)
slander /'sla:ndë(r)/ **n.** shpifje; përgojim; **vt.** shpif,
përgojoj, marr nëpër gojë
slang /slen/ **n.** gjuh. zhargon
slant /sla:nt/ **n.** pjerrje; anim; **vi.** pjerret, anon
slap /slep/ **n.** dackë; **vt.** qëlloj me shuplakë
slash /slesh/ **n.** 1. prerje; 2. varrë; **vti.** 1. pres, çaj me
(thikë, shpatë etj.); 2. rrah me kamxhik
slaughter /'slo:të(r)/ **n.** 1. therje (e bagëtisë); 2.
gjakderdhje, kasaphanë; **vt.** 1. ther (një kafshë); 2.
masakroj, bëj kërdinë
slave /sleiv/ **n.** skllav
slavery /'sleivëri/ **n.** skllavëri
sledge /slexh/ **n.** sajë; **vit.** udhëtoj me sajë; transportoj me
sajë
sleep /sli:p/ **n.** gjumë; **go to sleep** bie të fle; **put smb to
sleep** vë në gjumë; **get to sleep** më zë gjumi; **have a good
sleep** fle mirë; **vti.** fle, bie në gjumë; 2. merr, nxë (për të
fjetur)
sleeper /sli:pë(r)/ **n.** 1. njeri që fle; 2. traversë; 3. vagon
fjetjeje
sleepily /'sli:pili/ **adv.** përgjumësh
sleeping-pill /'sli:pinpil/ **n.** ilaç për gjumë
sleeplessness /'sli:plisnis/ **n.** pagjumësi
sleepless /'sli:plis/ **adj.** i pagjumë
sleepy /'sli:pi/ **adj.** 1. i përgjumshëm, i përgjumur; 2. i fjetur
sleet /'sli:t/ **n.** llohë; **vi.** bie llohë
sleeve /sli:v/ **n.** mëngë; **have something up one's sleeve** mbaj
diçka të fshehtë
sleigh /slei/ **n.** slitë
slender /'slendë(r)/ **adj.** 1. i hollë, hollak; 2. i hequr, i
dobët; 3. i pakët, i pamjaftueshëm
slice /slais/ **n.** 1. thelë; 2. fetë, rriskë; 3. pjesë; **vti.**
pres në feta, rriska, thela
slide /slaid/ **vi.** rrëshqas; **n.** 1. rrëshqitje (në akull,
dëborë etj.); 2. rrëshqitje (dheu); 3. rrëshqitëse; 3.
diapozitiv
sliding /'slaidin/ **adj.** lëvizëse, rrëshqitëse
slight /slait/ **n.** mospërfillje; **adj.** 1. i hollë; 2. i vogël,
i parëndësishëm; **not in the slightest** aspak; **vt.** shpërfill

slightly /'slaitli/ **adv.** pak, paksa
slim /slim/ **adj.** i hollë; 2. shtathollë; 3. i vogël, i pakët,
i pamjaftueshëm; **vit.** 1. hollohem; 2. dobësohem
sling /slin/ **vti.** 1. hedh; 2. gjuaj; 3. hedh, var; **n.** 1.
rrip; 2. gjalmë; 2. hobe
slink slink/ **vi.** iki, largohem vjedhurazi
slip /slip/ **n.** 1. rrëshqitje; 2. shkarje; lapsus; **a slip of
the pen (tongue)** shkarje e penes (gojës); 3. copë letër; **vti.**
1. shkas, rrëshqas; 2. iki vjedhurazi, pa u vënë re; 3. fus
shpej e shpejt pa u parë
slipper /'slipë(r)/ **n.** pantofël
slippery /'slipëri/ **adj.** 1. rrëshqitës; 2. i paqëndrueshëm, i
pabesë
slit /slit/ **n.** 1. çarje; 2. frengji
slither /'slidhë(r)/ **vi.** shkas, rrëshqas
slope /sloup/ **n.** 1. pjerrësi; pjerrësirë; 2. shpat i pjerrët;
vti. pjerr, anoj
slot machine /'slot mëshin/ **n.** automat, shpërndarës automatik
slow /slou/ **adj.** 1. i ngadalshëm; 2. prapa (ora); 3. i
ngathët; 4. i plogët, pa gjallëri; **adv.** ngadalë; **vit.** 1.
ngadalësoj; 2. vonoj; **slow up (down)** ul, ngadalësoj ritmin,
shpejtësinë
slowly /'slouli/ **adv.** ngadalë
slum /slam/ **n.** lagje e varfër
slush /slash/ **n.** llucë; dëborë e shkrirë
sly /slai/ **adj.** dinak, tinëzar, dhelparak
small /smo:l/ **adj.** 1. i vogël; **small change** kusur; 2. i
parëndësishëm; 3. shpirtvogël
smallpox /'smo:lpoks/ **n. mjek.** li
smart /sma:rt/ **adj.** 1. i bukur, shik, elegant; 2. i mençur, i
mprehtë; 3. i shpejtë; 4. i fortë, i fuqishëm
smartness /'sma:rtnis/ **n.** 1. elegancë; 2. mprehtësi
smash /smesh/ **vti.** 1. thyej, bëj copë-copë; 2. shpartalloj
(armikun); 3. godit fort; 4. përplas; 5. përplaset; **n.** 1.
thyerje; 2. përplasje (e makinës etj.)
smashing /'smeshin/ **adj.** i mrekullueshëm, fantastik, i
shkëlqyer
smear /smië(r)/ **vti.** njollos, ndot; **n.** njollë
smell /smel/ **vti.** 1. mban erë, kundërmon; 2. marr erë, nuhat;
smell at something nuhas; **smell of something** mban erë; **smell
smb (sth) out** gjej, zbuloj me nuhatje; **n.** 1. erë; 2. nuhatje
smelly /'smeli/ **adj.** që mban erë të keqe
smile /smail/ **n.** buzëqeshje; **vti.** buzëqesh, vë buzën në gaz
smith /smith/ **n.** farkëtar
smoke /smouk/ **n.** 1. tym; 2. pirje e duhanit; **vti.** 1. pi
duhan; 2. nxjerr, lëshon tym; 3. tymos, thaj në tym; 4.
nxjerr, largoj me tym. **smoked** /smoukt/ **adj.** i tymosur, i
tharë në tym
smoker /'smoukë(r)/ **n.** duhanxhi, pirës duhani
smoking /'smoukin/ **n.** pirja e duhanit; **No smoking** Ndalohet
duhani
smoky /smouki/ **adj.** 1. tymak; 2. i tymosur; 3. i tymtë
smooth /smu:th/ **adj.** 1. i lëmuar; 2. i qetë, i patrazuar
(deti); 3. i sheshtë; 4. i rehatshëm; 5. i ëmbël, i butë; **vt.**
1. sheshoj, shtroj; lëmoj; 2. **fig.** sheshoj, zgjidh
smoothly /'smu:thli/ **adv.** butë
smother /'smadhë(r)/ **vt.** 1. mbyt; 2. shuaj; 3. mbaj; 4.
mbuloj

smoulder /'smouldë(r)/ **vi.** digjet nën vete (zjarri)
smuggle /'smagl/ **vti.** 1. bëj kontrabandë; 2. fut kontrabandë
smuggler /'smaglë(r) **n.** kontrabandist, trafikant
snack /snek/ **n.** vakt i lehtë i ndërmjemë (ushqimi)
snag /sneg/ **n.** vështirësi, pengesë e paparashikuar; **come across a snag** has, ndesh një pengesë, vështirësi të paparashikuar
snail /sneil/ **n.** kërmill; **at a snail's pace** me hap breshke
snake /sneik/ **n.** gjarpër; **vi.** gjarpëron
snap /snep/ **vti.** 1. kafshoj; 2. kërcet, thyhet; 3. flas ashpër; 4. bëj një fotografi; **n.** 1. kërcitje, krismë; 2. ftohje e motit; 3. fotografi; 4. vrull, energji, gjallëri
snapshot /'snepshot/ **n.** 1. fotografi e çastit; 2. e shtënë kuturu
snarl /sna:rl/ **vti.** 1. hungëron (qeni); 2. i hakërrohem dikujt
snatch /sneç/ **vti.** rrok; kap; rrëmbej; **n.** 1. kapje; rrëmbim; 2. fragmente, copëza
sneakers /'sni:këz/ **n.** atlete
sneer /snië(r)/ **n.** 1. zgërdheshje; 2. vështrim përbuzës; **vi.** 1. zgërdhihem; 2. përqesh, qesh me përbuzje
sneeze /sni:z/ **n.** teshtitje; **vi.** teshtij
sniff /snif/ **vti.** 1. tërheq, thith hundët; 2. nuhat, thith me hundë; **n.** thithje
snip /snip/ **vti.** pres me gërshërë; **n.** 1. prerje; 2. copë e prerë
snooze /snu:z/ **n.** dremitje; **have a snooze** dremit; **vi.** dremit, kotem
snore /sno:(r)/ **n.** gërhitje; **vi.** gërhas
snow /snou/ **n.** borë, dëborë; **vi.** bie dëborë
snowball /'snoubo:l/ **n.** top dëbore; **play snowballs** luaj me topa dëbore
snowdrop /'snoudrop/ **n. bot.** lule bore
snowfall /'snouf:ol/ **n.** rënie dëbore; rreshje dëbore
snowflake /'snoufleik/ **n.** flok bore
snowstorm /'snousto:m/ **n.** stuhi bore
snowy /'snoui/ **adj.** 1. i bortë, me dëborë; **snowy weather** kohë bore; 2. i mbuluar me dëborë; 3. i bardhë si bora
snug /snag/ **adj.** i rehatshëm, komod
so /sou/ **adv.** 1. kaq; 2. kështu; ashtu; 3. gjithashtu; **so as to** me qëllim të; **so that** në mënyrë që; **conj.** për këtë arsye, prandaj
soak /souk/ **vti.** 1. njom, lag; 2. qullem, lagem; 3. hyn, futet; 4. thith
soap /soup/ **n.** sapun; **vt.** sapunis
soap-box /'soupboks/ **n.** kuti sapuni
soap-powder /'souppaudë(r)/ **n.** pluhur sapuni
soar /so:(r)/ **vi.** 1. fluturoj lart ; 2. ngrihen (çimet etj.)
sob /sob/ **n.** ngashërim, dënesë; **vti.** ngashërehem, qaj me ngashërim; **sob something out** tregoj me ngashërim
sober /'soubë(r)/ **adj.** 1. i esëllt; 2. i kthjellët (nga mendja); 3. i qetë, i përmbajtur
soccer /'sokë(r)/ **n.** futboll
sociable /'soushbl/ **adj.** i shoqërueshëm
social /'soushl/ **adj.** 1. shoqëror, social; 2. i shoqërueshëm; **social security** sigurimet shoqërore; **social work** punë sociale; **social services** shërbimet shoqërore; **n.** 1. mbledhje; 2. mbrëmje
socialist /'soushëlist/ **adj.** socialist

society /sĕ'saiti/ **n.** 1. shoqëri; 2. shoqëri, miqësi; 3. shoqatë

sock /sok/ **n.** çorape e shkurtër

socket /'sokit/ **n.** 1. zgavër; gropë; 2. **el.** portollambë; prizë

soda /'soudë/ **n.** sodë; **soda water** ujë i gazuar

sofa /'soufë/ **n.** divan, kanape

soft /soft/ **adj.** 1. i butë; 2. i butë, i ëmbël (zë etj.); 3. i lëmuar; 4. e lehtë, e dobët (era etj.); 5. e butë (klima etj.); 6. e butë, joalkoolike (pija)

soften /'sofn/ **vti.** zbut; zbutet

soft-hearted /,soft 'ha:rtid/ **adj.** zemërbutë, shpirtmirë

softly /'softli/ **adv.** 1. butë; 2. qetë; 3. lehtë

soggy /'sogi/ **adj.** 1. i njomë, i lagët; 2. e qullët (buka)

soil /soil/ **n.** tokë, dhe

soil /soil/ **vti.** 1. ndyj, fëlliq; 2. ndot; 3. njollos

soldier /'soulxhë(r)/ **n.** 1. ushtar; 2. ushtarak

sole /soul/ **n.** shuall (këpuce)

sole /soul/ **adj.** 1. i vetëm; 2. ekskluziv; 3. unik; 4. i veçantë

solemn /'solëm/ **adj.** solemn

solicitor /sĕ'lisitë(r)/ **n.** avokat

solid /'solid/ **adj.** 1. i ngurtë; 2. i fortë, i fuqishëm, i qëndrueshëm; **a man of solid character** njeri me karakter të fortë; 3. kompakt, i lidhur; 4. i njëzëshëm

solidity /sĕ'liditi/ **n.** 1. fortësi, qëndrueshmëri; 2. ngurtësi

solitary /'solitëri/ **adj.** 1. i vetmuar; 2. i vetëm

solo /'soulou/ **n. muz.** solo

soloist /'soulouist/ **n.** solist

solution /sĕ'lu:shn/ **n.** 1. zgjidhje (e një problemi); 2. tretësirë

solvable /'solvbl/ **adj.** 1. i zgjidhshëm; 2. i tretshëm

solve /solv/ **vt.** zgjidh, zbërthej (një problem etj.)

solvent /'solvnt/ **adj.** 1. tretës, solvent; 2. i aftë për të paguar, shlyer (borxhet etj.)

some /sam/ **adj.** 1. disa; 2. ca; 3. një pjesë; 4. rreth; **pron.** dikush; disa, ca

somebody /'sambëdi/ **pron.** dikush; **n.** njeri me rëndësi

somehow /'samhau/ **adv.** disi, në një farë mënyre

someone /'samwan/ shih **somebody**

somersault /'samëso:lt/ **n.** kollotumba; **vi.** bëj kollotumba

something /'samthin/ **pron.** diçka

sometime /'samtaim/ **adv.** 1. dikur; 2. ndonjëherë; 3. ndonjë ditë

sometimes /'samtaimz/ **adv.** 1. nganjëherë; 2. herë-herë

someway /'samwei/ **adv.** shih **somehow**

somewhat /'samwot/ **adv.** 1. paksa, pak a shumë; 2. deri diku

somewhere /'samweë(r)/ **adv.** diku

son /san/ **n.** bir

song /so:n/ **n.** këngë

son-in-law /'san in lo:/ **n.** dhëndër

soon /su:n/ **adv.** 1. shpejt; 2. herët; **sooner or later** herët apo vonë; **as soon as** menjëherë sa, posa; **soon after** fill pas, menjëherë pas; **sooner than** më parë se; **the sooner the better** sa më shpejt, aq më mirë

soot /sut/ **n.** bloze

soothe /su:dh/ **vt.** qetësoj, zbut, lehtësoj (dhembjen etj)

sophisticated /së'fistiketid/ **adj.** i sofistikuar
sore /so:(r)/ **adj.** 1. i dhembshëm; 2. i acaruar; i irrituar;
3. i prekur, i lënduar, i pikëlluar, i trishtuar
sorrow /'sorou/ **n.** 1. pikëllim, hidhërim, brengë; 2. vuajtje,
fatkeqësi; 3. keqardhje; **vi.** brengosem; pikëllohem;
trishtohem; hidhërohem
sorrowful /'sorouful/ **adj.** 1. i brengosur, i hidhëruar; 2. i
mjeruar
sorry /'sori/ **adj.** i hidhëruar, i brengosur; i pikëlluar; 2.
keqardhës, që i vjen keq; 3. i penduar; 4. i mjeruar, i
mjerueshëm; **I am sorry!** Më falni! **be (feel) sorry for smb** më
vjen keq
sort /so:rt/ **n.** lloj, soj, tip, klasë, kategori; **a sort of**
një lloj; **of a sort** njëfarësoj; **vti.** 1. ndaj; 2. zgjidh
soul /soul/ **n.** 1. shpirt; 2. frymë, njeri; 3. mishërim;
zemër; shpirt
sound /saund/ **n.** 1. tingull; tingëllim; 2. zë; **vti.** 1.
tingëllon, kumbon; 2. shqiptoj; 3. tingëllon, duket
sound /saund/ **adj.** 1. i shëndoshë, i shëndetshëm; **a sound
mind in a sound body** mendje e shëndoshë në trup të shëndoshë;
2. i bazuar, i mbështetur; 3. i plotë; 4. i mirë, i aftë, i
saktë
soup /su:p/ **n.** supë; **chicken soup** supë pule
soup-spoon /'su:pspu:n/ **n.** lugë gjelle
soup-plate /'su:ppleit/ **n.** pjatë e thellë
sour /'sauë(r)/ **adj.** 1. i thartë, i athët; 2. i thartuar; 3.
i pezmatuar, i vrertë; **vti.** 1. thartoj; 2. **fig.** thartohem
source /so:rs/ **n.** 1. burim (uji); 2. burim, pikënisje,
zanafillë; **a source of information** burim informacioni
south /saudh/ **n.** jug; **adj.** jugor; **adv.** në jug, drejt jugut
southerly /'sadhëli/ **adj.** jugor
southern /'sadhën/ **adj.** jugor
southward /'saudhwërd/ **adv.** në jug, drejt jugut; **adj.** jugor
souvenir /,su:vë'nië(r); 'su:vëniër/ **n.** suvenir, kujtim
sovereign /'sovrin/ **n.** sovran, monark; **adj.** sovran
sovereignty /'sovriniti/ **n.** sovranitet
sow /sou/ **vti.** 1. mbjell; 2. **fig.** mbjell, përhap; **sow the
seeds of hatred** mbjell farën e urrejtjes; **As a man sows so
shall he reap** ç'të mbjellësh, do të korrësh
sowing /'souin/ **n.** mbjellje; **sowing time** kohë e mbjelljeve
sowing-machine /,souinmë'shi:n/ **n.** makinë mbjellëse
soy-bean /'soië bi:n/ **n. bot.** sojë
spa /spa:/ **n.** llixhë, burim ujërash termale
space /speis/ **n.** 1. hapësirë; 2. kozmos; 3. vend; 4. vend
bosh, boshllëk; 5. interval
spacecraft /'speiskra:ft/ **n.** anije kozmike
spaceship /'speisship/ **n.** shih **spacecraft**
spacious /'speishës/ **adj.** i gjerë, i madh, që ka hapësirë të
madhe
spade /speid/ **n.** 1. lopatë; 2. maç
spank /'spenk/ **vt.** qëlloj me shuplakë (në prapanicë)
spanner /'spenë(r)/ **n.** çelës dadosh
spare /speë(r)/ **adj.** 1. rezervë; **spare wheel** gomë rezervë; 2.
i lirë; **spare time** kohë e lirë; 3. i dobët; 4. i pakët; **n.**
pjesë rezervë; **vti.** 1. fal; 2. kursej; 3. jap; 4. kushtoj
sparing /'speërin/ **adj.** i kursyer, kursimtar
spark /spa:rk/ **n.** shkëndijë, xixë

sparkle /'spa:rkl/ **n.** vezullim, shndritje; **vi.** vezullon, shndrit

sparrow /'sperou/ **n. zool.** trumcak, harabel

speak /spi:k/ **vti.** 1. flas; bisedoj; 2. flas, mbaj fjalim; 3. provon, dëshmon; **speak up** flas me zë të lartë; **speak for smb** flas në emër të; **speak of something** flet për; **speak well (ill) for smb** flas mirë (keq) për dikë; **so to speak** si të thuash

speaker /'spi:kë(r)/ **n.** 1. folës, bashkëbisedues; 2. orator

spear /spië(r)/ **n.** heshtë, shtizë; **vt.** shpoj, godit, plagos, vras me heshtë

special /'speshl/ **adj.** i posaçëm, i veçantë; **n.** 1. e veçantë; 2. gazetë, tren special

specialist /'speshëlist/ **n.** specialist

speciality /,speshi'eliti/ **n.** specialitet

specially /'speshëli/ **adv.** veçanërisht, në mënyrë të veçantë

specific /spi'sifik/ **adj.** i veçantë, specifik

specification /,spesi'fikeishn/ **n.** specifikim

specify /'spesifai/ **vt.** specifikoj, përcaktoj me hollësi

specimen /'spesimën/ **n.** 1. mostër; 2. kampion; 3. gjedhe

speck /spek/ **n.** 1. pikë, pikël; 2. grimcë

speckled /'spekld/ **adj.** pikëlor

spectacle /'spektëkl/ **n.** 1. spektakël; shfaqje; 2. pamje

spectacles /'spektëklz/ **n. pl.** syze

spectacular /spek'tekjulë(r)/ **adj.** spektakular

spectator /spek'teitë(r)/ **n.** spektator, shikues

speculate /'spekjuleit/ **vi.** 1. marr me mend; 2. spekuloj

speech /spi:ç/ **n.** 1. ligjërim; të folur; 2. fjalim, ligjëratë

speechless /'spi:çlis/ **adj.** 1. i pagojë, memec; 2. i hutuar

speed /spi:d/ **n.** shpejtësi; **at full speed** me gjithë shpejtësinë; **at a speed of** me shpejtësi prej; **vti.** 1. shpejtoj, nxitoj; 2. shpejton; **speed something up** shpejtoj, rrit shpejtësinë e

speeding /'spi:din/ **n.** tejkalim i normës së shpejtësisë

speedometer /spi'domitë(r)/ **n.** tregues i shpejtësisë

speedy /'spi:di/ **adj.** i shpejtë; a speedy recovery shërim i shpejtë

spell /spel/ **n.** 1. magji; 2. magjepsje; **cast a spell over smb** magjeps **spell** /spel/ **n.** 1. periudhë, interval, kohë; 2. ndërresë

spell /spel/ **vti.** 1. rrokjezoj; 2. shkruaj, shqiptoj shkronjë për shkronjë

spelling /'spelin/ **n.** drejtshkrim, ortografi

spend /spend/ **vti.** 1. shpenzoj; 2. harxhoj; 3. kaloj (kohën etj.)

spice /spais/ **n.** beharna, erëza

spicy /'spaisi/ **adj.** 1. pikant; 2. aromatik

spider /'spaidë(r)/ **n.** merimangë; **a spider's web** pëlhurë e merimangës

spike /spaik/ **n.** 1. majë; 2. thumb

spill /spil/ **vti.** 1. derdh; 2. zbuloj, nxjerr në shesh

spin /spin/ **vti.** 1. rrotulloj; 2. tjerr

spine /spain/ **n.** shtyllë kurrizore

spinster /'spinstë(r)/ **n.** lëneshë, grua e pamartuar

spiral /'spaiërël/ **adj.** spirale

spirit /'spirit/ **n.** 1. shpirt; frymë; 2. kurajë; 3. entuziazëm; 4. vrull, gjallëri; 5. gjendje shpirtërore; **in high spirits** në gjendje të mirë shpirtërore, në humor të mirë; 6. alkool; **pl** pije alkoolike

spirited /'spiritid/ **adj.** 1. i gjallë; 2. i vrullshëm
spiritless /'spiritlis/ **adj.** i pashpirt, i pajetë
spiritual /'spiritjuël/ **adj.** shpirtëror
spit /spit/ **n.** 1. pështymë; **vti.** 1. pështyj; 2. vjell zjarr
(pushka) 3. veson; 4. nxjerr (ushqimin)
spite /spait/ **n.** inat, maraz, smirë; **out of spite** nga inati;
in spite of megjithë, pavarësisht nga; **have a spite against
smb** kam një inat me dikë; **vt.** mërzit, zemëroj, inatos
spiteful /'spaitful/ **adj.** 1. inatçi; 2. keqdashës
splash /splesh/ **n.** 1. llokoçitje; 2. spërkë, stërkitë; **vti.**
1. spërkat; stërkit; 2. spërkatem; 3. llokoçit, llapashit
splendid /'splendid/ **adj.** i shkëlqyeshëm, i mrekullueshëm,
madhështor
splinter /'splintë(r)/ **n.** 2. cifël, ashkël; 2. spicë
split /split/ **n.** 1. çarje; 2. përçarje; 3. ndarje; 4.
shpërbërje; 5. e çarë; **vti.** 1. çaj; 2. shpërbëj, zbërthej; 3.
ndaj; **split up with smb** prishem me dikë
splitting /'splitin/ **adj.** therës; **a splitting headache**
dhembje e madhe koke
spoil /spoil/ **vti.** 1. prish (planet, pushimet etj.); 2.
prish, llastoj (një fëmijë); 3. prishet (ushqimi etj.); **n.
pl.** 1. plaçkat e (grabitura); 2. plaçkitje; 3. përfitime
spokesman /'spouksmën/ **n.** 1. zëdhënës; 2. folës
sponge /spanxh/ **n.** sfungjer; **vti.** laj me sfungjer
sponsor /'sponsë(r)/ **n.** sponsor; **vt.** sponsorizoj
spontaneous /spon'teiniës/ **adj.** spontan, i vetvetishëm
spool /spu:l/ **n.** 1. masur; 2. rrotkë, rrotëz; 3. bobinë
spoon /spu:n/ **n.** lugë
sport /spo:rt/ **n.** 1. sport; **go in for sports** merrem me sport;
2. **pl.** lojëra (sportive); 3. **pl.** takim sportiv; 4. zbavitje,
shaka; **say something in sport** them diçka me shaka; **make sport
of smb** vë dikë në lojë; **vti.** 1. luaj; 2. dëfrehem
sportsman /'spo:rtsmën/ **n.** sportist
sportswoman /'spo:rtswumën/ **n.** sportiste
spot /spot/ **n.** 1. njollë; 2. pullë; 3. puçërr; 4. vend; **on
the spot** në vend; aty për aty; 5. pikë (shiu); **vti.** 1. ndot,
njollos; 2. dalloj, shquaj; 3. veson
spotless /'spotlis/ **adj.** 1. i rregullt, i pastër; 2. **fig.** i
pastër (moralisht), i panjollë
spotty /'spoti/ **adj.** njolla-njolla
spout /spaut/ **n.** lëfyt (çajniku etj.)
sprain /sprein/ **vt.** ndrydh; **n.** ndrydhje
spray /sprei/ **n.** 1. spërkë, spërkël; 2. stërpikje; 3.
spërkatës, stërkitës; **vt.** spërkat
sprayer /'spreië(r)/ **n.** spërkatës; spërkatëse
spread /spred/ **vti.** 1. shtroj, shtrij; 2. hap; 3. lyej; 4.
shtrihet, përhapet; **n.** shtrirje, përhapje
spring /sprin/ **n.** pranverë; **adj.** pranveror, i pranverës
spring /sprin/ **n.** 1. kërcim; 2. burim; 3. sustë; **vit.** kërcej,
hidhem; **spring from something** buron, vjen, lind
sprinkle /'sprinkl/ **vt.** spërkat; **n.** spërkatje
sprout /spraut/ **n.** lastar, filiz; **vti.** mugullon; rrit(et)

spurt /spë:rt/ **vti.** rrjedh çurkë (uji, gjaku etj.); 2. shtoj (ritmin, përpjekjet etj.); **n.** vërshim, shpërthim i menjëhershëm

spy /spai/ **n.** spiun; **vit.** 1. spiunoj; 2. përgjoj

squabble /'skwobl/ **n.** zënkë; **vi.** grindem për gjëra të vogla

squad /skwod/ **n.** skuadër (ushtarësh etj.)

square /skweë(r)/ **n.** 1. katror; 2. shesh; **adj.** 1. katror; 2. kënddrejtë; 3. i rregulluar, i sistemuar; 4. i drejtë, i ndershëm; 5. i fortë, i lidhur; **vti.** 1. **mat.** ngre në fuqi të dytë; 2. drejtoj; 3. laj, shlyej; 4. barazoj; **adv.** 1. drejt; 2. ndershmërisht

square-built /,skweë(r) 'bilt/ **adj.** i lidhur; shpatullgjerë

squash /skwosh/ **n.** 1. ngjeshje, shtypje; 2. lëng frutash; **vti.** 1. shtrydh; 2. ngjishem, shtyhem; 3. shtyp (një kryengritje)

squash /skwosh/ **n.** kungull

squat /skwot/ **vi.** 1. rri galiç; 2. rri në bisht

squeak /skwi:k/ **n.** 1. piskamë; 2. cihatje; **vti.** 1. piskat; 2. kërcet

squeeze /skwi:z/ **n.** 1. shtrëngim; 2. shtrydhje; 3. ngjeshje, shtypje; **vti.** 1. shtrydh; 2. shtrëngoj; 3. shtyhem, ngjishem; 4. nxjerr me forcë

squirrel /'skwirël/ **n. zool.** ketër

squirt /skwë:rt/ **vit.** derdhet, çurkon (uji et.); **n.** curil, çurg

stab /steb/ **n.** goditje me (thikë etj.); **vti.** shpoj, godit me (thikë etj.)

stability /stë'biliti/ **n.** stabilitet, qëndrueshmëri

stabilize /'steibilaiz/ **vt.** stabilizoj; **stabilize prices** stabilizoj çmimet

stable /'steibl/ **adj.** i qëndrueshëm, i pandryshueshëm

stale /'steibl/ **n.** stallë

stack stek/ **n.** 1. mullar, qipi; 2. turrë, grumbull, stivë; **stack of som**ething një grumbull, një mori; **vt.** 1. vë mullar (barin); 2. stivoj; grumbulloj

stadium /'steidiëm/ **n.** stadium

staff /sta:f/ **n.** 1. shkop; 2. personel; staff-room dhoma e mësuesve; 3. **usht.** shtab; **vt.** siguroj me personel

stag /steg/ **n. zool.** dre

stage /steixh/ **n.** 1. skenë; 2. **fig.** arenë, skenë; 3. fazë, shkallë, moment; 4. etapë; **at this stage** në këtë fazë; **at a later stage** në një fazë të mëvonshme; **vti.** 1. inskenoj, vë në skenë; 2. organizoj

stagger /'stegë(r)/ **vti.** 1. më merren këmbët, eci si i pirë; 2. shtangem, habitem; **n.** marrje e këmbëve

stagnant /'stegnënt/ **adj.** i amullt, i ndenjur

stagnation /steg'neishn/ **n.** stanjacion, amulli

stain /stein/ **n.** njollë (edhe **fig.**); **vti.** 1. njollos, ndot; 2. **fig.** njollos; 3. ngjyros

stainless /'steinlis/ **adj.** 1. **fig.** i panjollosur, i pastër; 2. i pandryshkshëm

stair /steë(r)/ **n.** 1. shkelëz, këmbë shkalle; 2. shkallë; **at the foot (head) of the stairs** në fund (krye) të shkallëve

staircase /'steë(r)keis/ **n.** shkallë

stake /steik/ **n.** 1. furkë; 2. hu; shtyllë; 3. bast

stale /steil/ **adj.** bajat, i ndenjur

stalk /sto:k/ **n.** kërcell (i bimës, lules etj.)

stall /sto:l/ **n.** 1. grazhd; 2. banak; 3. kioskë; qoshk; 4. plate

stammer /'stemë(r)/ **n.** belbëzim; **vti.** 1. belbëzoj, më mbahet
goja; 2. them, shqiptoj duke belbëzuar
stamp /stemp/ **n.** 1. vulë; 2. përplasje e këmbëve; 3. pullë
(poste); 4. lloj; **vti.** 1. përplas këmbët; 2. vulos; 3.
stampoj; 4. ngjit pullën
stand /stend/ **vit.** 1. qëndroj më këmbë; 2. ngrihem më këmbë;
3. është, qëndron; 4. vë, vendos; 5. duroj, përballoj; **stand
aside** mënjanohem, rri mënjanë; bëj mënjanë; **stand by** sodit;
rri në gatishmëri; **stand by smb** përkrah, mbështes dikë; **stand
by something** i qëndroj besnik (fjalës, premtimit etj.); **stand
for** përfaqëson; duroj, toleroj; **stand out** spikat, bie në sy;
këmbëngul, vazhdoj të rezistoj; **stand over smb** i rri mbi kokë
dikujt; **stand up** ngrihem; **stand up for** i dal krah; **stand up
to** i bëj ballë; **n.** 1. ndalesë; 2. qëndrim, pozicion; 3.
mbajtëse; 4. qoshk; 5. qëndresë, rezistencë; 6. tribunë
standard /'stendërd/ **n.** 1. standard, nivel; **standard of
living** standardi i jetesës; 2. flamur; **adj.** standard
standing /'stendin/ **adj.** i përhershëm; që ka ende vlerë; **n.**
1. pozitë; 2. peshë; 3. zgjatje
standpoint /'stendpoint/ **n.** këndvështrim; pikëpamje
standstill /'stendstil/ **n.** ndalim, ndalje, ngecje në vend;
come to a standstill bie në amulli
staple /'steipl/ **adj.** kryesor; **the staple food** ushqimi
kryesor; **n.** prodhim (ushqim, artikull) kryesor
star /sta:(r)/ **n.** 1. **astr.** yll; 2. yll; **a five-star hotel**
hotel me pesë yje; 3. yll (kinemaje etj.); **a film star** yll
kinematografie
starch /sta:rç/ **n.** 1. niseshte; 2. koll
stare /steë(r)/ **vit.** 1. shikoj ngultas; 2. zgurdulloj sytë;
n. shikim i ngulët
starry /'sta:ri/ **adj.** 1. yllëzor; 2. i shndritshëm (nga
yjet); 3. i shndritshëm si yjet
start /sta:rt/ **vit.** 1. nisem; 2. filloj; 3. fillon; 3. ndez, vë
në funksionim (makinën etj.); 4. hidhem, kërcej përpjetë (nga
habia etj.); **to start with** pikësëpari; fillimisht; **start for**
nisem për; **start out** nis; nisem; **n.** 1. nisje; 2. fillim; 3.
sport. start; 4. hedhje, kërcim përpjetë (nga frika etj.);
from start to finish nga fillimi në fund; **make an early start**
nisem herët
starter /'sta:rtë(r)/ **n.** 1. startues; 2. lëshues (i motorit)
startle /'sta:rtl/ **vt.** 1. tremb, tromaks; 2. habit
startling /'sta:rtlin/ **adj.** 1. i habitshëm; 2. tronditës,
alarmues
starvation /sta:'veishn/ **n.** 1. uri; 2. vdekje nga uria
starve /sta:rv/ **vti.** 1. vuaj, vdes nga uria; 2. lë të vdesë
nga uria; 3. kam shumë uri; **starve to death** vdes nga uria
state /steit/ **n.** 1. gjendje; kushte; situatë; 2. shtet; **vt.**
1. shpall, deklaroj; 2. shpreh; 3. caktoj, fiksoj
statement /'steitmënt/ **n.** 1. deklaratë; 2. shprehje; 3.
raport, relacion
statesman /'steitsmën/ **n.** burrë shteti
station /'steishn/ **n.** 1. stacion (treni, autobusi etj.); 2.
stacion (televiziv etj.); 3. pozitë shoqërore; 4. vendndalim,
vendqëndrim, stacion (për autobusa etj.); **vt.** vendosem, zë
vend
stationary /'steishnëri/ **adj.** stacionar, i palëvizshëm
stationery /'steishnëri/ **n.** kartoleri; artikuj kartolerie
statistical /stë'tistikl/ **adj.** statistik, statistikor

statistics /stë'tistiks/ **n.** statistikë
statue /'stetju:/ **n.** statujë
status /'steitës/ **n.** 1. status, gjendje; 2. pozitë
stay /stei/ **vit.** 1. rri, qëndroj; **stay in bed** rri në krevat;
2. qëndroj si (vizitor, mik); 3. ndaloj, pengoj; 4. qëndroj,
përballoj, duroj; 5. shuaj (etjen etj.); **stay in** rri brenda
në shtëpi; **stay up** rri natën vonë; **n.** 1. mbështetje; 2.
ndalim, qëndrim; 3. qëndresë, durim
steady /'stedi/ **adj.** 1. i qëndrueshëm, i palëvizshëm; 2. i
rregullt; 3. i vazhdueshëm, konstant
steak /steik/ **n.** thelë (mishi, peshku)
steal /sti:l/ **vti.** 1. vjedh; 2. përvidhem; **steal away**
largohem vjedhurazi
stealing /'sti:lin/ **n.** vjedhje
stealthy /'stelthi/ **adj.** i fshehtë
steam /sti:m/ **n.** 1. avull; 2. **fig.** energji, forcë, fuqi; **vit.**
1. avullon, nxjerr avull; 2. gatuaj, pastroj me avull; 3.
lëviz (me avull)
steam-engine /'sti:m enxhin/ **n.** lokomotivë, motor me avull
steamer /'sti:më(r)/ **n.** avullore
steamy /'sti:mi/ **adj.** 1. i avullt; 2. i avulluar
steel /sti:l/ **n.** çelik; **adj.** i çeliktë
steep /sti:p/ **adj.** 1. i pjerrët, i rrëpirët; 2. i paarsyeshëm
steer /stië(r)/ **vti.** 1. drejtoj, manovroj, pilotoj; 2.
drejtohet, manovrohet
steering /'stiërin/ **n.** drejtim, komandim
steering-wheel /'stiërinwi:l/ **n.** timon
stem /stem/ **n.** 1. trung; 2. kërcell; 3. **gjuh.** temë, rrënjë;
vi. buron, rrjedh
step /step/ **n.** 1. hap; **step by step** hap pas hapi; **in the
steps of** në hapat e; 2. masë; **take steps to do something** marr
masa të bëj diçka; 3. shkallë; **vit.** eci, lëviz, shkoj; **step
aside** bëj mënjanë; tërhiqem nga një detyrë etj.; **step down**
jap dorëheqjen; **step in** ndërhyj; **step something up** ngre,
rrit, shtoj
stepchild /'stepçaild/ **n.** thjeshtër
stepfather /'stepfa:dhë(r)/ **n.** njerk
stepmother /'stepmëdhë(r)/ **n.** njerkë
sterile /'sterail/ **adj.** 1. shterp, beronjë (grua); 2. shterp,
e varfër (toka); 3. **fig.** shterp; 4. **mjek.** steril
stern /stë:rn/ **adj.** 1. i ashpër, i rreptë; 2. i egër, i
vrazhdë
stew /stju:/ **vti.** 1. ziej ngadalë; 2. pëlcas nga vapa; **n.**
mish i shterur
stewardess /,stjuë'des/ **n.** stjuardesë
stick /stik/ **n.** 1. shkop; 2. bastun; 3. shkarpë, karthje
stick /stik/ **vti.** 1. ngul; 2. ngjit; ngjitet; 3. vë, fut; 4.
i përmbahem, i qëndroj (premtimit etj.); 5. ngec; **stick at**
vazhdoj me këmbëngulje (një punë etj.); **stick something out**
nxjerr; **stick to something** i përmbahem; vazhdoj me ngulm;
stick by smb i qëndroj besnik dikujt; **stick together** qëndroj
bashkë, qëndroj i bashkuar
sticky /'stiki/ **adj.** 1. ngjitës; 2. mbytës, me zagushi
stiff /stif/ **adj.** 1. i ngrirë, i paepshëm, i palakueshëm; 2.
i trashë; 3. i vështirë; 4. formal; 5. e fortë (era, pija
etj.)

stiffen /'stifn/ **vti.** 1. ngrij, nguros, ngurtësoj; 2. forcoj
(moralin etj)
stifle /'staifl/ **vti.** 1. mbyt, zë frymën; 2. mbys; shtyp; 3.
shuaj (zjarrin)
stifling /'staiflin/ **adj.** mbytës
still /stil/ **adj.** 1. i qetë; i heshtur; 2. i palëvizshëm;
adv. 1. akoma, ende; 2. më, akoma më; 3. megjithatë
stilt /stilt/ **n.** këmbalkë
stimulate /'stimjuleit/ **vt.** nxit, stimuloj
stimulating /,stimju'leitin/ **adj.** stimulues, eksitues
stimulation /,stimju'leishn/ **n.** stimulim, nxitje, shtysë
sting /stin/ **n.** 1. thimth, thumb; 2. thumbim, pickim; 3.
djegie (nga pickimi etj.); **vti.** thumboj (edhe **fig.)**
stink /stink/ **n.** erë e keqe; **vit.** 1. qelb, qelbet, bie erë e
keqe; 2. qelb ajrin; 3. **fig.** bie erë
stir /stë:(r)/ **n.** 1. përzierje; 2. lëvizje, trazirë; **vit.** 1.
lëviz; 2. trazoj, përziej
stitch /stiç/ **n.** 1. qepje; 2. gojëz, ilik, syth
stock /stok/ **n.** 1. fond; 2. material; 3. furnizim; 4. gjë e
gjallë; 5. aksion; obligacion; 6. origjinë, prejardhje; 7
trung; 8 inventar
stock-broker /'stokbroukë(r)/ **n.** kambist; agjent i bursës
stock exchange /,stok eks'çeinxh/ **n.** bursë
stockholder /'stokhouldë(r)/ **n.** aksionar
stocking /'stokin/ **n.** çorape (grash)
stomach /'stamëk/ **n.** 1. **anat.** stomak; 2. lukth; 3. bark; 4.
fig. qejf, dëshirë; **have no stomach for** s'kam dëshirë të; 5.
oreks
stone /stoun/ **n.** 1. gur; 2. bërthamë e frutave; 3. gur i
çmuar; 4. gur i veshkave; **vt.** 1. qëlloj me gurë; 2. heq,
nxjerr bërthamën (nga frutat)
stony /'stoni/ **adj.** 1. i gurtë; 2. guror
stool /stu:l/ **n.** 1. stol; 2. jashtëqitje, nevojë
stoop /stu:p/ **vit.** kërrusem; përkulem; **n.** kërrusje; përkulje
stop /stop/ **n.** 1. ndalim; ndalesë; **come to a stop** ndalem; 2.
fund; **put a stop to** i jap fund; 3. **gjuh.** pikë; 4. stacion
(autobusi); **vti.** 1. ndaloj; 2. ndërpres; 3. qëndroj, ndalem;
4. mbaroj; 5. pushoj; 6. qëndroj (në hotel etj.); 7 pengoj;
stop smb from doing something pengoj dikë të bëjë diçka
stopper /'stopë(r)/ **n.** 1. tapë; 2. shtupë
stopping /'stopin/ **n.** mbushje e dhëmbit
storage /'sto:rixh/ **n.** 1. ruajtje; magazinim; depozitim; 2.
elektr. ngarkim, akumulim; 3. magazinë
store /sto:(r)/ **n.** 1. rezervë; 2. depo, magazinë; 3. dyqan,
tregtore; 4. sasi, fond; **vt.** 1. ruaj, rezervoj; magazinoj; 2.
pajis
storehouse /'sto:(r)haus/ **n.** magazinë, depo
storekeeper /'sto:(r)ki:pë(r)/ **n.** 1. magazinier; 2. **amer.**
shitës
store-room /'sto:(r)ru:m/ **n.** magazinë
storey /'sto:ri/ **n.** kat
storm /sto:rm/ **n.** 1. stuhi, furtunë, shtërngatë; 2.
shpërthim; 3. sulm; **take by storm** marr me sulm; **vti.** 1.
tërbohem; 2. shpërthej; 3. sulmoj, marr me sulm; 4. sulmoj
(me pyetje etj.)
stormy /'sto:mi/ **adj.** i stuhishëm (edhe **fig.)**

story /'stoːri/ **n.** 1. tregim, histori; 2. gojëdhënë; 3. përrallë; 4. rrenë

story-teller /'stoːritelë(r)/ **n.** 1. tregimtar; 2. rrenacak, gënjeshtar

stout /staut/ **adj.** 1. i fortë; 2. i bëshëm; 3. i vendosur, kurajoz

stove /stouv/ **n.** sobë, stufë

stovepipe 'stouvpaip/ **n.** tub sobe

stowaway /'stouëwei/ **n.** pasagjer klandestin

straight /streit/ **adj.** 1. i drejtë; a straight line vijë e drejtë; 2. i rregullt; **put (get) something straight** rregulloj; 3. i ndershëm, i çiltër, i sinqertë; **adv.** drejt; **straight away** menjëherë, përnjëherë

straighten /'streitn/ **vt.** drejtoj

straightforward /,streit'foːwërd/ **adj.** 1. i ndershëm, i sinqertë; 2. i drejtpëdrejtë

strain /strein/ **vti.** 1. ndej, tendos; 2. **fig.** tendos; **strain every nerve to do something** tendos çdo nerv për të bërë diçka; 3. sforcoj, mbilodh; 4. kulloj; 5. filtroj; **n.** 1. tendosje; 2. lodhje, sforcim; 3. ndrydhje

strainer /'streinë(r)/ **n.** 1. kullore, kullesë; 2. filtër

strait /streit/ **n.** 1. ngushticë; 2. **pl.** vështirësi, ngushticë

strand /strend/ **n.** 1. fill, fije (litari, floku etj.); 2. **fig.** fill (i tregimit etj.)

strange /streinxh/ **adj.** 1. i çuditshëm; 2. i huaj, i panjohur; 3. i padëgjuar; 4. i pamësuar

stranger /'streinxhë(r)/ **n.** 1. i panjohur; 2. i huaj

strangle /'strengl/ **vt.** mbyt (edhe **fig.)**

strap /strep/ **n.** 1. rrip; 2. fasho; **vt.** 1. lidh me rrip; 2. lidh me fasho

strategy /'stretëxhi/ **n.** strategji

straw /stroː/ **n.** 1. kashtë; 2. fije kashte; **catch at a straw** kapem pas fijes së kashtës

strawberry /'stroːbëri/ **n. bot.** luleshtrydhe

stray /strei/ **vi.** 1. shmangem; 2. gaboj, humb rrugën; **adj.** i humbur, arrakat; **n.** kafshë arrakate

stream /striːm/ **n.** 1. rrëke, përrua; 2. rrjedhje (gjaku etj.); 3. **fig.** rrymë **go with the stream** shkoj me rrymën; 4. mori, lumë; streams of cars lumë makinash; **vi.** 1. rrjedh; 2. lëkundet, valëvitet

streamlined /'striːmlaind/ **adj.** aerodinamik

street /striːt/ **n.** rrugë

streetcar /'striːtkaː(r)/ **n. amer.** tramvaj

strength /strength/ **n.** forcë, fuqi

strengthen /'strengthn/ **vt.** forcoj, fuqizoj

strenuous /'strenjuës/ **adj.** i mundimshëm, i lodhshëm, kapitës

stress /stres/ **n.** 1. shtypje; 2. presion; 3. theksim, rëndësi; **lay stress on** vë theksin në; 4. **gjuh.** theks; 5. stres, lodhje; **vt.** theksoj

stretch /streç/ **n.** 1. shtrirje; 2. hapësirë; 3. sforcim, tendosje; **vti.** 1. shtrij, zgjat; 2. ndej, tendos; 3. shtrihet, zgjatet; **stretch oneself out** shtrihem sa gjatë gjerë; **stretch one's legs** shpij këmbët

stretcher /'streçë(r)/ **n.** tezgë, vig

strew /stru:/ **vt.** 1. përhap; shpërndaj; 2. stërpik; 3. mbuloj;

strict /strikt/ **adj.** 1. i përpiktë, i saktë; 2. i rreptë

strictly /'striktli/ **adv.** rreptësisht; **Smoking is strictly prohibited.** Ndalohet rreptësisht duhani.

stride /straid/ **n.** 1. hap i madh; 2. ecje; **make great strides** bëj përparim të madh; **vit.** eci me hapa të mëdhenj

strike /straik/ **n.** 1. grevë; **be on strike** jam në grevë; **come (go) out on strike** dal në grevë; 2. goditje; **vti.** 1. godit, qëlloj; 2. shkrep, ndez; 3. bie (ora); 4. përplasem, godit; 5. sulmoj; 6. më lind, më shkrep (një mendim etj.); 7 më bën përshtypje; çuda, habitem; 8 bëj grevë

striker /'straikë(r)/ **n.** 1. grevist; 2. **sport.** gjuajtës

striking /'straikin/ **adj.** 1. i dukshëm, që bie në sy; 2. përshtypjelënës, sensacional, mahnitës

string /strin/ **n.** 1. spango; 2. tel (violine etj.); 3. varg (rruazash etj)

strip /strip/ **n.** brez, rrip (toke etj.); **vti.** 1. zhvesh; **strip off one's clothes** zhvesh, heq rrobat; 2. çmontoj

stripe /straip/ **n.** vijë, shirit, brez

striped /straipt/ **adj.** vija-vija

stroke /strouk/ **n.** 1. goditje; 2. tingëllimë; 3. **mjek.** goditje, pikë; 4. ledhatim, përkëdhelje; 5. lëvizje e duarve; **at a (one) stroke** me një goditje, me një veprim

stroll /stroul/ **n.** shëtitje; **go for a stroll** dal shëtitje; **vi.** shëtit

strong /stron/ **adj.** 1. i fuqishëm; 2. i shëndoshë, i shëndetshëm; 3. i fortë, i thellë; 4. i fortë, i qëndrueshëm; 5. e fortë (pije alkoolike)

stronghold /'stronhould/ **n.** kala, fortesë

structure /'strakçë(r)/ **n.** 1. strukturë, ndërtim; 2. ndërtesë, godinë

struggle /'stragl/ **n.** 1. luftë; 2. përpjekje, mundim; **vi.** 1. luftoj; 2. përpiqem, mundohem

stub /stab/ **n.** bisht (lapsi, cigareje etj.)

stubborn /'stabërn/ **adj.** kryeneç, kokëfortë

student /'st(j)u:dnt/ **n.** student

studio /'st(j)u:diou/ **n.** studio

study /'stadi/ **n.** 1. studim; 2. dhomë studimi; **vti.** studioj

stuff /staf/ **n.** 1. lëndë, material, substancë; 2. plaçkë, send; 3. stof leshi; 4. mbushje (e pulës etj.); **vt.** 1. mbush (jastëkun, pulën etj.); 2. ngjesh; rras; 3. ngjishem, dendem (së ngrëni)

stuffing /'stafin/ **n.** mbushje (e pulës etj.)

stuffy /'stafi/ **adj.** mbytës, i rëndë (ajri); 2. i mërzitshëm; 3. e zënë (hunda)

stumble /stambl/ **n.** pengim; **vi.** 1. pengohem; 2. më merren këmbët

stump /stamp/ **n.** 1. cung; 2. kërcu; 3. bisht (cigareje etj.)

stun /stan/ **vt.** 1. hutoj, shushat, shastis; 2. lë pa ndjenja

stupid /'st(j)u:pid/ **adj.** i trashë, i marrë, budalla

stupidity /st(j)u:'pidëti/ **n.** budallallëk, marrëzi

stupor /'st(j)u:pë(r)/ **n.** 1. shtangie, trullosje; 2. mpirje

stutter /'statë(r)/ **vit.** belbëzoj; **n.** belbëzim

sty /stai/ **n.** thark (derrash)

style /stai/ **n.** 1. **art. let.** stil; 2. modë; 3. stil, mënyrë

stylish /stailish/ **adj.** elegant, i modës
stylist /'stailist/ **n.** 1. stilist; 2. modelist
subconscious /,sab'konshës/ **adj.** subkoshient
subdivide /'sabdi'vaid/ **vti.** nënndaj
subdue /sëb'd(j)u:/ **vt.** 1. nënshtroj; 2. ndrydh, nënshtroj;
3. zbut
subject /'sabxhikt/ **n.** 1. temë, subjekt; 2. shtetas; 3. lëndë
(mësimore); 4. **gjuh.** kryefjalë; **adj.** 1. i varur, i
nënshtruar; 2. i prirur; /sëb'xhekt/ **vt.** 1. nënshtroj; 2. bëj
objekt të (kritikës etj.)
submarine /,sabmë'ri:n; 'sabmërin/ **n.** nëndetëse
submissive /sëb'misiv/ **adj.** 1. i nënshtruar, i përulur; 2. i
dëgjuar, i bindur
submit /sëb'mit/ **vti.** 1. nënshtroj; nënshtrohem; 2. shtroj,
paraqit (për diskutim)
subordinate /së'bo:dinët/ **adj.** 1. vartës; 2. i dorës së dytë;
3. **gjuh.** i varur; /së'bo:dineit/ **vt.** 1. vë në vartësi; 2.
trajtoj si më pak të rëndësishme
subordination /së'bo:di'neishn/ **n.** 1. vartësi; 2. nënshtrim;
3. nënrenditje
subpoena /së'pi:në/ **n.** fletëthirrje (për në gjyq)
subscribe /sëb'skraib/ **vit.** 1. pajtohem (në gazetë etj.); 2.
jap, kontribuoj (me të holla); 3. nënshkruaj (një peticion
etj.)
subscriber /sëb'skraibë(r)/ **n.** 1. pajtimtar; 2. nënshkrues
subscription /sëb'skripshn/ **n.** 1. nënshkrim; 2. pajtim; 3.
kontribut (në të holla)
subsequent /'sabsikwënt/ **adj.** 1. pastajmë; 2. vijues, pasues
subsidiary /sëb'sidiëri/ **adj.** 1. dytësor; 2. plotësues
subsidize /'sabsidaiz/ **vt.** subvencionoj
subsist /sëb'sist/ **vi.** jetoj, mbahem gjallë
subsistence /sëb'sistëns/ **n.** 1. jetesë; ekzistencë; 2. mjete
jetese
substance /'sabstëns/ **n.** 1. lëndë, material; 2. thelb,
esencë; **in substance** në thelb; 3. para; pasuri
substantial /sëb'stenshl/ **adj.** 1. i madh; 2. i fortë; 3. i
pasur; 4. real, i vërtetë; 5. lëndor; 6. i bollshëm
substitute /'sabstit(j)u:t/ **n.** 1. zëvendësues; 2. zëvendësim;
vti. zëvendësoj
substitution /,sabsti't(j)u:shn/ **n.** zëvendësim
subtract /sëb'trekt/ **vt. mat.** zbres, heq
subtraction /sëb'trekshn/ **n. mat.** zbritje
suburb /'sabë:b/ **n.** rrethinë, periferi
subway /'sabwei/ **n.** 1. nënkalesë, tunel i nëndheshëm; 2.
amer. metro
succeed /sëk'si:d/ **vit.** 1. kam sukses; 2. zëvendësoj; 3.
trashëgoj
success /sëk'ses/ **n.** sukses
successful /sëk'sesful/ **adj.** i suksesshëm
succession /sëk'seshn/ **n.** 1. vijimësi; radhë; 2. sërë, varg;
3. e drejta trashëgimore
successor /sëk'sesë(r)/ **n.** trashëgimtar, pasardhës
such /saç/ **adj.** i tillë; **pron.** i tillë; **as such** si i tillë
suck /sak/ **vti.** thith
sudden /'sadn/ **adj.** i papritur, i menjëhershëm, i befasishëm;
all of a sudden befas
suddenly /'sadnli/ **adv.** befas, papritur

sue /sju:/ **vti.** 1. padit; 2. kërkoj
suffer /'safë(r)/ **vit.** 1. vuaj, ndjej dhembje; 2. pësoj
(humbje, dështim etj.); 3. duroj, toleroj
suffering /'safërin/ **n.** vuajtje
sufficient /së'fishnt/ **adj.** i mjaftë, i mjaftueshëm
suffix /'safiks/ **n. gjuh.** prapashtesë
suffocate /'safëkeit/ **vti.** 1. zë frymën; 2. mbyt (duke i zënë
frymën)
suffocation /safë'keishn/ **n.** mbytje; asfiksi
suffrage /'safrixh/ **n.** e drejtë votimi
sugar /'shugë(r)/ **n.** sheqer; **vt.** sheqeros, ëmbëlsoj
sugar-basin /'shugë(r)beisn/ **n.** mbajtëse sheqeri
sugar-beet /'shugë(r)bi:t/ **n.** panxharsheqeri
sugar-cane /'shugë(r)kein/ **n.** kallam sheqeri
suggest /së'xhest/ **vt.** 1. sugjeroj; propozoj; 2. aludoj;
nënkuptoj; 3. i kujtoj, i sjell ndër mend
suggestion /së'xhesçn/ **n.** 1. sugjerim; propozim; 2. ide,
mendim
suggestive /së'xhestiv/ **adj.** sugjestiv; aludues
suicide /'su:isaid/ **n.** 1. vetëvrasje; **commit suicide** kryej
vetëvrasje; 2. **fig.** vetëvrasje
suit /s(j)u:t/ **n.** 1. kostum; 2. **drejt.** padi; 3. lutje,
kërkesë; **vti.** 1. më shkon, më ka hije; 2. është i
përshtatshëm, i pranueshëm
suitable /'s(j)u:tëbl/ **adj.** i përshtatshëm
suitcase /'sju:tkeis/ **n.** valixhe
suite /swi:t/ **n.** 1. komplet (mobiliesh); 2. komplet
(dhomash); 3. **muz.** suitë
sulk /salk/ **vi.** var buzët, vrenjtem, ngrysem
sulky /salki/ **adj.** i vrenjtur, i ngrysur
sullen /salën/ **adj.** 1. i vrenjtur, i zymtë; 2. i ngrysur
sum /sam/ **n.** 1. shumë; 2. mbledhje; llogaritje aritmetike; 3.
total; **in sum** shkurt, me dy fjalë; **vti.** 1. përmbledh; 2.
nxjerr shumën e përgjithshme
summarize /'samëraiz/ **vt.** përmbledh
summary /'samëri/ **n.** përmbledhje; **adj.** përmbledhës; **a summary
account** raport përmbledhës
summer /'samë(r)/ **n.** verë; **adj.** veror
summit /'samit/ **n.** 1. majë mali; 2. mbledhje, takim i nivelit
të lartë; **talks at the summit** bisedime në nivel të lartë
summon /'samën/ **vt.** 1. thërres (në mbledhje, gjyq etj.); 2.
mbledh; **summon up one's courage** marr zemër
summons /'samënz/ **n.** thirrje (në gjyq etj.)
sun /san/ **n.** diell
sunbathe /'sanbeith/ **vi.** bëj banjë dielli
sunburn /'sanbë:rn/ **n.** djegie nga dielli
Sunday /'sandi/ **n.** e diel
sunflower /'sanflauë(r)/ **n. bot.** lule dielli
sunlight /'sanlait/ **n.** dritë dielli
sunny /'sani/ **adj.** diellor, me diell
sunrise /'sanraiz/ **n.** lindje e diellit
sunset /'sanset/ **n.** perëndim i diellit
sunshine /'sanshain/ **n.** 1. dritë diellore; 2. ngazëllim,
rrezëllim (i fytyrës)
sunstroke /'sanstrouk/ **n. mjek.** pikë e diellit

suntan /'santen/ **n.** nxirje nga dielli
suntanned /'santend/ **adj.** i nxirë nga dielli
superb /s(j)u:'pë:rb/ **adj.** i madhërishëm, i shkëlqyer, i mrekullueshëm
superficial /,s(j)u:pë'fi:shl/ **adj.** i përciptë, i sipërfaqshëm
superfluous /s(j)u:pë:fluës/ **adj.** i tepërt
superintendent /,su:përin'tendënt/ **n.** mbikqyrës
superior /s(j)u:'piërië(r)/ **adj.** 1. i epërm, i sipërm; 2. superior, më i mirë; 3. më i lartë; **n.** epror
superlative /s(j)u:'pë:rlëtiv/ **adj. gjuh.** sipërore; **n. gjuh.** shkallë sipërore
superman /'s(j)u:pëmen/ **n.** mbinjeri
supermarket /'s(j)u:pëma:kit/ **n.** supermerkato
supernatural /,s(j)u:pë'neçrël/ **adj.** i mbinatyrshëm
supersonic /,s(j)u:pë'sonik/ **adj.** supersonik
superstition /,s(j)u:pë'stishn/ **n.** bestytni
superstitious /,s(j)u:pë'stishës/ **adj.** bestytnor, supersticioz
supervise /'s(j)u:pëvaiz/ **vti.** mbikqyr
supervision /,s(j)u:pë'vizhn/ **n.** mbikqyrje
supper /sapë(r)/ **n.** darkë
supplement /'saplimënt/ **n.** shtesë, shtojcë; **vt.** plotësoj
supply /së'plai/ **n.** 1. furnizim; 2. rezervë, zahire; 3. pajisje; **vt.** 1. furnizoj; 2. pajis; 3. plotësoj nevojat (kërkesat)
support /së'po:rt/ **vt.** 1. përkrah, mbështet; 2. mbaj (peshën, familjen etj.); **n.** përkrahje, mbështetje
supporter /së'po:rtë(r)/ **n.** përkrahës, mbështetës
suppose /së'pouz/ **vt.** 1. supozoj; 2. mendoj
supposed /së'pouzd/ **adj.** i supozuar; **be supposed to** supozohet të; **not be supposed to** nuk lejohet të
supposition /,sapë'zishn/ **n.** supozim, hamendje
suppress /së'pres/ **vt.** 1. shtyp; **suppress an uprising** shtyp kryengritjen; 2. mbys; 3. mbaj, përmbaj (dhembjen etj.)
suppression /së'preshn/ **n.** shtypje; represion
supreme /s(j)u:pri:m/ **adj.** suprem; më i larti; më i rëndësishmi
sure /shuë(r)/ **adj.** i sigurt; **be sure to** mos harro të; **make sure** sigurohem; **adv.** natyrisht, sigurisht; **for sure** sigurisht
surely /'shuërli/ **adv.** natyrisht, sigurisht, me siguri
surface /së:rfis/ **n.** sipërfaqe
surgeon /'së:rxhën/ **n.** kirurg
surgery /'së:rxhëri/ **n.** kirurgji
surgical /'së:rxhikl/ **adj.** kirurgjik
surname /'së:rneim/ **n.** 1. nofkë; 2. mbiemër
surpass /së:(r)'pa:s; së:r'pes/ **vt.** kaloj
surplus /'së:(r)plës/ **n.** tepricë; **adj.** i tepërt, suplementar; **surplus value** mbivlerë **surprise** /së'praiz/ **n.** 1. habi, çudi; **to my surprise** për habinë time; 2. befasi; **take smb by surprise** zë, kap në befasi; 3. surprizë, e papritur; **give smb a surprise** i bëj dikujt një surprizë; 4. sulm i papritur; **take something by surprise** marr me sulm; **vt.** 1. habit, çudit; 2. zë, kap në befasi
surprising /së'praizin/ **adj.** 1. i papritur, 2. i habitshëm, i çuditshëm

surprisingly /së'praizinli/ **adv.** çuditërisht
surrender së'rendë(r)/ **n.** dorëzim, kapitullim; **vti.** 1.
dorëzohem; 2. dorëzoj
surround /së'raund/ **vt.** rrethoj
surroundings /së'raundinz/ **n.** 1. **pl.** rrethinë; 2. mjedis,
ambient
survival /së'vaivl/ **n.** 1. mbijetesë; 2. mbijetojë, relikt
survive /së'vaiv/ **vti.** mbijetoj, mbetem gjallë
suspect /'saspekt/ **n.** njeri i dyshimtë; **adj.** i dyshimtë;
/së'spekt/ **vt.** dyshoj; vë në dyshim
suspend /së'spend/ **vt.** var; varet; 2. pezulloj, ndërpres; 3.
shtyj; 4. pezulloj (nga puna)
suspenders /së'spendërz/ **n. pl.** tiranda
suspense /së'spens/ **n.** ankth, gjendje që të mban pezull; **keep**
smb in suspense mbaj dikë pezull
suspicion /së'spishn/ **n.** dyshim, mosbesim; **above suspicion**
jashtë dyshimit
suspicious /së'spishës/ **adj.** i dyshimtë
suspiciously /së'spishësli/ **adv.** me dyshim
sustain /së'stein/ **vt.** 1. mbaj; 2. pësoj; vuaj; 3. mbaj
(gjallë); 4. mbaj, ushqej
sustenance /'sastinëns/ **n.** 1. mbajtje me ushqim; 2. të
ushqyer; 3. ushqim
swab /swob/ **n.** 1. tampon; 2. leckë, shtupë, sukull
swaddle /'swodl/ **vt.** 1. mbështjell me pelena; 2. mbështillem
(me batanije etj.)
swaddling clothes /'swodlin kloudhz/ **n. pl.** pelena
swallow /'swolou/ **n.** dallëndyshe
swamp /'swomp/ **n.** kënetë, moçal; **vt.** përmbyt
swan /swon/ **n. zool.** mjellmë
swarm /swo:m/ **n.** 1. mizëri; 2. luzmë; **vit.** 1. mizëron, zien
(nga njerëzit); 2. roitin (bletët)
sway /swei/ **n.** 1. kolovitje; 2. lëkundje
swear /sweë(r)/ **vti.** 1. betohem; 2. shaj
sweat /swet/ **n.** djersë; **vit.** djersit; djersitem
sweater /'swetë(r)/ **n.** 1. pulover; 2. triko
sweep /swi:p/ **n.** 1. fshirje; 2. lëvizje (e dorës etj.); **vti.**
1. fshij; 2. rrëmben, merr me vete; 3. përhapet, shtrihet
sweet /swi:t/ **adj.** 1. i ëmbël; 2. i freskët, i pakripur; 3. i
ëmbël, i këndshëm; 4. i dashur; **n.** 1. karamele, bonbone; 2.
ëmbëlsirë; 3. kënaqësi; 4. ëmbëlsi
sweeten /swi:tn/ **vti.** ëmbëlsoj
sweetheart /'swi:tha:rt/ **n.** i dashur, e dashur
swell /swel/ **vti.** 1. ënjtem; 2. mufatet, bymehet, fryhet; **n.**
1. ënjtje, fryerje; 2. xhungë
swelling /'swelin/ **n.** 1. ënjte; 2. xhungë
swerve /swë:rv/ **vit.** mënjanohem, shmangem, bëj mënjanë
swift /swift/ **adj.** i shpejtë
swim /swim/ **n.** 1. not; 2. notim; **vit.** 1. notoj; 2. noton,
pluskon; 3. vjen rrotull
swimming /'swimin/ **n.** not
swindle /'swindl/ **n.** mashtrim; **vti.** mashtroj
swindler /'swindlë(r)/ **n.** mashtrues, batakçi

swing /swin/ **n.** 1. lëkundje, kolovitje; 2. ritëm; 3. shilarës, kolovajzë; **vit.** 1. kolovit, lëkund; 2. lëkundem, kolovitem

switch /swiç/ **n.** 1. çelës (elektrik); 2. lëvizje; 3. fshikull, thupër; **vti.** 1. kaloj; 2. këmbej, ndërroj; 3. fshikulloj; **switch on (off)** hap (mbyll) dritën

switchboard /'swiçbo:rd/ **n. elek.** kuadër i shpërndarjes

swollen /'swolën/ **adj.** i ënjtur, i fryrë

swoop /swu:p/ **vi.** lëshohem

swop /swop/ **n.** shkëmbim, trambë; **vti.** shkëmbej, bëj trambë

sword /so:rd/ **n.** shpatë

swot /swot/ **vit.** studioj shumë

syllable /'silëbl/ **n. gjuh.** rrokje

symbol /'simbl/ **n.** simbol

sympathize /'simpëthaiz/ **vi.** simpatizoj

sympathy /'simpëthi/ **n.** simpati

symptom /'simptëm/ **n. mjek.** simptomë

syntax /'sinteks/ **n. gjuh.** sintaksë

synthetic /sin'thetik/ **adj.** sintetik

syringe /'sirinxh/ **n. mjek.** shiringë

syrup /'sirëp/ **n.** shurup

system /'sistëm/ **n.** sistem

systematic /,sistë'metik/ **adj.** sistematik

table /'teibl/ **n.** 1. tavolinë, tryezë; **lay the table** shtroj tavolinën; 2. ushqim; **keep a good table** ha mirë; 3. tabelë, pasqyrë; **table of contents** pasqyrë e lëndës; **vt.** shtroj (për diskutim)

table-cloth /'teiblkloth/ **n.** mbulesë tavoline, mësallë

table-spoon /'teiblspu:n/ **n.** lugë gjelle

tablet /'teblit/ **n.** 1. pllakë (përkujtimore); 2. **mjek.** tabletë

table tennis /'teibl tenis/ **n.** pingpong

table-ware /'teiblweë(r)/ **n.** takëm, komplet tavoline

tack /tek/ **n.** 1. thumb me kokë; 2. **det.** drejtim i anijes; 3. vijë politike; **vti.** 1. mbërthej me thumba; 2. ildis

tackle /'tekl/ **n.** 1. pajime; takëme; 2. **det.** sistemi i litarëve e makaravе; **vti.** 1. trajtoj; 2. përballoj; 3. merrem; 4. **sport.** ndërhyj (për të marrë topin)

tact /tekt/ **n.** takt

tactful /'tektful/ **adj.** me takt, i matur

tactic /'tektik/ **n.** 1. taktikë; 2. **pl. usht.** taktikë (edhe **fig.**)

tactical /'tektikl/ **adj.** taktik

tactless /'tektlis/ **adj.** i patakt

tag /teg/ **n.** 1. etiketë; 2. kokë (metalike, plastike e lidhëseve të këpucëve)

tail /teil/ **n.** 1. bisht; 2. bisht (i kometës, aeroplanit etj.); 3. ndjekës, gjurmues; **vt.** ndjek, i qepem dikujt nga pas

tailor /'teilë(r)/ **n.** rrobaqepës; **vt.** 1. pres e qep; 2. përshtat

take /teik/ **vti.** 1. marr; 2. kap; 3. mbart, çoj, transportoj; 4. marr; vjedh; 5. bëj; **take a walk** shëtis; 6. ha; pi; **take drugs** pi drogë; 7 pushtoj; marr; **take cold** marr të ftohtë; 8 marr, udhëtoj me; **take the bus** udhëtoj me autobus; 9 shoqëroj, përcjell; **take smb home** çoj dikë në shtëpi; **take smb aback** befasoj, zë në befasi; **take after smb** i ngjan dikujt; **take something apart** çmontoj, zbërthej; **take something away** heq, largoj; zbres, heq (një numër nga një tjetër); **take something down** shkruaj, mbaj shënim; **take someone or something for** marr dikë (diçka) për; **take something for granted** marr si të vërtetë; **take someone in** marr dikë në shtëpi; mashtroj; **take something in** ngushtoj, zvogëloj; marr punë në shtëpi; thith; përpij; **take it that** mendoj, besoj se; **take off** ngrihet (aeroplani); heq, zhvesh; **take someone off** imitoj; përqesh; **take something on** marr (një punë); marr përsipër; **take something over** marr në ngarkim; **take to something** jepem pas diçkaje; shkoj diku; **take to someone** pëlqej, më hyn dikush në zemër; **take up** zë (vend)

take-off /'teik of/ **n.** ngritje e aeroplanit

tale /teil/ **n.** 1. tregim; rrëfenjë; përrallë; 2. trillim

talent /'telënt/ **n.** talent, dhunti

talented /'telëntid/ **adj.** i talentuar

talk /to:k/ **n.** 1. bisedë, kuvendim; 2. llafe, thashetheme; 3. bisedë, ligjëratë; leksion; **vit.** 1. flas; 2. bisedoj; diskutoj; 3. flas, zotëroj (një gjuhë); **talk something over** e bisedoj diçka

talkative /'to:këtiv/ **adj.** llafazan, fjalaman

taker /'to:kë(r)/ **n.** 1. folës; 2. fjalaman

tall /to:l/ **adj.** 1. i gjatë; 2. i lartë

tame /teim/ **adj.** 1. i zbutur (për kafshët); 2. i butë, i bindur, i shtruar; 3. i mërzitshëm; **vt.** 1. zbut (një kafshë); 2. qetësoj

tan /ten/ **n.** ngjyrë kafe në të verdhë; 2. nxirje, pjekje nga dielli; **vti.** 1. regj lëkurët; 2. nxihem (nga dielli); 3. më zë dielli

tangerine /,tenxhë'rin/ **n. bot.** mandarinë

tangle /'tengl/ **n.** 1. ngatërrim; 2. rrëmujë, pështjellim; **vti.** ngatërroj; ngatërrohet; ngatërrohem

tangled /'tengld/ **adj.** i pleksur, i ngatërruar

tank /tenk/ **n.** 1. tank; 2. sternë, rezervuar; 3. cisternë

tanker /'tenkë(r)/ **n.** 1. anije, aeroplan cisternë; 2. autobot

tap /tep/ **n.** rubinet

tap /tep/ **vti.** 1. trokas; 2. prek, cek lehtë; **n.** trokitje; prekje e lehtë

tape /teip/ **n.** 1. shirit; 2. kordele; **vt.** 1. lidh me shirit; 2. regjistroj në shirit magnetik

tape-measure /'teip mezhë(r)/ **n.** metër shirit

tape-recorder /'teip riko:rdë(r)/ **n.** magnetofon

tar /ta:(r)/ **n.** katran, pisë; **vt.** shtroj me katran

target /'ta:rgit/ **n.** 1. tabelë, shenjë; 2. **fig.** objekt; 3. synim, objektiv

tariff /'terif/ **n. fin.** tarifë

tart /ta:rt/ **n.** 1. byrek me fruta; 2. turtë **tart** /ta:rt/ **adj.** 1. i athët, i thartë; 2. thumbues, therës

task /ta:sk/ **n.** detyrë; punë; urgent task punë urgjente; **vt.** 1. caktoj një detyrë; 2. sforcoj

taste /teist/ **n.** 1. shije; 2. gusto, parapëlqim; 3. shije (estetike); **vti.** 1. provoj (për shije); 2. ka shije; 3. ndjej shijen e

tasteful /'teistful/ **adj.** i bërë me shije, që ka shije

tasteless /'teistlis/ **adj.** i pashije, i zbarët, i pashijshëm

tasty /'teisti/ **adj.** i shijshëm

tatters /'tetërz/ **n. pl.** rrecka, zhele; in tatters me zhele

tattoo /të'tu:/ **n.** tatuazh; **vi.** bëj tatuazh

tax /teks/ **n.** taksë; **vt.** 1. taksoj; 2. vë në provë; tax sb's patience provoj durimin e dikujt; 3. akuzoj

taxable /'teksëbl/ **adj.** i tatueshëm

taxation /tek'seishn/ **n.** tatim

tax-collector /'tekskolektë(r)/ **n.** taksambledhës; taksidar

tax-free /,teks'fri:/ **adj.** i patatueshëm

taxi /'teksi/ **n.** taksi

taxpayer /'tekspeië(r)/ **n.** taksapagues

tea /ti:/ **n.** 1. **bot.** çaj (bima); 2. çaj

tea bag /'ti: beg/ **n.** qese me çaj

teach /ti:ç/ **vti.** jap mësim, mësoj dikë

teacher /'ti:çë(r)/ **n.** mësues, mësimdhënës

teaching /'ti:çin/ **n.** 1. mësimdhënie; 2. **pl.** mësime

teacup /'ti:kap/ **n.** filxhan çaji

team /ti:m/ **n.** 1. skuadër, ekip; 2. pendë, çift

teapot /'ti:pot/ **n.** çajnik

tear /teë(r)/ **n.** grisë, grisje; **vti.** 1. gris, çjerr, shqyej; tear something up gris; 2. shkëput; 3. shkul; 4. griset; 5. vrapoj me shpejtësi; 6. shqitem, shkëputem; tear oneself away from shkëputem, shqitem prej

tear /tië(r)/ **n.** lot; burst into tears shpërthej në lot

tearful /'tië(r)ful/ **adj.** i përlotur

tease /ti:z/ **vt.** 1. ngacmoj; 2. mërzit; 3. kreh, shprish (leshin)
tea set /'ti:set/ **n.** takëm çaji
tea-spoon /'ti:spu:n/ **n.** lugë çaji
technical /'teknikl/ **adj.** teknik; **technical terms** kushte teknike
technically /'teknikli/ **adv.** teknikisht
technician /tek'nishën/ **n.** teknik
technique /tek'ni:k/ **n.** teknikë; mjeshtëri
technological /,teknë'loxhikl/ **adj.** teknologjik
technology tek'nolëxhi/ **n.** teknologji
teddy bear /'tedi beë(r)/ **n.** ari lodër
tedious /'ti:diës/ **adj.** 1. i mërzitshëm; 2. i lodhshëm
teem /ti:m/ **vi.** 1. lëvrin, gëlon; 2. mizëron
teenager /'ti:neixhë(r)/ **n.** adoleshent
teens /ti:nz/ **n.** adoleshencë, mosha nga 13-19 vjeç
telegram /'teligrem/ **n.** telegram
telegraph /'teligra:f/ **n.** telegrafi; **vit.** telegrafoj
telephone /'telifoun/ **n.** telefon; **answer the telephone** marr, ngre receptorin e telefonit; **telephone booth** kabinë telefonike; **telephone call** thirrje elefonike; **telephone directory** libër telefonik; **vti.** telefonoj, marr në telefon
telescope /'teliskoup/ **n.** teleskop
television /'telivizhn/ **n.** televizion; **televison set** aparat televiziv
telex /'teleks/ **n.** teleks; **vt.** dërgoj (me) teleks
tell /tel/ **vti.** 1. tregoj; rrëfej; 2. jep informacion; 3. them, flas; 4. nxjerr një të fshehtë; 5. dalloj; shquaj; 6. përcaktoj; 7 urdhëroj; **can tell** mund të them; **tell someone off** shaj; qortoj; **there is no telling** kush e di kur;
teller /'telë(r)/ **n.** 1. rrëfyes, tregues; 2. tregimtar; 3. numërues i votave; 4. arkëtar banke
temper /'tempë(r)/ **n.** 1. natyrë, karakter, **temperament**; 2. gjendje shpirtërore; **fly into a temper** nxehem, inatosem; **in a bad temper** tërë inat; **in a good temper** gjithë humor; **keep one's temper** ruaj gjakftohtësinë; **lose one's temper** shpërthej, humb durimin
temperature /'tempriçë(r)/ **n.** temperaturë; **have (run) a temperature** kam temperaturë
temple /'templ/ **n.** faltore, tempull
temporary /'temprëri/ **adj.** i përkohshëm
temporarily /'temprërili/ **adv.** përkohësisht
tempt /tempt/ **vt.** tundoj, josh, ngas
temptation /temp'teishn/ **n.** ngasje, tundim, joshje
tempting / 'temptin/ **adj.** ngasës, tundues
ten /ten/ **n.** dhjetë
tenacious /ti'neishës/ **adj.** 1. i vendosur, këmbëngulës; 2. i fortë, i qëndrueshëm
tenancy /'tenënsi/ **n.** qiramarrje
tenant /'tenënt/ **n.** qiramarrës, qiraxhi
tend /tend/ **vi.** 1. prirem, kam prirje; 2. priret
tendency /'tendësi/ **n.** prirje, tendencë
tender /'tendë(r)/ **adj.** 1. i butë; 2. i dashur, i dhemshur; 3. i njomë; **tender age** moshë e njomë; 4. i ndjeshëm; 5. i dobët, delikat
tenement /'tenëmënt/ **n.** apartament, dhomë me qira

tennis /'tenis/ **sport.** tenis
tennis-court /'tenisko:rt/ **n.** fushë tenisi
tennis racket /'tenis rekit/ **n.** raketë tenisi
tense /tens/ **adj.** i tendosur, i nderë; **tense nerves** nerva të tendosura; **a tense atmosphere** atmosferë e nderë
tense /tens/ **n. gjuh.** kohë
tension /'tenshn/ **n.** 1. tendosje, shtrirje; 2. tension (mendor); 3. acarim, tension; 4. **elekr.** tension
tent /tent/ **n.** tendë, çadër; **pitch up a tent** ngre çadrën
tenth /tenth/ **adj.** i dhjetë; **n.** e dhjeta
term /të:rm/ **n.** 1. afat; 2. semestër; 3. **pl.** marrëdhënie; **be on good terms with** kam marrëdhënie të mira me; 4. term; 5. **pl.** kushte (të një marrëveshjeje); **come to terms with** arrij në marrëveshje me
terminal /'të:rminl/ **n.** stacion i fundit; **adj.** 1. i fundit, përfundimtar; 2. semestral
terminate /'të:rmineit/ **vti.** përfundoj; përfundon
termination /,te:rmi'neishn/ **n.** mbarim, përfundim
terminus /'të:rminës/ **n.** stacion i fundit (i trenit, autobusit)
terrace /'terës/ **n.** tarracë
terrible /'teribl/ **adj.** 1. i tmerrshëm; 2. shumë i keq; 3. shumë i madh, shumë i fortë
terribly /'teribli/ **adv.** 1. shumë; 2. tmerrësisht
terrific /të'rifik/ **adj.** 1. i tmerrshëm; 2. shumë i madh; 3. i mrekullueshëm
terrifically /të'rifikli/ **adv.** tmerrësisht
terrify /'terifai/ **vt.** tmerroj
territory /'terito:ri/ **n.** 1. territor; 2. fushë
terror /'terë(r)/ **n.** 1. terror; 2. tmerr; **strike terror into smb** i kall tmerrin dikujt
terrorism /'terërizëm/ **n.** terrorizëm
terrorist/ 'terërist/ **n.** terrorist
test /test/ **n.** 1. provë, sprovë; **put to test** vë në provë; 2. test, provim; 3. analizë; **test tube** provëz; **vt.** testoj, ekzaminoj
testify /'testifai/ **vti.** dëshmoj; dëshmon
textbook /'tekstbuk/ **n.** libër shkollor
textile /'tekstail/ **adj.** tekstil; **n.** tekstil
than /dhen/ **conj.** se, sesa **thank** /thenk/ **vt.** falënderoj
thanks /thenks/ **n. pl.** falënderim; **thanks for** faleminderit për; **thanks to** falë, në sajë të
thankful /'thenkful/ **adj.** mirënjohës
that /dhet/ **pron.** që, i cili; ai, ajo; **conj.** se; që; saqë; **adv.** aq, kaq
the /dhi:, dhë/ **def. art.** nyjë shquese
the /dhë/ **adv.** më; **the sooner the better** sa më shpejt aq më mirë; **all the better** aq më mirë
theater /'thiëtë(r)/ **n.** teatër
theft /theft/ **n.** vjedhje
their /dheë(r)/ **adj.** i tyre
theirs /dheërz/ **pron.** i tyre
them /dhem/ **pron.** ata, ato; atyre
theme /thi:m/ **n.** temë

themselves /dhem'selvz/ **pron.** vetë; veten
then /dhen/ **adv.** atëhere; pastaj; në atë kohë; **by then** në atë
kohë; **just then** pikërisht atëhere; **then and there** menjëherë;
from then on qysh nga ajo kohë
theoretic(al) /,thië'retik(ël)/ **adj.** teorik
theoretially /,thië'retikli/ **adv.** teorikisht
theory /'thiëri/ **n.** teori
there /dheë(r)/ **adv.** 1. atje; 2. në atë çështje; **there is
(are)** ka, është, ndodhet; **there he is!** ja tek është!
thereafter /,dheër'aftë(r)/ **adv.** paskëtaj, këtej e tutje
thereby /,dheër'bai/ **adv.** 1. me anën e kësaj; 2. në lidhje me
të
therefore /'dheërfo:(r)/ **adv.** prandaj, si rrjedhim, si
rezultat
thermometer /thë'momitë(r)/ **n.** termometër
thermos /'thë:mës/ **n.** termos
these /dhi:z/ **pl. adj. pron.** këta, këto
they /dhei/ **pron.** ata, ato
thick /thik/ **adj.** 1. i trashë; 2. i dendur
thicken /thikën/ **vti.** 1. trash, trashet; 2. komplikohet,
koklavitet
thief /thi:f/ **n.** hajdut, vjedhës
thigh /thai/ **n.** kofshë
thimble /'thimbl/ **n.** gishtëz
thin /thin/ **adj.** 1. i hollë; 2. i thatë, i hollë, i dobët; 3.
i holluar; 4. i rrallë; **vti.** 1. holloj; hollohem; 2. dobësoj,
dobësohem; 3. rrallohet
thing /thin/ **n.** 1. send, gjë; 2. **pl.** plaçka, tesha; 3.
ngjarje, rrethanë; 4. punë, çështje; 5. krijesë; **as things
stand** në këto kushte
think /think/ **vti.** 1. mendoj; 2. kam mendimin, jam i
mendimit; 3. besoj, më duket; 4. kujtoj; 5. gjykoj, quaj; 6.
synoj, kam ndër mend; **think about something** kujtoj, sjell
ndër mend; mendohem, rrah me mend; **think badly of** mendoj keq
për; **think highly of** çmoj, vlerësoj lart; **think something
over** peshoj, mendoj mirë; **think out** mendoj, gjej në mend
thinker /'thinkë(r)/ **n.** mendimtar
thinking /'thinkin/ **n.** mendim
third /thë:rd/ **adj.** i tretë
thirdly /'thë:rdli/ **adv.** së treti
thirst /thë:rst/ **n.** 1. etje; 2. **fig.** etje, lakmi, dëshirë;
vi. kam etje
thirsty /'thë:rsti/ **adj.** i etur, i etshëm (edhe **fig.**)
thirteen /'thë:'ti:n/ **num.** trembëdhjetë; **n.** trembëdhjetë;
adj. i trembëdhjetë
thirteenth /'thë:ti:nth/ **adj.** i trembëdhjetë
thirtieth /'thë:tiith/ **adj.** i tridhjetë
thirty /'thë:rti/ **n.** tridhjetë; **adj.** i tridhjetë
this /dhis/ **adj. pron.** ky, kjo; **this way** këtej
thistle /'thisl/ **n. bot.** gjëmbaç
thorn /tho:rn/ **n.** gjemb
thorny /'tho:rni/ **adj.** gjëmbor
thorough /'tharë/ **adj.** i plotë, i tërë
thoroughfare /'tharëfeë(r)/ **n.** rrugë kryesore
thoroughly /'tharëli/ **adv.** tërësisht, plotësisht

though /dhou/ **adv.** megjithatë; **conj.** megjithëse, sadoqë; **as though** sikur
thought /tho:t/ **n.** 1. mendim; 2. përkujdesje, vëmendje, konsideratë; 3. qëllim; 4. pikëpamje; 5. gjykim; 6. vlerësim
thoughtful /'tho:tful/ **adj.** 1. i menduar; 2. i vëmendshëm, i kujdesshëm
thoughtless /'tho:tlis/ **adj.** 1. i pakujdesshëm, i shkujdesur; 2. i pamenduar; i pamend
thousand /'thauzënd/ **n.** njëmijë; **adj.** i njëmijtë
thousandth /'thauznth/ **adj.** i njëmijtë
thrash /thresh/ **vti.** 1. rrah; 2. fshikulloj; 3. shqyrtoj; 4. mund thellësisht
thread /thred/ **n.** pe, fill; **vt.** shkoj perin në gjilpërë
threadbare /'thredbeë(r)/ **adj.** 1. i ngrënë, i vajtur; 2. **fig.** bajat
threat /thret/ **n.** kërcënim, kanosje; **carry out a threat** realizoj kërcënimin
threaten /'thretn/ **vti.** 1. kërcënoj, kanos; kërcënon; 2. paralajmëron
threatening /'thretnin/ **adj.** kërcënues
threateningly /'thretninli/ **adv.** kërcënueshëm
three /thri:/ **n.** tre, tri; **adj.** i tretë
threshold /'threshhould/ **n.** 1. prag; 2. **fig.** prag, fillim, vigjilje; **on the threshold of** në prag të
thrift /thrift/ **n.** kursim, ekonomi
thriftless /'thriftlis/ **adj.** dorëlëshuar, prishës, prisharak
thrifty /'thrifti/ **adj.** kursimtar
thrill /thril/ **vti.** 1. dridhëroj, rrëqeth; 2. dridhërohem, rrëqethem; **n.** drithërimë, rrëqethje
thriller /'thrilë(r)/ **n.** roman (film etj.) sensacional
thrilling /'thrilin/ **adj.** 1. ngjethës; 2. elektrizues
thrive /thraiv/ **vi.** lulëzon
throat /throut/ **n.** grykë
throb /throb/ **vi.** rreh, regëtin, pulson; **n.** rrahje, pulsim, regëtimë
throng /throun/ **n.** fron (i mbretit)
throttle /'throtl/ **vti.** mbyt (edhe **fig.**)
through /thru:/ **adv.** 1. tejpërtej; 2. krejt, plotësisht; **prep.** nëpër, përmes
throughout /thru:'aut/ **adv.** kudo, ngado, gjithkund; gjatë gjithë
throw /throu/ **vti.** 1. hedh, flak; 2. hedh, rrëzoj për tokë; 3. nxjerr, ngre; 4. hedh, gjuaj (topin); **throw something away** hedh, flak diçka; **throw oneself into** i përvishem punës; **throw somebody out** nxjerr përjashta; **throw something out** hedh poshtë, kundërshtoj; jap, lëshoj; **n.** hedhje
thumb /tham/ **n.** gisht i madh i dorës
thunder /'thandë(r)/ **n.** bubullimë; gjëmim; **vit.** 1. gjëmon, bubullin; 2. ushton, uturin
thunderstorm /'thandërsto:m/ **n.** stuhi, furtunë
Thursday /'thë:rzdi/ **n.** e enjte
thus /dhas/ **adv.** kështu, në këtë mënyrë
tick tik/ **n.** 1. tik-tak; 2. çast, moment
ticket /'tikit/ **n.** 1. biletë; 2. etiketë; 3. **amer.** listë e kandidatëve (për zgjedhje); **vt.** etiketoj, i vë etiketën

tickle /'tikl/ **vti.** 1. gudulis; gudulisem; 2. kënaq; **n.** guduli, gudulisje
tide /taid/ **n.** 1. baticë; zbaticë; 2. rrymë; rrjedhë; **go with the tide** shkoj me rrymën; **vt.** kapërcej (një vështirësi etj.)
tidy /'taidi/ **adj.** 1. i rregullt; 2. i pastër; 3. i konsiderueshëm; **vt.** rregulloj, vë në rregull
tie /tai/ **vti.** 1. lidh; lidhet; shtrëngohet; 2. **sport.** barazoj; **n.** 1. lidhje; 2. kravatë; 3. lidhëse; 4. **sport.** barazim
tie-pin /'taipin/ **n.** karficë kravate
tiger /'taigë(r)/ **n.** **zool.** tigër
tight /tait/ **adj.** 1. i shtrënguar; 2. i puthitur; 3. i papërshkrueshëm (nga uji etj.); 4. i tendosur; 5. i vështirë; 6. i ngushtë; **in a tight corner (spot)** në gjendje të vështirë
tighten /'taitn/ **vti.** 1. shtrëngoj; shtrëngohet; 2. tendoset
tights /taits/ **n. pl.** geta
tile /tail/ **n.** tjegull; **vt.** mbuloj me tjegulla
till /til/ **prep.** deri; **conj.** gjersa, derisa
till /til/ **vt.** punoj tokën
tillage /'tilixh/ **n.** kultivim, punim i tokës
tiller /'tilë(r)/ **n.** 1. bujk; 2. kultivues i tokës
timber /'timbë(r)/ **n.** 1. tra; 2. lëndë ndërtimi
time /taim/ **n.** 1. kohë; 2. periudhë; 3. çast, moment; 4. herë; 5. kohë, orë; 6. kohë, epokë; 7 **muz.** kohë; **at a time** në një kohë, njëkohësisht; **at one time** dikur; **at the time** atëhere; **at times** hera-herës; **for the time being** hëpërhë; **from time to time** nga koha në kohë; **in a few day's time** shpejt; **in time** në kohë; me kohë; **in good time** herët; **in no time** shpejt; **it's about time** është tamam koha; **have a good time** e kaloj mirë; **just in time** tamam në kohë; **kill time** vras kohën; **on time** në kohën e duhur; **spare time** kohë e lirë; **spend time** harxhoj kohën; **take your time** e marr shtruar; **time and time again** shpesh; **all the time** gjatë gjithë kohës; **at no time** në çast; **at the same time** njëkohësisht; **vt.** 1. caktoj, zgjedh kohën; 2. gjej kohën; 3. mat kohën
timekeeper /'taimki:pë(r)/ **n.** 1. kohështënues; 2. kronometër; kronometrist
timely 'taimli/ **adj.** që ndodh, bëhet në kohën e duhur
timetable /'taimteibl/ **n.** orar (i trenave, autobusëve etj.)
timid /'timid/ **adj.** i druajtur
timidity /ti'midëti/ **n.** druajtje
tin /tin/ **n.** 1. **kim.** kallaj; 2. kuti (konservash; **vt.** konservoj
tinned /tind/ **adj.** i konservuar; tinned meat mish i konservuar
tinfoil /tin'foil/ **n.** letër varak
tinkle /'tinkl/ **n.** tingëllimë; tringëllimë; **vit.** tingëllon; tringëllon
tin-opener /'tinopënë(r)/ **n.** hapëse (konservash)
tiny /'taini/ **adj.** i vogël
tip /tip/ **n.** 1. bakshish; 2. këshillë; 3. informacion; **vt.** 1. jap bakshish; 2. prek, cek lehtë; 3. tregoj (një të fshehtë)
tip /tip/ **vti.** 1. pjerr, anoj; 2. hedh, derdh; 3. përmbys; **tip out** derdh; **tip over** përmbys
tipsy /'tipsi/ **adj.** i pirë lehtë

tiptoe /'tiptou/ *n.* **(in) walk on tiptoe** eci në majë të
gishtave; **vi.** eci në majë të gishtave
tip-top /,tip'top/ *adj.* i shkëlqyer, i klasit të parë
tire /'taië(r)/ *vti.* 1. lodh, lodhem; 2. mërzit, mërzitem
tired /'taiëd/ *adj.* 1. i lodhur; 2. i mërzitur; **be tired of**
jam mërzitur me; **tired out** i lodhur, i këputur
tireless /'taiërlis/ *adj.* i palodhur, i palodhshëm
tiresome /'taiërsëm/ *adj.* 1. i lodhshëm; 2. i mërzitshëm
tissue /'tishu:/ *n.* 1. **anat.** ind; 2. shami letër; 3. pëlhurë;
tissue paper letër e hollë (për mbështjellje e paketim)
title /'taitl/ *n.* 1. titull (libri); 2. titull (nderi,
fisnikërie etj.); 3. **drej.** e drejtë (e zotërimit, pronësisë)
to /tu:/ *prep.* në; drejt; deri; nga
toad /toud/ *n.* zhabë
toast /toust/ *n.* peksimate, bukë e thekur; **vt.** pjek; thek
toast /toust/ *n.* dolli; shëndet; **drink a toast to** ngre një
dolli për; **vt.** ngre dolli për
tobacco /të'bekou/ *n.* duhan
tobacconist /të'bekënist/ *n.* duhanshitës, cigareshitës
today /të'dei/ *n.* dita e sotme; **adv.** sot
toddle /'todl/ *vi.* 1. çapitem; 2. shëtis
toddler /'todlë(r)/ *n.* fëmijë që ka nisur të çapitet
toe /tou/ *n.* gisht i këmbës; **from top to toe** nga koka në
këmbë; **tread (step) on sb's toes** shkel dikë në kallo
toffee /'tofi/ *n.* karamele
together /të'gedhë(r)/ *adv.* bashkë, së bashku, së toku
toil /toil/ *n.* punë e rëndë; **vi.** punoj shumë e gjatë,
robtohem
toilet /'toilit/ *n.* 1. tualet; 2. banjë, nevojtore
toilet paper /'toilit peipë(r)/ *n.* letër higjenike
token /'tokën/ *n.* shenjë, simbol; **as a token of** si shenjë të
tolerance /'tolërëns/ *n.* tolerancë, durim
tolerant /'tolërënt/ *adj.* tolerant, i durueshëm, i duruar
tolerate /'tolëreit/ *vt.* duroj, toleroj
toll /toul/ *n.* 1. taksë (për kalim ure, rruge etj.); 2.
humbje (në luftë, aksident etj.)
tomato /të'meitou/ *n.* domate
tomb /tu:m/ *n.* varr
tombstone /'tu:mstoun/ *n.* gur varri
tomorrow /të'morou/ *n.* e nesërme; **adv.** nesër
ton /tan/ *n.* ton
tone /toun/ *n.* 1. ton; 2. tingull; 3. zë; **vti.** 1. jap tonin;
2. zbut, ndryshoj tonin; 3. harmonizoj
tongs /tonz/ *n.* **pl.** 1. piskatore; 2. mashë
tonic /'tonik/ *n.* tonik; **adj.** tonik
tongue /tan/ *n.* **anat.** gjuhë; 2. gjuhë; **hold one's tongue** mbaj
gjuhën; 3. e folme
tonight /të'nait/ *n.* mbrëmje e sotme; **adv.** sot
tonsil /'tonsil/ *n.* **anat.** bajame; **have one's tonsils out** heq
bajamet
tonsilitis /,tonsi'laitis/ *n.* **mjek.** pezmatim i bajameve
too /tu:/ *adv.* edhe; gjithashtu; për më tepër; shumë; tepër
tool /tu:l/ *n.* 1. vegël, instrument; 2. mjet; 3. **fig.** vegël,
mashë

tooth /tu:th/ **n. anat.** 1. dhëmb; **have a tooth out** heq dhëmbin; 2. dhëmb (i sharrës etj.)
toothache /'tu:theik/ **n.** dhembje dhëmbi
toothbrush /'tu:thbrash/ **n.** furçë dhëmbësh
toothless /'tu:thlis/ **adj.** i padhëmbë
toothpaste /'tu:thpeist/ **n.** pastë dhëmbësh
toothpick /'tu:thpik/ **n.** dhëmbëkruese **toothsome** /'tu:thsëm/ **adj.** i shijshëm, i këndshëm
top /top/ **n.** 1. majë; **at the top of** në majë të; 2. krye; 3. kulm; **at the top of one's voice** me gjithë zërin; **on top** sipër; **on top of** mbi, sipër; 4. kapak; **adj.** 1. i sipërm; 2. maksimal
top /top/ **n.** fugë
topic /'topik/ **n.** temë, subjekt
topical /'topikl/ **adj.** aktual
topple /'topl/ **vit.** 1. bie, rrëzohet; 2. përmbys, rrëzoj
torch /to:rç/ **n.** 1. pishtar; **hand on the torch** dorëzoj pishtarin; 2. elektrik dore
tornado /to'neidou/ **n.** 1. uragan; 2. ciklon
torpedo /to:'pi:dou/ **n.** torpilë, silur; **vt.** siluroj
torrent /'torënt/ **n.** 1. përrua, rrëke; 2. **fig.** lumë, rrëke
tortoise /'to:tës/ **n. zool.** breshkë
torture /'to:çë(r)/ **n.** torturë; **put somebody to the torture** torturoj dikë; **vt.** torturoj
torturer /'to:çërë(r)/ **n.** torturues
toss /tos/ **vti.** 1. hedh; 2. lëkundem; 3. vërtitem, përpiqem; 3. hedh short; **toss up (toss for it)** hedh kokë a pilë
total /'toutl/ **adj.** 1. i plotë, i tërë, i tërësishëm, total; **n.** total, shumë e përgjithshme; **vti.** 1. nxjerr totalin; 2. arrin, kap shumën
totally /'toutëli/ **adv.** plotësisht, krejtësisht
touch /taç/ **n.** 1. prekje; 2. të prekurit (shqisë); 3. nuancë; 4. kontakt, lidhje; **keep in touch with** mbaj lidhje me; **lose touch with** humb lidhjet me; **out of touch with** i shkëputur nga; 5. dorë, stil; **vti.** 1. prek, çik; 2. **fig.** prek (ndjenjat); 3. ngacmoj, trazoj; 4. mallëngjej; 5. barazohem, krahasohem; 6. preket, i bie, e zë (një sëmundje etj.); 7 prek, trajtoj; **touch on (upon) something** trajtoj (një çështje); 8 prek, vë në gojë
touchable /'taçëbl/ **adj.** i prekshëm
touching /'taçin/ **adj.** prekës
touchy /'taçi/ **adj.** 1. që preket, fyhet lehtë; 2. sedërmadh
tough /taf/ **adj.** 1. i fortë, i qëndrueshëm; 2. i fortë, i fuqishëm, i paepur, i pathyeshëm; 3. i egër; 4. i pabërë, i fortë (mishi etj.); 5. i ashpër, i rreptë; 6. i vështirë; 7 kokëfortë
tour /tuë(r)/ **n.** 1. udhëtim; **a round-the-world tour** udhëtim rreth botës; 2. turne; **vti.** 1. shëtit (një vend); 2. bëj turne
tourism /'tuërizëm/ **n.** turizëm
tourist /'tuerist/ **n.** turist; **adj.** turistik
tournament /'to:nëmënt/ **n. sport.** turne
tow /tou/ **vt.** rimorkioj (anijen, makinën)
toward(s) /të'wo:d(z)/ **prep.** drejt; për; ndaj; nga
towel /'tauël/ **n.** peshqir, rizë; **vt.** fshihem me peshqir
tower /'tauë(r)/ **n.** kullë; **vi.** ngrihet, lartësohet

tower-block /'tauë(r) blok/ **n.** bllok grataçelash
town /taun/ **n.** qytet
town hall /,taun'ho:l/ **n.** bashki
townsfolk /'taunzfouk/ **n.** qytetarë
townsman /'taunzmën/ **n.** qytetar
toxic /'toksik/ **adj.** toksik, i helmët
toy /toi/ **n.** lodër; **adj.** lodër; **a toy car** makinë lodër
toyshop /'toishop/ **n.** dyqan lodrash **trace** /treis/ **n.** 1.
gjurmë; shenjë; 2. sasi e vogë; **vti.** 1. gjej, zbuloj; **trace
something back** gjej zanafillë, burimin, prejardhjen; 2.
rrjedh, zë fill; 3. ndjek, gjurmoj; 4. kalkoj
track /trek/ **n.** 1. gjurmë, tragë, vragë; **on the track of** në
gjurmë të; 2. kurs, udhë; 3. rrugë e ngushtë; shteg, monopat;
4. shinë, binar; 5. pistë; **vt.** gjurmoj; ndjek gjurmët e;
track smb (sth) down gjej duke gjurmuar
tractsuit /'treksju:t/ **n.** tuta (sportive) **tractor**
/'trektë(r)/ **n.** traktor
trade /treid/ **n.** 1. tregti; 2. zanat, profesion; **vit.** 1.
tregtoj, bëj tregti; 2. këmbej, bëj trambë
trade-mark /'treidma:rk/ **n.** markë e fabrikës
trader /'treidë(r)/ **n.** tregtar
trade union /,treid'ju:niën/ **n.** sindikatë
trading /'treidin/ **n.** tregti
tradition /trë'dishn/ **n.** traditë
traditional /'trë'dishënl/ **adj.** tradicional
traditionally /'trë'dishënëli/ **adv.** tradicionalisht
traffic /'trefik/ **n.** 1. trafik, qarkullim; **traffic jam**
bllokim qarkullimi; **traffic light** semafor; 2. kontrabandë,
tregti e paligjshme; **vi.** bëj tregti të paligjshme
trafficker /'trefikë(r)/ **n.** trafikant
tragedy /'trexhëdi/ **n. let.** tragjedi
tragic /'trexhik/ **adj.** tragjik
trail /treil/ **n.** 1. gjurmë; vazhdë; 2. gjurmë, erë; 3. rrugë
e ngushtë, shteg; **vit.** 1. tërheq, zvarrit; 2. çapitem me zor;
3. gjurmoj, shkoj pas herës
trailer /'treilë(r)/ **n.** rimorkio
train /trein/ **n.** 1. tren; **take the train** marr trenin; **catch
the train** kap trenin; **change trains** ndryshoj tren; **goods
train** tren mallrash; **passenger train** tren pasagjerësh; 2.
karvan; varg; 3. shpurë; **vti.** 1. ushtroj, mësoj, përgatit; 2.
stërvit; 3. drejtoj
trainer /'treinë(r)/ **n.** trajner
training /'treinin/ **n.** përgatitje; stërvitje; trajnim
traitor /'treitë(r)/ **n.** tradhtar
tram /trem/ **n.** tramvaj
tramp /tremp/ **n.** 1. zhurmë (e hapave); 2. shëtitje e gjatë;
3. endacak; **vit.** 1. eci rëndë; 2. endem, eci gjatë në këmbë
trample /trempl/ **vti.** shkel (edhe **fig.**); **trample under foot**
shkel, marr nëpër këmbë
tranquil /'trenkwil/ **adj.** i qetë
transaction /tren'zekshn/ **n.** 1. kryerje; 2. trajtim; 3. punë;
4. veprim, operacion (financiar)
transcend /tren'send/ **vt.** tejkaloj; kapërcej kufijtë

transcript /'trenskript/ **n.** 1. transkriptim; 2. kopje e transkriptuar; 2. kopjim

transfer /trens'feë(r)/ **vti.** 1. transferoj; 2. zhvendos; 3. transferohem; shpërngulem; 4. ia kaloj një tjetri (pasurinë); 5. kaloj, hedh; **n.** 1. transferim; 2. kalim

transform /trens'fo:rm/ **vt.** transformoj, shndërroj

transformation /,trensfë'meishn/ **n.** transformim

transformer /trens'fo:rmë(r)/ **n. elek.** transformator

transfuse /trens'fju:z/ **vt. mjek.** bëj transfuzion

transfusion /trens'fju:xhn/ **n.** transfuzion; **blood transfusion** transfuzion gjaku

transistor /tren'zistë(r)/ **n.** tranzistor; **transistor radio** radio me tranzistorë

transit /'trensit/ **n.** 1. tranzit; 2. kalim; **transit visa** vizë tranzit

transition /tren'zishn/ **n.** tranzicion, periudhë kalimtare

transitional /tren'zishënl/ **adj.** kalimtar, tranzicioni

transitive /'trensëtiv/ **adj. gjuh.** kalimtar; **transitive verb** folje kalimtare

translate /trens'leit/ **vti.** 1. përkthej; përkthehet; 2. shpjegoj, interpretoj; 3. kthej

translation /trens'leishn/ **n.** përkthim; **in translation** të përkthyer (jo në origjinal)

translator /trens'leitë(r)/ **n.** përkthyes

transliterate /trenz'litëreit/ **vt.** tejshkronjëzoj

transliteration /,trenzlitë'reishn/ **n.** tejshkronjëzim

transmission /trenz'mishn/ **n.** 1. transmetim; 2. transmision

transmit /trenz'mit/ **vt.** 1. transmetoj; 2. përçoj, përcjell

transmitter /trenz'mitë(r)/ **n.** 1. transmetues; 2. radiodhënës

transparent /trens'peërënt/ **adj.** 1. transparent, i tejdukshëm; 2. i qartë

transplant /trens'pla:nt; trens'plent/ **vti.** 1. përandit; artis; 2. transplantoj; **n.** transplantim

transplantation /,trenspla:n'teishn/ **n.** transplantim

transport /trens'po:rt/ **vt.** 1. bart, transportoj; 2. internoj, syrgjynos; **n.** bartje, transport

trap /trep/ **n.** 1. çark; 2. kurth, grackë; **fall into a trap** bie në kurth; **vti.** 1. bie në grackë; 2. kap, zë me çark

travel /'trevl/ **vit.** 1. udhëtoj; 2. lëviz, përhapet; **n.** udhëtim; **travel agency** agjensi udhëtimi

traveller (traveler) /'trevlë(r)/ **n.** udhëtar

travelling (traveling) /'trevlin/ **n.** udhëtim; **adj.** 1. shëtitës; 2. udhëtimi, i udhëtimit; **traveling expenses** shpenzimet e udhëtimit

trawler /'tro:lë(r)/ **n.** peshkatore (me tral) **tray** /trei/ **n.** tabaka

treacherous /'treçërës/ **adj.** 1. tradhtar; 2. i pabesë

treachery /'treçëri/ **n.** tradhti

tread /tred/ **vit.** 1. shkel; 2. eci; 3. shtyp; **n.** hap

treason /'tri:zn/ **n.** tradhti; **high treason** tradhti e lartë

treasure /'trezhë(r)/ **n.** thesar; **vt.** 1. ruaj; **treasure something in one's memory** ruaj në kujtesë; 2. çmoj, vlerësoj së tepërmi

treasurer /'trezhërë(r)/ **n.** thesarmbajtës

treasury /'trezhëri/ **n.** 1. thesar; 2. **fig.** thesar

treat /tri:t/ **n.** 1. kënaqësi; 2. qerasje; **vti.** 1. trajtoj; 2. shtjelloj; 3. **mjek.** kuroj, mjekoj, trajtoj; 4. quaj, konsideroj; 5. qeras, gostit; **treat somebody to something** qeras dikë me; **treat something as** quaj, konsideroj
treatment /'tri:tmënt/ **n.** trajtim, shtjellim; 2. **mjek.** trajtim, mjekim, kurim
treaty /'tri:ti/ **n.** 1. traktat; **peace treaty** traktat paqeje; 2. marrëveshje
tree /tri:/ **n.** pemë
trek /trek/ **n.** udhëtim i gjatë e i lodhshëm (në këmbë)
tremble /'trembl/ **n.** dridhje; **vi.** dridhem
tremendous /tri'mendës/ **adj.** 1. i madh; 2. i jashtëzakonshëm
tremor /'tremë(r)/ **n.** 1. dridhje; 2. lëkundje; **earth tremors** dridhje të tokës
trench /trenç/ **n.** 1. hendek, kanal; 2. llogore, transhe; **vti.** hap (kanal, llogore)
trend /trend/ **n.** prirje, drejtim, tendencë; **vi.** prirem
trespass /'trespës/ **vi.** 1. shkel, cënoj, dhunoj; 2. kaloj (kapërcej) kufirin; 3. shpërdor, shpërdoroj; 4. mëkatoj
trespasser /'trespësë(r)/ **n.** shkelës
trial /trail/ **n.** 1. provë; **put something to trial** vë diçka në provë; **take something on trial** marr diçka me provë; 2. proces gjyqësor; gjyq; **bring somebody to trial** hedh në gjyq; **put somebody on trial** hedh në gjyq; **on trial** në provë; në gjyq
triangle /'traiengl/ **n. gjeom.** trekëndësh
trianglar /trai'engjulë(r)/ **adj.** 1. **gjeom.** trekëndor; 2. trepalësh
tribal /'traibl/ **adj.** fisnor
tribe /traib/ **n.** 1. fis; 2. lloj; 3. racë
trick /trik/ **n.** 1. dredhi, mashtrim; 2. marifet, hile, rreng; **play a trick on somebody** i punoj dikujt një rreng; **vt.** mashtroj
trickery /'trikëri/ **n.** 1. mashtrim; 2. dredhi
trickle /'trikl/ **vi.** rrjedh, pikon, shkon çurg; **n.** çurg
tricky /'triki/ **adj.** 1. mashtrues, rrengtar, dredharak; 2. i vështirë, i komplikuar, delikat, me spec
tricycle /'traisikl/ **n.** triçikël
trifle /'traifl/ **n.** 1. vogëlimë, çikërrimë; 2. shumë e vogël (të hollash); 3. çikë, grimë; **vit.** luaj, tallem
trifling /'traiflin/ **adj.** i vogël, i parëndësishëm
trim /trim/ **adj.** 1. i rregullt e i pastërt; 2. i hollë, elegant; **vt.** 1. shkurtoj, rregulloj; 2. zbukuroj, stolis; 3. sjell në drejtpeshim (anijen avionin etj.); **n.** 1. rregull; 2. zbukurim
trimming /'trimin/ **n.** 1. zbukurim, dekoracion; 2. garniturë
trip /trip/ **n.** 1. udhëtim; ekskursion; 2. pengë; **vit.** 1. pengohem; 2. i vë këmbëzën; **trip someone up** pengoj, i vë stërkëmbësh dikujt
triple /'tripl/ **adj.** 1. i trefishtë; 2. tripalësh; **n.** trefish; **vti.** trefishoj; trefishohet
triumph /'traiëmf/ **n.** 1. triumf; 2. ngadhënjim; **vi.** triumfoj
triumphant /trai'amfënt/ **adj.** triumfues, ngadhnjimtar
triumphantly /trai'amfëntli/ **adv.** triumfalisht
trivial /'triviël/ **adj.** i vogël, i parëndësishëm
trolley /'troli/ **n.** 1. karrocë dore; 2. vagonetë; 3. tryezë me rrota
troop /tru:p/ **n.** 1. grup, turmë; 2. kope; 3. **pl. usht.** trupa

tropic /'tropik/ **n. gjeog.** tropik
tropical /'tropikl/ **adj.** tropikal; **tropical climate** klimë
tropikale
trot /trot/ **vit.** 1. vrapon trokthi (kali); 2. eci me hap të
shpejtë; **n.** trokth, trok
trouble /'trabl/ **n.** 1. shqetësim; 2. hall; 3. bela, telash,
bezdi; 4. trazirë, turbullirë; 5. çrregullim; shqetësim; 6.
mundim; **save trouble (save the trouble of)** kursen mundin e;
get into trouble futem në telash; **ask (look) for trouble**
kërkoj belanë; **take the trouble** marr mundimin; **be in trouble**
kam telashe; **go to trouble (take) trouble** fus veten në bela;
make trouble for krijoj telashe për; **vti.** 1. shqetësoj;
shqetësohem; 2. bezdis
troubled /'trabld/ **adj.** i shqetësuar
troublesome /'trablsëm/ **adj.** 1. shqetësues; 2. i bezdisshëm
trousers /'trauzëz/ **n. pl.** pantallona
trout /traut/ **n.** troftë
trowel /'trauël/ **n.** 1. mistri; 2. kunj
truant /'tru:ënt/ **n.** nxënës që vidhet nga shkolla; **play
truant** vidhem nga shkolla
truce /'tru:s/ **n.** armëpushim
truck /trak/ **n.** 1. kamion; 2. vagon mallrash
trudge /traxh/ **vi.** çapitem me zor
true /tru:/ **adj.** 1. i vërtetë; 2. i saktë; i përpiktë; 3.
besnik, i vendosur; 4. i vërtetë, i pastër; 5. i vërtetë,
origjinal; **come true** realizohet, bëhet realitet; **adv.** 1.
saktë; 2. çiltërisht
truly /'tru:li/ **adv.** 1. sinqerisht; 2. realisht, me të
vërtetë
trumpet /'trampit/ **n.** trombë; bori; **vti.** trumpetoj
trunk /trank/ **n.** 1. trung; 2. baule, sënduk; 3. feçkë (e
elefantit)
trunk-call /'trank ko:l/ **n.** thirrje telefonike interurbane
trust /trast/ **n.** 1. besim; **put trust in** i besoj; 2.
përgjegjësi; 3. mirëbesim; 4. trust; **vti.** 1. besoj; 2.
mbështetem, i zë besë; 3. shpresoj
trustee /tras'ti:/ **n.** 1. administrator besnik; 2. anëtar i
administratës së një enti publik
trustful /'trastful/ **adj.** besimplotë
trustless /'trastlis/ **adj.** mosbesues
trustworthy /'trastwë:rdhi/ **adj.** i besueshëm
trusty /'trasti/ **adj.** i besuar
truth /tru:th/ **n.** e vërtetë; **tell the truth** them të vërtetën
truthful /'tru:thful/ **adj.** 1. i vërtetë; 2. i sinqertë, i
ndershëm
try /trai/ **vit.** 1. provoj; 2. gjykoj; 3. lodh, sforcon; 4.
orvatem, përpiqem, bëj përpjekje; **try something on** provoj
(një veshje etj.); **try one's hand at** provoj aftësitë në; **n.**
1. orvajtje, përpjekje; 2. provë; **have a try at** bëj një provë
tub /tab/ **n.** 1. kade; 2. govatë
tube /t(j)u:b/ **n.** 1. gyp, tub; 2. tubet; 3. metro; 4. llambë
elektronike; 5. kamerdare (biçiklete, makine)
tuberculosis /tju,bë:kju'lousis/ **n. mjek.** turbekuloz
tuck /tak/ **vti.** 1. fut; 2. mbledh, mbështjell; **n.** palë, kind
Tuesday /'tju:zdi/ **n.** e martë
tuft /taft/ **n.** tufë; xhufkë
tug /tag/ **n.** 1. tërheqje; 2. rimorkiator; **vti.** 1. tërheq
fort; 2. rimorkioj

tuition /tju:'ishn/ **n.** 1. mësim; 2. pagesë për mësim privat
tulip /'tju:lip/ **n. bot.** tulipan
tumble /'tambl/ **vit.** 1. bie, rrëzohem; 2. shprish; 3. lëviz poshtë e lartë; 4. shëmbet, rrënohet; **tumble down** rrënohet, shkatërrohet; **n.** 1. rënie, rrëzim; 2. çrregullim
tumbler /'tamblë(r)/ **n.** 1. gotë; 2. akrobat
tumor /'tju:më(r)/ **n. mjek.** tumor
tune /tju:n/ **n.** 1. **muz.** melodi; motiv; 2. **muz.** akord, harmoni; **in (out) of tune** i akorduar (i çakorduar); **vit. muz.** akordoj; **tune in** sintonizoj (radion); **tune up** akordoj (një instrument)
tuner /'tju:në(r)/ **n.** akordues
tuning /'tju:nin/ **n.** 1. akordim; 2. sinkronizim
tunnel /'tanl/ **n.** tunel; **vt.** hap tunel
turban /'të:bërn/ **n.** çallmë
turbine /'të:rbain/ **n.** turbinë
turbulent /'të:bjulënt/ **adj.** 1. i vrullshëm, i rrëmbyeshëm; 2. turbullues, i papërmbajtur; 3. i harlisur, i harbuar
turkey /'të:rki/ **n. zool.** gjel deti, misërok
Turkish /'të:rkish/ **n.** 1. turk; 2. turqishte; **adj.** turk; **turkish delight** llokum; **turkish coffee** kafe turke
turmoil /'të:rmoil/ **n.** turbullirë, trazirë
turn /të:rn/ **n.** 1. rrotullim; 2. kthesë; kthim; 3. ndryshim; 4. radhë; 5. shërbim, nder, favor; 6. prirje, tendencë; **in turn** me radhë; **take turns at/take it in turns** bëj me radhë; **do somebody a good turn** i bëj një nder dikujt; **take a turn for the better** kthen për mirë; **by turns** me radhë; **vti.** 1. rrotulloj; rrotullohem; 2. kthej; kthehem; 3. bëhet, shndërrohet; 4. kaloj, kapërcej; 5. jap formën, formësoj; **turn against** kthehem kundër; **turn down** refuzoj; hedh poshtë; **turn in** bie të fle; **turn into** kthehet, shndërrohet; **turn off** mbyll (dritën, rubinetin etj.); **turn on** hap (radion, televizorin etj.); **turn out** dal; shndërrohet; shkon, zhvillohet; **turn out a light, etc.** mbyll dritën etj.; **turn out a place** boshatis, zbras; **turn someone out** nxjerr jashtë; **turn over** kthehem; **turn to** i drejtohem; **turn up** vij; arrij; shfaqem; **turn up one's nose at** përbuz, përçmoj
turncoat /'të:rnkout/ **n.** 1. renegat; 2. dallkauk
turner /'të:rnë(r)/ **n.** tornitor
turning /'të:rnin/ **n.** kthesë; **turning-point** pikë kthesë
turnip /'të:rnip/ **n. bot.** rrepë
turtle /'të:rtl/ **n. zool.** breshkëujёse
tutor /'tju:të(r)/ **n.** 1. **drejt.** tutor; 2. mësues privat; 3. pedagog; 4. ndihmës lektor në kolegj
tweet /twi:t/ **n.** cicërimё; **vi.** cicëron
tweezers /'twi:zëz/ **n.** piskatore
twelfth /twelf/ **adj.** i dymbëdhjetë
twelve /twelv/ **n.** dymbëdhjetë; **adj.** i dymbëdhjetë
twentieth /'twentiith/ **adj.** i njëzetë
twenty /'twenti/ **n.** njëzet; **adj.** i njëzetë
twice /twais/ **adj.** dy herë
twig /twig/ **n.** degëz, bisk
twilight /'twailait/ **n.** mugëtirë, muzg, mug
twin /twin/ **n.** binjak; **adj.** binjak

twinkle /'twinkl/ **n.** 1. vezullim; 2. shkëlqim, xixëllimë; **vi.**
1. vezullon, xixëllon; 2. shkëlqejnë, ndritin (sytë etj.)
twist /twist/ **vti.** 1. rrotulloj; 2. dreth, përdredh; 3.
shtrembëroj (fytyrën, kuptimin etj.); 4. kthehet; gjarpëron;
5. ndrydh, përdredh; **n.** 1. përdredhje; 2. shtrembërim; 3.
kthesë
twitter /'twitë(r)/ **vi.** ciceron (zogu); **n.** cicerimë
two /tu:/ **n.** dy; **two by two** dy nga dy
type /taip/ **n.** 1. tip, lloj; 2. shembull, model; 3. shkronjë,
gërmë; **vti.** daktilografoj
typewriter /'taipraitë(r)/ **n.** makinë shkrimi
typical /'tipikl/ **adj.** tipik
typist /'taipist/ **n.** daktilografist
tyrant /'taiërënt/ **n.** tiran

U

udder /'adë(r)/ **n.** gji, sisë (lope)
ugly /'agli/ **adj.** i shëmtuar
ulcer /'alsë(r)/ **n. mjek.** ulcerë
ultimate /'altimit/ **adj.** 1. përfundimtar; 2. themelor, bazal;
3. maksimal
ultimately /'altimitli/ **adv.** më në fund, së fundi
umbrella /am'brelë/ **n.** ombrellë, çadër; **under the umbrella of**
nën ombrellën e
umpire /'ampaië(r)/ **n. sport.** arbitër
unable /an'eibl/ **adj.** i paaftë, i pazoti
unaccustomed /,anë'kastëmd/ **adj.** 1. i pamësuar; 2. i
pazakonshëm, i pazakontë; **unaccustomed to** i pamësuar, i
paambientuar
unanimous /ju:'nenimës/ **adj.** i njëzëshëm
unanimously /ju:'nenimësli/ **adv.** njëzëri
unarmed /an'a:rmd/ **adj.** i paarmatusur
unashamed /,anë'sheimd/ **adj.** i paturp
unauthorized /,an'o:thëraizd/ **adj.** i paautorizuar
unavoidable /,anë'voidëbl/ **adj.** i paevitueshëm
unaware /,anë'weë(r)/ **adj.** i pavetëdijshëm
unawares /,anë'weërz/ **adv.** 1. befas, papritur; 2. padashur
unbearable /an'beërëbl/ **adj.** i padurueshëm
unbelievable /,anbi'li:vëbl/ **adj.** i pabesueshëm
unbreakable /,an'breikëbl/ **adj.** i pathyeshëm
unbutton /,an'batn/ **vt.** shkopsit, zbërthej kopsat
uncertain /an'së:rtn/ **adj.** 1. i pasigurt; 2. i ndryshueshëm
uncertainty /an'së:rtnti/ **n.** pasiguri
unchanged /an'çeinxhd/ **adj.** i pandryshuar
uncle /'ankl/ **n.** xhaxha; dajë
uncomfortable /an'kamfërtëbl/ **adj.** i parehatshëm
uncommon /an'komën/ **adj.** 1. i rrallë, i pazakontë; 2. i
jashtëzakonshëm, i shquar
unconcerned /,ankën'së:rnd/ **adj.** i shkujdesur, moskokëçarës
unconditional /,ankën'dishënl/ **adj.** i pakushtëzuar
unconscious /an'konshës/ **adj.** i pavetëdijshëm
unconsciously /an'konshësli/ **adv.** pa vetëdije
uncontrolled /,ankën'trould/ **adj.** i pakontrolluar
unconvincing /,ankë'vinsin/ **adj.** jobindës
uncover /an'kavë(r)/ **vt.** zbuloj, nxjerr në shesh
uncultivated /an'kaltivetid/ **adj.** 1. i pakultivuar; 2. **fig.** i
paedukuar; i pamësuar
undecided /,andi'saidid/ **adj.** i pavendosur
undeclared /,andi'kleërd/ **adj.** i pashpallur, i padeklaruar
undeniable /,andi'naibl/ **adj.** i pamohueshëm, i padiskutueshëm
under /'andë(r)/ **prep.** nën; poshtë; sipas; **adv.** poshtë
underclothes /'andëkloudhz/ **n.** ndërresa, të brendshme
underestimate /,andër'estimeit/ **vt.** nënçmoj, nënvleftësoj; **n.**
nënvleftësim, nënvlerësim
undergo /,andë'gou/ **vt.** përjetoj, kaloj; 2. i nënshtrohem
(operimit etj.)
undergraduate /,andë'gredjuët/ **n.** student i padiplomuar

underground /,andë'graund/ **adj.** i nëndheshëm; 2. **fig.** i
fshehtë, ilegal; **adv.** 1. nën tokë; 2. **fig.** fshehtas; **n.** metro
underhand /,andë'hend/ **adv.** fshehtas; nën dorë
underline /,andë'lain/ **vt.** theksoj, nënvizoj
undermine /,andë'main/ **vt.** 1. gërryej; 2. **fig.** shkatërroj;
minoj
underneath /,andë'ni:th/ **adv.** poshtë; **prep.** nën
undershirt /,andë'sh:rt/ **n.** fanellë e brendshme
understand /,andë'stend/ **vti.** kuptoj
understandable /,andë'stendbl/ **adj.** i kuptueshëm
understanding /,andë'stendin/ **n.** 1. intelekt; 2. mendje; 3.
marrëveshje; 4. mirëkuptim; **adj.** mirëkuptues
undertake /,andë'teik/ **vt.** 1. marr përsipër; 2. ndërmarr; 3.
zotohem
undertaking /,andë'teikin/ **n.** sipërmarrje; premtim
undervalue /,andë'velju:/ **vt.** nënvleftësoj
undervest /'andëvest/ **n.** kanotiere
underwater ,andë'wo:të(r) **adj.** nënujor, i nënujshëm
underwear /'andëweë(r)/ **n.** të brendshme (veshje)
undesirable /,andi'zaiërëbl/ **adj.** 1. i padëshirueshëm; 2. i
papërshtatshëm
undeveloped /,andi'velëpt/ **adj.** 1. i pazhvilluar; 2. i
parritur; 3. i papërpunuar
undo /an'du:/ **vt.** 1. zgjidh, liroj; 2. prish; rrënoj; 3.
zhbëj
undone /an'dan/ **adj.** 1. i papërfunduar, i pambaruar; 2. i
pazbërthyer
undoubted /an'dautid/ **adj.** 1. i padyshimtë; 2. i padiskutueshëm
undoubtedly /an'dautidli/ **adv.** padyshim
undress /an'dres/ **vti.** zhvesh; zhvishem
unearned /an'ë:rnd/ **adj.** 1. qyl, i fituar pa punë; 2. i
pamërituar
unearth /an'ë:rth/ **vt.** 1. zbuloj; 2. zhvarros
uneasy /an'i:zi/ **adj.** i shqetësuar
uneatable /an'i:tëbl/ **adj.** i pangrënshëm
uneducated /an'edjukeitid/ **adj.** 1. i paedukuar; 2. i
pashkolluar
unemployed /,anim'ploid/ **adj.** i papunë
unemployment /,anim'ploimënt/ **n.** papunësi
unending /an'endin/ **adj.** 1. i pambarim; 2. i përhershëm
unequal /an'i:kwël/ **adj.** i pabarabartë
unerring /an'e:rin/ **adj.** 1. i pagabueshëm; 2. i saktë
uneven /an'i:vën/ **adj.** 1. i parregullt, i thyer, i përthyer;
2. tek (numri)
unexpected /,anik'spektid/ **adj.** i papritur, i paparashikuar
unexpectedly /,anik'spektidli/ **adv.** papritur; papritmas
unfair /an'feë(r)/ **adj.** i pandershëm
unfaithful /an'faithful/ **adj.** i pabesë
unfamiliar /,anfë'milië(r)/ **adj.** i panjohur
unfashionable /an'feshnbl/ **adj.** që s'është i modës
unfasten /an'fa:sn/ **vt.** 1. zgjidh; 2. liroj; 3. zbërthej
unfavorable /an'feivërbl/ **adj.** 1. negativ; 2. i
papërshtatshëm, i pavolitshëm
unfinished /an'finisht/ **adj.** i pambaruar
unfit /an'fit/ **adj.** i papërshtatshëm
unfold /an'fould/ **vti.** 1. shpalos, hap; 2. shpaloset, hapet
unforeseen /,anfo:'si:n/ **adj.** i paparë
unforgettable /,anfë'getibl/ **adj.** i paharrueshëm

unfortunate /an'fo:çënit/ **adj.** fatkeq
unfortunately /an'fo:çënitli/ **adv.** fatkeqësisht
unfounded /an'faunded/ **adj.** i pabazuar, i pambështetur
unfriendly /,an'frendli/ **adj.** jomiqësor
unfulfilled /,anfu'fild/ **adj.** 1. i paplotësuar; 2. i parealizuar
unfurnished /an'fë:rnisht/ **adj.** i pamobiluar
ungrateful /an'greitful/ **adj.** mosmirënjohës
ungrounded /an'graunded/ **adj.** i pabazë, i pathemeltë
unhappy /an'hepi/ **adj.** 1. i palumtur, fatkeq; 2. i pafat
unhealthy /an'helthi/ **adj.** 1. i pashëndetshëm, shëndetlig; 2. i dëmshëm
unhurt /an'hë:rt/ **adj.** 1. i padëmtuar; 2. i palënduar
unidentified /,anai'dentifaid/ **adj.** i paidentifikuar
uniform /'ju:nifo:rm/ **n.** uniformë; **adj.** i njëtrajtshëm, uniform
uniformity /,ju:ni'fo:rmiti/ **n.** uniformitet, njëtrajtshmëri
unify /'ju:nifai/ **vt.** bashkoj, unifikoj
unilateral /,ju:ni'letërl/ **adj.** i njëanshëm
unimportant /,anim'po:rtnt/ **adj.** i parëndësishëm
uninhabited /,anin'hebitid/ **adj.** i pabanuar
unintentional /,anin'tenshnl/ **adj.** i paqëllimtë
uninterested /an'intrestid/ **adj.** i painteresuar
uninteresting /an'intrestin/ **adj.** jointeresant, i mërzitshëm
union /'ju:niën/ **n.** 1. bashkim; 2. lidhje; 3. shoqatë; 4. sindikatë; 5. union; 6. harmoni, unitet
unique /ju:'ni:k/ **adj.** unik, i vetëm
unison /'ju:nizn/ **n.** 1. harmoni, mirëkuptim; 2. **muz.** unison
unit /'ju:nit/ **n.** njësi (matjeje, ushtarake etj.)
unite /ju:'nait/ **vti.** 1. bashkoj; 2. bashkohem
united /ju:'natid/ **adj.** i bashkuar; **the United States of America** Shtetet e Bashkuara të Amerikës; **the United Nations** Kombet e Bashkuara
unity /'ju:niti/ **n.** 1. unitet, bashkim; 2. harmoni
universal /,ju:ni'vë:sël/ **adj.** 1. universal; 2. i përgjithshëm
universe /'ju:nivë:rs/ **n.** univers
university /,ju:ni'vë:siti/ **n.** universitet
unjust /an'xhast/ **adj.** i padrejtë
unjustifiable /an'xhastifaibl/ **adj.** i pajustifikueshëm
unkind /an'kaind/ **adj.** 1. keqdashës; 2. i panjerëzishëm
unknown /an'knoun/ **adj.** i panjohur; **n. mat.** e panjohur
unlawful /,an'lo:fl/ **adj.** i paligjshëm, i jashtëligjshëm
unless /an'les/ **conj.** në se ... nuk
unlike /an'laik/ **adj.** i ndryshëm; **prep.** ndryshe
unlikely /an'laikli/ **adj.** e pamundur; që s'ka ngjasë të
unlimited /an'limitid/ **adj.** 1. i pakufishëm; 2. i pakufizuar
unload /an'loud/ **vti.** shkarkoj
onlock /an'lok/ **vt.** 1. çel, hap; 2. zbuloj, nxjerr në shesh
unlucky /an'laki/ **adj.** i pafat
unmarried /an'merid/ **adj.** i pamartuar, beqar
unnatural /an'neçrël/ **adj.** 1. i panatyrshëm; 2. i shtirur
unnecessary /an'nesisëri/ **adj.** i panevojshëm
unnoticed /an'notist/ **adj.** i paparë, që s'është vënë re
unofficial /,anë'fishl/ **adj.** jozyrtar

unpack /an'pek/ **vti.** shpaketoj, hap
unpaid /an'peid/ **adj.** i papaguar
unparalleled /an'perёleld/ **adj.** i pashembullt, i pakrahasueshёm
unpleasant /an'pleznt/ **adj.** 1. i pakёndshёm; 2. i papёlqyeshёm
unpopular /,an'popjulё(r)/ **adj.** jopopullor
unprecedented /an'presidentid/ **adj.** i pashembullt, i paprecedent
unpredictable /,anpri'diktёbl/ **adj.** i paparashikueshёm
unproductive /,anprё'daktiv/ **adj.** joprodhues, improduktiv
unprofitable /an'profitёbl/ **adj.** i paleverdisshёm, jorentabёl
unpromising /an'promisin/ **adj.** jopremtues
unqualified /an'kwolifaid/ **adj.** i pakualifikuar
unquestionable /an'kwesçёnёbl/ **adj.** i pakundёrshtueshёm, i padiskutueshёm
unreasonable /an'ri:znёbl/ **adj.** i paarsyeshёm
unrefined /,anri'faind/ **adj.** 1. i parafinuar; 2. i trashё, i pagdhendur, i papёrpunuar
unreliable /,anri'laiёbl/ **adj.** 1. i pabesueshёm; 2. i paqёndrueshёm
unrest /an'rest/ **n.** 1. shqetёsim; 2. trazirё, turbullirё; 3. çrregullim
unsatisfactory /an,setis'fektёri/ **adj.** i pakёnaqshёm
unseen /an'si:n/ **adj.** i paparё
unselfish /an'selfish/ **adj.** vetёmohues
unsettled /an'setld/ **adj.** 1. i pavendosur, i pazgjidhur; 2. i paqёndrueshёm
unshakable /an'sheikёbl/ **adj.** i palёkundshёm
unskilled /an'skild/ **adj.** i pakualifikuar
unsociable /an'soushёbl/ **adj.** i pashoqёrueshёm
unstable /an'steibl/ **adj.** i paqёndrueshёm
unsteady /an'stedi/ **adj.** 1. i paqёndrueshёm; 2. i lёkundshёm
unsuccessful /,ansё'ksesful/ **adj.** i pasuksesshёm
unsuitable /,an'sju:tё:bl/ **adj.** i papёrshtatshёm
untidy /an'taidi/ **adj.** i çrregullt
untie /an'tai/ **vt.** zgjidh
until /an'til/ **prep.** deri; para; **conj.** gjersa
untimely /an'taimli/ **adj.** i parakohshёm
untiring /an'taiёrin/ **adj.** i palodhur
untrained /an'çreind/ **adj.** 1. i papёrvojё; 2. i pamёsuar, i pastёrvitur
untrue /an'çru/ **adj.** 1. i pavёrtetё; 2. i pabesё
untruth /an'tru:th/ **n.** pavёrtetёsi
unused /an'ju:zd/ **adj.** i papёrdorur
unused /an'ju:st/ **adj.** i pamёsuar
unusual /an'ju:zhl/ **adj.** i pazakonshёm, i veçantё
unwanted /an'wontid/ **adj.** i padёshirueshёm
unwelcome /an'welkёm/ **adj.** 1. i papёlqyer; 2. i paftuar
unwell /an'wel/ **adj.** i sёmurё; pa qejf
unwilling /an'wilin/ **adj.** mosdashёs
unwillingly /an'wilinli/ **adv.** pa qejf, pa dёshirё
unwise /an'waiz/ **adj.** budalla, i trashё
unworthy /an'wё:rthi/ **adj.** i padenjё, që nuk meriton
unwrap /an'rep/ **vt.** 1. shpaketoj; 2. shpalos
unwritten /,an'ritn/ **adj.** i pashkruar

up /ap/ **adv. part.** 1. sipër, lart; 2. çuar, më këmbë; **What's up?** Ç'ka? Ç'po ndodh?; **prep.** lart, përpjetë; **up the river** përpjetë lumit; **up and down** lart e poshtë; **up to** deri

upbringing /'ap,brinin/ **n.** 1. edukim; 2. rritje

update /,ap'deit/ **vt.** përditësoj

updating /,ap'deitin/ **n.** përditësim

upgrade /,ap'greid/ **vt.** 1. ngre në pozitë; 2. ngre lart, përmirësoj

uphold /ap'hould/ **vt.** 1. mbroj, mbështes; 2. ruaj, mbaj

upholster /ap'houlstë(r)/ **vt.** vesh (kolltukët etj.)

upon /ë'pon/ **prep.** në, mbi; **once upon a time** na ishte njëherë

upper /'apë(r)/ **adj.** i sipërm, i lartë

uppermost /'apëmoust/ **adj.** më i larti, mbizotërues

upright /'aprait/ **adj.** 1. i drejtë; 2. pingul; 3. i ndershëm

uprising /'apraizin/ **n.** kryengritje

uproar /'apro:(r)/ **n.** zhurmë, potere, trazirë, turbullirë

uproot /ap'ru:t/ **vt.** 1. shkul me rrënjë; 2. çrrënjos

upset /ap'set/ **vti.** 1. përmbys; përmbyset; 2. prish (planet); 3. trazoj, shqetësoj; **n.** 1. prishje, çrregullim; 2. përmbysje

upside down /,apsid'daun/ **adv.** përmbys, së prapthi

upstairs /,ap'steëz/ **adv.** në katin e sipërm; **adj.** i katit të sipërm

up-to-date /,ap 'të 'deit/ **adj.** i kohës, bashkëkohor, modern, i ditës

uptown /,ap'taun/ **adv.** në pjesën e sipërme të qytetit

upward /'apvërd/ **adv.** sipër, lart; **adj.** rritës, ngjitës, që shkon në rritje

urban /'ë:bën/ **adj.** urban

urge /ë:rxh/ **vt.** 1. nxit, shtyj; 2. ngut, shtyj; 3. këmbëngul; **n.** dëshirë e madhe

urgency /'ë:xhënsi/ **n.** urgjencë

urgent /'ë:xhënt/ **adj.** urgjent, i ngutshëm

urgently /'ë:xhëntli/ **adv.** urgjentisht

urine /'juërin/ **n.** urinë, shurrë

urn /ë:rn/ **n.** urnë

us /as, ës/ **pers. pron.** ne, neve

usable /'ju:zëbl/ **adj.** i përdorshëm

usage /'ju:sizh, ju:zizh/ **n.** përdorim

use /ju:s/ **n.** 1. përdorim; zbatim; **go out of use** del nga përdorimi; **make use of** përdor; **come into use** hyn në përdorim; 2. dobi, vlerë; **What's the use?** Ç'kuptim ka?; **it's no use** s'ka kuptim, është e kotë; /ju:z/ **vt.** 1. përdor; 2. harxhoj, konsumoj; 3. shfrytëzoj, keqpërdoroj; 4. sillem

used /ju:zd/ **adj.** i përdorur

used /ju:st/ **adj.** i mësuar; **be used to** mësohem me; **used to do something** më ishte bërë zakon të

useful /'ju:sful/ **adj.** i dobishëm

useless /'ju:slis/ **adj.** i pavlefshëm, i padobishëm

usher /'ashë(r)/ **n.** tregues i vendeve në teatër, kinema; **vt.** fut, shoqëroj

usual /'ju:zhuël/ **adj.** i zakonshëm; **as usual** si zakonisht

usually /'ju:xhuëli/ **adv.** zakonisht

utensil /ju:'tensl/ **n.** 1. vegël; 2. enë

utility /ju:'tiliti/ **n.** dobi, leverdi

utilize /'ju:tilaiz/ **vt.** përdor; shfrytëzoj
utmost /'atmoust/ **adj.** 1. më i madhi; 2. më i largëti; 3. më ekstremi
utter /'atĕ(r)/ **adj.** i plotë, i tërë; **vt.** 1. nxjerr, shqiptoj; 2. them, flas
utterance /'atĕrĕns/ **n.** 1. shqiptim, shprehje; 2. thënie; **give utterance to one's feelings** shpreh ndjenjat

vacancy /'veikënsi/ **n.** 1. zbrazëti, boshllëk; 2. vend i lirë, vakant

vacant /'veikënt/ **adj.** 1. i zbrazët; 2. i lirë, i pazënë; 3. i hutuar; 4. i zbrazët, bosh

vacate /vë'keit/ **vt.** 1. liroj; 2. lëshoj

vacation /vë'keishn, vei'keishn/ **n.** 1. pushime; 2. **amer.** leje; pushim; 3. lirim (i shtëpisë etj.); **vi.** pushoj

vaccinate /'veksineit/ **vt. mjek.** vaksinoj

vaccine /'veksi:n, vek'si:n/ **n.** vaksinë

vacuum /'vekjuëm/ **n.** vakuum

vacuum cleaner /'vekjuëm kli:në(r)/ **n.** fshesë elektrike

vacuum flask /'vekjuëm fla:sk/ **n.** termos

vague /veig/ **adj.** 1. i paqartë, i turbullt; 2. i pasaktë; 3. i pasigurt

vain /vein/ **adj.** 1. i kotë, i padobishëm; **in vain** më kot; 2. mburracak; 3. sqimatar

valid /'velid/ **adj.** 1. i vlefshëm; 2. i argumentuar, i bazuar

valise /vë'li:z, vë'li:s/ **n.** valixhe

valley /'veli/ **n.** luginë

valuable /'veljuëbl/ **adj.** i çmueshëm, i vlefshëm

valuables /'veljuëbls/ **n. pl.** gjëra të çmuara, arturina; bizhuteri

valuation /,velju'eishn/ **n.** vlerësim

value /'velju:/ **n.** 1. vlerë; 2. dobi; 3. **ek.** vlerë; 4. çmim; 5. kuptim; **vt.** vlerësoj, çmoj (edhe **fig.**)

van /ven/ **n.** 1. furgon; 2. vagon (mallrash)

vanilla /vë'nilë/ **n.** vanilje

vanish /'venish/ **vi.** 1. zhdukem; 2. humb, shuhet

vanity /'veniti/ **n.** 1. sqimë, fodullëk; 2. kotësi

variety /vë'raiëti/ **n.** 1. shumësi, llojshmëri, shumëllojshmëri; 2. variacion; 3. varietet

various /'veriës/ **adj.** i ndryshëm

varnish /'va:rnish/ **vt.** 1. lyej me vernik; 2. lustroj; **n.** 1. llak; 2. vernik

vary /'veëri/ **vti.** 1. ndryshoj; 2. ndryshon

vase /va:z, veis/ **n.** vazo

vast /va:st/ **adj.** shumë i madh, shumë i gjerë, i paanë

vault /vo:lt/ **n.** 1. kube; 2. qilar, bodrum

vault /vo:lt/ **n.** kërcim; **vti.** 1. kërcej; 2. kërcen

veal /vi:l/ **n.** mish viçi

vegetable /'vexhtëbl/ **n.** perime, zarzavate

vegetarian /,vexhi'teriën/ **n.** vegjetarian

vegetation /,vexhi'teishn/ **n.** bimësi

vehicle /'vi:kl/ **n.** 1. mjet transporti; 2. mjet (shprehës, komunikimi)

veil /veil/ **n.** 1. vello; 2. **fig.** perde; **vt.** 1. mbuloj me vell; 2. **fig.** mbuloj, fsheh

vein /vein/ **n.** 1. venë, damar; **be in the (right) vein** jam në ditë të mirë; 2. **fig.** damar, prirje, dell; 3. **gjeol.** damar, shtresë

velocity /vi'lositi/ **n.** shpejtësi **velvet** /'velvit/ **n.** kadife; **adj.** i kadifenjtë

veneer /vë'nië(r)/ **n.** 1. rimeso; **fig.** cipë, lustër; **vt.** vesh me rimeso

vengance /'venxhëns/ **n.** hakmarrje; **take vengance on** hakmerrem

vengeful /'venxhful/ adj. hakmarrës
ventilate /'ventileit/ vt. 1. ventiloj, ajros; 2. **fig.** përhap
ventilator /'ventiletë(r)/ n. ventilator
venture /'vençë(r)/ n. aventurë, ndërmarrje e rrezikshme; **at a venture** kuturu; **vti.** 1. rrezikoj; rrezikohem; 2. guxoj, marr guximin
verandah /vë'rendë/ n. verandë
verb /vë:b/ n. folje
verbal /'vë:bl/ adj. 1. fjalësor; 2. gojor; 3. i fjalëpërfjalshëm; 4. **gram.** foljor
verdict /'vë:dikt/ n. 1. vendim gjyqi; 2. gjykim, mendim
verge /vë:rxh/ n. skaj, buzë, cak, kufi; **on the verge of** në prag të; **vi.** 1. afrohem; 2. prirem, anohem
verification /,veri'fikeishn/ n. verifikim; 2. provë, dëshmi; 3. vërtetim
verify /'verifai/ vt. 1. verifikoj, sqaroj; 2. vërtetoj
verse /vë:rs/ n. 1. vjershë, poezi; 2. strofë; 3. varg
versed /vë:rst/ adj. i kënduar, i thelluar, që ka njohuri të thella
version /'vë:rshn/ n. 1. version; 2. përkthim
versus /'vë:sës/ prep. 1. kundër; 2. përkundrejt, përballë
vertical /'vë:tikl/ adj. pingul, i pingultë, vertikal
very /'veri/ adj. 1. tamam, pikërisht; 2. vetë; adv. shumë
vessel /'vesl/ n. 1. enë; 2. anije
vest /vest/ n. 1. kanotiere; 2. jelek
vet /vet/ n. **shkurt.** veterinar
veterinary /'vetrinri, 'vetërineri/ adj. veterinar
veto /'vi:tou/ n. veto; **put a veto on something** vë veton; **exercise the right of veto** ushtroj të drejtën e vetos; **vt.** vë, përdor veton
via /vaië/ prep. nëpër, nëpërmjet
vibrate /vai'breit/ vit. 1. dridhem, dridhet; 2. lëkundem, lëkundet
vibration /vai'breishn/ n. lëkundje, dridhje
vicar /'vikë(r)/ n. famulltar
vice /vais/ n. ves
vice /vais/ n. morsetë
vice- /vais/ pref. nën, zëvëndës
vicinity /vi'siniti/ n. 1. afërsi; 2. fqinjësi; **in the vicinity of** në afërsi të
vicious /'vishës/ adj. 1. i keq, i mbrapshtë; 2. i ashpër; 3. i egër; 4. i shthurur, me vese
victim /'viktim/ n. viktimë
victor /'viktë(r)/ n. fitues
victorious /vik'toriës/ adj. fitimtar
victory /'viktëri/ n. fitore
video recorder /'vidiou ri'kodë(r)/ n. vidioregjistrues
video tape /'vidiou teip/ n. shirit vidiokasete
view /vju:/ n. 1. shikim; 2. pamje, panoramë; 3. dukje, paraqitje, ekspozim; 4. mendim, pikëpamje; 5. qëllim; **with a view of** me qëllim të; **come into view** shfaqet; **in my view** sipas mendimit tim; **in view of** duke marrë parasysh; **on view** ekspozuar; **point of view** pikëpamje; **vt.** 1. shikoj, analizoj, shqyrtoj; 2. shoh, shikoj
viewer /vju:ë(r)/ n. shikues; **television viewers** teleshikues
viewpoint /'vju:point/ n. pikëpamje
vigorous /'vigërës/ adj. i fuqishëm, energjik

vile /vail/ **adj.** 1. i keq; 2. i poshtër, i ndyrë; 3. i turpshëm
village /'vilixh/ **n.** fshat
villager /'vilixhë(r)/ **n.** fshatar
villain /'vilën/ **n.** 1. maskara; 2. i poshtër; 3. shejtan, i prapë (fëmija)
vine /vain/ **n.** pjergull, hardhi
vinegar /'vinigë(r)/ **n.** uthull
vineyard /'vinjëd/ **n.** vreshtë
viola /'vaiëlë/ **n. bot.** manushaqe, vjollcë
viola /vi'oulë/ **n. muz.** violë
violate /'vaiëleit/ **vt.** 1. shkel; 2. dhunoj; 3. përdhunoj
violation /,vaië'leishn/ **n.** 1. shkelje; 2. dhunim
violator /'vaiëleitë(r)/ **n.** 1. shkelës; 2. dhunues
violence /'vaiëlëns/ **n.** 1. fuqi, forcë; 2. dhunë
violent /'vaiëlënt/ **adj.** 1. i fuqishëm, i fortë, i furishëm; 2. i madh, i fortë
violet /'vaiëlit/ **n. bot.** manushaqe
violin /,vaië'lin/ **n. muz.** violinë
virtual /'vë:çjuël/ **adj.** faktik, real, i vërtetë
virtue /'vë:çju/ **n.** 1. virtyt; 2. dëlirësi; 3. veti, aftësi; 4. avantazh; **by (in) virtue of** në sajë të, me anë të
virtuous /'vë:çjuës/ **adj.** 1. i virtytshëm; 2. e dëlirë, e ndershme
virus /'vaiërës/ **n. mjek.** virus
visa /'vi:zë/ **n.** vizë
visibility /,vizi'biliti/ **n.** dukshmëri, pashmëri
visible /'vizibl/ **adj.** i dukshëm
vision /'vizhn/ **n.** 1. pamje; 2. vizion; 3. vegim; 4. ëndërr
visit /'vizit/ **n.** 1. vizitë; **pay someone a visit** i bëj dikujt një vizitë; 2. eskursion; udhëtim i shkurtër; **vti.** 1. vizitoj, bëj vizitë; 2. qëndroj; 3. frekuentoj; 4. inspektoj; kontrolloj
visitor /'vizitë(r)/ **n.** vizitor
visual /'vizjuël/ **adj.** pamor, optik
vital /'vaitl/ **adj.** 1. jetësor; 2. i domosdoshëm; 3. i gjallë, vital
vitality /vai'teliti/ **n.** vitalitet, gjallëri
vitamin /'vaitëmin/ **n.** vitaminë
vivid /'vivid/ **adj.** 1. i shndritshëm; 2. i gjallë; 3. i qartë
vocabulary /vou'kebjulëri/ **n.** 1. fjalor; 2. fjalës; 3. fjalori (i një teksti, metode etj.)
vocation /vou'keishn/ **n.** 1. mjeshtëri, zanat, profesion; 2. prirje, tendencë
vocational /vou'keishnl/ **adj.** profesional
voice /vois/ **n.** 1. zë; **raise one's voice against** ngre zërin kundër; 2. mendim, pikëpamje; 3. zë, peshë, ndikim; 4. **gram.** diatezë; 5. **fon.** tingull; **vt.** 1. shpreh; 2. **fon.** shqiptoj
void /void/ **adj.** 1. bosh, i zbrazët; 2. pa; 3. **drej.** i pavlefshëm; **null and void** i pavlefshëm; **n.** boshllëk, zbrazëtirë
volcanic /vol'kenik/ **adj.** vullkanik
volcano /vol'keinou/ **n.** vullkan
volition /vou'lishn/ **n.** vullnet; **of one's own volition** me vullnet të lirë
volleyball /'volibo:l/ **n. sport.** volejboll
volume /'voljum/ **n.** 1. vëllim (libër); 2. **kim.** vëllim; 3. vëllim, sasi

voluntary /'volěntěri/ **adj.** vullnetar
voluntarily /'volěntěrili/ **adv.** vullnetarisht
volunteer /,volěn'tiě(r)/ **n.** vullnetar; **vt.** dal vullnetar
vomit /'vomit/ **vti.** 1. vjell; 2. nxjerr, vjell (tym etj.)
vote /vout/ **n.** 1. votě; 2. votim; **put something to the vote**
hedh ně votě; **cast a vote** hedh votěn; **vit.** votoj; **vote for**
(against) votoj pro (kunděr); **vote down** rrězoj me votim
voter /'voutě(r)/ **n.** votues, zgjedhěs
voting paper /'voutin peipě(r)/ **n.** fletě votimi
vouch /vauç/ **vi.** garantoj, hyj garant
voucher /'vauçě(r)/ **n.** 1. garant, dorězaněs; 2. faturě,
děftesě (pagese)
vow /vau/ **n.** betim, zotim, angazhim; **vt.** zotohem, jap fjalěn,
betohem
vowel /'vauěl/ **n.** zanore
voyage /'voiixh/ **n.** lundrim, udhětim (me vapor)
vulgar /'valgě(r)/ **adj.** vulgar
vulnerable /'valněrěbl/ **adj.** 1. i cenueshěm, i prekshěm; 2.
fig. i dobět; **vulnerable spot** pikě e dobět

wade /weid/ **vit.** eci, çaj me vështirësi (përmes borës, baltës etj.)

waffle /'wofl/ **vi.** llomotit, dërdëllit; **n.** llomotitje

wag /weg/ **vti.** 1. tund; 2. tundem; **the dog wagged its tail** qeni tundte bishtin; **wag one's finger at somebody** i tund gishtin dikujt

wage /'weixh/ **n.** 1. usu. pl. pagë, rrogë; 2. shpërblim; **increase (reduce) wages** rrit (ul) rrogat; **vt.** bëj, zhvilloj

wag(g)on /'wegën/ **n.** 1. karro, qerre; 2. vagon (mallrash)

wail /weil/ **vit.** 1. qaj, vajtoj, vë kujën; 2. **fig.** ulërin (era etj.); **n.** 1. vajtim, kujë; 2. ulërimë

waist /weist/ **n.** mes, bel

waistcoat /'weistkout/ **n.** jelek

wait /weit/ **vit.** 1. pres; **wait for** pres; **keep somebody waiting** lë dikë të presë; 2. shtyj; vonoj; 3. shërbej (si kamarier); **wait on somebody** i shërbej dikujt si kamarier; **n.** 1. pritje; 2. pritë; **lie in wait for** zë pusi

waiter /'weitë(r)/ **n.** kamarier

waiting room /'wetin ru:m/ **n.** dhomë pritjeje

waitress /'weiçris/ **n.** kamariere

wake /weik/ **vit.** 1. zgjoj; zgjohem (edhe **fig.**); **wake up** zgjohem (nga gjumi); **wake somebody up** zgjoj dikë; **wake up to something** kuptoj, bëhem i vetëdijshëm për; 2. zgjoj, ngjall, kujtoj

walk /wo:k/ **n.** 1. shëtitje; **go for a walk** dal shëtitje; 2. ecje; hap; 3. shëtitore; **vit.** 1. eci; 2. eci në këmbë, shëtit; **walk about** sillem vërdallë; **walk away from somebody** fitoj pa vështirësi (garën)

walkie-talkie /,wo:ki 'to:ki/ **n.** radiotelefon portativ

wall /wo:l/ **n.** mur; **run one's head against the wall** i bie murit me kokë; **with one's back to the wall** me shpatulla pas murit; **go to the wall** pësoj disfatë; **vt.** rrethoj me mur, mbyll me mur

wallet /'wolit/ **n.** kuletë

wallpaper /'wo:l peipë(r)/ **n.** letër për të veshur muret

walnut /'wo:lnat/ **n.** 1. arrë; 2. dru arre

waltz /wo:ls/ **n. muz.** vals

wander /'wondë(r)/ **vit.** 1. bredh, endem, sorollatem, vij vërdallë; 2. humb rrugën, drejtimin; 3. shpërqëndrohem

want /wont/ **n.** 1. mungesë; **for want of** për mungesë·të; 2. nevojë; **in want of** ka nevojë për; 3. dëshirë; 4. kërkesë; **vti.** 1. dua, dëshiroj; 2. duhet, kërkohet; 3. kam nevojë; 4. kërkoj; 5. duhet të; 6. mungon, është mangët

war /wo:/ **n.** luftë; **at war** në gjendje lufte; **declare war** i shpall luftë; **go to war** hyj në luftë; **wage war on** luftoj kundër; **the First (Second) World War** Lufta e Parë (e Dytë) Botërore; **civil war** luftë civile

ward /wo:d/ **n.** 1. pavijon; 2. tutelë

warden /'wo:dën/ **n.** 1. kujdestar; 2. drejtor; 3. gardian, rojtar (burgu)

warder /'wo:dë(r)/ **n.** rojtar (burgu)

wardrobe /'wo:droub/ **n.** gardërobë, dollap rrobash

ware /weë(r)/ **n.** 1. artikull; 2. **pl.** prodhime, mallra

warehouse /'weëhaus/ **n.** depo, magazinë

warfare /'wo:feë(r)/ **n.** luftë

warm /wo:m/ **adj.** 1. i ngrohtë; 2. i përzemërt, i dashur, i ngrohtë **vt.** 1. ngroh, nxeh; 2. **fig.** ngroh, i jap zemër

warmly /'wo:mli/ **adv.** ngrohtësisht
warmth /wo:mth/ **n.** 1. ngrohtësi, nxehtësi; 2. **fig.** përzemërsi
warn /wo:n/ **vt.** paralajmëroj
warning /'wo:nin/ **n.** paralajmërim; **adj.** paralajmërues
warrant /'worënt/ **n.** 1. urdhër, autorizim; 2. justifikim; **vt.**
1. justifikoj; 2. garantoj, siguroj
warship /'wo:ship/ **n.** luftanije
wart /wo:t/ **n.** lez, lyth
wash /wosh/ **n.** 1. larje, e larë; 2. lavanteri; 3. tesha për
larje; 4. ujë, lëng gështenjash; **vti.** 1. laj; 2. lahet; 3.
lahem; 4. lag; **wash up** laj pjatat; **wash down** laj me rrjedhë
uji; **wash off** heq, pastroj me të larë; **wash one's dirty linen
in public** nxjerr të palarat në shesh; **wash one's hands of smb
(sth)** laj duart me
washbasin /'woshbeisn/ **n.** legen
washing /'woshin/ **n.** 1. larje; 2. tesha të lara apo për t'u
larë
washing-machine /'woshin më'shin/ **n.** makinë larëse
washing-powder /'woshin paudë(r)/ **n.** pluhur larës
wasp /wosp/ **n.** grenzë
waste /weist/ **n.** 1. shpenzim, harxhim i kotë; 2. humbje;
waste of time humbje kohe; 2. mbeturina, mbetje; 3.
shkretëtirë; 4. djerrinë; **vti.** 1. shpenzoj, harxhoj,
harxhohet kot; **waste one's words (breath)** harxhoj fjalët
(frymën) kot; 2. shkretoj (tokën); 3. tretet, konsumohet;
adj. 1. djerrë (toka); 2. i papërdorshëm; 3. i panevojshëm
waste-basket /'weistba:skit/ **n.** kosh plehrash
waste pipe /'weistpaip/ **n.** tub shkarkimi
watch /woç/ **n.** 1. roje; 2. përgjim, vrojtim, survejim; 2.
patrullë; 3. ndërresë (rojesh); **keep watch** bëj roje; **keep
watch over somebody** survejoj dikë; **be on the watch** jam roje;
vti. 1. vështroj, shikoj; 2. vrojtoj; 3. kujdesem; **watch out!**
kujdes!; **watch out for** hap sytë për; **watch over** ruaj,
kujdesem
watch /woç/ **n.** orë dore ose xhepi
watchful /'woçful/ **adj.** vigjilent
watch /woç/ **n.** orë dore ose xhepi
watch-glass /'woç glas/ **n.** xham ore
watchman /'woçmën/ **n.** roje
watch-tower /'woçtauë(r)/ **n.** kullë vrojtimi
watchword /'woçwë:d/ **n.** parrullë (kalimi)
water /'wo:të(r)/ **n.** 1. ujë; 2. **pl.** ujëra territoriale; **by
water** me vapor; **get into hot water** fus veten në bela; **like a
fish out of water** si peshku pa ujë; **spend money like water** i
prish paret si ujë; **vti.** 1. ujis, vadis; 2. lag, spërkas me
ujë; 3. i jap ujë (kuajve etj.); 4. holloj me ujë; 5. njomen
(sytë etj.)
water-closet /'wo:të(r)klozit/ **n.** banjë; nevojtore
water-color /'wo:të(r) kalë(r)/ **n.** bojë uji
waterfall /'wo:të(r)fo:l/ **n.** ujëvarë
watermelon /'wo:të(r)melën/ **n.** shalqi, bostan
watering-can /'wo:tërin ken/ **n.** ujitëse
waterproof /'wo:të(r)pru:f/ **adj.** i papërshkueshëm nga uji
watertight /'wo:të(r)tait/ **adj.** hermetik, që nuk fut ujë
watery /'wo:tëri/ **adj.** 1. i ujshëm; i holluar; 2. i shpëlarë
watt /wot/ **n.** vat

wave /weiv/ **n.** 1. valë, dallgë; 2. **fig.** valë; 3. lëvizje, lëkundje; 4. permanent, ondulacion; **vti.** 1. valëvit; 2. bëj shenjë me dorë; 3. bëj permanent (flokët)

wax /weks/ **n.** dyllë

way /wei/ **n.** 1. rrugë, udhë; 2. distancë, largësi; 3. mënyrë; 4. gjendje; 5. drejtim, aspekt; **way of life** mënyrë jetese; **by the way** meqë ra fjala; **feel your way** gjej rrugën me të prekur; **find one's way** gjej rrugën; **lose one's way** humb rrugën; **force your way in** hyj me forcë; **be (get) in the way** pengoj, zë rrugën; **give way** lëshoj pe; thyhet, shkatërrohet; **a good way** goxha rrugë; **lead (show) the way** heq rrugën; **all the way** gjatë gjithë rrugës; **in a big way** në shkallë të gjerë; **go one's own way** bëj sipas kokës; **tell someone the way** i tregoj rrugën dikujt

wayside /'weisaid/ **n.** anë rruge; **adj.** që është anës rrugës

WC /,dablju: 'si:/ **n.** WC; banjë, tualet

we /wi:/ **pers. pron.** ne

weak /wi:k/ **adj.** i dobët; **weak point** pikë e dobët

weaken /'wi:kën/ **vti.** 1. dobësoj; 2. dobësohem

weakly /'wi:kli/ **adv.** dobët

weakness /'wi:knis/ **n.** 1. dobësi; 2. debolesë

wealth /welth/ **n.** 1. pasuri; 2. begati; 3. bollëk

wealthy /'welthi/ **adj.** i pasur

weapon /'wepën/ **n.** armë

wear /weë(r)/ **vti.** 1. vesh; 2. **fig.** marr, kam; 3. pranoj; 4. toleroj; 5. mbaj; 6. rron; 7 konsumoj; 8 prish; 9 ha; **n.** 1. veshje; 2. konsumim; 3. amortizim

weary /'weëri/ **adj.** 1. i lodhur, i këputur; 2. lodhës

weariness /'weërinis/ **n.** 1. lodhje; 2. këputje

wearisome /'wiërisëm/ **adj.** 1. i lodhshëm; 2. i mërzitshëm

weather /'wedhë(r)/ **n.** mot, kohë

weave /wi:v/ **vti.** 1. end; 2. thur; 3. gjarpëroj, gjarpëron

web /web/ **n.** 1. rrjetë, pëlhurë merimange; 2. **fig.** rrjetë

wed /wed/ **vti.** 1. martohem; 2. **fig.** bashkoj, kombinoj

wedding /'wedin/ **n.** 1. martesë; 2. dasmë; **wedding dress** rrobat e dhëndërisë, nusërisë; **wedding ring** unazë martese

Wednesday /'wenzdi/ **n.** e mërkurë

weed /wi:d/ **n.** bari i keq; **vti.** heq, shkul barërat e këqia

week /wi:k/ **n.** 1. javë; 2. ditët e javës; **week in, week out** çdo javë

weekday /'wi:kdei/ **n.** ditë jave

weekend /,wi:k'end/ **n.** fund jave; **at the weekend** në fundjavë

weekly /'wi:kli/ **adj.** javor, i përjavshëm; **adv.** çdo javë; **n.** e përjavshme (gazetë, revistë etj.)

weep /wi:p/ **vit.** qaj; **weep for joy** qaj nga gëzimi

weigh /wei/ **vti.** 1. peshoj; peshon; 2. **fig.** peshoj; **weigh one's words** peshoj fjalët; **weigh the evidence** vlerësoj dëshmitë faktike

weight /weit/ **n.** peshë; **put on (gain) weight** shtoj në peshë; **lose weight** humb në peshë; 2. gur peshoreje; 3. **fig.** peshë; rëndësi

weird /wiëd/ **adj.** 1. i panatyrshëm; i pazakontë; 2. i çuditshëm

welcome /'welkëm/ **adj.** i mirëpritur, i mirëseardhur; **you are welcome** s'ka për se; urdhëroni; **vt.** mirëpres; **n.** mirëpritje

welfare /'welfeë(r)/ **n.** mirëqënie

well /wel/ **n.** 1. pus (uji, nafte etj.); 2. **fig.** burim

well /wel/ **adv.** 1. mirë; 2. fort, mirë; 3. shumë; **as well** si dhe; gjithashtu; **as well as** si dhe; **do well** ecën mirë; **do well to do something** bëri mirë që

well-being /'welbi:in/ **n.** mirëqënie

well-bred /'welbred/ **adj.** i sjellshëm, i edukuar

well-known /,wel'nëun/ **adj.** i mirënjohur

well-off /,wel'of/ **adj.** i pasur

west /west/ **n.** perëndim; **the west** perëndimi, vendet perëndimore; **adj.** perëndimor, i perëndimit; **adv.** në perëndim

westerly /'westëli/ **adj.** perëndimor

western /'westën/ **adj.** perëndimor; **n.** uestern (roman, film etj.)

westwards /'westwëdz/ **adv.** në drejtim të perëndimit

wet /wot/ **adj.** 1. i lagur; 2. i lagësht; 3. **fig.** i pashpirt; **n.** shi; lagështirë; **vt.** njom, lag; **wet one's whistle** njom fytin

wetting /'wetin/ **n.** lagie, qullje

whale /weil/ **n.** balenë

wharf /wo:f/ **n.** skelë

what /wot/ **adj.** çfarë, cili; **pron.** çfarë; **what about?** sikur të; **what for?** për çfarë?

whatever /wot'evë(r)/ **adj.** cilido; **pron.** çfarëdo

wheat /wi:t/ **n.** grurë

wheel /wi:l/ **n.** 1. rrotë; 2. timon; 3. rrotullim; **vti.** shtyj, tërheq një mjet me rrota

wheel-barrow /'wi:l berou/ **n.** karrocë dore

wheel-chair /'wi:l çeë(r)/ **n.** karrocë për invalidët

when /wen/ **adv.** kur, në ç'kohë; **conj.** në kohën kur

whence /wens/ **adv.** nga, prej nga

whenever /wen'evë(r)/ **adv.** kurdoherë; në çdo rast

where /weë(r)/ **adv.** ku, në ç'vend

whereabouts /'weërëbauts/ **adv.** ku; **n.** vendndodhje

whereas /weër'az/ **conj.** kurse, ndërsa

whereby /weë'bai/ **adv.** nëpërmjet të cilit, me anën e të cilit

wherefore /'weëfo:/ **adv.** pse

wherein /weër'in/ **adv.** ku, në çfarë, në se

whereupon /,weërë'pon/ **adv.** dhe pastaj, paskëtaj

wherever /weër'evë(r)/ **adv.** kudo që

whether /'wedhë(r)/ **conj.** nëse, në qoftë se

which /wiç/ **adj.** cili; **pron.** i cili, të cilin

whichever /wiç'evë(r)/ **adj. pron.** cilido, secili

while /wail/ **conj.** ndërsa; kurse; **n.** kohë; **for a while** për pak kohë; **once in a while** rrallë; **vt.** kaloj (kohën)

whilst /wailst/ **conj.** ndërsa

whimper /'wimpë(r)/ **vti.** qaj pa zë, qaravitem; **n.** qaravitje

whine /wain/ **vit.** angullin, kuis; **n.** kuisje

whip /wip/ **n.** kamxhik; **vti.** 1. kamxhikoj; 2. rrah (vezën etj.)

whirl /wë:rl/ **vti.** 1. rrotulloj, vërtit; 2. kalon, lëviz me shpejtësi; 3. më vjen mendja rrotull

whisker /'wiskë(r)/ **n.** 1. mustaqe (të maces, miut etj.); 2. favorite, baseta

whisky,whiskey /'wiski/ **n.** uiski

whisper /'wispë(r)/ **n.** 1. pëshpëritje; 2. thashetheme; 3. fëshfërimë; **vit.** 1. pëshpërit; pëshpëritet; 2. fëshfërin

whistle /'wisl/ **n.** 1. vërshëllimë; 2. bilbil; **vit.**
vërshëllej; fishkëllen
white /wait/ **adj.** i bardhë; **n.** 1. ngjyrë e bardhë; 2. njeri i
bardhë; 3. të bardhët e (vezës, syrit)
whiten /'waitën/ **vti.** zbardh; zbardhem
whitewash /'waitwosh/ **vt.** lyej me gëlqere; **n.** sherbet
gëlqereje
whizz /wiz/ **n.** fishkëllimë (e plumbit); **vi.** fishkëllen
(plumbi)
who /hu:/ **pron.** kush, cili; i cili
whoever /hu:'evë(r)/ **pron.** cilido, kushdo
whole /houl/ **adj.** 1. i tërë, i gjithë; 2. i pathyer; 3. i
padëmtuar; **n.** 1. tërësi; 2. e tërë; **on the whole** në tërësi;
as a whole si e tërë
wholeheartedly /,houl 'ha:tidli/ **adv.** me gjithë zemër
wholesale /'houlseil/ **n.** tregti, shitje me shumicë; **adv.** me
shumicë
wholly /'houlli/ **adv.** tërësisht, plotësisht
whom /hu:m/ **pron.** cilin, kë
whose /hu:z/ **pron.** i kujt, i cilit
why /wai/ **adv.** përse; për ç'arsye
wicked /'wikid/ **adj.** i lig, i poshtër
wide /waid/ **adj.** 1. i gjerë; 2. i zgurdulluar; **adv.** 1. gjerë;
2. krejt; 3. larg (shenjës)
wide-awake /,waid ë'weik/ **adj.** syhapur
widen /'waidn/ **vti.** zgjeroj; zgjerohem
widespread /'waidspred/ **adj.** i shtrirë, i përhapur gjithandej
widow /'widou/ **n.** e ve
widower /'widouë(r)/ **n.** i ve
width /width/ **n.** gjerësi
wife /waif/ **n.** grua, bashkëshorte
wig /wig/ **n.** parukë
wild /waild/ **adj.** 1. i egër; 2. i ashpër; 3. i tërbuar; 4. i
papërmbajtur; 5. i stuhishëm; 6. primitiv, i paqytetëruar
will /wil/ **n.** 1. vullnet; 2. dëshirë; 3. vendosmëri; **vt.** 1.
dëshiroj; 2. urdhëroj, komandoj; 3. lë testament, lë
trashëgim; 4. ushtroj vullnetin, forcën e mendjes; **aux. v.** do
të
willing /'wilin/ **adj.** 1. i gatshëm; 2. i vullnetshëm
willingly /'wilinli/ **adv.** me dëshirë, me qejf
willingness /'wilinnis/ **n.** gatishmëri, vullnet, dëshirë
willow /'wilou/ **n.** shelg
win /win/ **vti.** 1. fitoj; përftoj; siguroj; 2. bind; 3. arrij
me vështirësi; **win someone over** bëj për vete; **n.** fitore
wind /wind/ **n.** 1. erë; 2. frymarrje; 3. gazra; **like the wind**
si era; **vt.** 1. nuhat; 2. më merret fryma; 3. çlodh
wind /waind/ **vit.** 1. dredhoj, gjarpëroj; 2. mbështjell, bëj
lëmsh; 3. kurdis; **wind something up** përfundoj diçka
windmill /'windmil/ **n.** mulli me erë
window /'windou/ **n.** dritare
window pane /'windoupein/ **n.** xham dritareje
windowsill /'windousil/ **n.** prag, pezull dritareje
windscreen /'windskri:n/ **n.** xhami i përparmë i makinës
windy /'windi/ **adj.** 1. me erë; 2. fjalaman
wine /wain/ **n.** verë

wineglass /'waingla:s/ **n.** gotë, kupë vere
wing /win/ **n.** 1. krah; 2. vende anësore; 3. **usht.** krah; 4.
sport. krah; 5. **av.** skuadrilje; **vti.** 1. fluturoj; 2. plagos
në krah (zogun)
wink /wink/ **n.** 1. shkelje e syrit; 2. çast; **in a wink** sa hap
e mbyll sytë; **vit.** shkel syrin, ia bëj me sy; **wink at**
something bëj sikur nuk shoh
winner /'winë(r)/ **n.** fitues
winning /'winin/ **adj.** fitues, fitimtar
winter /'wintë(r)/ **n.** dimër; **winter sports** sportet dimërore;
winter clothes rroba dimërore; **vi.** dimëroj; **adj.** i dimrit,
dimëror
wintry /'wintri/ **adj.** 1. dimëror, dimri; 2. **fig.** e ftohtë
wipe /waip/ **vti.** 1. fshij; 2. shkatërroj, zhduk nga faqja e
dheut; **wipe off** fshij; **wipe out** pastroj nga brenda; zhduk,
shkatërroj; **n.** fshirje
wire /'waië(r)/ **n.** 1. tel; 2. telegram; **vti.** 1. lidh me tel;
2. bëj instalime elektrike; 3. telegrafoj
wireless /'waiëlis/ **n.** radio
wisdom /'wisdëm/ **n.** 1. mençuri, zgjuarsi; 2. dije, dituri; 3.
urtësi
wise /waiz/ **adj.** 1. i ditur; 2. i zgjuar, i mençur; 3. i
matur; 4. i arsyeshëm
wish /wish/ **n.** dëshirë; **vti.** 1. dëshiroj; 2. uroj; **wish**
someone well uroj të jesh mirë; **wish for** dëshiroj, kam
dëshirë të
with /widh/ **prep.** me; me anë të; nga
withdraw /widh'dro:/ **vti.** 1. marr, tërheq; 2. tërheq, marr
mbrapsht; 3. tërhiqem; 4. **usht.** zmbraps, tërheq (trupat)
wither /widhë(r)/ **vit.** 1. fishk, fishkem; 2. thaj, thahem
withhold /widh'hould/ **vt.** mbaj, ruaj
within /widh'in/ **prep.** brenda; **adv.** brenda
without /widh'aut/ **prep.** pa; **without fail** patjetër
witness /'witnis/ **n.** 1. dëshmitar; 2. dëshmi, provë; **give**
witness dëshmoj; **vti.** 1. jam dëshmitar i; 2. dëshmoj; 3.
tregon, provon
witty /witi/ **adj.** i mençur, mendjemprehtë
wobble /'wobl/ **vit.** lëkund; 2. **fig.** nguroj, hezitoj
wobbly /'wobli/ **adj.** i lëkundshëm, që lëkundet
woe /wou/ **n.** 1. mjerim, trishtim, brengë; 2. e keqe
wolf /wulf/ **n.** ujk; **a wolf in sheep's clothing** ujk me lëkurë
qengji
woman /'wumën/ **n.** 1. grua; 2. femër
womb /wu:m/ **n.** mitër
wonder /'wandë(r)/ **n.** 1. habi, çudi; 2. mrekulli; **work**
wonders bëj çudira; **vit.** 1. habitem, mahnitem, çuditem; 2.
jam kureshtar, pyes veten
wonderful /'wandë(r)ful/ **adj.** i mrekullueshëm
wood /wud/ **n.** 1. dru (lëndë); 2. dru zjarri; 3. pyll
woodcock /'wudkok/ **n.** shapkë
woodcutter /'wudkatë(r)/ **n.** druvar
wooded /wudid/ **adj.** pyjor, me pyje
wooden /wudn/ **adj.** i drunjtë, prej druri
woodland /'wudlënd/ **n.** pyllnajë
woodman, woodsman /'wud(s)mën/ **n.** druvar
wool /wu:l/ **n.** 1. lesh; 2. fije, copë, rrobë (leshi)
woolen /'wulën/ **adj.** i leshtë, prej leshi; **n. pl.** stof leshi;
rroba leshi, të leshta

word /wë:rd/ **n.** 1. fjalë; **have a word with** flas me; **will not hear a word against** s'lë të thuash një fjalë kundër; **in other words** me fjalë të tjera; **the last word in** fjalë e fundit në; **word for word** fjalë për fjalë; **have words with somebody** bëj fjalë me dikë; 2. lajm, fjalë; **send (leave) word** dërgoj (lë) fjalë; 3. premtim, fjalë; **be as good as one's word (keep one's word, be true to his word)** mbaj fjalën; **break one's word** shkel premtimin; **vt.** 1. shpreh me fjalë; 2. formuloj

wording /'wë:rdin/ **n.** formulim

wordless /'wë:rdlis/ **adj.** i pafjalë; i pashprehur me fjalë

wordy /'wë:rdi/ **adj.** fjalëmadh, fjalëshumë

work /wë:rk/ **n.** 1. punë; **at work** në punë; **out of work** i papunë; **get to work** filloj punën; 2. vepër; 3. **pl.** mekanizmat, detajet e orës etj. 4. **pl.** uzinë, punishte; **vit.** 1. punoj; 2. punon, funksionon; 3. vepron; 4. drejtoj; 5. punoj, i jap formë; **work something out** llogaris; zgjidh; përpunoj

workday /'wë:rkdei/ **n.** ditë pune

worker /'wë:rkë(r)/ **n.** punëtor

working /'wë:rkin/ **n.** 1. minierë, galeri e shfrytëzuar; 2. punë, aktivitet, funksionim; **adj.** i punës, punues, punonjës; veprues

workman /'wë:rkmën/ **n.** punëtor

workshop /'wë:rkshop/ **n.** 1. punishte; 2. oficinë; 3. repart; 4. takim, mbledhje pune

world /wë:rld/ **n.** 1. botë; 2. gjithësi; **a world of** shumë

worldwide /'wë:rldwaid/ **adj.** botëror

worm /wë:m/ **n.** 1. krimb; 2. glistër; **vt.** 1. zvarritem; 2. trajtoj, kuroj (për krimba)

worn /wo:rn/ **adj.** 1. i grisur; 2. i këputur, i lodhur

worry /'wari/ **n.** shqetësim; **vti.** shqetësoj; shqetësohem

worried /'warid/ **adj.** i shqetësuar

worrying /'wariin/ **adj.** shqetësues

worse /wë:rs/ **adj.** më i keq; **adv.** më keq

worship /'wë:rship/ **n.** adhurim; **vt.** adhuroj

worst /wë:rst/ **adj.** (shkalla sip. e **bad**) më i keq; **adv.** më keq; **worst of all** më keq nga të gjithë

worth /wë:rdh/ **n.** vleftë, vlerë; **adj.** i vlefshëm; që ia vlen

worthless /'wë:rdhlis/ **adj.** i pavlerë, i pavlefshëm

worthwhile /wë:rdh'wail/ **adj.** që ia vlen

worthy /'wë:rdhi/ **adj.** i denjë, i merituar; që meriton

would /wud/ **modal v.** (past tense of **will**) do të

wound /wu:nd/ **n.** plagë; **vt.** plagos (edhe *fig.*)

wrap /rep/ **vti.** mbështjell; mbështillem

wrapper /'repë(r)/ **n.** 1. letër ambalazhi; 2. mbështjellëse

wreath /ri:dh/ **n.** 1. kurorë; 2. unazë, dredhë (tymi)

wreck /rek/ **n.** gërmadhë, rrënim, shkatërrim; **vt.** shkatërroj

wreckage /'rekixh/ **n.** 1. mbeturina; 2. rrënoja

wrench /renç/ **vt.** 1. shkul, tërheq me forcë; 2. përdredh, ndrydh; **n.** 1. tërheqje; 2. ndrydhje, përdredhje; 3. **tek.** çelës anglez

wrestle /'resl/ **vit.** 1. **sport.** mundem, bëj mundje; 2. **fig.** luftoj, ndeshem me; **n.** 1. mundje; 2. **fig.** luftë, ndeshje

wrestler /'reslë(r)/ **n.** mundës

wretched /'reçid/ **adj.** 1. i keq; 2. fatkeq, i mjerueshëm

wriggle /'rigl/ **vit.** përdredh; përdridhem

wring /rin/ **vt.** 1. shtrydh; 2. nxjerr me zor; 3. përdredh kokën (pulës etj.); **n.** 1. shtrydhje; 2. përdredhje

wrinkle /'rinkl/ **n.** rrudhë; **vti.** rrudh; rrudhem; **wrinkle up one's forehead** rrudh ballin; **be wrinkled with age** rrudhem nga mosha

wrinkled /'rinkld/ **adj.** 1. i rrudhur; 2. i rrudhosur

wrist /rist/ **n.** kyç i dorës

wrist watch /'ristwoç/ **n.** orë dore **writ** /rit/ **n.** urdhër ligjor (i shkruar); **writ for the arrest of somebody** fletarresti për dikë

write /rait/ **vit.** shkruaj; learn to write mësoj të shkruaj; 2. shkruaj (letër); 3. shkruaj (poezi, prozë etj.); **write something down** mbaj shënim

writer /'raitë(r)/ **n.** shkrimtar

writing /'raitin/ **n.** 1. shkrim; 2. të shkruarit; **in writing** me shkrim; 3. **pl.** shkrimet, veprat

writing paper /'raitin peipë(r)/ **n.** letër shkrimi

wrong /ron/ **adj.** 1. i gabuar; 2. i pasaktë; 3. i papërshtatshëm; 4. i padrejtë; 5. i keq **adv.** keq; gabim; **n.** 1. e keqe; 2. padrejtësi; **vt.** 1. keqtrajtoj; 2. gjykoj padrejtësisht

wrongly /'ronli/ **adv.** gabim

xerox /'ziëroks/ **n.** fotokopjim; **vt.** fotokopjoj
Xmas /'krismës/ **n. shkurt.** i **Christmas**
X-ray /'eks'rei/ **n.** rreze iks, rreze rëntgen; radiografi; **vt.**
bëj radiografi

Y

yacht /jot/ **n.** jaht; **vi.** lundroj, bëj gara me jaht
yard /ja:rd/ **n.** jard (= 0.9144 m)
yard /ja:rd/ **n.** oborr
yarn /ja:rn/ **n.** 1. pe, fill (leshi); 2. tregim, histori
udhëtimesh; **vi.** rrëfej përralla
yawn /jo:n/ **vi.** 1. më hapet goja, gogësij; 2. hapet; **n.**
gogësitje
year /jië(r)/ **n.** 1. vit, mot; **year in year out** vit pas viti;
all the year round gjatë gjithë vitit; 2. moshë
yearly /'jië:rli/ **adj.** vjetor; **adv.** çdo vit
yearn /jë:rn/ **vi.** 1. dëshiroj; 2. kam mall, më merr malli
yeast /ji:st/ **n.** 1. maja; 2. tharm
yell /jel/ **vti.** 1. bërtas, çirrem; 2. flas duke bërtitur; **n.**
britmë
yellow /'jelou/ **adj.** i verdhë; **n.** ngjyrë e verdhë
yelp /jelp/ **vi.** leh, kuis; **n.** lehje, kuisje
yes /jes/ **n.** po; **interj.** po
yesterday /'jestëdi;'jestëdei/ **n.** dje
yet /jet/ **adv.** akoma, ende; **as yet** deri tani; **conj.** por;
megjithatë
yield /ji:ld/ **vti.** 1. prodhoj, jap prodhim; 2. dorëzohem; 3.
bëj lëshime, lëshoj pe; **n.** prodhim
yoghurt, yoghourt /'jogë:rt/ **n.** kos
yolk /jouk/ **n.** e verdha e vezës
you /ju:/ **pers. pron.** ti; ju
young /jan/ **adj.** i ri; **n.** 1. të vegjlit; 2. të rinjtë
youngster /'janstë(r)/ **n.** i ri, djalosh
your /jo:ë(r)/ **adj.** yt, jote, e tu, tuaj, tuaja
yours /jo:z/ **poss. pron.** yti, juaji, jotja, të tutë, të tuat
yourself /jo:'self/ **pron.** veten; vetë; vetëm; **by yourself**
vetëm
youth /ju:dh/ **n.** 1. rini; 2. i ri
youthful /'ju:dhful/ **adj.** rinor

Z

zebra /'zi:brë/ **n.** zebër
zero /'ziërou/ **n.** zero; **zero hour** ora e sulmit
zig-zag /'zigzeg/ **n.** zigzak; **adj.** zigzak
zip, zipper, zip fastener /zip; zipë(r); ,zip'fa:snë(r)/ **n.**
zinxhir; **vt.** hap, mbyll me zinxhir; **zip up** mbyll me zinxhir
zone /zoun/ **n.** zonë
zoo /zu:/ **n.** kopsht zoologjik
zoological /,zouë'loxhikl/ **adj.** zoologjik
zoologist /zou'olëxhist/ **n.** zoolog
zoology /zou'lëxhi/ **n.** zoologji

GEOGRAPHICAL NAMES
(Emrat Gjeografikë)

ENGLISH - ALBANIAN

A

Abu Dabhi/ Abu Dabi
Accra/ Akrë
Addis Ababa/ Adis Abebë
Adriatic Sea/ Deti Adriatik
Afghanistan/ Afganistan
Africa/ Afrikë
Alabama/ Alabamë
Alaska/ Alaskë
Albania/ Shqipëri
Algeria/ Algjeri
Algier/ Algjer
Alma Ata/ Alma Atë
Alps/ Alpe
Altai/ Altaj
Amazon/ Amazonë
America/ Amerikë
Amman/ Aman
Amsterdam/ Amsterdam
Andes/ Ande
Andorra/ Andorrë
Angola/ Angolë
Ankara/ Ankara
Antarctic Continent/ Kontinenti i Antarktidës
Apennines/ Apenine
Appalachian Mountains, Appalachian/ Apalashe, Malet Apalashe
Arabian Sea/ Deti Arabik
Arctic Ocean/ Oqeani Arktik
Arctic Region/ Zona Arktike
Argentina/ Argjentinë
Arizona/ Arizonë
Arkansas/ Arkanzas
Arkhangelsk/ Arhangelsk
Armenia/ Armeni
Ashkhabad/ Ashkabad
Asia/ Azi
Asia Minor/ Azi e Vogël
Asunción/ Asuncion
Athens/ Athinë
Atlanta/ Atlantë
Atlantic Ocean/ Oqeani Atlantik
Australia/ Australi
Austria/ Austri
Azerbaijan/ Azerbajxhan
Azov, Sea of/ Deti Azov

B

Bab el Mandeb/ Bab-el-Mandeb
Bag(h)dad/ Bagdad

Bahrain, Bahrein/ Bahrejn
Baikal/ Bajkal
Baku/ Baku
Balkan Peninsula/ Gadishulli i Ballkanit
Baltic Sea/ Deti Balltik
Baltimore/ Baltimorë
Bamako/ Bamako
Bangkok/ Bangkok
Bangladesh/ Bangladesh
Barents Sea/ Deti Barenc
Beirut/ Bejrut
Belfast/ Belfast
Belgium/ Belgjikë
Belgrade/ Beograd
Bengal, Bay of/ Gjiri i Bengalit
Benin/ Benin
Bering Sea/ Deti i Beringut
Bering Strait/ Ngushtica e Beringut
Berlin/ Berlin
Bermuda Islands, Bermudas/ Ishujt Bermude
Biscay, Bay of/ Gjiri i Biskajës
Black Sea/ Deti i Zi
Bogota/ Bogota
Bolivia/ Bolivi
Bombay/ Bombei
Bonn/ Bon
Borneo/ Borneo
Boston/ Boston
Botswana/ Botsvanë
Brazil/ Brazil
Brazzaville/ Brazavil
Britain/ Britani
Brunei/ Brunei
Brussels/ Bruksel
Bucharest/ Bukuresht
Budapest/ Budapest
Buenos Aires/ Buenos-Ajres
Bulgaria/ Bullgari
Burundi/ Burundi
Byelorussia/ Bjellorusi

C

Cairo/ Kajro
Calcutta/ Kalkutë
California/ Kaliforni
Cambridge/ Kembrixh
Cameroon/ Kamerun
Canada/ Kanada
Canberra/ Kanberrë
Cape of Good Hope/ Kepi i Shpresës së Mirë
Cape Town, Capetown/ Kejptaun
Cape Verde Islands/ Ishujt e Kepit të Gjelbër
Caracas/ Karakas
Caribbean (Sea)/ Deti i Karaibeve
Carpathian Mountains, Carpathians/ Malet Karpate
Caspian Sea/ Deti Kaspik
Caucasus, the/ Kaukaz

Central African Republic/ Republika e Afrikës Qëndrore
Central America/ Amerika Qëndrore
Chad/ Çad
Chad, Lake/ Liqeni i Çadit
Chicago/ Çikago
Chile/ Kili
China/ Kinë
Chomolungma/ Xhomolungma
Colombia/ Kolumbi
Colombo/ Kolombo
Colorado/ Kolorado
Conakry/ Konakri
Congo, the/ Kongo
Copenhagen/ Kopenhagen
Corsica/ Korsikë
Costa Rica/ Kosta Rikë
Cote d'Ivoire/ Bregu i Fildishtë
Crete/ Kretë
Crimea, the/ Krime
Cuba/ Kubë
Cyprus/ Qipro
Czech Republic/ Republika Çeke

D

Dacca/ Dakë
Dakar/ Dakar
Damascus/ Damask
Danube/ Danub
Dardanelles/ Dardanele
Dar es Salaam/ Dar-es-Salam
Delhi/ Delhi
Denmark/ Danimarkë
Dnieper/ Dniepër
Dniester/ Dniestër
Dominican Republic/ Republika Dominikane
Don/ Don
Dublin/ Dublin

E

Ecuador/ Ekuador
Edinburgh/ Edinburg
Egypt/ Egjipt
Elbe/ Elbë
Elbrus, Elbruz/ Elbrus
England/ Angli
English Channel/ Kanali i Anglisë
Equatorial Guinea/ Guiena Ekuatoriale
Estonia/ Estoni
Ethiopia/ Etiopi
Euphrates/ Eufrat
Europe/ Evropë
Everest/ Everest

F

Falkland Islands/ Ishujt Falkland
Federal Republic of Germany/ Republika Federale Gjermane
Finland/ Finlandë
Florence/ Firence
Florida/ Floridë
France/ Francë

G

Gabon, Gaboon/ Gabon
Gambia/ Gambia
Ganges/ Gang
Geneva/ Gjenevë
Genoa/ Gjenovë
Georgetown/ Xhorxhtaun
Georgia/ Gjeorgji
Germany/ Gjermani
Ghana/ Ganë
Gibraltar/ Gjibraltar
Glasgow/ Glasgou
Gobi, the/ Gobi
Great Britain/ Britania e Madhe
Greece/ Greqi
Greenland/ Groenlandë
Guadeloupe/ Guadelupë
Guatemala/ Guatemalë
Guinea/ Guine
Guyana/ Guajanë

H

Hague, The/ Hagë
Haiti/ Haiti
Hamburg/ Hamburg
Hanoi/ Hanoi
Havana/ Havanë
Havre/ Havër
Hawaii/ Havai
Helsinki/ Helsinki
Himalaya(s), the/ Himalajë
Hindustan/ Hindustan
Hiroshima/ Hiroshimë
Ho Chi Minh/ Ho Shi Min
Holland/ Hollandë
Hollywood/ Hollivud
Honduras/ Honduras
Hong Kong/ Hong-Kong
Horn, Cape/ Kepi Horn
Hudson Bay/ Gjiri i Hudsonit
Hungary/ Hungari

I

Iceland/ Islandë
Illinois/ Ilinois
India/ Indi
Indiana/ Indianë
Indian Ocean/ Oqeani Indian
Indonesia/ Indonezi
Iran/ Iran
Iraq/ Irak
Ireland/ Irlandë
Israel/ Izrael
Istanbul/ Stamboll
Italy/ Itali

J

Jaffa/ Jafë
Jakarta/ Xhakartë
Jamaica/ Xhamaikë
Japan/ Japoni
Java/ Java
Jerusalem/ Jeruzalem
Jibuti/ Xhibuti
Johannesburg/ Johanesburg
Jordan/ Jordani

K

Kabul/ Kabul
Kamchatka/ Kamçatkë
Kansas/ Kanzas
Karachi/ Karaçi
Katmandu/ Katmandu
Kattegat/ Kategat
Kazakhstan/ Kazakistan
Kenya/ Kenia
Kiev/ Kiev
Kilimanjaro/ Kilimanxharo
Kinshasa/ Kinshasë
Kishinev/ Kishinev
Korea/ Kore
Kuril(e) Islands/ Ishujt Kurile
Kuwait/ Kuvajt
Kyoto/ Kioto

L

Lahore/ Lahorë
Laos/ Laos
Latvia/ Letoni
Lebanon/ Liban
Leipzig/ Lajpcig
Lesotho/ Lesoto
Lhasa/ Lhasa
Liberia/ Liberi

411

Libya/ Libi
Liechtenstein/ Lihenshtajn
Lima/ Limë
Lisbon/ Lisbonë
Lithuania/ Lituani
Liverpool/ Liverpul
London/ Londër
Los Angeles/ Los Anxhelos
Louisiana/ Luizianë
Luanda/ Luandë
Lusaka/ Lusakë
Luxembourg/ Luksemburg

M

Madagascar/ Madakaskar
Madrid/ Madrid
Magellan, Strait of/ Ngushtica e Magelanit
Malaysia/ Malajzi
Malta/ Maltë
Managua/ Managua
Manchester/ Mançester
Manhattan/ Manhatan
Manila/ Manilë
Marseilles/ Marsejë
Martinique/ Martinikë
Maryland/ Merilend
Massachusetts/ Masaçusets
Mauritania/ Mauritani
Mauritius/ Mauricius
Mecca/ Mekë
Mediterranean Sea/ Deti Mesdhe
Melanesia/ Melanezi
Mexico/ Meksikë
Mexico (City)/ Qyteti i Meksikës
Miami/ Majami
Michigan/ Miçigan
Milan/ Milano
Minnesota/ Minesotë
Minsk/ Minsk
Mississippi/ Misisipi
Missouri/ Misuri
Moldova/ Moldavi
Monaco/ Monako
Mongolia/ Mongoli
Montreal/ Monreal
Morocco/ Marok
Moscow/ Moskë
Mozambique/ Mozambik
Munich/ Mynih

N

Nairobi/ Najrobi
Namibia/ Namibi
Naples/ Napoli
Nebraska/ Nebraskë

Nepal/ Nepal
Netherlands/ Hollandë
Neva/ Nevë
Nevada/ Nevadë
New Guinea/ Guinea e Re
New Orleans/ Nju-Orleans
New York/ Nju-Jork
New Zealand/ Zelandë e Re
Niagara/ Niagarë
Niagara Falls/ Ujëvarat e Niagarës
Nicaragua/ Nikaragua
Nice/ Nicë
Nigeria/ Nigeri
Nile/ Nil
North America/ Amerika e Veriut
North Carolina/ Karolina e Veriut
North Pole/ Poli i Veriut
North Sea/ Deti i Veriut
Norway/ Norvegji
Nuremberg, Nurnberg/ Nuremberg

O

Oceania/ Oqeani
Oklahoma/ Oklahomë
Oman/ Oman
Oregon/ Oregonë
Oslo/ Oslo
Oxford/ Oksford

P

Pacific Ocean/ Oqeani Paqësor
Pakistan/ Pakistan
Palestine/ Palestinë
Panama/ Panama
Panama Canal/ Kanali i Panamasë
Paraguay/ Paraguai
Paris/ Paris
Peking/ Pekin
Pennsylvania/ Pensilvani
Persian Gulf/ Gjiri Persik
Peru/ Peru
Philadelphia/ Filadelfia
Philippines/ Filipine
Poland/ Poloni
Portugal/ Portugali
Prague/ Pragë
Pretoria/ Pretorie
Puerto Rico/ Porto Riko
Pyongyang/ Phenian
Pyrenees/ Pirenej

R

Red Sea/ Deti i Kuq
Republic of South Africa/ Republika e Afrikës së Jugut
Reykjavik/ Rekjavik
Rhine/ Ren
Rio de Janeiro/ Rio-de-Zhaneiro
Rocky Mountains/ Malet Shkëmbore
Romania/ Rumani
Rome/ Romë
Russia/ Rusi

S

Sahara/ Saharë
Sakhalin/ Sahalin
San Francisco/ San Francisko
San Salvador/ San Salvador
Santiago/ Santiago
Santo Domingo/ Santo-Domingo
Sao Paulo/ San Paulo
Sao Tomé and Principe/ Sao-Tome-e-Principe
Saudi Arabia/ Arabia Saudite
Scotland/ Skoci
Seine/ Senë
Senegal/ Senegal
Seoul/ Seul
Sevastopol/ Sevastopol
Shanghai/ Shangai
Siberia/ Siberi
Sicily/ Sicili
Singapore/ Singapor
Sofia/ Sofje
Somalia/ Somali
South America/ Amerika e Jugut
South Carolina/ Karolina e Jugut
South Korea/ Korea e Jugut
South Pole/ Poli i Jugut
Spain/ Spanjë
Sri Lanka/ Sri Lankë
Stockholm/ Stokholm
Sudan, the/ Sudan
Suez Canal/ Kanali i Suezit
Swaziland/ Suazilend
Sweden/ Suedi
Switzerland/ Zvicër
Sydney/ Sidnei
Syria/ Siri

T

Tadjikistan/ Taxhikistan
Taiwan/ Tajvan
Tanzania/ Tanzani
Tashkent/ Tashkent
Tbilisi/ Tbilis
Teh(e)ran/ Teheran
Tel Aviv/ Tel Aviv
Texas/ Teksas

Thailand/ Tailandë
Tibet/ Tibet
Tokyo/ Tokio
Toronto/ Toronto
Trinidad and Tobago/ Trinidad dhe Tobago
Tunis/ Tunis
Tunisia/ Tunizi
Turkey/ Turqi
Turkmenistan/ Turkmenistan

U

Uganda/ Ugandë
Ukraine/ Ukrahinë
Ulan Bator/ Ulan-Bator
Ulster/ Ulster
United Arab Emirates/ Emiratet e Bashkuara Arabe
United Kingdom of Great Britain and Northern Ireland/
Mbretëria e Bashkuar e Britanisë së madhe dhe Irlandës së
Veriut
United States of America, USA/ Shtetet e Bashkuara të
Amerikës
Urals, the/ Ural
Uruguay/ Uruguai
Uzbekistan/ Uzbekistan

V

Vatican/ Vatikan
Venezuela/ Venezuelë
Venice/ Venecie
Victoria/ Viktoria
Vietnam/ Vjetnam
Virginia/ Virgjinia
Vistula/ Vistulë
Vladivostok/ Vladivostok
Volga/ Vollgë

W

Wales/ Uells
Warsaw/ Varshavë
Washington/ Uashington
West Virginia/ Virgjinia Perëndimore
White Sea/ Deti i Bardhë
Wisconsin/ Viskonsin

Y

Yellow Sea/ Deti i Verdhë
Yemen/ Jemen
Yugoslavia/ Jugosllavi

Z

Zaire/ Zaire
Zambia/ Zambia
Zanzibar/ Zanzibar
Zimbabwe/ Zimbabve
Zurich/ Zyrih